Dominican Gallery

Cum permissu superiorum
Malcolm McMahon, O.P.
Prior provincialis Angliae

Dominican Gallery

Portrait
of a
Culture

Aidan Nichols, O.P.

First published in 1997

Gracewing
Fowler Wright Books
2 Southern Avenue
Leominster
Herefordshire HR6 0QF

ISBN 0 85244 393 5

Typesetting by
Action Typesetting Ltd, Gloucester, GL1 1SP

Printed by Cromwell Press
Broughton Gifford, Wiltshire, SN12 8PH

Contents

Foreword

In this fascinating book, Fr Aidan Nichols presents the writings of seven English Dominicans who flourished between 1930 and the Second Vatican Council. It is hard to imagine seven more different men, both in character and in interest. They were all theologians, but their theology was enriched by formation in a variety of disciplines. They included a Jungian psychologist, a calligrapher and printer, a Scripture scholar, a Byzantinist and archaelogist, a logician and a Dante scholar.

As the subtitle of the book suggests, they were all formed by, and contributed to, a common culture, which was Dominican, Thomist and English. But this was not the culture of a small Catholic ghetto, introverted upon itself. What made the writings of these men important in their time and of abiding interest, is that their theology was marked not only by strong doctrinal and philosophical convictions, but by a passionate interest in all human search for truth. Thomas Gilby described theology as 'the overspill of divine faith into all the levels of human reasonableness, its wit, humour, poetic imagination, sense of analogy, power of co-ordination, openness to be taught, and search for reason why, whence, how and what it is all about'

Contemporary western society is something of a cultural desert. There is, of course, great literary, and artistic creativity. We are blessed with wonderful novelists, musicians, painters and film makers. It is a time of extraordinary technological advance. As I write the little Sojourner is trundling across the face of Mars, sniffing at rocks. Despite so much that is rich and vital, we are culturally impoverished in that there is no common vision of what it is to be human, and of the destiny to which we are called. The only shared perception, the cultural glue of our time, is that of consumerism, which offers us a stunted and shrivelled perception of the human being, whose freedom is to choose between different products in the supermarket, and whose dream is to have a lot of money.

The cultural crisis of contemporary society was already evident when these seven Dominicans were most productive and it was a shared preoccupation for them all. They realised that this crisis was not merely social or political but in its deepest roots religious. For, as Christopher Dawson, who inspired so many of these Dominicans, wrote, 'A society which has lost its religion becomes sooner or later a society which has lost its culture.'

They did not reply to this crisis with a Thomism which was a neat theological system, offering answers to all possible questions. St Thomas was a man of the thirteenth century whose culture was, according to Gervase Mathew, marked by 'the power to receive and then transform'. Its fundamental philosophical and theological intuitions made it critically hospitable to every attempt to make sense of our world and our lives. This was why these Dominicans were so happy to enter into conversation and argument with all sorts of people: artists, philosophers, historians, politicians. In that sense it offered healing to a culture which was falling apart. Their Thomist theology, with its vision of all creation coming from God and returning to the Creator, offered a meeting place for so many partial insights into who we are and for what we are made.

In the words of Aidan Nichols, Gerald Vann believed that 'Thomas succeeded not only in unifying the "disparate elements of a complete culture" but also in finding the truth between various "contradictory theories" themselves generated by confrontation with the deepest problems the mind can know. [Gerald Vann] presents Thomas's achievement as, then, both synthesis and adjudication.'

What can these seven men teach us, as we face the challenge of sharing our faith in a society whose culture is even more impoverished than when they wrote thirty years ago?

First of all let us learn something of their confidence in daring to enter into debate with other people who claim some insight into the human condition. These Dominicans were men of strong theological and doctrinal convictions. They believed that they had a teaching to impart. They did not fear to roll up their sleeves and dive into argument. But this confidence did not make them bigoted or deaf to others. They dared to learn new disciplines, play with new theories, hazard a new approach. For the God who has spoken to us in the Word made flesh, offers a truth that is beyond our grasp and which we are always just at the beginning of understanding. In these wonderful words of St. Anselm, 'Truth is so vast and so deep that it cannot be exhausted by any man, nor has the Lord, who has promised to abide with his Church till the end of the world, ceased to impart his gifts'. So may these brothers teach us both a strong faith and an open ear, a confidence and an intellectual humility.

Secondly, their theology is always filled with a reverence for this created world. Their theology is not abstract, but helps them to delight in what they can see and hear and touch. It is down to earth, a theology that is profoundly incarnational. With Conrad Pepler it takes the form of a reverence for mother earth, to cultivate which is a form of *cultus*, and the ground of all culture. In Gervase Mathew it can be seen in his delight in Byzantine mosaics and Coptic wall paintings, his pleasure in human artefacts. In Thomas Gilby and all of these writers it is seen in his Aristotelian and 'primitive craving of mind for the whole real'.

Finally, if their faith brought them down to earth, it also propelled them up to heaven. They have a common conviction that all theology is ultimately mystical. Victor White writes that 'It is safe to assert that there was no great scholastic theologian who was not something of a mystic'. Theology is not merely an intellectual exercise, the articulation of coherent theories about creation and salvation. It belongs to our falling in love with God, our attempts to respond to the One who offers us His friendship. The sharp critical intelligence of the theologian should be that of 'a mind in love'. And so for them, doing theology has always to be underpinned by a life that has moments of silence, of that stillness which is necessary for true attentiveness. As Gerald Vann wrote 'Stillness is the womb of all great achievement'. If we are to have something of the confidence and openness of these seven Dominicans, and follow them in contributing to the renewal of contemporary culture, then we must recover the contemplative rhythm of their lives.

Fr Timothy Radcliffe OP
Master of the Order of Preachers

Preface

This book studies the culture of the English Dominicans in the period from 1930 to the Second Vatican Council. It does so through the writing and thinking of seven men, at once outstanding and representative – a series of portraits intended to capture the spirit of an age. Hence the title: *Dominican Gallery*. The *terminus a quo* is conveniently set by the fact that their earliest contribution to the Dominican 'house journal', *Blackfriars*, appeared in the opening year of the 1930s; the *terminus ad quem* is not so precise, since several of them survived the Council and continued to write. Their formation, intellectually and spiritually, was, however, already complete, and the post-conciliar ecclesial culture (if the phrase can be used of a highly disparate phenomenon) scarcely affected them.

The period in which these seven just men were, in all essentials, formed – the 1930s – was a fortunate one for English Catholics, and indeed for Catholic-minded Anglicans as well. They were in possession of an intellectual leadership equipped with a firm grasp of Christian dogma, the capacity to offer a learned apologetic, and confidence, both corporate and personal, about the world-transforming possibilities of the faith. In December 1939, Dorothy Sayers set out a 'rough draft of aims and intentions' for a series of books on a post-Second World War Christian reconstruction in England, to be called 'Bridgeheads'. 'We aim', she wrote, 'at the Resurrection of Faith, the Revival of Learning, and the Reintegration of Society.'[1] Although the opportunity was missed, and the cultural conjuncture which the event of the Second Vatican Council entered was, accordingly, unpropitious, the formula combining spiritual ardour, intellectual light and social zeal is not for that reason necessarily defective.

The English Dominican life and literary achievement of those formed in the inter-war years constitutes, in my judgment, the high point of the contribution of the Dominican Province to the culture of Church and society in England – and not only, it would seem, in mine. In her explosive biography of Eric Gill, Fiona McCarthy wrote of the English Dominicans at the time of Gill's first encounter with them as 'fashionable [but] not so fashionable then [in 1914] as they were to become later, when ageing Catholic intellectuals of the 1930s would write nostalgically of the Dominican leaven spreading through their generation...[2] Still, that charmed generation of friars (of the men whose work I shall be describing, Victor White was 28 in 1930, Gerald Vann 24, Thomas Gilby 28, Sebastian Bullough 20, Gervase Mathew 25, Kenelm Foster 20, Conrad Pepler 23) was not of course without preparation and – therefore – precursors, nor did it lack all posthumous influence and – therefore – successors. But the former had not the sophistication, the latter the integration, which the concept of a 'classical moment' in the history of ecclesial culture implies.

Though the point of time at which these seven figures were formed, humanly, spiritually, intellectually, is vital, since theirs was a cultural 'moment' unsurpassed in the history of the Catholic Church in England, the unity of their culture does not depend on that fact of chronology alone. Indeed, no common portrait of them would be possible that abstracted from their belonging to the life of a single religious order, in its English incarnation. For this reason, some account of the English Dominican background must be offered here – as well as an account of the English Catholic setting.

Scene-setting for an account of our seven individuals may be taken, then, in two stages.[3] First (Chapter 1), I will set out the process of 'formation' of an English friar of this period – something which will also enable me to give a rough sketch of the particular communities to which these seven men might be 'assigned'.[4] Although the English Province possessed, by the end of the Great War, or would acquire, in the course of the 1920s, houses outside England – one in Scotland,[5] and a number, chiefly small missions, in certain Caribbean islands and South Africa (where they boasted a more ambitious foundation in the Afrikaaner 'Oxford', Stellenbosch) – consideration of these will be strategically omitted. It is Englishmen in an English setting that I shall describe. This first chapter will end with an account of some of the disputed questions thrown up by the history of the English Dominicans and how, in the period, they debated them.

Secondly, in Chapter 2 on 'The Setting' for the writing activity of these seven figures, the state of Catholicism in England in the inter-war years must be, however cursorily, considered. This is a work of *pietas*, but it claims a wider audience than simply fellow-Dominicans or those linked by ties of friendship or spiritual affinity with the Order. The culture it describes was connected by a myriad ties to the wider culture of English Catholicism as a whole at an extraordinarily vigorous period of its history – with the stimulus provided by, among others, the artists Eric Gill and David Jones, the philosopher of history Christopher Dawson, the novelists Graham Greene and Evelyn Waugh (though the latter two entered little into the contemporary Catholic debate on general ideas).

That wider culture itself was by no means – as is sometimes ignorantly stated – self-confined to a 'ghetto Catholicism'. Its inhabitants could show deep interest in the work of a non-Catholic Christian like T. S. Eliot, or of a neo-pagan like D. H. Lawrence. Within this constellation to identify oneself with the distinctively English Dominican sub-culture was to take a particular stance, to commend an ethos and approach, to favour one series of emphases against another. Harman Grisewood, the most notable Catholic in the Reithian BBC, could cap an argument with Tom Burns, the leading Catholic publisher of the time, by adding, 'I am Thomist and Dominican, you are Ignatian and Jesuit'![6] So investigation of what it meant, in England, to be 'Thomist and Dominican' may throw light on the broader scene.

Finally, the themes and ideas expounded in the remaining seven chapters of this book possess, quite apart from the historical interest of their collocation, a value and fascination of their own. The key is perhaps to be found in some words in Grisewood's autobiography, where he contrasts the English Catholic intelligentsia of the first and second halves of this century:

> It is seldom remembered now that, whereas the intellectual interests of the second half of the century are social and political, the interests of the first half were far more inclusive. Earlier in the century the arts and the philosophy of history played an important part. We were concerned then with the continuance or establishment of an inclusive civilisation.[7]

The Catholic Christian, concerned as he or she is with the transcendent *politeia* – citizenship – of the heavenly Kingdom, is also keen that its colonies on earth shall be as all-embracing as possible. The work of the English Dominicans described in this book was a contribution to the sustaining and remaking of a Christian culture in this perspective. Their specific contribution was to keep the discussion theological: that is, to ensure that the re-creation of a culture in which they believed themselves to be participating would turn out a thoroughly *theocentric* affair. Such a *civilisation*, at once humane and divine, must be of interest to any *civis*, any citizen. Or so I believe.

I am grateful to Harman Grisewood who, alas, died while this study was still in production and – most especially – to Fr Bede Bailey, OP,

Archivist of the English Dominican Province, as also to Fr Fergus
Kerr, OP, prior of Blackfriars, Edinburgh, for their help with this
book.[8] Roger Ruston, as copy editor, made sagacious suggestions for
its improvement, which I thankfully acknowledge. Responsibility for
its judgments, and any remaining errors, must be mine.

Blackfriars, Cambridge
Pentecost 1997

Notes

1.   B. Reynolds, *Dorothy L. Sayers: her Life and Soul* (London: Hodder
     and Stoughton, 1993), pp. 307–8.
2.   F. McCarthy, *Eric Gill* (London: Faber and Faber, 1989), p. 134.
3.   The story of the English Dominican Province from 1221 to the end of
     the 1920s is briefly recounted in Appendix 1 of this book; 'The Pre-
     history of the Modern English Dominicans', pp. 407–417.
4.   For completeness' sake and the benefit of those readers interested in
     the later history of the English Dominican Province, a brief *aggiorna-
     mento* of the houses is included.
5.   For the return of the Dominicans to Scotland, see A. Ross, O.P., *Dogs
     of the Lord. The Story of the Dominican Order in Scotland* (Edinburgh
     1981), 'The Return of the Friars'.
6.   Harman Grisewood in conversation with the author on 21 August 1993.
7.   H. Grisewood, *One Thing at a Time. An Autobiography* (London:
     Hutchinson, 1968), p. 80.
8.   I hope the use made here of archival (and other) materials exemplifies
     the philosophy of archiveship offered by another Dominican archivist
     when she wrote: 'A rich memory introduces personalities and events
     which help build up a sense of identity and self-worth, and becomes a
     moment of encouragement and enlightenment and of love for a heritage
     rightly laid claim to.' Thus D. Horgan, O.P., 'In Our Keeping:
     Archives of the Congregation of Irish Dominican Sisters, Cabra',
     Catholic Archives, 14 (1974), pp. 60–64.

1

The English Dominican background

On Holy Cross Day (14 September 1898), a seventeen-year-old Stoneyhurst boy, the son of an Indian Army officer, began his pre-noviciate retreat and the launching (though he did not know it yet) of a new phase in the history of the English Dominican Province. Cyril Bede Jarrett by his four successive provincialates (1916–1932) formed the Province which the seven men to be described in this book entered. Fr Allan White, in an extended essay on Jarrett's impact, defined his policy as prior provincial in terms of four main aims:

> an increased involvement in the intellectual and academic centres of the country, the active engagement of the Province in the mission-ary work of the Church in the territories which formed part of the British Empire, the development of the preaching apostolate as exemplified in the establishment of the review *Blackfriars*, and the return of the Dominicans to Scotland.[1]

If, as Fr Allan reports, all these aims were realised, this implies what is vulgarly termed a 'power base', and this he identifies as a late nine-teenth century

> group of young men who wished to change [the Province's] ethos from that of a community of cultivated antiquarian curés, to that of a body of highly-educated, professional intellectuals in the forefront of theological research; amongst these was numbered Father Bede Jarrett.[2]

But this adjudication perhaps overestimates the degree to which pure theology – which must mean, first and foremost, for Catholicism, dogmatic or systematic theology – predominated in Jarrett's forward thinking. It is possible to suppose, alternatively, that his own range of writing, sustained if with difficulty, throughout his terms of office, must furnish a key to his ideal. There we find, in the first place, a series of forays into mediaeval social and intellectual history, and biography – *S. Antonino and Mediaeval Economics; Social Theories of the Middle Ages; Medieval Socialism; The Emperor Charles IV* (Luxemburg); a life of the late nineteenth-century Italian professor of Roman-Byzantine law Contardo Ferrini, beatified by Pope Pius XII in 1947;[3] next, there are the collections of homilies and ascetic conferences, and rounding it all off the *Dominicana*: his life of Saint Dominic, his annotated version of the *Lives of the Brethren*, a Dominican competitor to the Franciscan *Fioretti*, and his study of the English Dominican Province of the Middle Ages.[4] Given, too, that Jarrett's single most specific hope for the development of the Oxford Studium – the proposed chair of canon law – was itself ordered to the goal of fruitful exchange between the sacred sciences and the profane (like the late Walter Ullmann, he thought the canonical sources would throw light on the development of jurisprudential and political thought at large), it does not seem excessive to claim that his vision of English Dominican intellectual life of the future was not confined to philosophy and theology *stricto sensu* – though indeed it is impossible to imagine anyone so rooted in the Dominican tradition not requiring a thoroughly theological intelligence to be at work at all times.[5]

At any rate, the fruiting of the plants he tended, as this book will describe that, involved the saying of good, true and beautiful things about the whole range of culture. It was deeply informed, to be sure, by the revelation of which the Catholic Church considers her doctrine to be the transcription, and it gave a special value to the services afforded that revelation and doctrine by Thomism. It frequently turned to contemplate the life-giving *dogmata* of the Church in and for themselves. But its more characteristic approach was to ransack the treasure house of the Catholic tradition of past and present to illuminate the varied modes in which the Christian spirit can put itself forth in mentefacts and artefacts that are in different respects both the materials and the signs of God's Kingdom.

Their houses

In the period covered by this study, the noviciate – or year of initiation into the Order's way of life and tradition – took place, with a brief war-time intermission, at *Woodchester*, set as that priory was in an area of outstanding natural beauty in the Cotswold countryside. The offer by William Leigh in 1850 of Woodchester Park to provide for the Dominicans a church worthy of their Order constituted a turning-point in the fortunes of the Province.[6] The church had been built speedily, but in no slapdash way. Its architect was Charles

Hansom, younger of two brothers counted as among the finest Neo-Gothic designers in Britain. The first friars – Fr Augustine Procter and Br Lewis Weldon – arrived at St Mary's Hill, the residence set apart for them while the monastery was a-building, on 8 October 1850. Hansom was entrusted with the construction of the priory, but since it was the first purpose-built, fully-fledged priorial establishment to be created by the Dominicans in England since the Reformation, the plans were submitted for approval to the Master of the Order, Alexandre-Vincent Jandel, who 'was anxious that the monastic disposition of the building should conform to the demands of Dominican observance'.[7] It was finished in 1853, and raised to the canonical status of priory the following year, with the newly retired provincial, Fr Dominic Aylward – the choice of Jandel – as its first prior. Young men entering at Woodchester in the years between the First and Second World Wars would be conscious of a certain *éclat*. Robert Hugh Benson, son of archbishop Edward Benson of Canterbury, and author of novels both neo-Tudor and necromantic, chose to become a Catholic there. The contrasting figure of Cardinal Francis Bourne of Westminster, stolid but astute, was attracted, and even clothed in the habit, but did not persevere. Nor were the laity less striking. J. M. Capes, founder of the Catholic journal *The Rambler* which Newman had taken over with consequences trying to himself, had been a parishioner. So had Matthew Bridges, the hymn-writer, best known for his theologically and verbally magnificent paean to Christ: 'Crown Him with Many Crowns'. And in 1934, soon after our period opens, Woodchester's cemetery would receive the body of the most distinguished friar of the generations immediately preceding and following the Great War, Bede Jarrett, symbol of the Dominican renaissance.

What would the novices have studied? The edition of the *Constitutions* published in Rome in 1925 under the seal of the Dutch Master-General Louis Theissling, declares that novices are to be taught 'the history of our Order, especially the lives of our saints, as well as the spiritual writers of our school. They are to become practised in the chant and the ceremonies, and the more suitable ones at playing the organ.'[8] As well as studying the divine Office (the Liturgy of the Hours, according to the distinctive liturgical books of the Order of Preachers, a variant on the Roman rite), they were to ponder Scripture, and, more especially, to study and memorise the Pauline epistles: an early source records how St Dominic always carried the letters of the apostle of the Gentiles on his person. There were of course a hundred and one domestic duties to carry out in the running, without employed help, of a substantial priory with its own gardens. But, as the summary in the *Constitutions* suggests, the insertion into the Order's tradition was an undertaking of a predominantly spiritual and liturgical character.[9] As such it fitted in well with the hopes of William Leigh for making Woodchester Park a radiation point for Catholicism. Fr Edwin Essex wrote in his guide to Woodchester:

> Night and day the divine office was recited in the choir of the church; the full ceremonial of the liturgy was carried out in the sanctuary. This public and corporate worship, which has always been an essential part of the Dominican tradition, was the realisation of what the founder had in mind; the parish he had foreseen from the beginning was to enjoy the benefit of everything the Catholic Church had to offer, a spiritual ministry that nothing must ever be allowed to limit or hinder.[10]

The church was dedicated to the Annunciation of the Blessed Virgin Mary. At the centenary celebrations of the arrival of the Dominicans in Woodchester, Fr Hilary Carpenter, then Provincial, found this apposite:

> It was significantly dedicated to Our Lady of the Annunciation by men who realised to the full the implication of her consent (in the name of all mankind) to play her part in bringing the Incarnate Truth of God into the world of men. It has been the mother through whom a revitalised Province of the Dominican Order came into being and from whom have been born those great English Dominicans whose names have been household words.[11]

As in several Dominican houses flourishing during the years between the two World Wars (Oxford, Edinburgh, Cambridge) the building benefited from the stonemason's skill of Fr Aelred Whitacre whose work has the linearity of Gill's but not the crispness. Over the arch of the south porch is Whitacre's bas-relief of that Annunciation mystery – though here he was asked to copy the mid-Victorian original which had crumbled away.

The Woodchester novice, duly professed, would then proceed to the 'house of studies' (later, 'house of philosophy'): *Hawkesyard* Priory, near Lichfield, in Staffordshire. 'Hawkesyard Park' appears as a manor of the Rugeleys or Roughesleys in the reign of Henry III. The historic house visible today, however, belongs with that spate of gracious domestic construction by minor county families characteristic of the middle decades of the eighteenth century. Acquired by the Spodes, the celebrated Potteries porcelain-manufacturers, the brick mansion would be clothed in stone and laid out with gardens once famous. In 1885 the last Josiah Spode was received into the Catholic Church, together with his niece Helen Gulson, at nearby Stone, where

the English Congregation of the Dominican Sisters of St Catherine of
Siena, the most important of the nineteenth-century Dominican sister-
hoods in England, had its mother house. They became aware of the
friars while attending a parish mission at the chapel on their doorstep
in Rugeley. The exemplarily tonsured neo-mediaeval figure of Fr Pius
Cavanagh, from Holy Cross, Leicester, can hardly have predicted the
result of his *ferverini*. By Spode's testament, his property would pass
on his death, which happened in 1893, to his niece for the rest of her
natural life, but to the Dominicans thereafter. With that philanthropic
kenoticism of which Victorian converts were capable, she insisted on
anticipating this provision and retiring to a cottage in the garden. In
the autumn of the following year, accordingly, a trio of fathers, a
quartet of students of the Order, and a second trio of lay-brothers,
took possession. Not content with this self-denying ordinance, their
benefactress at once undertook the construction of new conventual
buildings, complete with church, in the Blakeian landscape – wood-
land framed by industrial canal and, eventually, cooling towers –
which formed the ample grounds. In 1898 the brethren transferred to
this 'designer priory', and the hall became the home of their apostolic
school. After various vicissitudes it would transmogrify into 'Spode
House', a retreat and conference centre run in close collaboration with
the Priory proper. In 1929 with the realisation of Jarrett's conventual-
academic project at Blackfriars Oxford, the studies were divided,
Hawkesyard remaining the house of philosophy but the practitioners
of the 'queen of sciences', the 'theologians', transferring to Oxford.
This would remain the division of labour in the Province until 1967.

What form did the philosophical studies at Hawkesyard take?
Conformably with the general norm of the intellectual life of the Order
in this period, the standard course commenced with logic, after which
the student embarked on 'natural philosphy', itself divided into two
main segments. Cosmology was concerned with the inanimate world;
psychology looked at animate things – and especially at the nature of
the human being. What held these two sub-divisions together was the
fact that both studied the general, abiding principles at work in man's
physical environment. Unlike contemporary natural science, whose
philosophical presuppositions are largely positivist, and which stops
short, then, with the data of observation and experiment, these disciplines stressed the need to interpret material reality in terms of the
common principles of thought: the elucidation of reality as such, the
realm of being. Continuing up the ladder of such neo-scholastic learning, the student friar then investigated epistemology – the varieties, and
validity, of knowledge. Thus equipped, he could tackle general metaphysics, which looked at the content, property and consequences of

reality at large. The crown of philosophy was natural theology, which looked into the existence and nature of the Cause of being – both first and last, Alpha and Omega. Lastly, he would descend from these empyrean heights to consider, in the light of God as the last end of man, his 'beatitude', the character of human activity as a means to that fulfilment in moral philosophy. All this took place within a highly structured conventual round from the first chanting of divine office in church at 5.30 a.m. through to 'lights out' at 9.45 p.m. Particular importance was given by the Dominicans to the solemnised form of Compline, with its daily procession down the church to the image of Mother and Child, the friars singing the *Salve Regina*.

The decline of vocations to the Order in England after the Second Vatican Council led to the decision in 1967 to reunite the studies – but this time at Oxford. Shorn of its conventual and liturgical glory, Hawkesyard-Spode proved in time unable to compete with the better appointed conference centres which various Catholic orders or organisations had developed elsewhere. In 1983 the decision was taken to sell the Spode-Gulson bequest. In an elegiac commemoration one of its most devoted lay supporters, the Dominican tertiary Professor Donald Nicholl remembered Spode as an exciting 'forum' for 'worship, study, debate, and, indeed, for virtually all that makes human life together worth-while'.[12] It was an omnium-gatherum for cardinals, calligraphers, Communists. Though the persons were always welcome, the eclecticism was sometimes suffered rather than chosen – for a conference centre must fill its available space. Such misgivings, combined with a certain dislike for rural living, compounded the financial factors already mentioned. Those with *pietas* were naturally embarrassed, however, when they recalled Spode's own words to the Dominican Provincial who received his bequest, that the 'lamp before the Blessed Sacrament' should never be extinguished.

Only the library was in good part preserved, through a judicious redistribution of its contents to the other houses. Certain liturgical adjuncts and *objets d'art* were also retained. The magnificent stone reredos, showing a 'tree of Jesse' blossoming in Dominican and English saints; the Father Smith organ built for Mr Spode, though its splendid case was originally at Eton; the fine glass, showing the Mother of God, with the saints of the Order, and the mysteries of the Rosary; the Ditchling Stations of the Cross (by Joseph Cribb), and the bodies of numerous brethren – as well as of Josiah Spode and Helen Gulson – were left behind.

The *Oxford* priory, to which after philosophical studies the young friar would proceed for theology proper, maintained a similar life-style to Hawkesyard (though without the possibility of such rural pursuits for the students as bee-keeping and the making of home-made preserves). The Oxford Blackfriars remains as the only survivor of the triumvirate of houses involved in the process of Dominican formation in this period. From the earliest years of his Dominican life Bede Jarrett had dreamed of a return to Oxford for the friars: a dream which became an informed aspiration with his matriculation in the University (through the Benedictine 'Hunter Blair's Hall', now St Benet's Hall) in 1904. Elected provincial in 1916 he had a unique opportunity vouchsafed to few: to make a dream come true. On 15 August 1921 – exactly seven hundred years after the arrival in Oxford of the first Dominicans under Gilbert of Fresney, both first prior of Oxford and first Provincial of England, the foundation stone of the new foundation was laid by Cardinal Bourne in the presence of the Downside historian-become-cardinal, Dom Aidan Gasquet, and 'many other notables'.[13] In 1929 the house became a full priory and its church, dedicated to the Holy Spirit, was duly consecrated. Its architecture, by Doran Webb, has been described as a 'Renaissance cum Gothic neighbour to the more fully Gothic Anglo-Catholic stronghold of Pusey House'. The wide nave and choir, flanked on the right by a threesome of tiny chapels was 'unadventurously late Perpendicular'. Yet in the words of the historian of post-Reformation Catholic church-building:

> One is surprised, in these days of more daring modernities, to know of the stir which Oxford's Blackfriars originally caused. But its simple furnishings, and its lack of coloured windows, were in their time an austerity of a primitive Cistercian stamp.[14]

Some of the elements of the common culture to be studied in this book are symbolised in such devotional objects as were placed therein: a figure of St Dominic by Eric Gill (and Stations of the Cross by Aelred Whitacre); a mediaeval Nottingham alabaster of the Annunciation; a seventeenth-century statue of St Thomas, portrayed with the insignia of a knight of the golden fleece – a gift to Jarrett from the Spanish king Alfonso XIII. (The head of the figure was irreparably damaged by vandals in the 1970s, and the entire statue consequently, removed from public view.) The choir-stalls, always too numerous for the number of residents, indicated the ambition to house eventually a population equal to the mediaeval priory in its prime (some ninety or so). A second quadrangle, intended to provide more cells as well as certain other common offices (distinctive common rooms for student-friars and lay-brothers, an infirmary with its own chapel, and so forth) remained unbuilt, for the money was never forthcoming, though a slender tower of study bedrooms, complete with gargoyle-like faces of prior and provincial, was added in the 1950s.

In this setting, then, the Dominican ordinand set about his business of acquiring the 'sacred sciences'. The subjects to be covered were dictated by the necessities of ordination training, and hence resembled closely those found in the seminaries and elsewhere. The difference lay in the habitual recourse of both teachers and students to the original texts of St Thomas, both in dogma and in moral theology. The direct contact with the world of high mediaeval theology in its most classical spokesman constituted an important expansion of intellectual sensibility; the peculiar excellences of Thomas's theological doctrine (not least his virtue-centred approach to ethics) were their own reward, and as regards the literary genre of the *Summa Theologiae* (the chief text in use) there are those who 'find themselves anachronistically attracted to the old layout, objections, *sed contra*, response, replies, the spaces in between providing the silence for reflection and anticipation'.[15]

Bede Jarrett was extremely clear-minded about what he wished the Oxford studium to be. *Pace* the fears of the supporters of Hawkesyard, it was by no means intended as a one-way traffic, where only the Dominicans would learn. Certainly he stressed that the student religious were to attend university lectures, and read for university degrees, the more necessary as 'there will be critical need in England in these following years for the best educated clergy'. But he was far from counselling such students to believe all they heard.

> We believe that in such surroundings the clerical studies will take on a new freshness, for one of the things which the young clerical students finds it difficult to realize is that his lectures and text books are ever likely to be of any use to him. Arius and Nestorius and even Luther seem so dead, that he finds it unreal to bother further with their principles or heretical systems. At Oxford he will soon see that the new modern thinkers are most often merely the old prophets reborn.

At the same time, the studium was to give to the university.

> We hope to be able to establish in the new priory after the fashion of the medieval Dominicans, a public course of scholastic philosophy and theology ... [to which elsewhere he added a proposal for a faculty of canon law] and to afford a place where also the best available Catholic talent of the country, Benedictine, Jesuit, Secular and lay, might give special courses on religion, history, natural science, and economics.

(In fact this last aspect – the notion of an integrated Catholic institute, more or less modelled on the *Instituts Catholiques* of France – was never realised, though in the early 1990s a lay initiative along these lines had on its committee the long-serving, but recently retired, Regent of Blackfriars, Fr Simon Tugwell.)[16] Lastly, Jarrett held it to be

> probable that a religious Order in Oxford, wearing the habit, and able to carry out in choir the monastic observances and chant, would be able to influence happily even the non-Catholic under-graduate in such a university, where still lingers so much fragrance of her Catholic past.[17]

On 1 January 1994, Blackfriars ceased to be merely 'an institution not being part of the University but having associations with it' (a clumsy formula, but the official one), and became a permanent private hall, based within, but not coterminous with the priory – which maintains its own identity and autonomy as a house of the Order. The change gave Blackfriars, *qua* hall, significant powers: to matriculate students on a very generous (and for graduate degrees, unlimited) basis; to present any lector, at the instigation of the Regent, for appointment to any faculty of the university; to advertise its academic events on university lists, and engage the university in promoting the lectures of Blackfriars' own visiting teachers.[18] It was a triumphant conclusion to sixty years of effort (and sometimes vicissitude) since Jarrett's death.

After ordination, the *coetus lectorum*, or gathering of the professors at Oxford, would determine whether a particular newly-fledged priest should be enrolled as a 'formal student', in order to continue more specialist studies within the Order with a view to professing himself – or go forth into one of the numerous 'non-academic' works of the Province, as the prior provincial might determine in the light of the needs of houses and missions at home and abroad. As a result of inheritance from the penal period and the new foundations of both the Victorian and the Edwardian – Jarrett – expansions, a considerable variety was to hand.

Among the communities that lay outside the process of formation, the oldest foundations were the parish houses of Hinckley, Leicester, London, Newcastle and Pendleton (Salford), of which the first had been deemed a priory (a house sufficient in size to support the choir office and to elect its own superior) only by a canonical fiction of the early nineteenth century. The towns of Hinckley and Leicester had been served by English Dominicans since 1734, when Fr John Clarkson was sent to Aston Flamville, the home of the Turville family, as chaplain.

The little village of Aston Flamville may be called the cradle of the renascence of the Dominican English Province where, from a single grain, like a grain of mustard seed, the present English Province of the Dominican Order has grown to a great tree.

So wrote the chronicler of *Hinckley St Peters* at the time of the building of its new (and quite hideous) church in 1958.[19] In 1765 the indefatigable Fr Thomas Norton bought a house and land there and opened the first chapel. There in 1846 the full habit was resumed for the first time in post-Reformation England, replacing the black leggings and jacket, closed at the neck by a white kerchief, of the recusant clergyman. But with the loss of its novices to Woodchester in 1850, and its 'apostolic school' to Hawkesyard in 1898, the house's subsequent life was reduced to that of a Dominican parish *simpliciter*, until the ending of the Order connection with its transfer to the secular clergy of the diocese of Nottingham in 1989.

The *Leicester* mission, served from Hinckley as it originally was, began its burgeoning with the construction of a small chapel by Fr Francis Xavier Chappell in 1800. In 1815 his health collapsed, and he retired to the English Dominicans' Continental redoubt at Bornhem, in Flanders (see Appendix 1, pp. 411–413) whence had come the Fleming Fr Benedict Caestryck, who now succeeded him as pastor, to good effect. A substantial church, dedicated, like Bornhem, to the Holy Cross, with a relic thereof brought from across the water, opened in 1819. The elevation of the house into a priory in 1882 ushered in something of a liturgical and evangelical *âge doré*. In the early years of the new century its music was noted for its excellence, and when the era of operatic Masses gave way to that of the less exigent revived plainchant, the accent shifted to a more argumentative form of apostolic outreach through an exceptionally thriving 'Catholic Evidence Guild', whose members benefited from the expertise of the best theologian of the pre-Jarrett period, Fr Vincent McNabb, prior at Leicester from 1908 to 1914. In 1931 a new choir, Lady chapel and transepts were built for the church; a nave of less worthy materials was added later.[20] Holy Cross continued, and continues, to serve as the central parish church of the city of Leicester, gradually attaching to itself the chaplaincies of, first, the University of Leicester, and then its *frère cadet*, the De Montfort University. The inexorable progress of university and polytechnic expansion, with the polytechnics in time re-formed (or at least re-named) as universities as the proportion of the British population in receipt of higher education multiplied, thus enabled a parochial commitment typical of the nineteenth-century situation of English Dominicanism to turn by degrees into a recognition of the primacy of preaching and teaching more compatible with the origins of the Order. The same process, but without renunciation of the parochial element, was visible elsewhere.

In *London*, Fr Augustine Procter had access, as Provincial, to the ear of Cardinal Nicholas Wiseman of Westminster who in 1861 formally invited the Dominicans to make a conventual foundation in the metropolis. Based on the former mission of Kentish Town, its parochial catchment extended beyond this settlement of the working (or unemployed) poor, up the tree-lined walk of Haverstock Hill towards impeccably bourgeois Hampstead, thus helping to fulfil Wiseman's dream that London, like Rome, might have a house of prayer as sentinel on each of its hills. Two years later Jandel, as Master of the Order, laid the foundation-stone in Wiseman's presence of a church eventually to be named for St Dominic but patterned on the fifteen mysteries of the Rosary, as a necklace of side-chapels, each dedicated to a Rosary mystery, framed sanctuary and nave.[21] The church actually built, unlike that whose foundation stone was laid, could be called a family undertaking: its architect, Charles Buckler, was brother to no less than three English Dominicans – Reginald, Edmund, Albert. A hall (later called the 'Aquinas Centre') and priory were finished first, the latter retrenched in the later 1980s to pay for its own renovation. Equipped with a Willis organ, St Dominic's was said to have been one of only four or five Catholic churches whose music Edward Elgar could tolerate. The parish itself was a social conglomerate, with the labouring poor as its largest element, though the acquisition of Hampstead Heath by the Metropolitan Board of Works in 1872 and the 1889 incorporation into that great park-land of Parliament Hill, set bounds to the development of urban sprawl.

Not, however, that pastoral and sacramental outreach totally dominated the lives of the friars. The library was conceived as a great ecclesiastical collection for the London of the future. On its basis, Fr Laurence Shapcote produced in the years 1911 to 1925 the first complete English translation of the *Summa Theologiae* of St Thomas, still used by many. The consecration of the priory church by Bourne in 1923, during Jarrett's lengthy reign as Provincial, followed on an important evolution at St Dominic's: the inauguration, by McNabb, with Jarrett's help, of London University Extension Lectures in the Aquinas Hall. Chiefly devoted to Scripture, they were quite possibly the first public Catholic theological lectures in England since the Reformation. In the later 1920s the priory was irregularly attended by a number of the Catholic *literati* of the period such as Maurice Baring, Hilaire Belloc and G. K. Chesterton.

In the North-west was *Pendleton* – St Sebastian's priory set amidst the Mancunian poor by the aesthete-psychologist André Sebastian Raffalovich in 1901, as an act of thanksgiving for his conversion.[22] Despite this exotic patronage (Raffalovich wrote what has some claim to be the first scholarly study of homosexuality – in French),[23] Pendleton was treated as something of a Cinderella. The discovery of dry rot in the woodwork enabled the church to be demolished and the conventual buildings patched up for other uses in the 1960s.

Similar in social setting but more fortunate in survival, across the Pennines lay *Newcastle*. Although recusant Dominicans had laboured in Northumberland at two adjacent missions, Hexham and Stonecroft, these were swept away by the severe retrenchment of the opening decades of the nineteenth century. When expansion was possible again after the second spring at Woodchester, the preachers arrived at Newcastle virtually by chance when a secular priest of the diocese of Hexham and Newcastle, the Revd Rodolph Suffield, took the habit of the Order in 1860. Conscious that the Dominicans wished to expand their apostolate, Suffield's bishop loaned them his parish of St Andrew's until they could create one of their own. Thanks to the zeal of Fr Antoninus Williams, an early novice at Woodchester, a church dedicated to St Dominic was opened in 1873, with archbishop Manning preaching on the Dominican devotion to dogma and Haydn's 'Imperial' Mass initiating another splendid choral tradition.[24] In 1882 the house was erected as a priory, though the conventual buildings, of a modest description as befitted such a poor area, were not finished until 1937. Suffield himself ended up as a Unitarian, evidence that the Province was by no means insulated against the chilling effects of theological and philosophical debate in late Victorian England. The historian of the parish enters a remark which could also be made, no doubt, of the other urban parish priories, Leicester, Pendleton, London, where not all was archiepiscopal divinity and the glories of the Viennese school:

> In effect [the Dominicans] concentrated on providing people with the comforts of religion, with an elementary education that would include religion, and a centre that would bring together Catholics in the neighbourhood – and not just a religious centre but one with dances, plays and various associations binding the community together.[25]

Laxton Priory in Northamptonshire was the last of the English houses to be created before our period opens: but it could also claim to be, in another sense, the most venerable, since as the site of the English Dominican school its pedigree went back to the middle years of the seventeenth century. To Jarrett, overseeing the purchase of the late eighteenth-century Laxton Hall in February 1924, and the transfer there of the Hawkesyard school, the new setting maximised the advantages of a close liaison of school and religious community, but minimised the disadvantages. That is, the presence of schoolboys would not disturb the even tenor of conventual life in a formal priory like Hawkesyard (where one father, moreover, doubled up as both head of the house of studies and headmaster). Yet the new school would still be within a priory setting, albeit a less ambitious one, and he proposed that boys and masters alike would sing Dominican Compline at the close of each day.[26] To those who objected that schoolmastering was no more a traditional Dominican apostolate than the running of parishes, the provincial had, in each case, some historical precedents to cite, albeit – it must be admitted – rather insubstantial ones. In point of fact, both were 'sports' thrown up by the peculiar history of the recusant community – although in the twentieth century, other provinces would acquire parishes at least, for reasons both good and indifferent. In the case of the school, however – or *schools*, for it eventually boasted a 'prep school' of its own – the 'traditionalist' argument eventually prevailed, bolstered by the socialistic hostility of the 1960s to independent education.

The only English house to be founded after the death of Jarrett, but fully within our period, was Blackfriars St Michael's, Cambridge, still happily surviving. Its origins were exceptional, for it was in a way a lay foundation. Two distinguished Tertiary members of the Order, Professor Edward Bullough and his wife Enrichetta, daughter of the celebrated Italian *tragédienne*, Eleonora Duse, designed and built the property with a view to its becoming a Dominican house on their deaths. When, after the First World War, Mrs Bullough returned to the practice of Catholicism, through the good offices of Vincent McNabb, she paved the way for the entry into the Church of her husband – hitherto a non-enthusiast for Christianity in the Masonic fashion – in 1923. Since other Dominicans had also been involved in the dual conversion (Sr Mary Monica Brooke-Milne of the Sisters at Stone, Staffordshire for Enrichetta, Bede Jarrett for Edward), they found the Order's lay oblateship a natural outlet for their new affections – the more readily as the renascent Thomism of the French Dominicans gave Bullough the intellectual framework he had been seeking.[27] Dr Elisabeth Stopp of Caius', Cambridge, has explained the symbolism, at once topographical and iconological, given architectural expression in the future priory.

In Bullough's thinking, St Michael's, situated at the top of the only hill that Cambridge boasts and not far from the Castle Mound, remnant of an ancient stronghold on the Via Devana, was to be the house integrating the Dominicans geographically, intellectually and spiritually, with the University of Cambridge. The house was dedicated to Michael the Archangel, not only because he traditionally has shrines on hill-tops but because he also has strong Italian associations, with Castel Sant' Angelo in Rome and Monte Gargano in the south. He was, too, and still is now, victorious in the great apocalyptic war in heaven and stood for the victory of truth – *veritas*, the Dominican motto – over evil and error. Characteristically enough, the Bulloughs provided a visual aid for this devotion in the shape of a relief sculpture of the archangel on the back wall of the fireplace in the library-sittingroom; it was exciting to gaze into the flames of a log fire on winter evenings and watch the winged figure of St Michael brandishing his spear to thrust down to a fiery hell Satan and all his wicked spirits.[22]

To this building would be added, after the Second World War, 'Howfield', the boyhood home of Archbishop Michael Ramsey of Canterbury. Described in less than flattering terms in a recent biography of the theologian-primate, its English understatement was the perfect complement to the Mediterranean gesticulation next door.[23] The two villas were joined by a piece of contemporary architecture during Fr Thomas Gilby's priorship in the early 1960s. Cambridge remained, however, a house in search of a role. The best that could be found for it was *domus scriptorum*, a 'house of writers'. The contemplative calm of its natural setting in a large garden *was* conducive to writing; yet writers cannot be produced to order, on a superior's command.

Evidently, between the strict observance of Woodchester, participation, however spectatorial, in a knees-up in the parish hall at Newcastle, the effort to control a school-room at Laxton, and commenting cantos of Dante for the University Press at Cambridge, certain significant disparities might be espied. And this brings us to the last section of our opening chapter, the themes of the Province's internal debate.

Their disputed questions

The Province has consisted, since its early Victorian revival, of a remarkably disparate collection of communities and individuals, at its best a freedom to be uniquely oneself in the chastened sense suggested by 'Pope Hadrian VII' in Frederick Rolfe's novel: 'Cultivate and help to cultivate individuality, at your own expense if possible, but never at the expense of your brother.'[24] Naturally, such an attitude also has its disadvantages where common life and collaborative enterprise are concerned. But the variety does not mean that all generalisation is impossible. In the broad movement of the Province's history, a wave of missioners has been succeeded by one of pastors-in-community, only to give way to a third roller of intellectuals and *spirituels*. The qualification needs noting, however, that neither of the previous waves should be taken fully to have spent itself, for lone friars still exist, as do *parochus* and curates in the parish priories, just as, conversely, the more recent emphasis on the intellectual life and spirituality is anticipated in various impressive figures of the pre-Jarrett Province. Another way in which to approach the constants in the modern history of the English Dominicans would be *via* the themes they took as the subject-matter of their 'disputed questions', themes that recur in different persons, different periods.

One, for instance, would be a debate about the relative merits of an ideal of observance (relevant to such matters as the quantity and quality of liturgical celebration, the role of silence, the wearing of the habit and various other monastic practices). For on the one hand there were those English Dominicans who wanted, in the Victorian period and the early decades of this century, what they termed 'strict' or 'primitive' observance (in the spirit, always, and according to the letter, often, of the *Primitive Constitutions*). The background was the tension caused in the Order at large by the disparity of its two revival ideals – that of its long-serving Master, Alexandre-Vincent Jandel, and that of its best-known figure, the refounder of the Province of France, and one time superior of Jandel, Henri-Dominique Lacordaire.[25] The disagreement, which came to a symbolic head over the issue of the night Office, turned on the question, Should the apostolate determine what level of ascetic and liturgical life is appropriate for a friar, or, should the ascetic and liturgical life of a friar form him for whatever apostolate he will be called to?[26] On such an apparent nuance, the future development of an ancient Order depended.

In the English Province, the proposal for a reformed house, operating on a strict interpretation of the Jandel *Constitutions*, was first aired in the early 1870s – following on the death of a much-loved provincial, Dominic Aylward, a Lacordairean. It had the support of two of the Province's major figures in that early period of its renaissance – one a writer, Bertrand Wilberforce (grandson of the great Evangelical opponent of the Slave Trade in the British Empire),[27] and the other, Albert Buckler, a 'professional' superior, and formulator of the Province's tradition of giving 'missions' (a form of regular parish renewal), that apostolic staple of the English Victorian Catholic revival and beyond.[28] Such initiatives received – curiously – no encouragement from Rome, however, and encountered stiff resistance in England. Although a trickle of friars tried their vocations in the highly Jandelian Province of Lyons (or with the Carthusians at Parkminster, a very different outcome for the contemplative impulse), and the idea remained alive throughout the 1920s and 30s, the coming of the Second World War (and wholly other preoccupations) found it no further advanced. In a later phase of the same debate, in the period following the Second Vatican Council, the term 'classical' observance might be preferred, so as to avoid connotations of rigorism or deliberate archaism. By that time, the whole discussion had moved 'leftwards', for to those who considered emphasis on the forms of conventual observance potentially inhibiting of the apostolate were added – in a specifically late twentieth-century perspective – others who found such 'structures' inimical to the spontaneity of persons and groups.[29] In a not very numerous Province, the traditional way in the Order of resolving this tension between the contemplative-monastic and apostolic-pastoral dimensions of the life – namely, by a combination of general observance with particular dispensations – was rarely practical. It presupposed communities of much larger size.

A second theme that crops up in scattered places would turn on the interpretation of that phrase 'apostolic-pastoral' itself. Historically, the Order's intended apostolate was a mission to teach Catholic doctrine. That need not be construed in terms consistently high-brow, for doctrine can be communicated, defended and explored at a variety of levels. Nor need it exclude a pastoral aspect: doctrine when applied became spirituality, and the Dominicans could boast a decent number of spiritual masters (and mistresses) among their saints and *beati*, as well as the writers of their school. Moreover, the preaching of the Word is meant to issue in a continuing conversion, and so the sacrament of Penance – hearing confessions, and the direction of penitents, had traditionally been included in the Order's apostolic self-definition. And what was this if not a pastoral task? The question remained, however, whether a Dominican was justified in devoting himself more or less full-time to a pastoral – and above all, a *parochial* – ministry in the Church.

The English Dominican parishes had grown out of the missions of the penal period; they were (depending on taste) a cruel or happy necessity of the reconstitution of English Catholicism on a normal canonical basis in the mid-Victorian era. But were they opportunities for, or obstacles to, the main mission, the presentation of Catholicism as a credible and viable religion to the minds and hearts of Englishmen (and women)? Bede Jarrett argued for their retention:

It was only with the greatest reluctance that the Religious undertook the business of parochial organization; yet though in some ways it may have proved a bar to the perfect observance of the full cloistral exercises, in other ways it has done good to all parties concerned. It has made seculars and Religious better acquainted with each other; and it has enabled the Religious to come into close relations with the working population and prevented them from becoming too remote from the conditions of daily life; not is it the least of the advantages of this arrangement that the faithful have an intimate knowledge of the Religious life.[30]

To friars worried about the untraditional nature of such an apostolate he could only cite the example of the thirteenth-century parish of Santa Maria sopra Minerva, in Rome, seat of the Masters of the Order from the 1380s to 1936 (and rather vaguer Polish precedents), suggest that parochial demand might reinforce conventual asceticism in something of the way long journeys on foot did in the Middle Ages, and appeal to the *de facto* conditions, from 1926 onwards, of the Dominican laws.[31]

The third theme is the most relevant to this study. Whatever the ideal character of the conventual observance which should distinguish communities of Preachers, and however much or little their preaching should issue in direct pastoral care of those who heard (or read) them, no one could disagree with the centrality of preaching – the mission to teach the faith – as such. An Order of Preachers without preaching would obviously be Hamlet without the Prince of Denmark. But what was to be the content – the substance – of this preaching? And if the answer to that were fairly evident – the Catholic faith – the question still arose of the conceptuality in which that faith was to be expressed, the apologetic strategies whereby it was defended, the nature of the studies which should prepare its communicators for their task, in a word the intellectual culture, from which, as out of a soil more or less nutritious, the activity of preaching could grow. The great theological faculties of England were either Anglican (Oxford, Cambridge, Durham) or Anglican and Nonconformist (London). The ancient Universities (Oxford and Cambridge) were also, in the opening decades of this century, the matrices of English philosophical life at its most sophisticated. They could provide a training in philosophical, linguistic, textual and historical tools hardly available elsewhere in the English portion of this island. But had the Dominicans suffered centuries of exile and the pinched existence of their nineteenth-century struggle for survival in order to be spared to do worship in the academic temples of the Protestant establishment? Evelyn Waugh, in explaining the high profile achieved by ecclesiastical affairs in the years immediately before the First World War, wrote:

> The Church of England was the religion of a governing class which then ruled a great part of the world. Her roots spread deep and wide in the established order, holding it together and drawing strength from it. Her fortunes were the concern of statesmen and journalists. The two older universities, despite all the secularism of the late nineteenth century, were still centres of theological energy.[32]

But had not the English Dominicans generous access, both in Thomism and in the native Catholic writers of the Edwardian period, to alternative springs of wisdom? For several decades, to be a Catholic intellectual in England meant being, in some respect, a disciple of Chesterton and Belloc.[33] The latter spoke

> with the weight of an age-old international order and the true Englishness of the past against the parochialism of British Protestantism and modern secularism ... They did at least present Catholic Christianity as a critique of and confrontation with the present order in Britain.[34]

That comment, whose terminology betrays the influence of the movements of *contestation* of the 1960s and later, is too negative in its concluding judgment. Rather, Belloc and Chesterton created a counter-pose to humanitarian positivism by illuminating the real nature of Christian civilization and exhibiting to reasonable opinion the conditions on which alone it could survive. Married to Thomism, both philosophical and theological, and benefiting from the latter's intellectual and ecclesial high standing,[35] could they not be midwives to the birth of a powerful 'local' theology that was also self-consciously linked to the *Catholica*, the universal Church beyond even the British Empire's bounds? The lector primarius at Hawkesyard wrote to the youthful Fr Kenelm Foster in 1938:

> The really intelligent are busy restoring the guilds, re-establishing the institution of property, recovering responsibility and personal fulfilment in craftsmanship, recalling the rational condemnation of usury and reviving the peasantries. The Leisure State is an offence to the nature and dignity of man, in whom there is freedom and responsibility, whose work should be personal, contemplative *praise*; perfected in adoration and fulfilment of the divine will.[36]

The question whether the house of studies should be located in the depths of rural Staffordshire (but with forays for the brightest students to Louvain) or relocated amid the urban academe of Oxford awoke these issues to life. A significant minority agitated to reverse the decision to make Oxford the chief house of studies until the Second World War. Led by such lectors as Austin Barker and Reginald Ginns, they lobbied Rome in the person of Master-General Stanislas Martin Gillet, who, after his visitation of the Province in 1932, indicated his acceptance of their viewpoint. Only the delay caused by the need to extend student accommodation at Hawkesyard, and to find some continuing rationale for Blackfriars Oxford which would justify the all-too-recent generosity of its benefactors, provided a space in which alternative counsels could prevail.[37] Michael Coren's description of Chesterton's death-bed goes some way towards explaining the passion with which some English Dominicans worked for the reversal of the Jarrett orientation to Oxford. Its references to Chesterton's (relatively) rural retreat, to Thomism and to the metropolis, too vast and varied as the latter was to be held in the gossamer chains of an upper-class scholarly Anglicanism, are the three points that make up the triangle.

> On June 12th [1936] Monsignor Smith, the parish priest, arrived at Top Meadow to anoint Gilbert with chrism and to give communion. Gilbert was partly conscious for the rite as he had been for brief periods over the previous two days. Father Vincent McNabb followed soon afterwards. He sang the Salve Regina over Gilbert, the hymn which is sung over dying Dominican priests; how appropriate for the biographer of St Thomas Aquinas, the jewel of the Dominican order. He saw Gilbert's pen lying by the side of the bed, blessed and kissed it and then returned to London.[38]

It was the achievement of the seven Dominicans whose work is set forth in this book that they managed by and large to have it both ways – at any rate in the sense that, while developing a specifically, and proudly, Catholic intellectual culture they also listened to, and addressed, other voices coming from other Englands and indeed other foreign parts than those with which hitherto English friars had had to do. It was their good fortune to live at a time of both peace and creativity in the Order and in the English Catholic Church. They profited both from this assurance and from this expansion of horizons.

Notes

1. A. White, O.P., 'Father Bede Jarrett, O.P., and the Renewal of the English Dominican Province', in D. A. Bellenger (ed.), *Opening the*

Scrolls, Essays in Catholic History in Honour of Godfrey Anstruther (Bath: Downside Abbey, 1987), p. 226.

2. Ibid., p. 221.
3. Ferrini attracted Jarrett not only because of a shared interest in the development of concepts of sovereignty and law but, even more fundamentally, through the idea of marrying 'science with sanctity': thus G. Anichini, in Ferrini's year of beatification, entitled his study of him *Un astro di santità e di scienza* (Rome: 1947).
4. *Medieval Socialism* (London: The People's Books, 1913; Burns, Oates and Washbourne, 1935); *S. Antonino and Medieval Economics* (St Louis and London: Herder, 1914); *Meditations for Layfolk* (London: Catholic Truth Society, 1915); *Living Temples* (London: Burns, Oates and Washbourne, 1919); *The Religious Life* (London: Faith Press, 1920); *The English Dominicans* (London: Burns, Oates and Washbourne 1921; 1937); *Life of St Dominic* (London: Burns, Oates and Washbourne, 1924); *Lives of the Brethren* (re-edited, with notes, London: Burns, Oates and Washbourne, 1924; 1955); *Social Theories of the Middle Ages* (London: Ernest Benn, 1926); *History of Europe* (London: Sheed and Ward, 1929); *Space of Life Between* (London: Sheed and Ward, 1930); *House of Gold* (London: Sheed and Ward, 1931); *Life of Contardo Ferrini* (London: Ouseley 1933); *Our Lady of Lourdes* (London: Burns, Oates and Washbourne, 1934); *Abiding Presence of the Holy Ghost* (London: Burns, Oates and Washbourne, 1934); *The Emperor Charles IV* (London: Eyre and Spottiswoode, 1935).
5. The idea of the Chair of Canon Law was greatly boosted by the support of the then Regius Professor of Civil Law, F. de Zulueta. But just this sort of close collaboration between Blackfriars and an Anglican/agnostic University was what would lead the Fathers of the Studium to complain to Rome of the imprudent character of Jarrett's eirenicism.
6. See Appendix 1, p. 414.
7. E. Essex, O.P., *Dominican Church and Priory, Woodchester* (Gloucester; n.d., but c. 1950).
8. *Constitutiones Fratrum Sacri Ordinis Praedicatorum* (Rome: 1925), p. 31. They would be modified in 1932, then appearing with the benediction of Theissling's successor, Stanislas Martin Gillet, after whom they would become known.
9. An autobiographical impression of the Woodchester noviciate of 1931, albeit a highly personal one, can be found in *My Dear Time's Waste* (Aylesford; Saint Albert's Press, 1966) by the Carmelite, Brocard Sewell (formerly Br Eric Sewell, O.P.). pp. 54–64.
10. E. Essex, O.P., *Dominican Church*, p. 17.
11. 'Sermon Preached at the Centenary Mass' in *A Dominican Centenary. Woodchester 1850–1950* (Woodchester, Glos.: n.d. but 1950).
12. D. Nicholl, 'The Closure of Hawkesyard and Spode', in the *Birmingham Diocesan Year Book, 1988* (Birmingham: 1989), p. 113.

13. 'Fr. H. C.' (Hilary Carpenter, O.P.), *Blackfriars, Oxford* (Oxford: n.d. but 1937).

14. B. Little, *Catholic Churches since 1923. A Study of Roman Catholic Churches in England and Wales from Penal Times to the Present Decade* (London: Robert Hale 1966), p. 185.

15. D. W. Hudson, 'The Future of Thomism: an Introduction', in D. W. Hudson and D. W. Moran (eds.), *The Future of Thomism* (Notre Dame: American Maritain Association, 1992), p. 7.

16. The project of founding a (general) Catholic Faculty of Theology and Philosophy at either Oxford or Cambridge goes back to Cardinal Bourne's speech of 3 August 1923 to the National Catholic Congress in Birmingham: see E. Oldmeadow, *Francis Cardinal Bourne* (London: Burns Oates and Washbourne, 1944), pp. 199–204. The opportunity to make such of St Edmund's House, Cambridge, an appendage of the Westminster Seminary at Ware (now Allen Hall), was lost in the 1960s and 70s.

17. Cited in K. Wykeham-George, O.P., and G. Mathew, O.P., *Bede Jarrett of the Order of Preachers.* (London: Blackfriars Publications, 1952) pp. 94–5.

18. B. Davies, O.P., 'Blackfriars *qua* Permanent Private Hall', circular letter of 10 January 1994 to all houses of the Province.

19. M. Harrison, O.P., *Hinckley St Peter's: Dominican Revival* (Hinckley: 1958), p. 5.

20. A. H. Kimberlin, *The Return of Catholicism to Leicester, 1746–1946* (Hinckley, n.d. but probably 1946).

21. For a description of its architecture and furnishings see *S. Dominic's Priory 1223–1923* (Ditchling: St Dominic's Press, 1923).

22. On whom see B. Sewell (ed.), *Two Friends. John Gray and André Raffalovich. Essays Biographical and Critical, with Three Letters from André Raffalovich to J.-K. Huysmans* (Aylesford: St Albert's Press, 1963).

23. See P. W. J. Healy, '*Uranisme et Unisexualité*: A Late Victorian View of Homosexuality', *New Blackfriars* 59.693 (1978), pp. 56–64.

24. G. Anstruther, O.P., *The Dominicans of Newcastle upon Tyne* (Newcastle, n.d. but 1948).

25. A. Archer, O.P., *St Dominic's Parish, Newcastle upon Tyne, 1873–1973. A History from the Point of view of the Parishioners* (unpublished n.d.), p. 9. Fr Archer used his oral-historical researches at Newcastle to present St Dominic's as a case-study of what the liberal-bourgeois post-conciliar reform in English Catholicism had swept away in his *The Two Catholic Churches A Study in Oppression* (London: SCM Press, 1986).

26. Tugwell and Bellenger, *Letters of Bede Jarrett*, p. 86.

27. M. Oakeshott, 'Edward Bullough', *The Caian*, XLIII. 1 (1934): this obituary essay contains a detailed account of his academic production. See also E. Stopp, 'Remembering Edward Bullough, 28.iii.1880 to 17.ix.1934.' This unpublished and undated

typescript is in the possession of Blackfriars, Cambridge.

22. E. Stopp, 'The Cambridge Setting', *New Blackfriars* 67.798 (1986), p. 409.

23. M. de la Noy, *Michael Ramsey. A Portrait* (London: Collins, 1990), pp. 27–9.

24. F. Rolfe, *Hadrian VII* (London: Chatto and Windus 1958 original edn, London: 1904), p. 165.

25. B. Bonvan, *Lacordaire-Jandel. Suivi de l'édition originale et annotée du Mémoire Jandel. La restauration de l'Ordre dominicain en France après la Révolution écartelée entre deux visions du monde* (Paris: Editions du Cerf, 1989).

26. These are the terms in which the issue is posed in a contemporary biography of the first novice-master of the revived province of France: E. Cartier, *Un Religieux dominican. Le R. P. Hyacinthe Besson. Sa Vie et ses lettres* (Paris: Poussielgue, et Fils, 1865), I. pp. 389–435.

27. H. M. Capes, O.S.D., *The Life and Letters of Father Bertrand Wilberforce of the Order of Preachers* (London and Edinburgh: Sands & Company, 1912[2]).

28. A. Buckler, O.P., *St Dominic's Mission Book* (London: Burns and Oates, 1876); idem., *Some Instructions for Giving Missions* (privately printed, 1885).

29. V. Walgrave, O.P., *Essai d'autocritique d'un Ordre religieux. Les Dominicains en fin de Concile* (Brussels: Editions du Cep, no date).

30. B. Jarrett, O.P., *The Church in England in 1922* (London: Catholic Truth Society, 1922), p. 11.

31. Tugwell and Bellenger, *Letters of Bede Jarrett*, pp. 167–8.

32. E. Waugh, *The Life of Ronald Knox* (London: Chapman and Hall, 1959), p. 105.

33. J. P. Corrin, *G. K. Chesterton and Hilaire Belloc: The Battle against Modernity* (London: Ohio University Press, 1981), p. 171.

34. T. Woodman, *Faithful Fictions. The Catholic Novel in British Literature* (Milton Keynes: Open University Press 1991), p. 22.

35. The symposium published by the Province (and held significantly at Manchester) for the sixth centenary of Thomas's canonisation gives an idea of this homegrown pre-Oxford scholarship. The Dominican contributions – Aelred Whitacre on Thomas's theology, Vincent McNabb on his mysticism and Hugh Pope on his exegesis show detailed and broad familiarity with the texts of Aquinas and his Baroque commentators – but no other reading. The two secular academic contributions – T. F. Tout on Thomas's place in history, and A. E. Taylor on his ethics derive from outside Oxbridge (Manchester and St Andrews respectively) and might be regarded as 'safe' – for the first was a historian of administration and institutional development, the other a professional Platonist and orthodox Anglo-Catholic. It would not have been possible to find a believing intellectual of the first rank at Oxford in this period. However, the book's publisher *was* Oxonian: Basil Blackwell. Thus A. Whitacre, O.P. et al., *St Thomas Aquinas* (Oxford: Blackwell, 1925).

36. Letter from Austin Barker, O.P., to Kenelm Foster, O.P., of 15 December 1938, English Dominican Archives. Italics original.
37. Tugwell and Bellenger, *Letters of Bede Jarrett*, pp. 185-6.
38. M. Coren, *Gilbert. The Man who was G. K. Chesterton* (London: Jonathan Cape, 1989), p. 2.

Select bibliography

A. Archer, O.P., *St Dominic's Parish, Newcastle upon Tyne. A History from the Point of View of the Parishioners* (n. p., n.d.).

B. Jarrett, O.P., *The English Dominicans* (London: Burns, Oates and Washbourne, 1921; 1937[2]).

A. H. Kimberlin, *The Return of Catholicism to Leicester, 1746–1946* (Hinckley, 1946).

C. Ryan, O.P., *A Guide and History of Hawkesyard Priory and Spode House* (Rugeley, 1962).

S. Tugwell, O.P., and Dom A. Bellinger (eds), *Letters of Bede Jarrett. Letters and Other Papers from the English Dominican Archives Selected by Bede Bailey, O.P.* (Bath, Downside Abbey, and Oxford, Blackfriars Publication, 1989).

A. White, O.P., 'Father Bede Jarrett, O.P., and the Renewal of the English Dominican Province', in D. Bellenger (ed.), *Opening the Scrolls. Essays in Honour of Godfrey Anstruther* (Downside, 1987), pp. 216–234.

Constitutiones Fratrum Sacri Ordinis Praedicatorum inchoatae in Capitulo Generali Provincialium Romae celebrate anno Domini 1924 sub reverendissimo patre Fr. Ludovico Theissling, magistri generali eiusdem Ordinis (Rome, 1925).

A Guide to Hawkesyard Priory and Church (Gloucester, n. d.).

Hawkesyard Priory and Spode House (Rugeley, 1956).

The Priory Church of Holy Cross, Leicester (Leicester, 1989).

Unpublished papers from the English Dominican Archive, 25 George Square, Edinburgh.

2

The English Catholic setting

An overall view

In 1920 there had been rather over two million Catholics in England and Wales. They were ministered to by a clergy some four thousand strong: double its figures in 1880. Four hundred thousand of their children received education in Church schools.[1] Their community was a complex, stratified affair. It was compounded of three main elements, the indigenous, recusant 'Old Catholic' element, at its strongest in west and north Lancashire, and County Durham; the massive Irish immigration, beginning before Victoria's reign opened but continuing in force throughout our period till it dwindled to a trickle in the 1940s and 50s; and the converts, of whom a minority constituted the nucleus for a Catholic intelligentsia.[2] The Old Catholics provided the socially most prestigious members of the Church, in the shape of the Catholic aristocracy and other landed families no less antique for lacking handles to their names. Their presence reassured those to whom it was important that to be Catholic was not to be non-English, and furnished the basis for an alternative genealogy of Englishness to that found in the Whig interpretation of history – or Protestant sentiment generally. It would be a mistake, however, to think of the recusant Catholics as consisting entirely of nobs and swells; in the traditional heartlands of recusancy, Catholicism was 'the healthy religion of a normally structured society'.[3] Moreover, in the English Midlands, where the Industrial Revolution had taken a more small-scale, but no less intensive or prosperous form, an indigenous Catholic middle class had already formed by the later decades of the eighteenth century. From the Old Catholics, the English Catholic community between the two World Wars inherited its major institutions: its seminaries, principal monasteries, and leading Catholic independent schools.

The Irish (or, as intermarriage proceeded apace, *Anglo*-Irish) gave

Catholicism what Anglicanism signally lacked and the Nonconformists would increasingly lose as the century progressed: a thorough rooting in the working class. It might even be said that it was the generous distribution of Catholicism among all the main social groupings of the inter-war years that made possible its conviction of a vocation to *change* England. Catholicism was a visionary, culture-transforming synthesis, made up of divine revelation and human wisdom, intended redemptively to finish and perfect society. But English Catholicism could take seriously a mission not just to 'convert' England but to baptise its culture in the plenary grace of the Gospel only because it was aware of its latent strength in such varied socio-economic strata.

The last strand in the weave of the community came from the converts, most of whom entered the Church through marriage, but some – and these the more influential – by a process of study and reflection on the state of contemporary thought and the contemporary world. Figures like the historian Christopher Dawson, the philosopher of mysticism Edward Watkin, the theological belletrist Ronald Knox will be considered, however briefly, in this chapter while Fr David Mathew, in his *Catholicism in England, 1535–1935*, would add, in his account of the years after the First World War, such additional names as those of the art historian E. W. Tristram, the lay theologian and critic G. K. Chesterton, and the novelist Compton Mackenzie – though the latter would probably have identified himself as a Scot.[4] They became Catholics because – and here generalisation is not too hazardous – they saw the Church of Rome as enjoying legitimate authority in matters of faith and morals, and as representing not only a wider Christendom than that which they had inherited but a wider *humanitas* as well.

The Church they entered had become, in its own terms, a more effective body than in the age of Victoria, crucial though that latter period was for its revival.[5] Its network of parishes and schools was systematically in place, their running, if more routinised, better adjusted to the efficacious catechesis, sacramentalisation and pastoral care of a growing population. As late as the 1950s, English seminarians in Rome could take pride in the thought of the peculiar compactness and vigour of their community, the close bonds which links clergy and people, the businesslike quality of parochial good management – and contrast the performance of the Latin lands.[6] If it was not a church notable for theological achievement (in marked contrast to, for instance, its cross-Channel neighbour in France) the Society of Jesus, in particular, was taking giant steps to redeem the situation, with such ventures as Heythrop College, Oxfordshire (eventually a 'Pontifical Athenaeum', able to confer papal degrees),

Campion Hall, a Permanent Private Hall of Oxford University, and the annual Catholic Summer Schools in theology at Cambridge. The collected papers of the latter, organised around the main themes of dogmatics and edited by the indefatigable Fr Cuthbert Lattey, S. J, constitute something of a multi-authored native *Summa Theologiae* of the 1920s.[7] Nor were there lacking individual priest-scholars of distinction among the diocesan clergy, such as the Orientalist and liturgist Adrian Fortescue,[8] and the metaphysician Canon D. B. J. Hawkins.[9] However, the real intellectual strength of the English Catholic Church would lie in what I shall call its 'theology of culture': its willed act of presence in the variety of domains – from art to politics – where its most illustrious converts were already fully at home. Despite the notable attempts to Anglicise (both literally and metaphorically) the philosophical and theological achievements of French Thomism (and these were certainly not without a wider resonance among the non-Catholic public), its main claim to the attention of posterity lies in this resolute endeavour to bring a Catholic sensibility to bear on cultural life. Without any depreciation of the supernatural uniqueness of revelation and dogma – on the contrary, it was the recognition of the metacultural status of Catholic Christian faith which made the enterprise possible – theological concern was focused chiefly on man as the culture-dwelling animal. What Professor Adrian Hastings says of the convert writers and thinkers of the inter-war years could be extended to the Catholic intelligentsia as a whole:

> They found in it [Catholicism] a sure framework for spiritual progress, literary creativity and political stability, but also for an ordered and coherent view of the world to replace the increasing intellectual and ideological confusion evident outside the walls.[10]

Their theological culture issued in a theology *of* culture, a theologically informed programme for culture's Christian revivification.

The seven friars whose work this book describes were products of this milieu and their literary work reflected its ethos and aims. In the 1930s the English Dominicans had consolidated their intellectual tradition (above all, at Blackfriars, Oxford) without damage to the spiritual and liturgical life which is, for a religious order of the patristic or mediaeval period especially, its vital underpinning and accompaniment. They were, therefore, well-placed to take advantage of the new sense of self-confidence which typified English Catholicism in that decade.

By the end of the 1930s, the English priesthood comprised well over five and a half thousand men, while the average annual intake of converts amounted to some twelve thousand. In the suburbs and country towns Catholic churches and chapels burgeoned, in many areas for the first time since the Reformation. Moreover, the somewhat oppressive feeling of being generally on the defensive – against Protestantism, whether refined or vulgar, or against Modernism, whether scholarly or journalistic, had given way to a greater serenity – and willingness to seize the initiative. We hear the note struck at the end of Maisie Ward's *Insurrection versus Resurrection*, written in 1937.

> The best Catholic thinkers of today are, like Newman, passionately orthodox. A Chesterton, a Claudel, realise that it is not by surrender to the passing enthusiasms of an hour that you really move men, that you really win them. The minor poet appeals to the little group, the genius speaks in the common speech of man and reaches the heart of the universe. The Modernist was like the minor poet: when he spoke of the modern mind he was thinking of a little group of Biblical critics or immanentist philosophers. But the Faith has a common speech to the heart of all mankind ...

The writer's father, Wilfrid, had been Newman's biographer, and a leading Liberal Catholic (but anti-Modernist) in the turn-of-the-century doctrinal crisis; her mother, Josephine, divided her energies between novel-writing and speaking for the Catholic Evidence Guild. Maisie herself was Chesterton's biographer while her husband, Frank Sheed, cofounded with her the Catholic publishing house named after them and was a lay theologian in his own right. Her testimony must count for something, therefore, when she concludes:

> The long siege is over ... For the siege implied coherent and successful human systems and a Church hemmed in and on the defensive. Today there are no such systems. Over against the Church stands chaos. The one great question that remains is which shall prevail – chaos or the divine order eternally established by God.[11]

It should not be thought, however, that the Catholic community in England was entirely of one mind and will. In *Catholicism in England, 1535–1935*, David Mathew was at pains to stress that the Church converts entered was far from being in all respects a disciplined phalanx who could be relied on to have but one judgment in all things. First, there was a marked division among English Catholics where matters political were concerned. The most prominent Catholics in public life – in administration and diplomacy as well as politics proper – were Conservatives. 'Sections' of the Catholic industrial population looked rather to Labour. Lastly, there were the less numerous, but highly vocal, adherents of a distinctively Catholic 'third way' in political judgment: the followers of Distributism, the adherents of the Land Movement, and, at the vortex of this activity the fascinating figure of Eric Gill with his proposals for a root-and-branch reform of the shape and ethos of industrial society. Secondly, among the factors making for disunity, Mathew placed the 'strain' occasioned between the gap between Catholic life in its moral dimension and 'an increasingly alien social ethic' – he meant in regard to what is coyly termed 'family morality', notably, divorce and contraception. While an earlier generation of non-Catholics in England maintained, beneath the surface, a distaste for Rome ultimately founded on Protestantism, whether residual or full-blooded, a new generation objected mainly to moral teachings of the Church once shared with Protestantism (and indeed humanism) at large. And here 'the use of marriage' (that is, contraception) bulked largest. *Plus ça change* ... an observer from the 1990s might well note.

> There was always a wall between us, but now it is crowned with glass. It is improbable that dissensions on such large questions as 'mariolatry' and papal infallibility would have the same effect of social disintegration as a divergent outlook on the most personal of all questions.[12]

The phrase 'social disintegration' gives pause for thought. What Mathew was thinking of was not so much any 'disintegration' of the unity of the Catholic body by internal dissent among those equally determined to remain Catholic on their different terms. He had in mind rather the lapsation – and so disaggregation from the social body of the Church – of Catholics whose will to remain attached to their Mother had been undermined by the pressure of a countervailing ethic in secular society. Concern with lapsation – 'leakage' – was neither unusual nor new. In the previous decade, a briefer survey by Bede Jarrett had recorded the impression that, while the flow of converts was increasing annually, the leakage of the lapsed was probably of comparable volume. Locating the causes in poor parental example, mixed marriages, attendance at non-Catholic schools, distance from Catholic churches and chapels, poverty, 'Sunday employments' and insufficient doctrinal instruction, Jarrett regarded the latter as the crucial factor.[13] The inter-war years had begun, after all, with a confident agnosticism settled firmly in the driving-seat of English society. The umbilical cord had not so much snapped as wasted away for those who, in the last analysis, set more store by what the papers say: 'The families who completely subordinate their religious interests are naturally carried slowly outside the Catholic Church.' But if that description is not a thousand miles distant from the state of English Catholicism some half century and more after Mathew's writing, in his very next statement the sense of déjà-vu is utterly dispelled. For Mathew goes on: 'On the other hand, a quality of greater determination, sometimes aggressive in its manifestations, is becoming characteristic of the manner in which Catholicism is held by the large majority of its adherents.'[14] Despite the epithet 'aggressive', this is intended as an approbatory statement ('the life and its implications have penetrated deep'). A more assured, and exigent Church than that which would succeed it in the 1960s, its presence was, for the 'born Catholic', hard to escape. The novelist Antonia White wrote of the Church in her barely fictionalised account of her childhood, *Frost in May*: 'Wherever she looked, it loomed in the background, like Fuji Yama in a Japanese print, massive, terrifying, beautiful and inescapable, the fortress of God, the house on the rock'.[15] Mathew rounded off his picture with a comment which goes far to explain the special place enjoyed by the English Dominicans in the new situation caused by this greater confidence on the part of the majority of the Catholic body. The 'Thomist philosophy', Mathew opined, was giving a background of depth to many English Catholics whose fathers 'seldom troubled themselves about such general questions'. For were not the Dominicans hereditary guardians of that 'philosophy'?

The intellectual life

The most important *salon* where such 'general questions' were discussed was that which convened at the house of Charles Burns, doctor and psychologist, in St Leonard's Terrace, Chelsea. It was described in a number of autobiographies, or biographies, of figures of the period, perhaps most fully in Christina Scott's life of her father, Professor Christopher Dawson. Here as in a kaleidoscope, a shifting galaxy of luminaries could be espied. Charles Burns himself brought a sympathy with the Viennese psychologists, but of no uncritical kind. His aim was to expel what was alien in their thought, while rendering their sanitising perceptions congenial. Tom Burns, Charles's younger brother, later to be editor of *The Tablet*, was a publisher with the Catholic house Sheed and Ward. Though his enthusiasm for the Neo-Thomists was later to be qualified, he played a part in making their work, and notably that of Jacques Maritain, known in England. Maritain's *Art et Scolastique* had already been printed in English translation by H. D. C. Pepler's St Dominic's Press at Ditchling, where it much influenced Eric Gill.[16] But as Burns discovered on forays in the Parisian *Quartier Latin*, beyond that slight volume lay 'a whole *opus*, an invasion of all my chosen fields of thought'.[17] Gaining Maritain's friendship, Burns met thereby the social thinker Emmanuel Mounier, the dramatist and philosopher Gabriel Marcel, and a host of other figures of the French Catholic revival. (Stanislaus Fumet, Henri Ghéon, Julien Green ...), the contributors, both imaginative and philosophising, to the series *Le Roseau d'or*. If later the French spiritual masters from de Caussade to Laberthonnière came to have more importance for Burns, his work of mediation nonetheless remained useful.

The poet and artist David Jones had a different mission. His work tried to re-relate his readers both to history and to their own human nature. In seeking the recovery of tradition, he aimed to foster not a sense of living in the past but of the past *living in us*.

> This sense of our past dwelling among us, not as a ghostly revival nor as documentation but as really present and as insistently demanding something of us, is communicated in the *Anathemata* over a vast range of what the poet calls 'our inheritance' ...[17]

though, as this critic points out, the lion's share of that patrimony is pre-Tudor and so pre-Reformation, a past (therefore) mediaeval, Germanic, Celtic and Roman, whose perspectives are integrated by the principal mysteries of the Christian narrative, the Incarnation and the immolation on the hill, as well as by the universal sacrifice of the Mass.[19] Taking Jones's principal work, the epic-like *Anathemata*, to be in the best and original sense a 'museum', or 'sanctuary of the Muses', David Blamires spoke of how the "devoted objects" are collected and arranged with care that is more than careful of their mere beauty: they are set to some purpose, to illustrate the "inward continuities" of man's life as a "maker" and as a spiritual being.'[20] Jones's awareness of the vital meanings recuperable in the artefacts and mentefacts of the past led him on indeed to make the further philosophical claim that man is in a highly distinctive sense *homo faber*, 'man the maker'. He is man the maker *of signs, homo significator* – and it is through the awareness of embodied significance that an animal may simultaneously be a spiritual subject. Conjoining word and image, for he worked not only as poet but also as calligrapher, illustrator, and engraver as well as in watercolour painting and drawing, Jones was peculiarly well placed to write about the relation of art to the Christian sacraments – themselves fusions of matter and form – as well as to the revelation made via a pattern of events and language which is their source. His entry, in the 1920s, into the ambience of the Dominican Order, via the tertiary Guild ('for those who make things with their hands') of St Joseph and St Dominic at Ditchling in Sussex makes him an especially important figure for our topic.

In the 'Preface' to *The Anathemata*, Jones singled out one man as, through his 'writings and conversation', the chief provider of the work's *materia poetica*. And this was the historian of culture Christopher Dawson, another regular participant in the Chelsea group.[21] Dawson was, in the period, its most influential member. Indeed, Eliot, on lecture tour in the United States, some time after the publication of Dawson's *Progress and Religion* and *The Making of Europe*, asked, in a peculiarly American question, who was 'the most powerful intellectual influence in England' at the time, is remembered as replying 'Christopher Dawson'.[22] Dawson, the offspring of minor Yorkshire landowners and clerical patricians from the Welsh Marches, had effectively determined on becoming a Catholic at Oxford, but delayed his reception (and a Catholic marriage) until ruffled family sensibilities could be smoothed. Academically brilliant but unplaceable – history, religion and literature were not only all but equally grist to his mill, Dawson's earliest professional work had been for the *Sociological Review*, the journal of Le Play House, a 'think-tank' inspired by the pioneering French sociologist Frédéric Le Play, whose six volume *Les Ouvriers européens* (1855) analysed social structures – from the Steppes of Russia to the North of England – in terms of 'work, place and folk'. To these Dawson would add 'religion', for he had already accepted the dictum of the Liberal Catholic John Baron Acton, Regius Professor of Modern History at Cambridge, that 'religion is the key of history'.[23]

Though his distaste for specialisation (together with high-profile Catholicism) made him academically difficult to employ, a post was eventually created for him as 'Lecturer in the History of Culture' at the University College of the South-West (later Exeter University) in 1922. The modest demands of his slight audience enabled him to begin work on a mammoth cultural history, provisionally entitled 'The Life of Civilisations': this was, after all, the age of Spengler and Toynbee,[24] It was also a period of Christian interest in the theology of history of an intensity unprecedented since patristic times.[25] The Byzantinist and liturgical theologian George Every, now archivist of Oscott College and a pupil of Dawson's, has explained the plan of his *chef d'oeuvre*.[26] *Progress and Religion* was intended as a summary synthesis of the entire work;[27] *The Age of the Gods* (the study which first gained Dawson celebrity for its deft interweaving of widely scattered archaeological materials so as to relate Europe's prehistory to archaic Asia) should have been its first volume.[28] A second, unfinished contribution on 'The Rise of the World Religions' was to follow. *The Making of Europe* counts as volume three,[29] with *Medieval Religion* as a part-publication of its successor.[30] The fifth and final volume – from the Enlightenment to the modern age – only saw the light of day in the shape of a posthumous fragment on the events of 1789 in France, with preface by Toynbee: *The Gods of Revolution.*[31]

Progress and Religion announces the principal theme of Dawson's enterprise. A society's vitality is bound up with its religion. He wrote elsewhere:

> The great civilizations of the world do not produce the great religions as a kind of cultural by-product; in a very real sense the great religions are the foundations in which the great civilizations rest. A society which has lost its religion becomes sooner or later a society which has lost its culture.[32]

A way out of the waste-land – this was what Dawson's work seemed to offer, at any rate in aspiration, and explains the attraction to him of Eliot who invited him to write for his journal, *The Criterion*, almost as soon as *Progress and Religion* appeared. But if, in Dawson's view, for sunlight culture needs to be open to the spiritual, it also requires rooting in the earth. This second, and complementary, conviction connects Dawson with D. H. Lawrence, whose view of sexuality as a cosmic mystery he shared.[33]

The Dawsonian formula 'the spiritual integration of culture' might well have served as a sub-title of the Dominican journal *Blackfriars* in this period – just as it could well have constituted the marching-orders of the seven individual friars to be discussed in these pages. After the Dawsons moved to Boars Hills, Oxford, in 1939 there was indeed mutual influence – notably with Victor White and Gervase Mathew.

If anyone in the Chelsea circle epitomised the desire for a new (Christian) Renaissance, synthesising the main elements of contemporary understanding within the total frame-work of a Catholic metaphysic, that person was Dawson's best friend, and the contributor of the fourth *Essay in Order*, Edward Watkin. Watkin, born near Manchester in 1888, was received into the Church while an undergraduate at New College, Oxford, in 1908 – at Downside, to whose contemplative interpretation of the English Benedictine ethos he remained permanently indebted (his son, Dom Aelred, became headmaster). Mysticism constitutes perhaps the commonest theme of his writing, though he himself regarded *The Philosophy of Form* as his most worthwhile work.[34] It tried to reconcile two epistemological approaches normally regarded as competing: the view, namely, that truth is attained by intuition, and the position which would have it that truth is found only through reasoning. Watkin claimed that thought is either intuition or the 'discrimination' of intuitions – thus linking the quantitative apprehensions of natural science on the one hand (abstract and clear intuitions) and those of aesthetic experience (dimmer, but more concrete intuitions) on the other. Whatever the merits of this proposal as a thesis in epistemology, its admirable holism of approach was typical of Watkin's Catholicism in general,[35] and of his 'essay in order' in particular.

The Bow in the Clouds is the Genesis symbol for the Noachic covenant, the guarantee of Israel's God, in his role as cosmic Lord, that his faithful love will always preserve the world on its foundations. More widely, then, the rainbow signifies 'the reflection of God in the many levels and forms of human experience, and the reality it has revealed and shall reveal hereafter.[36] The book considers the chief modes of human experience – from the physical sciences through their human counterparts to metaphysics; from life, through art and sexuality to religion – as so many colours on the spectrum. Beneath the first visible colour lies the ultra-violet of pure matter, the presupposition of natural science; above the last visible colour lies ultra-red, the mystical. The method is to ask the reader to

> interrogate impartially their own experience and the recorded experience of others. Is that experience justified, co-ordinated, harmonised and most adequately interpreted by accepting as objectively valid the forms of experience I have symbolised by these seven colours and those beyond violet and beyond red? I believe it is.[37]

The formula 'the recorded experience of others' stands for a host of witnesses whom Watkin summons to the stand: philosophers both ancient and modern (the pre-Socratics, Plato, Aristotle, Plotinus; the German Catholics Peter Wust and Max Scheler, the Russian Orthodox Nikolai Lossky, the Episcopalian Alfred North Whitehead); Church Fathers like Augustine and Pseudo-Denys; spiritual writers of various periods (Hildegard of Bingen; Mechthild of Magdeburg, Jan Ruysbroeck, Ramon Lull, Angela of Foligno; John of the Cross, Pascal, Augustine Baker, F. W. Faber, Friedrich von Hügel); poets such as Dante and Keats as well as the theoretician of poetry Henri Bremond; D. H. Lawrence, to whom a considerable section is devoted; the scientists Heisenberg, Jeans, Eddington; mediaeval metaphysicians of West and East (Thomas and Bonaventure; Shankara and Ramanuja); friends and acquaintances like Belloc and Dawson himself, Martin d'Arcy SJ, and the forerunner of Italian Christian

Democracy, then exiled to London, Don Luigi Sturzo. And not forgetting, for it holds a place of special honour, the Roman liturgy itself. All these voices are made eloquent, and the aim is nothing less than the making, in small compass, of a *speculum universale*, a 'mirror of all things'. Presenting human experience as God's rainbow – differentiated as the manifold which is the creation goes forth from God, but unified in relation to him, Watkin concludes by summing up the approach which, he thinks, alone can do that total experience justice. His statement could serve perfectly as a summary of the qualities that, cumulatively speaking, attach to the seven Dominican authors to be described in this book. The proper way to scan experience is:

> historic without being historicist, absolute yet relative, broad without being shallow, profound without being narrow, religious without being fanatical, contemplative but inspiring action in every sphere; it is individualist, because the individual is a unique communication and image of God, yet social, because only a community of spirits can reflect his multiplicity in unity; it renounces the world as end, to accept it as means; the spirit is 'hid with Christ in God', but the feet are firmly planted on earth; it combines the patience born of the contemplation of eternity with the activity which responds to the unique opportunity of the passing moment ...

And Watkin can conclude his evocation of the ethos of this Christian renaissance by writing:

> if it is theocentric, it is also humanist, for it sees in man God's likeness and temple; it is spiritual, yet values the body in which the spirit is incarnate, the material in which its ideas are forms of visible loveliness; its glance pierces to the darkness of matter below, sweeps through all the ranks and provinces of created being, material, biological and spiritual, and rises to be lost once more in the light of Godhead. In a word, it is Catholic.[38]

Nor was the aim merely, as we might say, Idealist: concerned with a just understanding, merely, of the intelligible connexions of things. As Watkin makes clear, the aim is a practical one, the construction of a new human order. Embodying the metaphysical order of being and value, this prospective society animated by Catholic Christianity can be termed 'image and prophecy of the Jerusalem which is above ... God's temple city'.

Then there were translators of distinction, who helped introduce an Anglophone audience to treasures of Catholic theology and literature from Continental Europe. Alick Dru was perhaps best known as a translator of Kierkegaard (Catholic philosophers and theologians were just beginning to take a serious interest in this Danish Lutheran opponent of Hegelianism around this time). But he also Englished Ghéon's study of Mozart, and major works by Henri de Lubac, Hans Urs von Balthasar and Adrienne von Speyr. T. S. Eliot wrote an introduction to his version of Josef Pieper's *Leisure. The Basis of Culture.*[39] His study of Charles Péguy, long matured, confirmed the well-foundedness of a favoured poet of *Blackfriars.*[40] With the Downside monk Illtyd Trethowan, he sought to replace the somewhat dessicated apologetics customary in English Catholic manuals with a more generous fundamental theology inspired by a contemporary of Péguy's, Maurice Blondel.[41]

Barbara Lucas, granddaughter of the matriarchal Edwardian Catholic poet Alice Meynell, translated novels by Léon Bloy (who had been responsible for Maritain's conversion from agnosticism), François Mauriac and the lesser known Yvonne de Bremond d'Ars, as well as studies of modern Italian painting and contemporary theatre – and later, the historical theology of the Oratorian convert from Calvinism Louis Bouyer. Her husband, Bernard Wall, put into English major works by Maritain, Marcel and, subsequently Teilhard de Chardin. He was, however, primarily an Italianist, with a major study of Manzoni to his credit (a writer who would engage the critical enthusiasm of the last of the Dominican authors to be studied here, Kenelm Foster).[42] Wall's interests were extremely wide-ranging and given expression in the journal of cultural affairs, *Colosseum*, which he founded – like many 30s journals, it would end ingloriously with the coming of War – as well as in an intellectual autobiography which mentions a number of the figures touched on in this book (including Victor White, Gerald Vann, Gervase Mathew).[43] His account of immediately post-Civil War Spain helps to explain the passionate disagreements of informed English Catholics on the issue.[44]

If Jones was the chief literary artist in the group, he had an interpreter of brilliance in the fourth of the translators René Hague. Hague would English a crop of intellectual fruits from French Catholicism — Marcel, de Lubac, Teilhard, but it was as elucidator of the often darkly riddling poetry of David Jones that his services were most demanded.[45] After Eric Gill's break with the cofounder of St Dominic's Press, Ditchling, Hilary Pepler, he found in Hague his closest collaborator. The printing press of 'Hague and Gill' would continue to use Gill's splendid type designs till its demise in 1956. Its production of Jones' *In Parenthesis* – probably the greatest poem produced by war in the English language – was both innovatory and fine.[46]

Gwendolin Plunket Greene, whose *Prophet Child* – a meditation on spiritual childhood as a necessary condition of all integral Christian seeing of the world in God – was dedicated to Jarrett, and carried one of Jones' unicorn woodcuts as its frontispiece, acted as a kind of spiritual mother to the set. Not for nothing was she the niece to whom Baron Friedrich von Hügel had written some of his most celebrated letters of spiritual direction. His presentation of Catholicism as at once institutional, mystical and intellectual, was formative for its outlook.[47]

Contemplativity, for von Hügel, was by no means to be associated with quietistic withdrawal from the city. These figures, accordingly, sought ways of influencing the wider world of public life and culture in England, though in no mere activist spirit. An important conduit of such influence was Harman Grisewood, already by 1936 Assistant to the programme organiser of the BBC, and, after the Second World War, Controller of its cultural service (the 'Third Programme'), and Director of the Spoken Word.[48]

The BBC could claim a premier position in the diffusion of English culture, not only in these islands, but through the proxy of its daughter organisations, in the over-extended British Empire beyond. But an older institution, the 'two Universities' – only Oxford and Cambridge could be meant – dominated that culture's presentation in the legislature, the professions, the civil service élite. The London Catholic intelligentsia maintained its own more modest links with the ancient Universities through the Jesuit Master of Campion Hall, Oxford, Father Martin D'Arcy. D'Arcy, the son of a West Country barrister, had arrived at Oxford as a Jesuit seminarian. Well prepared by the Society's tradition of classical studies, he carried off a series of glittering prizes thanks to his performance in *Litterae Humaniores*. He was simultaneously Master of Campion, the Jesuit permanent private hall, and a university lecturer in philosophy. Sought out by bright undergraduates under the spell – temporary or lasting – of Rome, he would appear at St Leonard's Terrace with a sprinkling in tow: the future poets W. H. Auden and Stephen Spender, the biographer-actor Robert Speaight. Despite his academic office, D'Arcy was not afraid to move across from the philospher's rostrum to the preacher's pulpit, holding that, in the generally perceived crisis of the post-Great War West, the welfare of souls comes first. The viewing of the world in the 'light of certain principles due to Christianity and Greek metaphysics and Roman order' was to D'Arcy the highest example of a believing necessary to human flourishing. In the relevant sense:

Belief is the natural end of beings possessing minds, and if they

allow their minds to suffer an eclipse, then, in the ensuing darkness, it is no wonder if the *gens lucifuga* of the soul, the creatures
of darkness, emerge ... The evil of unbelief is that it must shut its
eye to the forms and patterns of truth inscribed in the universe, and
retire to the inner sanctuary of the mind, there to rest in uncertainty, in the presence of a fugitive self and the broken idols of its
hopes.[49]

As a temporary expedient, so D'Arcy thought, the 'world of inner
feelings and experience' could substitute for 'external interests', just
as 'confidence in self so often succeeds the worship of God'. But in
the end psychology will prove a disappointing surrogate for religion
and metaphysics, petering out in faddism, pessimism and even barbar-
ianism. The conviction that the survival of the civilisation of the West
depended on its recovery both of the *philosophia perennis* and of the
Judaeo-Christian revelation itself, provides the key to D'Arcy's
prolific output. So far from threatening the integrity of the human, the
divine alone can nurture it towards its fulness: thus, in his study of
the philosophy and theology of history D'Arcy would see Christian
revelation as illuminating man and his 'slow development' as surely
as the vision of the sheet filled with birds, beasts and insects gave
Peter at Joppa 'a better taste for the things of nature and a more generous understanding of the Gentile world'.[50] So too, in his study of the
philosophy and theology of love, D'Arcy found charity not opposing
proper self-love but giving it fruition: for 'it is God who loves them
["self and intellect"] and gives them both increase. "Unarm Eros, the
long day's task is done"; in Agape is rest and everlasting life.'[51]

The London Catholic intelligentsia were primarily concerned with
what, in the 1960s came to be called 'indigenisation', the giving of a
local habitation and a name in England to the wider body of Catholic
thought. In particular they sought to incarnate in English culture – at
the level of philosophy, art, and social thinking – the insights of the
French Catholic revival, at once austerely Thomist and generously
humane as, by the 1920s, that had become. The influence of Jacques
Maritain, himself a pupil of the French Dominicans, was intellectually paramount, both through his writings and as mediated by
occasional visiting French Dominicans such as Pères Auguste
Maydieu and Marie-Dominique Roland-Gosselin. There was some
early interest in the social philosophy of the *Action française*, but
Maritain's *Things That Are Not Caesar's* was generally regarded as a
convincing rebuttal of that movement's claims to Catholic allegiance.[52]

But if France was the intellectual mainstay of the English Catholic intellectuals, another Latin country, across the Pyrenees, proved their Achilles' heel. The mid-1930s confronted them with the issue of Spain. Like most English Catholics they were by and large pro-Franco but unlike less well-informed opinion, far from favourable to the Franco excesses. Their opinions here were indebted to the convert poet and translator of John of the Cross, Roy Campbell.[53] However, this majority report failed to sway those who were horrified at any identification of the Catholic Church with the Franquist reaction: of these the most notable, and vocal, was Eric Gill. Gill will be dealt with in this study chiefly by way of presenting Fr Conrad Pepler, the Dominican son of his partner and friend Hilary. Like Martin D'Arcy, Gill was only an occasional conformist to the group's agenda of meetings. Still, he acted as a kind of elder statesman, if such a term can be used for one perpetually so dynamic and forceful. His conviction, largely achieved before the First World War opened, that art, philosophy and social politics are inextricably interrelated, and that the key to their unity belongs with religion, was the foundational *credendum* of the 30s Catholic intelligentsia.[54] He preceded them too in his discovery of the serviceable qualities of the thought of Aquinas, especially as presented by the French Neo-Thomists, in this re-conceiving of the world.

If the main non-Catholic participant in the Chelsea set was T. S. Eliot, in many ways its members echoed Eliot's basic themes: the reintegration of a fragmented cultural heritage, the overcoming of a diremption between thought and sensibility; the defence of the presence, within fine literature, of concepts drawn from metaphysics and religion, the reunion of rationality and mysticism, and the setting forth of the conditions for a new order in society, by way of a Christian sociology.[55] Swayed by Eliot's extraordinary prestige in the literary world of the day, they tended to suppose that the current of cultural history was flowing in their direction – towards a 'new Christendom'. The post-War world with its growing secularism, levelling democracy hostile to élite culture, and bureaucratisation, would prove a sad awakening.

This 'ministry of all the talents', considered as a corporate claimant for the intellectual leadership of English Catholicism was more impressive than anything that had preceded it – or would follow it. Not that it was all-embracing. It was unfortunate that, with the (brief) exception of Thomas Gilby, none of the younger intellectual and spiritual figures of the English Dominican renaissance lived in London. However, through articles and reviews in *Blackfriars* they were already familiar names. A more significant sign of non-inclusiveness lay in its relation (or, rather, lack of relation) with the Catholic renaissance (both Roman and Anglican) then proceeding in the senior of the ancient universities. It was not enthused by what it heard of the Oxford 'Inklings' one of whose members was the Oxford Dominican Gervase Mathew. With whatever justice, the London Catholic intelligentsia regarded this connection – C. S. Lewis, Charles Williams, J. R. R. Tolkien, *et al.* – as romantic, anti-intellectualist, insecure,[56] though they worshipped another Dominican of the Oxford house – Victor White – from afar. It is significant, for instance, that, despite their shared love of *mythos*, Jones and Tolkien never met.[57] But the Oxonians cannot be so quickly dismissed. If the Anglican renaissance of the Christian imagination in Lewis and Williams had its analogue in the work of J. R. R. Tolkien, its counterpart in the revival of apologetics should chiefly be associated with a figure more on the periphery of the Inklings – rather, a late Bellocian – Ronald Knox, then Catholic Chaplain to the University of Oxford.

Tolkien's fiction must, like that of Charles Williams, be seen as what it is: theologically saturated.[58] The imaginative modes of the two have much in common: stories of journey and quest, war between sons of light and sons of darkness, salvation-history. The tenor of their work, however, differs considerably. If Williams' is a 'romantic theology', where high points of affective and mystical experience are privileged,[59] that of Tolkien is a cosmic eschatology, concerned for all the realms of being and their destiny. Of Tolkien's fantasies, only *The Hobbit, or There and Back Again* was actually in print when the Second World War broke out, but *The Lord of the Rings* was being read aloud to the Inklings as he wrote it, from the late 30s on. It is at once ethically objective (there is but 'one Law for all creatures'), elegiac (for time and death are mighty powers), yet hopeful (for an ultimate 'eucatastrophe', a happy ending to end all endings). The Anglo-Saxon poem 'The Battle of Maldon' in Tolkien's translation includes the lines: 'The world withers/The wind rises/The candles are quenched./Cold falls the night.' Tolkien too affirms the mortality of men and ages, but the conviction of order at the heart of being which the responsible freedom of his reluctant heroes entails also allows him to hint at a joy beyond time, when in the words of Julian of Norwich, 'all shall be well and all manner of things shall be well'. For W. H. Auden, Tolkien's mythopoeic masterpiece passed supremely well the test of a good story, in that it persuaded its readers to face life neither with despair nor with false hopes.[60] To Gunnar Urang, the same work made Christian eschatology imaginatively credible again by offering what that commentor termed a 'phenomenology of hope'.

What is it like to face the approaching end and yet experience hope?
It is like encountering personal will rather than dealing with impersonal process. It involves something more like a decisive battle than
a continuous development, something cataclysmic rather than
gradual. It requires involvement in events, not detached contemplation. It reckons with real, malignant evil, not merely ignorance
or imperfection. It presupposes an ordering of the historical process
to some end. And it comes to be based on 'signs' and 'paradigmatic
events' within that history. Thus Tolkien has created an imaginative framework – nothing more explicit than that – for the Christian
experience of hope.[61]

The Inklings were too closely associated, perhaps, with the School of
English at Oxford to have formed a natural liaison with the more clas-
sically oriented Ronald Knox, down the road at the Old Palace as
Catholic chaplain from 1926 to the eve of war. Hastings calls him the
'showpiece' for the new intellectual confidence of English
Catholicism: 'brightest of all pre-war young men, most orthodox of
all priests'.[62] Chesterton had not been able to resist the obvious
comparison with an earlier Knox, main architect of the Protestant
Reformation in Scotland. 'Mary of Holyrood may smile indeed,/
Knowing what grim historic shade it mocks/To see wit, laughter and
the Popish creed,/Cluster and sparkle in the name of Knox.'[63] Knox's
career as an apologist had begun as an Anglo-Catholic, with *Some
Loose Stones*, a response to a corporate manifesto of Liberal Anglican
scholars, *Foundations*.[64] His search for religious certainty brought
him to the Church of Rome, a journey chronicled in *A Spiritual
Aeneid*. It was at Oxford that he began his written expositions of
specifically Roman Catholic faith: *In Soft Garments, The Hidden
Stream, The Belief of Catholics* and (with Arnold Lunn) *Difficulties*.
The stimulus of undergraduates was replaced, during the Second
World War, by the challenge of schoolgirls: the wartime exodus of
Londoners from the threat of *Blitzkrieg* had brought the human
contents of the Assumption Convent, Kensington Square, to the
country-seat of Knox's friends the Actons at Aldenham. The *Creed in
Slow Motion* and *The Mass in Slow Motion* were brilliantly imaginative attempts to present Catholic faith and devotion at a girl's level.[65]
Later in life, Knox considered his apologetic work born of too intellectualist a theory of the religious person: it was necessary, rather, to
combine 'the lucidity of St Thomas with the unction of Pascal'.[66] But
in practice, Knox had always tempered Neo-Scholastic and anti-
Modernist clarity with concern to speak to the heart, and set the bells
of previous experience ringing. His imagistic brushwork caught the

attention of those lacking a more philosophical bent, and could evoke an immediate response of recognition. As a former High Churchman, he was the beneficiary of an alliance between religion and imagination going back to the Caroline divines, and their near-contemporaries the metaphysical poets of the seventeenth century. The wedding of literary culture and theological expression is celebrated throughout his writings – it extends, naturally, to his translation of the Vulgate Scriptures, as well as to his *Enthusiasm*, (a study of what can happen to religion when experience is not informed by doctrine),[67] and that matrimonial union proved a happy one for Catholic apologetics in England.[68]

These Christian intellectuals were operating at an apparently providential time. The intensified economic and political pressures of the years after the Great War (the lion caged in Bolshevism, stalking the land in Fascism), together with the manifest human insufficiency of much in the artistic and philosophical worlds of the time (Formalism and Nihilism in aesthetics, logical positivism in philosophy), combined to raise the question, Is liberalism enough? In the novel form, Evelyn Waugh and Graham Greene were concerned simply to write good books – but the effect was that of an assault, mounted from different starting-points, on the complacencies of bourgeois liberalism: Waugh through the portrayal of a Catholic aristocracy whose sins are covered by acceptance of faith's paradoxes, Greene by attempting to see society through very different eyes, those of criminals and exiles. Looking back on the phenomenon of the English Catholic novel to mid-century, Fr Gerald Meath OP commented:

> Proust and Virginia Woolf are the products of a world which has been driven in on itself and condemned to self-conscious art because it has lost the pattern of God's planning. The loss of this sense means a loss of faith, and it has produced the excessive concern with techniques and experiment that is so common today and has made the modern novel etiolated and narrow ... [Catholic novelists'] greatest temptation may be to overemphasise the pattern, but undoubtedly their infallible method will be to keep out of God's light and allow him to appear through their 'mirrorings', and the last thing they will worry about will be 'edification'.[69]

The wider cultural context gave such writers the confidence they needed to persist in their literary strategies, rebarbative to modernism as these might seem. The 1930s witnessed what Hastings termed 'a breakdown of the agnostic consensus of the enlightened and ... the growing sense that a belief in supernatural religion really was an intellectual option for modern man.'[70] The novelist Compton Mackenzie summed up at the end of the decade:

> Communism or Fascism – they may be mutually destructive, but
> they are both expressions of distrust in the individualism which has
> made such a mess of the world. We are watching now, I fancy, the
> beginning of the end of an epoch which started with the renaissance
> and the Protestant Reformation and the discovery of America and
> the conception of England as an extra-European State.[71]

It was not, then, liberalism only – literary and cultural, social and
political – against which such writers defined themselves. The attempt
of the Papacy of John Paul II to outline a 'third way' outside the
camps of both socialism and capitalism was widely anticipated in the
period. As another wartime commentator remarked, apropos of the
genesis and development of Belloc's social philosophy:

> The rise of Socialism was not merely disastrous in itself, in that it
> harnessed many fine and disinterested minds to a false philosophy,
> but it also manoeuvred into the defence of the capitalist regime,
> almost the whole of those forces which should have been led in the
> attack on it.[72]

As so often, the episcopate was only dimly aware of the surges of
these creative stirrings in the Christian imagination, the Catholic intelligence. With the deaths of such late Victorian bishops as Henry
Edward Manning, John Cuthbert Hedley and William Robert
Brownlow, the age of the writing bishop was past.[73] Their worries lay
elsewhere. David Mathew's chief cause for complaint was directed
against the 'more sophisticated sections of the Catholic body'.[74] In the
'smart set' to whom Evelyn Waugh's Father Rothschild SJ, ministered
with such omniscience and discretion, Mathew discerned a frame of
mind of 'almost nominal Catholicism which is unwilling to move even
slightly against the stream', an 'erosion of indifference', an 'impatience with the clergy'. A later historian, Dr Edward Norman, called
the Catholic *ecclesia episcoporum* of this period 'a Church which had
become confident and routinized; splendid in its pastoral machinery,
but lacking the genius of inventiveness.'[75] Mathew's remarks do not
smack of over-confidence. But then again, he was hardly a typical
bishop. Certainly, the salon at St Leonard's Terrace would have
considered itself reformist. If pressed, they might have identified their
enemies as 'pietism' and 'separatism': a refusal to marry the heart's
devotion to hard thinking, on the one hand, and, on the other, a quasi-
sectarian indifference to the fate of the wider culture.[76]

But for the principal exception to Norman's strictures we must look
elsewhere: Mathew's study was finished in the year (1935) that the

safe but unexciting Cardinal Francis Bourne was succeeded at
Westminster by an archbishop, Arthur Hinsley, who would do much
for the revival of Catholic social thought. Hinsley was in that domain
both patron and facilitator of the work of Dawson and his younger
colleague Barbara Ward. The spread of Fascism well beyond the
confines of Italy in the later 1920s had been followed by the dizzy rise
of Hitler to the Chancellorship of Germany in 1933. Invited, initially,
by the *Catholic Times* to comment on 'The Church and the Dictators',
Dawson began to give serious attention to the role of the Church *vis-
à-vis* contemporary politics. *Religion and the Modern State* (1936)
proposed a choice between the 'mechanised order of the absolute
State' (whether nominally Fascist or Socialist) and a recovery of the
Christian elements in Western culture by way of a return to a spiritual order with a quite different ethos for civil society.[77] *Beyond
Politics* (1939) opined that the Church's greatest task in the service of
Western civilisation was the preservation of her own inheritance and
a refusal of instrumentalisation by any political movement, whatever
its name.[78] These works commended themselves to the newly
enthroned archbishop. Hinsley, aware that Dawson, had been refused
a Chair in the Philosophy and History of Religion at Leeds, owing to
(it would seem) anti-Catholic prejudice, and so was out of a job,
offered him two.

The *Dublin Review* had been founded by the first holder of the see
of Westminster, Cardinal Nicholas Wiseman; Dawson had already
written much in its pages, thanks to his good relation with his fellow-
convert editor, Algar Thorold, an expert on the history of mysticism
and son of the Anglican bishop of Winchester. Now it could be his
organ at a time of national emergency unparallelled since the
Revolutionary and Napoleonic Wars.

Sword of the Spirit, by contrast, was an organisation launched by
Hinsley himself, with a view to creating a new domestic and international order once peace had come again.[79] Its vice-presidency (Hinsley
himself being president) remained in Dawson's hands as long as the
cardinal lived. The movement's aim was to unite all men of good will
(but notably Christians) in a struggle against totalitarianism of both
Left and Right, and for the unity of the centre, what Dawson called
'principles far more vital than the issue of the Left/Right party dog-
fight'.[80]

In both cases, Barbara Ward – the future economist and human
rights activist Baroness Ward – was to be found at Dawson's side as
assistant editor at the *Dublin*, board member (and, effectively, administrator) at the Sword. Unfortunately, the other Catholic bishops (with
the exception of David Mathew) objected to what they considered the

ecumenical dalliance of Sword of the Spirit. Hinsley rejoined that the movement aimed at practical co-operation with a view to realising the papal social encyclicals – not at interventions in the realms of doctrine and discipline. Rome came down on the side of the collegial consensus. Father John Carmel Heenan, eventually his successor, commented shortly after Hinsley's death, with characteristic *suavitas*:

> In his moments of depression the Cardinal was sometimes inclined to believe that there was in some Catholic quarters a lack of good will. But he thought along these lines only in moments of depression. In his heart he knew that his position and personality enabled him to go much further along the road to co-operation than would be possible for other members of the hierarchy. They always spoke as diocesan bishops. Cardinal Hinsley often spoke as a national leader first. He did not of course ever make utterances incompatible with the dogmatic character of the teaching Church but often he spoke not as a bishop teaching his own flock but as a Catholic Englishman testifying to his sense of spiritual communion with Englishmen outside the fold.[82]

The decision to divide into Catholic and non-Catholic Branches inevitably made for loss of momentum – although by this time significant differences of opinion between Catholics and High Anglicans on the one hand, Broad and Free Churchmen on the other, over the issue of natural law, had already created difficulties.[83] After Hinsley's death in 1943, Dawson was removed from the *Dublin* editorship as (in effect) one too closely identified with the late cardinal's stand. However, their collaboration stimulated the writing of his *The Judgment of the Nations* (1942) with its plea for a post-war European unity,[84] while, as pointed out in a lengthy debate in *The Times* on 'Catholicism Today' in November 1949 the ten points of social and international order which the original Sword took as its agreed principles retained both validity and usefulness.[85] In the later transformation of Sword of the Spirit into the Catholic Institute for International Relations, a much greater professionalisation of social fact-finding was accompanied by a new focus of concern on human rights and their abuse – a concept at once wider and narrower than that of order, but recommended by the usage not only of international organisations but of the Papacy itself from the 1960s onwards. In the post-conciliar world, too, Catholic identity would prove harder to sustain.

Although the seven Dominican heroes of this study published much of their work after the Second World War, and in one case, as late as the 1980s, their formation, outlook and ethos was in all major respects set by the inter-war world. After the Second World War, English Catholicism was by no means as sclerotic and dull as is sometimes alleged. Institutionally, indeed, it went from strength to strength, and was strongly, even effortlessly, convinced of its future.[86] It continued to attract, in the war years and beyond, converts of the greatest intellectual distinction, whether prospective or already achieved: the philosopher Elizabeth Anscombe, the anthropologist E. E. Evans-Pritchard, the poet Edith Sitwell.[87] To some degree, however, it suffered a closing in of cultural horizons.[88] Its very success as a creator of new parishes, schools, missionary training houses, encouraged it to become more activist and clerical in orientation. As early as 1942 Dawson could be found complaining that 'a belief in effecting things by organization and formulas, etc., etc., [is] growing rather than lessening'.[89] The generosity of temper of an older generation, the conviction that Catholicism was, thanks to the renewing power of the supernatural for nature, a culture-transforming force of unlimited significance, was less in evidence now. 'If brilliance there was, it was largely the autumnal maturity of a generation formed well before the Second World War.'[90] It is to that brilliance, as irradiating in seven of the 'Jarrett Dominicans', that the rest of this book is devoted.

Notes

1. A. Hastings, *A History of English Christianity, 1920–1985* (London: Collins, 1986), p. 134.
2. For the background, see E. I. Watkin, *Roman Catholicism in England from the Reformation to 1950* (London: Oxford University Press, 1957); J. Bossy, *The English Catholic Community, 1570–1850* (London: Darton, Longman and Todd, 1975).
3. A. Hastings, *A History of English Christianity*, p. 133.
4. D. Mathew, *Catholicism in England, 1535–1935. Portrait of a Minority: Its Culture and Tradition* (London: Longmans, Green and Co., 1936), p. 251. Mackenzie was born in 1883 in West Hartlepool of a London-Scots father and an American mother, and did not visit Scotland till 1926. Such, however, was his energy, and the coincidence of his 'Alban' enthusiasm with the founding of the Scottish National Movement (also in 1926) that the Braid Scots novelist Lewis Grassic Gibbon, could soon parody his 'Scottish idea' as 'a Scots Catholic kingdom, with Mr Compton Mackenzie Prime Minister to some disinterred Jacobite royalty, and all the Scots intellectuals settled out on the land on thirty-acre crofts or sent out to re-colonise St Kilda for the good of their souls', cited A. Linklater, *Compton Mackenzie. A Life* (London: Chatto and Windus, 1987), p. 227.
5. E. R. Norman, *The English Catholic Church in the Nineteenth Century*

(Oxford: Clarendon Press, 1984).

6. A. Kenny, *A Path from Rome. An Autobiography* (London: Sidgwick and Jackson, 1985), p. 55.

7. Beginning in 1922 they continued publication till 1940.

8. J. G. Vance and J. W. Fortescue, *Adrian Fortescue. A Memoir* (London: Burns, Oates and Co., 1924).

9. Hawkins' work may be described as an attempt to commend to those raised in British empiricism the merits of scholastic philosophy and the service it could perform for Christian doctrine; see E. A. Sillem, 'Hawkins, Denis John Bernard, *New Catholic Encyclopaedia* 6, (New York, NY: McGraw-Hill Book Company, 1967), p. 945.

10. A. Hastings, *English Christianity*, pp. 279–80.

11. M. Ward, *Insurrection versus Resurrection: The Wilfrid Wards and the Transition*, II (London: Sheed and Ward, 1937), pp. 550–1.

12. Mathew, *Catholicism in England*, p. 253.

13. Jarrett, *The Church in England in 1922*, pp. 29–30.

14. Mathew, *Catholicism in England*, p. 253.

15. A. White, *Frost in May* (London: Penguin Books 1933). For Fr Victor White's role in bringing back this formidable lady to the Church see S. Chitty, *Now to My Mother* (London: Weidenfeld and Nicolson, 1985), p. 135.

16. J. Maritain, *Art et Scolastique* (Paris: Librairie de l'Art catholique, 1920); ET *The Philosophy of Art* (Ditchling: St Dominic's Press, 1923), with an Introduction by E. Gill.

17. T. Burns, *The Use of Memory. Publishing and Other Pursuits* (London: Sheed & Ward, 1993), p. 24.

18. H. Grisewood, *David Jones* (London: BBC Publications 1966), p. 13.

19. For other works on David Jones see D. J. Blamires, *David Jones, Artist and Writer* (Manchester: Manchester University Press, 1971); T. Dilworth, *The Shape of Meaning in the Poetry of David Jones* (Toronto: University of Toronto Press, 1988). Professor Dilworth is now preparing a study of Jones's painting which promises to be as exhaustive as this latter work is for the poetry.

20. Blamires, *David Jones*, p. 195.

21. M. D. Knowles, J. J. Molloy, E. I. Watkin, 'Christopher Dawson, 1889–1970', *Proceedings of the British Academy*, LVII, (1971), pp. 439–452.

22. C. Scott, *A Historian and his World. A Life of Christopher Dawson, 1889–1970* (London: Sheed and Ward, 1984), p. 210.

23. Ibid., p. 49.

24. O. Spengler, *Der Untergang des Abendlandes. Umrisse einer Morphologie der Weltgeschichte* (Munich: 1918–1920; 1922); A. Toynbee, *A Study of History* (London: Oxford University Press, 1934–1961, 12 vols.)

25. J. M. Connolly, *Human History and the Word of God. The Christian Meaning of History in Contemporary Thought* (New York and London: 1965).

26. Scott, *A Historian and his World*, pp. 82–83.
27. C. Dawson, *Progress and Religion. An Historical Enquiry into the Causes and Development of the Idea of Progress and its Relationship to Religion* (London: Sheed and Ward, 1929).
28. C. Dawson, *The Age of the Gods. A Study in the Origins of Culture in Prehistoric Europe and the Ancient East* (London: J. Murray, 1928).
29. C. Dawson, *The Making of Europe, An Introduction to the History of European Unity* (London: Sheed and Ward, 1932).
30. C. Dawson, *Medieval Religion and Other Essays* (London: Sheed and Ward, 1934).
31. C. Dawson, *The Gods of Revolution* (London, Sidgwick and Jackson, 1974) With an introduction by Arnold Toynbee.
32. C. Dawson, *The Dynamics of World History* (New York: 1957), p. 128.
33. C. Scott, *A Historian and his World*, p. 94. Cf C. Dawson, *Christianity and Sex* (*Criterion Miscellany* No. 13, London: Faber and Faber, 1930).
34. E. I. Watkin, *The Philosophy of Mysticism* (London: Grant Richards, 1920); *Poets and Mystics* (London: Sheed and Ward 1953); *The Philosophy of Form* (London: Sheed and Ward, 1935; 1938; 1950).
35. E. I. Watkin, *The Catholic Centre* (London: Sheed and Ward, 1939) gives this holism a theocentric and doxological rationale: following the French Carmelite spiritual theologian Elizabeth of the Holy Trinity, 'Catholic praise; has its 'circumference' in the utmost limit of creation and its 'centre' in God, p. 247.
36. E. I. Watkin, *The Bow in the Clouds. An Essay towards the Integration of Experience* (London: Sheed and Ward, 1931), p. 3.
37. Ibid., p. 7.
38. Ibid., pp. 151, 152.
39. J. Pieper, *Leisure. The Basis of Culture* (ET London: Faber and Faber, 1952).
40. A. Dru, *Péguy* (London: Harvill Press, 1956); cf. *Blackfriars*, XXVIII. No. 333 (1947), with essays by Robert Speaight and Liam Brophy.
41. A. Dru and I. Trethowan (ed.), *Blondel's 'Letter on Apologetics' and 'History and Dogma'* (London: Harvill Press, 1964).
42. B. Wall, *Alessandro Manzoni* (Cambridge: Bowes and Bowes, 1954); and more widely, *Italian Life and Landscape* (London: Paul Elek, 1950–1); *Italian Art, Literature and Landscape* (London: William Heinemann 1956); *A City and a World. A Roman Sketchbook* (London: Nicolson 1962). Worth mentioning here are his Vaticanological explorations in *Report on the Vatican* (London: Weidenfeld and Nicolson 1956) and (with his wife) *Thaw at the Vatican* (London: Victor Gollancz 1964).
43. B. Wall, *Headlong into Change. An Autobiography and a Memoir of Ideas since the Thirties* (London: Harvill 1969). This took further the comments in *These Changing Years. Notes on Civilisation and Revolution* (London: Harvill 1947).
44. B. Wall, *Spain of the Spaniards* (London: Sheed and Ward 1938). The

editorial policy of *Blackfriars* favoured the *de jure* (Republican) government; soon after the war ended, however, there emerged from Blackfriars, Oxford, John-Baptist Reeves' *Dominican Martyrs in Red Spain* (Oxford: n.d. but 1939), which gives an account of thirty-one Dominicans who apparently died for the faith, including the former Master of the Order Bonaventure Garcia de Paredes.

45. R. Hague, *A Commentary on the 'Anathemata' of David Jones* (Wellingborough: Christopher Skelton, 1977). See also Hague's *Dai Greatcoat. A Self-portrait of David Jones in his Letters* (London: Faber and Faber, 1980). Hague also reconstructed from fragments a poem cycle left unpublished on Jones' death in *The Kensington Mass* (London: Agenda Editions, 1975).

46. B. Wall, *René Hague. A Personal Memoir* (Wirral: The Aylesford Press, 1989), pp. 17–19.

47. G. P. Greene, *The Prophet Child* (London: Longmans, Green and Co., 1935); *Two Witnesses. Personal Recollections of H. Parry and F. von Hügel* (London, 1930); F. von Hügel, *Letters from Baron Friedrich von Hügel to a Niece* (London: Dent, 1928; 1950); *The Mystical Element in Religion as Studied in St Catherine of Genoa and her Friends* (London: J. M. Dent, 1923, two volumes).

48. H. Grisewood, *David Jones. Artist and Writer* (London: BBC Publications, 1966); *One Thing at a Time. An Autobiography* (London: Hutchinson, 1968); *The Painted Kipper. A Study of the Spurious in the Contemporary Scene* (London: C. A. Watts and Co., 1970).

49. M. D'Arcy, *The Nature of Belief* (London: Sheed and Ward, 1931), pp. 33–4.

50. M. D'Arcy, *The Sense of History, Secular and Sacred* (London: Faber and Faber, 1959), p. 283.

51. M. D'Arcy, *The Mind and Heart of Love. Lion and Unicorn: A Study in Eros and Agape* (London: Faber and Faber, 1945), p. 330.

52. J. Maritain, *La Primauté du spirituel* (Paris: Plon, 1927); ET *The Things That Are Not Caesar's* (London: Steed and Ward, 1930). The point of the (original) title was that *Action française* asserted 'La politique d'abord!', holding that, only when a proper ordering of civil society had been restored in France could the religious question usefully be addressed. Both 'sides' made appeal to Thomism, something rather obscured in A. Maydieu, O.P., 'The Influence of St Thomas on French Politics', *Blackfriars* XXVIII. 330 (1947), pp. 395–405. Only Eliot, exempted by his Anglicanism from attention to papal *volte-faces*, never withdrew explicit allegiance to Maurras. 'Throughout his life, Eliot would continue to support Maurras, and his philosophy was to enter the fabric of Eliot's own concerns', so P. Ackroyd, *T. S. Eliot* (London: Cardinal, 1984), pp. 41–2.

53. R. Campbell, *Light on a Dark Horse. An Autobiography, 1901–1935* (London: Hollis and Carter, 1951), pp. 308–47.

54. M. Yorke, *Eric Gill. Man of Flesh and Spirit* (London: Constable, 1981), pp. 73–98.

55. S. Spender, *Eliot* (London: Fontana Collins, 1975). On Eliot's new Christendom writing, see *The Idea of a Christian Society* (London: Faber and Faber, 1939); *Notes towards the Definition of Culture* (London: Faber and Faber, 1948); and R. Kojecky, *Eliot's Social Criticism* (London: Faber and Faber, 1971).

56. The title of Gareth Knight's study *The Magical World of the Inklings* (Shaftesbury: Element Books, 1990) might confirm such views. But the author, who confines himself to an account of Tolkien, Lewis and Williams (together with the interpreter of English Romanticism Owen Barfield) explains that by 'magic' (which Williams, certainly, had once practised) he means simply the mythopoeic use of the human imagination. None the less, Knight is a professional student of *esoterica* and his book is sometimes docketed by retailers as 'New Age', a movement with perhaps more adherents in the England of the 1990s than New Christendom! To a certain degree Eliot linked the Chelsea group to the Inklings. For his admiration for Williams, see his 'The Significance of Charles Williams', The *Listener* 36, 936 (19 December 1946).

57. W. Blissett, *The Long Conversation. A Memoir of David Jones* (Oxford: Oxford University Press, 1981), p. 16.

58. H. Carpenter, *J. R. R. Tolkien. A Biography* (London: Unwin Paperbacks, 1978); N. D. Isaacs (ed.), *Tolkien and the Critics* (London: 1969).

59. C. S. Lewis explained: 'A romantic theologian does not mean one who is romantic about theology but one who is theological about romance, one who considers the theological implications of those experiences which are called romantic. The belief that the most serious and ecstatic experiences either of human love or of imaginative literature have such theological implications, and that they can be healthy and fruitful only if the implications are diligently thought out and severely lived, is the root principle of all his work.' See 'Preface', *Essays Presented to Charles Williams* (London: Oxford University Press, 1947), p. vi. For further enlightenment, there is M. McDermott Shideler, *The Theology of Romantic Love* (New York: Harper, 1962) and *Charles Williams: A Critical Essay* (Grand Rapids, Mich: Eerdmans, 1966); G. Cavaliero, *Charles Williams, Poet of Theology* (London: Macmillan 1983), and for a comparison of Williams, Lewis and Tolkien, G. Urang, *Shadows of Heaven* (Philadelphia: Pilgrim Press, 1971).

60. W. H. Auden, 'Good and Evil in The Lord of the Rings', *Critical Quarterly* 10 (1968), pp. 138–42.

61. Urang, *Shadows of Heaven*, p. 122.

62. A. Hastings, *English Christianity*, p. 282.

63. *The Collected Poems of G. K. Chesterton* (London: Cecil Palmer 1927), p. 15.

64. B. H. Streeter (ed.), *Foundations. A Statement of Christian Belief in Terms of Modern Thought* (London: MacMillan, 1912).

65. R. A. Knox, *Some Loose Stones* (London: Longmans, 1913); *A Spiritual Aeneid* (London: Longmans, 1918); *In Soft Garments. A Collection of Oxford Conferences* (London: Burns Oates, 1942); *The*

Hidden Stream. A Further Collection of Oxford Conferences (London: Burns Oates, 1952); *The Belief of Catholics* (London: Ernest Benn, 1927); *Difficulties. Being a Correspondence about the Catholic Religion between Ronald Knox and Arnold Lunn* (London: Eyre and Spottiswoode, 1932); *The Creed in Slow Motion* (London: Sheed and Ward, 1949); *The Mass in Slow Motion* (London: Sheed and Ward, 1948).

66. R. A. Knox, *Proving God* (London: The Month, 1959), p. 43.
67. R. A. Knox, *Enthusiasm. A Chapter in the History of Religion, with special reference to the Seventeenth and Eighteenth Centuries* (Oxford: Clarendon Press, 1950).
68. M. T. Walsh, 'Ronald Knox the Apologist', *Priests and People* 2, 10 (1988), pp. 401–4.
69. G. Meath, O.P., 'The Catholic Novel', *Blackfriars*, XXXII 281 (1951), p. 609.
70. A. Hastings, *English Christianity*, p. 291.
71. C. Mackenzie, *West to North* (London: Rich and Cowan 1942), p. 297.
72. D. Jerrold, 'The Influence of Hilaire Belloc', in D. Woodruff (ed.), *For Hilaire Belloc. Essays in Honour of his Seventy-second Birthday* (London: Sheed and Ward, 1942), p. 11.
73. P. Hughes, 'The Bishops of the Century', in G. A. Beck, A.A. (ed.), *The English Catholics, 1850–1950* (London: 1950), p. 192.
74. Mathew, *English Catholicism* p. 259.
75. E. R. Norman, *Roman Catholicism in England from the Elizabethan Settlement to the Second Vatican Council* (Oxford: Oxford University Press, 1985), p. 109.
76. Their criticisms of the weaknesses of many clergy and laity in this regard, as well as – it must be conceded – their failure to note some careful distinctions worked out in the theology of the Schools (the laymen among them had no formal theological training), could make relations with ecclesiastical censors unpredictable. For Watkin's experience, see M. Goffin, 'Fighting under the Lash', *Downside Review* 113. 392 (1995), pp. 203–18.
77. C. Dawson, *Religion and the Modern State* (London: Sheed and Ward, 1936).
78. C. Dawson, *Beyond Politics* (London: Sheed and Ward, 1939).
79. For Hinsley's role, see J. C. Heenan, *Cardinal Hinsley. A Memoir* (London, Burns Oates and Washbourne 1944), pp. 182–210. The movement took its title from that of his BBC Radio broadcast to the nation on 10 December 1939, see ibid., pp. 87–88.
80. Cited C. Scott, *A Historian and his World*, p. 139.
81. For an example of her thinking in this period, see her 'The Incarnation and the Human Order', *Blackfriars*, XXI 24a (1940), pp. 694–700.
82. Heenan, *Cardinal Hinsley*, p. 209.
83. See below, Chapter III.
84. C. Dawson, *The Judgment of the Nations* (London: Sheed and Ward, 1942).

85. Letter of 8 November 1949 by Professor A. C. F. Beales, author of *The Catholic Church and International Order* (Harmondsworth: Penguin, 1941). For the ten principles, see Heenan, *Cardinal Hinsley*, pp. 180–81.
86. Hastings, *English Christianity*, pp. 473–5.
87. For the wider patterns of conversion, see S. Gilley, 'Loss and Gain: Conversions to Catholicism in Britain, 1800–1914', *The Ransomer*, XXXIII. 3 (1994), pp. 16–29.
88. The difference in tone is detectible in the French collection of essays by exclusively English (and Scots) Catholic authors: D. Mathew *et al.*, *Catholicisme anglais* (Paris: Editions du Cerf, 1958), for example at p. 55.
89. In R. Hague (ed.), *Dai Greatcoat. A Self-Portrait of David Jones in his Letters* (London and Boston: Faber and Faber, 1980), p. 112.
90. Hastings, *English Christianity*, p. 487. Anscombe and Evans-Pritchard (other names could be mentioned) are, evidently, exceptions to this rule.

Select Bibliography

P. Ackroyd, *T. S. Eliot* (London: Cardinal, 1984).

D. Attwater, *A Cell of Good Living. The Life, Works and Opinions of Eric Gill* (London: Geoffrey Chapman, 1969).

D. Blamires, *David Jones. Artist and Writer* (Manchester: Manchester University Press, 1971).

M. Branson & W. Heinemann, *Britain in the 1930s* (London: Weidenfeld & Nicolson, 1973).

T. Burns, *The Use of Memory. Publishing and Further Pursuits* (London: Sheed and Ward, 1993).

H. Carpenter, *J. R. R. Tolkien. A Biography* (London: Unwin Paperbacks, 1978).

H. Carpenter, *The Inklings* (London: Unwin Paperbacks 1981).

J. P. Corrin, *G. K. Chesterton and Hilaire Belloc. The Battle against Modernity* (Athens [Ohio]: Ohio University Press, 1981).

J. Coventry, 'Roman Catholicism' in R. Davies (ed.), *The Testing of The Churches, 1932–1982. A Symposium* (London: Epworth Press, 1982).

T. Dilworth, *The Shape of Meaning in the Poetry of David Jones* (London and Toronto: University of Toronto Press, 1988).

R. L. Green and W. Hooper, *C. S. Lewis. A Biography* (London: Collins, 1974).

H. Grisewood (ed.), *Epoch and Artist. Selected Writings by David Jones* (London: Faber and Faber, 1959).

A. M. Hadfield, *Charles Williams. An Exploration of his Life and Work* (Oxford: Oxford University Press, 1983).

R. Hague, *A Commentary on the Anathemata of David Jones* (Wellingborough: Christopher Skelton, 1977).

R. Hague (ed.), *Dai Greatcoat. A Self-Portrait of David Jones in his Letters* (London: Faber and Faber, 1980).

A. Hastings, *A History of English Christianity, 1920-1985* (London: Collins, 1986).

A. Hastings, (ed.), *Bishops and Writers. Aspects of the Evolution of Modern English Catholicism* (Anthony Clarke: Wheathampstead, 1977).

F. McCarthy, *Eric Gill* (London: Faber and Faber, 1989).

C. L. Mowat, *Britain between the Wars, 1918-1940* (Chicago: University of Chicago Press, 1955).

E. Norman, *Roman Catholicism in England from the Elizabethan Settlement to the Second Vatican Council* (Oxford: Oxford University Press, 1985).

P. A. Schakel, *Reason and Imagination in C. S. Lewis* (Grand Rapids, Michigan: Eerdmans Publishing Company, 1984).

C. Scott, *A Historian and his World. A Life of Christopher Dawson, 1889-1970* (London: Sheed and Ward, 1984).

R. Speaight, *Ronald Knox the Writer* (London: Sheed and Ward, 1966).

S. Spender, *The Thirties and After: Poetry, Politics, Panorama* (1933-75) (New York: Random House, 1978).

A. N. Wilson, *C. S. Lewis, A Biography* (London: Collins, 1990).

T. Woodman, *Faithful Fictions. The Catholic Novel in British Literature* (Milton Keynes: Open University Press, 1991).

M. Yorke, *Eric Gill. Man of Flesh and Spirit* (London: Constable, 1981).

3

Victor White

Henry Gordon White was born in Croydon in 1902, and baptised in the Church of England, of which his father was a clergyman. After reception into the Catholic Church he received the habit of the Order at Woodchester in 1924. (He had earlier tried his hand with the secular clergy at the English College in Valladolid.) His basic studies were completed at Hawkesyard, where he was ordained priest in June 1928. After a year of further study at Louvain (a quite common phenomenon, thanks to the Flemish connections of the English Province, see Appendix, p. 412), he went to Oxford in 1929 when the priory was opened. In the following year he became a lector in theology there, and remained at the Oxford Blackfriars until 1954, teaching at various times both dogmatic and moral theology as well as Church history. Fr Victor's theological touch was outstandingly sure, but his theological outlook – a Thomist sensibility deliberately attuned to a wider culture – was perfectly typical of the English Dominicans these studies will describe. We shall shortly see, through passing his work in review, what that might mean. This judgment requires, however, one qualification and that an extremely important one. The exceptional element lay in the influence on his thought of Carl Gustav Jung, the Swiss depth psychologist. In Jung Fr Victor would find not only a surprising source of theological illumination but also, in the end, a hostile and barely reconcilable interlocutor whose enmity was only just overcome, through the intervention of Mother Michael of the Carmel of Presteigne, by the time of his death.

Adrian Cunningham, of the University of Lancaster, writing of Fr Victor's relations with Jung, calls their meeting, indeed, a 'fateful encounter'.[1] While it is important not to let the 'Jungian controversy' totally dominate an account of Fr Victor's own theology, it has to be conceded that it was, biographically speaking, the most important single factor in his Dominican life. In the late 30s he encountered Jungians for the first time at an Oxford group where clergy, psychol-

ogists and others met to discuss common themes, under the chair-
manship of John Layard, himself both anthropologist and Jungian
analyst. (Layard and his wife Doris had been trained as psychotherapists by Jung himself. They were eventually to become Catholics.) A
more personal involvement began, through the good offices of Donald
Mackinnon, the Scottish Episcopal philosophical theologian, when in
1940 Fr Victor initiated, with Layard, a Jungian analysis of himself.
In a fragmentary memorandum, now in the possession of the English
Dominican Archive, which describes his search for enhanced self-
understanding, he maintains a proper realism as to just how much
light is available to us – by *any* procedure – in this world.

> It is difficult to know where to begin this story, for I do not yet
> know where it is going to end. Perhaps I shall never know; perhaps
> it never does end. And until I know the end, I shall never know its
> real beginning. For even were I to introduce the story with a weari-
> some complete autobiography, still I should not begin from the
> beginning. I should have to go much further back than the limits of
> my conscious memory will take me; back to infancy; back to the
> womb; back to my parents; back to their wombs and their parents
> and so ad infinitum. Back, perhaps, to palaeolithic and anthropoid
> ancestors, back to Eden, back to primaeval swamps, back to the
> Mind of God. And that is just what, as yet, I cannot do. I cannot
> know the beginning until I know the end; and when I know the
> End, I shall know Everything.

In 1945, with the war ended, Fr Victor began a correspondence with
Jung which lasted until 1959.[2] In its course, he became regarded,
somewhat to his own irritation, as the house theologian of the Jungian
movement – an etiquette whose own uncertain implications led to the
abrupt cancellation of his appointment as Regent of Studies of the
Province. When the Master of the Order, Emmanuel Suarez, was
killed in a motoring accident in the summer of 1954, the Provincial,
Fr Hilary Carpenter, who distrusted these arcane sources of wisdom,
saw his opportunity, and used the intermission in office-holders in
Rome to have the appointment set aside.[3] All unknown to his
brethren, the turn of affairs was made more painful for Fr Victor by
its following hard on the heels of a personal struggle over his vocation, as revealed in private letters to Jung.[4] The situation was acutely
embarrassing but eventually – at any rate, at the institutional level –
resolved.

Ever since the late nineteenth-century *éclat* of Woodchester –
spread abroad not least by Jandel – had encouraged the Dominicans
of the Californian Province to send their students thither for part of

their training, the English and Californian Provinces had been in sporadic communication. The solution found was for Fr Victor to spend a year on the Pacific seaboard of America, until the *débâcle* of his non-appointment became stale news. When he returned in March 1955, to Blackfriars, Cambridge, it was for the last years of his life. An accident on a motor cycle in April 1959 did nothing to inhibit the development of a cancer which killed him – by way of thrombosis – on 22 May 1960. Some would consider that he had legitimate griev-ances over his treatment by the Order (yet no religious order has a duty to offer its members 'a career'). His death, however, seems to have been serene. As one of his pupils reported:

> Whatever his human anguish about the difficulties of his position, he appears to have died without bitterness, his last words being 'Dear God, take me', as widely reported to her friends by Mother Michael of the Blessed Trinity, on the authority of Mrs Ginsberg, who was present.[5]

The breakdown of his friendship with Jung saddened these last years. The crisis in their relation turned on Fr Victor's evaluation of Jung's study *Answer to Job*, something I will consider in due course. Here it may simply be noted that, on the book's republication as part of Jung's *Collected Works* in English translation Fr Victor – barely two years before his death – described it scathingly in these words:

> The editors call it provocative, but we are uncertain what it is intended to provoke. Were it not for the preface, we might read most of it as a straight religious satire in the line of Voltaire, France and Shaw's *Black Girl* ... The preface may appease the indignation of the devout reader when it assures us that the 'God' or 'Yahweh' – who is the book's protagonist and victim – is not God or Yahweh at all, but a psychological image or archetype. But this can only baffle other readers, rather especially if they are also psychologists. For while they may have learned that the human psyche can project images, and the ego may become more conscious of them, they will find it hardly intelligible that an image should (as does 'Yahweh' in this account) itself project and become conscious – let alone create the world and become incarnate.

Deploring Jung's reduction of the 'high tragedy' of the biblical Book of Job to 'banal melodrama', Fr Victor concludes cuttingly with the remark that Jung's *Answer* constitutes a perfect candidate for 'a Freudian interpretation, in terms of the author's own personal psychology and parental relationships'.[6]

In April 1960, Jung, once apprised by Mother Michael of the imminence of Fr Victor's death, wrote to offer him his peace, declaring himself convinced of his 'sincere and human loyalty', and even saying that, were he younger and fitter he would attend his deathbed. He had a Mass offered for the repose of his soul on the first birthday after his death, 21 October of that year. Fr Victor had remarked humorously enough that it was all very well Jung complaining he had disapproved of part of his work – given the trouble the Dominican had brought on himself for approving of most of it!

I have said that Jungianism – or, better, a Catholic and Thomistic appropriation of Jung's insights – was not the only passion of Fr Victor's life. Two other causes may be mentioned. His anguish of soul in 1940 did not, it may be surmised, turn entirely on inner-psychological factors. He was much shaken by two events. One was on a vast scale: the approach of war and the challenge it brought to those Catholics who, having sought a Thomistic renascence of social morality, and a Distributist recasting of the social substance, now saw these hopes frustrated with the coming of a quite different agenda. In May 1940 Fr Victor initiated a major correspondence in the *Catholic Herald* of London, then under the distinguished control of Count Michael de la Bedoyère. While admitting the danger of contributing 'wantonly' to a division of public opinion, and careful not to implicate the Order as a whole (or indeed 'any of my fellow-Dominicans'), Fr Victor proposed that Catholics should: refuse co-operation in any method of warfare which involves the slaying by direct intention of non-combatants; hold themselves bound to resist all forms of 'hate propaganda'; publicly make plain their distrust of the Soviet alliance, and disapproval of a war whose effect would be 'to extend atheistic Communism in the event either of victory or defeat'; require that all reasonable means of peaceful settlement of territorial dispute (Danzig and the Corridor; Djibouti, Tunis and Suez) be manifestly exhausted; ask of Government what concrete end or settlement to war they envisaged, in the case of victory, and declare a preference for any form of *physical* evil to any kind of moral. As he wrote:

> If the dilemma should arise, we must prefer any suffering and humiliation to the committing of sin ... our very love for our country demands that we should prefer even national humiliation, defeat and foreign domination itself to a war which is morally evil and contrary to the law of God in its end or its methods or its moral circumstances. We believe that national honour is far less compromised by the former than by the latter, and that it will indeed be enhanced by the former if undergone for the avoidance of the latter. While we believe non-resistance to be a counsel and not a precept,

we believe also that counsels are preceptive when their only alternative is sin.[7]

It was soon pointed out by a contributor to the debate (R. J. Dingle) that the law makes no provision for what Fr Victor had in mind: the conscientious objection it foresees must be to war *per se*, not to the political objects or consequences of a particular war. The clause was intended for Quakers, Tolstoyans and Christadelphians whose doctrines in these matters differed greatly from those of the Catholic Church.

In a speech to the Oxford University Society of Christian Socialists in the wartime winter of 1942, he commented with some bitterness:

> The workers of the world consider that they have very much more to lose than their chains. So far from uniting for world socialism they are blowing each other to pieces, if not with positive enthusiasm then at least with docility and effectiveness. Race and blood, custom, self-preservation, mere inertia and gregariousness, have proved far more powerful factors of union and division than the international payroll.[8]

And if the laying bare of the fallaciousness of Marxism-Leninism provided some compensation ('The historical dialectic, we are discovering, writes with very crooked lines indeed'), the fact remained that the coming of a more humane and truly theocentric society in the West was no further advanced. Looking to Ditchling, the Laxton Distributists, and the Iona of the Presbyterian George McLeod as models, Fr Victor ended with a moving appeal for strategic withdrawal.

> No Christian can postpone Utopia, or the life of the children of the Kingdom, to the remote and undefined future; it must be proclaimed and exemplified here and now – and no one will find that more difficult than the Christian in politics in the narrower sense. All should, I think, recognise the fact that there are times when the most effective way to contribute to the aims of Christian politics is the exemplification of Christian life lived in the greatest possible independence of the existing political and economic set-up and the whole productive and distributive apparatus which it organises.

After all:

> It was in this manner, in the Dark Ages, in the hermitages and monasteries, that the windows of this world were left open to eternity, that from them later eternity could radiate into time and make

possible the recovery of any sort of culture, justice and kindness.
There are times when, on a long estimate, the really effective way
to 'muck in' is to 'muck out'.

These words signal the abandonment of the hope which, as a
convinced student of Maritain's *Humanisme intégral*, animated him in
the 1930s for a 'new Christendom', analogically related to the old.[9]

The last of Fr Victor's enthusiams which warrants mention is
ecumenism, the movement for the reunion of Christians, and the event
of 1940 which added to the uncertainty of that time of his life: an invitation from Dom Bede Winslow, monk of Ramsgate, to take part in
an English Chevetogne, a 'monastery of union' on the pattern of the
Belgian Benedictine foundation at Amay-sur-Meuse, working for the
reunion of, in particular, separated Eastern Christians with the
Catholic Church. Discreet 'conversations' between the English
Dominicans and the Fathers of the Anglican 'Society of the Sacred
Mission' had been pioneered by Fr Henry St John, OP, a former
Anglican clergyman of squirearchical background who was, from
1928 to 1954 headmaster of Laxton. Later these would diversify as to
the composition of the Roman and Anglo-Catholic teams,[10] but insofar
as they are represented in Fr Victor's papers, they remained definitely
the 'Laxton conversations' with 'Kelham' – the Society's mother-
house and convenient sobriquet.[11]

Although the Laxton conversations awakened Fr Victor to the possibilities of ecumenism, the interlocutors stubbed their toes on the issues
that, fifty years later, would set definite limits to post-conciliar
ecumenical advance in relations between the Catholic Church and
Anglicanism. Thus we find that 'The OP suggestion that agreement
could be reached upon the statement 'Revelation is embodied in apostolic tradition' was accepted by SSM with the rider 'Provided that
Holy Scripture is a safeguard *sine qua non* for *de fide* definition.' Or
again:

> From the SSM point of view, as it appeared to us, *de fide* defini-
> tion is regarded rather as a last line of defence against heresy.
> SSM, moreover, deprecate the multiplication of definitions as prej-
> udicial to Christian unity. OP, whilst fully appreciating that point
> of view, would consider the development of dogma from the orig-
> inal deposit of revelation and the rational formulation of this
> development as necessary in the life of a growing and developing
> Church.[12]

Increasingly, however, Fr Victor looked not so much to Anglicans as
to the Christian East. If his study 'The Background to Papal

Infallibility', a response to some remarks of the Oxford Anglican Professor Clement Webb, was printed in the Anglo-Papalist journal *Reunion* in 1937, by 1942 we find 'Western and Eastern Theology of Grace and Nature' originating as a paper read to the Orthodox and Anglican Fellowship of SS. Alban and Sergius and published in the organ *Sobornost*. There he wrote:

> The East and the West are both very sick; each, I believe, from the hypertrophy of its own virtues and for lack of complementary and counterbalancing unity with the other. To us, both of East and West, this terrible, sacrilegious schism must become so intolerable that we are ready and eager and determined to pay the heavy price which must be paid to atone for our rending of the Body of Christ. It is not that we can pay the criminal price of infidelity either to authentic Eastern Orthodoxy or to authentic Western Catholicism. Rather must each rediscover that authenticity in its common origin, and be more faithful to its integral and unsullied tradition, the tradition of the Church of the Seven Councils.[13]

Around the same time, he was also writing for *Eastern Churches Quarterly*, the pioneering journal for the English Catholic study of the Christian East, founded by Bede Winslow in 1936. Growing out of a supplement to the Prinknash Benedictine journal *Pax*, the E.C.Q. was pervaded by the ethos of its creator, of whom Elizabeth Fry, his collaborator, wrote, 'There was, under the undemonstrative exterior, a bit of a love-affair with Eastern Christianity'.[14] During the later 1930s Winslow strove to create the ecumenical monastery to which Fr Victor became strongly attracted. Fry describes the project in these words:

> It was to be exclusively Latin, unlike Amay – he [Dom Bede] never really believed in Westerners taking or using Eastern rites, apart from exceptional cases of a very deep vocation. It was to work primarily by the Benedictine means of a liturgical and contemplative and laborious life – it was to be an agricultural community. Secondarily, it was to work through hospitality and be the source of the E.C.Q., and a centre of ecumenical interest and information.[15]

In Christmastide 1940, we find Fr Victor writing to John Layard reporting the nightmarish dreams that visited him in the period of waiting before the Dominican Provincial would give him an interview on this topic: his proposed entry into the 'Winslow community'.[16] The difficulty of getting the 'right personnel' is cited by Fry as a major contributory reason for the project's failure; yet it must be 'taken as the model' for how Winslow believed that 'work for unity could best be done'.[17]

Fr Victor's attraction to the Christian East, and to work for its reconciliation in no way implied any *insouciance* towards the Western heritage – as, regrettably, is sometimes the case. More specifically, he argued powerfully for an Orthodox reassessment of scholasticism. He pleaded with their representatives not to 'recoil too hastily from this scholastic terminology until you have first mastered the meaning it had for the greater schoolmen'.[18] In an age of metaphysical decline, such discourse could only become debased coinage. Moreover, the scholastic theologian in his concern to 'extract and to safeguard the intelligible meaning' to be found in the symbols of divine revelation seeks to serve them, not destroy them.

> These high mysteries taken in isolation are patient of interpretations which are destructive of other high mysteries, equally integral to the *analogia fidei*, to the fullness of the faith, and of great hurt to the souls for which Christ died.

Thus, just as the Fatherhood, Sonship, breathing and flesh-taking of God became in the patristic and conciliar discussion of the Greek East the subjects of terms like *phusis, ousia, hypostasis, perichoresis, idiomata*, so in the Latin West, 'cause' and 'effect', 'substance' and 'accident', *qualitas* and *habitus, gratia activa* or *gratia passiva*, have become linguistic aids to Catholic Orthodoxy with regard to 'our membership of Christ's body, and our deification through identity with the God-Man...' And this is highly germane to the first of Fr Victor's works we shall explore.

A view of scholasticism

Fr Victor's approach to the world of Christian scholasticism, which formed the principal intellectual matrix of the English Dominicans at the start of our period, is most succinctly expressed in the little study entitled *Scholasticism* which the Catholic Truth Society included, curiously, in a series of 'Studies in Comparative Religion'.

He opens with an assertion of both the unity and the pluralism of scholastic thought. By and large the Christian scholastics possessed 'a certain unity of outlook, an agreement on certain fundamental assumptions'. But this *Gemeingut* or common inheritance does not of itself make scholasticism a system – as its name might, misleadingly, imply. The 'ensemble of the highly variegated speculation of the mediaeval schools' was something 'very heterogeneous': in more modern terminology, 'pluralistic'. Fr Victor defines his subject, accordingly, in these terms: 'the sum of the learning and the specula- tion, and of the multifarious systems of thought which were taught and debated in the schools of the Middle Ages or which, surviving and developing after that period, had their origins therein.'[19] So under- stood, Christian scholasticism merits cultural, philosophical and religious respect: *cultural* respect, for the schoolmen salvaged crucial elements of the inheritance of Greece and Rome, transmitting precious remnants of antiquity in 'more vital if less lovely forms', and in so doing determining the 'distinctive form which European culture assumed'; *philosophical* respect, for both the content of scholastic thinking and its methods – especially today when 'clearly defined methods of thought and exposition have become something of a lost art'; *religious* respect, since it constituted in its own day and (in numerous Catholic educational institutions) since the 'vehicle whereby the revelation of God through Jesus Christ is principally expressed, taught, penetrated, systematised'. It is on the latter that Fr Victor will lay – as is proper for a theologian – most weight.

His account of the pre-scholastic period of Western theology is chiefly indebted to one English and one German source: Christopher Dawson, whose importance for the English Catholic Culture of the 1930s has already been signalled, and Martin Grabmann, the prodi- giously learned historian of scholasticism, whose work at the Ludwig-Maximilian University in Munich is today commemorated in the Martin Grabmann Institut of mediaeval theological history there. Fr Victor explains that the 'extreme conservative traditionalism' of the post-patristic period slowed down the tempo of theological work, while the barbarian incursions simultaneously lowered the cultural level of the Latin West. In the monastic schools, which perpetuated the pedagogical tradition of the late antique schools of rhetoric, *ratio* – the conscious application of dialectical method – might be applied to some point of doctrine here and there, but *auctoritas* – the deploy- ment of authorities from Scripture to the Fathers – was king. What was missing was the use of *ratio* as 'a recognised instrument for pene- trating and co-ordinating the whole corpus of Christian doctrine'. When people decided to do *that*, scholasticism was born.

And in Fr Victor's view, that birth had one midwife: the Benedictine monk Anselm of Canterbury. This judgment is decisive for the picture Fr Victor is painting. It means that scholasticism is not the coming-of-age of theological reason in its autonomy; it was revo- lutionary without being rebellious. Its *ratio*, however it be described, cannot be defined over against *auctoritas*. For:

Anselm was second to none of his contemporaries in his profound reverence for authority and tradition. He was possessed of a singularly vivid sense of the divine character of the Church's teaching-authority and that of the Holy See and of Holy Scripture. He had the highest esteem for the teachings of the ancient Fathers and especially for his beloved Saint Augustine. It was not in his acknowledgement and reverence for *auctoritas* that Anselm differed from his predecessors and contemporaries. It was in the *use* which he made of authority that he was an innovator.[20]

And, with Grabmann, Fr Victor believes that the crucial difference was this: patristic study, for Anselm, was a *stimulus to further investigation*.[21] As Anselm himself puts it so simply in his treatise *De fide Trinitatis et de Incarnatione Verbi*:

The days of a man's life are numbered, and those holy doctors were not able, within the short span of their lives, to say everything that might be said. Truth is so vast and so deep that it cannot be exhausted by any mortal man; nor has our Lord, who has promised to abide with his Church till the end of the world, ceased to impart his gifts.[22]

Here we find Fr Victor in the process of setting out a theological agenda (no less!) for his readers, and hence, implicitly, for the Order to which he belonged, in its English context. And that agenda is neither (with theological Modernism) deconstructionist nor (with the most unimaginative of contemporary neo-scholasticisms) merely repetitive, but 'constructionist' in both preserving tradition (a *sine qua non*) and building upon it.

There are various aspects to this. First, there is the (anti-rationalist) conviction that *ratio* is not a means to belief but a necessary instrument for penetrating the inner meaning of the truths which (by faith) Catholic Christians believe. Secondly, there is a repudiation of a purely intellectualist account of how faith is led to *intellectus*, 'understanding' (for that was Anselm's brief description of theological reason at work, *fides quaerens intellectum*, 'faith seeking understanding'). As Fr Victor cites from the *Monologion*: 'It is clear that man must concentrate *all* his powers to the contemplation, understanding and love of the supreme Good.'[23] Thirdly, Fr Victor commits himself to the cause of scholastic *ratio* insofar as it is systematising, co-ordinating, synthetic. And this turns out to have two aspects, one *organic*, the other *analogical*.

By employing methodical dialectic for the attainment of a deeper and more embracing understanding of all aspects of particular dogmas [Anselm] was led to see their essential interrelation one with another, and the essentially organic character of the corpus of Christian doctrine. The analogies of supernatural and natural truths became apparent to a degree which had not been appreciated hitherto.[24]

And those are, indeed, the great steps forward for which Catholic tradition will always be indebted to scholastic thought.

If we are to understand the particular twist which Fr Victor attempted to give to the scholastic tradition as it existed among Dominicans in his lifetime, it is vital to recognise the pivotal role he allotted to Anselm. His eye is always – and balefully – vigilant for what he terms the 'left-wing scholastics'. Appealing to the work of the German Dominican Heinrich Seuse Denifle, he insists that authentic scholasticism is always open to the mystical dimension of Christianity.[25] For him, not only Albert and Thomas but also Bonaventure, the Victorines, William of St Thierry, Rupert of Deutz and even St Bernard were at one and the same time mystics *and* scholastics.

It is safe to assert that there was no really great scholastic theologian in the Middle Ages who was not something of a mystic, and, what is more remarkable, there was scarcely a mystic or saint during this period who was not to some extent a scholastic theologian.[26]

But the Latin Christian achievement was unthinkable without the Greeks. As Fr Victor points out, St John Damascene's *On the Orthodox Faith* served as inspirational model for the scholastic renaissance of the West, while the translation of the whole of Aristotle's *Organon* – the 'new Aristotle' of the thirteenth century – not only improved but 'crystallised' the dialectical technique of *ratio*. 'Scholasticism' here means, above all, 'high' scholasticism – the golden age whose sun-king was Aquinas. His account was especially indebted to Père Antonin-Dalmace Sertillanges' *S. Thomas d'Aquin et son oeuvre*, a study translated by a member of the Province, the historian Godfrey Anstruther, in 1933. But just as Fr Victor's praise of *ratio* is, in Anselmian fashion, no detraction from *auctoritas*, so his enthusiasm for the reception of Aristotle at the moment of the Thomist high noon is not intended as any repudiation of Plato: hitherto the 'loving nurse' of Christian philosophy. He goes out of his way to praise Plato for:

his theism, his other-worldliness, his vindication of the primacy of the spiritual against earthly values, his insistence on the reality and worth of personality and personal experiences, on moral conversion and ascesis as the condition of spiritual realization, on the immortality of the soul ...[27]

How could this catalogue ever be bettered? Thanks to the transmission of the works of Aristotle 'from Athens to Alexandria, from Alexandria to Syria' and thence, absorbed into the Muslim world, through north Africa to Spain, the Christian mind was able to make use of a yet more powerful intellectual instrument. For Aristotle had 'got to the heart of things, [he] had laid the foundations of an eternally valid metaphysics, had laid bare the inner meaning of reality and the ultimate structure of being.' In more measured language, Aristotle could give Catholic theology what, to this date, it lacked: 'a sound metaphysical framework and, to some hitherto unsuspected extent, a rational justification'. In all this, St Albert's contribution was – for Fr Victor, following, once again, Grabmann – distinctly provisional. It was insufficiently 'orderly or methodical'. Fr Victor's hero is, without a doubt, St Thomas.

In his paean to St Thomas, Fr Victor both undergirds and goes beyond his positive evaluation of scholasticism as a whole. *Undergirds*, because his Aquinas is *par excellence* the intellectual saint. Yet *goes beyond*, because 'his work was something utterly new and unique, which transcended the most ambitious aims of the Scholasticism of the past'. How so? Though his supreme life-work was the revelation of the ultimate harmony of supernature and nature, he also recognised the autonomy, within its own province, of purely natural reason.[28] And here Fr Victor departs from his general account of scholasticism by stressing the novel features of Thomas's intellectual production *vis-à-vis* the (already innovatory) project of scholasticism at large. For Thomas not only insisted on the most authentic texts, he also recognised the varying degrees of authority which those texts commanded. At the same time, he set about the 'simplification and rejuvenation' of the scholastic technique itself, which, at the hands of his predecessors, had sometimes become end where it should resolutely have remained means.

All of this touches on *method*; but what of *content*? Fr Victor's attempt (it can be no more!) to encapsulate St Thomas's thought in a nutshell also sums up his own abiding theological convictions. And philosophically (first) these are:

> that the object of our thought is Being: the metaphysical world of essences, causes, purposes, and laws, which lies beyond the world of appearances; that it can attain the inmost structure of finite reality and that it can argue to the existence and attributes of infinite God, transcendent and immortal.

And to this optimistic philosophy is added an equally confident theology:

The theological foundation is the conviction, guaranteed by God himself, that over and above, but interpenetrating, this metaphysical realm, there is a boundless Supernature, the Triune God revealed to man in Christ, to the sharing of whose life, through grace here, in glory hereafter, man is called and destined.

Nor is this all. For – and here is the axiom which enabled Fr Victor (and, implicitly or explicitly, all the English Dominicans described in this book) both to appropriate and to take further the cultural materials they found present at hand in their theological work –

over and above this is the conviction that these two orders of nature and supernature – the first the object of reason, the other of faith – are in reality one, owing their unity and cohesion to the one God from whom all proceeds and to whom all tends.

And this made possible, then, in St Thomas, the synthesis of the whole body of truth (human and divine) which with 'a daring undreamed of by his predecessors' he 'made it his life-work to construct and express'. Fr Victor in his turn gives expression to a vision of Thomas so exalted that few, even, of committed Thomists can follow him to the heights, when he remarks:

His work is ... the final fruit of mediaeval Scholasticism, in which Scholasticism transcended itself. St Thomas occupies a unique position between the mediaeval and the modern world. The mediaeval world had never attained that breadth of clear vision which could contain the Heaven and the Earth in the range of a single glance. The modern world has lost it.[29]

This is overstated; yet its hubris helped to launch a culture on its voyage.

Closely relevant to Fr Victor's presentation of Thomist scholasticism are his essay on 'Holy Teaching' – Aquinas's concept of theology, and the brief commentary on the saint's *De modo studendi* which served as the inaugural lecture of the academic year 1944–45 in the study houses of Hawkesyard and Oxford. Fr Victor opens *Holy Teaching* by drawing attention to an important, though not easily accessible, study which brings together all the main texts whereby people in the past have set forth their understanding of what theology, for Thomas, was.[30] He cannot compete in completeness with the Dutch Jesuit van Ackeren's account (it was sufficiently ecumenical to carry a preface by the protagonist of Christian Reunion Père Yves Congar!) – and yet a fresh look may have something to be said for it.

Fr Victor stresses the 'kerygmatic, evangelistic or pastoral' rather than 'academic, speculative or scholarly' concept of theology subjacent to St Thomas's account.[31] But, as he at once admits, so rare is Thomas's use of the *word* 'theology', that such a claim must seem somewhat hardy. In fact, in the introduction to the *Summa Theologiae* we encounter the word but twice: once when Thomas wants to distinguish his own use of it from that of Aristotle – for whom it meant 'first philosophy', that is, metaphysics, something clearly distinct from what is going on in the '*holy* teaching' Aquinas is talking about – and once when Thomas pauses, merely, to give the word's derivation, 'talk about God'. Fr Victor's evaluation turns in fact on his belief that the *Summa Theologiae* is a teacher's handbook, and the 'beginners' in *sacra doctrina* not first-year theological students at all but anyone who is starting to understand the Catholic faith.

> The task of the *catholicae veritatis doctor* is ... to encounter *all* men, beginners no less than the proficient, leading them from what they know and accept to what they do not of the universal truth. And the whole purpose of the *Summa* will be to assist him in this task. In other words, its whole orientation is evangelistic, 'pedagogical', and ... it is 'scientific' only to the extent that scientific and logical methods may serve this evangelistic concern.[32]

If this be true, then a number of hoary old chestnuts about the *Summa Theologiae* as an ABC for new boys will have to be lain in a drawer. Its difficulty is, in point of fact, no less (but no more) than that of high mediaeval theology at large.

Nevertheless, St Thomas hoped that its order would prove pedagogically well-adapted: his 'treatment and arrangement' will be governed by the claims of the '*ordo disciplinae* – the order of learning, pedagogical method', rather than by the interests of '*ordo investigationis* – the professional investigator.' And *teaching* for Aquinas means the 'leading-out' (*e-ducatio*) of the mind of another from what it knows and accepts to what it as yet does not'. In the case of *this* teaching, however, both subject and object are *sacra*, in the strict sense of 'divine'. 'God only is the Teacher and the Taught – the Doctor and the doctrine – in this *sacra doctrina*: the rest of us are its *doctores* only as the instruments for the imparting of a *veritas* which he alone strictly knows.' Our investigation of God's revealed mysteries will take the form, accordingly, not of establishing their *être* (*that* they exist) but their *raison d'être* (*why* they exist), namely the purpose which this or that act of divine 'free-giving' is meant to fulfil.

Revealed mysteries are the order of the day because God's destining man to a completion or fulfilment beyond his grasp is 'solely the gift of his grace, and therefore known to God alone'. And this *salus*, 'salvation', Fr Victor interprets – revealing at this juncture the connection with his *psychological* interests – as "health", "weal", "well-being", 'vital integration", here as well as hereafter'. On the divine teaching, then, 'depends the whole weal of man which is in his God'. This firm – indeed passionate – conviction explains Fr Victor's attitude to the Modernist crisis and its aftermath, for the effects of that seismic shock still reverberated in the period of his writing. Reviewing Maude Petre's *Von Hügel and Tyrrell: The Story of a Friendship* for *Blackfriars* he felt that the Modernist *grande dame* had missed the point.

> Tyrrell, Loisy and the rest were condemned not because they sought a 'fuller recognition on the part of the Church of the social, historical and scientific demands of the modern mind', but because they reached and held tenaciously to doctrines which falsified the inmost meaning of the Christian Scriptures and Creeds.[33]

The spiritual and intellectual revival in inter-war Catholicism which Miss Petre believed to be the 'lineal descendant and inheritor' of Loisy and Tyrrell resulted, rather, in Fr Victor's view, from the 'ruthless extermination of the naturalistic philosophy of religion which they substituted for supernatural theology'. Though the 'pettiness' and 'anguish' which accompanied the anti-Modernist reaction are deeply to be regretted, even more deplorable was the existence of that to which anti-Modernists were reacting.

He had devoted a good deal of thought to the topic by way of preparing his paper for the Laxton Conference with the Anglican monks of Kelham in the previous year. In his paper on 'Authority, Revelation and Infallibility', he remarked that

> The story of the rise and fall of Roman Catholic Modernism will remind [a Catholic] that it is possible to attain a considerable degree of verbal agreement with orthodox creeds and dogmatic utterances and even, indeed, with large tracts of the *Summa* of St Thomas, while the facts which the creeds proclaim and which the *Summa* presupposes may be freely denied or held in question.

This was how the Modernists 'contrived to combine orthodoxy and liberalism'. And appealing to the French Dominican Ambroise Gardeil's *Le Donné révélé et la théologie*, he summarised and appropriated the latter's reply to Tyrrell in the words 'Experience may be the stuff of knowledge, but it is not knowledge, and does not convey truth unless it be reflected on by the mind'. And he echoed this remark in a statement made towards the end of his life on the same topic:

The question of truth or error arises only in the judgment, in some affirmation or negation about it. The onlooker by the Jordan, or on the mount of Transfiguration sees only what he sees. The 'voice from heaven' says something about it; and what it says is no less than 'This is my beloved Son'.[34]

Accepted in faith, this 'revelational fact' already declares what Nicaea and Chalcedon will formulate as dogma: the *homoousia* of Jesus with the Father. Not that the original revelatory experience is always given in explicit propositions, for more customarily these are lacking. But dogmas are continuous with such 'experienced facts about experienced facts': they too state what is revealed, being called forth by the original experience of revelation and the need to 'describe, communicate and understand it, truthfully and not erroneously'.[35] Here Fr Victor's Thomist emphasis on truth and on mind as the faculty of the true helped him to keep a firm hold on the integrity of doctrine at a time when the waters of modern sentimentalism were rising higher.

Not that this implied, of course, that Fr Victor was averse to *all* rethinking of the gospel in more contemporary categories. It was simply that the rethinking must be faithful, a genuine re-presentation of the same message. He offers an *exemplum* in an existentialist idiom in *Holy Teaching*.

The *veritas catholica* is no mere *conformitas intellectus cum re* (this is only the indispensable preliminary, which itself demands the voluntary 'leap' of faith from the self-sufficiency of human consciousness into utter confidence in the Unseen and the Unknown); for the *res* itself is presented not as an already intelligible idea, form or essence, but as end. And because it is an end, it is realised, becomes real and true, not just by its conscious acceptance as an idea (*fide sola*), but must be really achieved, 'created' out of the 'nothingness' – the indetermination – of freedom. Or, in St Thomas's own, pre-existentialist words, it is attained only by *intentiones et actiones*. 'Be ye doers of the Word, and not hearers only.' But there can be no such doing without hearing: the *sacra doctrina* announces the old, old story, and the timeless and eternal too; but not just for scientific scrutiny or serene contemplation, but as end and means, as a challenge, as something not yet done, and demanding to be done, by '*intentiones et actiones*', by purpose and action. And only in the measure in which it is *done* is it saving and healing *truth*. Only so is it 'needed', and only so does it meet the needs of the learner – the disciple – who is all mankind.[36]

The point which this particular example of *relecture* serves is one made in more Hellenic terms by Aquinas himself when he denies that *sacra doctrina* can be reduced to either the 'speculative' or 'the practical' *tout court*. The divine knowledge transcends the distinction found in the human sciences between what concerns objectivity for its own sake, and what directs subjective action. Accordingly, the *sacra doctrina* which is an 'imprint' of this knowledge, also transcends and comprehends both. And casting an eye on his own Jungian investigations, Fr Victor comments that

> our present-day understanding of the psychological function of symbols and beliefs may help us to understand how eminently practical and inherently salutary are such seemingly 'speculative' treatises as those on the Trinity, the Incarnation, the Eucharist.

Incidentally, this is not the only Jungian allusion in *Holy Teaching*. The two ways in which St Thomas thought that correct judgment might be formed in theology, through study and rational processes, on the one hand, and 'inclination' or 'connaturality' on the other, are likened to Jung's functional distinction between 'intellectual judgments' and 'feeling judgments'. Which is the more appropriate for learning purposes will often turn on the 'typology' of the learner.

In conclusion: Fr Victor's presentation of *sacra doctrina* is at once supernaturalist and pragmatic. 'Supernaturalist' because he strongly underlines how Thomas values reasoning processes in theology not for any prospect of somehow 'improving' upon revelation – for example, by making its content more 'scientific'. On the contrary, revelation is already, just because it is supernatural, unsurpassable fulness, and all extraneous disciplines or procedures in its regard derive simply from the needs of human frailty, so as the better to manifest its content to limited minds. 'Pragmatic' because with Thomas he stresses the desirability of adapting theology to the 'vital needs of every class of actual and potential disciple'. He thus links St Thomas to St Dominic, and the wider project of an *ordo praedicatorum*.

> The *sacra praedicatio* for St Dominic did not primarily mean the recitation of monologues from church pulpits to a silent and captive audience of the faithful ... The greater part of his *praedicatio* consisted not of monologues but of dialogue, of long and gruelling discussions with Albigensian leaders, often in public and with lay and even heretical judges and assessors, sometimes lasting weeks on end. And when, so rapidly, he dispersed his small band of brethren into the great urban and university centres of Europe, it surely was not only to teach but also to learn; or, more exactly, just because it was to teach and evangelise, it was to learn what and

how men of their time were thinking, what were their needs, and where they were to be met.[37]

Unlike the *Summa Theologiae*, the *De modo studendi* is addressed not to teachers at large, in the context of the whole Church, but to an individual student, in the context of his cell. In his *Letter to Brother John*, Thomas advises the gradual contemplative appropriation of the truth which the neophyte friar is bursting to learn. Against such *curiositas* he recommends *studiositas* – a controlling of the innate desire of the mind to know, for 'the intellect, being immaterial, cannot be forced, and while the divine Sophia will give herself to humble souls, she will not be raped'.[38] Fr Victor's commentary on the *Letter's* opening section appeals to Thomas's treatise *On Truth* to clarify what is here unspoken. In Thomas's view of education (a modification of Socrates'), truth cannot be imposed from without; it can only grow from within through my own activity: hence the importance of measuring that activity aright. And this explains why, as we shall see, the lion's share of a letter claiming to answer the question, How should I study? actually deals with an apparently different question, How should I *live*?

Not that the teacher's role is nugatory: the existence of the *Summa Theologiae*, as explained by Fr Victor, persuades otherwise. Words, as the 'conventional signs of ideas already attained by other minds', are vital. They are not, however, an end in themselves. And Fr Victor dwells on this point to issue a warning against an inflated, as it were idolatrous attitude to the work of the Angelic Doctor:

> Woe betide us when we mistake the signs for the signified; when we study the *Summa* instead of studying God and his creation with the assistance of the *Summa*. Woe betide us when we put any human teacher in the place which belongs to God alone, giving to his utterances that unqualified assent which belongs only to the humble obedience of faith in the First Truth.[34]

Yet Thomas modifies Socrates' portrait of the teacher as midwife, in that he could never have said, as Socrates is made to say in the *Theaetetus*, 'There is no wisdom in me'.[40] On the contrary, the teacher proposes to the student (the order of premisses to conclusions': 'The Thomistic teacher ... must himself know his stuff'.

Thomas's actual advice to Brother John is overwhelmingly ascetic and ethical: it concerns silence, prayer, the keeping of the cell, fraternal charity, for all of these dispose to theological wisdom. Contemplative silence as the proper background for study makes sense because God 'alone teaches within man and as the Supreme Teacher'[41]

– the silence involved must, then, be not only exterior but interior in the quieting of the emotions. In any case, the worshipful subjection of the mind to God safeguards the student against intellectual pride. 'Consciously directed, collaborative friendship', typical of good community spirit, serves study, enabling interchange and preventing criticism from being resented, whereas to be avoided are the disruptive effect of *familiaritas*, which Fr Victor paraphrases as 'strange, overwhelming, absorbing personal attractions and repulsions'.

There then follows a passage where St Thomas meets in advance the criticism later made of scholasticism as a useless system of appeal to authorities: 'Do not heed by *whom* a thing is said, but rather *what* is said you should commit to memory.' For Fr Victor, members of the Dominican Order cannot be too thankful that 'the highest voices in the Church summon us to the feet of such a teacher', and yet the very fact that Dominicans are Thomas's pupils closes off to them all 'facile ipsedixitism.'

'Truth is the good of the intellect': this Thomistic axiom was Fr Victor's guiding star in his exegesis of the *De modo studendi*. The fruits of St Dominic's contemplation would not have been useful to others unless they had first been good in themselves – an allusion to the Letter's peroration, which, in one of the horticultural metaphors beloved of Scripture, speaks of seed putting forth foliage, blossoms and – eventually – grapes, in the vineyard of the Lord of Hosts. Fr Victor's final work plays with that couplet Eros/Agape, which had so appealed to Martin D'Arcy as a way of speaking of the complementary tasks of nature and supernature in Catholic theology. If our intellectual longing (like Brother John's) is to be satisfied, that can only be because

> the infinite, all-devouring Eros is met ... by the gracious self-giving of the Infinite in Agape. Then alone can our intellect know even as it is known, no longer *in aenigmate* ['through a glass in a dark manner'], in the slow, tedious business of collecting and collating sense-experience, the search for *media demonstrationis* ['means of proof'], but 'face to face'.[42]

Doctrinal foundations

How, with these convictions about the value of Christian scholasticism in general and the thought and example of Aquinas in particular, did Fr Victor lay the doctrinal foundations for his own contribution to Catholic thought? Essays written from the 1930s onwards and gathered together in *God the Unknown* enable us to formulate an answer.[43] Leaving aside the account of the 'theologian's task', already touched on, those essays may conveniently be brought under four heads: Fr Victor's *de Deo*, or theology of God; his *de Christo*, or theology of the Incarnation; his *de gratia*, or theology of salvation, and his *de ecclesia*, or theology of the Church.

First, then, how did Fr Victor present the fundamental approach of Catholic theology to the mystery of God himself? He was a distinctly *apophatic* theologian: emphasising God's infinite exceeding of all man's concepts and images, he could echo Thomas in repeating Denys the Areopagite's axiom in the *Mystical Theology* that the most perfect union with God is union with the utterly Unknown.[44] It is not enough to say that our knowledge of God is inadequate and indistinct. Thomas will assert that of our cognition of the angels – of whom, he thinks, we can never know what distinguishes one from another. But God lies outside all categories and classes of being, just as he is beyond any possibility of being imagined or conceived.

This does not of course imply that Fr Victor – or Thomas Aquinas, or Denys – was agnostic about the fact *that* God is. It is *what* he is, not that he is which is the mystery. Through the existence of other things – a rather multifarious collection of other things, 'all sorts of happenings, changes, productions, things, values, strivings', we can prove that there *is* that which human beings call 'God' or 'the Divine'. The famous 'Five Ways' to the existence of God, in Fr Victor's careful formulation:

> enable us to know not the being or existence of God (*Dei esse*), but only that what men call God is, or exists (*Deum esse*). They show that *unless* there is some unknown ground or source ... on which everything ultimately depends, then nothing could ever exist or happen at all. This is not to say ... that God is an 'explanation' of the universe, for we cannot 'explain' what is to some extent known by what is unknown. But we do claim that if there were no God, there could not be anything else.[45]

Throughout his doctrinal theology, Fr Victor is aware simultaneously of two interlocutors: the philosophical (and normally agnostic) critic on the one hand, and, on the other, the full-bloodedly dogmatic (but anti-Catholic) Neo-Orthodox Evangelical theologian of the school of Karl Barth. For in the English intellectual world of the later 30s, 40s and 50s, non-theistic philosophy (generally some form of logical positivism) and Barthian theology were the most determined schools with which Catholic divinity had either to treat or to do combat.

He stresses, *vis-à-vis* the philosopher, the epistemologically modest character of the 'proofs of God's existence': they do not establish the reality of 'any *a priori* conception of God', for they leave what *Deus* is a mystery, demonstrating solely that 'the mystery, which we can only even name "from effects", truly is'. The *quinque viae* lead to a 'learned ignorance', whereby we affirm 'there is an Unknown', encompassing *en route* the demolition of conceptual idols and misleading preconceptions of the Divine (what Thomas calls *Deus secundum opinionem*, as distinct from *Deus secundum naturam*). As we have seen, Fr Victor is even reluctant to use the phrase 'the *existence* of God' in this context, for 'existence' means having a place in reality's domain, whereas God both transcends and includes all reality. And where the *Oxford English Dictionary* leads, the neo-scholastic manuals follow. There 'existence' is described as 'that whereby something is outside its causes', but the God to which the Ways lead 'has no causes to be outside of, and he cannot be *extra* anything'. However, these *caveats* should not be taken to imply that Fr Victor's confidence in the Five Ways was shaky: these 'ways' show that 'the affirmation of this Unknown is a true and logically necessary affirmation'. He will later go on to explain how, on their basis, fuller discourse about God is possible, and takes place.

But Fr Victor must take another tack *vis-à-vis* the Barthian, a theological animal less frequently sighted (unfortunately) now than then. He had a great, if qualified, admiration for Barth's achievement and its subversive effect on the confidence of theological liberalism among the Protestant churches. Here at last was an ecumenical interlocutor with whom one might do business.

> To the immense influence of Karl Barth, however unfavourably we may judge it in certain respects, is due a more widespread realisation that genuine Christian unity can be achieved only on the basis of uncompromising loyalty to the Truth which is the Word of God in Christ Jesus, that there is no unity in the one Lord which is not unity in one Faith.[46]

Fr Victor had, too, an interior sympathy with the ground of the Barthian objection to natural theology – concern for any compromising of the transcendent integrity of revelation – though not with the objection itself. He believed one could, in Pascal's words, 'hold both ends of the chain' – and a reference to Pascal is apposite, for his *testament* is perhaps the most celebrated formulation of the contrast between the 'God of the philosophers' and the 'God of Abraham, Isaac and Jacob', the God of scriptural revelation. Fr Victor replies (in defence of Thomas's provision of philosophical proofs in his *Summa Theologiae*) that a duality of *rationes cognoscibiles* – 'knowablenesses', found through faith and reason respectively, does not mean there are two 'Gods'. 'The *media*, in the Light of which they respectively make their affirmations, are quite distinct, and though they sometimes reach the same conclusions, it is consequently to other 'knowablenesses' of God they attain.' But why should the dogmatic theologian – which is how St Thomas presents himself – be interested in the 'medium' proper to philosophical divinity? Basically, Fr Victor offers two elucidations. First, the philosophical deployment of thinking can help to unpack the content of *sacra doctrina*: divine relevation in its transmission in the Church. Not that *the revelation* itself is deficient – on the contrary, it is altogether luminous, but *our minds* are. Secondly, there is a missionary imperative at work in the incorporation of the Five Ways within the body of St Thomas's work. Aristotle had considered an opponent of metaphysical principles who will say nothing reasonable in his own defence to be no better than a vegetable, whereas should such a one offer actual arguments refutation is possible, and so the metaphysician's mission can proceed. Similarly here:

> if the opponent of articles of faith, says St Thomas, grants nothing in revelation, then it is impossible to argue with him on the basis of revelation. But he is not on that account a vegetable. Reason remains available; and to the extent that faulty reasoning constitutes his arguments against faith, then the 'teacher of Catholic truth' can and should, on the basis of reason, set out to resolve them.[47]

Moreover, Thomas never suggests that a rational 'preamble to faith' is required in principle from every believer (as some later Thomists have maintained). Such exercises are, on the contrary, intrinsically necessary only for those who 'believe nothing divinely revealed'.[48]

So far Fr Victor has done little in the way of 'naming' God: indicating language which might be used of him. But his apophaticism does not prevent him from appropriating the little treatise on 'the divine Names' which Aquinas included in the *Prima Pars* of his *Summa Theologiae*. Not because we know the Unknown, but because we can perceive finite existents and reason about them, it transpires that 'certain concepts can be truly predicated concerning it, by way of inference from finite existence ("causality"), transcendence of finite existence ("excellence") or denial of finite existence ("negation").'[49] And those three moments in a sequence of thinking – inferring from the created order to its Ground, but in a way that recognises the superabundance of being which makes that Source unlike all its effects – is summed up in the Thomist idea of analogy, and more specifically, the strict analogy or 'analogy of proportionality' on which Fr Victor concentrates in his essay 'Talk about God'.

In speaking, for example, of a 'healthy mind', one uses such analogy on the implicit formula, A:X::B:X – in other words, 'as the body is sound in its way, so the mind is sound in its'. Utilised *in divinis*, such a device of thinking, found endemically as it is in our ordinary language, proves eminently serviceable:

> When I say, 'God is good', do I mean by 'good' the same as when I say, 'That cake is good'? No indeed. I mean that as goodness can be predicated in its own poor and limited way of this cake, *so* it can be predicated of God in his own infinite way. My meaning in the use of the same term is quite different, yet connected by a proportion of its proportions to its respective subjects. I cannot indeed comprehend positively what goodness means as applied to God; but I know, thanks to my use of the analogy of proportionality, that my affirmation that God is good is valid and true. If I do not denude my concept of goodness of all the imperfections inherent in finite goodness and then apply it thus to God, I shall indeed be a blasphemer or an anthropomorphist; but much of the task of the theologian consists in that purification of concepts in order that they be applied validly but still analogically to God.[80]

Before leaving the topic of Fr Victor's fundamental theology of God it should be stressed that, appearances to the contrary notwithstanding, his was far from being an aridly intellectualist approach which left nothing for the volitional, cordial, conative dimensions of man's being – for will, heart, desire. He accepts St Thomas's view that some sort of knowledge of God is implanted in our hearts, in that we naturally and necessarily desire our own good and indeed bliss. Desire for God, and love of him, is implicit in every desire and every love – though we know it not. But since 'to know' means *to know that we know*, until we are shown how our bliss can only be in God, we do not innately know God – any more than someone who sees a shape loom up in the fog can be said to 'see Peter' until he sees it is Peter that he is seeing. Still, this 'confused' knowledge of God connatural to the soul will be vital to Fr Victor in his theologically-aware psychology – of which more anon. It is surprising that he did not make this point to counter the (very severe) charge of 'theoretical atheism' which Dom Illtyd Trethowan of Downside launched against the apophaticism of Fr Victor's *De Deo*.[51] Eirenically, the latter apologised for his 'meagre' account of St Thomas's proofs, and assured the Benedictine writer that, in his view, 'the *viae* are, in fact and intention, much more like the embodiment of our apprehensions in a form of discourse, which [you] advocate, than the question-begging syllogistic concoctions which both [you] and I deplore.[52]

Fr Victor's Christology is more accurately described as an account of the Incarnation of the Word – for he left no full account of the *acta et passa Christi*, the deeds and sufferings of the God-man, without which a true Christology is unthinkable. In *God the Unknown*, Fr Victor's comments on the Incarnation are found in the twofold context of, first, a benevolent account of the Platonist tradition in metaphysical thought, and, secondly, a miniature dialogue with the religion of India, the greatest of the 'non-Abrahamic' faiths (Judaism, Christianity, Islam). In both respects we overhear him establishing a conversation with cultivated non-Catholics, without, however, surrendering any of the claims to uniqueness of Christian dogma. And this is something only a culture conscious of its own divine foundation, as well of a certain human depth and richness, can do.

It is sometimes thought that Dominicans, and Thomists generally, because they are Aristotelians must somehow be opposed to or at the least suspicious of Platonism. Nothing could be further from Fr Victor's mind. Without a view of the world as 'symbol' – as, in a generalised sense, a 'sacrament' or 'a transcendental world of pure intelligibility and immateriality', belief in the Incarnation of the Logos can scarcely get underway. Though Plato did not originate such a 'sacramental' *Weltanschauung*, for it belongs tacitly with primitive man's 'mystic participation' in natural powers and phenomena, he gave it theoretical formulation, just at the moment when the human psyche was emerging to reflective existence – at any rate so far as the historical experience of the West is concerned. For Fr Victor believed

> it can be shown, and in the view of the present writer shown conclusively, that the acosmic and negative features of the Platonic tradition, and indeed of Plato himself, are but secondary corollaries, imperfectly apprehended, of a positive vision in which we must find the real core of Plato's teaching and the living thread of continuity which underlies the Platonic tradition. And that core of truth, that positive vision and the attitude of mind which it fosters, so far from being anti-sacramental, is precisely and in the highest degree sacramental.[53]

Fr Victor writes with palpable sympathy for the reservations of a traditional theologian like St Bonaventure *vis-à-vis* the 'Aristotelian renascence' in this context. By his doctrine of the exemplar Ideas, the archetypes of everything in this world, Plato had pointed the way towards the Logos. And moreover, as the Myth of the Cave in the *Republic* shows, he knew he was in the shadows, awaiting illumination, whereas the very completeness and autonomy of Aristotle's philosophy, theistic though it might be, 'precluded the entry of the

Word'. It was St Thomas's masterstroke that he fused to perfection the Platonic with the Aristotelean traditions, things which before had at best brushed each other *en passant*. Above all, Thomas showed how, though Aristotle may have refuted the notion of the Ideas as separate entities, or some particular argumentative strategy in their defence, his corpus can carry no 'conclusive weight against the ideas as such' or (and this is the more important point, theologically) 'against the contention of Christian Platonism that they are ontologically identical with the Divine Substance'. 'He showed that Christian Platonism required Aristotle to justify its own doctrines with logical and metaphysical rigour as well as to save it from the acosmic errors of pagan Platonism.' By relocating the Ideas as God's perception of his own multiple 'imitableness' in an actually multiple creation, Christian Platonism saved Aristotelianism, conversely, from that 'philosophical immanentism and unbalanced "this-worldliness" of the pagan Aristotelians which were so justifiably alarming the pastors and masters of Christendom.'

The universal relevance of the Logos of God, one in his divine simplicity but not unrelated to multiplicity owing to the 'office' performed by the Ideas,[54] is, then, clear enough. But can the same be said of the man Jesus in whom the faith of the Church finds the Logos incarnate? In 'Incarnations and the Incarnation', Fr Victor turned his mind to the matter of the uniqueness of Jesus Christ. Though disclaiming any specialist knowledge of the Indian (Hindu) Scriptures he none the less drew attention to them, for 'it would seem to be the case that it is in India that the issues have been most clearly reflected upon and formulated'. He begins from what seems *prima facie* the outright contradiction between New Testament faith in the one and only Incarnation, given in and with the 'child of Mary', on the one hand, and, on the other, the teaching on a succession of divine descents or avatars put into the mouth of Krishna in the fourth book of the *Bhagavad Gita*, the Vaishnaivite classic of the sixth century BC.

Fundamentally, Fr Victor tries to soften the force of this shocking contrast while simultaneously preserving intact whatever is necessary to the 'scandal' of the Gospel. Thus, the succession of avatars can remind the Christian reader of the divine Spirit who 'spoke through the prophets', for the seers of Israel, as 'proclaimers and teachers of his yoga' (the Torah) might be seen as manifestations of the transcendent but indwelling God. And if indeed the *Gita*, like the Upanishads, teaches the presence of the 'supreme and unborn Lord in the heart of all things ...', for Christian theology too God is most intimately present to all beings by reason of 'the very dependence of each and all on him for whatever being they have'. Moreover, by grace God can be present in human beings in a still more interior way: 'as the known in a knower, and the beloved in the lover'.[55] All of which leads Fr Victor to conclude that 'If the divine presence in man, or any of its varying manifestations, are to be called incarnations, then an orthodox Christian can have no objection to a multitude of incarnations.'[56] But in a sense this only makes more acute the need to answer the question, what, then, is *the* Incarnation? The 'very centre of the message committed to the Church' is that God is now not merely *manifested to* man, or *become present in* human beings, but actually *is* one of us. And the implications of this, in Fr Victor's mini-Christology, are twofold.

First, it forced the Church to rethink the doctrine of God as the One-and-Two, and eventually – for the relation of Jesus with the Father is not conceivable for the New Testament without the Holy Spirit – the One-and-Three. Although the Vedantist idea of the three divine attributes of being, knowledge and bliss might be thought of as a trinitarian foreshadowing, nonetheless 'reflection on the Incarnation and the *Homoousios* has compelled the Church to statements about the Divinity which could otherwise never be reached.'[57] More specifically, it enabled her to transcend, in her religious hold on God, the duality of Absolute and Relative, One and Many, which India could never overcome.

A Western reader may be pardoned for supposing that the non-dualism of Sankaracharya and the dualism of Madhvacharya succeed only in asserting one of these pairs of opposites by suppressing the other; and he may ask whether the 'Qualified Non-dualism' of Ramanuja achieves more than an uneasy compromise. He cannot wonder at this; for without the questions raised by the Incarnation, the *Homoousios* and the Trinity, God is indeed Absolute and not Relative, indeed one and not many, or alternatively relative (to the phenomenal universe) and many – or one of many – and not one. But the Christian theologian may say *neti, neti* even to this fundamental dualism. His God transcends even the opposition 'absolute-relative' for his one absolute God is also two and three by 'subsistent relations'.[58]

And the second service which the Gospel of the unique Incarnation can perform for India lies in the idea of divine-human communion which the mode of that Incarnation – the union at once without division and without confusion, of the divine and human natures in the person of the Word – made possible.

In Christ, and in the Church's dogmas of his two distinct natures in one Person, the Christian finds the divine solution to the puzzle which haunts the Upanishads, and indeed all profound religious contemplation ... To become divine is now to become fully human; to become fully human is to be divine.[59]

The Catholic Christian may sometimes be more aware of the divinity of Christ, sometimes more conscious of the humanity, but he knows that the two are complementary, not competitive, and that the way to divinisation lies in the most complete identification with the hominisation of the Word, as he takes our humanity on the way of the cross into glory.

And the upshot is that, for Fr Victor, and here he believes – surely correctly – that he speaks for Catholicism as such, other avatars and manifestations are valid 'only to the extent that they portray him in whom the unity and duality of God and man is supremely realised'. Though the narratives of the Hindu (and Buddhist) Scriptures may point an incarnational moral, the incorporation of a figure of Christ into the temples of these faiths will not satisfy the Christian. To have 'employed Christ for a time as a chosen object of *bhakti* [devotion]' is not what being a Christian means.

To see how Christ is pivotal, and not merely exemplary, for the God-world relation, there can be no better subject of meditation than the mystery of the Atonement – and it is to Fr Victor's soteriology that, for that third building-block of his 'doctrinal foundations', I now turn.

Fr Victor was perfectly aware that no full account can be given of the Christian understanding of salvation without a close attention to the *story*, at once historical and symbolic, of the suffering and death of Jesus Christ. Of the Passion narratives of the gospels he wrote:

It would be instructive ... to show how those very incidents which strike us as the most poetic and mythological, which display the closest resemblances to the archetypal ritual pattern, are inextricably interwoven by the evangelists with down-to-earth existence at its most personal and individual, its most prosaic and even squalid; and it is precisely in and through this that they see the transcendent mystery.[60]

The 'myth' of the dying and rising god, type of the Saviour in a wide variety of cultures is here earthed, and in being thus empirically fulfilled, ceases to be simply itself.

Just because it has been lived and died out in fact and history, consciously and voluntarily, the myth is not destroyed but fulfilled; its endless repetition is broken together with its unconscious, compulsive power. Indeed, in becoming fact it ceases to be mere myth.

And it does so by transforming the nature of the God-world relationship, both in reality and for thought. It is the task of exploring this change that dogmatic theology sets itself, and on this level do Fr Victor's reflections proceed. The Atonement brings together numerous strands in the doctrine of salvation: grace and nature, the Word of God and natural law, the various dimensions in the theological concept of *justitia Dei*, God's 'justice'. Like the cross itself, it gathers into one the four corners of the world. And if an account of the significance of the Lord's saving death can be so compendious, that is because 'the *theologia crucis* of my master, St Thomas Aquinas' furnishes 'an account of the subject in which the truth in all other accounts is respected, their inadequacies supplied, and their seeming antinomies resolved.' Fr Victor comes to this (to the historian of theology at first sight puzzling) conclusion by treating the entire *Summa Theologiae* as a tacit treatise on the Atonement. Thus for instance the whole of the First Part of the *Summa* could be regarded as an essay on the two terms (God and man) to be 'at-oned' on Calvary. More specifically, its sections on the relation of God's mercy and justice throw light on how the salvation won on the cross can be at once acquittal and satisfaction, while what Thomas has to say there about God's love, and notably its creative quality, is highly relevant to the mediation of grace and forgiveness by the crucifixion. The treatise on the Trinity, similarly, helps to explain how the Atonement is also our filial adoption, and the restoration of the divine image in us, while the questions on our original creation are essential to an understanding of our re-creation by way of Christ's victorious death and rising again. On what the Second Part has to offer a theology of the Atonement, Fr Victor's concise account may speak for itself:

> Its subject matter is man as the image of God and the realisation of that image in so far as man's activities and endeavours are to be directed to, and consummated in, 'one-ment' with God, his last End as well as his Creator, and it is essential that we should master this if we would correctly understand the doctrine of the Third Part which, as the *consummatio totius theologici negotii* [climax of the whole affair of theology] expounds how that 'one-ment', destroyed in principle by sin, is re-established by Christ. In the Second Part also will be found such indispensable preliminaries as an exhaustive analysis of how sin mars the divine image and destroys the ground of man's primordial 'one-ment' with God, of how law both aids and hinders the regaining of that 'one-ment', of how divine

grace – *really* healing and transforming because of the creativeness of divine love, and hence no legal fiction or extrinsic imputation – is unconditionally necessary for that 'one-ment' and ever increases it by the faith, hope and love which it engenders in our spiritual faculties.[61]

Comprehensiveness is the key-note of Fr Victor's soteriology. He presents the saving work of Jesus Christ *both* (with Barthians) as the divine answer to a divine question (to wit, God's 'free and secret will to destine man for a oneness with himself which infinitely transcends all creaturely capacities and all possible human deserts'), *and* (with those Thomists who laid special weight on the natural law tradition of investigating the human condition by human means) as the divine answer to a human question at the same time. For the primordial, God-given oneness of man with God (reflected in the doctrine of man as God's image), was the 'source and centre' of something much more down-to-earth:

a oneness of man also upon the 'natural' and empirical level – firstly of the individual within himself inasmuch as all his constituent elements with their variety of function are subordinated to his spirit, which in its turn is subordinated to God; secondly of human society inasmuch as from this interior and God-centred harmony of its components arises the perfect harmony of men among themselves in the achievement of perfect community; and thirdly of men, both individually and socially, with the rest of creation.[62]

But these unities and harmonies are now dislocated. And with these dislocations – whose facticity the reader of any newspaper might verify – salvation must also deal.

If Fr Victor devoted what might seem a disproportionate amount of attention to these aspects (the disease explaining the remedy, as well as, with Barth, the remedy explaining the disease), the reason was not simply that he believed these ruptures in right relationship to be important. He also thought it incumbent on him to attempt an explanation to Evangelical Christians of why Catholics were willing to approach them via such concepts as 'nature', 'reason' and 'natural law', thus introducing what Barthians (and, one might add, traditional Lutherans) would regard as 'fallen' concepts into the ambit of the pure Word of God. He ascribed the disappointing outcome of wartime collaboration between Protestants and Catholics on the social questions raised by Sword of the Spirit, and its local analogues, the 'Christian Councils', not so much to Roman feet-dragging as to a draughty theological gap in the wall of the common house. The 'common ground' which all sides thought to find in (doctrinally unproblematic) social co-operation has turned out to be 'the very battlefield of the Reformation', namely, the 'connecting link between the divine order of salvation revealed through faith in the Word of God and the "natural man" '. In his essay 'Word of God and Natural Law', Fr Victor summed up his own attempts to assuage Protestant anxieties in this matter during a series of ecumenical encounters at St Deiniol's Library, Hawarden, in the course of the Second World War.[63]

His apologia makes, essentially, two points. First, he clears aside as based upon an elementary error the notion that natural law, as understood by St Thomas, takes its origin from the creature in its autonomy. While law in its largest sense is the 'preconception' or 'pattern' of ordered activity, and therefore the product of mind (since only mind can 'order', that is, *correlate*), in the case of *cosmic* order the mind in question can only be divine.

> Natural law is the rational creature's participation of the *lex aeterna*, the mind of God. It is the rational creature's own knowledge of his purpose as manifested in his nature and in the exigencies of his nature, and of the manner in which that end of his nature is to be attained by the means at its disposal. It is a *derived* knowledge – a participation for it exists primordially on the divine mind of the God who made the nature and the end and the means.[64]

Natural law, then, is a reading – limited, it is true, but within its limits, valid – of the divine purpose for the world. Thus, referring to the Tén Words of the revealed Torah:

> When we maintain that the content of these Commandments is 'materially' of natural law as well as Commandments of God, we mean that both God in his tables of stone, and God manifesting his purpose to us in our own nature as it should be scrutinised by our own reason, are talking of and forbidding the same acts. (Not indeed in the mode and motivation of the implementing – *modum faciendi* – but in the act itself which is forbidden – *substantia actus*.)

The believer will have the advantage over the non-believer, through his or her fuller awareness of the sanctions, the subjective certitude, the range of motivation and the wider significance attaching to these precepts – and that will bring Fr Victor to his second point. But for the moment what he wishes the Evangelical to see is that 'the Lord in the Bible and the 'natural' man, the believer and the unbeliever, are both talking about the same thing: in the not-committing murder, adultery, theft and the rest there is an *Anknüpfungspunkt* [a point of contact] between the Word of God and natural law.' And secondly, although the bare use of intellect analysing the 'merely *humanum*', could not tell me of God's gracious predestining of mankind to share his own inner-trinitarian life through Jesus Christ, nevertheless this deification of the *humanum*, overcoming as it does the limitations not only of sinfulness but also of creatureliness, and known to me by faith in the Word of God alone, is not irrelevant to the body of truth available by natural law. And the reason for *that* is that grace aims at the transformation of the human being in his or her entirety.

> The question between us, as we Catholics see it, is not what justifies but *what is justified*. The Catholic answer is emphatic: *Man is justified*, and he will stress every one of those three words. It is *man*, the finite and reason-endowed creature, in his very nature, who is justified. He *is* justified; justification is a real predicate really pertaining to him, thanks to God's re-creative love – he is not merely called and accounted just. Finally, man is *justified* – i.e. rendered truly just and righteous (however imperfectly and initially only) in the eyes of God and in fact.[65]

And in a *tour de force* of exposition, Fr Victor draws connections between different aspects of the Council of Trent's decree on justification to show that it is precisely because Catholicism believes in justification by divine grace alone that it so emphatically denies salvation by faith alone, without works of love. Because it is *man* who is justified, grace, in its perfecting of human nature, 'postulates' works done under grace. It is *by* such works that God 'enables us to fulfil our place in the divine order and attain under God, our God-given end'. Of course:

> Non-killing, non-stealing cannot justify us, whether accomplished at the behest of reason or of revelation. After justification, they can forward the Christian life and merit further grace and glory, only to the extent that they come from grace and God-given supernatural charity. Nevertheless, they are an essential, integral and indispensable part of the way to glory. And that, not merely on account of some arbitrary whim of Jehovah, but because their non-observance is contrary to our own nature whose perfection is itself effected by grace and as the condition of glory.[66]

And in a nuanced discussion, Fr Victor also underlines the relevance of obedience to natural law (or the attempt of it) for man *prior to* justification likewise. On the one hand, the 'habitual natural-law-breaker' has vicious habits which will impede prevenient grace to which 'unnatural' living must constitute, *prima facie*, an obstacle. On the other hand, just as the virtues of the reasonable man can induce a sense of self-sufficiency, and, tainted by pride, become *vitia splendida*, so the 'very criminality of the criminal may reveal to him his impotence and his need of divine assistance'. The chasm between what the Gentiles do and what they would do reveals the need for merciful grace no less clearly among them than does among Jews the disparity between the ethical provisions of the Torah and Israelite moral practice.

As Fr Victor suggests elsewhere, the idea of justification and the general concept of justice are interrelated, and both are ultimately subsumed under that of the Last Judgment.[67] Man's original condition Catholic divinity calls original *justice*, because it entailed a 'balanced harmony and proportion'. In the Fall, the human will 'by sundering its own proper subordination to the Divine Lordship and defying the Divine Justice [in claiming *more* than its due] brings about a disorder, an injustice, a lack of balance and proportion within the *humanum* itself ...' This is something which Fr Victor speaks of in terms at once biblical (the wrath of God's justice), Hellenic (*hybris* calling forth *nemesis*) and Indian (as breeding an 'inevitable karmic process ... from the very nature of things as God made them'). Justification by Christ appears then as a *new justice* in which by faith the 'vertical right relation' (with God) is re-established, leaving the 'karmic' (finite) consequences of sin to be resolved, whether terrestrially or purgatorially. Only eschatologically, with the Last Judgment, itself the definitive act of justice (for *judicare* means *ius determinare*, to judge is to determine the due), will Christ's new order of harmony and justice be fully established. On that 'day' not only will sin be abolished, but its temporal consequences will also cease for the redeemed, since, in the words of the Johannine Apocalypse, 'the former things have passed away' (Revelation 21.4). St Thomas by no means accepted all the elements in Anselm of Canterbury's soteriology of 'satisfaction' for injustice done, but he allowed the theme of satisfaction, none the less, its own *just* place, for, in Shakespeare's words:

> no man well of such a salve can speak
> That heals the wound, and cures not the disgrace.[68]

In making Aquinas's soteriology his own Fr Victor claimed for it the best of both worlds in the age-old conflict between 'subjective' and 'objective' views of Christ's atoning work. For the subjective or exemplarist school, whose mediaeval master was Peter Abelard, the

Saviour 'achieves our at-one-ment' through the persuasive force of his love and example', because this engenders like dispositions in use. Thomas Aquinas, too, in the *Tertia Pars*, opens his account of the atoning purpose of the Incarnation by recalling

> that teaching of Scripture and of the Fathers according to which God, by becoming man and suffering with man and for man, supremely gives ground for our faith, confidence to our hope, enticement to return so unsurpassable a manifestation of his boundless love, and example of all those virtues which flow therefrom and which transform our attitude in our dealings with God and with our fellow-men.[69]

But – by contradistinction to Abelard, and his disciples among the Anglican Modernists of Fr Victor's day, St Thomas does not treat this 'exemplary causality' as merely a matter of moral influence, but as an expression of the divine creativity. The loving-kindness revealed in the saving death is the 'source' and 'motor' as well as the 'object' and 'motive' or 'the love whereby he permits us to join our love with his'.

But there is more. The setting of the Atonement is not a pastoral idyll where we, ourselves innocent, are but given greater grounds for joy. The new order Christ brings to the world has to 'take full account of the whole situation which sin has introduced'. Man's relation with his centre destroyed, the divine image shattered (though not obliterated), man has become 'the subject of conflict and tragedy, the microcosm a microchaos'. A rich variety of terms expresses the divine response, on the tree of the cross, to the various human needs which sin introduced into the world.

> It is *reconciliation* inasmuch as it re-establishes the basic relationship with God that sin had destroyed; it is *forgiveness* and *acquittal* inasmuch as, by that re-establishment, sin itself (*culpa*) is annihilated; it is *heaven-opening* and *hell-closing* inasmuch as it recalls us to our eternal destiny, removes the obstacles thereto, and so abolishes that eternal loss of God (*poena damni*) which is the first consequence of sin; it is *deliverance* inasmuch as it frees us from the enslavement of creatures and to the domination of the powers of evil which sin brings in its train; it is *redemption* inasmuch as it transfers us from that enslavement and re-establishes us as the free friends of God; it is *sacrifice* inasmuch as, by the unstinting oblation of the anarchic Self (St Paul's 'old man') it consecrates us to God and reintegrates us into the divine community; it is *meritorious* inasmuch as it disposes our human nature for the reception of the divine gifts; it is *satisfaction* inasmuch as our Saviour, by

himself under-going the penal consequences of sin (*poena sensus*), delivers his members from their liability (*reatus*) to them.[70]

Fr Victor stresses, however, that this liberality of vocabulary and theme does not rule out the predominance in Thomas's soteriology, of a 'leading idea'. The latter he identifies, in fact, as the *love* of God. In what Newman called his 'wisest love', God chose that 'method of salvation which, though most costly to himself, most fully supplied our human needs'. Fr Victor sees this instanced with particular delicacy in the 're-orientation' St Thomas gave the notions of merit and satisfaction in this context. Through Christ as New Adam, encapsulating our humanity within himself, we receive God's gifts not as beggars, 'humiliated and ashamed' but 'on a basis of equality, of payment and desert'. Just what could so easily degenerate into a 'sordid legalistic commercialism' of both doctrine and piety stands forth, at Thomas's hands, as a sublime manifestation of the divine graciousness and courtesy.

Two important footnotes must be added before Fr Victor has finished. First, salvation is provided; it is not given away. Christ's sufferings are 'substitutionary' for ours, but *not* in the sense that they are 'actually efficacious to us independently of our subjective disposition and co-operation': only through our own faith, and the sacraments of faith in which we participate, are the effects of the Passion brought about within us. We must be, through the sacraments, and above all the Mass – that 'simple and God ordained rite of the sanctification of the bread and wine and their transformation into the Realities which they signify' – configured to Christ in his life and death, so as to share his triumph.

Secondly, salvation is present here and now; but not entirely so. The fulness of Christ's work is reserved for the end of time. However, and returning in the end to the debate between the disciples and opponents of Karl Barth:

> If the humanitarian, purely immanentist 'Left Christianity' of an older generation is a treason to the supernaturalism and eschatologism of the Gospels, the exclusively transcendentalist 'new orthodoxy' of a younger generation which has no message for the natural and historical order but to condemn it, is no less a treason to him who went about doing good, healed not only sin but the temporal effects of sin, and bade us pray and work for the coming of his Kingdom on earth.[71]

Fr Victor's ecclesiological contribution – the last of our quartet of 'doctrinal foundations' – was marked by his participation in the ecumenical movement, still a novelty, as that was, for Catholics in his period. Not for nothing was he the translator of Yves Congar's epoch-making *Chrétiens désunis*, and the sole English Dominican convened to Le Saulchoir, the great studium of the province of France, for a colloquy of Congar's with separated Christians as the storm clouds gathered in 1938.[72] Welcoming the spread of the Octave of Prayer for the Unity of Christendom (originally an Episcopalian venture) to the Catholic Church as elsewhere, Fr Victor found it a salutary beginning for a new ecumenism which would avoid the mistakes of the old (the historical gamut of which stretched in his view from Mary Tudor's attempt to rebind England to her ancient ecclesiastical allegiance, at the one end, to the Faith and Order movement of early twentieth-century ecumenism at the other). Those earlier attempts had been vitiated, he believed, both by an excessively political concern with 'temporal expediency or purely human idealism', and by the absence of any widespread consent of the faithful.

> Both these factors, the intrusion of the political and the absence of popular support, may well have contributed to the impermanence of the Marian reunion in England; they were certainly conspicuous in the breakdown of the Reunion of Florence, the 'Conversations' of Santa Clara, Bossuet, Leibnitz – perhaps in part those of Malines, Lausanne, Stockholm, Edinburgh, Oxford.[73]

The prayer of the Octave is neither indebted to the civil power nor confined to *savants* and hierarchs. Moreover, its sublime object is not simply the restoration of the 'lost continent' of Christendom

> in defensive alliance against all other pre-Christian and post-Christian continents, but nothing less than the unity of all mankind, of the whole world, in Christ Jesus. The unity of the Church means nothing less than universal brotherhood through identification with the Son of God, whereby God becomes our Father in the unifying life of the Spirit of Love.[74]

That goal is so stupendously ambitious that the only means 'scientifically commensurate' with it is prayer. At the same time, only through prayer can this particular objective of intercession be understood. Concerned that some forms of appeal for the closing of ranks in the interests of shoring up Christendom could be said to ape secular, and even totalitarian, politics, Fr Victor warned that, without the interior peace and unity that comes from participation in the communion of the trinitarian Persons, the external unity which is right and proper as the visible sacrament of that sharing will prove spurious and perhaps even pernicious.

The integrity of society is dependent upon the integrity of the personality, and the integrity of the personality is dependent upon grace, upon relationship with God, upon integration into the Trinity through the absorption of the anarchic self into the Self of Christ.

And prayer simply *is* that desirable 'relational event' whereby we 'accept and deepen our filial relationship to God, and in so doing discover his Fatherhood and its consequence, the brotherhood of man'.[75] Schism would be impossible were there not somewhere a 'self-assertion of the members over and against Christ their head', and here Fr Victor does not exclude the possibility that Catholics, rightly believing the Chair of Peter to be the divinely appointed centre of unity for the whole Church, may yet show signs of the *spirit* of schism – through a failure to crucify the unregenerate self with its destructive prejudices and false complacency.

A quarter century and more after the promulgation of the charter of Catholic ecumenism – the Decree *Unitatis redintegratio* of the Second Vatican Council – much seems prescient in Fr Victor's account. His insistence that the Church is primarily a mystery of communion, yet one endowed with the means of sacramental expression in a visible society, sketches out in advance that Council's own ecclesiological scheme. His conviction that whereas

the truths which are expressed by our dogmatic formulas may be indeed absolute and immutable – we should sin against unity itself were we to compromise on *them* ... the formulas themselves ... are relative [while] ... *our* understanding of their content, and of its correlation in *analogia fidei*, has always been limited and often subject to further penetration and even revision

sums up in advance the approach made to issues of doctrinal conflict by the happier 'agreed statements' of the 'bilateral dialogues'. At the same time, alas, his troubled prophecy of a race of professional ecumenists, divorced from both the hierarchs and the 'rank and file', and 'identifying' more with each other than with their churches has proved far from inaccurate and his fear that the 'unionist' idea might end by spawning the 'chimaera of a brand-new syncretist world-religion composed artificially and eclectically of bits of all religions' (one thinks of the *later* work of the Camaldolese monk Dom Bede Griffiths) far from groundless. Nonetheless, he thought, 'a world-religion the world must have', for if a 'world-community' be the answer to the 'present world-chaos', that community must be founded on a 'personal relationship to that which transcends society if society is not itself to become a tyrannical impersonal deity'. *All* human beings, since they are potentially members of Christ, are possible members of Christ's Body likewise. Nor is that possibility remote or abstract, for the 'activating principle, the Power of Christ and his Spirit, is everywhere present'. The offer is open to all, but compels none.

Fr Victor held to the common scholastic doctrine that membership of the Church flows from the sacramental 'character' conferred by baptism. The sanctifying grace of that rebirth in the life-giving waters makes over the recipient to the Lordship of the Holy Spirit, the church's divine 'Soul'. But belonging to the Church – the social 'Body' which that Soul animates, turns on the power to both impart and receive whatever pertains to the social life and worship of the Church on earth. Yet because the Church is, on her divine side, a mysterious communion of supernatural life, as well as, on her human side, a visible society endowed with all the means for self-perpetuation which any society requires, complete membership of her must be at once 'internal' and 'external'.

This thought fructifies in a proliferation of distinctions in a typical neo-scholastic manual *De ecclesia*: distinctions which Fr Victor by no means found redundant. It may be *useful* to distinguish between those who are members of the Church 'perfectly and completely', holding a flawless internal and external unity with her; 'completely but imperfectly', in external communion but with an imperfect internal adhesion of mind and will; 'perfectly but incompletely', with 'material' – that is, unwitting – heretics in a state of grace; 'incompletely and imperfectly', when such Christians lack divine grace; or 'perfectly only' which is the case of catechumens prior to baptism, and those innocently excommunicated, since these two groups are blessed with both faith and grace. Fr Victor's own emphasis lies on finding the just mean between excess and defect in how we treat the visible society of the Church. He was in no doubt that Christ had, of set purpose, left such a Church in the midst of human history on earth.

> Precisely because he invites mankind to *become* a Church, he also *founds* or *institutes* that Church as a visible, grace-bearing and grace-imparting society. The Good Shepherd commits his sheep to Peter; he, the supreme Prophet, charges his Apostles and their successors to teach with his authority and in his name; he, the supreme Priest, empowers them to re-enact his sacrifice and to impart the visible and social means of grace which he has instituted; he, the supreme King, authorises them to govern and co-ordinate his members as a visible, harmonious organism.[76]

It is noteworthy that this Christological ecclesiology uses a variant of the key-idea of the threefold office prophetic, priestly, kingly, of

Christ, and in dependence on Christ, the Church, which would only enter the Catholic dogmatic tradition two years later, in the encyclical *Mystici corporis* of Pope Pius XII.[77] Clearly it would be infidelity to minimise the significance of the Church's visibility, thus constituted by Christ. As Fr Victor writes: 'A union with Christ that does not issue in fellowship with his fellows, which does not benefit from, nor is fostered by, the means which he has ordained, is at best a tenuous and incomplete union.' At the same time, we must not exaggerate: sharing in that visible society's social and liturgical activities is but the 'means and the *consequence* of union with Christ and ever-deepening identification with him'.[78] And he sums up in a perfectly balanced formula:

> As there can be no complete and fulfilled *external* union with the visible Church which is not fulfilled in progressive internal union with its Head, so there can be no complete *internal* union with the Head which does not issue in external adhesion to, and participation in, the life of the Body.

The 'Head' here is of course the undying, invisible Lord of the Church, Jesus Christ. But Fr Victor felt obliged by the dialogue he maintained with the Church of his own baptism, to enter sympathetically into Anglican difficulties about the human icon of that transcendent Head, the Roman pontiff, and more specifically, the latter's claim to infallible teaching authority.[79]

The Petrine office, on the Catholic view, is one organ – only one, but an important one – of that 'infallibility with which Christ endowed his *Ecclesia*'. Whether such *was* Christ's intention and action is in the last analysis a question 'of fact and one which cannot be settled by interdenominational negotiation'. However, Fr Victor was convinced that the reticence and resistance of most Anglicans to the 'papal claims' derived not from historical queries about the mind of Jesus and the practice of the early Church but from misconstructions of the notion of *magisterium* (teaching authority) in general, and, more primary still, of the manner in which God has 'revealed himself and his mighty salvation to us'.

A teaching authority is nothing without doctrines to convey, and doctrines are unstatable without propositions, so the question which formulates itself must be: 'What have propositions, that lowly form of linguistic utterance, to do with the everlasting health offered humankind by the living *personal* Word of God?' How can the Catholic gainsay the obvious validity of Karl Barth's Evangelical dictum that Christian truth is not so much language at all as 'what God has done, will do and is doing'?[80] Or how may he or she deny the justice of Michael Ramsey's High Anglican assertion, in his splendid study *The Gospel and the Catholic Church*, to the effect that 'Truth is uttered in God's redemption through Christ, and men learn the truth through repentance as well as intellectual processes, and apprehend the truth in their life as well as in their thinking.' There is no gainsaying or denying to be done – simply the remarking that

> If the Christ-fact is to be lived – just because it is fact, and historic fact – it must be communicated to us, and accurately communicated. It is not enough for our salvation that God should have dealt in such or such wise with his people; it is necessary that those historic dealings should be *related* to me if they are to have for me any redemptive value. It is not enough that Christ should have lived and died and risen; if I am to realise all that in myself I must *know* it and who he is. Nor can I do the will of God unless his will in my regard be made known to me; I cannot receive his grace unless I be told what means he has appointed for its reception.[81]

Christ the Word is not language, but the truth of God embodied in our flesh; and yet words, whether spoken or written, remain indispensable for the conveying of the Word made flesh to others.

Moreover, because the revelation completed in Christ is a universal revelation, intended for all, the Gospel story demands its own 'extension and communication', its world-wide reproduction; hence the office of teaching in Christ's name and place 'belongs to the very essence and purpose of the Church'. Not that the apostles, to whom this task fell, became oracular mediums, but they were so divinely assisted as to be 'rendered incapable of teaching error in exercising their apostolic function of teaching the revelation of Christ to the nations'. And while the ambit of the apostolic preaching is confined to what has been 'received from the Lord', that signifies no mere 'gramophonic reproduction of the Master's words', but an authoritative exploration of the 'whole rich, inexhaustible content of divine Revelation in its limitless potentialities of development, application and explanation.' And Fr Victor goes on to affirm that quite apart from Christ's own promise, at the end of the Gospel according to St Matthew, to accompany his 'apostolate' throughout all subsequent time, the 'continued existence of such [an] infallible authorised teaching office' is so integral to the essence of the Gospel that 'it can never fail the Church of God'.

> The growing Church should, if need arise, be able to say with unerring authority which inferences drawn from the original message are, and which are not, authentically part and parcel of the universal

faith; what is, and what is not, substantially identical with the original message. She should be able to condemn, with absolute assurance, beliefs which are contrary to or inconsistent with the faith once delivered to the saints. This is what we claim when we say that the Church, when she definitely lays down that such and such a statement is or is not part of the Catholic faith, is infallible.[82]

The rest is easily told. The inheritors of the mission of the apostles (if such are to be found on earth) can only be the historic episcopate, and if one asks, 'Which set of them?' the answer must be, in conformity with Catholic understanding of the primacy of Peter, 'that alone is to be held the authentic collective episcopate which is in peace and communion with the Chair of Peter at Rome.' The judgment of that episcopate, moreover, is not yet ecumenical and fully binding – nor, therefore, infallible – until it receives the approbation of the Petrine office-holder 'in whom we believe the highest degree of apostolic authority to reside'. Furthermore, because of the ecumenical extent of the Roman bishop's pastoral charge, concerned as this is with the peace and welfare of all the 'Churches', and not simply his own, Catholics hold the pope to be a 'competent organ' of that same infallible teaching office, such that, if need arise, he may himself declare that a given doctrinal belief is indeed the faith of the universal Church – even without assembling a council for that purpose. Fr Victor, writing in 1937, considered that his own period was one when that strategy might impose itself, for the time was one of easy communications yet difficult political conditions for many Catholic bishops. The dogmatisation of the glorious assumption of the Blessed Virgin Mary (an event he, like his mentor Jung, treated as of global significance) would verify his prediction that in the future the defining power of the Roman pontiff might be more widely used; of a new, ecumenical Council, however, he foresaw nothing.

Psychology and the Church

Jung's foreword to *God and the Unconscious* provides a helpful orientation for the reader who wishes to gain a brief overview of those concepts in his psychology which would prove most useful to Fr Victor in his own 'analysis' of, and 'therapy' for the psyche not so much of an individual patient as of a *corporate culture*. Jung uses the opportunity of addressing a specifically Catholic and theologically-informed audience to make a number of points. First, the psychologist's investigation of the dream life of his patients makes

clear the relation between dream motifs and 'mythologems' or mythological archetypes, forms. Such mythologems express, for Jung,
processes in the unconscious; they are not 'inborn representations',
but '*modi* without definite content',[83] yet their relation to the mytholo-
gies found in human culture cannot be overlooked. Secondly, the
difference, from the standpoint of the empirical psychologist, between
the mythological and the religious is simply that whereas the former
belongs to a largely obsolete, archaic, petrified collection of sacred
forms, the latter retains its living, intense, numinous appeal. This
argues nothing for the objective transcendental validity of religion, but
everything where the 'spiritual atmosphere' of the 'psychic economy'
is concerned. Thirdly, the 'collective representations' found outside
the analyst's consulting room, in the shared world of public culture,
are vital for the patient, who must relate his individual discoveries in
treatment to the corporate life of humanity. Were he, on the contrary,
condemned to be a pure individualist, nursing the private truth analysis has yielded, he would remain 'neurotic, unrelated, and estranged
from his social group'. Precisely because of the religious, or at any
rate mythopoeic, character of the archetypes, some collaboration
between psychologists and theologians is therefore required. As Jung
put it:

> The medical psychotherapist cannot in the long run afford to over-
> look the existence of religious systems of healing – if one may so
> describe religion in a certain respect – any more than the theolo-
> gian, in so far as he has the *cura animarum* at heart, can afford to
> ignore the experience of medical psychology.[84]

At the same time, Jung takes the opportunity to rub in the fact that his
preferred concepts may be philosophically monstrous, and thus theological non-starters: for such ideas as the archetype or psychic energy
are but *Hilfungsmittel*, auxiliaries to medical practice, while his rejection of the definition of evil as a 'privation of the good', if soundly
based, is so only for the empirical realm.[85] It was indeed over this
disputed question that Fr Victor and he would go, painfully, their
separate ways.

When we turn, however, to the opening essay of *God and the
Unconscious* – intended as this was for the first chapter of a never to
be written comprehensive treatise on the soul from every possible
standpoint, a Casaubon-like 'Key to all Psychologies', we soon
discover that Fr Victor's primary concern is not with the individual
patient who, for his healing, may need to be re-related to a wider
environment, but with the total *Lebensraum* of modern Western souls
at large. Images of the divine have changed and changed again in

human history, but never before in general culture has there been so marked a twilight of the gods, the 'passing away of all forms, and of the very Formless itself'.[86] But whereas in the age of Nietzsche, the death of God might be welcomed as man's salvation not by but from religion, today a new, more chastened enlightenment is less sanguine. Rationalist philosophy, anthropology, comparative religion, biblical criticism, the physical sciences and, finally, Freudian depth psychology may have combined to hammer nails into religion's coffin – the last most thunderously of all with its claim that gods (like demons) are but 'illusory by-products of the conflict between our inward instinctual drives and the demands of our environment'. But, alas, the victory is Pyrrhic. Not only does contemporary physics return both everyday certainties and yesterday's science to a state of unintelligible chaos, forcing us, in its league with the new astronomy, to an 'unprecedented asceticism of intellectual abnegation', but technological power has begun the process, with the atom-bomb, of dis-integrating the cosmos under the supremely ironic code-word of its erstwhile divine Integrator, 'Operation Trinity'.[87] Moreover, even 'creedless scientists' grow alarmed at the moral consequences of the slow retreat of religious belief. Writing in the 1930s, R. B. Cattell had already reported that

> Psychologist and social scientist lose their militant attitude to religion when they realize that all their forces may well be needed to reestablish some order in the city they have so successfully besieged. The intellectual world is full of 'post-war' problems from this enormous cultural conflict, but perhaps the everyday world is even more distressingly aware of imminent emotional famines and pestilences arising from the intellectual readjustment.[88]

And Cattell, in the course of constructing his own 'scientific' religion of the 'Theopsyche' (which presumably philosophically naive effort Fr Victor gently leaves to one side) catalogues the 'boredom, and misuse of energy, vacillating loyalties, false goals, fruitless conflicts and despair' which come from the collapse of the 'system of order and morality' once sustained by traditional faith.

In this context the attractiveness of Jung's psychology to a Catholic priest and Dominican friar was twofold. First, Jung denied that, despite the scepticism of the predominant intelligentsia, the acid of secularism had corroded irremediably deep. Resources remained that could still be tapped by the present and future. He rejected as naive the notion that merely declaring invalid some form of faith is to become psychologically free of its effects. The Judaeo-Christian inheritance constitutes a 'definite form of adaptation to inner and outer experience'; it has moulded a similarly definite form for civilisation itself. No intellectual change of opinion could have so obliterating an effect on the emotional processes, much less on the unconscious itself.[89] But secondly, and even more importantly, Jung queried whether the psychologists really *had* shown how the religious 'illusion' is created and sustained.[99]

In 'The Gods Go A-Begging', Fr Victor considers the first of these points.[91] He suggests that, by analogy with the law of the conservation of energy in the physical world, psychic energy is never lost or annihilated. And thus the *libido* poured into or extracted from religion in previous generations remains pent up, seeking an outlet.

> Being deprived of divine beings, we shall find that, willy-nilly, we are in practice attributing omnipotence to a State, a Leader, a Party, a relation, a neighbour, or that we ourselves are behaving as if we were God Almighty, or are the victims of inscrutable forces within against which our conscious wills and endeavours are powerless.[92]

The human mind, deprived of its heaven above and hell beneath, will wish to make surrogates on earth – and Fr Victor found examples of such hells in the concentration camps, and such pseudo-heavens in the modern romantic marriage or partnership, in which human beings deified as gods and goddesses ('I adore you') inevitably become demons and their homes hells. The gods may be dead, but they will not lie down. For Jung, as a clinical practitioner, many neuroses derive from the fact that, out of a 'childish passion for rational enlightenment' (though abuse does not take away use where Mistress Reason is concerned!), 'people blind themselves to their own religious promptings'.[93]

In 'The Unconscious and God', Fr Victor begins a two-part assessment of the validity of Freud's reduction of religious belief to the status of a (hitherto quasi-universal) neurosis. Of course the idea of the unconscious does not begin with Freud by a long chalk. Dreams, automatisms, the rebounding of 'forgotten' experience or unrecognised desires on human behaviour, alternating personalities and abnormal or paranormal psychological manifestations of many kinds had been known from time immemorial: what was new, in the late nineteenth century, was the 'deliberate application of experimental method to the study of such phenomena'.[94] What was *relatively* new in the same period was the concept (and name) of the unconscious or subliminal self as their agent, source or, at the very least, generic label. Actually, Fr Victor was not content with the usual text-book account of how this key-idea surfaced in the history of psychology as a discipline. The clinical study of repression – defined as the 'unconscious dismissal from the mind of experiences, emotions and ideas which it has failed to assimilate' – in the generating of psychoneurosis and psychosis was pursued independently in France, Switzerland and Austria in the *fin-de-siècle* period. But earlier nine-teenth-century Idealism and Romanticism had anticipated the main outlines of the idea itself. Fr Victor found congenial the study *Psyche* by the Saxon physician-philosopher C. G. Carus who, in complete disregard of pathological psychology, had already reached not only the more important of Jung's conclusions but even much of Fr Victor's own attempted re-integration of them with the *philosophia perennis*.[95] Thus Carus described the unconscious as the supra-indi-vidual source of consciousness, known only through its effects. It is furnished with primordial images, the subjective expression of that which, objectively is nature, and, seen transcendentally, is some sort of participation in the life of the Creator himself. At the same time, Carus praised Aristotle and Aquinas for not confining their philo-sophical psychology to conscious mentation. Unlike many of their successors, they realised that the psyche is not only conscious: consciousness is its instrument not its entire being. If Schelling's Idealism was a significant influence here, Romantic writers and artists a-plenty reacted in relatively independent ways against the Enlightenment over-valuation of consciousness. Indeed Fr Victor virtually *defined* Romanticism as 'an upsurge from the neglected unconscious', whence came 'first the activity and imagery' of the unconscious, and then 'the idea and the name itself'.[96] He took Blake, Shelley, Keats and Coleridge to be the equivalent of the German and French Romantics of whom the critic Albert Béguin wrote:

> Romanticism revives several ancient myths, that of the universal unity and the *Anima Mundi*; and it also creates several more: that of the Night, which is the Guardian of the Treasure, that of the Unconscious as the sanctuary of our hallowed communing with the Supreme Reality, and that of the Dream which transfigures percep-tion, and in which every image becomes a symbol, and all language becomes mystery.[97]

Whatever its historical origins, few psychologists, save for a handful of behaviourists, dispute the utility of the idea. Without it, involun-tary mentation (such as dreams) and what Fr Victor calls the 'seeming purposiveness of non-conscious biological functioning' are hard indeed to fathom.[98] The most important question so far as the relation between the unconscious and (belief in) God is concerned, must be that of its *boundaries*. If banishment or repression accounts for all unconscious contents (as early orthodox Freudianism averred), then

the psyche is 'a closed system, all of whose contents could be mech-
anistically explained in terms of the individual's life-history, and at
least theoretically analysable until there was no "unconscious" left.'
'God' would then be nothing but a projection of desires banished or
fears repressed: Freud's own view in *Totem and Taboo* and *The
Future of an Illusion*. Yet in *Moses and Monotheism* Freud himself
made a startling admission: accepting that the unconscious includes
memory traces of the experience of former generations, he blew apart,
albeit with the tiniest stick of gelignite, the closed confines of the individual psyche. And outlining his own view that the unconscious is a
'boundary concept' (*Grenzbegriff*) for that which, by definition, our
consciousness cannot penetrate yet which frequently 'behaves as if
endowed with consciousness' not to speak of 'intelligence and
purposeful volition', Fr Victor appointed the third-century North
African divine Tertullian as patron of his further explorations of this
theme. In the *De testimonio animae*, Tertullian had sought a common
ground between Christian and non-Christian, and had found it in
certain contents of the soul. Tertullian, in directing sophisticated
pagans to seek within the realities that Christian salvation addresses –
God, the demons, sin and guilt, heaven and hell, conflict and immortality – had shown how

> the involuntary and spontaneous speech and behaviour even of the
> most sceptical mind – its uncontrolled and unpremeditated phan-
> tasies, prayers, curses and feelings – persist in testifying to its
> belief in these things even in spite of doubts and denials of
> consciousness. Stated in the language of today, his appeal is
> precisely to the spontaneous, automatic expressions of the uncon-
> scious as against the sophistications of the spoiled and 'educated'
> conscious ego.[99]

Fr Victor's critique of Freud does not consist solely in the point,
already made, that the theory of repression is asked to bear too
implausibly heavy a burden when all the possible contents of the
unconscious are loaded on its back. For, further, there is the question
as to whether 'function and purpose' as well as historic causation
might be manifested in those moments when the dark recesses come
briefly into conscious light. In the scientific and philosophical climate
of Freud's Vienna, a mechanistic methodology and a programmatic
atheism were built into Freudian psychoanalysis from the start. Such
presuppositions are the target of Jung's withering remark, apropos
both Adler and Freud in *Modern Man in Search of a Soul* that their
methods 'actually hinder the realization of meaningful experience'.[100]
Nowhere is this clearer than in the diverse concepts of *libido* held by

the three schools. The key to Jung's attraction for Fr Victor – despite, especially in his early period, the former's highly ambivalent *personal* attitude towards religion, can be found in the teleological twist he gave to Freud's idea of man's earliest psychic energy as sexual, indeed incestuous, through and through. His *Wandlungen und Symbole der Libido* was directed to showing 'how the undifferentiated *libido*, originally in the infantile state wholly absorbed in the parental relationship, is by religious symbols, rites and beliefs, weaned from the parents and transformed into creative and atoning power.' And Fr Victor continues admiringly:

> An immense erudition, covering the myths and religions of widely differing levels of culture, re-enacted in the case-histories of contemporary and often quite 'non-religious' patients, is brought to bear to support and illustrate this general thesis; but perhaps nowhere does Jung succeed in establishing his conception more satisfactorily than in his recurrent studies in this book of the unique significance from the psychotherapeutic standpoint of the teaching, life, death and resurrection of Jesus of Nazareth.[101]

Jung inverted Freud, as Marx once had Hegel. For the aim of the *libido* is not pleasurable impregnation of the mother for its own sake, but return to the womb: that is, rebirth. Union with the mother is not the reality of which the symbols of myth and ritual are but coded tokens; rather such union is *itself the symbol* of 'inward rebirth and baptismal regneration into life more abundant'.

In holding that, in the religions, the spiritualising power of *libido* exists 'raised to a system',[102] Jung indicated his view that the bounds of the psyche are not entirely individual. Fr Victor summed up this aspect of his work, the value of which, for the repristinising of biblical and patristic symbols in a renewed Christian culture he found himself scarcely able to overestimate, in the following statements:

> The ontogenesis of the psyche is a 're-echo' of a phylogenesis; the contents of the unconscious are not limited by the acquisitions of the individual's lifetime; behind them lie dormant the experiences of the race; it includes collective as well as personal elements. Behind submerged 'memories' of events in the individual's lifetime lies a racial heritage manifested in archetypal figures. Behind the particularized physical mother's womb lies the archetypal womb of the Great Mother of all living; behind the physical father the archetypal Father, behind the child the *puer aeternus*; behind the particular manifestation of the procreative sexual libido lies the universal creative and re-creative Spirit. The second of all these

pairs appears now, not as a phantasy-substitute for the first; but rather does the first appear as a particular manifestation and symbol of the second.

Jung has in fact, and even in spite of himself, given a point to Tertullian's *anima naturaliter christiana* such as has never been exhibited with such clearness before.[103]

And Fr Victor points to the theological propriety of linking Jung's undifferentiated and open-ended *libido* to St Thomas's teaching on human nature's 'natural desire' for God; the figure of the archetypal Mother to the patristic teaching on the divine nature (as distinct from the Trinitarian Persons)[104] and the 'terrible' and 'benign' aspects of the same maternal archetype to fallen Eve and Mary, the new Eve, respectively.

And this particular way of putting the divergence of the two schools over the *libido* idea suggests another major disagreement, which Fr Victor would touch on in a discussion of Sir James Frazer's anthropological treatment in *The Golden Bough* of the mythopoeic motif, so crucial to Christianity, of the 'dying god'. The point concerns the status of the *symbol*.

Freud seems to have viewed the symbol *only* as a source of disguised, and usually disagreeable, information for the resisting consciousness. Jung has that it was very much more than that; that it was the very instrument which, just because it was polyvalent, transformed consciousness itself and thereby the sick personality.[105]

Taking Jung's work not, however, as an apologia for European Christendom but as a challenge to it, it fell to Fr Victor to attempt a demarcation of the 'frontiers' separating (and joining) theology and psychology.[106] He found that to many specialists in both psychological practice and theology a hermetic division of the two 'saves a great deal of trouble'. A dichotomous application of the distinction between nature and supernature provides an air of respectability to cover sloth. But soul and psyche are not two different entities; they are two words for the same entity, while salvation and health are not two totally different realities but have their overlap and common ground.

Not that Fr Victor found unintelligible the well-informed priest's reasons for caution in the face of Jungianism at large. One could hardly overlook such factors as: Jung's lack of theoretical system, his preoccupation with the erratic and eccentric aspects of religion suggested by the pathology of his clients, and his tendency, under the influence of Rudolf Otto's *The Idea of the Holy*, to locate the essence of religion in its most primitive raw material. Fr Victor concurs in these judgments to the extent of wishing that the analytical psychologist would learn from the theologian how a 'developed religious and worshipful active attitude, involving rational and voluntary decision', differs from magic and superstition. In particular, he retained a healthy suspicion of Jung's excessive sympathy for gnosticisms, both ancient and modern, concurring in the judgment of one of his own correspondents, the Jewish convert to Catholicism Karl Stern, that Jung's work could lead only too easily to 'some sort of non-committal mysticism, a mysticism without discipline'.[109] And while regretting that some of the patristic opponents of Gnosticism were not better psychologists – for the absorption in *gnôsis* may be seen as the 'revenge of introverted feeling and intuition' on an 'unprecedented differentiation of extraverted thinking and sensation' which typified the Hellenic achievement,[108] Fr Victor finds himself unable to dissent from the negative reaction of the Church of the Fathers to a movement characterised by an esoteric sectarianism, so matter-hating that 'absorbed in his lightsome world of phantasy, the world of fact was *his* [the Gnostic's] shadow'. Whereas Jung treated gnosis – the enlargement of consciousness by the mastery of surrounding mystery – as superior to the faith of the institutional Church, Fr Victor briskly reverses this ranking.

> While gnosticism has no room for faith, faith has room indeed need, for gnosis. Gnosis cannot be a substitute for faith, but the possession of gnosis is part and parcel of the gifts to the faithful *Ecclesia*. In the Body of Christ are many members, each with their several functions: and those of the gnostic are among the most honourable. Without the intuitive understanding of what in faith she believes, the Church herself would be incomplete – uncatholic. But it is gnosis *in* faith, not in despite of faith; and it is for the benefit of the whole body and not only for the individual member. Gnosis is not supreme: it must be ruled by Faith and Hope and Charity and the greatest of these is Charity.[109]

Once these principles are recognised, the Church can own her contemplatives and mystics, and even 'her alchemists and cabbalists' – but always on condition that none claim by these titles a perfection superior to that of the *plebs sancta*, the common people of God. Despite his robust claim that Jungian psychology has demonstrated the 'relevance of faith and practice to the needs and workings of the human psyche', Fr Victor was, therefore far from ready to abandon all criticism of Jung's thought as base ingratitude to one who had rendered such signal service.

Such an attitude would in fact trivialise the epistemic claims both of faith and of analytic psychology. So, just as Fr Victor had defended, over against Barth, the possibility of a two-pronged approach to God through faith and reason, invoking the Thomist concept of diverse yet compatible *rationes cognoscibiles*, here too he insists that 'every science must be met on its own ground and understood only in the light of its own premises and observations' 'Must be *met*': but will the meeting be all sweetness and light, or may there be elements of friction, even collision?

Certainly, there may be, and were – and not only the ones just cited. Thus, for instance, Fr Victor entered reservations about Jung's treatment of the Holy Trinity, where, despite his willingness to enter into 'theological intricacies', he 'misses much of what ... the worship of the Trinity (over against polytheism or monism) means even psychologically to the simple Christian'; his lack of interest in divine transcendence – the affirmation of which, as a complement to divine immanence, is 'a psychological fact of immense importance and influence'; and (returning once again to matters trinitarian) his failure to see in the Athanasian doctrine, where the Absolute finds itself transcended in the union of Absolute and Relative, the 'supreme "reconciling symbol" which sanctifies relationship itself. And, as already signalled, Jung's attempt to introduce evil into God – as a reality that cannot be overlooked when we are imaging the archetype of the Source itself – found in Fr Victor a resolute opponent. In a lengthy footnote, which resumes and expands their exchange of opinions in the years 1949 to 1951, he summed up what he termed that discussion's 'inconclusive and nugatory results' with the bald declaration:

> 'Jung has our keenest support and sympathy in deploring the minimizing of evil which leads to its repression, with its devastating results for the individual psyche and for society; but we are unable to find any evidence that the conception of the *privatio boni* has contributed to this. On the other hand, we are unable to find any intelligible, let alone desirable, meaning in such fundamental Jungian conceptions as the "assimilation of the shadow" if they are not to be understood as the supplying of some absent good (e.g., consciousness) to what is essentially valuable and of itself "good".'[110]

Some private notes in the English Dominican Archive express his anxieties about *Answer to Job*. Whether Jung wills it or no he is 'forever the Father of analytical psychology'; no work of his, then, can be other than an authoritative representation of the teachings of his school. Hence the problem the book has created for those who are 'known as supporters and advocates of it' – like, of course, Fr Victor. The psychological counsel of *Answer to Job* is that it is 'God', not myself, who is internally divided, moody, capricious and purposeless. Consequently, evil is an irreducible constituent of reality to be accepted – not, as a privation of reality, to be 'made good'. Jung's God is seemingly for ever evil, but in my consciousness (*gnosis*) of this fact he may 'become more reasonable and amiable'.

Fr Victor faced two kinds of resultant anxiety. One was for the welfare of those henceforth to be treated on this basis by Jung's disciples. 'By example if not by precept', the book proposes to ignore *personal* psychology (heredity, environment, upbringing, the personal shadow) which is deemed banal, uninteresting and obvious in comparison with the myth. But secondly, he was worried about the specifically religious and ecclesial consequences. 'The correct (because Jung's) way of dealing with the problem is by a highly emotion-charged ridiculing of the 'good' God, his witnesses and devotees, with no undue care for accuracy or for its consequences.'[111] He added, If these are *not* the psychological implications of *Answer to Job* – implications which may be and in fact are being drawn from it, what else *could* be? In effect, Jung has inverted the earlier psychology of all schools, including his own.

> What psychologists have hitherto considered to be primitive, infantile reactions and neurotic projections now have the highest sanction as the correct solution of problems – and indeed the highest wisdom. The criticism by non-Jungian psychologists that the collective unconscious becomes an escape mechanism for personal psychology appears to be confirmed. Indeed, psychology itself is reduced back to mythology: conscious realization of the myth is now the *summum bonum* to which even *sanitas* must be subordinated. Criticism by empirical results in terms of 'cure' and mental health are no longer valid as applied to this 'way of integration'. It is not yet clearly stated that realization of the myth (or at least belief in it) is a *sine qua non* for being an 'analytical psychologist'; but the question must arise, and be answered.[112]

Moreover, the book threatens to put into reverse the stupendous breakthrough of Indo-European man to a true concept of the divine.

> About 500 B.C. something happened to our fathers and our Culture. Plato's Idea of the Good, Aristotle's all-blissful, all-knowing *Theos*, the Vedanta's realization of the Atman without attributes or with the attributes of Being-Knowledge-Bliss, the whole Greek search for the One beyond the Many and the

Opposites, precisely Job's heroic encounter and healing, and Yahweh's self-vindication (as related in the *Bible*) have delivered us from the evil and unconscious Gods, and make any such projection impossible.

Henceforth we cannot know the cruel God otherwise than *as* a projection – and so 'precisely *not* what we call God, or the standard and measure of all things'. Of course the Christian will, of all people, find Jung's approach the most problematic (Fr Victor means, in the light of the Atonement wrought for man by God himself), though he may be all the more willing than most to experience the darkness and evil in himself, and the darkness in his own apprehension of God.' Jung has reversed the theological maxim, orthodox in relation to particular human sin, *Omne bonum a Deo, omne malum ab homine*. Ascribing all evil to One who is other than humanity no doubt will bring great relief to some; but 'the adherent of the Old Gospel finds ... this Evangelium ... poisonous'.

Fr Victor's anger with Jung is palpable. He is 'far more than the Pope to Catholics'. The latter 'claims only to be protected from teaching error in certain strictly specified circumstances. But the Pope only believes; Jung does not need to believe, he *knows* – and has said so. He is 'integrated' – and again has said so.'[113] And as to the writer of these notes, he foresaw an eventual 'agonising re-appraisal of his position *vis-à-vis* analytical psychology'.

If then *Answer to Job* was a potential disaster for those in therapy, for the intellectual integrity of those Catholic Christians who had welcomed Jung's work, and, not least, for human *culture*, it was with relief that Fr Victor turned to less conflictual areas. The most fruitful terrain for theological/psychological collaboration lay, he felt, not with the doctrine of *God* at all, but with the doctrine of *man*. For the Tridentine dogma of intrinsic rather than imputed justification, grace really heals and reintegrates fallen nature – and can this be without psychological effect? And summarising the Catholic doctrine of human nature – created, engraced, fallen, redeemed – Fr Victor summarises the character of the justified man's 'holy warfare' when he writes:

Man's fallen and disintegrated condition, the disorder of desires (*concupiscentia inordinata*) and the lust of spirit against flesh and of flesh against spirit, must be humbly accepted if they are to be transmuted. There is no way back to the innocence, harmony and irresponsibility of Eden, and any attempt to find one's way thither through escapist phantasy and idealism is to reject the way of Christ, as Jung has rightly seen. There is no escape from world, flesh and devil; they are to be renounced only by being faced and overcome.[114]

And citing the mediaeval English mystic Walter Hilton (whom we shall encounter later in the context of Fr Conrad Pepler's spiritual theology), Fr Victor explains that the first step on the way to reintegration – conformation with Christ – is acceptance of the 'shadow'. Grace does not, for Hilton, rid us of the shadow, but prevents its domination. To the *proficiens*, in Hilton's words: 'the soul is not borne *in* the shadow, though he feel it; but *he* beareth *it*. For through grace he is made mighty, and strong for to bear his body and all the stirrings of it, without hurting or defiling of himself.'[115]

For a sane doctrine of man, capable of drawing in the positive insights Jung could offer but also filling out the *lacunae* in his thought, Fr Victor turned for philosophical assistance to the two writers who would have figured most prominently in philosophical anthropology at Hawkesyard, Aristotle and Aquinas. He believed in fact that practical psychology would eventually have to come to terms with philosophy – nay, with metaphysics: the difference between subjective and objective in, for example, the analyst's treatment of 'projection' is but one example where an evaluation of what is 'really there' cannot be avoided. And though the miniature treatises known as the *Parva Naturalia* show Aristotle to have been acutely interested in empirical phenomena, not least psychological events and their interrelation, it is for his ability to create a 'comprehensive framework' for the 'general principles and potentialities' which observation suggests that we most need him. Beginning from the datum of ordinary language, that what distinguishes a living – that is, ensouled – organism is self-movement (at least, for plants, in the form of self-nourishment, self-repair, self-reproduction), Aristotle came to the conclusion that the soul is not so much 'a complete "it" [as] that *by* which we live, *hô zômen*', the 'formal, determining constituent principle of a living compositum'. Rigorous metaphysic and dialectic combined with the empirical data of that soul-body composite's vital processes to warrant an analysis of its life in terms of *dunamis*, 'potency', on the one hand, and, on the other, *energeia*, 'act', 'activity', 'actualisation') or *entelecheia*, 'completion'. The same vocabulary is pressed into service to indicate how subject and object are unknowable except in function one of another.

> When I think, I think things, and in that thinking both 'I' and the 'things' emerge, on reflection, as potencies to one unique and identical act of knowing and being known. Subject and object are not

ultimate *a prioris*: they are conscious data which presuppose a pre-
conscious identity, a *participation mystique* in the deepest sense.
Thought is precisely that act in which, in experiencing the 'not-I',
I experience my ego, and from which I infer the human psyche
itself. But an act of psyche it is, by definition and it is in that vitally
important sense that Aristotle knows that, while the first function
of the psyche is to animate the body, its wider functions are indeed
all embracing ... The human psyche, by its powers of *nous* [intel-
lect] and *aisthesis* [sense] both makes and becomes the whole
world.[116]

Although at first Aristotle's hesitations about the immortality of such
a soul rendered his anthropology suspect to Christian thinkers, the fact
that, for him, the whole man (and not just a part of the human being)
comes within psyche's remit guaranteed that Catholicism would eventually recognise his wisdom – to the point, at the Council of Vienne,
of stigmatising the denial of his fundamental definition of the soul as
heresy. It was tailor-made for a Gospel whose central message was
'that of man's psycho-physical integrity – the message of health
(*salus*) wrought in and through the flesh and the hope of glory through
the resurrection of the body. Only that Gospel could make sense of
man's destiny, if Aristotelianism were true. St Thomas, 'with the
Bible in one hand and Aristotle in the other', showed how that Gospel
'could meet the inherent insufficiencies and contrarities which
Aristotle had analysed and exposed'. Aristotle's havering on the question, Is *nous* – immaterial mind – a divine reality, transiently present
to soul, or only relatively godlike, and an aspect of soul (and hence,
though, its guarantor of immortality), could only be ended by the
advent of revelation.

> Without the faith of the 'People of the Book', that man is made in
> the image of God and not vice-versa, the problem is indeed a diffi-
> cult one to resolve. The revelation of creation will enable St
> Thomas to distinguish clearly between the indwelling, uncreated
> God, the source of all truth and knowledge, and the godlike, but
> finite, created intellect which is essentially and only a potentiality
> of the psyche, the latter in its turn being individuated by the body
> of which it is the form. In so doing he can reconcile the implica-
> tions of both of Aristotle's sets of observations without
> inconsistency.[117]

An anthropology without an ethics is but a torso. In Fr Victor's eyes,
Aristotle has most of the pieces of the jigsaw of rational ethics, but he
cannot arrange them – not surprisingly since merely natural morality

must, for the concrete human person, be incomplete. The purpose of Aristotelian moral practice is such good living as is humanly practicable – for the body as well as the soul, in a city with others. And yet he holds at the same time that man's bliss lies in 'the highest activity of his highest part exercised on the highest objects and with the maximum of perfection and permanence' – an aristocratic, intellectualist, self-sufficient, godlike ideal. But Christian revelation confirms the rumour which the *Nicomachean Ethics* report but hurry past:[118] human fulfilment is a divine gift which resolves these antinomies.

> The end, the fulfilment, which God has destined for man – the eternal divine life dwelling in him as a free gift of divine love – can be known only by God and communicated by his revelation, and can be attained only by the power and grace of the indwelling Spirit given by God through Christ: the Christ who attains the immortal life of soul – *and* body by first accepting the death which is their separation.[119]

So far not much has been said in this connection about the unconscious; the theme, in its Aristotelo-Thomist guise, enters with the subject of, precisely, *revelation*. If in an apparently authentic detached fragment, Aristotle remarks on the pagan mysteries that they require a receptivity to inner experience (*pathein*), not active engagement in study (*mathein*), St Thomas will treat the cognitive processes that revelation involves as 'no grasping (*mathein*) but an experiencing (*pathein*)'. They turn out to contrast sharply with the procedures of 'directed thinking', but not to be for all that wholly beyond the limits of rational investigation.

St Thomas's notion of revelation as a form of understanding is coterminous with his account of prophetic inspiration, found above all in the *De veritate* and the *Secunda Pars* of the *Summa Theologiae*.[120] As Fr Victor explains, for Aquinas the distinguishing mark of prophetic knowledge lies in its remoteness from normal cognition; prophets see things which others do not see. Thus for Thomas, a prophet is not primarily one who 'forth tells' – for all use or proclamation of prophecy, whether by speech, writing, gesture or dramatic action, is a secondary question'; nor is he one who 'foretells' – though foreknowledge is by no means atypical of prophetic vision, since after all the future is 'peculiarly remote and opaque to ordinary conscious apprehension, in contrast to the present or the past'. While the possible materials of prophetic knowledge are limitless, and include, then, the field of natural perception and reason: '*within* that field the prophet will see something which our connatural faculties cannot see, and he sees it by means other than those of the consciously directed employment of those faculties.'[121] In this experience the subject is seized by an 'inbreathing', *inspiratio*, which Thomas will also call a 'touch', *tactus* – whether or not the prophet simultaneously retains the normal use of their own faculties. Here grace is fully *operative*, whereas in the choice of expression for prophetic knowledge it will be *co-operative* simply – in one of those careful distinctions beloved of Latin theology which Fr Victor elsewhere urged the Orthodox not to dismiss with an impatient wave.[122]

So far Fr Victor has not specified the nature of the 'remoteness' which is annulled in the sheer happening of a knowledge originated neither consciously nor willingly. St Thomas, contrasting supernatural prophecy with what he held to be *one* of its possible conduits – an arcane but entirely natural formation of powerful images within the depths of the imaginative faculty, takes its far horizon to be nothing less than the eternal. Whether the supernatural prophet is aware of it or not, he is 'concerned with the things of time only from the standpoint of eternity'.

> While the natural *propheta*, at his best, is concerned with future good or bad 'fortune' as predetermined by the 'Fates' – the mechanical laws of cause and effect immanent in nature (*karma*) – the supernatural prophet is concerned with the ultimate designs of the Author and Finisher of men and stars.[123]

His 'sources of information' are not, as with the 'natural visionary', predetermining factors in finite reality contemporary with himself, but issue from the infinite God to whom all events are an eternal Today. Whereas the natural prophet sees something present that is significant of the future, his supernatural counterpart sees something present whose significance lies in eternity. And this includes the commonplace and humdrum: for ordinary events can possess eternal relevance in God's designs for his people's *salus*, their health and welfare. 'For there to be revelation there must be perception, not merely of the historic occurrence of the Crucifixion or the Empty Tomb, but also and principally of their *meaning* in the eternal designs of God.' Though the Word has been made flesh, prophetic understanding is still required to identify his presence in the man Jesus; to supply for the ignorance of his Incarnation among those millions whom Aquinas (who knew less of them) called *homines in silvis*, the 'men of the woods'; and to facilitate (through the Gifts of the Holy Spirit) the mystical experience of Christians.

God and the Unconscious was widely noticed. Canon D. J. B. Hawkins wrote in *The Tablet* that while much of Jung's psychology is plainly nonsense, yet 'if any of it is not nonsense, it is of greater importance than the departmental observations of experimental and physiological psychology in the nineteenth century'. Adapting some comments of the satirical novelist Thomas Love Peacock on Byron's *Manfred*, Hawkins wondered how the 'heterogeneous mythological company' of depth psychology could originally have met, and expressed his preference for an Aristotelian psychology of the unconscious in terms of powers, habits and dispositions but sporadically manifested in overt acts.

> If the cesspool theory of the unconscious mind be taken as Freud's way of recognising original sin, it needs to be complemented by a redemptive doctrine of the way in which divine grace seizes and modifies our latent powers in the direction of good.

Hawkins applauded Fr Victor for embarking on the critical purification of depth-psychological language. 'Questions and theories assume their proper proportion only when they are precisely formulated.'[124] Writing in the *Oxford Magazine*, V. A. Demant, then professor of Moral and Pastoral Theology in the University, and a high churchman, called the book the best confrontation yet between theology and analytical psychology – 'and it is the more interesting to meet a scholar of the allegedly most rationalist school of theology welcoming the discoveries of the psychologist most critical of intellectualism'. 'Father White means his readers to see that knowledge of the psyche can be used to appropriate the richer influences of Christianity which has with us today become over-cerebralised, verbalised and moralised.'[125]

This was easier for an Anglican to say than a Catholic. Charles Burns, whose Chelsea salon was so important to the flow of ideas among the English Catholic intelligentsia, admitted in *The Dublin Review* that a 'plea for a kind of "communication" of the Faith to the psyche of modern man, which is ... more by way of myth and symbol' might lead the unwary on to 'dangerous ground – near to the *Grenzbegriff* of Modernism', but felt that Fr Victor 'constantly brings us back to *terra firma*'.[126]

That thin ice was in the vicinity no one denied. But was Fr Victor skating over it? Warning voices from across the Atlantic suggested as much. Writing in *The New Scholasticism*, Raymond McCall deplored the degree of the English Dominican's acceptance of the Jungian theory of the collective unconscious and its archetypes, which he lambasted as 'a monstrous combination of scientific Lamarckianism with philosophical Averroism and a totally improbable fiction.' The author of *God and the Unconscious* had closed his eyes to too much in Jung that was scientifically and philosophically untenable. The

partial similarities he had traced failed to prove that Jung's affinities
with Catholicism were greater than with 'Rosicrucianism, Theosophy,
Zoroastrianism or Zen-Buddhism'.[127] His tone was echoed in an
extended assessment of the book by Dom Gregory Stevens in
Theological Studies. While welcoming many of Fr Victor's 'sound
observations' on the need for a *rapprochement* between modern
psychology and Catholic thought, the reviewer offered various strictures on the book's implied integration of Thomism and Jung.
Querying the elevation of the collective unconscious to the status of a
'basic religious phenomenon' and disputing the identification of
Jung's *libido*, or formless psychic energy, with St Thomas's 'natural
desire for God' (it was more like plain *appetitus*), Dom Stevens
reserved his sharpest comments for Fr Victor's attempt to come to
terms with the fundamental Jungian symbol of the self as a 'quadernity', not Trinity, through the incorporation of Marian motifs. 'Such
weird "integrations", if not decidedly detrimental to religion, are of
very little value, and taken without qualifications smack of pantheism
or, at least, of a reduction of religion to the level of the symbolic.'[128]
If four years later the Master of the Order, Fr Michael Browne, asked
for the book to be withdrawn (in fact it was already out of print), at
least the English Provincial, Fr Hilary Carpenter, took the opportunity to make amends for his scuppering of Fr Victor's regency by
paying tribute to his qualities as a religious as well as his passionate
adherence to the *sana doctrina* of St Thomas.

In point of fact Fr Victor had already answered these criticisms in
an address of 1957 to an international Congress in Spain.

> Realizing, as theologians seldom do, the urgency of the problem,
> Jung has felt it incumbent upon him to try to fill the vacuum
> himself, admittedly (as he repeatedly confesses) in somewhat
> amateurish fashion. Four dogmas especially have engaged his atten-
> tion: those of the Trinity, the Incarnation, the Mass together with
> Transubstantiation, and the Assumption of our Lady. His treat-
> ments of these dogmas will certainly be misread if it is not clearly
> understood that they are primarily concerned, not with their theol-
> ogy, but with their psychological *function*: their salutary or
> insalutary effects on the psyche. But even if this limitation be care-
> fully borne in mind, and notwithstanding the many profound
> insights which his treatments of them contain, it must be said that
> he has not correctly and completely grasped the Catholic Church's
> understanding of any one of them. It ill becomes a theologian to
> reproach Jung for some mistakes in his own field, especially if he
> himself has neglected his call for more expert assistance; but the

unfortunate fact remains that Jung not seldom brands as heretical what has every appearance of orthodoxy, and as orthodox what certainly is serious heresy.[129]

And singling out for special attention Jung's views on the psychological ill-suitedness of trinitarian (as distinct from quaternian) symbols, Fr Victor asserts that the Church's dogmatic formulae 'precisely safeguard the faithful against those dangers which Jung believes to follow' when the former, rather than the latter, 'reign supreme in the psyche'.

> For the Church's teaching insists, on the one hand, that the Triune God is utterly transcendent – *increatus, immensus, aeternus* – and that in Him alone is complete equality and *homousia* of Utterer and Uttered. On the other hand, that *imago Trinitatis est in anima secundum mentem tantum* – the image of the Trinity is in the human soul in regard only to its purely spiritual operations. The formulas thus ensure that the Three in One in its perfection is *not* to be taken as a pattern of human completeness and behaviour, but contrariwise as an object of differentiated adoration; even though it is (as St Augustine saw) the prototype of the psychological dynamism of cognition and conation.[130]

And Fr Victor would devote the latter 50s, the last years of his life, to perfecting a Catholic reception of those elements in Jungianism which, once dogmatically as well as humanely, evaluated, could work towards the *salus* – the health and salvation – of both culture at large and individual souls.

Soul and Psyche – a reworking of his Edward Cadbury lectures in the (non-denominational) theology school of the University of Birmingham – was the posthumously published result. If it largely confirms the positions Fr Victor took in *God and the Unconscious* it also adds some fresh elements which can be noted here.

While in *God and the Unconscious* Fr Victor's primary emphasis lay on what the Catholic Church might take from a purified Jungianism by way of assistance in the creation of a psychologically healthful culture which would dispose to salvation, *Soul and Psyche* marks a certain shift of register. Emboldened by what he saw as a crisis of confidence among psychiatrists and psychotherapists – on the European Continent if not in the Anglo-Saxon world, he offered Catholicism as the true revelation of healing Good which psychology, in its self-deceiving *weltanschauliche Neutralität* would reject at its peril. Those who set themselves up to speak for the good of the human psyche can hardly prescind entirely from all conception of man's nature, mode of existence and eventual destiny.[131] On the other hand, analytical psychology, insofar as it claimed to be an empirical science, could hardly be expected to make a leap of faith of which only the whole person would be capable. It could, however, become more comprehensive in the data it recognised, more phenomenologically attuned to the Bible and Church tradition of which, as practised by Jung himself, it not infrequently spoke. The result would be a more equal partnership in which (Catholic) Christian beliefs and practices could be 'correlated' with psychological experience and hypothesis – to the benefit of the latter.

For, so far from accepting Jung's claim that religious dogma (as distinct from symbolism) constitutes a defence mechanism against immediate, individual experience (however this be defined), Fr Victor maintained stoutly that 'creeds and doctrines', while providing a yard-stick for the measuring of such experience, also 'tend rather to expose the believer to immediate experience than to shield him from it'. Dogma is a translation of the direct experience of the original recipients of revelation, an experience which, through the pressure of that same revelation as transmitted via Bible and tradition, generates an equally direct experience – specifically Christian experience – in those who believe. Thus whereas the symbol (whether scriptural, sacramental, or otherwise theological) has a 'power of transforming and integrating psychic energy which can be possessed by no conceptualised scientific theory or credal statement alone', the dogmas perform as 'divinely guaranteed descriptions of that with which the Catholic Christian's direct experience has to do'. The faith which is mediated in different but complementary respects by both symbol and dogma presupposes and gives a 'new amplitude to the archetypal experience [as described by Jungians, q.v.], even though in so doing it will dethrone it from any claim that may be made for it to primacy'. And in thus humbling both ego-consciousness and the unconscious, revealed faith does a power of good. As well as tending powerfully to eradicate the tendency of the human animal to treat itself as God almighty, the faith which reaches us in the *enuntiabilia* of dogma enters the mind as *veritas salutifera* – healing truth.

It is not an academic fondness for precision, let alone an idolatry for mere words, that has prompted the Church's dogmatic definitions or her passionate condemnations of heresies, but her concern for the *salus humana* – human health and wholeness. It is in this light that we should understand such pronouncements as those opening words of the Athanasian Creed, which may otherwise seem so monstrous: 'Whosoever wills to be *salvus* (i.e. healed, whole, saved), before all things it is needful that he hold that Catholic faith [i.e. the faith which is for all]; unless he keep it whole and undefiled, without doubt he will perish in eternity.'[132]

Heresy destroys living relationship with God ('in eternity'), or to put it in Jungian terms, in the realm of the timeless archetypes.

But in this case why are not orthodox Christians supremely well-integrated persons and so walking demonstrations of the truth of the Gospel, not least to practising psychiatrists? One reply is that saving truth does not occupy a vacuum: it may have to contend with the obstacles provided by personal, hereditary and environmental factors. Again, the very possession of such truth gives rise to problems of adaptation in a society and culture, organised and animated, respectively, by very different principles and values. But these considerations, though valuable, do not yield the whole story. Medically, a definition of health is not easy to come by – not only in terms of mental health where many who are strikingly well-adjusted to their milieu may, from the standpoint of the realisation of their aims as human beings, be much sicker than many neurotics, but even in those of physical health, for 'feeling fine' is compatible with serious disease and death is not only biological life's end-result but its 'end-intended' or completion.[133] For Jung, successful treatment did not mean the elimination of suffering but realized 'individuation' – that is, the person's conscious relation to powerful items of the unconscious hitherto his master. And the individuation process already displays a 'pattern of life through death' – something which Fr Gerald Vann will take as the *leit-motif* of his spiritual theology (see Chapter 4). And there is here an intimation that the problem of health and wholeness will not be fully resolved this side of the grave. More positively, Fr Victor argues that since, for Catholic Christianity, it is original sin which is chiefly responsible for the 'disorganization' and 'sickness of nature' which afflict all human beings in various ways, sanctifying grace, which is the divinely provided 'cure' for that illness is the only way to health. But sanctifying grace is a *process*, and one that works itself out in some strange ways – as the lives of the saints bear witness.

> Sanctifying grace is, by God's mercy, still available to fallen, disintegrated man. And, on this Thomistic showing, its function is still to perfect, and to bring health and wholeness to human nature, and this precisely by restoring its centre of cohesion in God. Baptism brings forgiveness and the rebirth of the life of grace which the original sin had lost. But it does not automatically restore the prototypal integrity ... For sanctification since the fall, is no longer a

given *fait accompli*, but a process. Just because sanctifying grace perfects nature, and nature as it actually is in its disintegrated condition, it must progressively integrate the whole of it, and this includes its sicknesses and mortality. The integration of death, and of the death-dealing elements, is now an essential part of holiness, as it is of wholeness and health. It must be a painful process, the way of the cross, the integration of the evil which is precisely the privation of the original wholeness and of the particular disorders which are consequent on that privation. Following the example set supremely by Christ, the consequences of sin and of history, direct and indirect, are now the very condition of sanctification; the stage on which the drama must be played.[134]

From which it follows that the presence of neuroses and even psychoses in the souls of the righteous is nothing to wonder at. Wholeness is the work of grace – hence the triumphant proclamation of the resurrection as 'joy to the whole world' by the early (and contemporary) Church. Yet that gift of gracious wholeness is eschatological and thus more an object of the theological virtue of hope than something to be experienced fully in this life. And so the presence of involuntary affliction whether of body or soul does not argue against the presence of such grace. Indeed, it may be through just such disorders that the life of grace operates: that St Thérèse of Lisieux's attacks of scrupulosity, no less than her tuberculosis, were among the media whereby God's holiness took deeper hold on her total personality.

The sanctifying grace bestowed through Christ and his Church is not the same, however, as religion *tout court* – for there human, and therefore distorting, factors may creep in. The practical workings of religion are – whether fortunately or unfortunately – of great importance for it is

in and through his religious practices that [the human being] will find his theophanies, his images and conceptions of Divinity, and although these practices may be accompanied by verbal instruction and intellectual apprehensions, his understanding of them will normally be conditioned by his actual religious experiences.[135]

Hence the crucial role played in the practical exercise of Catholicism by the *image*, whether in the wider sense of the sign-system of the liturgical cultus, or in the narrower sense of the individual icon or artwork, or in the more primordial sense of the symbolization of divine and sacred figures on which these turn.

The aim of religion is that people should make of their lives 'a harmonious service of God, stabilized, integrated, differentiated and matured through their specifically religious observances'. For this to happen, an image or set of associated images must have the power to 'constellate' the whole personality and to activate its potential for development and growth. A true symbol will be able to do this for both conscious and unconscious contents. If it is to present what demands the 'total service of religion', it must manifest the Infinite, for theologically, 'total surrender (*latreia*) to anything less than the Infinite is idolatry' – whose effect according to the Hebrew prophets is the degrading of the idolater to the likeness of his idol. We have seen how, in his paper to the Madrid Congress Fr Victor presented the trinitarian symbol in this light, arguing that the threefold image shows forth uncreated transcendence, whereas the quarternary images beloved by Jung represent the longed-for wholeness of man's created being. This he now reaffirms: 'The emanation of the fourfold by way of creation is wholly distinct from the timeless begetting of the Second and the breathing forth of the Third in identity ... of being with a distinction solely of mutual relation ...'[136]

The function of the ternary image of the Triune God, psychologically considered, is not to furnish an image of human wholeness, then, but to provide a validation of both the 'static' and the 'dynamic' aspect of existence from within the Source of all reality.

> Where such a revelation of God prevails, the absolute and the relative, the static and the dynamic, being and becoming, the unlimited and the limited, the particular and the universal, the individual and the social, are all alike holy and all have their divine prototype.

For on the one hand, the 'Unity preserves the psyche from that disassociation which goes with polytheism', while the 'Trinity of the Unity preserves it from that other-worldly contempt for the relative, the dynamic, the distinctive and the individuated' which frequently follows both from transcendental monism and from an undifferentiated monotheism.

But the image of the Holy Trinity does not stand alone; it is never found save in some kind of conjunction with that of the incarnate Son, whose own image *is* quaternary, for his symbol is the four-armed cross, which the Jewish-Christian writer Hermas in his treatise *The Shepherd* re-imagined in comparing Christ with a great square stone, lying in a plane wide enough to include the whole world. The 'Four is thus indeed brought into the Life of the Three, without the Three in any way becoming Four, or the Four being obliterated by the Three, the creature by the Creator'. This the christological doctrine of the two natures united in a single trinitarian Person carefully guards.

It might have been expected that this distinction between the ternary symbolism of the Uncreated and the quaternary of the created, would have enabled Fr Victor to deal simply and straightforwardly with the criticism that the *feminine* archetypes are missing from Christian imagery as thus far presented. Although he will indeed invoke the figure of the Blessed Virgin Mary as integral to the quaternity of redeemed humanity, he felt it important to allow some space for the feminine within the Christian conceptuality, and iconography, of God himself. He argued that the undifferentiated divine Essence includes the prototype of motherhood – and that this affirmation may be made without any calling into question of the revealed masculine symbols for Father, Son and Spirit. The Essence, after all, though it may not be separated from the Persons, can be contemplated apart from them. And following the cue of the Russian Sophiologist Sergei Bulgakov, Fr Victor sees our blessed Lady as

> not *only* a fellow-creature, but also a unique created revelation of the uncreated Wisdom. This Wisdom is the Divine Being itself, which is unbegotten in the Father, begotten in the Son, 'breathed' in the Holy Spirit; and, though changeless Being in the Godhead, is yet refracted in ever-changing forms, in the Becoming of creation.[137]

At the Incarnation, so Fr Victor wrote in his essay in commemoration of Pope Pius XII's definition of the dogma of Mary's glorification in 1950, the three divine persons assumed a created human *nature* into hypostatic union with the Person of the Son; at the Assumption of the Virgin, they assumed a human *person* into the glory of the Godhead. The distinction, he believed, preserved one from any taint of 'mariolatry' while permitting the image of the blessed Mother to work its sanitising influence in Christian lives. For it makes clear that the mysteries of Christ are mysteries of the *Redeemer*, prototypes, exemplary causes, of the processes in which we must share for our redemption; the mysteries of Mary are mysteries of the *redeemed*, first and supreme effects of God's saving work through Christ.

> There seems to be some strange rightness in the portrayal of this reunion in splendour of Son and Mother, Father and Daughter, Spirit and Matter: in the gracious bending of the Divine Persons to crown the Woman, even (if our contemplation take a more ethical turn) in this exaltation of lowliness and simplicity.[138]

And because Mary's body was the '*mater materia*, from which the divine Spirit, in fashioning the Body of Christ, fashions the new cosmos', Fr Victor felt confident in proclaiming the *culturally regenerative force of the Assumption dogma.*

The arts and sciences of matter have one after another been banished from the Temple and the Church which begot and reared them. It is not long since laboratory and oratory were synonymous, the dividing line between prayer and chemistry was hardly discernible, and temple and theatre were hardly distinguishable. Medicine and the healing of mind and body, no less than the arts of love, have become wholly secularised; the dance driven from the sanctuary to the *Palais*. Religion has become a speciality, occupying but a small section of the *minds* only of a dwindling section of humanity: the rest of human activity, spiritual, mental, creative, emotional, carnal, is, by the common consent of believer and unbeliever alike, accounted secular and profane ... In the vogue of yoga, the growing interest in ancient paganism and modern oriental cults, may perhaps be discerned the yearnings of matter for spirit and spirit for matter, the ending of this unnatural divorce. They are yearnings which, if we are heedful, we can hardly fail to hear within 'ourselves also who have the first-fruits of the Spirit', and to which the Assumption of our Lady should summon us to find our own answer, for ourselves and our posterity.[139]

Notes

1. A. Cunningham, 'Victor White and C. G. Jung. The Fateful Encounter of the White Raven and the Gnostic', *New Blackfriars* 62. 733–34 (July–August 1981), pp. 320–34.
2. The correspondence, released only in 1990 by the *Jung Erbengemeinschaft*, is to be edited by Mr Cunningham.
3. The story is told in more detail in A. C. Lammers, *In God's Shadow. The Collaboration of Victor White and C. G. Jung* (New York: Paulist. 1994) – a work which, from a thorough knowledge of Jungian psychology, traces both the collaboration and the controversy.
4. Letters of 8 November 1953 and 4 March 1954, cited in ibid., pp. 94–95.
5. Fr Aelred Squire to Dr Lammers, 3 August 1987, as cited in her study, *In God's Shadow*, p. 113.
6. 'Jung on Religion', *National Review* for 19 April 1958, p. 375.
7. 'Catholics and War. The Principles Involved', *Catholic Herald*, 1 May, 1940.
8. 'When is a Christian Socialist?', p. 12, English Dominican Archives.
9. 'Christendoms, New or Old?' *Blackfriars* XIX. 224 (1938), pp. 795–804.
10. H. St. John, O.P., *Essays in Christian Unity, 1928–1954* (London: Blackfriars Publications, 1955), pp. xvi–xvii.
11. A brief account in B. and M. Pawley, *Rome and Canterbury through*

four Centuries. A Study of the Relations between the Church of Rome and the Anglican Churches, 1530–1973 (London and Oxford: Mowbrays, 1974), pp. 320–21. The conversations were eased by the considerable presence of Anglican Thomism at Kelham: see A. Mason, *SSM. History of the Society of the Sacred Mission* (Norwich: The Canterbury Press, 1993), p. 176.

12. 'Laxton Discussion, O.P. and S.S.M., Appendix', p. 2, English Dominican Archive.

13. 'Western and Eastern Theology of Grace and Nature', *Sobornost* (1942), reprinted in *God the Unknown and Other Essays* (London: Harvill Press, 1956), pp. 145–56.

14. W. J. B. Fry, 'Memoir of Dom Bede Winslow', in A. H. Armstrong and E. J. B. Fry, *Re-discovering Eastern Christendom. Essays in Commemoration of Dom Bede Winslow* (London: Darton, Longman & Todd, 1963), p. 7. For the spirit and programme of the journal, see his 'Integral Catholicism and the E. C. Q.', *Eastern Churches Quarterly* VI. 4 (1945), pp. 66–77, which draws on Père Yves Congar, O.P., and Dom Clément Lialine, of Chevetogne, and 'The General Principles of the E. C. Q.', ibid. XIII, 3–4 (1959), pp. 7–8.

15. Ibid., p. 9.

16. Letter of 29 December 1940 to John Layard, English Dominican Archives.

17. E. J. B. Fry, 'A Memoir of Dom Bede Winslow', p. 9.

18. *God the Unknown and Other Essays*, p. 147.

19. *Scholasticism* (London: Catholic Truth Society, n. d.), p. 2.

20. Ibid., p. 7.

21. M. Grabmann, *Geschichte der scholastischen Methode*, I. (Freiburg: Herder, 1909), pp. 269–70.

22. *De fide Trinitatis et de Incarnatione Verbi*, preface.

23. *Monologion*, 68. The italics are, evidently, White's.

24. *Scholasticism*, p. 10.

25. See M. Grabmann, *P. Heinrich Denifle, O.P. Eine Wurdigung seiner Forschungsarbeit* (Mainz: Kirchheim & Co., 1905).

26. *Scholasticism*, p. 11. See his three part *Blackfriars* essay on 'Thomism and Affective Knowledge', XXIV 274 (1943), pp. 8–16; XXIV 277 (1943), pp. 126–31; XXV 294 (1944), pp. 321–28, Lammers takes this as the key to an appreciation of Fr Victor's theological project; his aim was a Thomism grounded in St Thomas' writings which would be consistent with knowledge generated by subjective experience – in her own phrase, 'the warrants of experience'. *In God's Shadow*, p. 41.

27. *Scholasticism*, p. 16.

28. Hence the *guarded* welcome Fr Victor gave Henri de Lubac's *Surnatural. Etudes historiques* (Paris: 1946), writing: 'His conception of the 'divine exigence' and of the 'natural desire' compels him to deny the very possibility that God could have created man without grace and a super-natural destiny, a possibility which St Thomas expressly, albeit

quite casually, affirms. Père de Lubac would have been on firmer ground had he confined his criticism of later theologians to their quite disproportionate and sometimes invalid use of a methodological concept of abstract and unrealized possibility. We have already said something, and other critics have said far more, of the unsoundness (at least from the standpoint of logical coherence and as an interpretation of St Thomas) of his own peculiar thesis on this point; but it would be unfortunate if this were to distract attention from the importance of his negative criticism of much post-Tridentine theological development.' 'The Supernatural', *Dominican Studies* II (1949), p. 69.

29. *Scholasticism*, pp. 25–26.
30. E. van Ackeren, S.J., *Sacra Doctrina. The Subject of the First Question of the 'Summa Theologica' of St. Thomas Aquinas, with an Introduction by Yves M. J. Congar*. (Rome: Catholic Book Agency, 1952).
31. *Holy Teaching. The Idea of Theology according to St Thomas Aquinas* (London: Blackfriars, 1958), p. 4.
32. Ibid., p. 7.
33. 'An Orthodox Heresiarch?', *Blackfriars* XVIII. 213 (1937), p. 915, citing M. D. Petre, *Von Hügel and Tyrrell: The Story of a Friendship* (London: Dent, 1937), p. 2.
34. 'Authority, Revelation, and Infallibility', English Dominican Archives.
35. *Soul and Psyche* (London: Collins and Hervill, 1960), p. 89. Ibid., p. 88.
36. *Holy Teaching*, p. 12, with an internal citation of James 1.22.
37. Ibid., pp. 21. 22.
38. *How to Study, being the Letter of St Thomas Aquinas to Brother John, De modo studendi* (Oxford: Blackfriars, 1947), p. 20. The ascription to Aquinas is contested.
39. Ibid., pp. 15–16.
40. *Thaeatetus* 150c.
41. *De Veritate* XI. 1.
42. *How to Study*, p. 40, citing 1 Corinthians 13.12.
43. *God the Unknown, and Other Essays* (London: Harvill Press, 1956).
44. Ibid., p. 16; cf. *Summa Theologiae* Ia, q. 12, art. 13, ad i.
45. Ibid., p. 18.
46. Ibid., p. 169.
47. Ibid., pp. 43–44.
48. *Summa Theologiae*, Ia, q. 1, a. 8.
49. *God the Unknown*, p. 50.
50. Ibid., p. 31.
51. I. Trethowan, 'Christian Atheism', *Downside Review* 75. 242 (1957), pp. 325–37, where in fact Fr Edward Sillem's critique of Berkeley's proof of God's existence is the chief object of Dom Illtyd's anxieties.
52. V. White, O.P., E. Sillem, Dom I. Trethowan and Editor, 'The Knowledge of God', *Downside Review* 76. 242 (1958), p. 14.
53. *God the Unknown*, p. 63.

54. A term Fr Victor draws from the sixteenth-century Dominican theologian Cardinal Cajetan: the Ideas are multiple *secundum munus ideandi*, i.e. precisely in their *function* as ideas.
55. *Summa Theologiae* Ia, q. 8. art. 1.
56. *God the Unknown*, p. 86.
57. Ibid., p. 89. The *homoousios* is of course the teaching of the Council of Nicaea (325) that the Son is 'one in being with' the Father.
58. Ibid. '*Neti, neti*': Sanskrit for 'Not this, not that'.
59. Ibid., p. 92.
60. *God and the Unconscious* (London: The Harvill Press, 1952), p. 226.
61. Ibid., p. 100.
62. Ibid., p. 103.
63. Ibid., pp. 116–132. The literary precipitate can be found in A. R. Vidler and W. A. Whitehouse (eds.), *Natural Law. A Christian Reconsideration* (London: SCM Press, 1946).
64. Ibid., p. 121.
65. Ibid., p. 127.
66. Ibid., p. 128.
67. 'The Concept of Justice in St Thomas Aquinas' in ibid., pp. 133–44.
68. Sonnet 34.
69. *God the Unknown* p. 103, with reference to *Summa Theologiae* IIIa, q. 1. a. 2, and q. 46, a. 3.
70. Ibid., pp. 106–107, with copious references to the *Summa Theologiae, Tertia Pars*.
71. Ibid., p. 111.
72. E. Fouilloux, *Les catholiques et l'unité chrétienne du XIXe au XXe siècle. Itineraires européens d'expression française* (Paris: Le Centurion, 1982), p. 243.
73. *God the Unknown* p. 159.
74. Ibid., p. 161: the coherence of the thought with the celebrated opening clausula of *Lumen Gentium*, the Dogmatic Constitution of the Second Vatican Council on the Church, is noteworthy.
75. *God the Unknown*, p. 165.
76. Ibid., p. 181.
77. 'A variant', because in Fr Victor's version all three seem subordinated to a superordinate pastoral office, which he mentions first.
78. Ibid., p. 181. Italics original.
79. 'The Background to Papal Infallibility', in ibid., pp. 188–205.
80. Cited ibid., p. 190.
81. A. M. Ramsey, *The Gospel and the Catholic Church* (London: Longman, Green & Company, 1936), cited ibid., p. 191.
82. Ibid., pp. 195–96.
83. C. G. Jung, 'Foreword', *God and the Unconscious* (London: The Harvill Press, 1952), p. xxii.
84. Ibid., p. xxii.
85. Lammers, however, considers that Jung's determination to 'know only the soul' amounts to a 'psychomonism' for which only what has inner

value for the subject is accounted real: *In God's Shadow*, p. 22, drawing on the analyses of M. Nagy, *Philosophical Issues in the Psychology of C. G. Jung* (Albany: SUNY, 1991), pp. 63–79.

86. *God and the Unconscious*, p. 2.
87. The official name for the explosion of the first such bomb in the deserts of New Mexico.
88. R. B. Cattell, *Psychology and the Religious Quest* (London: Nelson, 1938), p. 42.
89. C. G. Jung, *Psychological Types* (ET London: Kegan Paul, Trench, Trubner & Co., 1938), p. 230.
90. For a more pessimistic account of the possibility of integrating Jungianism with Catholic Christianity, see R. Noll, *The Jung Cult: Origins of a Charismatic Movement* (Princeton: Princeton University Press, 1994), which situates Jung in the late nineteenth-century German and Swiss-German neo-pagan revival, pervaded as this was by a Nietzschean cult of personality, obsession with the occult – in which eroticism, mysticism and neophilia joined forces, and, most especially, the influence of the zoologist and monist Ernst Haeckel, who sought to restore health to the psyche of Western man by cutting through centuries of Judaeo-Christian 'underbrush' (Noll's term) in order to reach the promised land of a pre-Christian, impersonal psyche and there be revitalised.
91. *God and the Unconscious*, pp. 13–22.
92. Ibid., p. 16–17, with reference to C. G. Jung, *The Secret of the Golden Flower* (ET London: Kegan Paul, Trench, Trubner & Co. 1942), pp. 112–13.
93. C. G. Jung, *Modern Man in Search of a Soul*, (ET London: Kegan Paul, Trench, Trubner & Co., 1933), p. 77.
94. *God and the Unconscious*, p. 24.
95. On his work, see C. Bernoulli, *Die Psychologie von Carl Gustav Carus und deren geistesgeschichtliche Bedeutung* (Jena: E. Diederichs, 1925).
96. God and the Unconscious, p. 32.
97. A. Béguin, '*Art romantique et la rêve. Essai sur le romantisme allemand et la poésie française* (Marseilles: Editions des Cahiers du Sud, 1937), p. 98, cited *in God and the Unconscious.*
98. *God and the Unconscious*, pp. 35–36.
99. Ibid., pp. 38–39.
100. C. G. Jung, *Modern Man in Search of a Soul*, p. 263.
101. *God and the Unconscious*, p. 52.
102. C. G. Jung, *Psychology of the Unconscious* (ET London: Kegan Paul, Trench, Trubner & Co., 1919), p. 139.
103. *God and the Unconscious*, p. 56–57.
104. He knew of the Russian theologian Sergei Bulgakov's conceptualisation of that uncreated *ousia* by reference to the (female) Old Testament figure of Wisdom.
105. *God and the Unconscious*, pp. 221–22. Some further remarks by way of (critical) appreciation of Jung's view in *Soul and Psyche. An Enquiry*

into the Relationship of Psychotherapy and Religion (London: Collins and Harvill Press, 1960), pp. 65–75.

106. Cf. also 'The Common Ground of Religion and Psychology', in *Soul and Psyche*, pp. 11–31.

107. K. Stern, 'Religion and Psychiatry', *Commonweal* for 22 October 1948.

108. *God and the Unconscious*, p. 196.

109. Ibid., pp. 210–11.

110. Ibid., p. 76.

111. 'Problems arising from the Publication of Answer to Job', English Dominican Archive.

112. Ibid. The anti-Jungian critique of the idea of the collective unconscious mentioned here had been cited against Fr Victor's own *God and the Unconscious* by Norman Cohn in his review of the work in *Twentieth Century* for May 1953.

113. 'Problems arising from the Publication of *Answer to Job*,' op. cit. Dr Lammers suggests that the strength of Fr Victor's feeling on this matter owes something to a displacement of anger on to Jung for the *débâcle* over the Regentship in 1954: 'Finding himself cut off by his religious superiors because of his work with Jung, in his rage he cut himself off from Jung, who was his chief alternative source of emotional and intellectual support.' *In God's Shadow*, p. 112. The somewhat contradictory evidence she cites as to Fr Victor's attitude to his original passionately harsh comments on the book, 'Jung on Job', in *Blackfriars* for July 1955, gives a degree of plausibility to her view. On the other hand, the substantive issue (the goodness of God) is hardly a *bagatelle*.

114. *God and the Unconscious*, p. 79.

115. Cited ibid., p. 80; see also Fr Victor's *Walter Hilton. An English Spiritual Guide* (London: Guild of Pastoral Psychology, 1944).

116. Ibid., p. 99.

117. Ibid., pp. 100–101.

118. *Nicomachean Ethics*, 1099b 13.

119. *God and the Unconscious*, p. 105.

120. More precisely, *De veritate* 12, and IIa IIae, qq. 171–174.

121. *God and the Unconscious*, p. 114.

122. 'Western and Eastern Theology of Grace and Nature', in *God the Unknown*, pp. 145–53.

123. *God and the Unconscious*, p. 130.

124. *The Tablet*, 3 January 1953.

125. *Oxford Magazine*, 10 February 1953.

126. *Dublin Review* 227 (1953), pp. 79–83.

127. *New Scholasticism* 28 (1954), pp. 240–243. Fr Thomas Gilby, no mean scholastic himself, had already, however, drawn attention to elements in Thomism open to ideas of the unconscious: thus 'Vienne and Vienna', *Thought* XXI, 80 (1946), pp. 63–82.

128. *Theological Studies* 9 (1953), pp. 505.

129. 'Dogma and Mental Health', in *Conducta religiosa y salud mental. VII Congreso catolico-internacional de psicoterapia y psicologia clinica. Madrid, 10–15. 9. 1957* (Barcelona: Antibioticos, S. A., 1959), p. 99.
130. Ibid., p. 100.
131. *Soul and Psyche*, p. 41.
132. Ibid., p. 91.
133. Ibid., p. 173, citing V. von Weiszäcker's *Der kranke Mensch: eine Einführung in die medizinische Psychologie* (Stuttgart: Fromman, 1951).
134. Ibid., pp. 185–86.
135. Ibid., p. 192.
136. Ibid., p. 109.
137. Ibid., pp. 139–40, with reference to S. B. Bulgakov, *The Wisdom of God. A Brief Summary of Sophiology* (London: Williams and Norgate, 1937), p. 179.
138. 'The Scandal of the Assumption', *Life of the Spirit* V. 53–54 (1950), pp. 199–200.
139. Ibid., p. 210, with an internal citation of Romans 8.23.

Works by Victor White

'Spengler Views the Machine Age', *Blackfriars* XIII. 142 (1932), pp. 7–22.
'Scholasticism', in E. C. Messenger (ed.), *Studies in Comparative Religion* IV (London: Catholic Truth Society, n.d., but 1934).
'Faith', *Blackfriars* XVIII. 202 (1937), pp. 34–41.
'Doctrine in the Church of England', *Blackfriars* XIX. 216 (1938), pp. 163–76.
'Faith in the Church of England', *Blackfriars* XIX. 217 (1938), pp. 250–63.
'Christendoms, New or Old', *Blackfriars* XIX. 224 (1938), pp. 795–804.
'Reunion in Catholicity', *Blackfriars* XX. 230 (1939), pp. 370–74.
'Wars and Rumours of Wars', *Blackfriars* XX. 231 (1939), pp. 403–413.
'War and the Early Church', *Blackfriars* XX. 234 (1939), pp. 643–54.
'The Works of Dr Darwell Stone', *Blackfriars* XXII. 253 (1939), pp. 188–197.
'The Effects of Schism', *Blackfriars* XXIII. 263 (1942), pp. 49–58.
The Frontiers of Theology and Psychology (London: Guild of Pastoral Psychology, 1942).
'Thomism and Affective Knowledge' I, *Blackfriars* XXIV. 274, (1943), pp. 8–16; II, ibid. XXIV. 277 (1943), pp. 126–31; III, ibid. XXV. 294 (1944), pp. 321–28.
Walter Hilton. An English Spiritual Guide (London: Guild of Pastoral Psychology, 1944).
'St Thomas Aquinas and Jung's Psychology', *Blackfriars* XXV. 291 (1944), pp. 209–219.
Psychotherapy and Ethics (London: Newman Association, 1945).
The Letter of St Thomas Aquinas to Brother John, 'De Modo Studendi', Latin

Text with Translation and Exposition (Oxford: Blackfriars Publications, 1947).

'The Aristotelian-Thomist Conception of Man', *Eranos-Jahrbuch 1947, Band XV, Der Mensch* (Zürich: 1948).

'The Analyst and the Confessor', *Commonweal*, 23 July 1948.

'St Thomas's Conception of Revelation', *Dominican Studies* I (1948), pp. 3–34.

Notes on Gnosticism (London: Guild of Pastoral Psychology, 1949).

'Satan', *Dominican Studies* II (1949), pp. 193–98.

'The Supernatural', *Dominican Studies* II (1949), pp. 62–73.

'The Scandal of the Assumption', *Life of the Spirit* V. 11–12 (1950), pp. 199–212.

'Recent Contributions to Psychology', *Blackfriars* XXXII. 378 (1951), pp. 419–27.

'Buddhism Comes West', *Blackfriars* XXXII, 381 (1951), pp. 585–90.

God and the Unconscious (London: Harvill Press, 1952).

'The Dying God: Pagan, Psychological and Christian', *Blackfriars* XXXIII. 383 (1952), pp. 60–66.

'The Dying God: Pagan, Psychological and Christian: Differences', *Blackfriars* XXXIII. 384 (1952), pp. 113–122.

'Four Challenges to Religion' I, 'Freud', *Blackfriars* XXXIII. 385 (1952), pp. 170–74; II, 'Jung', ibid. XXXIII. 386 (1952), pp. 203–207; III, 'Frazer', ibid., XXXIII. 387 (1952), pp. 250–53; IV, 'Marx', ibid., XXXIII. 388–89 (1952), pp. 317–22.

'Religious Tolerance', *Commonweal*, 4 September 1953.

'Charles Gustave Jung', *Time and Tide*, 23 July 1955.

'Jung on Job', *Blackfriars* XXXVI. 420 (1955), pp. 52–60.

'Kinds of Opposites', *Studien zur Analytischen Psychologie C. G. Jungs. Festschrift zum 80. Geburtstag von C. G. Jung*, I (Zurich: 1955).

God the Unknown (London, Harvill Press, 1956).

Holy Teaching. The Idea of Theology according to St Thomas Aquinas (Blackfriars Publications, 1958).

'Some Recent Studies in Archetypology', *Blackfriars* XL. 470 (1959), pp. 216–19.

'Theological Reflections', *Journal of Analytical Psychology* V (1960), pp. 147–54.

Soul and Psyche. An Enquiry into the Relationship of Psychotherapy and Religion (London: Collins and Harvill Press, 1960).

4

Gerald Vann

Lawrence Samuel Vann was born at St Mary Cray in Kent in August 1906. When he was thirteen he was sent to the Dominican school at Hawkesyard, under the direction of a revered, if sharp-tongued, head-master, Fr Jerome Rigby.[1] By the time of the school's removal to Laxton (1924), Fr Gerald was already a Dominican novice, aged seventeen, at Woodchester. That autumn he returned to Hawkesyard for his studies in philosophy and part of those in theology: he was one of the first student friars to receive tuition at the shining new Blackfriars at Oxford. With the exception of a year at the Angelicum in Rome to gain the lectorate in theology (he wrote it on a topic highly suggestive for his later spiritual theology, 'On the Mystery of the Most Holy Trinity as the Archetype of Human Life'), he stayed at Oxford for five years, taking in his stride a degree in the Honours School of English Literature *en route*. But he was not to teach in the house of studies. After his Oxford degree he returned to his old school, now elegantly ensconced in the Georgian mansion of Laxton Hall. He would remain there – latterly as superior, and then head-master – for eighteen years. Indeed, Fr Gerald's post-Laxton life in the Order – short spells at Cambridge and Edinburgh, and then the last painful months struggling with cancer at Newcastle, up to his death there on 14 July 1963 – were something of a postlude. Though he continued to write, and his celebrity as a spiritual theologian to grow, he was not in demand as a preacher and broadcaster to the extent that characterised the Laxton years. Most importantly, he did not regard his schoolmastering as *faute de mieux*: on the contrary, he was able to work out a theology and spirituality of education which informed much of his writing for adults as well. With his close friend Fr Sebastian Bullough, and Fr Henry St John whom he succeeded (after a brief interval) as headmaster, he produced, in fact, a Dominican and Thomist Concept of what educating little boys is all about. And this both followed from, and fed, a devotion to the particular institution, which had been founded by Cardinal Howard in Bornhem in the Spanish Netherlands at the end of the 1650s (see Appendix 1) and whose mobile and somewhat chequered history he wrote for its tercentenary celebrations.[2]

It would not be the worst introduction to his work to describe how he saw the Laxton setting, where the lion's share of it was produced. (Only *On Being Human* preceded it, though half a dozen of his twenty-two books lie on its further side.) Fr Gerald opens by declaring that helping the young grow up is among the most difficult and delicate of tasks.

> To the outside it may all seem very simple:
> you assemble a group of people competent to teach this or that subject and capable of keeping order; you draw up your timetable; *et voilà*. The insider knows that these are not the most important ingredients in school life; he knows too that while he and his colleagues, individually, may influence their pupils deeply for good or ill, the greatest influence of all may well be that of 'the school' itself: he can indeed console himself with the thought that if the spirit of the school is a wise and good one it will cover a multitude of inadequacies and follies on his part.[3]

'Wise and good': the non-historical sections of *Blackfriars School* – and, furthermore, much of Fr Gerald's *oeuvre* as a whole, consist in exploring what those two epithets may entail.

Not that the historical segments of the essay are meant to be irrelevant to this ethical and theological quest. For in the first place, the Dominican spirit which a Dominican school must surely embody cannot be stated without reference to the Order's foundations. Fr Gerald presents this in terms of three saints and a *beatus*, with special emphasis on the last. St Dominic himself represents the imperative to 'absorb' reality – by rational means, but not by them alone, and to communicate the result, as wisdom, to others. St Albert stands for a 'vast and fearless intellectual curiosity'. St Thomas embodies intellectual integrity, but also the exalting of wisdom – both of the human spirit and of the Holy Spirit – above knowledge. Bl Jordan of Saxony, Dominic's first successor as Master of the Order, and the author of some remarkable letters of spiritual friendship to women which Fr Gerald would publish in a version of his own in the following year,[4] is treated as a model on account of qualities not usually associated with boys' boarding schools. He was 'a great administrator and man of affairs, but he is constantly referred to as *dulcis*, gentle, sweet-natured; he was famous for his kindness, his informality and his gaiety ...'[5] and, as we shall see later, these qualities are to be conceived as crucial aspects of that evangelical '*caritas* which alone gives wisdom to human love and experience'.

Nor does the pertinence of the past stop there, for the austerity of the (pre-1962) Dominican Mass-ritual and the Thomistic strategy of evaluating all contemporary problems and modes of thought in the light of a *philosophia perennis*, these too are instructive, and notably of a concern for getting down to essentials.

What, then, was the educational ethos which, as a schoolmaster-friar, Fr Gerald invoked? In a word, it was *sapiential*. Leisure, stillness; exploration, but with a sense of direction; independence, but without disorderliness; informality and gaiety, even: these were the chief components of his ideal. In particular, he stressed – and looked back across the centuries to the sixth-century achievement of Cassiodorus, that schoolmaster of the ancient West in decline, for corroboration – that without contemplative leisure no culture of spiritual worth can be. Citing words of his own in *The Water and the Fire*, written during his brief sojourn at Blackfriars, Cambridge,

> We are all aware of the frenzied tempo, the confusion, the activism, of modern life, its hatred or fear of silence and stillness. Education could set itself to combat this state of affairs; but in fact it is itself too often determined by the prevailing atmosphere; and becomes itself a frenzied rush, a scramble for examination marks, for degrees and diplomas; it becomes itself so utilitarian that it defeats its own essential ends; it may provide a great deal of information, it can hardly hope to be a royal road to a deep and vivid culture.[6]

So what is to be done? Fr Gerald set out four *desiderata*. First, the child must refind roots in nature, the rhythm of life and the cycle of seasons – something only possible if school is in the country, or at least a convincing piece of *rus in urbe*. Secondly, the child needs a sense of 'home – the last refuge of civilisation', and that only a home*ly*, small-scale and informal environment can provide. Thirdly, he ought to become aware of 'humanity's great universal symbols' by 'a *modus docendi* which shall address itself to the mind as a whole', of which an example appears to be:

> It is good to know what science has to tell us of the sun, but not if the knowledge destroys for us the 'great purring lion', the sun-god who goes down at night into the sea to be re-born next day at dawn ...

Fourthly – and here a specifically Thomist stress on *distinguer pour unir* comes into its own, the child will be well served by education only if all the levels of the personality are addressed at once distinctively, yet in such a way as to render them a harmonious unity. Thus:

> The development of the body is important not as an end in itself but as part of the development of the whole personality to fullness of life; the senses need to be developed and trained but again not to an independent life but to the whole personality's awareness of and connaturality with the true, the good and the beautiful. The same is true of the emotional level; which if wisely trained can serve the spirit by adding its powerful drive to the search for truth and goodness, but which otherwise can either come to dominate the personality to the eclipse of mind, or, on the other hand can lead, through suppression and atrophy, to a desiccation and frustration which will warp the whole personality.[7]

But all this is ultimately in the service of a religious education: humane certainly but with the only true humanism, that of the cross, which means:

> not the pursuit of a pagan, a profane culture in one department with religious belief and practice in another, but a culture impregnated, in-formed through and through with the love of God and an understanding of the purpose and the pity of God.

'Love', 'purpose', 'pity': these will turn out to be crucial terms in Fr Gerald's soteriology, and therefore in his theodicy, his defence of the goodness yet almighty power of our Maker.

But then like the headmaster he had been, Fr Gerald ends with an eye to parents of prospective Howardians, claiming that those at least of his *desiderata* which can be assured by human skill are realised at Laxton, and its preparatory school, Llanarth: the stress on free time and silence and the cultivation of the arts (and the decidedly unSpartan attitude to sport); the beauty of place – the one school with its 'Wilderness, its old walled-garden, its magnificent beeches', the other set amid the green-grey of the Welsh hills; the familial quality of a community where friars and boys intermingle.

Education is the seedbed of culture; yet it would be wrong to give the impression that Fr Gerald's preoccupations focused on one small school, even if it could be regarded as a blessed plot, a privileged locus for realising a Thomistic vision of nurture. Christian unity and global peace were wider aspirations. In 1936 he had begun to participate in the Laxton conversations. The profound grasp of Catholic ethics – in no legalistic but a truly evangelical spirit – which his contributions showed brought him to the awareness of Anglicans beyond the circle of the Society of the Sacred Mission. In the course of 1941, Dorothy Sayers, Dantist, playwright, creator of Lord Peter Wimsey and, not least, Christian apologist, sent him her memorandum on 'Consent among the Churches'.[8] This note on the 'Possible Formation of a Statement of Oecumenical Doctrine based on the Highest Common Factor of Consent among the Christian Churches' was not aimed, as were the 'agreed statements' of post-conciliar ecumenism, at a state of 'organic union'. The latter is probably a chimaera, at any rate short of the Second Coming, whereas Sayers' document was directed at an objective at once more limited and more practical.

From the fact that Fr Gerald agreed to take responsibility for the section on ethics in the proposed 'Statement', it appears that he shared Sayers' aim and approved her means. It was her conviction that a recognisable 'oecumenical Christian tradition' (namely, of generally accredited dogma) exists, and that, at any rate, its enemies can recognise it. On this she meant to build. She pointed out that lowest common denominatorism lacks all intellectual integrity.

> Teachers who take their work seriously realise that to teach the 'Bible' without any definite theological or philosophical purpose is to treat it with a frivolity which would not be tolerated in the handling of any secular subject, and those who have preserved a proper professional integrity rightly refuse to have anything to do with it ... Intelligent educators further realise that it is absurd to take the Lowest Common Denominator of 'Christian' agreement as a basis for instruction as, e.g. 'To believe in God and follow the teachings of Christ in a spirit of love'; since all such vague formulae achieve agreement only by refusing to define their terms. ('What is 'belief'? What is meant by 'God'? What are the theological implications of the title 'Christ'? What did he teach?) 'The simple Gospel' is also a question-begging phrase since 'the Gospel' was by no means simple to those who first heard it, and can only be made so by ignoring the greater part of it.[9]

The only proper procedure is ecclesial, doctrinal, theological. But at this point, a further problem arises: the existence, within Anglicanism and the Free Churches, of numerous 'Christians' (Sayers prefers to call them 'Jesuanists') who repudiate crucial aspects of orthodox oecumenical dogma, notably where the divinity of Christ is in question. 'There is more difference of essential doctrine between a 'Jesuanist' Anglican and an Anglo-Catholic than there is between Dr Whale and the Pope'. Alliance of Christians and 'Jesuanists' on the basis of a purely philanthropic engagement in the world has been tried and found wanting. Christian ethics, once divorced from divine authority, can offer no convincing argument for their superiority to rivals; it is impossible to detach the ethic of Christianity from a 'mythology' which makes no sense unless Jesus Christ was God; capitulation to this approach is in effect surrender to 'Jesuanism' and so fails to attack the secular philosophies at the 'present point of collapse: i.e. their assumption that salvation is of man'. The Creeds ecumenically interpreted in all their theological implications are what should be taught as the meaning of Christianity in the nation's schools – and this would provide an intellectual challenge as substantial as that of studying Shakespeare or biology.

What she sought – and what Fr Gerald was evidently prepared to sign, was not a statement by the 'actual heads' of the separated communions ('impracticable and perhaps undesirable'), but a statement drawn up and approved by 'representative and responsible clergy whose opinions are of weight with their own people'.

Fr Gerald's other concern, in the years immediately before and after, as well as during the Second World War, was international peace. In 1936/7 he founded a 'Union of Prayer for Peace', the object of which was to create around the world a body of Catholics pledged not only to pray for peace but also to study and make known in their own circle the teaching and tradition of Catholicism on social and international amity. Approved by the Holy See (it could hardly object!), this 'Union' continued for a number of years into the post-war era. Fr Gerald kept scrupulous lists of the 'pledgers', both British and foreign, and the prayer-cards in various languages which the Union overseas put forth. Like Fr Victor he was not a pacifist *tout court*; but, taking his cue from certain statements of Pope Pius XI which spoke of modern warfare as little better than mass murder, he considered that, *in present conditions*, organised non-violent resistance was the only ethical course to follow.

> Modern warfare [he wrote in 1939] is purely and exclusively destructive, and destructive of everything that is good in our world. And the most inexplicable argument for its justification is that which urges the possibility of having to fight to preserve our civilization, for we should lose, through anarchy or dictatorship, all that we value, without even the consolation of knowing ourselves innocent of inflicting injustice on others.[10]

He was perfectly willing to subscribe to the doctrine of the 'just war' *in abstracto*, but there was, he thought, such a thing as using eternal truths as a pillow to go to sleep on. Though (evidently) the hope that a second general European conflagration might be averted proved groundless, Fr Gerald's study *Morality and War* was not without influence. It made more common coin in circles beyond English Roman Catholics – or any kind of Christian for that matter – the scholastic theory of just warfare, both as to *ends* and as to *means*.

> *Bonum ex integra causa*, as the scholastics expressed it: a thing is good only if it is integrally good, good in all its elements. We shall not content ourselves with discovering that there is still something worth fighting for; since the essence of the problem consists in understanding in what sense we may legitimately speak of fighting at all. We shall not content ourselves with discovering whether there are legitimate methods of fighting; because the essence of the problem consists also in understanding for what objects it is permissible to fight at all.[10a]

How he portrayed the ethos of a humane-Christian civilisation we shall in due course discover. He *began* his writing career at the other end of the creation-Creator polarity, not with man but with God, and, more specifically, with the central subject of orthodox divinity: the Holy Trinity.

The trinitarian archetype

The Holy Trinity is, so Fr Gerald's lectoral thesis argued, the 'archetype of human life'. Following the customary theological doctrine of Latin Christendom since Augustine, there is a kind of vestigial image of the Trinity shimmering in all creatures. Though certain ancient philosophers 'as it were by its shadow and from afar' glimpsed this truth, lacking the 'contuition' of the mystery of the Trinity (an intuition of the triune God in, with and by means of perception of the pattern of finite being), they could not fully grasp it. But the New Testament revelation enables us to see that creatures are *from* the Father – as our 'principle, to whom we recur [or return]', *through* the Son – as the 'form which we follow', and *in* the Holy Spirit – 'by whose grace we are reconciled' to our Maker.[11]

Where the theologies of the Latin Church may legitimately diverge is in the *perspectives* from which they view the mirroring of the endless trinitarian mystery in the little mystery of the creature. Fr Gerald's starting point is *fecundity* – and not in the biological sense alone, for, citing the early twentieth-century philosopher Henri Bergson, each moment of our life where we play the artisan is a kind of creation. From the actuality which it enjoys, every creature always tries in some sense to progress, evolve, perfect itself, in such a way that it is a kind of craftsman of its own being, *artifex entitatis*. This takes numerous forms, both interior – growth in self-understanding, and exterior – in the making of works of every kind of 'art'. And with the Dominican neo-scholastic P. Hugon, Fr Gerald sees in the procession of the Word and Spirit from the Father a perfect fruitfulness which in creatures is reflected only with multitudinous *im*perfections.[12] From Heraclitus to 'Hermes Trismegistus', the pagans have surmised something of this mystery. Divines like Richard of St Victor brought forward 'congruent' (as distinct from demonstrative) reasons for believing in the Trinity along these lines: for it cannot be that the Supreme Good should lack a superabundant overflow into a communion of love.[13]

And after a brief conspectus of all the trinitarian heresies of Church history, seen in the light of John of St Thomas's maxim that they can be divided into two kinds – those which falsely infer unity of Person from unity of Essence, and those which, on the basis of the diversity of Person's wrongly deny the consubstantial oneness of the Essence[14] – Fr Gerald offers an exposition of the way St Thomas used the idea of the divine 'processions' to show how a Trinity of really distinct Persons can be in one concretely existing Essence.[15] Here as elsewhere Aquinas showed himself a profoundly biblical theologian, for his conceptually elaborate theology of the processions is, in the last resort, a meditation on the implications of two Johannine statements, on the coming forth of Jesus from God, and that of the Spirit of truth from the Father (John 8.42; 15.26). And drawing not only on such austerely conceptual schoolmen as Cajetan and Billot, but also on the aestheticians of the French Catholic revival, and notably Jacques Maritain and Paul Claudel, Fr Gerald represents St Thomas's intuition that the Word of the Father must be a Word which 'brings forth Love', *Verbum spirans Amorem*, since knowledge can never be perfect unless the will also is happily united with it.[16] The union of love that the spiration of the Holy Spirit brings about *is* the perfect fecundity of God.[17]

Since God is the *artifex* of all that is, the inner-Trinitarian processions must be highly relevant to that gracious outflowing of his productivity which is the creation. Fr Gerald cites approvingly Maritain's dictum in *Art et Scolastique*: 'If in the work of creation, the Word was the art, then the Spirit was the poetry.'[18] But, before pursuing the analogy between the divine Artist and the human, he pauses to underline the sense in which the comparison limps. Because art is, in the words of Jean Cocteau in *Le Rappel à l'ordre*, 'knowledge enfleshed', some object is always presupposed to the artist's understanding. Artists always have their raw materials, be these as lowly as the vocabulary of line and colour provided by the world around them. But the divine intellect and will – the God whose being is fruitful in the generation of the Son who is the Word and the Spirit who is Love, and who as the Creator is never other than this Father, Son, Spirit – do not simply *recognise* the goodness in things and loving it; rather, by loving it they *make it to be*.[19] And before leaving the doctrine of the immanent Trinity, Fr Gerald adds another thought which confirms the dissimilarity. Thanks to the divine simplicity – the fact that God *is* all he *has*, the divine fruitfulness must be the unchanging, 'intransmutable' possession of life. And lest anyone should consider such *immobilitas* a defect, he warns, in the words of Fr Vincent McNabb, that 'only a fool' would take the monk's immobility for aridity, 'silence for empty-headedness'. In the unmoving actuality of the processions is the tumultuous dynamism of eternal life to which we are assimilated by grace. With creatures, perfection is increased by degrees in 'as it were a rectilinear progression', whereas in God 'all remains within'.

We see the Deity, the undivided Trinity, 'fruitful in processions, distinct in personalities, a consortium of social relations, one having all that another has, not acting without another, reigning with the others in mutual felicity.'[20]

According to St Thomas's commentary on Job 26.13 where, in the Vulgate, the wisdom writer speaks of the divine creative activity as the work of God's 'spirit' and 'hand', in this text there 'appears, in the production of creatures, the Trinity of persons'. On the scholastic axiom whereby *omne agens agit sibi simile* – every agent acts in a fashion reminiscent of itself – we should expect the Trinity to be 'represented' in all of their creaturely works. For Aquinas there are vestiges of the Trinity even in irrational creatures, since these bear the marks of the Son/Word in their intelligible form and of the Spirit/Love in their internal order.[21] But in the rational creature, which is capable of producing its own 'word' and 'love' – spontaneously originated intellectual and volitional activity, we find more than a *vestige*. Here, and above all where those capacities are turned towards union with their divine Archetype, we are dealing with an *image* of the trinitarian life. Thanks to sanctifying grace, recreating the natural image from within, the procession of the divine Persons is represented not only in the rational creature's going forth from God but also in her return to him.[22] When by grace human beings give habitual hospitality to the divine persons in their 'mission', and are joined to God as those who 'enjoy' him, the ensuing love and wisdom make them the fullest image of the Trinity there can be – until, at any rate 'in the fatherland we reach the image of resemblance by perfect fruiting'.

So far this is all good Thomist Augustinianism. But Fr Gerald makes a more original contribution to theological tradition when he goes on to speak of the innumerable lights these truths make to play over life. From their range he selects three. *First*, the life of the Trinity is social: it is, in Richard of St Victor's words *concordialis caritas et consocialis amor*; a 'concordial charity and a consocial love'.[23] Whence it follows that all ethics are social; no individual can be 'good' outside the 'consortium' of human beings. This fact is made most plain in the founding of Christ's Church where we become one body and are required to live by one spirit. The centre of ecclesial life is not *sui-conscia*, 'self-consciousness', but the sacrifice of the Mass as the 'common act and oblation of the Mystical Body'. And in a delightfully unexpected reference (for Neo-Scholastic divinity) Fr Gerald furnishes his own translation from the English of S. B. James' *Adventures of a Spiritual Tramp*. The Catholic Church, to that convert, was *sublimatio domesticitatis*.[28]

Secondly, the trinitarian life is the expression of the divine Artist; by its impress, accordingly, man too can delight in producing, by skill and craft. Whereas human beings are meant to find happy joy in their work, artisanship of all sorts (and Fr Gerald echoes Eric Gill in taking the term 'art' to cover many kinds of making, of which the fine arts are but a few[25]) has degenerated into, on the one hand, the 'handmaid of commerce' and, on the other, mere mental distraction. Fr Gerald had an embryonic intuition about the interrelation of divine and human creativity as a privileged locus of trinitarian 'imaging' which would come to full term a decade later in Dorothy L. Sayers' wonderful study *The Mind of the Maker*.[26] In the play she wrote for the 1937 Canterbury festival of Christian drama, the closing words, given to the archangel Michael, express what Barbara Reynolds calls 'her new vision'.

> Children of men, lift up your hearts. Laud and magnify
> God, the everlasting Wisdom, the holy undivided
> and adorable Trinity.
> Praise Him that He hath made man in His own
> image, a maker and craftsman like Himself, a
> little mirror of His triune majesty.
> For every work of creation is threefold, an
> earthly trinity to match the heavenly.
> First: there is the Creative Idea; passionless,
> timeless, beholding the whole work complete
> at once, the end in the beginning; and this
> is the image of the Father. Second: there is the

> Creative Energy, begotten of that Idea, working in
> time from the beginning to the end, with sweat and
> passion, being incarnate in the bonds of matter; and
> this is the image of the Word.
> Third: there is the Creative Power, the meaning of
> the work and its response in the lively soul; and
> this is the image of the indwelling Spirit.
> And these three are one, each equally in itself
> the whole work, whereof none can exist without
> other; and this is the image of the Trinity.[27]

What *The Zeal of thy House* had presented thus imagistically in the course of a piece of theatre, *The Mind of the Maker* would work out not without verbal icons, but by a more systematic integration of speculative intellect with devout imagination. Still, the vision panned out from an insight perfectly comparable to Fr Gerarld's as when, in the 1940 essay *Begin Here*, she argued very simply that, because the Creator created man in his image we are never so truly ourselves as when we are creating something. Sayers made that argument central to a book she conceived as a war-time message to the nation, a call to bring good out of the evil of war.

> Six years before Hiroshima and Nagasaki she could still believe that war was not an ultimate catastrophe, because it tests the foundations of culture and destroys old habits and mistakes to clear the way for a new beginning, which she insisted had to be based upon a Christian understanding of work as an image of divine creativity.[28]

The third sense in which the mystery of the Holy Trinity illuminates human activity concerns its archetypical integration of unity and plurality. The One in Three 'solves' the problem of the one and the many which has eluded philosophers hitherto. Nor is this simply a matter of speculation, for, as Fr Gerald writes: 'life reaches its perfection inasmuch as it brings a multitude of things into unity, with everything being ordered to one goal, returned to one source, where everything is seen in one reality, everything loved in one object.[29] Insofar as the human soul, through supernatural contemplation, 'finds, out of distinctiveness and multiplicity, the unity of truth', to that degree the trinitarian likeness is perfected in her. For this the soul needs the gifts of wisdom and understanding. Otherwise the complexity of the act of faith's object, its obscurity and the question of the direction where progress in such 'action' lies would defeat the contemplative integration, echoing the Trinity, of the one and the many. Faith is not only about the Creator; it is also about creatures. As St Thomas remarks, beatitude 'to a certain extent consists in the due use of creatures and an ordered love in their regard.[30] Or, as Fr Gerald puts it: 'The love of creatures is changed, not taken away; it does not cease to be human, it begins to be divine.[31] The love-knowledge that grace engenders in the heart enables us to relate the many goods to the One who alone is good. It gives us new eyes with which to see relations otherwise elusive or hidden; and it renders us hospitable to our divine Guest – for, with the sending of the Son and the Spirit the Holy Trinity is present to the soul not simply by the 'presence of immensity', as Thomists call the creative divine causality at work to sustain all things, but by their absolutely own presence'. Son and Spirit come to the soul, in the grace of the former and the gifts of the latter, so that, in Aquinas's words, through 'such instruction of the mind' the intellect may 'break forth into the affection of love'.[32] Or, citing some words of Fr Vincent McNabb: 'The seer finds the world a unity of thought; the mystic finds the world a unity of love'.[33] This statement may be expanded in the light of the foregoing: the image of the Trinity in our humanity goes from glory to glory only when

> the mind, by wisdom, and love makes progress towards a single loving perception of Deity, unifying and amassing in this one Truth all creatures, all the articulable truths at its disposal, and everything that is comprised in what Augustine called 'this most ample and immense commonwealth of the whole creation'.[34]

The theme of 'Man's Response to the Trinity' would remain a leitmotif of Fr Gerald's work. Though he adopted a less formally Scholastic way of rehearsing it, his conviction that 'the doctrine of the Trinity is of immediate practical importance to us'[35] remained the same. It shows that which otherwise would be unknowable: 'what man's total response to God is meant to be, and how, in the totality of that response, man himself is made whole.' That movement toward wholeness and holiness turns out, on investigation, to betray a 'sacrificial pattern'.

The sacrificial pattern

The title of Fr Gerald's study of the sacrificial pattern of Christian living – *The Paradise Tree* – is not explained, yet the reference is not arcane once the book is digested. Against the background of the natural symbolism of trees (as the initial citation from Job has it, 'A

tree hath hope; if it be cut it groweth again and the boughs thereof
sprout'), and with echoes of the Garden of Eden, the 'paradise tree'
is the lifegiving cross. As Fr Gerald wrote in his study of the Fourth
Gospel:

> Again and again the events of the Passion re-state in dark and cruel
> form the symbols which originally portrayed the joy and innocence
> of paradise, but in so doing they lead us onwards, and not only
> indicatively but effectively, to the other paradise, the eternal life
> and joy of heaven.[36]

The book is a diptych. 'The Mystery' deals with the fundamental
Christian pattern of life-through-death as found in the 'Christ-life', the
commandments and the sacraments 'The Mystery in the Mass' is a
commentary on the liturgical unfolding of the Roman rite (with side
glances to the Dominican Use) in the perspective already suggested.

The opening section of *The Paradise Tree* concerns itself with the
relation between certain crucial symbolic archetypes – found not only,
in the style of C. G. Jung, in the psyche, but also, after the manner
of the Rumanian phenomenologist of religion Mircea Eliade, in the
myths and rituals of religion everywhere – and the special, indeed
unique, history of Judaeo-Christianity, seen as the preparation for and
entry of the uncreated divine Word into the time and space of his own
creation.

In an age marked by 'an appalling hypertrophy of the masculine
over the feminine aspects of living ... of go-getting activities over
poetry and prayer and the pursuit of wisdom',[37] the Church must learn
to re-actualise the potential of *symbolic* thinking: thinking made possible, that is, by the power of the great archetypes on which her faith
draws. Only the imagination, where these images have their home,
can, in Eliade's words 'see the world in its totality'.[38] And, citing
Jung: where religion (which should be the custodian of symbolic
truth) offers only a mere reiteration of dogma, or ethics for ethics'
sake, or a 'humanization of the Christ figure coupled with inadequate
attempts to write his biography',[39] it appears singularly unimpressive.
As Fr Gerald states the point in his own terms: 'Without a living
contact with Christian symbols dogma can very easily become stale
and sterile, the meaning rubbed away as from a worn penny.'[40] Here
he could appeal for theological support to the German Jesuit patrologist Hugo Rahner, brother of the more famous dogmatician Karl. In
'The Christian Mystery and the Pagan Mysteries', Hugo Rahner had
called Christianity a religion of grace at once disclosed and hidden in
sacramental symbols: mysteries of which 'God alone is the mysta-
gogue and hierophant.'[41]

But Fr Gerald must confront the obvious objection that the general utility, or even psychic necessity, of images and symbols as expressions of the real is one thing; the validity of the distinctively Christian symbols, with the unique truth-claims to which they are attached, is quite another. His answer is that the ancient universal symbols furnish a natural (and perhaps unconscious) prolegomenon to the acceptance of their revealed Judaeo-Christian counterparts. Somewhat in the spirit of G. K. Chesterton's *The Everlasting Man*, he points out that this congruence of the Church's Gospel with the myths of antiquity does not derogate from its plausibility. What better way for the divine Spirit to work than to make generally appreciated myth become specific fact?

> Whereas all the myths, profoundly true as they are psychologically, are quite obviously in the realm of fantasy, not of history, the story of Christ is inescapably real and matter of fact, pegged down to precise dates and places and human agencies. The pattern is there, indeed, but at long last made flesh; the struggle is a very real one; the ordeal is brought about by human greed, cowardice, hate, cruelty; the boon, the elixir, is offered here and now, day by day.[42]

And as these latter words suggest, Fr Gerald has already decided which of the ramifying mythological creatures and narratives of the past are to be deemed central. With the assistance of the American student of comparative mythology Joseph Campbell, he outlines a 'monomyth' which, in a variety of guises (Campbell spoke in the title of his best-known study of 'The Hero with a Thousand Faces') recurs in a multiplicity of cultures.

The argument proceeds in two stages. First, Campbell had vaunted the superiority of comedy over tragedy: the happy ending, seen as a transcending – not contradiction – of the tragedy of man, was anciently regarded as 'of a higher rank than tragedy, of a deeper truth, of a more difficult realization, of a sounder structure, and of a revelation more complete'.[43] The disclosure of the dark way from tragedy through to comedy is the highest office of both fairy tale and myth itself. But secondly, he had found the essence of comedy in the eventual triumph of the stricken hero over his vicissitudes. As Fr Gerald sums up what is, for him, the quintessential 'mythocomic' pattern:

> The hero leaves his home and adventures forth into the dark kingdom, often the dark waters; there he encounters an adversary, often a dragon or serpent, and there is a struggle between them ending in death, often that of the hero himself. In any case, having arrived at the nadir of the mythological round and undergone his

supreme ordeal he gains his reward; his triumph may be represented as a *hieros gamos* or sacred marriage with the goddess-mother of the world, or as his recognition by and atonement with the father-creator, or as his own divinization or apotheosis: intrinstically it is an expansion of consciousness and therewith of being (illumination, transfiguration, freedom). The final work is the return (resurrection); the hero brings back with him the elixir which restores the world.'[44]

It is *this* 'pattern' which the uncreated Word underwrites in his saving Incarnation and Atonement, the two chief doctrines which control all Catholic teaching. He came to live out the pattern in an efficacious manner, so that in future it should no longer be 'the expression of an unfulfilled yearning but something that men would be able to live out, effectively, in their turn'. And so Christianity is essentially different from the mythical religions insofar as, for the former, historical events are themselves transfigured into hierophany, the revelation of the sacred. And yet the Christian mystery is not for all that without connection to the mystery religions of paganism, since the God-man Jesus Christ was obliged to speak in images intelligible to human beings.

Fr Gerald thus arrives at a beautifully nuanced position whereby dogma and symbol are, in different ways, each necessary for the health of the other:

> We need dogma to prevent us from straying, in our apprehension of symbol, into strange paths – and the history of mysticism shows how strange such paths can be; on the other hand we need the vitality of symbol to prevent us from coming to find that doctrine and dogma have become for us dead things, dry bones.[45]

How does the 'pattern' work itself out in the 'Christ-life'? For the Roman liturgy of Christmas, it was 'while all things were held in quiet silence and night was in the midst of its course that the Father's almighty Word leapt down from his eternal throne'. The traditional notion that the stable of Bethlehem, location of the birth of the man assumed by the Logos, was fashioned from a *cave* enabled Fr Gerald to underline this theme of the darkness God made his own as man. The pagan mysteries too were enacted at night, and not infrequently in cave settings. Christmas speaks of the self-emptying of the Word incarnate, and of his homelessness. And looking ahead to both the hidden life and the public ministry of the Lord, Fr Gerald both qualifies this dark picture and reaffirms it.

True, as a child he had the love and care of his parents and as a man he had friends and followers, just as in the myth the hero has his helpers; the journey is not all darkness; his human experience must have included joy of an intensity beyond our imagining; his joy in the beauty of Nature, for instance, must have been not only infinitely more intense, as an aesthetic experience, than any we could know, since it included the joy of the artist in his art-work, for 'all things were made by him'; but it is darkness and loneliness which preponderate; he knew the loneliness caused by a lack of understanding, for we read that first his parents, despite their love, and then his followers, again and again failed to understand, and though as a child he knew the shelter of home he would have to leave it and go alone to meet his adversary.[46]

In the symbolic theology of the mysteries of the life of Christ – for it is no less! – presented in *The Paradise Tree* there are two moments of glory on the way, before the hero reaches journey's end. The Epiphany and the Transfiguration each stand as preface to tragedy: the sorrows of Christ's infancy, in the first case, with the Gospel accounts ending in a report of the 'anguish of mind' of his parents when they lose the child Jesus in the Temple, and, in the second, the sorrows of the adult protagonist of the ministry with, as their crisis-point, the anguish of the agony in the garden.

In his account of the Epiphany, Fr Gerald lays equal weight on the historical event – the facts, as an historical exegete such as Père Lagrange, whom he cites, might construe them, and on the later legendary refinements (for instance the royal status of the magi, or their number). History and legend are, in such matters, at parity, psychologically speaking, and moreover the legend belongs to history – to what a contemporary theory of the history of culture might call *Wirkungsgeschichte*, the history of the active influence of an event – through the gradually accumulating product of the belief and cultus that follow from it.

In line at once with history and legend, then, he presents the magi as representing all humanity – either as the traditional Western trio (the three races descended from Noah) or in the Byzantine twelve (the twelve tribes, and the twelve signs of the zodiac arranged around their central sun). Priest-kings, they:

bow down before the Child who is priest and king and God, and they lay before him the symbols of power and of glory but also of the mortality he has chosen and will later on deliberately choose again when Satan would have him choose power and glory alone ...

In them humanity symbolically renounces its claim to be able to offer sacrifice of itself. Instead, it salutes in them the new Adam who alone could offer in his flesh the true sacrifice. In so doing – and here Fr Gerald looks ahead to the second part of *The Paradise Tree*, his interpretation of the rite of the Mass – the central figure of the Epiphany would institute a sacrifice (the Eucharist) that could be humanity's, through the Church, as well as his own.

But the priest-kings of legend are also the 'wise men' of the historical tradition, and here too they can be seen as confecting a sacrifice. They submit the world's wisdom to the folly of God's infancy; plunging the 'illusory light of merely human brilliance into the darkness of the cave'. But, despite his archetypology, and conviction that all human beings must practise the 'self-naughting' of the mystics, Fr Gerald does not cease to be Thomist in his respect for man's science. And so he adds:

> The new wisdom does not mean the destruction of the old, it means the destruction of the arrogant self-sufficiency, and therefore the falsehood, of the old. Plato and Aristotle are not foolishness, but to think that Plato and Aristotle are enough is foolishness, They are not enough, and all the wisdom of the world is not enough, unless wedded to the folly of the Cross.

The same life-through-death motif which is *The Paradise Tree's* keynote is heard when we move on to the episode of the finding in the temple. The twelve-year-old boy – the *puer* – is common in myth and poetry (the young Dionysus, the Eros of Hölderlin), often associated with the paradise garden. He expresses, in Fr Gerald's terms, 'humanity's longing for ... the joy and beauty and freedom of heaven'. At the same time, the *puer* stands for separation: at the apogee of childhood, adolescence makes its baleful beginning, and with it a parting from, especially, the mother. George Bernard Shaw wrote querulously to abbess Laurentia McLauchlan of Stanbrook of the inconsiderateness of the boy Jesus in giving his mother the slip while he stayed to argue with the doctors of divinity.[47] The criticism is misplaced, through a confounding of levels of seriousness. A harsh lesson, though it may need long pondering, must sometimes be given directly, and therefore hurtfully. And that lesson is: 'He must leave his father and go alone on his dark journey to his Father: the mystics tell us with one voice that we must do the same.'

The Baptism of Christ is the consequence. Fr Gerald begins his account by drawing attention to the English idiom 'to go west' – meaning to perish or disappear, already attested in the age of Chaucer.

As the sun goes down into the darkness of the western ocean, so Christ goes down into the baptismal water and then into the dark kingdom of the dead, the 'sombre caverns of the underworld' as a Syrian baptismal liturgy puts it; so in the Christian rite of Baptism the neophyte goes down into the dark waters and there renounces Satan ... who dwells in the dark west, and he turns instead towards 'Christ the king of light, who comes from the east like the sun and brings him the illumination of Baptism'.[48]

Yet the darkness is also illumination inasmuch as going down into death is the necessary condition of being reborn. The darkness may be the night experienced by many mystics, or it may be, more prosaically, medical or financial crisis, the loss of those we love, self-doubt or some moral collapse – and Fr Gerald adds that sin itself, and its consequence, estrangement from God, can lead to deeper encounter with him wherever there is sincere repentance. The pre-Conciliar Liturgy for the baptism of adults speaks of the neophyte as 'wandering in doubt and uncertainty through the night of this world'. But then, coming up from the waters, new clothed in white garments and bearing a lighted candle, he turns to the altar – the east, the *Sol invictus*, for the new life has begun. All this is a start, not an ending.

Baptism is not to be thought of as just a rite to be once performed and then forgotten: it is the initiation of the pattern, and the pattern must be repeated again and again, for the Christian life is a series of deaths and rebirths ... Every time the penitent goes into the darkness of the confessional the pattern is repeated; but also, as we have seen, every entry into any form of darkness can be a repetition of the same theme, a baptism journey leading to a renewal or an enriching of life, a strengthening for the *agôn*, the struggle with the adversary.[49]

In christological terms, that struggle must be, in the first place, the mystery of the temptation in the wilderness. Strengthened by solitude and fasting – immemorially ancient means of preparing for moments of illumination or the beginning (or renewal) of great activity, the incarnate Word faced his ordeal. Whereas his temptation lay in following a path to resounding messianic success, suggested by the adversary, rather than the one mapped out by the Father with its accompanying agony, ours is the Devil's playing on the evil propensities within us. Yet there is also continuity: we too have powers, albeit puny, to use or abuse. Whoever prefers power, wrote Jung in *Symbols of Transformation*, *is* possessed by the Devil.

Fr Gerald uses the Genesis story of the wrestling of Jacob with an angel to throw light on the episode of the temptation. With the coming of dawn, the angel ceases to be an opponent and becomes a giver of blessing, and an oracle of Jacob's future greatness. So God allows the Christian to be tempted, not only to remind of weakness, and preserve from presumption, but also to

> harden and strengthen us, to be ready for whatever struggles the future may hold. As we are led to think of Christ's human nature as coming exalted, 'filled with the Spirit', from his Baptism, so we may think of him coming with human soul more poised, more calmly assured of its own strength, perhaps even with human mind (in its 'experimental' workings) more vividly and clearly aware of the way which lay before him, from his encounter with the dark angel. And as though to underline the victorious issue to the struggle which had gone on within him, we are told of darkness succeeded by dawn, of how the dark angel withdrew from him and angels of light came and ministered to him.[50]

As already announced in his discussion of the Epiphany, the Transfiguration of Christ is the moment of glory before the final gathering of the storm. Fr Gerald's exegesis is a piece of highly original spiritual interpretation, centering on Peter, James and John seen as types or *aspects of the self*. Human inconsistency, he suggests, derives from the fact that

> within the ontological unity of the personality there is a psychological multiplicity, there are several, perhaps many personalities; and perhaps we are not always capable of predicting which of these personalities, in any given situation, will take charge, or whether it will be in fact the right one.

Within the unity of the self, there may struggle a boisterous, impetuous Peter, liable to act even when action is pointless; a James, inadequate in face of responsibility, and taking refuge in sleep when action is required, and, finally, a John, with the unspoilt quality of childhood about him but also (and not unconnected with this), the capacity to be an eagle, a seer. Our true resources, as a crisis may show, can be buried so deeply that we fail to draw on them: perhaps moments of near-despair are given so as to awaken the John-figure, who, though now he sleeps, will go in the end with Jesus to his Passion and cross. And just as, psychologically, we need to integrate our various personalites into completeness, so theologically the one thing necessary is that we must be, whether active or inactive 'under the governance of the wisdom and will of God'.

As the 'Great Week' in the life of the Redeemer opens, Palm Sunday seemed to Fr Gerald a peculiarly clear instance of the 'pattern'. Jesus is moved, gladdened, touched, by the heartfelt homage of the people at his entry ('I tell you, if they should keep silence, the stones will cry out instead'); yet almost immediately 'As he drew near, and caught sight of the city, he wept" (Luke 19.40). The human unwillingness to accept this same ambivalence in experience (*toutes proportions gardées* – we are not the Redeemer!), derives, it may be, from a continuation of the 'childhood concentration of consciousness' which, on the one hand, refuses to allow moments of happiness to be spoiled by the intrusion of gloomier ideas, truths, realities, and on the other, insists on excluding from moments of misery any comforting thought that might rob us of unadulterated self-pity. All must be white, or black. And so the deepest joy – the one that is close to tears – is lost to us. Sacramental absolution is the paradigm of this,

> The load is lifted, and with it the sense of being lost, the loneliness; but the joy does not annul the sorrow; rather, the joy and sorrow become fused into a single thing, for which we have no name unless perhaps it be love.

And the sequel, the story of Holy Week, shows how sorrow and joy may increase together. The 'lifting up' is the crucifixion; at his trial Jesus proclaims his kingship, yet he is crowned with thorns; the darkness over the earth at his death coincides with the dawning of the new dispensation, as the temple veil is rent – symbol of the new accessibility of God to us; and the cry of dereliction and God-forsakenness 'neither contradicts nor is contradicted by the cry of triumph, *Consummatum est*'. Thus the purple of the Church's liturgical celebration of both Passiontide and Lent, while it denotes penitential days and seasons, also connotes imperial pomp and majesty – in the manner of Venantius Fortunatus's hymn to the tree of the cross, *Vexilla regis*, 'Tree of beauty and splendour, adorned with kingly purple'. Lastly, at the Easter Vigil, darkness and light come together, for about this mother of all vigils the deacon's praise of the candle (the *Exsultet*) sings, 'Of it is written, the night shall shine as the day'. So too for those who live from the power of these mysteries:

> The fulfilment we hope for is the eternal light which is also eternal rest; but even here on earth, *in via*, where there is both light and darkness, where sometimes it is darkness that seems to predominate, but where in any case we perhaps learn best how to live when we welcome and absorb reality in its *chiaroscuro*, even here it is light that must predominate in our minds since it is light that is ultimate, not darkness ... [51]

But that ultimate radiance is not available to us without our personal self-insertion into the sacrifice of Christ. Citing the Anglican Non-Juror William Law, there can be no true repentance until we see our deformity and are terrified by it: we must with Christ 'cross the brook Cedron and sweat drops of sorrows', not 'keep all things quiet in us by outward forms and modes of religion'.[52] In the sacrificial pattern, each person is 'his own load'. As in the Hiawatha myth of the North American Indians, described by Jung, we are to 'wrestle with ourselves in order to create ourselves', and this we can only do by 'shouldering our whole burden, our whole being, and carrying it to the place of sacrifice, the sepulchre, the cave'.[53] Even the shadow side must be integrated (shades of Jung again), inasmuch as – witness the Pentecost petitions of the *Veni sancte Spiritus* – we 'do not pray that the ignoble in us be destroyed but that it be cured and ennobled'.

The same pattern – what Fr Gerald calls the sacrificial 'monomyth' – recurs when we consider the Commandments, the Ten Words which play so large a part in both Jewish and Christian ethics. Fr Gerald interprets the Commandments in the light of Paul's Letter to the Romans, insisting that the Law (which they sum up) is 'indeed a way of life but not a way to life': the latter is found only through faith in Christ which prevents our transgressions of the Law from leading toward despair. The sense of sinfulness typical of the saints, though it be deep, vivid, anguished, never quenched their hope and joy. More widely, Fr Gerald combines Paulinism with the language of contemplative vision (*theôria*) beloved of the Greek fathers, and, finally, a stress on what would later be called the 'narrative' quality of Christian revelation.

> In our approach then to the ten commandments the primary emphasis must be not on works to be achieved but on a *theôria*, a perception of the God whom we thus approach, and on the attitude of heart and soul which that *theôria* is to awaken in us, in other words, on faith in the Pauline sense. And the *theôria* demands its setting: the story of God's love and mercy as revealed in Old and New Testaments.[54]

The recounting of the narrative certainly owes something to Fr Victor's old mentor, Jung, The 'Spirit-Mother', brooding over the chaos at the start of Genesis brings forth a world of distinct and lifesome forms, the abode of the *puer aeternus* but not yet of the saints for 'between the two lies the whole of history, the whole of the process of re-integration ... in and through Christ' of man with God, matter with spirit, the elements of the psyche with each other, humankind with nature. Fr Victor, in a letter of spring 1958, warned Fr Gerald off the attribution of feminiity to the Holy Spirit (the only authorities, he claimed, were 'rather notorious heretics').

Actually, I think that if one is looking for femininity in God – as distinct from his motherly opera *ad extra* – one must look to the undifferentiated *Essentia-sapientia* and not to the distinct Persons. But that's another thing that hasn't been worked out yet – though Ruysbroeck and other mystics seem to hint at something like it. And as Jung himself says, the gnostic feminine Holy Ghost looks like a hangover from the rational pagan Father-Mother Child triad which is quite pre-Trinitarian.[55]

And indeed we hear no more of feminine trinitarian persons in *The Paradise Tree*, which is probably just as well.[56] What we *do* hear of, in these ethical sections of the study, is the goal of perfection – rather than perfectionism. Fr Gerald counsels a 'humble realism', which will avoid all wasting of life through futile yearnings, as well as damaging life by 'rage or pique'; instead, the Christian must accept life according to God's designs for him or her, and, rendering life back to God in sacrifice, have confidence that he will 'make us whole'.

The sacrificial pattern reaches its climactic manifestation in the Mass – which is, precisely, *the* 'Holy Sacrifice', though Fr Gerald pauses briefly to consider its adumbrations in the other sacraments. The entire sacramental life comes to a focus in the Holy Eucharist: the sacrifice of the altar. Treating the liturgy under two heads – the Mass of the Catechumens, up to and including the reading of the Gospel, and the Mass of the Faithful, Fr Gerald finds in both the 'universal sacrifice-pattern'. In each part, offering to God is followed by a giving from God. In the Mass of the Catechumens, what is humanly offered is the Church's prayer of confession and praise, and what is divinely given is revealed truth in the written Word of God. In the Mass of the Faithful what is humanly offered is bread and wine, leading up to the human, but also more than human, offering of the Mediator, Jesus Christ, and what is divinely given is the life of that same Victim, the personal Word of God, in holy communion. Through the sacramental signs the past act of redeeming sacrifice on Calvary becomes effective for later generations; at the same time, the Christian people must draw intelligently, by reflection, on the source of salvation thus opened up for them, making it into conscious relationship with God. Thus the question 'Is the Eucharist a sacrifice or a memorial' is ill-posed. The Mass must be both, for it relates us to the historical event of the Redemption, itself unique and already accomplished, but so that we may make Christ's sacrifice our own, and become its co-offerers.

And taking the reader through the course of the Roman Liturgy (with frequent asides to its Dominican variant) Fr Gerald offers a

mélange of historical and spiritual wisdom to help him or her appreciate the pattern – the *shape* – of the liturgy.[57] It is, by and large, a
biblical theology of worship that he provides – but interspersed with
references to Scripture come judicious citations of Jung on the transformation symbolism of the Mass, to the Church doctors and spiritual
theologians, to the poetry of François Villon and the artworks of
Michelangelo and Donatello. Even D. H. Lawrence's comments on
the 'naturalness' of the ancient liturgy in *Apropos of Lady Chatterley's
Lover* are pressed into service, though Fr Gerald immediately adds a
caution against a naturalistic reduction of the Eucharist which would
see it as but the confirmation of cosmic rhythms, rather than their
redemption by a theological ethic founded on the grace of Christ's
Resurrection.

> If we thus see the Mass (as the supreme moment of the whole
> liturgy) in its natural setting, we must also and still more see Nature
> in the setting of the Mass: Nature hallowed and quickened and
> blessed through the Mass, Nature (including human nature, the
> body and the soul) made fruitful through the Mass, so that man-in-
> Nature, being 'loosed from the law of death' need no longer 'bring
> forth fruit unto death', but can 'bring forth fruit to God', having
> received that living water which becomes in him a 'fountain of
> water springing up into life everlasting'.[58]

While Fr Gerald makes use of the prayers and gestures of the Mass
to lay out a rich array of teaching on ethics and spirituality as well as
credal doctrine, he returns again and again to his primary theme: the
transfiguration of time by its taking up into eternity through union
with the sacrifice of Christ. Take for instance this comment on the
Supplices prayer, after the Consecration, which asks that Christ with
his angels, may offer to the Father our poor prayers and offerings in
unison with his infinite self-offering.

> The jewel in the lotus is eternity-in-time; now we have in the
> Lamb, the altar, the incense, the angels, time being caught up into
> eternity ... So, through Christ, the sacrifice ends for man in the
> *hieros gamos* or mystical union of the Church with its divine
> Bridegroom; in men's at-one-ment with their Father, becoming
> again as children, God's children and co-heirs with Christ; in the
> 'divinization' of man in the sense that he is given divine Life
> through the sacrament, given the boon (*inchoative*, as St Thomas
> would say) of eternal life with 'that expansion of consciousness and
> therefore of being' which consists of living not only in time but in
> eternity, not only in this world but in God, illumined by the self-

revealing of God transfigured by the divine fire, and obedient to the law conceived in terms of love, free – from the bondage of sin and law alike – in the 'liberty of the sons of God'.[59]

He closes, naturally enough, with the moment of communion after which the Roman Liturgy so abruptly ends. The holy communion brings home to us with unparalleled force the glorious destiny of our psycho-physical make-up. Since it means the receiving of Christ's flesh and blood into our own, how can we 'fail to love what that divine flesh and blood have come to hallow and make his own'? The final expression of the sacrificial pattern is not complete, however, with the recitation of that text which puts it in a nutshell. And this is the 'Last Gospel', whose excision from the Roman rite Fr Gerald foresaw and deprecated. For in the Johannine Prologue we celebrate the Word who is at once creative and enabling, who exemplifies the pattern and makes possible its reproduction in others. In the first place, he *reveals* the Godhead:

> first through the unfolding of the total cosmological process in which the 'living God' is ever active, then, within that process, through the shadowy perceptions vouchsafed to mankind as a whole and enshrined by mankind in a mythology; then, more directly, through the mouths of the prophets of the chosen people; and finally and perfectly through the coming of the Word himself to dwell among us and, by his living and dying among us, to give us life, that 'more abundant' life which is life eternal.

And in the second place, he prescribes the terms on which we can enter into the Godhead's life.

> He is also the mandatory Word, dwelling among us to show us the Way which is himself but at the same time giving us his command to follow the Way which is himself. For the Word is the pattern, and the pattern is the *lex eterna*, the eternal law, and that law is light and life for us; and, as his supreme commandment makes clear to us, law and light and life are alike love, and it is to love that we have to give testimony as we go through our journey in the world ... Before we can act we must have sight, we must enter into mystery, we must enter, so far as is possible *in huius saeculi nocte*, in the darkness of this world, into glory.[60]

It is to his Passion mysticism of the sacrificed Lamb, a spiritituality based on the glory Christ won on the Cross, that we must now turn.

The Passion of Christ

Fr Gerald returned again and again to the Passion of Christ – a theme central to the traditional spirituality of the Order, as manifested in, for instance, such contemplatively gifted figures as Blessed Henry Suso (d. 1366) and St Catherine de' Ricci (1522–90). He was always concerned to draw spiritual sustenance for the reader from meditation on that central mystery of the Gospel – sustenance, often enough of a very practical kind. The spiritual and the pastoral, to his mind, coinhered.

With the lyrical tone that is characteristic of his writing, he speaks of the 'love-story' which is the history of God's relations with mankind, entering on its climax 'in a garden'.[61]

> They came to a garden, and it was night. The little walled enclosure, remote from the city, the silvery olive trees, the disciples sleeping: everything is still. Stillness is the womb of all great achievement: the immobility not of inaction but of intense energy ... If we want to watch with Christ and live with Christ we must first learn to be still.[62]

The prayer of Christ in Gethsemane is not the 'negation of activity', but the necessary condition of all worthwhile action. Without prayer, the deepest wisdom and love are inaccessible. And the content of Christ's prayer in the garden is that he may do the Father's will – something Fr Gerald relates closely to the concept of the 'sacrament of the present moment', borrowed from one of his favourite sources, the seventeenth-century French Jesuit Jean-Pierre de Caussade, who defines it somewhere as 'willing what comes to us by God's order'. Clinical though that may sound, it is transmuted in Fr Gerald's version:

> A saint can fear his destiny and want to escape it; he can pray to be released from it; he can be heartbroken because of it; but because he is a saint he puts all his fears and his prayers and his sorrows into God's hands: not my will but thine be done. And it is by doing *that* that he shows how much he loves God; it is because he does *that* that he becomes a perfect instrument for God's purposes, becomes filled with power, the power that can help to save and heal the world. For the only thing that can heal the world is love.[63]

Visiting a sick friend, doing our ordinary work, facing some pain or trial: all of these, once done as sacraments of God's will, can become mighty instruments in the fulfilling of his love-story. Doing little things for God regularly is better than attempting grandiose things from time to time. And, germane to the original Lenten context of his 'The Agony in the Garden', Fr Gerald stresses here that freely adopted penances have as their aim our ascetic training for dealing with the penance that comes to us anyway, through life itself.

> Behind all the particular forms of self-denial that we may choose for ourselves, behind and far deeper than these, there is precisely the self-denial of taking fully and whole-heartedly what the moment brings to us of vexation or labour – the people who put heavy demands on our patience, the work that is hard and unrewarding, the duty that has no appeal for us – of taking all these as they come to us and accepting them fully and turning them fully into the acts of love which they ought to be.[64]

Not that what the 'present moment' entailed for the Redeemer in Gethsemane was itself in any sense a 'little thing'. Fr Gerald reminds his readers of Newman's evocation of the unique mental suffering of the Lord on the eve of his Passion, of how he was 'sickened', 'crippled', 'stifled', by the dread, dismay, sense of guilt and 'mount of sins' intuited in his forthcoming universally redemptive death.[65] And indeed, he adds to Newman's searing account a further consideration of his own, which is almost brutally expressed: Christ's 'knowledge that it would all to some extent be in vain, to some extent be futile'. He is referring to the deficient responsiveness of human beings to the atoning sacrifice:

> In this scene, which is ultimate love unfolding itself in what seems like ultimate tragedy, that answer is given, that love is given; and yet he was despised and rejected, he *is* despised and rejected; and for many it is as though it had never been, and for many of us Christians it is in practice as though it had never been.[66]

The episode in the garden is brought to a close by Jesus's arrest, thanks to Judas's betrayal. Though the betrayal *with a kiss* by Judas is archetypal for the sins of Christians in particular (for they are the followers and friends of Christ), Fr Gerald considers a variety of other kinds of betrayal which Judas's action focuses, and grotesquely crowns. There was the 'sudden change of heart' of the Jewish crowd, which showed up their earlier allegiance to Jesus as skin-deep. From this he draws the lesson that Catholic Christians cannot afford to let their knowledge and love of God remain on the surface of their lives – merely emotional, or purely routine, but 'dig down deep, and find God in the very depths of the spirit'. Else at the first hint of ridicule, or argument against the faith, or agitation against the Church, they are unlikely to stand firm. And the vehemence of the people's betrayal ('His blood be upon us and upon our children!') shows the speed with which apostasy, once begun, can proceed. Secondly, the Passion narratives present the betrayal of the 'priests and scribes', those learned in the cult and the law. It was those who ought best to have understood the credentials of Jesus who sought most fervently to destroy him – a warning of the possibility of culpable blindness. Through the process psychologists call rationalization, we 'persuade ourselves into thinking there are solid reasons for doing what we want to do, when really in our hearts we know the reasons all point the other way.'[67]

Thirdly, there is the betrayal by Peter and the rest of the Eleven, afraid for their skins (in the garden) or discomfited by social embarrassment (in the courtyard of the high priest's house). In many small ways, Christians betray the Lord by fear of losing popularity, face, employment, friends, pleasurable experiences: 'I tell you, I never set eyes on the man.' But for Catholics, who belong most intimately to the household of the faith, the betrayal of Judas remains the chief criterion for sins both of commission and omission (and in the latter category, Fr Gerald mentions especially the corporal works of mercy, as found in the Parable of the Great Assize). But his conclusion, as always, is pastorally 'upbeat'. Pointing out that the Saviour gave the new commandment of charity immediately after he had predicted the betrayal and Judas had departed, Fr Gerald goes on:

> If we betrayed him – as indeed we all have – then we can find no better way to tell him of our sorrow and to repair as far as possible the damage done, than by fulfilling that commandment. For so we share not with the betrayers but with the betrayed; not with what they did, but with what he came on earth to do: we share in his healing of the world.[68]

The scourging at the pillar inspired Fr Gerald to a rather full theological exegesis of this scene in the Passion story. Actually, for him it is a triptych: the stripping of Christ, his flagellation, and, finally, the crowning with thorns. These he links in turn to Jesus' poverty; his 'redeeming chastity', and his obedience. Deprived even of his garments, Jesus enters complete poverty; in his scourging various spiritual writers have seen a special atonement for the way human beings let the flesh rule them, rather than they the flesh; and by means of the mockery of his kingship, in 'setting aside his rule and accepting this ultimate rebellion from his creatures', the Word made flesh manifests his perfect obedience to the Father's will. And such poverty, chastity, obedience on the part of the Church's Head must be elements in the following of Christ, then, for all her members (not simply for religious, who are called to practise them in a special fashion).

How so? Christian discipleship entails or at the least strongly recommends a simple, modest way of life, and in this sense *poverty* – for which Fr Gerald cites the customary ascetic explanation down the ages. Whether through fear or loss or the amusements it can buy, wealth makes it easy to be absorbed by the things of the world, and forget God. And yet poverty of spirit means more than this. Touching as it does all our gifts – charm, beauty, wit, intelligence, artistic creativity, it forbids us, in the language of the Parable of the Prodigal Son, to take them to a far country away from God, and enjoy them there, forgetful of that other life which is our home. The apostolic counsel to use the things of this world as though we were *not* using them means that 'we must not try to love them apart from God, apart from God's will, apart from the thought that they are God's gifts to us, and a gift that may be withdrawn.' Saints like the *poverello* of Assisi give up not the love of everything but its proprietorship (in every sense of that word), and this enables their love so to expand that it can include all things, becoming all things to all men – and indeed to all creatures, a point which enables Fr Gerald to refer to the love of many saints for animals.

Chastity too is for all Christians, and Fr Gerald has a particularly ample idea of it. It is training the senses to play their part in the search for the true, the good and the beautiful. For the passions distort vision, derail judgment. Chastity of heart requires he warns, labour, self-denial, suffering, so it is internally related to the Passion of Christ.

Lastly, *obedience*. The Word emptied himself in obedient love by his original *kenôsis*, when he assumed human nature. But now, in a further stage of humiliation, Christ is 'robbed of what was his right precisely as man', namely, his human kingship. But the obedience which accepts such humiliation was what 'won the world back to love'. In our case, too, a parallel obedience turns all the virtues into the stuff of love and worship, so that 'morality finds its fulfilment by becoming religion'.

And so the way of the cross begins. As with the Latin Church's Stations of the Cross, which include a memorial of Jesus' meeting with 'his afflicted Mother', Fr Gerald pauses to consider the encounter of the Lord with Mary. In 'The Stillness of Mary', he sketches out some motifs given fuller expression in a study of the *Mater dolorosa*, entitled *The Seven Swords*. In *The Pain of Christ and*

the Sorrow of God, the key-note is struck by some words in Dorothy
Sayers' revival of the Passion Play genre in *The Man Born to be King*:
'We have no need of words, my son and I.' And if the silent sympathy – literally, 'co-suffering' – in the heart of Mary can go directly to
the heart of Christ, so, thanks to the God-man's transcendence of the
normal categories of space and time, the *pietas* of the modern
Christian, worlds apart though he is from the Jesus of history, can
enter into the spiritual energy exerted in Christ's Passion and form a
conduit for its mediation to others. From all of which Fr Gerald draws
the conclusion that there is never *nothing* we can do: even loving
thinking about another's troubles can redeem. And furthermore, only
if action and philosophising about the world's ills – to name the two
other chief modes of our co-involvement with suffering humanity –
draw a Marian quality from the still centre of Christ's work on the
cross will they be of any abiding value.

The Seven Swords enlarges the picture in terms of the traditional
devotion of the 'Seven Dolours' of the Blessed Virgin. The soul-pierc-
ing 'sword', prophesied by Symeon for the mother of the messianic
child in St Luke's gospel turned out to be a seven-bladed instrument
of torture, as devout reflection on the gospels excogitated seven ways
in which Mary could be said to share, through various incidents in
those narratives, the messianic travail which is the birth-pangs of a
new world. Illustrated by eight images from the painting of El Greco,
the book develops the insight that Mary's *Magnificat* was not the
'expression of a swiftly passing mood', for 'the sword is always there,
but so is the song'.[69] Fr Gerald's answer is that, as the 'Mother-
Maiden', Mary could embody apparently opposite sets of qualities
which confer on her a 'richness' that is a lesson for others. Mary's
life is a song, simultaneously, of innocence and experience. As
Mother, Mary knows in her own body, through a knowledge of the
'mysteries of good and evil', what great things the Almighty has done
for her. As Maiden, she has implicit trust in the God she loves, even
before the trust has been justified by experience'. Put negatively,
Mary is sullied neither by possessiveness nor by self-regardingness:
in avoiding these snares of respectively, motherhood and virginity
(archetypally, experience and innocence), she becomes a mirror of
wisdom for the Christian life.

> We can hope to imitate Mary, not only in her motherhood, but in
> her enduring girlhood, her enduring strangeness to evil, even
> though our story hitherto has been a story of squalor. For indeed
> Christianity is precisely the religion which redeems humanity's
> squalors.

And citing the Easter antiphon, *Valde Mane sabbatorum* ['Very early in the morning, on the first day of the week'], he goes on:

> *Valde mane*: the night seems so long and so relentless, the darkness so black and impenetrable, but swiftly in the end the light comes ... *Valde mane*: and in a moment the rose-red shaft of dawn strikes the open door of the tomb; and there in the garden is the Presence, radiant of eternity; and soon his mother will hear, will meet him, and no longer remember the anguish, for joy that her Son is reborn into the world, and that all humanity with him is reborn to a new heaven and a new earth.[70]

But this is to anticipate the journey's end to which Fr Gerald's Passion meditation is conducting us. Certainly, however, he never sunders the cross from the resurrection as his account of the crucifixion itself would demonstrate. His theology of the cross combines, as every 'adequate' theology of the Atonement must, two factors: the subjective and the exemplary, on the one hand, the objective and sacrificial on the other.

> Had there been no sin, we should not have known that immense revelation of the depths of love which is the Cross; and, for our part, we should not have known the human response to it, we should not have been capable of that depth of love and understanding which only sorrow can bring us.[71]

But the cross does not simply reveal the love and pity of God *vis-à-vis* human sorrow and pain. As 'made sin' for our sake, the Incarnate Son took upon himself the 'agony of emptiness and horror that is final separation from God', knowing this, however, not as the lost do, passively, and with hatred for the light, but actively, as 'the final act of sacrifice, and therefore as the last and thickest pall of darkness that precedes the dawn.' The dying cry of the Saviour, *Consummatum est*, is accordingly a shout of glory: he has overcome the world.

That triumph was won 'between two thieves'. From the one who blasphemed him, Fr Gerald draws the moral that 'there can be a state of soul against which Love itself is powerless because it has hardened itself against Love'. The repentant thief bears a different message down the ages: 'We never exhaust the infinity of Love.' In his repentance, evidently, since he is promised Paradise 'this day', he became immediately ready for God; his was the perfect contrition.

> At the end it is said we shall be judged on love. You cannot of course say, 'Then I need not bother about sins: it will be all right as long as I love God.' Our Lord told us; if you love me, keep my

commandments. The more you love God, the harder you will try not to sin. If you try not at all it means that you love not at all. But the trying is all. We are never to be depressed and hopeless about past failures: we are meant to make them the material of a deeper love.[72]

And the secret is forgetting ourselves and looking to Christ, on the psalmist's principle, 'My eyes are ever on the Lord. To receive the healing power of the salvation that flows from the Crucified we must be absorbed 'not in self-analysis and self-culture but in adoration'.

And that adoration speaks most wondrously to our condition when we realise that the One we adore is, in a certain sense, the *suffering* God. Fr Gerald was too good a Thomist to fall into a facile theopaschism which would admit evil, in the guise of suffering, into God. Nonetheless, he states '*God* suffered'. And he explains:

> That does not mean that the divine nature underwent a diminution and became subject to evil. But it does mean that *in* the divine nature there is a quality, to speak *humano modo*, of which the human quality of pity and compassion is the expression and, so to say, the evocation.[73]

God's actual redemptive sharing in the misery of the human situation is done through the humanity of Jesus. But it is the 'expression of the deeper and permanent mystery in the Godhead, the will-to-share ... that which Christ on the Cross took to himself and made his own and in his glorification turned into glory'. Taking the apparent antinomy of justice and mercy, identical in God, as his model, Fr Gerald speaks of compassion and triumph as mysteriously one in the Godhead. And if in human love here and now there is occasionally a far-off hint of this divine condition (for 'the same thing can cause sorrow for the suffering which it is and joy for the enrichment and deepening of being which it brings about', the experience of the blessed, as conceived and imagined by theologians and poets respectively provides a fuller sketch. Just as for St Thomas the glorified soul's longing for the resurrection of her body is compatible with beatitude for it is 'welcomed as part of the total love-story' as well as certain of fulfilment, for Dante the compassion of Beatrice is 'proper to the blessed ... to those who have telescoped means and end, who see the issue in the struggle, who see the good, which is love, emerging from evil and the evil only in terms of that triumphant good.' In the God revealed on Calvary, 'the imperfections of joy and sorrow as we know them' are, then, 'transcended in the fulness of creative and redeeming love'.

But how is that fulness to express itself in our life together here below? This is the question Fr Gerald addressed in his best-known book, *The Divine Pity*, which starts out from that charter of the life of the Kingdom, the *Sermo Domini*, Jesus' *Sermon on the Mount*.

A spirituality of social blessing

If Jesus' Sermon on the Mount is at the heart of New Testament ethics, then the beatitudes embody the ethos communicated in that discourse. The crucial importance of the beatitudes for Christian morality has been noted ever since Augustine. St Thomas, whose ethics are always integrated with his spirituality, considered the beatitudes in connection with the gifts of the Holy Spirit, those points where our freedom and God's grace are most intimately co-operative for individuals among the messianic people. Fr Gerald takes a step further by linking beatitudes, gifts and the *sacraments*, those corporate actions whereby the Church is constituted and built up. In thus supplying an explicit ecclesiological dimension lacking in Aquinas, Fr Gerald could also sketch out a social vision, for the Church, as the supernatural commonwealth of Christians must also be – in certain crucial respects, at least – the icon of a Christian society.

Fr Gerald opens with a eulogy on the creatures of the cosmos as engaged in the unconscious praise of the Creator. In nature's symphony man must join in the song with his own immortal voice, and also to 'help with his husbandry the song of the lesser creation, and to raise it by his awareness and his loving worship of God to a more explicit sharing in the prayer of Christ ...[74] More important still, in the human creature, the music has become discordant, out of tune. Owing to the world's ignorance and malice there is redemptive work to be done if its sweetness is to be restored. This is why the great contemplative saints – Paul, Catherine of Siena, Teresa of Avila – have followed up rapture by throwing themselves into the world, and Fr Gerald speculates that Lazarus of Bethany, raised from the tomb by the voice of Christ, was not ever afterwards dreamy and preoccupied. The *Cautelas* of St John of the Cross, with their warnings against the love of creatures, might seem to count against these points, but, invoking Maritain, Fr Gerald shows how the great Carmelite doctor has been misunderstood through a failure to distinguish between a radical destruction of the reality of our feelings for things and persons (which would be *in*human), and a radical renunciation of our 'proprietorship and purely natural exercise of' those feelings – all with the intent that 'a greater love will vivify them' (which is *super*human).[75] Just as to ignore the needs of the world would be to miss the whole purpose of the human life of Christ, so to suppose that we can work for the world as Christians without becoming identified with Christ would be to miss the entire reason why that human life could only be the incarnation of a divine person. Though Fr Gerald writes from out of a powerful conviction that the Church is endangered by a self-centred piety which forgets its duties to the world, his invocation of the Sermon on the Mount is far from manifesting a 'horizontal turn', or preoccupation with *les realités terrestres*, as much 'secular theology', conscious of the same danger, would positively boast of doing in the 1960s and afterwards.

> It might be true to say, take care of contemplation – make sure that it is fervent, assiduous, and wholly *God-centred* – and action will take care of itself, the redemptive work will inevitably follow in one form or another; but the reverse would certainly not be true. What is the purpose of the grace of God, the sacramental system, the whole dynamism of the supernatural life, but to enable us to know God, to love God, to serve God? ...
>
> To be poor in spirit, to be meek, to be clean of heart; all these things denote an attitude of soul towards the world; but primarily they denote an attitude of soul towards God ... Yes, we must long, and pray, and work, to be filled with the love of our neighbour; but first of all, above all; we must long and pray and work to possess the one thing necessary, the substance of life everlasting, the thing whereof this other, when it is strongest and deepest, is the expression and derivative ...[76]

Could there be a clearer statement of relative priorities? As the Roman critique of liberation theology forty years on would insist: there is no social gospel, but the one gospel has its social implications, which are (in Fr Gerald's words) its 'expression and derivative'.[77]

How, then, do the beatitudes carry such social entailments? St Thomas's definition of them does not seem, in this respect, encouraging: 'Certain excellent works of virtue under the impulse of the Gifts of the Holy Spirit, whereby we approach the goal of eternal happiness, and have a foretaste of it even in this life.'[78] Even when Fr Gerald adds his own rider that *Christian* virtue builds into the pagan concept of moral mastery a humility which 'preserves in the strength of the grown man the heart of the child', it is difficult to think we are much advanced. Really, the introductory chapters of *The Divine Pity* offer a *general* spirituality which can contextualise what follows. The chief clue – no obvious one – to how the beatitudes relate to social action comes with these lines:

The life and power are offered; but we do not acquire them by passively waiting, but by the hard work of obedience and prayer. So, as we think over each of the beatitudes in turn we shall think also both of the sacraments which bring us the different kinds of energy that we need, and of the attitude required of us if the energy is to be used – an attitude expressed on the one hand by the gifts of the Holy Ghost and on the other by the various types of prayer.[79]

'The life and power' here are, first, a *life* worthy of humanity and (therefore) a shared divine life, and, secondly, a *power* to see, love and treat the world in a 'familial' fashion. It is the *forms of that life* and the *capacities of that power* that the beatitudes reveal: these are their 'social implications'.

The Divine Pity will consider the beatitudes, then, as the revelation both of the command and of the potential to treat the world in a particular way. It will also indicate how, through life in the Church, we have resources that enable us to realise the command and actualise the potential. These are the sacraments, which, however, for their own right use require from us appropriate dispositions. Fr Gerald links them to those subtle facilities in the soul's relation with God which Aquinas calls the gifts of the Holy Spirit, as well as particular kinds of prayer – the most basic form that relation takes. And because he treats the beatitudes as themselves constituting an ascending order, without, however, the higher ever leaving the lower behind, the entire pattern, as he presents it, must also be a process, a cumulative growth. This is, then, a highly wrought scheme, and perhaps – to change the metaphor from metal to paint – too tight a frame for his canvas.

At the cost of (inevitably) even greater compression, let us encapsulate its content. The first beatitude, poverty of spirit, Fr Gerald links with the gift of fear, the prayer of devotion, and the sacrament of baptism. Poverty of spirit means treating persons and things as what they are: *God's* creatures, not ours. They are, then, 'to be used or enjoyed ... to become possessions – only within the framework of his will'.[80] The gift of fear gives us a sense of awe precisely at this distinction – in fact, an abyss – between the creature and the Creator. Fr Gerald calls such fear:

> not only compatible with but an essential element in our divine sonship ... the *condition* of love as of wisdom; for it is what makes us teachable; and so we have to guard it and labour to deepen and intensify it, till it can become, in the end, a part of heaven's unending hymn of praise and glory.

Such reverent adoration is the beginning of the 'prayer of devotion', which is not a matter of pleasant feelings but of

> filling the mind with the thought of God's goodness and man's helplessness: of God's goodness, because this thought brings forth love in us; of our own helplessness, because this excludes presumption, and brings us back again to the humble docility of the child.

Baptism belongs here because the first sacrament is a mystery of rebirth into the Kingdom as a child of God; one filled, consequently, with the power both to be and to do good in the world. The societal implications of the first beatitude, then, lie in the reverent, benevolent, non-grasping way an agent bathed in its light will live in the world.

'Blessed are the meek, for they shall possess the land.' The 'meekness' of this second beatitude can be joined with the gift of piety and authentic *pietas* in prayer, and all of these with the sacrament of confirmation. For Fr Gerald, evangelical 'meekness' consists in applying poverty of spirit to the self, and more especially to the inner life of virtue. It is the habitual acknowledgment of our own insufficiency, and the consequent need for salvation. Meekness confers the only power that can be wielded without fear of damaging others, and that because it is 'a power which is *received*, and received only by the humble who can put on Christ'. And the gift of piety adds to the sense of creatureliness instilled by the gift of fear a new dimension: one of the loving, trustful service of God – and of all human beings inasmuch as they belong to God. For St Thomas, Fr Gerald reports, this gift leads us to help those who are distressed; it is peculiarly equipped to drive out those vices which destroy the human family unity: envy, jealousy, and, so the English Dominican author adds, all the 'minor' forms which carelessness about charity can take, from tale-bearing and malicious gossip to priggishness and vulgarity, ingratitude and humourlessness, secretiveness and indiscretion. The prayer of piety responds to God as 'dear Father', but does so by choice in the company of the family of God, one's brethren. We should pray in the family and as a family: those unrelated to us by blood may be, above all in the Mass, our Christian *cognati*. The second sacrament, confirmation, is the mystery which fits us to be full members of that family of the Church. As a personalisation of Pentecost, the grace of confirmation is growth, fire and strength in the Holy Spirit, given not only for the individual's spiritual maturity but also that he or she may take up their active responsibilities in the 'family life' of Church and world. But here Fr Gerald thinks primarily not of social activism, or the uses of the spoken word, for the man who does a great deal may be a nuisance, the world tires of argument.

The supreme task of today is a question of being: because it is a question of bringing back to the world the direct *experience* of the power of love in the world; it is a question of bringing it face to face with the immensity of the Paraclete, the Strengthener, filling and shining through the bodies of men.

'Blessed are they that mourn for they shall be comforted.' In the constellation of the third beatitude Fr Gerald places the gift of knowledge and single-mindedness in prayer, while relating both of these to the sacrament of penance. Here we enter more deeply into the depths of Christian redemption. To be 'responsible', for the disciple of Jesus, entails a willingness to share in redemptive suffering. It is 'not only that you must not be intemperate and selfish in your desires, but that you must ready, if need be, to set aside your desires altogether, and even to choose discomfort and sorrow'. But such readiness carries the Lord's promise of sorrow's turning into joy *even on earth*.

To share more and more deeply in the all-inclusive love and sympathy and suffering of God is indeed to have sorrows, but to have sorrows that are turned immediately and inevitably into joy because they are the stuff of vision and understanding and love, and in the glory of the vision and the love they glow with fire.

St Thomas had already linked this beatitude with the gift of knowledge – for this spiritual knowledge leads us to mourn over the way we have allowed creatures to distract us from God, through our enjoying them apart from, and even in opposition to, him. The gift utterly dethrones the pleasure-principle but draws us to judge everything in the world as his 'handiwork and habitation'. Its workings are typically observed in

a poor peasant woman, unable to read or write or understand abstruse matters, but startling you by the deep penetration and the sureness of touch with which she judges human affairs and motives and duties in the light of divine truth ...[81]

Intuitively, we become single-minded about praying, judging aright what growth in prayer will mean for us at this time or that. 'The gift of knowledge should help us, neither to throw over from laziness a habit of formal meditation which is useful to us, nor to cling to it, through lack of courage, when it is really a hindrance.' And similarly, it will direct us to appropriate 'stuff' – subject-matter – for meditation and prayer.

And because this gift helps us in our judgements about God, about creatures, and about the way to God (not least through prayer), the sacrament to which it is most closely connected must be that of penance.

> It is so easy to forget the Presence, to isolate things from their own wholeness, and so either to idolize them or to batten on them. That is why, when we think over our attitude to created things, we have need of sorrow and repentance; not because we have loved excessively, but because we have not loved sufficiently, we have been selfish and so have not loved aright.[82]

Through docility to the Holy Spirit, the discipline of the confessional and its attendant sorrow, which seem dark things, give us light- and large-heartedness – a renewal of life and freedom saving us from self-centredness and so isolation from God. The negative pole of penance changes into its positive, enabling us the better to 'love and serve ... God's family ... for his sake and in his sight'. In other words: *blessed* are those who mourn.

The fourth beatitude calls down blessing on those who 'hunger and thirst after justice' and requires consideration of the gift of fortitude, the prayer of petition and the sacrament of the Holy Eucharist. Although this fourth beatitude has been given especial prominence in the post-conciliar period through the reception accorded to the Council's *Pastoral Constitution on the Church in the Modern World* by liberation theologians and others, Fr Gerald's assessment of it both anticipates and differs from that of 'justice and peace' activists today. It anticipates the later reading in that he regards the beatitude as an exhortation to 'social justice'; it differs from many subsequent interpretations by treating it as not only that. What we should hunger and thirst for is 'righteousness' in the widest sense: namely 'the realization of God's goodness in the world; with all our hearts we should want that goodness to be expressed and apparent in everything that is in the world, and in everything that is done in the world.' A social conscience is not a work of supererogation added to a Christian conscience by way of supplement. The love of neighbour that the Gospel requires is, among other things, the 'love that is an insatiable desire for justice'. Justice is the minimum we can wish for others with the will of benevolence; and its contravention, when we seize what we can for ourselves without consideration for the rest of the human family, is yet another way to isolation from God and man alike. And although Fr Gerald advocates a reconceptualising of justice in terms of the rights of God, first and foremost, he will have no cross preached at point of bayonet: 'To be just is to do things justly – the manner is important as well as the deed, the means as well as the end.' But the beatitude does not stop there. It also concerns the upbuilding of the life of the *Church* – its thought and love, the integrity and beauty of its worship, and its practical charity to those outside. And realistically Fr Gerald warns that the one who responds to this beatitude is well-advised to have appropriated its predecessor, to be a 'mourner'. It is not wise to be zealous until we have learned how to mourn, until the 'idea of discomfort and suffering for the sake of love has lost its terrors ...'

Not surprisingly, the gift most readily related to the fourth beatitude is fortitude. More originally, Fr Gerald treats that gift as the divine antidote to 'lukewarmness', itself a 'state of soul like the physical condition we call being run down, a state in which you may catch anything'. For not only does this gift infuse courage and strength to sustain danger and difficulty. Equally important, it generates the lively confidence that all such dangers and difficulties will be overcome – beyond our death if need be.

> There is a tendency in any age like our own, a *fin du siècle* period when the world has grown stale, for people to be ready to argue and discuss and perhaps accept a conclusion to the discussion, abstractly, but never to let this conclusion affect the conduct of real life. Perhaps it is the vice especially of the 'intellectual'. Fortitude can give us precisely the motive force that is lacking: it rejuvenates ...[83]

And not only that, for it also gives a boundless trust which underlies the 'almost arrogant prayer of petition of the saints'. Helpfully on a subject many find itself 'difficult', Fr Gerald goes on:

> We pray not against the framework of providence but within the framework of providence. We pray because prayer is one of the forces, the energies, which govern events in the world – as many other non-material things, modes of thought and will and desire, govern events in the world. We pray because in the design of providence this prayer may be foreordained to contribute to the bringing-about in the world of this event rather than that; and so we pray always with the *fiat voluntas tua*, not my will but thine; and if the immediate object of the prayer is not to be granted us, still the prayer can never be pointless, can never be wholly unfulfilled, because every prayer which is thus conditional is a prayer for the good of God's family, and in that sense will be heard.

Such petitionary prayer is correlative to fortitude: fortitude is required to sustain it, but fortitude needs the sense of the undergirding presence of God which this prayer gives.

The prayer for the daily bread which gives strength for the daily task is answered in the sacrament of the Eucharist. The power the Mass brings implies a social responsibility; the daily task is always in some sense a common task. The grace of this sacramental sacrifice is given for the sake of unity. Causing us as it does to live in Christ, it reforges not only unity for a human family but also 'something of the unity of all creation, since it is the whole of creation which it sanctifies'. Sacrifice is an anthropological necessity, because it is part of the creature's nature to express that dependence on its Creator which the prayer of petition implies; but the Mass is 'the summary and the fulfilment of all the sacrifices of all the races of the world because the thing offered is Him who is All in all.' But the eucharistic sacrifice is also a sacrament, the means *par excellence* whereby the redemptive act becomes operative, day by day, in the world. And this is closely relevant to the beatitude from which we began:

> God is everywhere, is All in all. But here you have a new, a redemptive presence: it is the redeeming Christ who through the Mass is still with the earth to save and heal and bless it, who through the Mass can walk again the lanes and fields of England, who through the Mass visits the slums and tenements, and weeps now over the battlefields and bombed cities as once over Jerusalem ... This redeeming ... power is able, if only we will use it, not only to transform into spiritual splendour the squalors and sufferings begotten of injustice, but still more to overcome in the end the spirit of evil which produces the squalors ...[84]

The fifth beatitude, 'Blessed are the merciful for they shall obtain mercy', gives Fr Gerald's study its title: *The Divine Pity*. With this he joins the gift of counsel, the 'prayer of sorrow', and the sacrament of the last anointing. As with J. R. R. Tolkien's fictional narrative in *The Lord of the Rings*, pity is central to Fr Gerald's social spirituality. Pity considers first the needs of outcasts, of waifs and strays; it is humble and reverent, not patronising and condescending; it is unsentimental, not closing its eyes to culpability, and the reality of evil; it is redemptive, healing, strengthening, building up. It provides an 'ocular demonstration of the Gospel'.

> Live this beatitude, learn to make your whole life an expression and fulfilment, a channel, of the divine pity, and [non-Christians] will forget all they have heard, they will forget all they have learnt from their history books, because they will be able to look into your heart and see [Christ's] glory, the glory of the only begotten of the Father, full of grace and truth.

The gift of counsel is concerned with the divinely appropriate means to reach given ends. Because it guides one in dealing with the most agonising of all practical problems – the problem of pain – it can only be closely relevant to the practice of pity. Without counsel, pain can lead to self-pity, or at least self-concentration; with it, our suffering can be turned into a 'greater love and service of the family'.

And the prayer that belongs here is, in a phrase of Fr Gerald's coining, the 'prayer of sorrow': prayer which is a contrite expression of our solidarity with the world's guilt and our responsibility for its pain.

> The essence of all the evil in the universe is the attempt of the creature to repudiate its dependence and become a god: the only way in which this evil can be overcome and turned into good is by reversing this movement and reasserting our creatureliness: and this we can only do by repentance and sorrow.

In Christ's renewal of our souls, we become 'part of that universal process whereby the omnipotent pity makes all things new'.

Although Fr Gerald was perfectly aware, along with Latin theology at large, that the sacrament of the last anointing need not be literally 'last', since one of its purposes is to restore to health the sick man, he deals with it here, in relation to the consummate beatitude of mercy inasmuch as anointing disposes the gravely sick person for entry into glory. To think of this last crisis in life is to wish to be prepared for it, and so to be better equipped in coping with the *diurnitas* of the good life, its day-to-day demands. It is right to pray, as ancient litanies do, to be spared a 'sudden and unprovided death', but even this must be left to God's will. The essential thing in all *memento mori* is 'to fear his justice, but to lift up our hands to his mercy'.

The penultimate beatitude has it that 'Blessed are the clean [or 'pure'] of heart, for they shall see God'. In its light Fr Gerald considers the gift of understanding, the prayer of 'wonder' and the sacrament of marriage. In Thomas's exegesis of the beatitudes, the first five concern the conditions for acquiring beatitude, the life of happiness when we shall *see*. By contrast, so Fr Gerald points out, the last two set forth 'those effects of the life of action which immediately dispose a man to the life of vision'. And the first of these is the quality which perfects a man in himself for that life: purity of heart. Under this heading, he looks at temperateness of flesh, and temperateness of mind. And these turn out to concern at one and the same time God's creatures and God himself. Temperateness of flesh

> safeguards and perfects the life of the senses, and therefore of the whole personality; for the purpose of the life of the senses is to enable us to know and love and become one with God's creatures

and through them to be led to God – all God's creatures, but human beings especially – and so to have our own being immeasurably enlarged.

Temperateness of mind eschews all twisting of the truth, every form of wishful thinking and self-deception, as well as all projecting of human limitation, by faulty theologising, on to God. Intemperate too are debased forms of worship which turn the adoration of God into self-indulgence. In point of fact, Fr Gerald appeals to the cathartic effect of faithful liturgy as a transparent example of how purity of heart comes about. If the liturgy's first and supreme purpose lies in giving worship to God, it also 'has the additional purpose of cleansing the mind and heart and whole personality'.

This beatitude, in its exigence, sums up all those mentioned so far. Fr Gerald summons his readers to pray that

> detachment and meekness and mourning, the hunger for God's justice and the power of pity, may all together give us that temperateness towards things and towards truth which will recover for us our power of vision, and so make us fit for the Vision.

And if cleanness of heart fits us for the God-given experience of the revealed mysteries of the Gospel, the gift of understanding draws the soul into a secret place where, undistracted by irrelevant imaginings she can learn to search the depths of God. Fr Gerald sums up the theological tradition he inherited by speaking of this gift as providing 'a sense of the certitude of the things of faith, a sense of the inner meaning of the scriptural account of the divine mysteries, a sense of the infinite perfection of God and the nothingness of man, which bring it quiet.' And with that prayer of 'quiet' in the Presence (the vocabulary is particularly associated with St Teresa of Avila), Fr Gerald associates what he calls the prayer of wonder: a 'still, wordless gaze of adoration'. Hinted at in the serene humility of the long drawn out endings of the plainsong alleluias (and elsewhere, for instance in Beethoven's last quartets), this prayer is already a beginning of beatitude. Though such prayer is not, by definition, a means to anything, it cannot but overflow into an action that saves, heals, consoles.

It may seem a far cry from such (at any rate, interior) cloisters to the sacrament of marriage, yet the key to the latter lies in 'making sex part of the totality of love, and love part of the totality of worship'. Married love is the normal way in which to love and worship God, and serve Church and world. Because it is a life-work it escapes romanticisation. It is not an affair of glorious moments, but a lifetime's achievement.

You have first of all the making of the unity of man and woman; and this is itself an endless process. On the physical level there is need of gentle adjustment of the two wills that there may be real peace and fulfilment; in the sphere of mind there is the long and laborious process, not indeed of coming to agree on every conceivable issue, but of reaching a real and stable sympathy of mind, a real unity on great issues, a real mutual complementing of the two different ways of thought; finally there has to be the unity of the deep personal will, not again that there can ever be a complete agreement of desire in every superficial and transient issue, but that beneath the surface-differences there may be a solid core of unity which nothing can shake.[85]

And if this interpersonal unity of the couple is not built in a day, the same is true of the widening circles to which that unity points: the family, and, beyond the family, the neighbour who may come to its hearth. Fr Gerald's view of marriage is certainly no *egoisme à deux*; on the contrary he stresses its missionary vocation, The Catholic family:

must be for the world a visible demonstration of the religion of love; and that it will be, first of all, by its own unity and peace; but the unity and peace must turn outward, must radiate love and light and the homage of service, so that the home may be, not only something that others can admire, but a hearth to which they can always come and be welcome, and sit and be warm.

And he sees the religious community, as an analogue of the family thus conceived, and capable of description in familial terms without loss of its apostolic dimension. The energies of celibate religious should be turned to the 'wider opportunities of their family life', which means *both* 'the creative work of the cloister itself' *and* the 'creation of a wider and wider circle of love and pity and strengthening influence in the world about them'.

The last beatitude reads: 'Blessed are the peacemakers, for they shall be called the children of God.' Here one can meditate on connections with the gift of wisdom, the prayer of union, and the sacrament of priesthood. For Aquinas, the love of peace is that quality in our relations with our fellows which disposes us in an immediate fashion to the life of vision. But this is no mere matter of group dynamics: 'You have the tranquillity of order ... when you have within you the re-integration of God's order; when you are reborn in the Spirit and so made whole, and made whole because restored to the status of a son of God.' Wisdom makes us like the Son, who is the uncreated

Wisdom of the Father. So this gift of the Spirit is a *sine qua non* for peace-making divine children.

Though this chapter forms the contemplative climax of *The Divine Pity*, for the gift of wisdom enables us to judge all things by their 'highest causes', and the prayer of union entails, at least for a while, the 'oblivion of everything except the supreme Reality', Fr Gerald, true to his principle that the highest graces give us most contact with the lowliest things, never loses his foothold on the earth. 'God has care of us', and taking 'the long view about everything': these simple statements and qualities are the hallmark of souls who come thus far. The spiritual doctrines of 'indifference' (Ignatius Loyola) and 'abandonment to divine Providence' (Jean-Pierre de Caussade) can be misunderstood. It is a question of *how* to care.

> In the mind of God ... we must not suppose that things come to be or pass away ... that there the flower fades and ceases to exist, the dead animal is lost as it is to the world of time. For us there is inescapably the torment of the finite mind; but we are given this gift of wisdom to help us to see *quasi oculo Dei*, to have in our finite way a dim perception of the way of the mind and the heart of God ... [86]

The *abandon* involved must be taken as a pun: the attitude of loving gratitude to God for *all* he sends produces a profound carefreeness. In Dante's words, *la sua voluntade è nostra pace*, 'his will is our peace'. Such peace, and its diffusion, is the vocation of every Christian, but only by taking the cues offered by all the beatitudes that have gone before shall we have within us that Will which is our peace. And if we are given this supreme prayer – the prayer of union, which is a beginning of beatitude even in this life, an apprehension of the Godhead as immediate Object of knowledge and love within us, it is as 'a sharing in Christ's eternal adoration of the Father, and therefore as a sharing also in his redemption of the world'.

And this is why Fr Gerald must finish with a reference to the sacrament of priesthood. In the icon which is the ministerial priest, the faithful can glimpse, as in a mirror, their common priesthood but brought to a unique focus. Now if the ministerial priesthood, whose climactic action is the office of offering the Mass, is a privileged means of access to understanding the royal and universal priesthood of all the baptised then the latter must understand their own vocation as not active merely, but also (and even primarily) contemplative. Thinking of the attempts of Church hierarchy to galvanise the Christian energies of the laity in the social order Fr Gerald remarks: 'If the phrase "catholic action" is interpreted as meaning that the way to serve the Church is to be endlessly active and to let contemplation take care of itself, then the glory of the common priesthood must necessarily be lost.' Redemptive action there must be – as the service of a love rooted in contemplation spreads light and joy in the world. There are no limits to the extent and modes of such action precisely because of the 'divine *immensitas* of charity'. The tasks of the common priesthood change, however, with the changing circumstances of the world. And so a 'spirituality of social blessing' must be conscious of the culture in which it has to work. It is to Fr Gerald's Thomist perception of culture that we will, in conclusion, turn.

A Thomist theology of culture

What I will call Fr Gerald's 'Thomist theology of culture' is barely intelligible without some indications as to how he saw Aquinas himself. His beautifully printed *Saint Thomas Aquinas*, whose preface offers grateful acknowledgement to E. I. Watkin's *The Catholic Centre* as well as to Christopher Dawson and the French Thomist historian of mediaeval philosophy Etienne Gilson,[87] is admirably suited for this purpose. For, in addition to offering a biography of 'the man', it makes no bones about the fact that it takes up a distinctive perspective on 'the work'.

Fr Gerald presents recourse to the wisdom of St Thomas in the context of a West which, tossed between conflicting views and theories, 'bears every appearance of drifting pilotless to destruction'. Writing in 1940, he remarks in criticism of, respectively, liberal humanism and National Socialism:

> The West is decadent – and the deepest decadence is to be found in those circles which loudly proclaim the youthful vigour and purity of their way of life; but it will hardly recover its lost vitality unless it can rightly diagnose the causes of its disease.[88]

Presenting Thomism in the light of the word-painting, in St Luke's gospel, of Martha and Mary, epitomes of the active and the contemplative lives, Fr Gerald finds the key to its contemporary relevance in its synthesis of contemplation and action – but with contemplation always first. Citing Ananda Coomaraswamy, the Hindu philosopher and art-critic much admired by Gill and Jones, Fr Gerald regards a sapiential metaphysics (the *sanatana dharma* of Indian tradition) as the *sine qua non* for any civilisation worthy of the name, and the 'true contrast' of cultures to lie between mediaeval Europe and Asia, on the one hand, and the modern world on the other.[89] And calling as witness

Victor White's claim in *Scholasticism* that for the great schoolmen, and St Thomas pre-eminently, 'scholastic' and 'mystic' are complementary, not competitive, terms, Fr Gerald maintains that, had only the Thomist synthesis of science and wisdom prevailed, it: 'would have carried Europe forwards, integrating its scientific discoveries, its humanist preoccupations, its political and economic evolution, into an organic whole ...'[90]

Instead, there transpired a disintegration of culture, where these various activities progressively ceased to enlighten each other, and to find their identity through their contribution to man's overall good and end. The nominalism of Ockham, the mentalism of Descartes, the materialism of Hobbes; the economics of *laissez-faire* and the 'monstrosity of art for art's sake' which follows 'necessarily from the brutality of an artless industry' mark stages in a decline whose crucial step is the denial that the 'process of perfection must be subsumed under a deeper, and at first sight, paradoxical, quest: the quest for self-loss in God.' A due order was lost to view, such that only the first term remained of a formula for perfection which Fr Gerald states as

> the perfection of body; the perfection of mind; the perfection of heart, will; achieved in unity and hierarchy; issuing in the expression of personality, of vision, in creative work; and finding God and therefore a new earth, a new self, through the loss of self in mysticism and worship.

Though Fr Gerald's mind was too subtle to remain content with the enunciation of a jeremiad, and he lightens his list of woes with generous reference to the many blessings of science and technology, as well as to the increment of philosophical wisdom which has come even from the exploration of cul-de-sacs, he shared, and indeed quoted, Christopher Dawson's foundational credo that: 'a society which has lost its religion becomes sooner or later a society which has lost its culture.'[92]

And in any case the chief desideratum is not to mourn the past but to shape the future: by rediscovering the religious metaphysic in which alone we can 'integrate our experience, and our mastery, of the relative'. And here, while no doubt the 'Thomist world-view' leaves much still to be done, its adoption means that thinking 'can be begun without fear of sterility'. Providentially, Thomas lived at a moment when the diverse heritages of East and West were present together, so that materials were to hand for a 'theandric' synthesis of human thought with divine. Upbringing, environment, temperament, fitted the Dominican doctor to be the mouthpiece for a truth that was not provincial but universal. Action and contemplation, humanism and self-loss, the world and God, these apparent antinomies, perplexing and even triggers for descent into chaos, he disclosed as held together in a beautiful order: *splendor ordinis*, the beauty of truth. The mode of presentation, expressive language, and identification of 'subordinate problems' with which a metaphysic must deal will change; yet a metaphysic which is essentially 'of its time' is not metaphysic at all.

Thomas succeeded, for Fr Gerald, not only in unifying the 'disparate elements of a complete culture' but also in finding the truth between various 'contradictory theories' themselves generated by confrontation with the deepest problems the mind can know. He presents Thomas's achievement as, then, both synthesis and adjudication. It can be both because a view of the real as a whole can enable individual problems to find their 'functional place' in that whole's organic unity. To grasp what the historical St Thomas did involves appreciating the profundity of the disputed questions which his materials posed, along with the complex disparity of the elements in which they are expressed. Enumerating those problems and factors, Fr Gerald writes:

> There was, first of all, of course, the Christian revelation, viewed so to say in abstraction from the varying ways in which its truth was applied to the realm of reason and nature. Secondly, there were the currents of Jewish thought, as embodied in the Christian religious tradition, and also as expressed in the thought of the Jewish philosopher. Thirdly, there was the influence of Platonism and Neo-Platonism, present with many variations in Augustine, Porphyrius, Boethius, the pseudo-Denys, Avicenna. Fourthly, the anti-rationalist theologism of the Augustinians. Fifthly, the anti-religious rationalism of the Averroists. Sixthly, Aristotle himself, as presented in the literal translations from the Greek of such men as William of Moerbeke. Seventhly, the legacies of Roman and Judaeo-Christians law, as yet unsynthetized; and the Roman-legal attitude of mind. Eighthly, the humanist cult of letters, and the legacy of classical poetry. Ninthly, the development of a mystical tradition in which Eastern and Western sources combined. Tenthly, the idea of knowledge not primarily as a means to practical achievement, not as an epiphenomenon of life, but as the highest kind of life, in which, however, the intellect could not be viewed in abstraction from the heart, the will. Finally, the recognition of the organic character of Christian truth; and the idea, implicit in it, of a universal synthesis to include the whole universe of being, natural and supernatural, human and divine.[93]

Because of the comprehensiveness Thomas set out to attain in his
account of the universe of being, he was naturally drawn to make use
of every means for the apprehending of truth. Reason and faith,
philosophy and theology, remain distinct yet inter-penetrate: 'Between
the modes of knowledge there is continuity as well as solidarity.[94]
Rational and intuitive touch and greet each other, for the Thomist
psychology investigates not only the nature and function of reason, but
how, even in this life, the limitations of reason are partially overcome'.[95] Thomas's affirmation of the mystical – one thinks here of his
remarks on the suprarational mode of knowing in faith in general, and
on the intellectual gifts of the Holy Spirit (knowledge, understanding,
wisdom, counsel) in particular, does not signify the breakdown of his
philosophic-theological synthesis, but the goal to which that synthesis
would lead.

And the enduring value of that synthesis – which was destined, alas,
to 'become the exclusive concern of a caste and ... lose contact with
the world', but whose hour, Fr Gerald thinks, may yet strike – is
twofold. First, it has an *intra*-ecclesial significance, inasmuch as
authentic Thomism can combine the rational interpretation of
Christian truth typical of post-Renaissance Catholicism with the intu-
itional interpretation typical of Eastern Orthodoxy. If the Benedictine
ecumenist Dom Clément Lialine, monk of Chevetogne, is right to find
in the Russian theologians of the nineteenth and twentieth century a
common desire for a new Christian anthropology, where affection and
cognition, sensibility and intelligence are held together in amity, then,
so Fr Gerald thought, St Thomas may be the man the 'Neo-Orthodox'
are seeking.[96] But secondly, the Thomist synthesis has an *extra*-eccle-
sial significance, for society and culture at large.

> If the East feels the need of an anthropology constructed, so to say,
> from above, from the plenitude of theology, the West can at least
> be said to feel the need of an anthropology constructed from below,
> from the tattered remnants of natural human instincts and intuitions
> of the good and the true; an anthropology which would at least take
> count of the whole man; and of the destiny of the whole man; take
> account of the value of personality, and of the need of the person-
> ality for a vital relationship to something other and greater than
> itself ...[97]

And if, in the dread warfare in which Europe was convulsed as Fr
Gerald wrote, the democratic West and the Communist East might be
ranged together as rationalists of different types, while the National
Socialist and Fascist powers could be considered upholders of the
rights of instinct, the West:

will be saved only by the subsumption of what is true in both under the *unum necessarium*, in which the accent is once again put upon the dependency of the creature on the power of the Creator, the self-oblation of the creature in love to the Creator, and the need of making all action an emanation from and an expression of the contemplation by the creature of the Creator.

In his essay 'The Policy of Integration', Fr Gerald took the side of Maritain in maintaining that the Catholic Christian is bound in any case to an 'integrationist view of the relation between the Church and the worlds. That is, while, certainly, the Christians cannot give their soul (including intelligence) to the world, they must still make themselves one with their environment, even when – or precisely because – that environment must be radically altered if Christianity is to flourish'.[98] Here he took his cue from Gwendoline Greene's *The Prophet Child*, with its claim that what believers should 'hate' is the evil *within themselves*, whereas the Godless world beyond they should love, overcoming its evil by good. Fr Gerald proposes the following programme:

> We shall in the first place try rationally to separate the good from the evil in the civilization in which we live ... we shall then fight the evil, making ourselves one with what is good ... we shall not separate ourselves from, but on the contrary unite ourselves with, society as a whole; knowing that while we can expect the fullness of realization of our 'somewhat of possibility' only in and through that society, we have towards it a duty to perform, an influence to make operative, and that this task can only be accomplished through the direct contacts, the sympathy, the intrinsic unity, which come of a common life.[99]

So far as theology is concerned, 'integrationism' thus defined, means, in Fr Gerald's view, the creation of a living Thomism in the world at large – for which purpose he wished to see nuclei of laypeople who did not so much know scraps of Thomism as 'think Thomistically' in an habitual fashion. So far as sociology is concerned, the building of a 'new Christendom' will entail, not 'the mere rehabilitation of the traditional views of Catholics and the expulsion of all other achievement, [but] the reassessing and criticism of the former, the adoption and, where necessary the Christianizing of the latter.'[100] – a formulation in which Fr Gerald is indebted to Maritain's *Humanisme intégrale*. The renascent Christian society which, imbued with the optimism of the 30s Catholic intelligentsia, he hoped to see, would differ from the neo-mediaevalism of the nineteenth-century Catholic revival by being an 'end in its own order', rather than an integration of that order with the supernatural end of man in an explicit – and thus sacral and sacramental – way. At the same time, however, it would constitute an analogous realisation of the same principles which had animated the historic Christian civilisation at its best. As Maritain, so Vann: the 'integral' humanism, open to the divine, of a new Christendom is conceptually unthinkable without the Thomist patrimony. Hence an account of 'Politics and the Thomist Order' becomes imperative.

The *principia suprema* which mediaeval Thomism could marshal as criteria for public policy, derive, in Fr Gerald's presentation, from three sources: Aristotle, Paul, Augustine.

> The Aristotelean notion of political society as condition of the good life, based upon the principle that man is a social animal, had been reinforced and transfigured by the Christian principle of membership of Christ's Mystical Body, and the consequent portrayal by Augustine of the City of God – a society at once natural and supernaturalized.[101]

The break-up of the Thomistic synthesis, reaching its climax in the sixteenth-century Reformation (as interpreted by the Anglican historian of economics R. H. Tawney), destroyed the perception of society as an organism, a 'communion of classes', varying in their interests, yet united by mutual obligations issuing from their relationship with a common end. The recognition of shared supra-economic and supra-political norms and authorities fades, leaving the human city a joint-stock company in which the 'liabilities of the shareholders are strictly limited'.[102] With Hobbes, the ethical is divorced from the political, for only when egoism realises the need for civil society if peace and commodious living are to be secured and premature death avoided does reason propose the renouncing of natural rights by reciprocal agreement. With Locke, the absolutism of the sovereign is replaced by that of the individual, for Lockeians have no thought for the common end of society: men 'merely seek in it the security necessary for their own individual ends'.[103] The majority rule which Locke regarded as practically necessary became in Whig hands an electioneering slogan for oligarchy. Fr Gerald preferred early nineteenth-century Tories to Whigs whose rejection of patriarchalism was particularly ill-timed in a period when industrial revolution exposed the small man to unparalleled social disaster. The collapse of the *anciens régimes* of continental Europe and of Britain stimulated a renewal of absolutism in different forms: Spencer's organism theory, where the individual cell has no independent personality in the

State-organism; Hegel's view of political society as an aspect of the Absolute in its movement towards its own perfection – and hence without goals beyond its own subsistence; Communism and Fascism in their shared tendency to deny all natural rights to individuals, so exhaustively does the party-State or *Volksstaat* suck ontological substance from them.

And here Thomism drives its middle course between individualism and collectivism, not through *compromise* but via *synthesis*. First, for Thomism, man is *by nature* a social animal: the idea of a free contract, therefore, falls, though the particular forms of social arrangement might, at least theoretically, be the result of voluntary agreement. Secondly, while in some respects individuals must tailor their lives and activity to the common good, in other respects social coexistence has as its own end the flourishing of individual persons. As persons, citizens are not parts of the whole, but *sui juris*: they 'have a perfection to compass which is personal to themselves'. Fr Gerald finds the term 'function' a key one in Thomist political theory.

> Society is for it an organism wherein each member has his function and therefore his duties to the whole community; duties which, as the *bonum commune* varies – for it will be a very different thing in time of prosperous peace and in time of war and famine – will demand more or less sacrifice and make possible to a greater or less degree the identification of the individual perfection with that of the whole. On the other hand, the citizens are persons, and the society therefore as a whole has the duty of respecting, safeguarding and positively promoting the personal good of each citizen. And as these mutual responsibilities are dictated not by utilitarian agreement but by natural law – the demands of human nature as such – their sanction is a moral sanction: the citizen is morally bound to further the interests of society, the State to further the interests of the person.[104]

And just as the Thomist metaphysic provided a post-hoc synthesis of a rich diversity of elements in pre-existing ways of thought, so the Thomist theory of the human city sketches out in advance a synthesis of elements yet to come into being when Thomism itself was born. Thus:

> With Spencer [the 'Thomist politic'] holds that the State is an organism, though refusing to allow that individuals are no more than cells in the organism. The principle of *functional* society emerges. With Plato's *Republic* and all communisms and collectivisms it holds that the end of the society is greater than the ends

of the individuals who compose it, while refusing to admit that the
State is omnicompetent and supreme. The principle of *social ethic*
emerges. Even with Hegel's pantheism it has this affinity, that it
views the evolution of the society as a process of divinization – the
working out of the divine idea in the material of human relationships – the principle of common striving after the *bonum commune*
emerges. With the *Contrat Sociale* of Rousseau it has this much in
common: that while denying the thesis that society is the outcome
merely of convention, and the pseudo-mystic deification (political
pantheism) of the General Will, it can see in the latter postulate the
truth that there *ought* to be a general will, if not in the sense understood by Bosanquet (as a real or higher as opposed to an apparent
or lower satisfaction of individual wills – Rousseau was not as
subtle as this) at least in the sense of a striving after a common
objective more divine than that of the will of each. With Hobbes
and Locke it holds that the State must protect and safeguard the
citizens' perfection; but it will not narrow the scope of State action
to this negative policy – what Bosanquet calls the hindering of
hindrances – alone, or enlarge non-interference to mean social irresponsibility and political atomism. To the principle of
non-interference with the personal end of the individual and safeguarding of individual rights it adds the duty on the part of the State
of fostering, actively, the individual's perfection by assuring him
the necessary material environment.[105]

And to this quotation, whose effortless mastery of its subject-matter
surely justifies its length, may be added Fr Gerald's attempt to
'compare and contrast' Thomism with the three ideological giants of
his day: Communism, Liberalism, and Fascism.

Thomism is fundamentally opposed to Communism in its denial of
personal end and rights, its State-absolutism, but at one with it in
its search for unity and a common goal. It is fundamentally opposed
to liberalist individualism on the grounds of its social irresponsibility, its denial of the supremacy of moral law, its denial of the
rights of the society against the individual but at one with its assertion of the validity of personal ends. Against Fascism it denies the
omnicompetence of the State, but welcomes the corporative idea as
expressive of its own principle of function.

Turning from the analysis of theories to the prescription of action, Fr
Gerald suggested that what world society needs is at once more formal
unity – by which he meant a 'single conscience in which there will be
room for all that is best of the civilizations already existing to reside

in harmony', and less standardisation or regulation of the life of persons and localities. In some regards centralised control is necessary and beneficent, but more primary is – in words of Disraeli, whose political novels Fr Gerald treats as springs of wisdom – that parochial polity of the country which secures to every labourer a home. And not a home only, but, by way of expansion of the vision of 'Young England', 'a safeguard and a setting for the increase of his soul'.

Becoming wise

There is a pathos about much of Fr Gerald's writing which seems to reflect the man. Fr Sebastian Bullough wrote in his tribute to him:

> There was a sadness about Fr Gerald beneath the genuine gaiety and the fraternal bonhomie which his brethren knew and enjoyed so well. Perhaps it was just this – that his own personal understanding brought the pain upon him, an understanding ... of the whole problem of mankind's hunger for love, or of mankind's self-satisfaction without it, or contentment with the false love that is selfishness. Gerald Vann saw these things and felt them deeply, and he also saw that he was powerless to help, beyond remaining a voice crying in the wilderness and having compassion on the multitude. He saw that the problem could only be solved by obedience to God, that man's hunger for love could only be satisfied by understanding God's love of mankind, and that only thus could man be led away from selfishness and led to the true human love of other men. And in his humble wisdom, he saw himself among the starving multitudes who had need of this compassion.[106]

There were certain consonances here with a figure of many centuries before on whose 'wisdom' he had chosen to write: Boethius, the Late Antique philosopher whose local cultus (at Pavia) was officially recognised by the Papacy in 1883.[107] Like Fr Gerald, Boethius combined an eye perpetually on the eternal world with a love of little things, whether human or simply earthly. Helen Waddell wrote in her *Wandering Scholars*:

> It was fortunate for the sanity of the Middle Ages that the man who taught them so much of their philosophy ... was of a temperament so humane and so serene; that the *maxime scrutator magnarum rerum*, 'mightiest observer of mighty things', who defined eternity with an exulting plenitude that no man has approached before or

since, had gone to gather violets in a spring wood, and watched with sore heart a bird in a cage that had caught a glimpse of waving trees and now grieved its heart out, scattering its seed with small impotent claws.[108]

One could easily tabulate similarities: Boethius was 'a lover of beauty and wisdom and all that we mean by the humanities'; 'no stranger to the *Lacrimae rerum*, the tears which lie at the heart of things'; he had 'something of the Greek exaltation of friendship'; his humanity was 'always apparent', enlivened by 'quiet touches of humour'; for him, philosophy was the love of wisdom precisely as (citing the *Consolation of Philosophy*) 'that living thought which is the cause of all, and which is self-subsistent, God'.[109]

Fr Gerald noted that the 'Philosophy' who visited Boethius in the Ostrogothic king's dungeon, there to lead him to Wisdom, was personified as a woman. He emphasised the significance of a 'feminine' attitude to reality – and found it adumbrated in three contemporary writers, all lay Christians, the Russian Orthodox Nikolay Berdyaev, the French Catholic, Jean Guitton, and, a figure we have already met, E. I. Watkin. In his study of Dostoevsky, Berdyaev speaks of a mediaeval world worshipping a transcendent God and his cosmic order, a Renaissance world dethroning both so as to worship instead a 'god' purely immanent in humanity, and a coming third age in which the true God is refound as now both transcendent and immanent, the redemptive God who is, therefore, disclosed 'in the squalors of humanity, the dark waters, out of which he will bring new light and new life through sharing in them'. Jean Guitton suggested that the remnant of Christendom is approaching an 'age of Mary' (indicated by the numerous Marian 'appearances' of the nineteenth and twentieth centuries) in which the influence of the Mother of God will assume new proportions. Watkin proposed a doctrinally corrected form of the trinitarian scheme of world-history initiated by the thirteenth-century Calabrian abbot Joachim of Fiora, with an age of the Holy Spirit not superseding that of the Son but completing it, as Pentecost the Passion. In this orthodox version of Joachimism, the phrase 'the age of the Spirit' would signify that

> within the reign and rule of the Word over the world, there is to come a time when the influence of the Paraclete will be more intense than before: when Christianity – love of God, obedience to God – will become more and more *inward*: a contemplative age, therefore, dominated more and more completely by the inward motivations of charity and the Gifts ...[110]

And symbolically – archetypally – these three, the 'mother', the 'waters', and the 'spirit', are intimately connected: without the receptive femininity they signify 'there can be no hope for our survival as a civilisation'. It was a contemplative renaissance which, above all, Fr Gerald sought:

> To think of the mother, the spirit, the water, is to think of inwardness: the Mother kept all these words in her heart; the Spirit is the indwelling Spirit who instructs the hearts of men; the waters lap you about, the waters of death, but become within you the waters of life, springing up into life everlasting.

Notes

1. G. Vann, O.P., 'A Sermon Preached at the Burial of Father Jerome Rigby, O.P., at Hawkesyard Priory, 8 April 1948', *Life of the Spirit* III. 25 (1948), pp. 5–8.
2. *Blackfriars School, 1659–1959* (Hinckley, n. d. but 1959).
3. Ibid., p. 1.
4. *To Heaven with Diana! A Study of Jordan of Saxony and Diana d'Andalò with a Translation of the Letters of Jordan* (London: Collins, 1960). The lengthy introduction, pp. 9–57, is essentially a study of Christian friendship. For the originality of the letters as a statement of monastic friendship between a man and a woman, see B.P. McGuire, *Friendship and Community. The Monastic Experience*, 350–1250 (Kalamazoo, Mich.: Cistercian Publications, 1988), pp. 394–98.
5. *Blackfriars School, 1659–1959*, p. 2.
6. Ibid., p. 13.
7. Ibid.
8. Copy among the Vann papers in the English Dominican Archive. On her attitude to the Church of Rome, the 'authorised' biographer comments, 'Though Dorothy never became a Roman Catholic, it is very noticeable in her correspondence that she accorded much more respect to Roman Catholic priests than to the clergy of the Church of England', J. Brabazon, *Dorothy L. Sayers, The Life of a Courageous Woman* (London: Victor Gollancz, 1981), p. 69. But perhaps Sayers *could* be considered as within the SSM 'circle': at any rate, it appears to have been a letter from Fr Herbert Kelly, the founder of Kelham, in praise of her play about mediaeval Canterbury, *The Zeal of thy House*, which started her off on her career as a theological apologist: thus B. Reynolds, *Dorothy L. Sayers; her Life and Soul* (London: Hodder and Stoughton, 1993), p. 287.
9. 'Consent among the Churches', I. 5.
10. *Common Sense, Christianity and War* (= Pax Pamphlets No. 6, London, James Clarke and Co., 1939), p. 8.

10a. *Morality and War* (London, Burns, Oates and Washbourne, 1939), p. 12.
11. 'De SS. Trinitatis Mysterio Humanae Vitae Archetypo', (Dissertation, Pontifical College at St Thomas Aquinas, Rome, 1921), pp. 1–2. Fr Gerald suggests here that 'comparative religion' can also furnish signs and shadows of the Trinity from the data of the non-Judaeo-Christian faiths.
12. P. Hugon, *De Deo Trino* q. 2, a. 1.
13. Richard of St Victor, *De Trinitate* III. 2.
14. John of St Thomas, *Commentary on the 'Summa Theologiae' of St Thomas, In Primam partem*, q. 27, disp. 12, a. 1.
15. 'De SS Trinitatis Mysterio', pp. 13–53.
16. *In Libros Sententiarum* X. 1. i.
17. 'De SS. Trinitatis Mysterio', p. 30; cf. St Thomas's *In Libros Sententiarum* X. 1. iii, and St Bernard of Clairvaux's *Sermons on the Song of Songs* 8.3.
18. J. Maritain, *Art et scolastique* (Paris: Librairie de l'Art Catholique, 1920), p. 164.
19. 'De SS. Trinitatis Mysterio', p. 34.
20. Ibid., p. 54.
21. *De Potentia* IX. 9; *De Veritate* X. 7.
22. *Super libros Sententiarum I.* xiv., 2, ad ii.
23. Richard of St Victor, *De Trinitate* IV. 20.
24. 'De SS. Trinitatis Mysterio, p. 59.
25. He depended here on Gill's 1925 essay 'Art and Religion', published in the review of the Prinknash Benedictines *Pax* for 1925.
26. D. L. Sayers, *The Mind of the Maker* (London: Methuen and Co., 1941; 1947[9]).
27. Cited from B. Reynolds, *Dorothy L. Sayers, Her Life and Soul* (London: Hodder and Stoughton, 1993), p. 285.
28. M. Brunsdale, *Dorothy L. Sayers. Solving the Mystery of Wickedness* (New York: Berg Publishers, 1990), p. 146.
29. 'De SS. Trinitatis Mysterio', p. 63.
30. *Summa Theologiae*, IIa.IIae, q. 9, a. 4, ad iii.
31. 'De SS Trinitatis Mysterio', p. 68.
32. *Summa Theologiae* Ia q. 43, a. 3, ad ii.
33. V. McNabb, O. P. 'Seer and Mystics', *Hawkesyard Review*, (1911), cited in 'De SS. Trinitatis Mysterio', p. 80.
34. Ibid., with a reference to Augustine, *De Trinitate* III. 6.
35. 'Man's Response to the Trinity', in *The High Green Hill* (London: Collins, 1951), p. 57.
36. *The Eagle's Word. A Presentation of the Gospel according to St John with an Introductory Essay* (London: Collins, 1961), p. 107.
37. *The Paradise Tree* (London: Collins, 1959), p. 12.
38. A reference to M. Eliade's *Images et symboles* (Paris: Gallimard, 1952), p. 24.
39. C. G. Jung, *Symbols of Transformation* (= *Collected Works* 5; London: Routledge and Kegan Paul, 1956), p. 225.

40. *The Paradise Tree*, p. 16.
41. H. Rahner, 'The Christian Mystery and the Pagan Mysteries' in J. Campbell (ed) *The Mysteries: Papers from the Eranos Yearbooks* 2 (London: Routledge and Kegan Paul, 1955) p. 367.
42. *The Paradise Tree*, p. 19.
43. J. Campbell, *The Hero with a Thousand Faces* (New York: Meridian Books, 1956), p. 28.
44. *The Paradise Tree*, p. 18.
45. Ibid., p. 25.
46. Ibid., pp. 27–28.
47. The Benedictines of Stanbrook, *In a Great Tradition* (London: John Murray, 1956), p. 250.
48. *The Paradise Tree*, pp. 37–38, citing H. Rahner, 'The Christian Mystery and the Pagan Mysteries', pp. 395, 399.
49. Ibid., pp. 40–41.
50. Ibid., p. 44.
51. Ibid., p. 54.
52. Quoted from S. Hobhouse (ed.), *Selected Mystical Writings of William Law* (London: C. W. Daniel Company, 1938).
53. *The Paradise Tree*, pp. 55–56.
54. Ibid., p. 64.
55. Letter of 26 March 1958, English Dominican Archive. The reference is to Jung's 'A Psychological Approach to the Dogma of the Trinity', in *Psychology and Religion: West and East* (= *Collected Works*, 11; E London: Routledge and Kegan Paul, 1958), pp. 107–200.
56. Indeed, Fr Gerald appears to have accepted Fr Victor's correction in much these terms, for we later find him remarking that 'if we bring together the two ideas of Mother and Spirit as in some way identified in the Godhead we are wise to think of Spirit, not in any trinitarian sense, but simply as the term "Spirit of God" is used in the Old Testament', *The Paradise Tree*, p. 271. And the mystery of the divine motherhood he finds embodied in the 'whole being' of Mary: ibid., p. 294.
57. The reference is to the great Anglican liturgiologist Dom Gregory Dix; but Fr Gerald's comments on the history of the Roman rite are chiefly indebted to the Innsbruck Jesuit Josef Jungmann.
58. *The Paradise Tree*, p. 263, with internal citations of Romans 7. 4–6 and John 4. 14.
59. Ibid., p. 237, with a reference back to p. 18 of his own work.
60. Ibid., pp. 290–91.
61. *The Pain of Christ and the Sorrow of God* (London: Blackfriars Publications, 1947), p. 7.
62. *The High Green Hill* (London: Collins, 1951), pp. 36–37.
63. *The Pain of Christ* pp. 8–9.
64. Ibid., pp. 13–14. All but the last of the essays in this collection were originally given as Lenten sermons in Westminster Cathedral in the spring of 1947.

65. Words taken from the speech of the Angel of the Agony in Newman's *Dream of Gerontius*.
66. *The High Green Hill*, p. 32.
67. *The Pain of Christ*, p. 20.
68. Ibid., p. 23.
69. *The Seven Swords* (London: Collins, 1952), p. 19.
70. Ibid., p. 78.
71. *The Pain of Christ*, p. 44.
72. Ibid., p. 56.
73. Ibid., p. 66.
74. *The Divine Pity. A Study in the Social Implications of the Beatitudes* (London: Sheed and Ward, 1945), p. 4.
75. Ibid., pp. 5–8, citing J. Maritain, *Les Degrés du savoir* (Paris: Désclee de Brouwer, 1932), pp. 903–904.
76. *The Divine Pity*, pp. 12–13.
77. Congregation for the Doctrine of the Faith, *Instruction on Christian Freedom and Liberation* (Vatican City: 1986).
78. Cf *Summa Theologiae*, Ia IIae q. 69.
79. *The Divine Pity*, p. 19.
80. Ibid., p. 22. Things are to be used, persons enjoyed: the celebrated distinction of *uti/frui* pioneered by St Augustine.
81. Ibid., p. 70.
82. Ibid., p. 76.
83. Ibid., pp. 96–97.
84. Ibid., p. 102.
85. Ibid., p. 148.
86. Ibid., p. 159.
87. Fr Gerald makes conspicuous use of Gilson's *Reason and Revelation in the Middle Ages* (New York: Scribner's, 1938) and *The Unity of Philosophical Experience* (New York: Scribner's, 1938), as well as *The Philosophy of Saint Thomas Aquinas* (ET Cambridge: Heffer and Sons, 1924).
88. *Saint Thomas Aquinas* (London: Hague and Gill, 1940), p. 2.
89. A. K. Coomaraswamy (ed.), 'René Guénon: Sacred and Profane Science', *The Visva-Bharati Quarterly* (November 1935), p. 1, cited in *Saint Thomas Aquinas* pp. 7–8.
90. *Saint Thomas Aquinas*, p. 15.
91. Ibid., p. 27. In expounding the *secunda pars* of the *Summa Theologiae*, Fr Gerald will speak of man's perfection as reached 'through the actualization, in unity and hierarchy, of all the potentialities of his many-levelled life, all minor perfections being subsumed under the first and principal which is the possession by the spirit of the vision of God, or, in this life, in which man can attain an inchoate beatitude, of such knowledge and love of God as is possible', ibid., p. 129.
92. C. Dawson, *Religion and Culture* (London: Sheed and Ward, 1948), p. 233; cited in *Saint Thomas Aquinas*, p. 32.
93. *Saint Thomas Aquinas* pp. 95–96.

94. Ibid., p. 111. Fr Gerald cites a telling comment of the historian of mediaeval philosophy Maurice de Wulf in this respect: 'The prohibitive attitude adopted towards philosophical conclusions threatening or contradicting a dogma is merely a particular case of the general law of solidarity': *History of Medieval Philosophy* (London: Longmans, 1926), II., p. 30.
95. *Saint Thomas Aquinas*, p. 151, with reference to T. Gilby, O.P., *Poetic Experience. An Introduction to Thomist Aesthetic* (London: Sheed and Ward, 1934).
96. *Saint Thomas Aquinas* pp. 156–59, with reference to C. Lialine, O.S.B., *De la Méthode irénique* (Amay: Prieuré d'Amay-sur-Meuse, 1938), pp. 62, 53.
97. *Saint Thomas Aquinas*, p. 166.
98. *Morals Makyth Man* (London: Longmans, Green and Co., 1938), p. 127; cf. J. Maritain, *Lettre sur l'Indépendance* (Paris, 1935).
99. *Morals Makyth Man*, p. 127, citing G. P. Greene, *The Prophet Child* (London: Longmans, Green and Co., 1935), p. 120.
100. *Morals Makyth Man*, p. 130. Here he was inspired by Fr Mark Brocklehurst's creation of an Aquinas Society for a far from élite audience at Holy Cross, Leicester. Fr Mark's insight into the unitive function of the Thomist synthesis underlies Fr Gerald's *Saint Thomas Aquinas*, as its preface admits.
101. *Morals Makyth Man*, p. 142.
102. R. H. Tawney, *Religion and the Rise of Capitalism, A Historical Study*, (London: John Murray, 1937), p. 189.
103. *Morals Makyth Man*, p. 145.
104. Ibid., p. 150.
105. Ibid., pp. 148–49.
106. *Gerald Vann* (privately printed, n. d., but 1963, without pagination).
107. *The Wisdom of Boethius* (London: Blackfriars Publications, 1952; = Aquinas Paper No. 20).
108. H. Waddell, *Wandering Scholars* (London: Constable, 1927), pp. xxvi–xxvii.
109. *The Wisdom of Boethius*, pp. 6, 7.
110. Ibid., p. 9.

Works by Gerald Vann

'De SS. Trinitatis Mysterio Humanae Vitae Archetypo' (Rome: Diss. Pontifical College of St Thomas Aquinas, 1931).
'St Thomas and Humanism' I, *Blackfriars* XIII. 148 (1932), pp. 395–402; II, ibid., XIII. 149, (1932), pp. 467–76.
On Being Human (London: Sheed and Ward, 1933).
'The Ethics of Modern War', *Blackfriars* XVII. 201 (1936), pp. 900–906.
'Diversity in Worship', *Blackfriars* XVIII. 202 (1937), pp. 47–51.

'Humanism and the Claims of God', *Blackfriars* XVIII. 204 (1937), pp. 171–82.

'The Psychology of War-mongering', *Blackfriars* XVIII. 213 (1937), pp. 887–904.

Morals Makyth Man (London: Longmans, Green and Co., 1937; reprinted as *Morals and Man*, London: Collins, 1960).

'Ends and Means', *Blackfriars* XIX. 214 (1938), pp. 23–27.

'Introduction to Thomist Politics', *Blackfriars* XIX. 218 (1938), pp. 323–37.

'Contrition and Action', *Blackfriars* XIX. 225 (1938), pp. 875–83.

Morality and War (London: Burns and Oates, 1939).

Of his Fullness (London: Burns and Oates, 1939).

'The Jews', *Blackfriars* XX. 231 (1939), pp. 414–19.

Saint Thomas Aquinas (London: Hague and Gill, 1940).

'Patriotism and the Life of the State', *Blackfriars* XXI. 238 (1940), pp. 16–32.

'Mr Eliot and the Idea of a Christian Society', *Blackfriars* XXI. 239 (1940), pp. 119–22.

'Obedience and Freedom', *Blackfriars* XXI. 247 (1940), pp. 580–92.

'Education and Art', *Blackfriars* XXII. 257 (1941), pp. 426–35.

'Man the Maker', *Blackfriars* XXIII. 264 (1942), pp. 90–95.

'The Human Person', *Blackfriars* XXIII. 270 (1942), pp. 339–45.

'Prayer and Politics' I, *Blackfriars* XXIII. 272 (1942), pp. 418–25; II, ibid., XXIII. 273 (1942), pp. 456–62.

The Heart of Man (London: Geoffrey Bles, 1944).

'*Mystici Corporis*: The Fullness of Catholic Life', *Blackfriars* XXV. 290 (1944), pp. 163–72.

The Divine Pity (London: Sheed and Ward, 1945; reprinted under the same title, London: Collins, 1956).

'Fatima and the People's Theology', *Blackfriars* XXVI. 303 (1945), pp. 206–212.

Eve and the Gryphon (London: Blackfriars Publications, 1946).

His Will is our Peace (London: Sheed and Ward, 1947).

The Pain of Christ and The Sorrow of God (London: Blackfriars Publications, 1947).

Awake in Heaven (London: Geoffrey Bles, 1948).

The Two Trees (London: Collins, 1948).

The Seven Swords (London: Collins, 1950).

The High Green Hill (London: Collins, 1951).

The Wisdom of Boethius (London: Blackfriars Publications 1950, = Aquinas Paper, No. 20).

The Water and the Fire (London: Collins, 1953).

Stones or Bread (with the Revd. P. K. Meagher, London: Collins, 1957).

The Paradise Tree (London: Collins, 1959).

The Son's Course (London: Collins, 1959).

Blackfriars School, 1659–1959 (Hinckley, n. d. but 1959).

To Heaven with Diana (London: Collins, 1960).

The Eagle's Word (London: Collins, 1961).

'Myth, Symbol and Revelation', *Blackfriars* XLII. 494 (1961), pp. 297–311.
The Missal Step by Step. A First Mass Book (with D. A. Young and P. Quail, illustrator, London: Burns and Oates, 1963).
Moral Dilemmas (London: Collins, 1963).

5

Thomas Gilby

Thomas Gilby was a Birmingham lad, born on 18 December 1902, whose parents became Catholics while he was still a boy. Sent to the Oratorian school, St Philip's, he evidently embraced his new faith with enthusiasm, because he presented himself to the Order before his seventeenth birthday, in September 1919. His theological (and philosophical) aptitude were already evident at Hawkesyard, and, following in the steps of a goodly number of English Dominicans since the founding of Bornhem (see Appendix) he was invited to carry out further studies at Louvain, where he was awarded a doctorate in 1929. The original idea had been that he would teach apologetics at Hawkesyard – the ancestor of today's 'fundamental theology', it was the only course in Catholic divinity as such taken by the Order's students at the philosophical stage of their intellectual formation. In 1931, however, Bede Jarrett called him to Oxford to teach moral theology and in the following year, when Jarrett himself was residing at Oxford as prior and editor of *Blackfriars*, Fr Thomas found himself editorial assistant for the latter into the bargain. Their collaboration was the easier in that Fr Thomas sympathised fully with Jarrett's policy of humane orthodoxy. In 1934, with the former Provincial's death, he found himself in a somewhat exposed position, as the more rigorist spirits in the Province made their influence felt. Removed from Oxford in 1935, he taught for the nuns of the Society of the Holy Child Jesus at their teachers' training college in Cavendish Square: a central London location which, paradoxically, gave him all the more opportunity to spread his own gospel through lectures and spiritual conferences. He became well-known to the group of Catholic writers and thinkers who met, as the nearest thing in London to a *croyant* Parisian *salon*, at Charles Burns's house in St Leonard's Terrace, Chelsea.[1] Assigned to Cambridge on the eve of the Second World War, Fr Thomas soon preferred action as a naval chaplain. Thus began a lifetime's romance with the sea, which found literary expres-

sion in a naval and military anthology, *Britain at Arms*,[2] and a different sort of outlet in his periodic post-war cruises on the yacht of his
publisher, Sir Oliver Crosthwaite-Eyre. When the war ended, the
Admiralty offered him the post of 'Principal Naval Chaplain, R. C.'
which, conscious of his obligations to the Province, he declined.

The 1950s were his *decennium mirabile*. Initiated by his study of
Thomistic method, *Barbara Celarent*,[3] and an exposition of scholastic epistemology and ontology, *Phoenix* and *Turtle*,[4] a flood of
Gilbyan Thomism proved the early promise of *Poetic Experience*,[5] a
short essay on Thomist aesthetics, to have been no isolated shower.
There followed judicious selections of St Thomas's prose, both philosophical and theological,[6] and two major studies of Thomistic social
and political theory, in the general style made familiar by the comparable work in France of Jacques Maritain.[7] These grave works – at
least in import, for the Gilbyan touch was light – were interrupted by
Up the Green River, a novel whose subject was the attempt by a
Midlands priest of the early Victorian period to found a colony for his
parishioners in the chaotic conditions of post-Napoleonic Spanish
America.[8]

When in 1958 Fr Thomas's friend Fr Henry St John was elected
Prior Provincial he suddenly found himself elevated to the superior-
ship at Cambridge and given the directorship of a revived 'Blackfriars
Publications' so that he could take in hand a great project. And this
was the editing of a new bilingual (English and Latin) version of the
Summa Theologiae of St Thomas, drawing on Thomist scholars from
around the English-speaking world, with a mandate not only to translate the text into fair modern English, but also to provide a scholarly
apparatus of references and notes, together with rather fuller aids to
students in the form of leisurely introductions and appendices where
important points – historical, philosophical and theological – could be
developed at greater length. Fr Thomas would be general editor of the
whole series, while in the upshot no less than thirteen of its sixty
volumes fell to his hand throughout. At last, the idea of Blackfriars,
Cambridge as a *domus scriptorum*, 'house of writers', came into its
own. In 1965 the Master of the Order, Anicetus Fernandez, awarded
him the mastership in sacred theology as a recognition of this
herculean labour.

Owing to the temporary setback in Thomist studies caused by the
post-conciliar crisis (thirty years later the situation is more encouraging, as for instance the appearance of an American essay collection on
the future of Thomism indicates),[9] the sales of the Gilby *Summa* were,
however, fluctuating. Like a number of the more interesting and
unconventional figures in the pre-conciliar Province, Fr Thomas

found his programme of moderate liberalisation overtaken by events. The desire to soften the asperities of an over-harsh ecclesiastical régime, and to water a somewhat desiccated scholasticism, remained in his eyes an entirely legitimate aspiration. But the onset of ecclesial and theological incoherence in the immediate wake of the Second Vatican Council was another question.

It is instructive that he, whose writing on the use of marriage had suffered at the hands of Order censorship, and was only published, belatedly, under a pseudonym,[10] should have made his last contribution to *New Blackfriars* a (low-key) defence of Paul VI's letter on the control of births, *Humane Vitae*.[11] As early as 1931, Fr Thomas had recognised that there is a 'case against contraception built on prejudice, prudishness, priggishness, convention', while also propounding a 'philosophical principle by which contraception may be tested and found wanting'.[12] Whereas both the killjoy and the sensualist regard pleasure as a thing-in-itself, it is in reality the healthy *accompaniment* of human acts.

> Pleasure sought apart from its proper subject is an anomaly ... Here the flower is plucked from the tree which alone can give it life. The natural momentum of a living activity is arrested, the rhythm interrupted, the harmony outraged. These, which seem at first sight merely poetical or physiological criticisms are really, I think, a swift and instinctive compression of the underlying principles of a sane philosophy of pleasure.[13]

In his account of the 'Catholic Background to Sex', it was explained that *Morals and Marriage* had been written pseudonymously 'solely in deference to the judgment of an authority, and not from fear of any irregularity of doctrine ...'[14] The reason for the hesitations of 'authority' are surely to be found in the account of the 'safe period', whose delimitation had been scientifically established only five years earlier, thanks to simultaneous gynaecological research in Austria and Japan.[15] Fr Thomas's judgment that 'when medical science authoritatively settles the fact of periodical sterility – if it has not already done so – the consequence will be that lawful advantage may be taken of it for purposes of birth control in certain cases', had already caused nervousness in the Province. The reasons are not entirely clear, since Pope Pius XI's encyclical on these matters, *Casti Connubii*, of 1931, had already taken this point – which was in any case in complete continuity with the established moral doctrine that conjugal intercourse was in no way interdicted for the naturally sterile. Probably the anxiety was that the general dissemination of information – as distinct from counsel given on an individual basis by doctors and priests –

would lead to irresponsible recourse to such naturally infertile periods. Certainly, Fr Thomas's book was a wholly straighforward, if unusually well-expressed, account of the traditional teaching. If it insisted on the Church's full acceptance of 'rational birth-control *as an end*' – for 'the very institution of marriage is a method of birth-control, since it limits procreation to those conditions in which a child will be cared for ... [16] it also maintained that 'considering, therefore, the biological nature of sex and the divine command of fruitfulness, there is a general obligation on married people to have as many children as they reasonably can'. The question remained, of course, of the force to be given there to the word 'reasonably'. While his position seemed laxist to many of his brethren in the 1930s, by the late 1960s the boot was on the other foot. His statement that

> Though temperamentally reluctant to draw the conclusion arrived at by the Encyclical [*Humanae Vitae*], I am sufficiently convinced that it follows from principles soundly established by reason and Revelation, and faithfully represents and applies the constant tradition of the Church that sexuality is never to be taken as an exclusively inter-personal value[17]

offended those Dominicans of the post-conciliar period who had taken up, often in public, a diametrically opposed view.[18] But such a reversal of fortune echoes a wider pattern in Catholic theology as the names of Jean Daniélou, Hans Urs von Balthasar and Henri de Lubac testify.

Fr Thomas sent the proofs of the penultimate volume of his *Summa* – the last was that of the indexes – to the printers in 1975, and died satisfied on 29 November of that year. Leaving his secular *divertissements* aside, the four chief subject-matters engaging his interest were scholastic philosophy; the mind of St Thomas; aesthetics, and social theory.

Scholastic philosophy

Two studies of scholastic philosophy – one centring on 'dialectic', the nature of argumentation, and the other on epistemology and ontology, the theory of knowing and being, emerged from Fr Thomas's study in quick succession in 1949–50. 'Study' is hardly the word for the first: *Barbara Celarent* (the whimsical title comes from a piece of scholastic doggerel listing the nineteen valid forms of syllogism) was written in the midst of his wartime experience as a naval chaplain on active service: more specifically, during the pursuit by HMS *Renown* of two leading German ships of the line, *Scharnhorst* and *Gneisenau*, in the

Arctic Circle. To hand was nothing but a 'miniature *Summa Theologica*', but, as the author's aim was the description of 'a habit of mind and method', an elaborate scholarly apparatus would have been, in any case, out of place. Fr Thomas's introduction tells us indeed a good deal about his authorial aims at large. He proposes to render scholasticism current by making it enjoyable. In a sea-going metaphor: 'A swing and a breeze from outside might be welcome where the conventional demeanour is rather stiff and the atmosphere often close'.[19] Keeping to a minimum any use of technical terms, yet eschewing the kind of simplification that loses half the point, Fr Thomas proposed to explain the dialectical tool-kit of Aquinas's thought itself: 'a general design offering violence to none of the details of experience – nothing human strange to me, a claim that could not be urged without extravagance for some ideologies'. His St Thomas has the sweep of an encyclopedist, the depth of a mystic, the finesse of a logician, yet is also, in a phrase of Lewis Mumford 'in no derogatory sense ... a master of platitude'. Treating Aquinas as fun: this was Fr Thomas's novel contribution to the English Dominican culture. If Aristotle had regarded *eutropelia*, playfulness, as a virtue, a point developed by some fathers of the Church,[20] and Aquinas had compared play with wisdom, in deference to the biblical book of that name,[21] then Fr Thomas could propose to conduct philosophy like sport. *Amateurisme* alone, in the conditions of modern culture, can unite science and letters, and, after all, 'a smile is no enemy to truth'.

Barbara Celarent considers in turn some key ideas in the scholastic presentation of logic, 'critical philosophy' or epistemology, rational psychology, and scientific method, and concludes with an account of the scholastic disputation, in use (admittedly in a late, baroque-scholastic, form) in the Dominican study-houses of Fr Thomas's day and still offered, as a model of formal debate, to appreciative audiences as late as the 1980s. The book centres around procedures for discovering truth in an ongoing philosophical conversation: hence its absorption in the central logical forms, in 'rules, figures and moods', ranging as widely as the 'practice of myth, analogy and the convergence of probabilities'.

That this is no manualist treatment of, in the first place, logic, emerges soon enough from Fr Thomas's manner of commending his subject. Logic is part of the 'courtesy of conversation', belonging with the Thomist virtues of friendliness and pleasantness, for 'without ease, modesty and exactness, men cannot dwell together'.[22] 'There will be no rebuilding from the ruins around us unless we begin from the personal integrity of exact thought: humanly speaking, there is no other foundation for civilization, nor for religion'. Logic is the 'art and science of thinking correctly, especially on subjects that admit of cogent demonstration'. While admitting that 'new' – i.e. post-Aristotelian – forms of statement and inference have been developed, Fr Thomas stoutly defends the utility, indeed indispensability, of the old 'proemial' logic, a logic of premises and conclusions. Logic helps us not to mistake ejaculations for explanations, intuitions for demonstrations, particular instances for general rules, yet it must not be allowed to run by itself with nothing to bite on, like a racing car with the engine in neutral. 'Logic alone will not provide the sense of reality, nor even the zest for discovery. It has no special message in comparison with living literature, it is like the book of the film of the book.' It is the most extreme of all abstractive procedures whereby we extract some aspect from the world (for a good reason), leaving the concrete whole, which alone fully concerns us, in momentary shadow. Logic is, then, no more and no less what Aristotle called it: *organon*, an instrumental means, not an end.

> One specialized instrument must be limited to one job. General intelligence, it is true, has the quality of being an all-rounder, but this does not come from overloading, but from a strong and flexible central control, the power of co-ordination and adaptation, of seeing the analogies linking apparently disparate things, of resolving the anagrams of reality, of taking logic into dialectic.[23]

Despite the variety of formal objects, all activities are, it is true, at work on the same material object, the 'common stuff worked up and elaborated in different fashions', the world experienced through the senses. And so philosophers, like statesmen, have a duty to keep open the customs posts that mark the frontiers of all the 'sciences', allowing morals, economics, politics, psychology to 'comfort and borrow from one another', while even theology, the sciences' queen, may be corseted into a court code unless 'nourished from humane biology, graced by literature, and tempered by a sense of history'. The Thomist philosophy offers a law that is polite not despotic ordering yet respecting disparate elements. And yet all these recommendations to seek connections must not overthrow the vital principle that each science begins by minding its own business.

Logic's business is not to decide whether final propositions are true but whether they are conclusions. Or better, bearing in mind its instrumental quality, 'Correctness is the form, but truth is the intention'. Logic compares with soda-water, made to a formula; dialectic (concerned with the material logic of content) resembles champagne, irresoluble into all its elements.

To the extent that a quasi-geometrical morphology can be exposed, a mathematical logic can also be exercised, but a humane discipline of experience also calls for a lively dialectic that will give grace and measure to liberal thought, not harsh and crabbed, but 'musical as is Apollo's lute', curling with the ebb and flow of intelligible being.[24]

To grasp that being by thought Fr Thomas commends the 'temperate realism' of Aristotle and St Thomas. The world is a 'pattern of real kinds composed on a common ground and repeated and multiplied in many individuals'. Such *realismus mitigatus* is a true synthesis between nominalism, with its relish for the facts of experience, and ultra-realism, whose universal forms remain constant and certain, though now brought close to the physical-scientific world. Our awareness of the kinds of things there are composes the 'first intentions' of mind, its first readings of the sensuous world, whereas by 'second intentions' our intelligence forms *entes rationis*, 'notional' or 'logical' beings such as genericity and peculiarity which can only exist in the human reason, as conditions of meaning, though they have a remote foundation in reality. In Fr Thomas's preferred example, 'As the Dormouse said to Alice, "You say things are much of a muchness – did you ever see such a thing as a drawing of a muchness?"'.'

It is from our resources in the interlocking worlds of real and logical being that we think: defining objects, making judgments about their relations, and generating conclusions about them through argumentation. Holding that mind is part of natural reality, St Thomas soars above subjectivism, seeing concepts as sympathies, *passiones animae*, in which knower and known become one.[25] 'Through its passion or affection the mind conceives a similitude or likeness. The form is not opaque but transparent; the mind does not stay there, but looks through it to the thing that is signified.' An idea is a beckoning or pointing; more like a non-misleading image than we might think, it is a *sign*. 'By affirming that ideas are natural signs we break out of ourselves and find company' in the world about us. It is the strength of ideas and meanings that they can be communicated – they are 'social and civilized of their nature'. By contrast, images and experience cannot enter fully into psychological commerce; their compensating advantage lies in their personal quality.

Consider the Catholic Church merely as a contemporary organization without ranging to periods that have passed and regions that have been lost: despite the great variety of religious experience, wealth of diverse cultures, gradation of moods and contrasts of individual types, even differences of theological accents, there is a unity in a common dogmatic and disciplinary idea. Sensation and emotions pass away, but thoughts and meanings endure with logic as their bone.[26]

And among these 'thoughts and meanings' the scholastic philosopher pays particular attention to *analogy*. Fr Thomas's account begins from the idea of the 'distributive whole', while unlike the 'collective whole', denotes both all the members of a class *and* each one of them singly. So with distributive ideas:

Some may be applied in exactly the same and unvarying sense to the particulars they comprise, in which case they are called univocal or identical notions; whereas others may be applied according to some resemblance or association, more or less profound, in which case they are called analogical or analogous notions. The degree of the likeness will mark the difference between true and forced analogy.

Such is the interrelatedness of even heterogeneous things that affinities abound.

They start at the level of ordinary idiom, as when we say as right as rain and as fit as a fiddle, or speak of icebergs calving; they state a likeness in such pleasant lines as

Happy convents, bosomed deep in vines,
Where slumber abbots, purple as their wines;

they lie at the heart of poetry, and, what is more to the point, are engaged by the philosopher as soon as he gets past the quasi-mathematic categories of the natural sciences and touches the everlasting myths. They are deep and far-ranging, lively and venerable, promising and variable, beckoning to heaven and recalling to earth.[27]

Based on different 'strengths of being', analogies express the 'sliding rhythms beneath set terms'. The simultaneous continuity and discontinuity of everything in the creation, and of the created with the Creator – who, however, lies beyond *all* categories – this is the foundational principle of natural theology, and analogical thinking serves it well.

But *cui bono*? Whom will this scholastic dialectic serve? Fr Thomas knew that he wrote at a time when the advances of specialisation in the experimental sciences had disturbed the 'universal balance of wisdom' at which the great scholastics aimed. The need for a 'higher directing knowledge', he thought, had never been greater.

The particular sciences offer no deep explanation of our world unless they are taken into a general philosophy; our emptiness, as

well as our precariousness, is displayed unless we match our clev-
erness with a wisdom that will demand contemplation; the mastery
of technique leads to a new and frightful barbarism unless
controlled by a humane philosophy and this can be completed only
by a theology: you are not my brother or sister, or even my neighbour, unless God is our father and lord.[28]

It was to address this need that Fr Thomas produced the second part
of his philosophical diptych, *Phoenix and Turtle*, where he commends
certain conclusions – and not simply methods – of the scholastic
philosophy.

Here the impetus was also naval: a discussion about the meaning of
life with an engineer in the neighbouring bath-tub while sailing in
convoy off the African coast. And the philosophical formulation of
that most comprehensive of all questions turned out to be: 'Is there a
universal operation order, an enduring and fundamental philosophy,
perennial and wider than a provincial episode, ascertainable without
much scholarship about its history?' Or, put in more patriotic style,
and with the implication that the scholastic *philosophia perennis*
continued to provide, in England, a basic framework of reference long
after the Reformation:

> Are they still valid, the ideas we have inherited from Judea,
> Greece, and Rome; the assumptions of the men who built Salisbury
> Cathedral and the Royal Crescent at Bath, who flocked to the *Globe*
> and improved the breeds of English sheep, who marched with
> Marlborough from the Meuse to the Danube, and who blockaded
> the French in Brest through months of winters' gales?[29]

(The last reference was a little unchivalrous, given that Fr Thomas's
inspiration was self-confessedly three Gallic Catholics: Léon Noël,
Jacques Maritain, and the Dominican Marie-Dominique Roland-
Gosselin, professor at Le Saulchoir.)

What Fr Thomas claimed to have found in scholasticism was –
naval metaphors again – a 'general chart'. Warning against indifference to modern developments of knowledge through a misplaced
mediaevalist nostalgia (for that age disappeared when 'the illuminated
manuscripts went flying like butterflies about the streets of
Malmesbury'), he advises recourse to a philosophy that can 'shape
and quicken our thoughts', enabling ordinary men and women to
discern 'meanings that are true without much qualification' on the
basis of 'meditation on the common run of experience'. Such a
general chart will have one virtue in particular that is relevant to our
own times, rather than human time at large. Anticipating the 1950s

debate between C. P. Snow and F. R. Leavis on England's 'two cultures' (scientific and literary), a scholastic philosophy can bridge that gap. 'Unless we are careful the split is now opening out, that schizoid weakness of modern life and thought, when the large and generous conclusions are non-rational and scientific conclusions are pared to points too fine for flesh and blood to feel'. The theoretical validity of the natural sciences cannot be had without some more general science, just as their beneficent application is impossible without good will. That analogy suggests a parallel criticism of the practice of the arts: picking up a theme in the critique of culture in late industrial society found in a different form in Eric Gill and his Dominican supporters, he remarks: 'The arts have been mechanical rather than liberal, and in consequence whole regions of Europe have been devastated, and not only by explosives. Look at the buildings, listen to the music, taste the food.'

Fr Thomas's project – to convince his readers that they both should and can make an approach to 'what is enduringly and impersonally true' is then tested against three objections: first, that to the scientific temper, it is otiose; secondly, that to the poetic temper it is the enemy of vitality and movement; and thirdly, that to the temper of the reasonable man it bites off more than it can chew. He prefaces his defence, however, with a few words of attack. The movement he represents is not without its supporters: originally – and this is a confession which may have embarrassed (but can hardly have surprised) some English Dominicans of the period, its 'political' strength lay in its links with *Action française*. Fr Thomas writes, coyly, 'an *action française*', but there can be little doubt of his meaning. 'Rallying the main tradition of classical thought is the summons to order and the defence of the West, the call to salvage what remains of past European greatness, especially the customs of those parts most affected by Roman rule.'[30] Though by 1950 the papal excommunication of *Action française* for its exploitation of Catholicism in the service of an essentially pagan ideal of order was a dead letter (it had been withdrawn by Pius XII), these words testify to one major source of scholasticism's appeal in the Francophone Europe of the early twentieth century. Since then, Fr Thomas some-what hurriedly adds, the movement's appeal has widened, and includes anti-sentimentalists, opponents of pan-biologism as an explanation of human affairs, those who find property the antidote to slavery, and devotees of the 'cult of symmetry'. And lest we find that too narrowly Conservative an agenda (Fr Thomas admits its special appeal for 'those who travel first-class on the railways'), all of us, no matter which values we place first in political ethics, must admit civilisation's need for a common grammar and code: agreed first principles of pure and practical reason alike.

But back to those objections. To a scientist claiming self-sufficiency for his own discipline, Fr Thomas declares:

> A particular science, though analysing its own proper relationships and permitting confident sweeps in its own medium, has never criticized its own postulates, still less the ambient medium of thought and intelligibility itself, and never can.

Such pretensions to autonomy are nothing but covert professions of the positivist faith. They leave the theoretical constructions of science an inverted pyramid teetering unsteadily on an invisible point. Still, Fr Thomas considers that the positivist challenge does scholasticism good, for a general philosophy, which should be tight-packed with experience, can end up merely 'large but empty' if not ceaselessly fed with facts. To philosophical realists, facts are precious: as things they are 'form-bearers'. And in the course of dealing with this first objection, Fr Thomas introduces that key word of all scholastic metaphysics: *being*. What, he asks, is reality in the raw, antecedent to scientific fact? He answers:

> We might refer to it as x - the unknown quantity, or rather, the unknown before quantity, for even quantity is imagined as extending something ... [But] *being* is a better term than x, more traditional and in its way more modest; it is but the participle of *is* and that to begin with is a more diffident word than *has* and vaguer than any letter of the alphabet.[31]

Yet being is no thin gruel. The notion of it pervades each fact and thought. Nothing can be humanly conceived save as a manifestation of being. Metaphysics is, consequently, humble yet strong: 'like the Rule of St Benedict [is] for those who seek the life of perfection'.

The second objection is launched from the side of the poet. Fr Thomas's strong attraction to aesthetics - and to the imaginative literature at which he tried his hand - ensured that this objection would reach its mark, and sting. He believed that the perennial philosophy could be presented in a way that would engage sensibility at its most deeply felt - however rarely this happened in practice.

> Its truth should be passionately apprehended and imaginatively expounded, and the effect should be of oratory, and perhaps of song. The aspiration of the philosopher is to know the maker and the making; to feel the pulse of being and suffer the *passio entis*; to know, not with the brain alone, but through every cell.

Yet though 'the Idea should be focused with the Images', the philosopher's task remains other than the poet's. He wants to find the most general meaning, even at the cost of seeming to sacrifice penetration to range. Their 'gesture is to everything and their deference to nothing less than to being in each and every manifestation', whether grandiose or humble.

The third objection has to do with humility, and the claim that metaphysicians lack all sense of the essentially limited character of the mind's light. Remembering, no doubt, the Thomistic adage that 'nothing is in the intellect that was not first in the senses', Fr Thomas responds by stressing the materialism of his intellectuality. 'The heart of metaphysics ... beats in unison with sensation; only minds embodied can be metaphysical minds.'

Though the unpretentious titles of the chapters of *Phoenix and Turtle* (after 'The Metaphysical Mood' come some all-important 'Vague Certainties' not to be shaken by 'Bugaboos') might disguise the fact, Fr Thomas's real subject is as austerely ontological – the 'isness of being' – as any treatise by Maritain or (among the non-scholastics) Martin Heidegger. What we have to think about is, first, 'is', and, secondly, 'is not': these are thought's aboriginal counters.

> Being is not an assumption, as will be seen later; the first meaning in the first motions of our mind, it cannot be dislodged. We cannot unthink it; we cannot think without it. We do not find it by sifting the evidence, for it is in all the evidence.[32]

By a meditation on how to approach being, Fr Thomas entices the reader to the affirmation of 'Eternal Mind', not simply as the condition of possibility for thinking, but as conferring the power of existence on whatever is. The conditions of possibility for objects (this way of thinking shows a certain influence of Kant on Fr Thomas's scholasticism, presumably acquired at Louvain, not Hawkesyard) are that, first, objects can be thought of, and, secondly, they can be thought of as able to be. The 'inner coherence of certain objects of thought' makes it appear that, as it were, 'our thoughts have been thought beforehand'.

> Whenever a necessity is discovered we are recalling what already is, a truth not just decided on once upon a time by an intelligence somewhere, an intelligence which has since turned to other matters, but a truth in a supreme intelligence that holds all the forms of our knowledge, past present and to come.[33]

'It's a poor sort of memory that only works backwards', remarked the White Queen in one of Fr Thomas's philosophical texts of predilection,

Alice in Wonderland. But the 'intrinsic coherence of the ideal possible' falls within the 'amplitude of being' – and here we return to the authentic ontological accents of historic scholasticism. The 'First and Transcendental Real' is not the 'topmost and directing part of a multiple scheme' but 'the total cause of everything'.

> In saying that an essence is *an able to be* more is meant than that it is able to be an essence. That would be tautology. What is meant is that it is able to have existence. Essence is an object of knowledge, but existence engages love. These are the two sides of a single created reality: that it can be known and that it can be made. It is an essence because of the divine mind thinking it, an existent because of the divine will crowning it with reality.[34]

'Substances are more ultimate than schemes.' It is, then, to the God who is 'an artist first and an engineer afterwards', that Fr Thomas directs his reader.

Phoenix and Turtle does not leave the reader with a firm hold on the main theses of the *philosophia perennis* in its Thomistic form. Fr Thomas was too taken up with describing the methods of scholasticism – and so, in part, retracing ground already covered in *Barbara Celarent*, as well as defining – in effect, redefining, in more humane terms – its ethos. The principal impression one takes from the book is in fact the humanity, and generosity, of Fr Thomas's epistemology. 'The mind has hearing as well as sight, it should listen to rhetoric while it observes the figures of argument'; the things 'adumbrated in myths may be stronger than the intelligibilities signified by the rational forms': these are typical statements. The technical terms of the scholastic philosophy 'should be treated like notes of music or lines of poetry, able to transport us beyond our powers of criticism'. Few Thomists of his period, or any other, spoke in this vein. Pressed for a justification he would surely reply that 'a dialectic of imagination and sympathy must be applied before existents disclose their lively meaning'. In other words – and here there appears the characteristic emphasis of specifically Maritainian (and, even more acutely, Gilsonian) Neo-Thomism on the priority of ontology over epistemology, being over knowing: the richness of what exists positively calls for such a warm and liberal theory of what it is to know. 'Real substances cannot be neatly fitted into an arrangement of counters'; 'we look for things, not merely for a written voucher'. And the ultimate ground of this fascination with beings in their wondrous actuality is stated by Fr Thomas's favourite 'metaphysical poet', John Donne –

If I should aske the Basiliske, how camest thou by those killing
eyes, he would tell me, Thy God made me so; and if I should aske
the Slowe-worm, how camest thou to be without eyes, he would tell
me, Thy God made me so. The Cedar is no better a glasse to see
God in, than the Hyssope upon the wall; all things that are, are
equally removed from being nothing; and whatsoever hath any
beeing is by that very beeing, a glasse in which we see God, who
is roote, and the fountaine of all beeing.[35]

The mind of St Thomas

For a clue to how Fr Thomas saw the distinctive mind-set of his
sainted namesake, the introductions to his two Aquinas anthologies are
instructive. The philosophical collection contains some happy
comments on the holy doctor's personality. Pointing out that few
major writers have been so niggardly in furnishing biographers with
data, Fr Thomas goes on:

> An impersonal and self-effacing disposition is suggested but not
> much more of his character, except that he was singularly free from
> bad temper in controversy, took an interest in everything, found
> nothing incongruous in the works of nature, and combined an
> immense reverence for his predecessors with an originality eased,
> and perhaps sometimes disguised, by the traditional phrases he
> adopted.

And it fits Fr Thomas's presentation of Thomism as placing abstract
thinking at the service of concrete experience that he concludes:

> The tales of his absent-mindedness testify to his powers of abstrac-
> tion: that he was remote and ineffectual is not confirmed by the
> consultative demands made on him by rulers of Church and State,
> nor by his interests when he lay dying – a treatise on aqueducts, a
> commentary on the *Song of Songs*, and a dish of herrings.[36]

The special value of the two anthologies – explaining no doubt their 80s
reprinting[37] – lies in the fact that texts are quarried not from the two
Summas alone, but from the entire range of Aquinas's work. As Fr
Thomas says, the philosophy of the saint – surprising as this may seem
– is to be sought in, among other places, his mystical and biblical
works.[38] The reason is that Aquinas possessed a 'ranging and commu-
nicative mind', which allows ideas deployed in one realm of thought to
be 'shot through with likenesses from another'. The famous principle
of analogy is not an epistemic instrument for framing general laws, but

stands for 'a complexion of being itself, revealing the kinship in difference of all things ...[39]'. Thanks to the wonderful interconnectedness of
the contents of St Thomas's mind – and the even more marvellous inter-
relations of nature and supernature which those contents reflected, for
him 'natural philosophy is written in the theological scene'. This does
not mean, however, that all attempts to extract a genuine philosophy
from Thomas's corpus are in vain. On the contrary:

> It *is* possible to perform an excision of the purely rational organs
> incorporated in the living unity, and find oneself then faced with a
> prospectus of pure philosophy, coherent, consistent, and as complete
> as can be expected; an independent prolegomenon to belief which
> may be of special, and even urgent, interest to those who find them-
> selves alien to the official organization of Christianity.[40]

But if human nature without grace can be conceived (though in the
historical reality of God's plan it has never, thus autonomously,
existed), grace without human nature is unthinkable. It would be the
Cheshire Cat's smile without its body. For grace – after creation,
God's 'second gift' – is precisely

> the entrance of God's intimate life into human beings, possessing
> them and shaping them to himself, but modified by the conditions
> of their creatureliness. It is their habitual intercourse, largely inar-
> ticulate, in the society of the three Blessed Persons, and as *theirs*
> responds to the nature of human intelligence, human volition,
> human sensation, human emotions, and even human physique.[41]

It was Fr Thomas's conviction that the ethos of Thomism as a theology had been misconstrued. Just because it was 'officially
recommended for the professional training of the officials of Latin
Christianity' – the Western Catholic clergy – who are 'matter-of-fact
rather than romantic', Thomism has been falsely rendered as though
it were a 'legal code'. But in the Summas and, more still, in the *opus-
cula* and commentaries of the authentic St Thomas will be found not
only a rational metaphysic but also a mind open to other modes of
truth – the mythopoeic, the allegoric and the historical. Concentrated
though his intellectual powers were on meaning, nonetheless the exis-
tent, rather than the essence, is for him the primary object that is there
to be understood. And so 'his theology is not a study of how certain
abstract ideas can be inter-related, but the account, furnished to the
believing reason, of God's deeds with men.' Through half a century
of study and teaching, Fr Thomas's conception of Thomism, while
filled with subtlety and nuance in its inner grain, remained impres-
sively rock-like – dare one say 'Petrine'? – in its outer stability. He

never retreated from the position he took in his earliest public work –
a review article on Martin D'Arcy's *Thomas Aquinas*. There, concurring with D'Arcy's distinguishing of St Thomas's rationalism from the
Cartesian absorption in 'clear and distinct ideas', he described
Thomist thought as

> a living synthesis of nature and mind; a metaphysics which is not
> the neat ordering of concepts – the Dutch interior Mr Bertrand
> Russell once took it to be – but a real relation with things; frag-
> mentary and detached by the limitations under which the mind at
> present works, but not on that account untrue; prone, perhaps to
> distort; but always aspiring to that perfect union with all that is real
> in the face to face vision of the Absolute ...[42]

Almost fifty years later he made a (posthumously published) attempt
to convey Thomism in a nutshell:

> The development is continuous from philosophy into a theology that
> is rooted in this world but open to and vivified by the Word of God
> ... It observes a tidal movement of ebb and flow from creatures
> and the Creator. Yet though the world shows forth his glory, and
> Thomism is committed to a demonstrable theism, carefully steering
> its course by the aid of analogy between anthropomorphism and
> agnosticism, or even the old *theologia negativa*, its theology is set
> above all on God for himself, not as the integrator of the
> universe.[43]

And he adds to the commonplace that, for Thomists, grace builds
upon nature the further thought that a major supplementary theme for
the school (especially after the Reformation) is the intrinsic effica-
ciousness of grace:

> Free will is seen as operating within God's universal causality with
> respect to all existence and action from beginning to end, and as
> contributing nothing that is entirely the creature's own except sin
> ... It is noteworthy how unanxious was the spirituality that fed on
> their doctrine of grace, and how full of joyous abandon to the will
> of God. Their moral theology remained comparatively immune
> from the legalisms that dominated the age of casuistry; to be happy
> rather than to be dutiful is man's final purpose, and duty itself is
> more a matter of equity than a code.

A generously conceived Thomism seeps into Fr Thomas's descriptions
of both theology and ethics in the same *Encyclopedic Dictionary of
Religion* from which these citations are drawn. He defines theology at
large as 'the overspill of divine faith into all the levels of human

reasonableness, its wit, humour, poetic imagination, sense of analogy, power of co-ordination, openness to be taught, and search for reason why, whence, how, and what it is all about.' Understandably, then, animals cannot be theologians, 'though occasionally you come across some that wear the air'.[44]

The kind of understanding that should issue from this overflow is

> the insight that comes from affinity, such as is wrought in us by the gifts of the Spirit, understanding, knowledge and wisdom. And this will be supplemented by the theological effort to listen to the resonances in God's creation, to catch glimpses of how things hang together, of taking the truths of faith into 'profane' experience and conversely, of being open-minded and ready to grasp analogies, of being sturdy and spirited about difficulties, in short, of being a person of distinct uncommon sense. Such a discipline will give a synoptic view, rare enough for an individual to attain to, but easier in the team-thinking of the Church.

And on ethics, where he favoured the virtue-centred approach typical of Thomism he spoke of the moral or acquired virtues as the 'City of Reason', opening up a 'measured course for right living in this world, while the supernatural or infused virtues are 'the City of God already present', counted among the endowments of sanctifying grace. And pointing out how neither Aristotle nor the Fathers nor St Thomas had treated them woodenly as screened compartments (for Aristotle prudence unifies them; for the Fathers they interpenetrate; for Aquinas charity quickens them and brings them alike to their goal), he attempts his own brief statement: they are 'like shorthand headings to show the versatility of the good life'.[45] But Fr Thomas's writings on ethics could never stay within naturalistic morals for long. *Homo sapiens* has 'the smell of a race both cursed and blessed beyond the comprehension of a eupeptic humanism'.[46] What he wrote of 'Roman Catholic theology' at large was profoundly true of his own thought:

> Moral good is a teleological notion to start with [i.e. goodness sets up a relation to an end, an intermediate or penultimate end, it may be, itself subordinated to a further or ultimate one], but the treatment soon becomes transmoral or the discourse moves into the dimensions of grace and theological virtues and living in Christ, and the final effect is eschatological rather than ethical.[47]

The virtue of the saints is therefore central to Catholic ethics, for 'the heart of the matter is the depth of the being in love with God and the range of the being in love with the friends of God'.[48]

These articles provide excellent summaries of the spirit in which he approached the thirteen volumes of the bilingual *Summa Theologiae* whose general editorship was his greatest life-work. In the opening volume, crucial for setting the tone of the rest of the series, it will not surprise us that the 'health warning' which prefaces Fr Thomas's appended essays on the very first question of the *Prima Pars* reads:

> Before anatomizing the *Summa* be advised that it composes a living whole pressing forward in a continuous movement which, except for purposes of schematization, should not be arrested in sets of scholastic 'stills' ... Its arguments are less like a progressive series of theorems than like waves merged in the ebb and flow of the tide, the grand Platonic sweep of the whole work which follows the *exitus* and *reditus* of Creation – the going forth of things from God and their coming back to him, the setting out and returning home, the first birth in which we are possessed by God and the second birth from which he is possessed by us. For the *Summa* is more than a great monument to theism: it is the orchestration of the Christian mysteries in perennial reason, in which the God of the philosophers is not pitted against the God of Abraham, Isaac and Jacob, or against the Father revealed in Christ.[49]

In his exposition of the main presuppositions and constituents of Aquinas's account of 'Christian Theology', Fr Thomas covers all the main topics which the historical theologian would expect: the method, style and temper of the *Summa Theologiae*: the concepts of *sacra doctrina*, theology as science (with more than a passing nod to the great French historian of mediaeval theology, Père Marie-Dominique Chenu); revelation, natural-and-supernatural, doctrinal development, the *Summa* and the Bible, the senses of Scripture, biblical inspiration. But more quintessentially Gilbyan is the essay – interposed among this richness – on 'The Dialectic of Love in the *Summa*'.

> Variously inflected according to the context in the *Summa*, the burden is constant that the mind can be loaded with knowledge deeper and wider than the forms represented in clear consciousness and that a reaching out to a thing, *appetitus*, *orexis*, distinct from the intaking movement of cognition, acts as the principal influence in effecting a union of knower and *thing*-known too intimate to be evaluated in rational terms. This perception ... is introduced here because the living discourse of Christian theology moves in the world of grace and depends on a loving intercourse with divine things, so much so that without devotion theology is like the faith from which it starts, which if *without works is dead*.[50]

Fr Thomas took for his own, after this lengthy preamble (the appended essays amount to over one hundred pages), the volumes on *God's Will and Providence*; *Creation, Variety and Evil*; *Purpose and Happiness*; *Psychology of Human Acts*; *Principles or Morality*; *Law and Political Theory*; *Consequences of Faith*; *Prudence*; *Justice*; *Temperance*; and *Well-tempered Passion* – with as something of an afterthought, perhaps, *Holy Communion*.[51] Doubtless the vagaries of a general editorship would explain in part this selection of themes; but not, I think, entirely so. For it also reflects Fr Thomas's abiding sense that the moral life is a most significant part of the life of grace which itself represents God's concrete will for the world; while, by the same token, ethics are mere *disjecta membra* until taken up into the concourse of God's redeeming will for the human species, and the universe of which it is the crown, in Jesus Christ. Thus, on the most 'dogmatic' of all topics he writes:

> Predestination is meaningless if it is not seen as the total inclusive act of redemption, which has a history and which reaches down to each man and by which each is related to the sacrifice of the Cross. As it is revealed in Christ, God is recognised as the One who loves in freedom, and who by his gracious decision invites men to himself in Christ.[52]

And then again, on introducing the Christian ethics of Aquinas:

> It is not until he reaches the virtues that St Thomas begins to get into his stride as a moral theologian, not until he reaches the Gifts and Fruits of the Spirit, the Beatitudes and the Gospel Law that it lengthens, not until he has dwelt on the activities of faith, hope and charity, the greatest of these, and has taken them into our living and dying and rising again with Christ can he be said to be nearing the end of his half-completed course.[53]

A Thomist aesthetics

The sub-title is perhaps too grand. Fr Thomas's aim in *Poetic Experience* – his contribution to the influential Sheed and Ward series *Essays in Order* – is to ask how a more concrete and immediate experience than that given us through *conceptual* understanding is possible. What he calls 'poetic experience' is an affair not only of the artist and the poet but also of the lover and the friend, as well as the devotee of nature. Knowing things by way of a 'process of abstraction and judgement and reasoning' may be the statistically normal way of doing things but it is unsatisfactorily circuitous. And so:

> This essay enquires whether a more direct way of knowing is open to us, and whether real things can be immediately and nobly experienced in themselves, without the go-between of abstraction, representation and argument; whether, in short, we can intimately possess things, not only thoughts about them.[54]

Fr Thomas's interlocutor will be his eponymous namesake, the reason being that Thomas Aquinas, as a philosopher-saint, was not only a thinker but a man in love with reality, and notably its noblest portion, persons. An account of 'Thomist aesthetics' could well be (and perhaps would more naturally be) an ontological kind of enquiry, exploring the ground of the lovable in the pouring forth of being by the Creator. Fr Thomas eschews this approach, however, in favour of a more epistemological search for the contours of a 'field of experience'. His will be an investigation of metaphysical psychology, following from a hunch that 'by grouping some elements of St Thomas's philosophy round the question of immediate and lyrical experience, a convergence will appear, not unfavourable to the claims of the poets.'

The book proceeds by, first, setting out the problem to be addressed – how can the mind directly appropriate some reality? – and, second, resolving it. As we shall see, the resolution Fr Thomas offers lies in following up hints dropped by Aquinas on three apparently disparate topics: the influence of love on knowledge, the soul's immediate consciousness of itself, and the experience of grace.

Fr Thomas's self-set problem is that rational activity, however necessary and in its way admirable, suffers from the vices of its virtues. It is concerned with generalities ('universals'), not particulars; it classifies everything it encounters into types and specimens (whereas in reality it is 'not the form that exists but the composite, which is determined by the form as a certain kind of thing'); its thoughts and notions (though they be considered not as objects of knowledge *per se* but as media in which things are known) are proxies for things, rendering the mind not so much a participator in the life of other realities but their spectator; it fails to satisfy mind, which was made to feed on the substance of things, made 'for Being without reserve'; and lastly it is too much our creation, too fully within our control. It lacks ecstasy. And in all these respects, 'poetic knowledge' – the spellbinding cast by a scene, person, symphony or 'the drive of a yacht in a high wind' (we remember Fr Thomas's nautical enthusiasms) – stands as reason's contrast, as noted already by Plato (*nous* over against *dianoia*), Denys (*pathein* rather than *mathein*), Keats (sensation and thought), the French historian of spirituality and literary theorist Henri Bremond's *moi* as the interiority of *je*, Claudel's *anima,* not *animus*. Last but not least there is St Thomas's *mens*, which is more than *ratio*, and Newman's contrast of the real with the notional. These count for much with Fr Thomas for, if Aquinas is incomparably his most frequently cited source, it is in the perspective of Newman, above all, that the Gilbyan Aquinas is viewed. As the *Grammar of Assent* makes clear, no fusing of abstractions, however numerous, can generate the concrete. But if Newman's epistemology furnishes the interpretative scheme within which Thomas Gilby reads Thomas Aquinas, the hermeneutical traffic is not all one way. Hawkesyard scholasticism admonishes the shade of the Oxford cardinal when we read that 'a distinction should be the occasion of making a complement, not an exclusion, and the philosopher must resist the temptation to deepen the divisions we have just indicated'.[55]

Logic reflects the abidingness of eternity, but grows monotonous. Individual experience echoes eternity's freshness, but does not endure. Taken as reciprocally corrective, they foreshadow a time when mind will enjoy perfect possession without threat of satiety, and novelty without menace of loss. Here Fr Thomas can cite, suggestively, the dictum of the nineteenth-century French Dominican orator Henri-Dominique Lacordaire to the effect that God 'is eternal youth'.

Fr Thomas wants to do justice, with the poets' help, to the 'dear realities of a moment', without abandoning the architectonic power of the metaphysician's structured vision of being at large. In the spirit of Chesterton, he will fight off a 'philosophical prussianism' that would erect a monumental system by clearing away the 'little living things'. For it is the latter knowledge, not the former, that is more divine. According to Aquinas, God 'regards first the individual distinctions of things, not their common denominators'.[56] Just as mystical experience is more than the callow neophyte's 'sensible consolation', so poetic experience may transcend a mere 'gush' of emotion. *Poetic Experience* depends indeed on a sustained analogy between poetic and mystical phenomena, its author recommending to philosophers the same kind of procedures when examining the poets as canonists and theologians use (*mutatis mutandis*) when testing the mystics.

His first step in establishing this analogy is to show how love can affect knowledge. Because the mind 'desires to hold substance immediately and completely, and will not rest until it does', it follows that not a monologue but a dialogue – a 'dialectic' – of both knowledge and love is involved in our encounter with the real. Underlying all mental activity, more primordial than conceptualisation, and more fundamental than all conscious wishing, willing and choice, lies the inborn appetite of mind (as of every power) for its own perfect actualisation. And this means, in mind's case, for perfect union with being. Beauty – to advert momentarily to that key term of aesthetics – is, for Aquinas, that which, on seeing, pleases – but it would be entirely to misconstrue his sense to take this as a question, essentially, of holding our affections. The latter is a consequence, an entailment: the crucial point is that the beautiful quietens the 'primitive craving of mind for the whole real'. The point is confirmed by a consideration of will – appetite as elicited by some good presented through the intellect. Unlike 'natural appetite', the activity of will is always conditioned by the prior state of the understanding. Yet here too we are speaking of a faculty that 'wants the substance rather than the meaning: the thing, not the thought of the thing.'[57] To the intellect, the object is a meaning; to the will it is a magnetic power. This is why love can outstrip knowledge, why a thing can be 'immediately loved though mediately known'.[58] But because mind and will are not two parallel 'tentacles twirling out of the soul', but rather influence and even *contain* one another, a question then arises. Given mind's innate desire for the poetic fact (the concreteness of real being), cannot will do something to bring mind to the concrete in immediate (as distinct from conceptually mediated) recognition?

From Aquinas's philosophico-theological corpus, two types of positive reply are forthcoming. First, the will by its own efficient causality can impel the mind to know. This is not merely a matter of a kick-start: by providing the interest which is knowledge's soul, will's causal power 'not only starts, but sustains and shapes the character of the effect'. And this forces mind to find, so far as it can, the concrete. Or as St Thomas puts it, 'Love may be said to discern, by causing discernment in the reason'.[59] Nor is this all. For, in the second place, love can not only work *upon* knowledge, but work *into* it – thanks to formal or exemplary causality, since this penetrates and transforms the act of knowledge from within. By a passion for the concrete, love redounds on mind, engendering in it not so much the rational judgment which is intellect's native act as a knowledge by affinity or sympathy. Thus a lover of a virtue may know the scope of that virtue not by ethical thinking so much as by a profound connaturality with the virtue in question. Fr Thomas points out, however, that with few exceptions of whom the great eighteenth-century Spanish divine John of St Thomas is chief, Thomists have failed to develop this point – except where, as in mysticism, its possible exemplifications are sacred, not secular. Newman, without a formal scholastic training, took John's point: some things are not so much learnt as *grown into*. And Fr Thomas defends himself from possible criticism on the point by high-and-dry Thomists:

Grace builds on nature, and its activities imitate and complete natural processes. Is it extravagant, then, to look for a natural closeness of experience which is prolonged and uplifted by grace into the mystical experience? The supernatural life of man has not a complete and separate existence of its own apart from nature, and it is right to expect a natural correlative even to the highest activities of grace. The theologians assume as much by attempting to expose the psychological structure of mystical acts.[60]

And in any case, just as for *Gestalt* psychology, the object to which one reacts is always a concrete whole, so for St Thomas the principle that does the acting *vis-à-vis* any object is neither mind nor will taken by themselves but the complete substance.[61]

The second building-block for a 'metaphysical psychology of the concrete' which Fr Thomas draws from the tradition of the schools is St Thomas's doctrine of the reflexivity or self-consciousness of mind. Though St Thomas is Aristotelean in his account of how we know the world around us by the searching intellect working through the life of the senses, he is Platonist in his epistemology of our inner awareness. When a spiritual reality becomes immediately present to mind, its quasi-presence through concepts is superfluous. But this is precisely what happens with our own self-consciousness.

The mind is not inert in the order of knowledge, it is charged with itself, and only awaits release in order to be aware of itself. This release is produced by its activity, 'the mind knows itself in its action', and notably, in its movements of love.[62]

The soul is always 'borne in mind' in a way that other things are not. Corresponding to such immediate self-knowledge is a cognate love of self by the soul, and love and knowledge here fuse, providing us with 'an urgent sense of the existence of a present and personal reality, a possession which doubles the soul's real identity with itself.' What has this to do with aesthetics? Simply this, that it shows *mens* rather than *ratio* in action, and furnishes an *analogy* for other possible forms of concrete knowledge.

Thirdly, Fr Thomas considers Aquinas's account of mystical experience, and asks whether this may not point to the possibility of what he has called 'the poetic experience' likewise. The angelic doctor's guiding principle is that whatever is in the mind really (*per essentiam*) and not merely by way of representation (*per similitudinem*) may be immediately experienced; it is known – in Fr Thomas's rendering of Platonist and Augustinian vocabulary – 'memoratively', by a habitual intellectual holding. By his causal power as our Creator God is already present in every creature at the springs of its being, but by grace he becomes present to rational creatures elected by him in a more intimate way which Gregory the great terms a presence 'by hospitality'. 'The soul turns to God in welcome, knowing and loving him through his effects within it.' Now this interrelation of God and man in grace is habitual, which means, *inter alia*, that it need not be explicitly recognised. The life of grace can unfold without much in the way of conscious experience. However, and conformably to the general position of the Dominican school, Fr Thomas holds that some such experience – and hence a mystical knowledge of God – is to be expected, given at any rate what he calls (somewhat vaguely, it is true) a 'favourable situation' as well as the working of the gifts of the Holy Spirit, those endowments, given *in nuce* in confirmation which facilitate the co-operation of the faculties of the baptised person in welcoming the divine Guest. Here God is known by 'sympathy': the mind does not so much *reflect* divine truths as *live* them.

Here then the presence of God, causing in the receptive soul a desire for himself, leading to a recognition of his relation with it appears to exhibit what we can describe as a 'structural isomorphism' with that other case Fr Thomas has investigated: the self-presence of mind to itself which, through activity, issues in self-awareness. This may be our clue, then, to concrete knowledge at large – and so to the poetic experience.

For an account, at once explanatory and descriptive, of poetic experience requires three things: positing some kind of 'immediate presence of the concrete real' to the mind; setting forth the nature of the 'activity which awakens the consciousness of that presence', and suggesting the 'characteristics of the [poetic] experience' itself, both through *de*duction from the nature of the activity and by *in*duction from what poets themselves have said.

But just these three stages are what analysis of self-consciousness and mystical knowledge disclose. Corresponding to the stage of *presence* 'we have seen how the concrete may be joined to the mind at the beginning of knowledge, the individual thing not indeed regarded as a particular determination in space-time, but as a substance'. And with the stage thus ready, the poetic experience can be triggered by a 'visitation' – whether this be divine, angelic (demonic) or simply the result of a 'happy combination of circumstances releasing the pent-up sensibility of the mind', may be left an open question. In the third stage, the mind thus made alert experiences poetically – and here Fr Thomas can only adopt the lyrical mode.

The mind is obscurely but irresistibly made aware of the concrete real with which it is charged. The beauty of some particular object – a poem, a passage in Bruckner, seas and skies, some human grace – pierces the entanglements of appearances and holds the mind's raptured and complete attention. Every resource is brought into play: the natural appetite for a physical union, the will's desire for the individual impelling the mind to a closer possession and inform-ing it with a deeper realization, the fusion of mind and sense to perceive the singleness and wholeness of a splendid particular. There is no sense of distance or separation from the thing, such as attends purely conceptual knowledge. All the activities of the self are loosed in enjoyment, unanimous in a single activity which breaks through the framework of aspects enclosing our ordinary rational activity, and which experiences for a moment or longer a reality that is really possessed. Now is the mind most alive, and at peace; the thing is present, held and delighted in.[63]

Hence the particularity of the poetic experience: which incidentally, explains its resistance to re-expression in terms of philosphical repre-sentation at large; hence, too, its sense of the concrete – so much more difficult a notion than the abstract, for the concrete 'is more than the sum of its parts – impossible to bare its individuality by the dissec-tions of reason and tabulate its constituents' and hence, finally, its closeness. If conceptual knowledge requires a certain strategic distance, thus allowing us to survey a range of relevant materials, in poetic experience the maxim 'Draw [an object] close and it becomes blurred' loses its validity.

And so Fr Thomas's conclusion is:

There is this likeness between poetry and prayer, that just as infused contemplation cannot be reduced to the regimen of an ascetical life, so also the poetic experience cannot be reduced to the mental training. The effect is greater than the cause.[64]

The poet Elizabeth Jennings seized on this point in her account of *Poetic Experience*. She concluded from Fr Thomas's book that, within the 'learned fabric of Aquinas's thought', he had revealed the meeting-point of poetry and prayer.

He has given poetry a central and high place in human experience; he has shown how its moments of revelation are not simply amazing flashes out of darkness but are, on the contrary, the whole of man transcribing or responding to the most important function of life – knowing by loving and loving by knowing, grasping the whole of an experience, not to possess but to be possessed, using the senses and emotions not denying them, releasing the mind from cold abstractions to free it for direct and close knowledge. This is the mystic's achievement and the poet's vocation.[65]

A Thomist politics

Fr Thomas's chief forays into the realm of Thomistic political theory take a rather different, but by no means incompatible, line from that essayed by Fr Gerald. Gilby had declared of his namesake:

St Thomas wrote in Latin, but delicate rounded apprehensions and supple turns of argument move beneath his curt and repetitive style, angular like his pointed Gothic script. The idiom of his thought is Greek; sometimes it almost sings. His discourse is a rhythmic response to things striving to ends, rather than gravely resting in their appointed places.[66]

Fr Thomas's aim was to draw out this underlying 'supple' intellectual melody in the clipped scholastic prose. Some might feel that the laudable desire to acquit St Thomas of a rigorist aridity in thought and expression tempted him to exaggerate the difference between the appearance of the text and the reality of the ideas. Writing impressionistically, as he often does, about the text in its context, we take away more readily the genial impression than the actual public doctrine – though the main lines of the latter are certainly there to be found in the two major studies, *Between Community and Society*, and *Principality and Polity*.[67]

It may surprise the later reader that in the pair of terms crucial to Fr Thomas's first politological study, 'community' has primitivist, and, to a degree, negative connotations whereas those of 'society' are chiefly eschatological, and overwhelmingly positive. The State, or what in non-Gilbyan parlance would be deemed 'civil society' – St Thomas's *civitas* or *regnum* – falls 'between' these two. 'Political science is the study of civilized styles of living together, which do not emerge until after the stage, studied by *scientia œconomica*, when the human mass is still a cluster of family and tribal groups.'[68] 'Community' is the group-life investigated by ethnology, social anthropology, and psychology, cultural history and comparative religion; vital though it may be as the material matrix of civilisation it remains too immured within the biological, and hence the forced, to be a suitable sobriquet for the humane city. At the other end of the spectrum of the human ascent through ever deepening and widening forms of consciousness and freedom lies 'society' – the spiritual association of those destined, by nature and grace, to be to each other eternal companions. Such spiritual friendship is realized through the *magnum sacramentum* of Christ and his Church, and lies beyond the politological, in the realm of theology proper.[69] And yet the metaphor of the spectrum misleads, for in Fr Thomas's presentation, pure community and pure society are themselves abstractions, for human beings 'can never be so consolidated' (in the communitarian mass) that they 'cannot be dispersed', nor are they ever so subtilized' (by spiritual society) that 'material processes cannot move them'.

> The pure community, or City of Force, and the pure society, or City of Freedom, are not, therefore, separable as complete human situations; a man is not to be mistaken, from excess of science, for a speciment of a pure community member, nor, from a deficiency of science, for a person unique and away on his own ... The human community ascends to the conditions of the human society through political institutions: the life of the spiritual society flows back into the depths of the material community.[70]

The ever-moving spiral reproduces in miniature the life of the individual, 'merged in nature through lust and death, yet promised an eternal partaking through the deeds of his flesh'[71] There is, then, distinction but not separation: a capitally Thomist point.

In the State, neither the appetites issuing from community nor the aspirations towards spiritual society receive a free rein; rather are they yoked together by discipline, both legal and political. Both, then are present, and active – 'just as unconscious knowledge and ecstasy are latent in rational discourse, even in mathematics'.[72] It behoves the State not to separate them too drastically, on pain of the common people ceasing to be at home in the civil order, on the one side, and the élite feeling no cause for pride on the other. It is, in Fr Thomas's view, a strength of Aquinas's approach to the philosophy of the *polis* that it would hold both ends of the chain: for the material cause of the State is the instinctual group, joined by local loyalties, while its final cause lies in promoting the life of friendship, and hence in a communion which adumbrates the City of God. Liberal humanism between, say, the 1840s and the 1920s, was so (temporarily) successful that it scarcely needed to speculate about the prior conditions and further implications of political flourishing; but now this sort of fuller analysis is needed. And the main reason for the new urgency – apart from considerations of the defective ideologies abroad – would seem to be a collapse of social cohesion.

The grace of original righteousness, with which human nature was

Bede Jarrett

Victor White

Gerald Vann

Thomas Gilby

Sebastian Bullough

Gervase Mathew (right), with David Mathew (centre)

Kenelm Foster

Conrad Pepler

created, was bestowed to brace compounds of mind and matter that
tended to disintegrate, not from the weakness and poverty, but from
the strength and richness of their parts. If organisms contain cells
that strain to go pirating away on their own, then clusters formed
by human beings living in communities will be no more compact,
for they are larger and looser, and their elements are dogged
centres of self-interest.[73]

If the Americanisation of culture, and what would later be called
'consumer materialism', are bogus ways of generating such coherence, then Fr Thomas hoped that the application of 'social conceptions
formed from widely differing traditions in the thirteenth century by a
philosophy distrustful of clumsy alternatives' would, in mediating
between 'functional duties and personal rights', hit the mark.

In point of fact, the account of the origins of the conceptual build-
ing-blocks of St Thomas's political theory in *Between Community and
Society* is not only discursive but diffuse. (It would be of little use to
an undergraduate student of the history of political thought.)
Summarised in the introduction to the work, the sources only receive
sustained attention in its sequel *Principality and Polity*. There the four
influences at work – Augustinian theologians, Roman law, mediaeval
culture, and Aristotelean philosophy – are laid out with much greater
system and a fuller scholarly apparatus. The provision of a synopsis,
not merely for the discussion of such materials, but for Fr Thomas's
explanation of what Aquinas did with them, helps the student to
understand where the text is taking him – particularly necessary as the
slightly confusing typographical practice of giving each page, and not
simply each chapter, its own subject-heading, is carried through from
the first volume to the second. *Principality and Polity* strikes the
reader as lucid and well-organised, but it lacks its predecessor's mean-
dering charm.

Essentially, it treats St Thomas's politology as the classical statement of the developed form of his own sources; and in so doing
Principality and Polity explains the genesis of Fr Thomas's own ideas
in *Between Community and Society*, for these are a representation of
what he considered Aquinas's most genial intuitions.

For Fr Thomas the good State is not so much the just State as the
civilised State; or rather, the concept of justice must be entertained in
so wide-ranging a sense (that which is, in a variety of ways, 'due') that
it comes to coincide with the notion of civilisation itself. Like the well-
tempered family, the healthy State will combine respect for distinct
personalities with the 'warmth of merging and belonging', thus producing 'a mingling of freedom and dependence, of adventure and security,

of private enterprise and common guarantees'. A number of factors come together in the happy political community. First, since the best law is custom enforced (rather than governmental edict), *tradition* is of vital importance, not least in advanced societies.

> Well-established authority ... will hesitate to displace ancient and immemorial customs by new-fangled regulations, or to substitute for old ways a brand-new constitution, tested by frequent plebiscite, after the fashion of nineteenth-century liberal revolutionaries. For one reason, nature as manifested in custom is freer, more flexible, and adaptive to circumstances than are such rigid artifices of law; for another, in politics, as in music, painting, and architecture, style possesses little lasting vitality when it offers pure form. Neither civic good sense nor social justice alone can produce loyal and devoted attachment.[74]

Secondly, the fortunate State is one in which individuals are readily disposed to enter into *amicitia utilis* – agreements with strangers to the family group by which, despite the lack of kinship bond, they consider themselves bound. The historian of mediaeval society Paul Vinogradoff regarded the history of *contract* as the greatest contribution of town life to the development of law.[75] Just so the typical political man of St Thomas's writings is the *civis*, for that fuller community of the *bourg* with its fairs and markets, and later the mercantile cities, has, through voluntary association, special opportunties for practising civility. Aquinas did not regard the State as an artificial concern, originating in such contract, as though it were a firm for trading, and yet he considered that a shared *jus* implies the distinction and independence of persons – and to that extent a multiplicity of free associations, generating a certain pluralism within its unity.

Thirdly, then, a well-organised State will manifest partnership and co-operation, an over-organised one the abrogation of individual responsibility. For the State is 'the entire human commonwealth' – not just the legal organ of government, much less (in the modern context) the 'party which has captured it'.[76]

> The political man, the typical citizen, in whom should meet influences from below through the archaic symbols of his race, and influences from above through the commands of a heavenly society, may become fixed in isolation between the two, rootless and hopeless, neither an animal nor a spirit, but a complex of conventions, a creature of the State, a man without country on earth or in heaven, a displaced person, his rights precarious, never loved just

as he stands, but docketed under a number and expended on some scheme. [77]

Co-operation entailed agreed reasonableness in social life; the *senior pars* was more weighty than the mere numerical majority. Fr Thomas found the colleges of the *Studium*, that new 'third estate' of thirteenth-century Christendom, to be its exemplars.

Fourthly, the flourishing State requires some form of clerisy, and, linked with this, the intelligent apprehension of an objective order of things. A 'body of clerks' must attempt to set out fundamental laws, as revealed by God or discovered by reason, in a consistent system of obligations and duties: its significance will lie, in good measure, in the setting of bounds to what government may do. The difference between tyrant and king turns on the question for respect for *law*:

> Positive and purely political law has its proper independence, yet without operating in an enclave: all the sciences should mingle together, and so should the arts; in law, the eternal runs into the provisional, and positive law applies the lasting natural law to works of the statesman's art. Obviously to such a theory law is a more comprehensive concept than it is to modern specialist legalism, to which law is the command of the human sovereign and an 'unjust law' a contradiction in terms.

To the State confidence is more necessary than obedience; and rulers will be trusted if they respect standards not of their devising. Wippo's proverb, *legem servare, hoc est regnare*, expressed the authentically constitutional spirit of early mediaeval government, despite the lack of formal constitutions, measuring all the acts of the legislative and executive powers. Certainly St Thomas in his *de regimine principum*, was far from admiring paternal absolutism. Unlike Fr Gerald, Fr Thomas, if asked to choose between Country and Court Party, would opt for the Whig.

> Altogether there are good grounds for calling St Thomas the first Whig, if a Whig is a man who believes that social and political life should be run according to a reasonable constitution, and who reserves to himself the right of deciding to break it in cases where the ordinary rules do not apply.

In actual fact, it is difficult to 'place' Thomas Aquinas in terms of the debates of Stuart England, because, in company with his contemporaries at large, he gave little thought to the question of how rightful political authority is set up. As Fr Thomas himself points out, Aquinas was less concerned with the political form of the constitution than with the need to safeguard the common good. The question of who is the *publica persona* in whom the State subsists impersonate, and what is his constitutional warrant, does not appear to have exercised him.[78] Enough to know that the tacit consent of the people is required. Despite his lack of enthusiasm for the canonists, he would have found in their company (rather than among the civilian lawyers) some upholders of the view that the people's concession of power to the prince may, in extreme circumstances, be revoked – and Fr Thomas liked to think that Aquinas's teaching on the force of custom among a free people, with its implication of 'an aboriginal and active right in the community taken as a whole', had inclined him to share their view.

His discussion ends on a characteristic note: the correspondence between a Spanish priest-theologian and Admiral Collingwood, then commanding the British fleet in the Mediterranean, after Napoleon's kidnap of the king of Spain and his heir, the prince of the Asturias, and their removal from the country. Collingwood had supported the priest:

> If, by taking the Spanish Princes out of the country, Buonaparte thought he has dissolved the only power which could lawfully oppose him, he was mistaken; for on the removal of the Princes, the sovereign power reverted to the source from which it sprung – the people; and the act of their delegates is legitimate sovereignty.[79]

It was a pity that Fr Thomas's ruminations on the conditions and spirit of a humane social order, furnished with decent political forms and conducive to the flourishing of many virtues, were rather lost to view in the wave of enthusiasm for Marxian socialism characteristic of the avant-garde of the English Dominicans between the Second Vatican Council and the general collapse of Marxism as an intellectual force in the late 1980s. But perhaps they may yet see their day.

The novel *Up the Green River* may be taken as a diverting footnote to Fr Thomas's thoughts on the human city. The young priest who is its protagonist, an Irishman born of 'Castle Catholics' and trained in Spain but working as a missioner in a diocese of the English Midlands in the 1850s, broods on his lot as pastor in a smokey town of the late Industrial Revolution.

> What was he doing? In effect it amounted to giving the last sacraments – preparing human beings to leave this world for another hereafter, trying to keep alive within them a private life on the margin of an industrialism to which they did not belong, but which gave them money but little pride of vocation. Surely they could

enjoy a better world now, surely the temporal should not repel but merge into the eternal.[80]

By a chain of events not always easy to follow, the 'Revd Richard French' leads a motley group of his Anglo-Irish parishioners to settle in a South American territory needing population for its development. Enclosed by a loop of the 'Rio Verde', wedged between the 'Republic of Liberadoria' and the 'Empire of New Algarves', it would appear to be a lightly fictionalised Oriental Republic del Uruguay – as that small State was known in English at the period in which the novel is set.[81] Its consul general, writing to Lord Clarendon in his capacity as Lord-Lieutenant of Ireland in 1849 to appeal for subjects of the British Crown as settlers there, had in fact described it as virtually uninhabited, and yet so attractive that:

> it, as well as the countries beyond it, which have been visited by the officers of Her Majesty's Navy, have been the constant subject of their wonder, their admiration and their praise. My Lord, there is not an admiral, a commodore, nor a captain in her Majesty's service who has been in these countries to whom I do not refer you, perfectly confident that they will bear out my assertion, when I declare that in climate as in soil, they may be regarded as the very finest portions of the globe.[82]

And the *Dublin Review*, in reporting the four-year 'Siege of Monte Video' to which the territorial claims of Argentina had led, expressed its own opinion that the 'affairs of the River Plate' should be better known in the United Kingdom of Britain and Ireland. 'To all who are seeking the solution of the question, 'Which is the most desirable place for emigration', it [the question of Uruguay] is one of vital, nay, of transcendental importance.' The editor of the *Liverpool Times*, Thomas Baines, had indeed already proposed the region as a desirable haven for the excess population of the swollen industrial cities in 1845.[83] The narrative of the emigration in Fr Thomas's novelistic form enables him to indulge his pleasure in everything connected with 'messing about in boats', and also to poke a good deal of fun at the spectacle of political theory and practice unencumbered by the virtue of *prudentia* – as found among the warring parties of the Exalted Progressists and Radical Revolutionaries. Not that the Clerical Conservatives appeared to engage his affections either, and one is left supposing that the authorial voice, in its descriptions of the abortive expedition, supported rather the Liberal Reformists, though these were

not a large and influential party, being composed of men from the middle-class inspired by the doctrines of the Enlightenment, who were disliked by the Right because they were not gentlemen and desired to curtail clerical privilege, and by the Left because they believed in the responsibilities and rights of property. Fray Felipe shrugged. 'They are our Whigs, but then, you see, there are not enough of them unfortunately.'[84]

Had Fr Thomas known more of the world of Germanophone Catholicism, its literature and scholarship, he would have been able to point out that the European Enlightenment of the eighteenth century was not always the enemy of the Catholic Church. As it was, he had to remain content to interpret Thomist social philosophy by reference to his own distinctly Augustan temperament. The virtues of civility, he thought, were often conspicuous by their absence in the representatives of more showy philosophies, of Left or Right. As I recall, he once remarked at Blackfriars Cambridge, in a sermon for children, 'Kingfishers are beautiful birds; but they foul their nests'.

An unrepentant Thomist

Fr Thomas lived to see Thomism go out of fashion in Catholic divinity, but did not survive quite to the point of its incipient return to favour. He remained unrepentant. In letters to Fr Kenelm Foster (on whom more anon), in the turbulent year, for both Church and State, of 1968, he declared that 'current theology is suffering from adolescent pimples ... Some of the new is awfully shoddy',[85] and ascribed a good deal of the 'intellectual rebellion' against authority among the clerics to 'an ill-repressed Oedipus Complex'.[86] In the more reflective context of his contributions to the *Encyclopaedic Dictionary of Religion* he wrote:

What is sometimes called liberalism among contemporary Catholic theologians to some extent re-enacts the crisis that faced the Reformation churches, particularly in Germany, nearly a century ago and shook their philosophism, pietism and revivalism. It may be considered as part of the backwash of the Modernist movement, or as among the results of biblical criticism not easily reconcilable in detail with old securities, or as a reaction against Hellenic rationalism and Roman rationalism which perpetuate a somewhat facile antithesis of law and liberty, or as an accompaniment to the specialization and decentralization of the religious sciences, or as a heightened emphasis on the command to love coupled with lessened attention to the full range of particular demands which love may make, or as a disposition to be content with intellectual agnosticism, or as a prophetic and charismatic response to a kerygma that ventures out into an unknown outside our control and unratified by authority.[87]

If so, Fr Thomas found it 'romantic and radical' rather than 'classical and whig'. Fr Conrad Pepler wrote of him in a memoir of 1975:

> In his early years Fr Thomas had been regarded by many as a dangerous 'innovator' who used the great Doctor of the Church as a tool to unbalance the seating of the stony traditionalists. He was certainly a progressive, as for example in his teaching on marital ethics and his guarded acceptance of the 'Safe Period'. But for a number of years before his death, with his staunch adherence to St Thomas he had been very much of a traditionalist – at least in the eyes of those who had reduced St Thomas to being one among many from his previous position, in the Order at least, as one above many. Fr Thomas himself was, I would say, always a progressive in the sense that his lively and enquiring mind was always developing from the principles he had established in his earlier studies. But he remained a Thomist and so faithful to the Dominican tradition in which we were all reared.[88]

Notes

1. See the references to him in T. Burns, *The Use of Memory, Publishing and Further Pursuits* (London: Sheed and Ward, 1993), pp. 63, 141.
2. *Britain at Arms. A Scrapbook from Queen Anne to the Present Day* (London: Eyre and Spottiswoode, 1953).
3. *Barbara Celarent. A Description of Scholastic Dialectic* (London: Longmans, Green and Co., 1953).
4. *Phoenix and Turtle. The Unity of Knowing and Being* (London: Longmans, Green and Co., 1950).
5. *Poetic Experience. An Introduction to Thomist Aesthetic* (London: Sheed and Ward 1934).
6. *St Thomas Aquinas: Philosophical Texts* (Oxford: Oxford University Press, 1951); *St Thomas Aquinas: Theological Texts* (Oxford: Oxford University Press, 1955).
7. *Between Community and Society* (London: Longmans, Green and Co., 1953); *Principality and Polity* (London: Longmans, Green and Co., 1958).
8. *Up the Green River. A Novel* (London: Eyre and Spottiswoode, 1955).
9. D. W. Hudson and D. W. Moran (eds.), *The Future of Thomism* (Notre Dame, Indiana: 1992). The Jesuit historian of Thomism, G. A. McCool, in a prefatory summary, concludes that with the displacement

of Descartes and Kant from centrality in philosophy at large, the main cause of the 'schism' between Gilson's 'pure' Thomism and the revisionist 'transcendental' Thomism of Maréchal is overcome, as also that, in the less theologico-phobic atmosphere of much modern philosophy the connection of Thomas's philosophy with his theology is no longer a bugbear.

10. 'T. G. Wayne', *Morals and Marriage* (London; Longmans, Green and Co., 1936, reprinted 1952.)
11. 'The Encyclical Abstraction', *New Blackfriars* 50. 582 (1966), pp. 94–102.
12. 'Pleasure-extract', Blackfriars XII. 135 (1931), p. 603.
13. Ibid., p. 606.
14. *Morals and Marriage*, p. x.
15. L. J. Latz, *A Discussion of the Physiological, Practical and Ethical Aspects of the Discoveries of Drs. K. Ogino (Japan) and H. Knaus (Austria) Regarding the Periods when Conception is Possible and when Impossible* (Chicago, Latz Foundation, n.d.), itself discussed in Fr Thomas's 'Natural Birth Control', *Blackfriars* XIV. 155 (1933), pp. 128–35.
16. *Morals and Marriage*, p. 54.
17. 'The Encyclical Abstraction', p. 97.
18. After a quarter-century, the well-foundedness of his position is more apparent; see e.g. J. E. Smith, *Humanae Vitae. A Generation Later* (Washington: Catholic University of America Press, 1991).
19. *Barbara Celarent*. p. ix.
20. H. Rahner, *Man at Play* (ET London: Burns and Oates, 1965).
21. *De hebdomadibus*, prologue; cf. Wisdom.
22. Ibid., p. 3, citing *Summa Theologiae* 2a 2ae, q. 114, a. 2, and q. 109, a. 3.
23. Ibid., p. 18.
24. Ibid., p. 33.
25. Ibid., p. 50, with reference to Aquinas's commentaries on Aristotle's *De anima* and his *Peri hermeneias*.
26. Ibid., p. 61.
27. Ibid., pp. 81–82.
28. Ibid., p. 250.
29. *Phoenix and Turtle. The Unity of Knowing and Being*, p. x.
30. Ibid., p. 8. Cf. A. Laudouze, O. P., *Dominicains français et Action Française 1899–1940. Maurras au couvent* (Paris: Editions ouvrières, 1989).
31. Ibid., p. 13.
32. Ibid., p. 23.
33. Ibid., p. 143.
34. Ibid., p. 145.
35. Cited ibid., pp. 24–25.
36. 'Introduction', *St Thomas Aquinas. Philosophical Texts*, p. xiii.
37. By the Labyrinth Press, Durham, North Carolina, 1982.

38. 'Preface', *St Thomas Aquinas. Philosophical Texts*, p. v.
39. 'Introduction' in ibid., p. xx.
40. Ibid., p. xxi. Italics added.
41. 'Introduction', *St Thomas Aquinas. Theological Texts*, p. xi. Italics original.
42. 'Father D'Arcy's St Thomas Aquinas', *Blackfriars* XI. 129 (1930), pp. 761–62.
43. 'Thomism', in P. K. Meagher, O. P.; T. C. O'Brien, and C. M. Aherne, S. S. J. (eds.) *Encyclopedic Dictionary of Religion, O – Z* (Washington: Corpus Publications, 1979), pp. 3253–54.
44. 'Theology', in ibid., pp. 3497–99.
45. Virtue, in *Encylopedic Dictionary of Religion, O – Z* , pp. 3679–80.
46. 'Guilt', in ibid., *A – E*, pp. 1585–86.
47. 'Good', in ibid., pp. 1521–22. The same article points that whereas a mere means to an end is only *bonum utile*, useful good, any genuine end, albeit subordinate, is *bonum honestum*, a value, something of objective worth, and *bonum delectabile*, a delight, which gives subjective fulfilment. The distinction is between the good in itself and the good as enjoyed.
48. 'Heroic Virtue', ibid., *F – N*, pp. 1655–66.
49. 'Structure of the *Summa*', in St Thomas Aquinas, *Summa Theologiae. Volume I, Christian Theology, Ia. 1* (London: Eyre and Spottiswoode, 1963), p. 43.
50. 'The Dialectic of Love in the *Summa*', in ibid., p. 124, with an internal citation of James 2.17.
51. These constituted, of the series cited above, respectively; volumes V; VIII; XVI; XVII; XVIII; XXVII; XXXII; XXXV; XXXVII; XLIII; XLIV; XLIX, published between 1966 and 1975.
52. 'Introduction', *St Thomas Aquinas, Summa Theologiae. Volume 5, God's Will and Providence, Ia. 19–26* (London: Eyre and Spottiswoode 1966), p. xxiv.
53. 'Introduction', *St Thomas Aquinas, Summa Theologiae. Volume 18, Principles of Morality, Ia. Iiae., 18–21* (London: Eyre and Spottiswoode, 1965), p. xxi.
54. *Poetic Experience. An Introduction to Thomist Aesthetic*, pp. 1–2.
55. Ibid., p. 12.
56. Ibid., p. 15, with reference to *Summa Contra Gentiles*, III, 63, and *Summa Theologiae*, Ia, q. 47, a. 1.
57. Ibid., p. 34. Cf St Thomas's *Quaestiones disputatae de Veritate*, 22, 12: 'The will is taken up with things as they are in themselves, the intellect with them as they are in a spiritual manner in the soul.'
58. Idem., *Quaestiones de Caritate*, 2, ad 12.
59. *Summa Theologiae*, IIa IIae, q. 47, 1, ad i.
60. *Poetic Experience*, p. 44. Fr Thomas is thinking here of such works as Père Ambroise Gardeil O. P.'s *La structure de l'Ame et l'expérience mystique* (Paris: Librairie Victor Lecoffre, 1927).
61. *Poetic Experience*, pp. 46–51.

62. Ibid., p. 53, with an internal citation of *Summa Theologiae* Ia, q. 87, art. 1, ad i.
63. Ibid., pp. 78–79.
64. Ibid. pp. 92–93.
65. E. Jennings, 'Voices of Explanation', in idem., *Every Changing Shape* (London: André Deutsch, 1961), p. 215.
66. *Between Community and Society. A Philosophy and Theology of the State*, p. 62.
67. *Between Community and Society*, and *Principality and Polity. Aquinas and the rise of State Theory in the West*.
68. *Between Community and Society*, p. 75, with reference to Summa Theologiae, IIa IIae, q. 47, a. 1 and q. 50, a. 3.
69. 'The social philosophy of the Middle Ages was overshadowed by a theology of the Last Things, *de novissimis*, and so, in studying it, we may be like Maine de Biran, who began with Condillac and ended with the Gospel of St John', ibid. p. 78.
70. Ibid., pp. 78–9.
71. Ibid., p. 79; see Gilby, 'The Genesis of Guilt', *Proceedings of the International Congress on Mental Health* (London: 1948).
72. *Between Community and Society*, p. 91.
73. Ibid., p. 1.
74. Ibid., p. 240.
75. P. Vinogradoff, 'Customary Law', in *The Legacy of the Middle Ages* (Oxford: Oxford University Press, 1938), p. 311.
76. *Between Community and Society*, p. 246.
77. Ibid., p. 246.
78. Ibid., p. 277. The prince '*curam populi habet et eius personam gerit*', IIae, q. 90, a. 3, ad ii.
79. G. L. N. Collingwood, *A Selection from the Private and Public Correspondence of Vice-Admiral Lord Collingwood* (London: James Ridgway, 1824), p. 433.
80. *Up the Green River* (London: Eyre and Spottiswoode, 1955), p. 45.
81. The book's frontispiece declares 'This story is not entirely unfounded on fact.'
82. Cited in 'The Siege of Monte Video', *Dublin Review* XXVI (1849), pp. 35–59.
83. T. Baines, *Observations on the Present State of the Affairs of the River Plate* (Liverpool; Times, 1845).
84. *Up the Green River*, p. 191. I am grateful to George Every of Oscott College, Birmingham, for help in making the identification of 'Aranda of the Conquerors'.
85. Letter of 1.4.1968, English Dominican Archives.
86. Letter of 28.1.1968, English Dominican Archives.
87. 'Liberal Theology', in P. K. Meagher, O. P., T. C. O'Brien, and C. M. Aherene, S. S. J., (eds.) *Encyclopedic Dictionary of Religion*, F–N, (Washington; Corpus Publications, 1979), pp. 2114–16.
88. C. Pepler, O. P., 'Memoir' for 1975, English Dominican Archives.

Works by Thomas Gilby

'Father D'Arcy's St Thomas Aquinas', *Blackfriars* XI. 129 (1930), pp. 748–61.

'Thomism for the Times', *Blackfriars* XIII. 147 (1932), pp. 340–53.

'Pleasure-extract', *Blackfriars* XIII. 151 (1932), pp. 602–607.

Poetic Experience. An Introduction to Thomist Aesthetic (Essays in Order 13, London: Sheed and Ward, 1934).

Morals and Marriage (by 'T. G. Wayne', London: Longmans, Green and Co., 1936, reprinted 1952.

'Thought, Volition and the Organism', *The Thomist* 2 (1940), pp. 1–13.

'Vienna and Vienna', *Thought* 21 (1946), pp. 63–82.

'St Thomas and Politics', *Dominican Studies* II (1949), pp. 280–84.

Barbara Celarent. A Description of Scholastic Dialectic (London: Longmans, Green and Co., 1950).

Phoenix and Turtle. The Unity of Knowing and Being (London: Longmans, Green and Co., 1950).

St Thomas Aquinas: Philosophical Texts (Oxford: Oxford University Press, 1951).

Between Community and Society (London: Longmans, Green and Co., 1953).

Britain and Arms. A Scrapbook from Queen Anne to the Present Day (London: Eyre and Spottiswoode, 1953).

St Thomas Aquinas: Theological Texts (Oxford: Oxford University Press, 1955).

Up the Green River. A Novel (London: Eyre and Spottiswoode, 1955).

'Science in Holiness', *Life of the Spirit* XI (1957), pp. 345–57.

'Having our Faculties', *Life of the Spirit* XI (1957), pp. 499–510.

'Mysticisms', *Life of the Spirit* XII (1957), pp. 210–17.

Principality and Polity (London: Longmans, Green & Co., 1958).

'The Play of Grace', *Life of the Spirit* XIII (1958), pp. 263–70.

'The State as Guardian of Morals?', *Blackfriars* XL. 466 (1959), pp. 23–29.

'The Crimination of Sin', *Blackfriars* XLI. 479 (1960), pp. 53–611.

'First and Seconds in Sex', *Blackfriars* XLI. 483 (1960), pp. 272–83.

'Not All That Anomalous', *Blackfriars* XLI. 486 (1960), pp. 402–408.

'Contraception revised: Reflections on a Spreading Argument', *Blackfriars* XLIII. 502 (1962), pp. 156–60.

'The Summa in the Sixities', *New Blackfriars* 46. 532 (1964), pp. 6–10.

'Faith of the Fathers' *New Blackfriars* 51. 596 (1970), pp. 165–69.

'Civilised Violence', *The Month* 5 (1972), pp. 168–75.

Numerous articles in P. K. Meagher, O.P., T. C. O'Brien and C. M. Aherne, S.S.J. (eds.), *Encyclopaedic Dictionary of Religion* (Washington: Corpus Publications, 1979).

Thomas Gilby, as General Editor of a new commented translation of *St Thomas Aquinas, Summa Theologiae*, published under the 'Blackfriars' imprint but by conjunction with Eyre and Spottiswoode of London and the

McGraw-Hill Book Company of New York, contributed the following specific volumes:

1. *Christian Theology* (1a, 1), 1964.
5. *God's Will and Providence* (1a, 19–26), 1967.
8. *Creation, Variety and Evil* (1a, 44–49), 1967.
16. *Purpose and Happiness* (1a 2ae, 1–5), 1969.
17. *Psychology of Human Acts* (1a 2ae, 6–17), 1970.
18. *Principles of Morality* (1a 2ae, 18–21), 1966.
28. *Law and Political Theory* (1a 2ae, 90–97), 1966.
32. *Consequences of Faith* (2a 2ae, 8–16), 1975.
36. *Prudence* (2a 2ae, 47–56), 1974.
37. *Justice* (2a 2ae, 57–62), 1975.
43. *Temperance* (2a 2ae, 141–54), 1968.
44. *Well-tempered Passion* (2a 2ae, 155–70), 1972.
59. *Holy Communion* (3a, 79–83), 1975.

6

Sebastian Bullough

Fr Sebastian entered the world as Halley Edward Duse Bullough at Cambridge in 1910, the son of Edward Bullough and Enrichetta Bullough, née Marchetti. His background was definitely European. His paternal grandparents, John Bullough and Alicia Schmildin, were respectively Lancastrian and Swiss. His father was born and grew up in the mediaeval lakeside town of Thun in the Bernese Oberland, but the Bullough family fortune, based on manufacture in Accrington, enabled him to be educated at the prestigious Vizthum Gymnasium at Dresden. There he met his future wife, the child of the unsuccessful marriage of the Italian *prima donna* Eleonara Duse (she introduced Ibsen's theatre into Italy) and her fellow-actor Tebaldo Marchetti (or Checchi – his stage-name). Edward Bullough was by the time of their marriage in 1908 already Cantabrigian through and through. He had matriculated at Trinity College in 1899 and read for the Mediaeval and Modern Languages Tripos, taking his degree in 1902. And then, as Dr Elisabeth Stopp has described the work of Bullough *père*, he settled for

> a life of teaching and research in Cambridge, supervising for his own and for other colleges, learning new languages – Russian, more especially, but also Italian, Spanish and even Chinese. His main field of study was, however, that of aesthetics which he approached mainly from the psychological and even physiological point of view, conducting experiments at the Cambridge Psychological Laboratory and publishing a number of distinguished papers.[1]

Their topics bear out Dr Stopp's report: they concerned such matters as the perception and appreciation of colours, the idea of 'psychical distance' in art appreciation, the relation of aesthetics to psychology, and of 'mind and medium' in art. In 1912 he was elected to the Drosier Fellowship at Gonville and Caius. Meanwhile the family

(Leonora, later Sister Mary Mark O.P. had been added to Halley) moved into No. 6, Huntingdon Road, directly facing Buckingham Road, the cul-de-sac where Edward Bullough would later build Blackfriars St Michael's, the future Dominican priory in Cambridge, and Fr Sebastian's last Dominican home. He was appointed University Lecturer in German in 1920.

In 1923 Bullough was received into the Catholic Church by the celebrated Jesuit writer and preacher Cyril Martindale,[2] and soon made his mark as a professional Catholic layman. Professor C. N. L. Brooke wrote of him in the relevant volume of the University's official history: 'He played something of the role among the Catholic academic community that Baron Anatole von Hügel and Lord Acton had played in an earlier generation.'[3] In other words, one of leadership and the conferring of lustre, respectively. Edward Bullough was joint president of the British Federation of University Catholic Societies, and, in 1928 President of Pax Romana, the world-wide co-ordinating body of such national networks. No doubt the administrative expertise he had gained in his work for the Government Committee on Modern Languages, 1916–18, and his assistant secretaryship of the Royal Commission on Oxford and Cambridge Universities, 1919–22, stood him in good stead. He played a major part in establishing Fisher House, the home of the Catholic Chaplaincy to Cambridge University,[4] and would doubtless have been gratified to see the succession of Dominicans who, from the late 1970s onwards, have served as chaplains there. Meanwhile, Edward Bullough's Italian interests, displayed in *Cambridge Readings in Italian Literature* and *Italian Perspectives*, increasingly got the better of the German, and he was appointed to the chair of Italian in 1933.[5] Before his untimely death within a year of becoming professor, he had been able to translate Etienne Gilson's *Le Thomisme* – a fine product of the Thomist Revival in France – under the title *The Philosophy of St Thomas Aquinas*, and with a preface by Fr Vincent McNabb.[6]

With such Catholic and Dominican intensity in his background Halley Bullough stood little chance to escape. He had received an Anglican christening at Little St Mary's during the period of his mother's indifference to Catholicism, but on her reconversion had undergone conditional baptism at Our Lady and the English Martyrs, emerging from the font as no longer Halley (he had been named for the comet, curiously,) but Hugh Dominic. Sent to Laxton for his schooling, he entered the friars' noviciate at Woodchester in September 1931 – on the same day that his sibling Leonora entered that of the Dominican sisters at nearby Stroud.[7] He evidently became devoted to the place, as witness 'The Woodchester Story', a narrative

chain of letters from the time of its foundation, which he edited.[8]
When his father succumbed to septicaemia at Bath, his body was taken
for burial to the priory, since Br Sebastian was there; Enrichetta
would join him in the grave on the same Gloucestershire hillside in
1961. Alone, she had made over the Italianate house to the Order in
1938; it was a kindness that the Provincial authorities assigned her
only son to the new foundation, in order that he should be near her.
Accordingly, he read Hebrew and Aramaic in the University rather
than, as otherwise intended, at the Dominican biblical school in
Jerusalem.

Lacking his father's conceptual gift, Sebastian Bullough was
nonetheless a gifted, if methodologically idiosyncratic, teacher. The
milieu of his teaching varied staggeringly, in the way only a religious
order committed to a variety of works could encompass: from the
schoolroom at Laxton, and its equivalent for little boys at Llanarth, to
the studium at Oxford and, finally, the Cambridge faculty of Oriental
Languages. Blessed with his father's easy temperament, he appears to
have loved it all. His last years were saddened, however, by the
demolition of the Dominican liturgy and its associated observances.
He died on 30 July 1967 at the convent of Stone, where Leonora
Bullough was a Dominican sister, and was buried at Cambridge, with
– as his official obituarist remarked:

> The bishop of Northampton celebrating the full Latin Liturgy of the
> Mass and the brethren burying him with the traditional Dominican
> rite. It did not seem to have been arranged. It seemed to happen
> that way and he would not have had it otherwise.[9]

The goal of art

It was no doubt Edward Bullough's interest in the psychology of
aesthetic perception which led Fr Sebastian to take as his research
topic, once released from the common round of priestly study, 'The
Goal of Art'. His Latin treatise *De finalitate artis*, submitted for the
qualification of lector in the Order at its Roman college in 1939,
belongs to a very different world from the psychological aesthetics of
his father. It is a work of the Thomist Renaissance (frequently called
nowadays the 'Third Scholasticism', the 'Second' being that of the
Counter-Reformation period). With that revival Edward Bullough had
been, as we have seen, sufficiently sympathetic to translate Gilson's
Thomisme, yet his own intellectual formation, method and manner
were of a very different kind. Fr Sebastian's bibliography carries no

mention of his father's work. His chief sources were – aside from Aristotle, Augustine and Thomas, with Cajetan and John of St Thomas not far behind – those figures in the neo-scholastic movement who had attempted a Thomist theory of art, notably: the American Dominican Leonard Callahan's *A Theory of Esthetic*; Fr Thomas Gilby's *Poetic Experience*; Eric Gill's *Beauty Looks after Herself*; Jacques Maritain's *Art et Scolastique*; Maritain's joint study with his wife entitled *La situation de la Poésie*; and *Art et Apologétique* by the French Dominican Antonin-Dalmace Sertillanges.[10] To these should be added two notable 'manuals' of the time, the Benedictine Joseph Gredt's *Elementa philosphiae*, and the Dominican Benoit-Henri Merkelbach's *Summa Theologiae Moralis*.[11] There were some sports: the English aesthetician Roger Fry's *Vision and Design* stresses primarily the plastic qualities and formal relations found within the artwork, and the positivistic thinking of the late nineteenth-century French writer Hippolyte Taine's *Philosophie de l'Art* is no more than an aesthetic naturalism, where environment is all. The *Führer zur Kunst* of the enormously prolific German critic Heinrich Lützeler, founder of the *Jahrbuch für Aesthetik und allegemeine Kunstwissenschaft*, is the work of a self-consciously Catholic author, but not a Scholastic one.[12] Fr Sebastian had also made use of the occasional publications of a Roman entity, housed at the Gothic Dominican priory of Santa Maria sopra Minerva, and intended to arouse interest in the sacred arts – the *Institutum Beato Angelico* (which still exists): papers by two successive Italian 'Masters of the Sacred Palace' (an office now known as 'Theologian of the Pontifical Household'), Mariano Cordovani and Aloysius Ciappi bulk large here.[13] Lastly, and an apparently thematic outsider – but it was a topic never far from his thoughts – there was the French Dominican Paul Philippe's *Le rôle de l'Amitié dans la vie chrétienne*.[14] Both Ciappi and Philippe were raised to the cardinalate by pope Paul VI. Philippe should not be confused with the two Dominican brothers-by-blood Marie-Dominique Philippe, founder of the order of apostolic monks called the Communauté de Saint Jean, and Thomas Philippe, co-founder, with M. Jean Vanier, of L'Arche, the movement for the handicapped, and thesis-father of *De finalitate artis*.

How did Fr Sebastian approach the topic of the 'intrinsic purpose' (*finalitas*) of art? In his preface, he points out that his investigation is relatively novel, in that little has been written from a theological and ethical point of view about art (in the tradition of the schoolmen, he means). At the same time, such a study is appropriate, and that for three reasons: first, 'we' (Dominicans, or perhaps Catholic Christians) are surrounded by artefacts, and notably, where beauty is concerned, cultic images, and it is important to be able to 'reprobate the bad and choose the good'; secondly, many bright people frequently discuss art and beauty, so preachers (or Catholics) should be equipped with *principles* to orient them in such debates; thirdly, 'by the consideration of the beautiful, the mind is raised up to the sublime and godly'.[15]

Although Fr Sebastian appears to have completed only a 'first book' of his treatise on aesthetics, that book includes all he had to say about the *artwork in itself*.[16] The 'immediate' or 'proximate' end of the activity of artistic making can only be the work itself: for artistic skill is the 'right reason of makeable things'. Such a sharp focus on the artwork in its own integrity of being (though that being is an ingathering of relations to wider aspects of the real) links the neo-scholastic aesthetics to which Fr Sebastian subscribed with the 'phenomenological school' of such influential post-war aestheticians as Mikel Dufrenne.[17]

Fr Sebastian's Neo-Thomism is announced at the outset when he begins his enquiry by pressing into service the fourfold Aristotelian analysis of the 'causes' of a thing, commended, we have noted, for its general philosophical serviceableness, by Fr Thomas Gilby. Anyone can recognise that the artwork would be impossible without the 'habit' of artistic making; without this capacity – and the cultural practices which it presupposes and prolongs – it would have no potential to be. That must be considered, therefore, as the 'efficent cause' of the work of art. But secondly, there is the question of its own purpose or 'final cause', and this Fr Sebastian locates in the integrity or perfection of the work, as willed by the artist. Next, we come to its 'formal cause': the factor of factors which make the work what it is; for the author, this is the topic of the *image*. In the Aristotelo-Thomist analysis of the nature of things there is always a quadernity of perspectives in which causality is viewed. What place is there for the last of these – 'material causality' – in Fr Sebastian's scheme? In actual fact, he simply subsumes it under the exemplary or formal causality of the image. On reflection, he points out, the 'material' from which an artwork arises is *experience*, while the 'matter' about which artistic activity revolves is *the subject of the work*: and both of these enter into the *constitution of the image*.

The artistic 'habit' is the quality in the agent which gives him or her the capacity to work well at the fashioning of artworks. It is an inclination at once to see, to grasp and to work in a certain manner. Consonant with his Thomist inheritance, Fr Sebastian stresses the crucial role of the intellect, for it belongs to mind to *order* things, and yet of course here mind must be married to hand since art is essentially an 'exterior work'. Citing Eric Gill, 'Art is deliberate skill, skill with mind behind it.'[18] It is not as such knowledge, yet it is *quaedam sequela cognitionis*, a kind of 'following' of knowledge. The expressive image in a work of art follows on a multiplicity of intellectual images ('mental words', the terminus of knowledge in Thomistic epistemology) drawn from a variety of acts of understanding. The artistic image concentrates a more diffuse understanding of reality and gives it a focused expression. Moreover, the exemplary image which the artist will render an artefact is not the image of something known so much as it is the image of *something to be made*. The complex inner word of the artist becomes artefact, not the token of an idea. Here we find a Neo-Thomist author curbing his intellectualism at the thought of the materiality of a thing, its shaping in the media of paint, wood or stone. For successful – nay triumphant – artistic making we do not need to be professional aestheticians: 'beauty looks after herself'.

The beautiful is a special *ratio*, or perspective on, the good.[19] And the good is – depending on context – some kind of 'whole thing', *totum*, which satisfies appetite, for appetite is never satiated except by some sort of plenitude. Perfect realities move the subjects drawn to them by the motion of love, and more precisely by that kind of love which goes out to things for their own sake, the love of friendship. What is thus loved *also* gives us happiness – yet that is not *why* it is loved. The beautiful is nothing other than the good when apprehended as wonderful. The beautiful is always the wondrous, which is not to say that it must necessarily be morally edifying, as the wife of Lot discovered when, transfixed by the sight of flaming Sodom, she became, as the folk-tale in Genesis 19 records, a pillar of salt. Fr Sebastian also notes the connections of the beautiful with the other 'transcendentals' – the true, and the one, for the lover of the lovely grasps its reality and form (related to *verum*), as well as its integrity (related to *unum*). The adage that beauty is what 'when seen, pleases' has nothing to do with subjectistic hedonism: rather does it signify the objective power to give repose to man as a conative, desiring being, when it falls on his mind's eye. 'Seeing' for the ancients and the mediaevals is ever an intellectual affair. And Fr Sebastian interprets the three Thomistic attributes of beauty – *integritas, proportio, claritas*, – from the starting-point of the idea of the beautiful as a perfect totality: 'integrity' is thus *radix pulchritudinis*, the shoot of beauty, requiring the integration of parts into a whole and hence 'proportion', and manifesting itself by way of delight to the mind, and so 'clarity'. The contemplation of the beautiful exercises at once all the chief powers of the human animal as a creature of sense and spirit: the beautiful delights both mind and senses, according to their kinds, it

arouses love in the will while the 'sensitive appetite' finds it delicious
and the spring of joy. Here Fr Sebastian could cite the words of his
confrère in *Poetic Experience*: 'The experience of earthly beauty [is]
the release of the whole being into activity and delight.'[20] He distinguishes 'speculative contemplation', where the mind occupies itself
with some perceived truth, from 'affective contemplation', which
arises from the friendship-love which goes out to some intrinsic good
desired for itself. Of the latter, the loving contemplation of God is the
supreme example, but Fr Sebastian is happy to cite as another instance
man's drawing to the beautiful. That too can cause 'ecstasy' – though
but for a brief moment, such is the inherent imperfection of all earthly
goods. With an evident reference to Gilby's aesthetics Fr Sebastian
calls such a condition, where a man finds himself displaced from his
normal centre on account of love, *experientia poetica*. He stresses that
such an experience may be close to that of tears, for the beautiful
arouses nostalgia for 'the beauty and perfection of things eternal and
unending'. Coming down from the heights, he adds that a useful thing
can also be beautiful – not exactly 'through its own utility' (*per
propriam utilitatem*) and yet 'because it is useful' (*quia est utile*), that
is, well-proportioned to its own purpose. Fr Sebastian, who had still
to develop his Laxton propensity for motor-cycling, took a locomo-
tive as his prize specimen here. The thought is Eric Gill's though one
doubts whether the case-study would be.

Concentrating his discussion on the beautiful in art, Fr Sebastian
defines the image as a 'likeness-bearing re-presentative sign'. Such
images may be intentional, mental, but until they undergo the change
of life which comes with embodiment in the physical realm, they are
hardly art. The 'exemplary image', entertained in the imagination, is
already, however, something *sensibile*, in a way sensuous – the image
is never an *idea*. At the same time, the image is not so entirely particular and concrete that it loses all intelligibility. Something universal
lingers, and hence the image is never merely brute fact. Moreover,
the image always points on to some further reality, even though as
perhaps with music, this may be that of 'pure proportions', considered apart from all matter. It may also be a reality beyond this world,
for the imagination may picture more perfect being than what is given
here below. At the same time, the humus of image-making is experience, whence impressions pass into the 'treasure hoard of memory' –
which is not to say that such impressions may not be much modified
by the 'interior movements of the soul'.

The exemplar image cannot with integrity remain sheerly interior.
What for the artist is vocational necessity has for the metaphysician a
binding force of its own. First, just as goodness is naturally self-diffu-

sive, so the beautiful must seek to pour itself out, to declare itself (a philosophical pun on the two senses of the Latin *clarum* lies behind the text here). Secondly, the human being is a sensuous creature, which does not live on (interior) word alone. For the whole man to delight in the image, both mind *and* sense must be involved. Thirdly, the embodiment of image as art 'fixes' the flux of the imagination, just as authors write so that they may understand the more clearly. And lastly in the very act of artistic making the mental image becomes in a marvellous way fertile: it so grows that the embodied image is always vastly more significant than its exemplar origin. In making, a variety of relevant images fructify – which is why a portrait will be superior to a photograph, while at the same time the contours – the 'grand lines' of the art-work clarify – which is why a masterpiece differs from a sketch. As in poetry verbal assonance or metrical exigency can suggest a word or a new image, so too in homiletic (evidently classified among the arts by this member of the Order of Preachers), one image or one argument will lead on to another. Not that such chains of events are enclosed within a deistic world: God himself can inspire the formation of exemplar images, since he is the 'greatest and best of all makers'. This the ancients glimpsed in the mythopoeic language of their 'muses'. And in any case, the artistic process – which does not simply imitate nature, though it takes its materials from her, is a quasi-creative act. It brings into being something *novel* – and as such participates in a fashion (*quasi*) in the creativity of God. It is the metaphysical marvel of matter that it is docile to the induction of new forms, as Michelangelo's famous statement about the statue hid in a block of marble would testify.

The climax of the study concerns the beauty of the image. Fr Sebastian has already suggested, in his discussion of the exemplar image, how the latter is always wanted for itself, on account of its own goodness, and how it tends on account of its *claritas*, 'radiance', to its own self-manifestation, for *claritas* is nothing other than the *declaribilitas rei pulchrae*, the 'declareability' of some lovely reality. There could, however, be another *ratio pulchritudinis* – at once ground of beauty and reason for ascribing it – and this would consist in a due proportion between an image and some outstanding goodness to which it was ordered. Here *use* – *utilitas* – might, in appropriate circumstances, itself confer beauty. Moreover, some internal proportion in the image, or peculiar quality of its materials, might also be relevant to the language of beauty in its regard.

But turning to yet another *ratio*, not hitherto mentioned – the *christological* – Fr Sebastian approaches the conclusion of his treatise. He points out that an image not only represents some reality; more, it may be said to be that very reality – in the representative mode. A perfect representation of even an highly imperfect reality has beauty because the relation between image and imaged establishes an onto-logical truth which possesses its own authority. 'And this beauty is that which is most proper (*maxime propria*) to the image as such.' But if that can be said even of the image of something vile (one thinks, for example, of Picasso's painting of an atrocity of the Spanish Civil War, *Guernica*), what must be the case when the reality represented is *itself* beautiful? The supreme beauty of an image will be the instance where what is represented is itself supremely glorious. And here, in an astonishing anticipation of the theological aesthetics of the Swiss dogmatician Hans Urs von Balthasar, Fr Sebastian can conclude:

> Among all lovely things on earth, the human body is pre-eminent, because, where creatures are concerned, it is maximally perfect. And yet the divine Beauty infinitely surpasses it. But just that Beauty in some fashion appeared on earth in the humanity of Christ, as the psalm has it, 'Deus Dominus et illuxit nobis'. The man [Jesus] Christ, since he is the most perfect human being, and in him the very Beauty of God shone out, is the loveliest reality that can be representatively imaged. Furthermore, he is most beautifully represented in his act of supreme loving – that is, in his Crucifixion and precious Death. The image of the Crucifix is, then, the highest thing in the realm of images.[21]

The crucifix, therefore, stands as the frontispiece of his *libellus*, 'little book', because it makes present the loveliest thing eye ever sees, as the traditional 'Prayer before a Crucifix' (which he cites), confesses.[22]

De finalitate artis, therefore, not only cites, ingenuously, by way of copious illustration of its arguments, the Vulgate version of the Scriptures. It also debouches in a conclusion based on biblical theology. It is to Fr Sebastian's work as an exegete that we must now turn.

Holy Writ

The Latinity of *de finalitate artis* was not Fr Sebastian's sole linguistic accomplishment, for he had a firm grasp on the biblical languages (as also on that useful adjunct to, especially, *Old* Testament study, Syriac).[23] But though in the last years of his life he taught Hebrew and Syriac on behalf of the University department of Semitic languages at Cambridge, he was perfectly content to decant his knowledge of Scripture to the boys of Laxton School. Indeed, he regarded

the teaching of the Bible to the young as among the noblest forms of
intellectual apostolate available in the Order. In a programmatic statement on 'Scripture at School', he wrote that, on the supposition that
education's function is to produce a Christian man, the study of
Scripture holds, evidently, a central place.

> Now in order to be a Christian, there are certain things that a man
> must know and believe, and these things are contained in God's
> revelation. During the education of a Christian, therefore, an
> acquaintance with the two channels of revelation, Canonical
> Scripture and Defined Tradition, and a knowledge of their contents,
> are not only paramount but essential. A man cannot profess the
> Christian Faith unless he knows something about it; still less can
> he adequately pray to an unknown God. And a Christian who does
> not pray is a Christian only in name for prayer is the manifestation
> of the Love of God, and this is the greatest and the first command-
> ment upon Christians.[24]

Lest it be thought that Bible and dogma constitute two totally self-
contained and parallel 'channels' of revelation, Fr Sebastian was at
pains to point out that, the more both Scripture and doctrine are
studied, 'the more it becomes plain that the words of Scripture lie at
the root of the Church's Theology, and correspondingly that the Bible
only becomes clear in the light of the Church's teaching.' (In the
Catholic schools of the time, however, and not unreasonably, given
the special difficulties attaching to the assimilation of ancient texts,
Christian Doctrine – 'Religious Knowledge' – and Scripture study
were normally distinct subjects in the curriculum.)

Fr Sebastian's concept of Scripture study was indeed nothing if not
holistic. Biblical study is not intended primarily to stock the mind with
facts but with understanding how the God who in many and various
ways spoke of old to the fathers through the prophets has now spoken
to us by his Son (Heb. 1.1). Thus, the teacher is to present the Old
Testament as 'looking forward to the New, not only in Messianic
prophecy but also of course much more generally in the preparation
both spiritual and material of the people of Israel'. And similarly, in
exploring the New Testament Scriptures, the pupil should be led to

> understand the trend of our Lord's teaching, and what in it was new
> to the world, to grasp the significance in revelation of various facts
> of the Gospel, and what great doctrines are implied therein, and to
> notice ... the connexion between the Life of our Lord and our
> pupils' everyday liturgical experience ...[25]

And the same concern with seeing the wood in the trees makes Fr

Sebastian insist that, in the study of Paul, the student should not get tied up in problems of detailed chronology or the topography of Asia Minor, fascinating though these may be, but concentrate rather on two things: Paul's careful diversity of apostolic tactics when addressing Jews and Gentiles respectively (presumably in Acts), and the ampler illustration of the Christian message which his letters provide. Only after the outlines are well established in the child's or the young person's mind is it pedagogically right to introduce the finer points of exegesis, whether historical or theological. For Fr Sebastian, this is done, even then, not for its own sake but simultaneously to clarify and to stimulate interest.

His approach would today be called 'post-critical': by no means, as we shall see, contemptuous of the critical approach to the text, but insistent that the text's full meaning can only be disengaged on the presuppositions made by the Church in canonising: a christological, and, in the last analysis, trinitarian scrutiny of Scripture. Twenty years before the Second Vatican Council, Fr Sebastian's account would more than satisfy the demand of christocentricity made by that Council's Dogmatic Constitution on Divine Revelation, *Dei Verbum*: 'The centre of the Biblical revelation is the Person of Christ. The Old Testament prepares the way of the Lord, and the Apostolic writings preach Christ to the world.'

Fr Sebastian's Grand Plan for communicating Scripture to youth consisted in an interweaving of the gospel narrative with the principal segments of the Bible, the latter constantly invited to illuminate the former. Its pattern was: '1. Gospel story. 2. Old Testament. 3. Gospel in more detail. 4. Apostles and Early Church. 5. Higher Gospel exegesis. 6. Apostolic writings.' Once *les grandes lignes* of Scripture were grasped, a foundation was laid that could be built on by a devout intelligence, granted the tools of study, in later life.

He left contributions to each of his three interlineated segments of Scripture: Old Testament; history of the apostolic Church; the apostolic writings. His *Five Minor Prophets*[26] includes his own translation of the short books of Obadiah, Micah, Zephaniah, Haggai and Zechariah: it is notable for its attempt to represent the stress values of Hebrew poetry by means of Gerard Manley Hopkins' 'sprung rhythm' – which, he noted, Hopkins had claimed as 'the rhythm of the old English verse, such as Piers Plowman ... gone out of use since Elizabethan times as a recognised poetical form until the present age'. Obadiah is not a prophet who can be presented attractively: his message is the terrible power and justice of God. Fr Sebastian's tranlation well captures its biting tone:

> If thieves came to thee, if raiders of the night,
> Would they not steal their fill?
> If grape-gatherers came to thee,
> Would they leave a remnant? (Obad. 5)

His note on the 'day of the Lord' in verse 15 of this shortest of all books of the Hebrew Bible (only 21 verses) was praised by Dr Raphael Loewe in the *Jewish Chronicle* as 'a model of what an editor should provide for a sixth-form schoolboy or lay student'. (That review of *Five Minor Prophets* – from a Semitist Bye-Fellow of Caius, Edward Bullough's old College – lauds the 'open-mindedness' of Fr Sebastian's editorial treatment, and calls the study 'a challenge to Anglo-Jewish educationists to produce something equally good for domestic use'.)[27]

Micah provides more propitious materials for Fr Sebastian's commentary. First, let us have an example of his translation of the rhythmic prose which in this book – unlike Obadiah's – alternates with oracular poetry. The prophet's lament over Judah's ubiquitous sinfulness, notably in matters of social justice, will serve.

> Alas for me. For I am become like the last harvests of summer, like the gleanings of a vintage – not a bunch of grapes to eat, not an early fig as my soul desired. The pious man is perished from the land, and upright among men there is none; they all lie waiting for blood, each man ensnareth his brother with a net. Both hands are set to do evil, and exceedingly well; the prince maketh his demands, and the judge also, for bribery; and the grandee speaketh the caprice of his own soul; and they entangle the good as a briar, the upright as a hedge. (Mic. 7.1–4)

The influence of Distributism on the English Dominicans of his generation can perhaps be discerned in Fr Sebastian's presentation of Micah as the 'country smallholder', speaking with feeling about those who 'cast a measuring-line upon a plot of land'.[28] Not that there is any trace of a socially reductionist presentation of the prophets in this exegete: for him, Micah sees the whole problem of existence in terms of man's abandonment of God; the mainspring of his preaching is the loving trust in God's mercy which bursts forth at the book's end in 'a passage rivalling the piety of the Psalms'. Above all, bearing in mind the christocentric character of Fr Sebastian's concept of exegesis, it was Micah's inspired privilege to see in Bethlehem the 'place whence the eternal Ruler of Israel would come forth'.

Zephaniah's self-dating to the reign of Josiah, combined with the prophet's own claim to royal kinship, and the congruity of the book's message with the themes of the Josianic reform (623–609), leads Fr Sebastian to attempt (unusually) a wider critical hypothesis of his own, seeing the writer as 'enlisted' by the king as an agent of his religious policy. But once again such theses are secondary to an exposition of the spiritual substance of the work: nowhere in the Old Testament 'is God's love for Israel expressed in terms so tender and so radiant'.

The study of Haggai can dispense with speculative theorising about origins, for each of his four oracles are precisely dated. Fr Sebastian, with a realistic sense of what communal and cultural identity require, sympathises with Haggai's stress on the urgency, some seventeen years after the first exiles had returned, from Babylon, of a rebuilding of the Jerusalem Temple – 'essential for the preservation of the Hebrew nation that was marked off from all others by their worship of Jehovah'. But that Temple is, more importantly, when the whole biblical canon is surveyed, a messianic figure, a type of the Messiah's community, the universal Church where all the nations shall come to adore.

> Thus the Temple of Jerusalem, the Church of Christ and the Sanctuary of Heaven, are through all the Scriptures seen with a single prophetic glance – a 'compenetration' of images – and the material work of placing a 'stone upon a stone', so strongly urged by Haggai, assumes a new and spiritual importance when taken together with the significant use of the same phrase ... by Christ in his prophecy of the undoing of the man-made Temple to make way for the spiritual Temple of the Church of Christ.[29]

Lastly, on Zechariah, Fr Sebastian holds to the unity of authorship of this dislocated work, treating its two halves as a diptych produced by the prophet in, respectively, young manhood and old age. The messianic aura which surrounded Zerubbabel as restorer of the Temple worship fades in Zechariah's middle age, not least owing to the new insecurity of the Persian Empire whose benevolent shade had enabled Zerubbabel's work. A chastened prophet now 'looks forward through the trials and tribulations of future history to the happiness of the Messianic age, identified mysteriously at the end with the 'Day of Jehovah', which will be a day of everlasting light.'[30] Throughout, Fr Sebastian's notes suggest helpful emendations of the Masoretic text of the Hebrew originals, on the basis of other ancient sources or of the scholarly conjectures of 'moderate' critics.

Such points would escape the boys of Laxton for whom Hebrew was not a curricular possibility. But Fr Sebastian's studies of Acts and of the 'apostolic writings' (that is, the New Testament Letters together with the Johannine Apocalypse) are models of accessible *vulgarisation*. The preface to *The Church in the New Testament* makes plain that this is definitely *ecclesial* exegesis.

> In order to see the Bible as a revelation, and particularly in relation to the Church, it is important that the student should see the links between the Bible and the present living organism of the Church, hence we have made frequent mention of liturgical practice and doctrines as understood both in New Testament times and now, and we have constantly amplified our biblical study with the examination of history and tradition outside the inspired books.[31]

It could also be called an exercise in neo-patristic exegesis, for Fr Sebastian claims to be covered by the mantle of patristic style, defined as a 'mixture of text ... paraphase, précis and explanation'. Though not a commentary, he believed that few points of history and doctrine relevant to Acts had been left out. He justifies the use of fairly frequent Greek, and even of occasional Hebrew and Aramaic (!) for fourteen-year-olds, by the consideration that experience shows this works as a stimulant of interest. (For those less linguistically precocious, one imagines that the illustrations from the old masters, or contemporary photographs of places, would have afforded welcome relief during such periods in class.) Like a certain school of New Testament exegesis today, Fr Sebastian emphasised the seamless web of historical continuity which joins the apostolic to the sub-apostolic age, though in his closing peroration such unity is also treated as meta-historical, through the mystery of the Eucharist.

> When we realise the continuity of the Church from the Apostles, through Ignatius and his fellow-bishops whom he visited and wrote to and wrote about we then can say with more understanding that the Church is not the only One, Holy and Catholic, but also in the deepest way Apostolic: 'Et in unam, sanctam, catholicam et *apostolicam* Ecclesiam', as we sing in the Credo. And in the Canon of the Mass, before the Consecration, we join ourselves in prayer, in the *Communicantes*, first of all with the Mother of God, the Queen of Apostles and Martyrs, and then with Peter and Paul and all the other Apostles, and then with the successors of Peter in Rome, Linus, Cletus, and Clement and finally with many other bishops and Martyrs. And after the Consecration, in the prayer *Nobis quoque peccatoribus*, we ask that to us sinners also may be granted some share and company with the Holy Apostles and Martyrs, among whom are specially mentioned Stephen, Matthias, and Barnabas (of whom we read in the Acts) and Ignatius, into whose

heavenly company we ask to be admitted. For the Sacrament of the Eucharist not only binds together all the Christians who partake of it at the same time, but also binds together all the Christians of the past, the present and the future; by the Eucharist we are brought not only together among ourselves, but brought into unity with the very Apostles themselves and their first devoted followers: 'For we, being many, are one bread, one body, all that partake of one bread'.[32]

The same principles are at work in its successor textbook *Saint Paul and the Apostolic Writings*. Fr Sebastian considered the epistles, with the Apocalypse, to be the 'crown and conclusion of the whole Scriptural revelation', because, as he explained,

> they contain not only St John's mysterious view into the future (both in heaven and on earth), and include the very last echo of God's direct Revelation to the Apostles (The Epistles of St John), with which the 'deposit of Faith' is competed, but they represent the labours of the Apostles in establishing Christ's Church in earth and in teaching Christ's new commandment to the world; they contain some of the sublimest teaching in the Bible and lie behind so much of the normal teaching of the Catholic Church on Faith and Morals.[33]

Warning against too much recourse to secondary literature, he argued that such works 'only exist to illuminate [the text's] obscurities and to define the circumstances of writing', and, so far as at least the first of these questions is concerned, the text alone will at any rate frequently be 'plain' when studied in the light of the 'supernatural mother-wit' that every Catholic possesses from the doctrinal and moral teaching of the Church and the daily partaking in her worship.

This passion to integrate Scripture as completely as possible in the Catholic organism explains how what is in many ways an admirable monument to lightly born New Testament scholarship can boast a most exceptional set of footnotes: thus the metaphor of the Church as a building in 1 Corinthians reminds the commentator of Bede Jarrett's *Living Temples* (meditations for boys), the *mia elpis* of Ephesians 4 is referred to the Act of Hope in the *Penny Catechism*, and the mention of one Pudens in Second Timothy sparks a train of thought running through the Roman church of Santa Pudenziana (possibly of Pudens' *gens*) to Cardinal Bourne who had been given its 'title' by Pope Pius X! On the other hand, if Catholic exegetes are the principal sources used (including from an older generation Hugh Pope and M. J. Lagrange, and among the *moderni*, Ceslaus Spicq and E. B. Allo, all

Dominicans), Fr Sebastian was by no means above drawing on the
great Anglican exegetical tradition of such figures as J. B. Lightfoot,
E. G. Selwyn, B. F. Westcott as well as the Scottish Presbyterian Sir
William Ramsay, to whom, however, Pope Leo XIII had awarded his
gold medal for services to Christian scholarship in 1893.

And if he was capable of shining both as a higher critic and as a
populariser of an exegesis at once historical and ecclesial, he also
turned his hand to the use of Scripture for *lectio divina*. Though that
term is not commonly found among Dominicans, the reality to which
it refers – the meditative reading of Scripture – is of course perfectly
familiar. *Meditations in Advent* and *Meditations in Lent* fall into this
category.

Taking the first Sunday of Advent as the beginning of the Church's
year, Fr Sebastian opens his *Meditations in Advent* with that day's
Introit from Psalm 24. He describes its sentiments as 'the proper
beginning of any human undertaking: an expression of complete trust
in God'. His *lectio* is a theological dramatics; a study in the theatre
of tension:

> The urgency of waiting climbs through the four weeks: *Excita,
> Domine, potentiam tuam et veni* – Stir up thy power and come;
> *Excita corda nostra ad praeparandos unigeniti tui vias* – Stir up our
> hearts to prepare – on the second Sunday; through the ember day
> Masses with their prophetic visions, to the climax of expectation on
> Christmas Eve: *Mane videbitis gloriam ejus* – Tomorrow you shall
> see his glory. And then in the Mass at dead of night, 'the people
> that walked in darkness have seen a great light' – as if none of us
> present had ever seen it before ... We know that what we are now
> watching happened hundreds of years ago, but we want to live it
> through again, knowing that the elemental truth of the drama has
> its power to sway our lives.[34]

Advent's second week is begun by a liturgical paraphrase of Isaiah 30,
which Fr Sebastian translates:

> O people of Sion,
> Behold thy Lord cometh
> To save all the world.
> O joy of thy heart
> At the sound of his voice,
> The voice of his glory.[35]

Here his meditation is a tissue of biblical texts on the joy of salvation;
and his message is the universal mission that falls to the Church as
her role in the theodrama.

The *goyim* of the Hebrews represented to the faithful people of Judah all those myriads of humanity who 'knew not God', who knew not how to worship the Lord of all, as they did by his merciful revelation ... The Christian, long schooled in the love and service of God, has this desire in his heart, that those who know not this service should learn to share it with him. Jesus, convert England; Jesus, convert the world. What does this mean, but the desire that all men, the nations, the *goyim*, should come to share our treasure?[36]

The third Sunday, *Gaudete* or Mid-Advent, takes its leit-motif from the Pauline summons to 'rejoice always' in Philippians 4. The Liturgy recaptures the exultant character of Paul's expectation of the coming Parousia of the Lord, for 'There is a special fullness in the rejoicing that follows upon anticipation, and in the anticipation itself there is a kind of restrained and silent happiness.' The most striking feature of this meditation is its use of an analysis of plainsong melodies to interpret the interconnections of the various New Testament episodes;

Here is the Alleluia in purple vestments, and in purple turned for a moment to rose, to give us courage; and the Alleluia in rose is the same melody as the silver Alleluia of the Ascension, the final triumph of the Risen Christ, *homo in fine temporum*, in heaven, yet with the marks of his pain; the same melody as the red-hot Alleluia of Pentecost, when the Apostles' doubts and anxiety and sadness were turned to love and courage and perseverance by the strength of the Spirit.[37]

For the last Sunday of Advent, in the Lectionary of Pope Pius V, St Luke presses into service the great Isaian prophecy of the voice crying in the desert which all the evangelists will use in characteristically different ways, to speak of the mission of John the Baptist. Fr Sebastian follows the ancient tradition of spiritual interpretation of this text by applying it 'tropologically' – existentially – to ourselves. 'If only we can prepare the Lord's highway within our own dryness, with trust that he can renew the face of the earth, the steep becomes a level, the scree becomes a plain.'

And so to Christmas. Here the lection from Isaiah 4 – 'a Boy has been born unto us, a Son has been given us' – for the Mass of Christmas Night sets the tone. The 'beloved Babe of Bethlehem' – if at Christmas we fail to understand him better, 'the festivities have been in vain, and vain were the weeks of waiting'. The point of love for the holy Child is to elicit in the heart a readier response to the 'consuming act of love that was the redemption of mankind upon the Cross'. Fr Sebastian had already noted that, in the liturgical space, as we greet the new-born King, the Crucifix is already present. Now, closing his meditation on the Nativity with Sedulius's 'delightful' hexameters on the Virgin Mother, *Gaudia matris habens*, he reminds his readers that Mary of Nazareth too had her Holy Week and Calvary. Only so could she have become, by participation in the Resurrection victory of her Son, *Königin des Weltalls* ('Queen of all the world', a reference to the Marian apparitions at Heede in 1939–40).

This insistence on linking the Incarnation with the Passion makes for a smooth transition to the Lenten meditations he published four years later. On the first Sunday of Lent the Gospel tells of the Lord's retirement into the desert for his time of preparation for mission, while in the city of Rome, the stational church for the Liturgy of that day is St John Lateran, the 'great church of St John the Baptist, the man of the desert'.[38] Fr Sebastian interprets the wilderness settings of the gospel by reference to Jerome of Bethlehem's eulogy of the para-doxical fertility of the desert for Christians, in Letter 14. *O desertum Christi floribus vernans*, 'Dear desert, fresh with the flowers of Christ!' Though the (physical) desert is arid and monotonous, it casts a spell which draws travellers to return. Retirement, meditation, peni-tence: these things change us in spirit. There *is* bitterness here: the first halting-place for the Israelites after the Red Sea was the place they called Mara, because the water was bitter (Exod. 15.23). But, with a reference to the redemptive Passion of Christ, which is the goal of Lent, 'God was good and showed them a tree, and when this tree was cast into the water, the water was turned to sweetness.'

For the second week of Lent, Fr Sebastian concentrates on the introits of the Mass. The Sunday's resumes Psalm 24, 'Be mindful, O Lord, of thy mercies'. Over against the bitterness of Mara were the twelve fountains of Elim, their good water signalled by the 'noble clump' of the seventy palm-trees which the children of Israel espied from a distance (Exod. 15.27). In Christian experience, God provides moments of consolation, giving assurance of his 'underlying mercy'. Similarly, the archetype of that experience in the life of Christ, the moment of the Transfiguration – the Gospel of the Second Sunday of Lent in both pre- and post-Conciliar Lectionaries – was for the apos-tles 'a consolation in their fear and depression and a raising of their hopes and an assurance of Christ's ultimate victory.' And just as, in the desert of this world, the grace flowing through the Church, embodied in Mary, brings life and refreshment, so today's stational Mass is at Santa Maria in Domnica, 'that lovely little church on the Caelian, with the *navicella*, the fountain in the form of a ship, bring-ing water to the dry piazza outside'.[39]

The third Sunday, by contrast, deals with hazards, for its Gospel is about the restless, perambulatory and desirous 'unclean spirits' (Luke 11.24–26). When the people of Israel were tempted by the demons of frustration and resentment to stone Moses, the Lord enabled him to draw forth water from the rock at Horeb, to curb at once their thirst and their anger (Exod. 17.1–7). Echoing the prayer to 'Holy Michael archangel' (his parents' favourite devotion) then said at the end of Low Mass, Fr Sebastian appeals to the protective 'Rock' of Christ against the 'wicked spirits who wander through the world for the ruin of souls', warning his readers by the bye that the demons, like all evicted lodgers, are always watching, once turned out, for a chance to return in strength. In the spiritual life, slacking does not mean marching on the spot, but retreating.

On Laetare – Mid-Lent – Sunday, the Church momentarily relaxes the 'stern violet of Lent into the lighter rose colour of the dawn ... a reminder that the sunrise of Easter will indeed come'. The Mass readings are the Feeding of the Five Thousand, in the version of St John, counterposed with Paul's teaching in Galatians about the fulfilment, and super-fulfilment, of the Law (Gal. 4.22–5.1). The God who in Exodus rained down manna for his people and bade Moses make a 'tabernacle', a 'tent' for his indwelling presence, has his Word become flesh in Mary, *arca foederis*, the 'ark of the covenant' – and dwell among us. Both symbols – manna and tent – are united in the eucharistic tabernacle of a Catholic church, where the incarnate Son draws men to the Father through his eucharistic gifts. And if, for the fourth-century Greek doctor Gregory of Nyssa, Moses entered on Sinai into the 'cloud' so as to know God and become his friend, that divine friendship is the aim both of the Incarnation and of the Church's Lent.

The fifth Sunday in the old Lectionary, the first of Passiontide, concentrated on the coming sacrifice of Christ, and Fr Sebastian considers this under the enigmatic sign, in the Book of Numbers, of the Serpent raised up in the wilderness: a figure of Christ crucified which Jesus applies to himself in the Fourth Gospel (Num. 21.4–9; John 3.14–15). Fashioned, perhaps, from the copper mined in both ancient and modern times at Phunon (Kharbet-Fenan), healing came, for this simple 'sacrament' of the Old Law, purely by looking. 'It is the way of looking that counts, and looking at him who was "lifted up"'.

And if the wilderness wanderings of ancient Israel are to be our biblical accompaniment during the liturgy of Lent, then what better text to take for Palm Sunday, when Jesus the Messiah enters Jerusalem on a donkey, than the other wonder of *Numbers*: Balaam's

ass (Num. 22.1–24.25)? If it took the biblical archetype of the talking
animals of C. S. Lewis's *Narnia* stories to make a pagan soothsayer
see sense, the entry of Israel into the Promised Land, which he facilitated, is captured only in a riddling mode by Christ's entry into
Jerusalem (the 'Faithful City that was to turn upon him'). 'But we
must understand our task and go in with our King and Master.'[40]

Fr Sebastian's final Old Testament type is the crossing of the Jordan
by Joshua – whose Hebrew name is the same as that of Jesus. If
Joshua was bidden to take off his shoes, so as to know by intimate
contact the earth of the Holy Land – holy because there the world's
salvation would take place – so the Christian, come through the waters
of baptism, which are the sacramental mediation of Christ's Passover,
must be conscious of the high calling and privilege which is his.

> Josue led them in, following the priests with the ark through the
> water, past the place where Jesus would be baptised. [And citing
> Origen of Alexandria:] 'When you come to the water of baptism,
> led by the priest, you enter the Land of Promise, and Jesus takes
> over from Moses and becomes your leader on your new journey'...
> When we tread in the footsteps of Josue who is Jesus, it is all holy
> ground, never to be defiled by the vanities we renounced with the
> fleshpots of Egypt, the very desire for which has been purged out
> of us by the desert and the last traces washed away by the Jordan.[41]

And so the land of Israel, sacred, in the last analysis, because it is a
figure of that 'place' which is man's communion with God in Jesus
Christ, opens out for us a never ending vista: the call is to go further,
not just in terms of moral growth but of growth in holiness as well.
This brings us to our next topic in Fr Sebastian's *oeuvre*.

Saints and heroes

Fr Sebastian had a considerable grasp of the history of sanctity in the
Order. Three typescript retreats in the possession of Blackfriars,
Cambridge – 'The Character of St Dominic' (1961), 'History of the
Order' (1953), 'Dominican Saints' (1954) – concern *au fond* the
history of Dominican holiness. In them, so to say, historiography has
become hagiography and vice versa, with the theological aim of
drawing out the Order's nature as a school of holiness.

Comparing Dominic with Francis, Fr Sebastian draws a sharp
contrast between a seigneurial figure – 'born in the manor-house, then
University and priesthood', and a bourgeois one. Citing an early
Franciscan source which describes in unflattering terms the post-

conversion appearance of the seraphic father ('He looked so dishev-
elled, they thought he was crazy'), he insinuates that St Dominic, if
not necessarily debonair, was always adequately turned out. For him,
poverty was simply 'a question of not using to excess'.[42] Dominic's
way of loving God was mediated through the desire to instruct people,
making his path of holiness a decidedly cooler affair than that of
ardent Francis. Fr Sebastian emphasised Dominic's capacity to lead
and legislate (it is vital, he thought, to know what one *wants* in the
spiritual life), and, as a counter-balance, his 'genius for friendship'.
Here he interprets the fragmentary evidence about Dominic's early
companions – William Claret, Bertrand of Garrigues, Matthew of
France, Peter Seila, Thomas of Toulouse, in the light of a central
theme of Jarrett spirituality. While admitting that Dominic's apostolic
ideal is lodged in the impersonal format of the Primitive
Constitutions, Fr Sebastian refuses to sever this from a personal sanctity which was linked to that mission by an – in memory, extremely
powerful – supportive prayer. Witness the early antiphon, *O spem
miram*. In his own free translation:

> It was a wonderful thing, the way he raised hope in the hearts of
> those who stood around him as he died, by promising that in the
> next life he would continue to help them. Make it come true, O
> Father, what you said, that you would continue to support the
> brethren with your prayers. There were many extraordinary things
> done for bodily ailments on earth, bring to us now, with Christ's
> help, the remedies for our ailments of the spirit.[43]

The picture is filled out in Fr Sebastian's 'History of the Order' where
other themes are brought into play: notably the trust in God which
gave Dominic a spirit of daring in his venture (and above all in the
gamble on rapid expansion which his early dispersion of the original
group involved), and the enthusiasm or devotion with which
Dominicans should regard study and intellectual life in general, as
well as the liturgy. And here the 'age of St Thomas' was vital, for
that mid-thirteenth-century zenith saw the Order's hitherto somewhat
fluid academic and liturgical life take crystalline form in Thomism and
the creation of the prototype liturgical books of its use by Humbert of
Romans.

Not that any of this guarantees the continued burgeoning of sanctity
unless institutional life stimulates, and houses, fervour. In the century
which connects the mastership of Munio de Zamora, deposed owing to
'detraction' in 1290, to the accession of the reforming Master Raymund
of Capua in 1385, Fr Sebastian found a slow descent into mediocrity,
the atmosphere of which was relieved only by occasional flares of –

significantly – *solitary* holiness: the 'rather solitary genius, Henry Suso' ... 'the great preacher, working alone, Vincent Ferrer'.[44] The increasing emphasis in these notes falls – by way of admiring choice – on the two principal reforming movements in the Order's history, from the fourteenth and nineteenth centuries respectively.

So far as the *mediaeval* Observantine reform is concerned, Fr Sebastian ascribed its power to St Catherine (who actually died before it gathered momentum). She was 'indirectly the cause of saving the Order'. Her understanding of the reforming Master, Raymund of Capua; her inspiration of him, and the support she promised after her death, made it possible. In an essay on 'Catherine the Dominican', published in *Blackfriars* he substantiated this claim in some detail.[45] Although Raymund's predecessor, Elias of Toulouse, had already embarked on a tightening up of the personal poverty of the friars, the news, around 1375, that pope Gregory XI might make him a cardinal, prompted Catherine to write to the pontiff, asking that he might appoint for the Order 'a good and virtuous man as our vicar, since the Order has need of it, having become too much of a wilderness'.[46] She wrote similarly to the archbishop of Otranto: 'Our present need is for a fearless surgeon who will wield the straight steel of holy justice; so much ointment has been used so far, that the limbs are nearly rotten.'[47]

Elias did not become a cardinal, but with the pope's death in 1378, and the disputed papal election which produced the 'Great' Schism of the West, the Order divided into two obediences – Avignon and Rome – leaving those faithful to the *Roman* pope without a canonical head. A fortnight after Catherine's death, and apparently predicted by her – to judge from a report of Bartholomew Dominici of Siena, as well as a comment in her own Letter 373, Raymond was elected Master of the Roman obedience by the Bologna General Chapter of 1380. And Fr Sebastian comments on this juncture:

> The schism had saddened the last two years of Catherine, who had worked so strenuously for the *santo passagio* or transfer of the papacy back to Rome, and had supported so keenly the Roman Urban VI. But now her spirit would live on in her friend Raymund, whom she used to call *padre e figliuolo dolcissimo* ['sweetest father and little son'] and who was now at the head of the Order. What was he going to do to bring the Order back to its former glory from being 'too much of a wilderness'?[48]

Raymund's scheme for reform turned on the creation of 'convents of observance' – which no one was obliged to join but where, likewise, no one was prevented from going. The model for such houses, Fr Sebastian thought, was furnished by a local reform, inaugurated by Catherine's women disciples, the monastery of the Second Order (enclosed nuns) at Pisa. Clara Gambacorta and Maria Mancini, with five others, moved from the house of the Pisan Dominicanesses at Santa Croce to the new foundation of San Domenico, with a charter for conventual reform consisting of five points: the absence of personal possessions and of a living room of one's own; regular attendance at choir; habitual silence in the house; strict enclosure. Only the last of these was irrelevant to their brethren in the First Order. Raymund recognised here the beginning of the realisation of Catherine's hopes. The notion that reform and renewal might 'infect' a Province by the creation of such a model house was probably turned into law at the Vienna General Chapter of 1388 (its *Acta* have perished), for some such arrangement is reflected in Raymund's decree of 1390 and a bull of Pope Boniface IX in 1391. The beauty of the scheme, in Fr Sebastian's eyes lay in 'the gentleness of the method':[49] while reforming, the less good elsewhere is tolerated in charity. 'Note that Raymond's scheme was so devised as *not to break charity*, but to have its effect gradually, to appeal to the young and enthusiastic.'[50]

Fr Sebastian also noted the role in the reform of (once again) *friends*, not only among the women but also with the men. This was especially clear in Italy, where John Dominici, the first 'vicar' of the reformed houses and Laurence of Ripafratta, their first novice-master, had befriended the nuns of Pisa, while in 1405–6 they managed to attract to the Order in its reformed guise the friends Antoninus of Florence and John of Fiesole, better known as 'Fra Angelico'. If the first priory to be built specifically as a house of the reform was Fiesole, it was at San Marco in Florence, under Antoninus's priorship that Fra Angelico created in wondrous images the most stunning testament to its spiritual power. One senses in Fr Sebastian's account a love for the beauty, both of appearance and of spirit, of which Italy is capable – something to which his Italian ancestry doubtless predisposed him but which also linked him to a persistent English literary passion, not least of his period. In *Aaron's Rod*, D. H. Lawrence had written:

> Sunlight, lovely full sunlight lingered warm and still on the balcony. It caught the façade of the cathedral sideways, like the tip of a flower, and sideways lit up the stem of Giotto's tower, like a lily stem, or a long, lovely pale pink and white and green pistil of the lily of the cathedral. Florence – the flowery town ... the red

lilies. The *Fiorentini* the flower-souled. Flowers with good roots in the mud and muck, as should be: and fearless blossoms in the air, like the cathedral and the tower and the David.[51]

Fr Sebastian concluded his essay on Catherine's Dominicanism:

Raymund's reform of the Dominican Order is an important phenomenon in monastic history. In all the older Orders there have been periods when the first fervour had declined, and it was humanly inevitable that this should be so. In most cases reformed branches or congregations began and frequently developed into juridically distinct bodies. But with the Dominicans the legal constitution of the Order from the beginning was such that any splintering from the juridical unity under the Master General (apart from the temporary division during the schism) was unthinkable. Raymund's scheme was therefore essentially a reform from within; in most provinces the whole province gradually became 'observant', and the process was virtually complete within a hundred years.

If that statement is too generous in its ascription of ubiquity, Fr Sebastian could turn it, in another context, into suasive exhortation to his fellow Dominicans:

When observance is an accepted thing, as now, let us treasure it, and never despise it. It is our means of realising the ideal – whatever share it may be, and even when it is hard or wearisome, it is heroic and beautiful.[52]

It should not be thought, however, that his concept of the Dominican Order was narrowly restricted to the issue of regular (or monastic) observance, for this is traditionally regarded, rather, as a *means* to the Order's goal. As the Constitutions in vigour at the time of his writing declared:

The means established by the most holy patriarch [St Dominic] for reaching our goal are: besides the three solemn vows of obedience, chastity and poverty, the regular life with its monastic observances, the solemn recitation of the divine office, and the assiduous study of sacred truth.[53]

The goal, then, is distinguished from its means:

Our Order is known from the beginning to have been specially instituted for the sake of preaching and the salvation of souls. Consequently, our study must aim principally at this, that we might be useful to the souls of others.[54]

'Zeal for preaching', preaching as one's 'normal job', 'getting *veritas* across to the world', these brief formulas punctuate Fr Sebastian's writing on Dominicanism. He evidently entertained the possibility that one rather unconventional Dominican – Savonarola – might be a saint, redeemed and sanctified by preaching. So aflame was the fifteenth-century Florentine friar for the conversion of the Christian city that he found himself unable to halt in the atrium of the papal court – and therefore denounced that also! Moreover, he points out that '*all* the *beati* and Saints of the seventeenth century [Order] were ... either missionaries or the fruits of the missions in the New World'. Still, that efflorescence would not have been possible, he thought, without contemplation, which he defined, in brief, as 'looking at God – not necessarily "swept to the angels" – but the dedication of ourselves [to prayer] with real conviction'.[55]

Fr Sebastian's robustly traditional view of the Order, influenced by his sympathy for the Observantine movements which mark its history, show through well in the *responsa* he sent to Rome by way of answer to the Master of the Order's 1967 'Questionnaire' on the shape of its post-Conciliar reform. In a terse Latinity he declared St Dominic to have 'founded a monastic Order whose members are, so to speak, "preaching monks",' from which it follows that 'the monastic life is of the essence of the Order'. Contemplating and transmitting to others the fruits of contemplation suggests that the 'testimony' of which the conciliar decree *Perfectae Caritatis*, on the Renewal of Religious Life, spoke so eloquently is, in the Dominican case, 'both by the monastic life and by preaching, and by the two equally'.[56] Any tampering with the traditional status of the four 'essential means' to preaching – the vows, the regular life with its monastic observances, the divine Office, and study, would, he thought, reduce the Order to the status of an early modern 'Congregation'. The classical conventual life, learnt in the years of formation, 'becomes afterwards habitual, and a rock of strength for the apostolate'. He thought that the 'observances' had a significance for their own in terms of apostolic witness: silence over against the cacophony of modern life; fasting over against its excessive comfort, the enclosure over against the contemporary world's unrestrained *mores*. He spoke to the situation of two groups within the Order in particular: its students and lay-brothers. On the first, while he was keen that those who already received a solid formation in Catholic theology should study in secular universities, the latter were no places for the initial studies. The glory of the Order's traditional formation was the 'confluence of study, community and liturgy' in a house numerous enough to make the celebration of the liturgy and the keeping of monastic observance possible 'with full dignity'. And as to the co-operator brothers:

> Our priory is like a city, whose citizens vow themselves to serve God and bear witness to the world, working for the salvation of souls. The greater part of this commonwealth carry out preaching and teaching formally and professedly. But, so as to sustain the total life of the city, others are administrators of goods – co-workers – and these simultaneously bear witness ... through the monastic life, yes, but also as sharing in an apostolate which is fruitful though not sacerdotal.

And Fr Sebastian envisaged that, in the post-Conciliar period, the brothers of the Order could lead a popular or parochial liturgical office, more suited to the less highly educated faithful (on the analogy, presumably, of the Little Office of the Blessed Virgin, and various devotional para-liturgies) thus permitting the full continuance of the monastic Office of the priestly and choir brethren which 'by its venerable tradition and intrinsic beauty carries a special power of witness and draws the more intellectual (as they are called) of the faithful'. For the solemn liturgy of the Order is 'the most precious part of our monastic life', as well as a source of 'consolation and edification' to many of the faithful. 'It would be deplorable if our common prayer were reduced to a vulgar order.' And notably, 'if the Latin language is renounced, so is the chant'. The rejection of 'our rite and especially of our chant would do irreparable harm',[57] as would the abandonment of St Thomas as the Order's main theological inspiration, 'the rock from which we are hewn'. 'The true "progressive" goes forward from the past into the future, ever mindful of his inheritance.' On the issue of poverty, Fr Sebastian thought that, for Dominicans, it really meant 'living modestly', since, for them poverty was directed chiefly to 'the witness of personal abnegation and the freedom to preach to men and woman of every condition'. In all these matters, he considered the link with the Order's contemplative nuns essential – and reminded the Master of the Order of their role in stimulating the Raymundian reform.

These comments are the more valuable in that Fr Sebastian showed himself no mere defender of a *status quo*: he thought it highly desirable, for instance, to introduce tutorials or supervisions on the Oxbridge model, as part of Dominican education, as well as to rationalise the Roman faculties, including of course the Angelicum, as constituent colleges of a single papal University.

An overall view

Fr Sebastian had a rare opporunity to draw together the various aspects of his Catholic and Dominican interests when commissioned by Penguin Books to contribute a general study of 'Roman Catholicism' to their series of 'Pelican Originals'. The 'Jarrett succession' is evidenced in the Greek quotation which prefaces the work: *monon timion te kai erasmion ... to philon genesthai Theô* – (The only thing that is really worthwhile ... is to become God's friend) – a citation from the *Life of Moses* by the fourth-century Cappadocian father Gregory of Nyssa.[58] Since the body of the text was completed by August 1962, before the Second Vatican Council had opened, and in going to the press there was time to add only an appendix on its formal procedure[59] (and a dedication to pope John XXIII, who died in the wake of its first session), Fr Sebastian's book might be said to have been out of date before it reached the shops. The timing was certainly unfortunate; but, as the decades since the close of the Council accumulate, and the need to garner the wisdom of *all* the Catholic generations becomes ever more acute in a sustained crisis for Catholicism that sees no general abating, the sin of being 'pre-conciliar' becomes ever more venial.

The book falls into five parts: the vocation of the Christian; the faith of the Christian; the life of the Church; the holiness of the Church; and 'the Church in the World' – a title adventitiously prophetic of the Council's Pastoral Constitution *Gaudium et Spes*, though, significantly, the first 'world' to which Fr Sebastian would relate the Church is that of *letters*. His remit was obviously one of sticking to the common doctrine, expounded in a manner as little personal as possible, and if this reduces the attracting power of *Roman Catholicism*, it also enables it to possess a representative quality.

Fr Sebastian opens by citing the 'traditional English Catholic Catechism', based as that is in part on the Doway Catechism of 1649. These opening words of the humble 'Penny Catechism' would certainly have been familiar to Fr Sebastian's Catholic readers in 1963:

Q. Who made you?
A. God made me.
Q. Why did God make you?
A. God made me to know him, love him, and serve him in this world, and to be happy with him for ever in the next.[60]

While his exposition of this text does justice to the elements in it open to reason to establish (the existence of God, the immortality of the rational soul), his stress falls emphatically on getting over to the reader the idea of special revelation and its salvific intention.

> The whole purpose of Catholic faith and practice, of which this small book is attempting to provide an outline, is to lead man to the realization in this life of his supernatural vocation, and of the fulfilment of that vocation in the next; to bring man to what the theologians call a 'state of grace', or a state of friendship with God upon earth, and so to a 'state of glory', or the eternal company of God in the world to come; to show man the way of 'justification' through Christ our Lord, and man's response to God's invitation to friendship, which leads him to 'eternal salvation'; and therefore, in short, to teach men to think as Christians, and so to lead their lives on earth as Christians, on the road to man's homeland with God in heaven.[61]

Only in the fulness of friendship with God will the human person find the 'whole fulfilment' of their nature: hence the vital urgency of grasping the notion of revelation, which is, at least in part, the only possible bearer of the good news about man's destiny. Echoing Fr Victor's exposition of Thomas's thought, Fr Sebastian insists that while revelation is the true word of God, the 'articles of faith', in which the Church, at her Councils, has summed up the witness of Scripture, are man's word responding in faith to the divine Word.[62] That revelation, as given to apostles and prophets is frequently couched in symbol and image, comparable with the language both of poetry and mysticism in their attempts to express the heights of experience, respectively human and divine. Hence the irreplacable role of Church authority. Only a living voice, whose timbre is assured by God in Christ, can 'guarantee' the words of Scripture and, moreover, ensure they are rightly understood.

The remainder of the book's account of the 'Christian vocation' are taken up with a sketch of the ethical practice of the Catholic Church, seen as specified in the Ten Words (or Ten Commandments) as further interpreted by the twofold love-command (love of God, love of neighbour). The Commandments draw attention to forms of moral evil and good in action; their biblical order attests the 'primacy of the spiritual' (a phrase of Maritain's), they begin with the service of God, and go on with the service of neighbour.

The longest section of this highly compressed work is that which takes as its subject the faith of the Church. Its structure is rather unusual. An opening chapter on 'The Authority of Christ' provides a tiny commentary on the whole of the Apostles' Creed. Two further chapters consider Bible and dogma as refractions of that authority, while the bulk of the section contemplates the Mass, and the other sacraments, as expressions of the Christ-life in the Church. Next, Fr Sebastian investigates eschatology, as the final goal of that life. An entire chapter on the topic of indulgences interrupts the sequential flow (doubtless because so many potential converts from other varieties of Christianity found it worrying). Finally, what has been said so far is recapitulated in reference to Mary who unites the end to the beginning, the Assumption, the mystery of hope *par excellence*, to the 'proto-gospel' of Genesis, the first glimmering in redemption history of divine salvation.

If Fr Sebastian's biblical expertise somewhat ran away with him in the comparatively full account of such matters as the formation of the canon of Scripture, theories of biblical inspiration, and the choice of English translations,[63] the doctrinal summaries are stark, though the baldness is occasionally relieved by a lush *aperçu*. Thus, for instance on the dating of the saving death *sub Pontio Pilato*:

> It is a remarkable thing that all generations of Christians have been for all these centuries singing in church the name of an obscure civil servant: the reason, surely, for its inevitable inclusion, is to underline the historicity of the event, for there is nothing more everyday and documentary than the name of a government official.

More telling for Fr Sebastian's approach to Catholicism is the mysterious and sacramental understanding of how 'the Life of Christ in the Church' is passed on. Its heart is the Holy Eucharist, which he discusses twice: as communion, in the midst of the seven sacraments, but as sacrifice by way of indicating 'the very centre of the Christian religion'.[64] If Christ as *pontifex* rebuilt the bridge between God and man, making peace by the blood of his cross, the holy sacrifice is what enables individual Christians to participate in that once-for-all offering of Calvary.

> The Mass is Christ's own redeeming sacrifice, performed once upon Calvary, but, as at the Last Supper, now in his mercy thrown open to man's participation in the offering. The whole point of Christ's gesture at the Last Supper was to include his friends in the offering of the sacrifice to be completed on Good Friday, and by his command to 'do this, to enable successive generations to be included.

Indeed, without the Supper, the death on the tree would not have been a true sacrifice: though Christ *could* have made the offering of his death sacrificial by a purely private intention, he did not in fact do so. He 'meant' his death not mentalistically but ritualistically, so that the disciples might not only understand it but actually share it, in an act of public communion.

To this Fr Sebastian links the very being of the Church – here anticipating the 'ecclesiology of communion' which has made such a mark on the official documents of the Roman church since the Second Vatican Council. The Mass is the sacrificial prayer of Christ inaugurated in the upper room, and continued before the Father until he come. He invites his members to share that prayer by partaking in his body, so that 'through him, with him, in him' (a phrase from the doxology which concludes the Roman Canon) they, though many, may be one body, for they all share the one bread (a reference to 1 Corinthians 10.17).

The only context adequate to understanding the sacraments at large is, likewise, the mystery of Christ's salvation. Divine filiation, friendship with God, new life in Christ: these are the key terms in which Scripture expresses our justification by the Father, redemption by the Son, sanctification by the Holy Spirit. But here the question arises, how does each person receive God's 'favour' – either at the 'initial rebirth' or 'in the preservation of the new life that is consequent upon the friendship'?

> Now although the power comes from God's grace, it is obvious that there must be a moment of the man's acceptance, and for man in his earthly state as a creature of sense some external sign is necessary to reassure him of the intangible inner reality: an external act that *signifies* the bestowal of God's grace and the man's receiving it.[65]

The (seven) sacramental signs are Christ's way of showing to human intelligence, and imagination, the reality of his grace. They constitute a spiritual replication of natural living, whose rhythms include 'one-off' events (such as, most obviously, birth itself), as well as actions (like the taking of nourishment) repeated every day.

Though Fr Sebastian is concerned, in this plain man's guide to Catholicism, not to be original, occasionally 'disputed questions' in the Church's theology oblige him to take a view. Thus we find him espousing Cardinal Cajetan's idea that, for children who have died before baptism could be administered, their parents' desire for that baptism creates the channel the divine power uses in bringing their offspring baptism's effects.[66] On the vexed question of the distinctive aim of confirmation, he produces the careful formula:

> ... the bestowal of a special grace of the Holy Spirit, bearing fruit in adult life (which may or may not have begun) in the divine strength necessary for leading a life in close friendship with God.

At Baptism a person has become a friend of God: at Confirmation (as the name suggests) he is made into a firm friend. A person who has been confirmed, perhaps years ago, reminds himself from time to time of the power that lies within him in virtue of his Confirmation, perhaps hardly realized and only too rarely brought to bear upon the problems he encounters.[67]

Fr Sebastian's theology of the interrelation of the Last Supper and the cross, already mentioned, he borrowed from the French Jesuit Maurice de la Taille whose *Mysterium Fidei* of 1921, disliked by Vincent McNabb, greatly influenced David Jones.[67] He presents sin, in the context of the sacrament of penance, as a 'disassociation from [Christ's] atonement before the heavenly Father', seeing confession as chiefly concerned to restore people, then, to divine friendship. 'Mortal sins' are those that kill such friendship dead; venial sins he compares to the 'rough words and gestures' that may come between friends, straining friendship, but with no thought of abandoning it. Fr Sebastian shows how such sins are none the less proper material for this sacrament, a point found difficult by many.

> Such things are indeed offences against the friendship, and do require the thought 'I am sorry'. Thus the sacrament of Penance, though not here restoring a broken friendship, is with the help of contrition bringing back the fulness of joy in friendship, or in theological terms an 'increase of grace'.

It is surprising that a Dominican theologian can present the sacrament of Holy Order in terms of the priestly (sacramental) and pastoral (juridical) dimensions of the Church's life, but without mention of the prophetic – the preaching of the Word! At the same time, however, he moved towards the Second Vatican Council's defintely un-Thomistic conviction that the episcopate is the fulness of ministerial priesthood, and held out an olive branch to Anglicans by treating the effects of Order (and thus of the Eucharist and penance also) as available, even without a valid rite, via the 'desire of the recipients'.

> Thus even if the Catholic sees Anglican Orders as invalid, this by no means suggests that he sees them as meaningless; on the contrary, their very meaningfulness to Anglicans, and the working through them of God's grace, is a warrant of the true desire.

In line with the multifaceted deployment of the crucial idea of *friendship* in *Roman Catholicism*, Fr Sebastian treats marriage – that other sacramental life-way – as a special kind of friendship, indeed a 'summit of friendship', crowned by a physical intimacy to which 'not all friends are called'.

Consideration of the sacrament of anointing – generally called in Fr Sebastian's period (but not by him) the 'Last Anointing', *Extrema Unctio*, ushers in an account of eschatology, the Last Things. Though, as his emendation of the common interpretation of the Latin title suggests, he readily grants that the anointing of the sick, with its effects not only of healing of mind (Council of Florence), consolation of spirit (Council of Trent) but also elimination of the 'relics' of sin (Trent likewise), *can* be followed by physical recovery, Fr Sebastian treats it as more usually a sacrament for the final crisis.

> Many people, stricken by a sudden or violent death, will not be able to receive this sacrament, but it is the normal desire of every Catholic to receive it, if possible, at the crisis of being about to pass into the unknown.

It is doubtful whether he would have followed the later trend in 'pastoral' liturgy to treat the journey of death as unproblematic, and a Requiem Mass as an occasion for pashcal rejoicing. He found the unknown journey a 'terifying dream', and the main concern of the Catholic burial service to be praying for the departed's good estate in the life to come. Not that biblical, credal and magisterial pronouncements leave us entirely uninformed, and here he concentrated upon 'individual' eschatology, especially in the light of Pope Benedict XII's decree on the vision of God of 1336, though setting his discussion in the wider context of hope in the 'general' resurrection. The face-to-face intuitive vision of the divine Essence alone can slake human desire, satisfy the 'intellectual creature'. But as the Apocalypse of John warns, there shall not enter there 'any thing defiled' (Rev. 21.27). And this raises the topics of hell and purgatory.

The Lamb of God, in taking away human sin, simultaneously plants in human hearts what Augustine called the 'seed of glory', which is to flower in the reciprocal friendship of man with God in heaven. However, it takes two to make a friendship, and 'he who destroys the seed will be unable to behold the flower'. Destroying the seed means persevering in a deliberate state of enmity with God, refusing his friendship to the end. This privation of heaven is what we call hell. But, as with the contrast of mortal and venial sin, there can be blemishes (merely) on that friendship, requiring a restoration of the perfect innocence given in baptism. And such cleansing of the spirit is what we call purgatory – something Fr Sebastian elucidates with the help of Newman's *Dream of Gerontius*, a poem about a Catholic Everyman's dying. And 'Who is to say which souls have reached

eternal bliss, and which are undergoing cleansing and needing intercession?' It is indeed appalling presumption to claim to know this,
even in the choice of colours for vestments, symbolically saturated as
such tones are in the Latin rite. What the Church of the ages bids is
that we should surround souls with pleas for rest and light, in their
utterly new condition of existing. Here too the vexed question of
indulgences finds its place, with Fr Sebastian stressing apophatically
that 'it is only God who can weigh [their] value'.

His account of the faith of Christians ends with Mariology, in a
patristically attuned evocation of Catholic belief about and devotion to
the Mother of the Saviour, making good use, incidentally, of Oriental
references, and notably texts from the Byzantine liturgy. On the floor
of the church at Long Sutton, Lincolnshire, one can still see the
English mediaeval invocation which sums up her place, next to the
Redeemer. 'Jesus mercy, Lady help': Fr Sebastian's epitome of her
role.

In dealing with the 'Life of the Church' he confines himself, somewhat oddly, to matters of worship and governance, leaving mission
and social service to 'The Church and the World'. The two subjects
he *does* treat, liturgy and government, are united in his account of the
Church's magisterium for, while the highest office of Church authority is interpreting divine revelation by the declaration of dogmatic
truth, the communion (*koinônia*) that binds into one body all who
accept Christ's authority on earth means that 'Liturgy must be regu-
lated by obedience', an obedience given, furthermore, in other areas
to those who 'command in his name'. A forthright account of the
infallibility of the episcopate gathered under its papal head (or, in
special circumstances, of the pope alone) reminds us, however, that
such definitive guidance of Christians can only be exercised 'with
regard to matters of faith and morals, i.e. what we must believe and
do for salvation, and not with regard to any purely mundane details
of human existence.'[69]

Fr Sebastian devotes far more space to a consideration of the many
Eastern liturgies of the Catholic Church than would be expected in a
book of this length: a vital testimony to the principle that liturgy,
though always requiring rubrical discipline by its celebrants,[70] need
not, for all that, be uniform. Noting, though still smaller than a man's
hand, the rise of liturgical reform in the Western church, he cautions
against too whole-hearted a subscription to its trends. The more
contemplative mode of quiet assisting at Mass of the 'recent past' is
as valid as any form of communal prayer aloud; central to the revival
is the renewal of the chant, by a 'restoration of the dignity of the
ancient melodies, and a deeper understanding of their value'. Fr

Sebastian's remarks on the objects of craft which surround the Catholic liturgy – images, music, fabrics, vessels, incense, and the church building itself – are highly redolent of Ditchling. In a sentence which Gill might have formed, he affirms that all these things 'are governed by liturgical laws, and the work of the artists and craftsmen who make these "liturgical things" is obedient work'. All these comments retain their force and value – unlike his portrait of Church government, which has been rendered antique by the reform of the Roman curia, and the Canon Law (both Western and Eastern) under the post-conciliar popes. Commenting on his work in the pontificate of John Paul II, it certainly sounds ironic to find him saying that anyone who knows Rome would instinctively feel that only one brought up within, or near, that 'most Italian of traditions' would 'fill the place properly'. And if there is a touch there, derived perhaps from his maternal ancestry, of pride in Italy as a Catholic culture, Fr Sebastian ends his account of the papacy by arguing for a legitimate triumphalism in papal style. Periodically pruned as its ceremonial splendours have been (and Church reform was, as he recognised, on the cards as he wrote), its forms remain 'the natural expression of men's enthusiastic reverence and acclaim for one who ... commands the obedience in things of the spirit of more millions than any other man, and wields an authority that is not his own, but is of Christ.'

Such things are, however, tangential to Christian holiness, Fr Sebastian's penultimate section. His chapter on prayer consists in a brief exegesis of the Our Father, followed by an explanation of the main Hours of the liturgical day, and, as a tailpiece, the Rosary. The combination of Scripture, liturgy and devotion seems especially Dominican. Given the form of the *Pater*, the prayer of petition is naturally prominent, though he notes the significance of Blessed Henry Suso's approach to the prayer, taking its petitions in reverse order. (Thus one begins with the 'elementary elimination of evil and temptation in our lives' and finishes with 'what is ultimate and yet primary, the adoration of God as "our Father"'.) None the less – and in accordance with the 'amicitial' or 'philiac' character of his theology (if one may be permitted such Greco-Roman neologisms!), his fundamental understanding of prayer is as the 'practice of friendship ... with God'. For the sanctification of the day Fr Sebastian recommends the lay recitation of at least part of the Liturgy of the Hours: he reminds his readers of the splendid Books of Hours which grace many museums; these have humble variants today. He also recommends the Rosary, and not just as the 'Poor Man's Psalter' since 'many of the most learned find solace in those simple forms, and realize the enrichment gained from the frequent, brief and measured meditation upon the greatest events of history.' Prayer helps moral action, which is turn conduces to sanctity, and eventually, in the saints, to perfection. The terms of this formula give us the remaining chapter headings of the section.

The account of distinctively Christian morality would have benefited from, for instance, the biblical and Thomist materials of Fr Gerald, for it restricts itself to the Church's interpretation and application of the precepts of the moral law, in her capacity as that law's custodian. Gaining a fuller picture of the Christian life must await his chapter on 'Christian Sanctity', which draws on a quartet of articles in the English Dominican journal of ascetical and mystical theology, *Life of the Spirit*, published some few years previously.[71] As the title of the original essays makes clear, his preferred approach is *historical*.

> In the long history of the Church's teaching there have been many masters of 'the spiritual life', that is, there have been many who have shown to Christian men and women the way of the ascent of the spirit towards God. All through that history the masters have drawn upon God's revelation in Scripture and grown to a deeper understanding of it, and as the centuries passed, they have learnt from their predecessors and built up a great heritage of spiritual wisdom.[72]

Beginning with Clement of Alexandria, Fr Sebastian presents a synergistic doctrine of growth into perfection, which entails both God's drawing of the person through loving contemplation to himself, and the human effort to master the passions and avoid the sinful self-seeking which impedes the ascent to God. Indeed, he finds the distinction between 'asceticism' and 'mysticism' to lie not in a chronological schema whereby we pass, hopefully, from the first to the second, but in exploration of what these twin dimensions, divine and human, of this co-operative process involve.

> These two sides of the one problem have been labelled by the theologians *mysticism* on the one hand, that is, the laying open of the spirit to the direct influence of God, and on the other hand *asceticism*, 'training or discipline', by which a man with God's help schools himself in moral virtue avoids sin, and deliberately turns his thoughts towards God.[73]

Elsewhere he points out that the sharp demarcation, not to say dichotomy between the two which is sometimes met with has no sanction in the *oeuvre* of St Thomas. There the gifts of the Holy Spirit link the human work of self-perfection through the virtues (ascetical theology) with God's work in the soul (mystical theology), grace building upon nature and the love of God excluding whatever is contrary to Christian perfection.[74] So far as the modern debate on the matter in the Catholic theology of the first half of this century is concerned, Fr Sebastian was influenced by the posthumous *Theologia Spiritualis* of the Jesuit, Père de Guibert of which an English translation had appeared in 1954: at de Guibert's hands, the separation becomes a harmless distinction within a whole.

Fr Sebastian's concise history of spirituality could and did profit from the substantial tomes published on this newcomer to the circle of the sacred sciences in his lifetime. Marcel Viller, of the Society of Jesus, had founded the great *Dictionnaire de Spiritualité* (still proceeding in its alphabetical fascicules) in 1937. It placed on a more professional basis the discoveries of such researchers as his fellow-Jesuit Emile Pourrat, whose *Histoire de Spiritualité* had begun to appear in 1918, two years after the inception of the Abbé Bremond's monumental *Histoire du sentiment religieux en France*. Meanwhile, at the Roman institute of the Orientalium, the indefatigable Père Irenée Hausherr, also of the Society, had commenced his series of still valuable monographs on the Eastern spiritual tradition.

Fr Sebastian has his own heroes and heroines chosen from among the *galère* which these works display. The Fathers are foundational, with the Cappadocians and Augustine central pillars. Gregory of Nyssa's apophaticism, with its emphasis on a cloud of unknowing, has as its goal the divine-human communion of friendship, while his brother Basil, as organiser of monastic life helped form the perfect setting for testing this teaching. Looking far ahead, Fr Sebastian commented

> The history of spiritual teaching has always been closely connected with the practice of spiritual perfection, namely with the history of monasticism, for indeed one of the salient features of the *devotio moderna* was the organization of the spiritual life in such a way that it does not depend any more upon the external profession of monastic life ... but rather builds up outside the monastery and in the world the spirit that governs monastic life, so that in a sense, the devout Christian, while pursuing spiritual perfection, leads a monastic life in the world *nella cella del cognoscimento di sè* ['in the cell of self-knowledge'] as St Catherine of Siena ... says in the first chapter of the *Dialogo*.[75]

And as for Augustine, his precious contribution was the placing of the whole enterprise under the sign of *amor Dei*, as charity begins, progresses, becomes great and perfect.[76] Other patristic luminaries are not neglected, especially among the greeks where Origen, Evagrius and Diadochus of Photike are singled out for praise. Fr Sebastian admits the enormous influence in the West of Denys the Areopagite, whose tripartite scheme of 'turning round' (*epistrophê*) to the Creator by way of purification (*katharsis*), illumination (*ellampsis*) and union (*henôsis*) became classical, and had caught up with the scholarly rediscovery of Maximus the Confessor who, as he puts it 'summarized the teaching of the Eastern masters with a new particular emphasis on the Person of Christ, who unites all things in himself, as the Church unites many within herself.'[77]

But of course the Western mediaeval development (in which, as a Dominican, Fr Sebastian would naturally have some moral and emotional investment) is unthinkable without the Western reception of East Christian spirituality – via John Cassian especially. (His *Conferences* were particularly appreciated by the early Dominicans.) Fr Sebastian is eloquent in praise of the contemplative tradition sprung from the *Rule* of Benedict whose 'wonderful freedom' in the practice of prayer he singles out for comment: from it came St Gregory's more reflective theory of contemplation, elaborated with help from Augustine, Anselm's union of affective prayer with scholastic theology, Bernard's passionate mysticism, as well as major figures of the sixteenth-century *devotio moderna* in Italy and Catalonia, and such turn-of-the-century masters as John Cuthbert Hedley and Columba Marmion. Among women theologians of the spiritual life Fr Sebastian anticipates later twentieth-century interest in Hildegard of Bingen.

He treats the Parisian Victorine school as a forerunner of the Dominican approach of the high middle ages: study, meditation and prayer being inseparable features of a single life. Fr Sebastian regards the spirit of Victorine theology as later embodied in their fellow-Augustinian the Franciscan minister-general Bonaventure, whose mysticism also recalls that of St Bernard. His account of St Thomas concentrates on the gifts of the Holy Spirit (an emphasis, this, of Fr Gerald, as we have seen), for it is by the action of these gifts ('qualities or habits', as Aquinas remarks, 'by which a man is made ready to be obedient to the Holy Spirit') that grace can build on nature.[78]

It is characteristic of Fr Sebastian's miniature history of spirituality that he does not care to draw well-defined boundaries between its various 'schools', recognising the high degree of mutual borrowing which their members practised. Thus he finds a close 'association', at least, between Albert the Great and the German Benedictine mystics, notably Mechthild of Magdeburg; from Albert the mystical theology of Denys the Areopagite percolated down to the Dominican Rhineland mystics (Eckhart, Tauler, Suso) – yet these were also affected by the work of the Flemish Augustinian Jan Ruysbroeck. Relishing the 'exact theological terms' in which Catherine of Siena embodied her mystical experience, Fr Sebastian can also approve the unassuming qualities of Ruysbroeck's fellow-Augustinian the English mystic Walter Hilton and the 'primitive quiet prayer' of the Byzantine Hesychasts who were his contemporaries. (He notes, however, of Gregory Palamas, the fourteenth-century 'doctor' of Hesychasm, that 'certain doctrinal consequences of his teaching remain an obstacle between East and West'.)

Devotio moderna, already touched on, is, in the strictest sense, a Netherlands school of spirituality which looked to Gerard de Groot (died 1384) as its founder. But in Fr Sebastian's view 'modern devotion', taken *au sens large*, commands the entire subsequent development of mainstream Latin Catholic piety. Ignatius of Loyola 'developed the key-ideas of the *devotio moderna* into something new and conquering, so that the piety of the whole post-Tridentine Church came under their influence, transformed and renewed by his brilliant spirit.'[79] Loyola sent three balls spinning through the firmament of Catholic piety: first, the deliberate adoption of systematic meditation; secondly, by way of a more marked stress on the three stages (purificatory, illuminative, unitive) of spiritual life, a tendency to detailed 'mapping' of its journey, of which St Teresa of Avila will provide the most egregious example; and thirdly, emphasis on the first, foundational, purgative stage as a *sine qua non* to be long inhabited through 'methodical prayer and the careful cultivation of virtue'.[80]

But if Fr Sebastian was tempted to depreciate the 'modern devotion' for its hostility to 'youthful exuberance', and coldness about theology (so different from its Victorine forebears), he was restrained by the thought that its main elements were far from 'something new that broke upon the world with Gerard de Groot'. The three stages or ways of prayer stand forth already in St Bonaventure, and are the structuring principle of the *Mystica Theologia* of the late thirteenth-century Carthusian Hugh of Balma. It was to Bonaventure and his Franciscan contemporary David of Augsburg that Gerard de Groot and his disciple Florentius Radewijns turned for instruction, and the crucial Ignatian term 'the Exercises' appears in the title of the latter's work: *Tractatus de Spiritualibus Exercitiis*. The *Modus Meditandi* of Luigi Barbo, reforming abbot of Santa Giustina at Padua, offered itself as a legitimate development of St Benedict's *lectio divina*, and through his fellow-abbot García de Cisneros of Montserrat, most probably influenced the newly reborn St Ignatius. Fr Sebastian, despite the burden of sometimes acrimonious rivalry between the Order of Preachers and the Society of Jesus (above all, in the theology of grace), writes with great respect of the Ignatian *Exercises*, seeing their main points in the twofold technique of 'particular *examen*' whereby faults are traced and corrected, and the 'exercise' itself – methodical meditation.

Consonant with the most influential Dominican sub-school of his day, that of Reginald Garrigou-Lagrange, Fr Sebastian is really more interested, however, in the Carmelite mystics of Spain's *siglo d'oro*. The represent 'the culmination of Catholic teaching on this ascent to perfect union with God'.[81] Teresian and Sanjuanist teaching is aligned with that of St Thomas by the claim that the basic principle of the first is 'that perfection consists in a complete conformity to the will of God', – a 'working out' of the fundamental principle of the second that Christian perfection 'depends upon the union with God which is charity'.[82] Teresa and John of the Cross are presented attractively as complementing each other in the way that friends should – a reference to her practical and autobiographical gifts, his poetic and theological insight.

None the less, while Fr Sebastian writes convincingly of the Carmelite doctors, his heart is given to another 'couple' with whom his account ends. François de Sales and Jeanne-Françoise Fremiot de Chantal introduce us to no different mystery, but more gently, less alarmingly. *Douceur* even or especially toward ourselves may seem too easy a virtue yet *la vie dévote*, to which the 'gentleman saint' would lead us is no less than the wondrous third mansion of St Teresa, where 'we should occupy ourselves, if we can, by gazing at him who is gazing at us, *en que mire qu le mira* ...'[83] Pray as you can, not as you cannot, is Fr Sebastian's last word, bearing in mind the urgency of the question: since, to cite Teresa again, *Es la puerta la oraciòn* ... 'Prayer is the door by which God can enter the soul'.[84]

Fr Sebastian's picture of sanctity draws on these materials, since holiness will naturally include prayerfulness. An identikit of the saint will tell us, better than any formal definition, what holiness means.

> It means primarily that the person loves God above all things and serves him with all his heart; that in his love of God he loves his fellow creatures; that he has learnt, at least in some measure, to gaze at God's greatness and goodness and to speak with God 'as a man is wont to speak to his friend', that is, to practise prayer and some measure of contemplation; that he is uniting himself in this life to God's will; that he is taking seriously his service of God and therefore as far as possible keeps himself from sin and temptation.[85]

If history throughout its post-Pentecostal course can provide examples of men and women conspicuous for their sanctity, Church authority has none the less a grave responsibility to see to it that 'none but those of genuine and certain sanctity should be put before the faithful as models of Christian living or surrounded with tokens of public honour'. Even without the mediaeval and modern 'canonisation' process – a term which may denote the identification of a saint as a 'yardstick' for holy living or, alternatively their inclusion within the official 'list' of holy persons – some kind of discernment would have to be practised.

Beginning with the martyrs (Fr Sebastian records the scrawled appeals to them in the catacombs – *petite, rogate*), the instinct of the faithful has been to venerate models of self-dedication, and, assured that they have been found worthy to receive the vision of God, to seek the assistance of those who are ever before his Face.

It is that *saeculum*, 'the Church in the *World*', which remains to be discussed before *Roman Catholicism* closes. Fr Sebastian places under that rubric all the works of the Church *ad extra*: expounding Scripture, explaining Christian doctrine, providing personal spiritual direction at retreats or days of recollection. Maintaining Christian scholarship, responding to scientific discovery and technological innovation, proclaiming justice in Christ's name through the principles of her social teaching in the political and commercial worlds, working for the reunion of separated Christians (and especially as corporate communities, *ecumenically*) with herself; witnessing in missionary endeavour to the nations who as yet know not Jesus Christ. Although Fr Sebastian did not enjoy the benefit of having the documents of the Second Vatican Council on these topics at his fingertips (they were not composed), both his selection of areas of concern, and the temper (at once doctrinally firm and humanly generous) in which he treats them fit perfectly well with the Council's ethos: a fact which argues for that body's largely confirmatory role of the more alert Catholicism of the late 1950s. The Gospel 'is to be preached to all men, and moreover in their own idiom and in terms of their own traditions.' The best of the Council is there is a nutshell. The closing words of *Roman Catholicism* are no less emblematic of Fr Sebastian's spirit:

> However this may work in the mercy of God, every Christian desires all other men not only to 'see the salvation of God', but to share with him the treasure of the Christian faith, as fully as possible to know of its richness, and with full awareness to understand what friendship with God in this life can mean, so that consciously and joyfully they may be able to say at the end, 'Come, Lord Jesus'.[86]

Notes

1. E. Stopp, 'Remembering Edward Bullough, 28. 3. 1880 to 17. 9. 1934', Typescript in the possesion of Blackfriars, Cambridge.

2. Martindale told Bullough on the eve of his reception, by way of expression of the culture-transforming vocation of the Church, 'In the long run, the whole world ought to be nameable his Church, because of the vital harmony established through all levels of creation', 'A Text for the Times', *New Blackfriars* 46.532 (1964), p. 34.

3. C. N. L. Brooke, *A History of the University of Cambridge, Volume IV, 1870–1990* (Cambridge: Cambridge University Press, 1993), p. 434.

4. M. N. L. Couve de Murville and P. Jenkins, *Catholic Cambridge* (London: Catholic Truth Society, 1983), p. 125.

5. E. Bullough, *Cambridge Readings in Italian Literature* (Cambridge: 1920); idem., *Italian Perspectives* (Cambridge: 1933): this last was in fact his inaugural lecture.

6. E. Gilson, *The Philosophy of St Thomas Aquinas* (E T Cambridge: Heffer, 1929).

7. A scene in a railway carriage described by B. Sewell, *My Dear Time's Waste* (Aylesford: St Albert's Press, 1966), p. 51.

8. 'The Woodchester Story, Being a Series of Letters and Documents Preserved in the Dominican Archives at Woodchester, illustrating the History of the Beginnings of the Woodchester Mission during the years 1846–1851, Collected and Set to Order by Br Silvester Humphries, O. P., edited by Sebastian Bullough O. P'

9. 'Father Sebastian Bullough, 1910–1967', *Acts of the Provincial Chapter of the English Province* (Newcastle: 1970), p. 23. Northampton was the diocesan: the see of 'East Anglia' had not yet been created.

10. L. Callahan, *A Theory of Esthetic according to the Principles of St Thomas Aquinas* (Washington: The Catholic University of America, 1927); T. Gilby, *Poetic Experience* (London: Sheed and Ward, 1934); E. Gill, *Beauty Looks After Herself* (London: Sheed and Ward, 1933); J. Maritain, *Art et Scolastique* (Paris: Librairie de l'Art Catholique, 1920); J. Maritain and R. Maritain, *La situation de la Poésie* (Paris: Descleé de Brouwer 1938); A.-D. Sertillanges, O.P., *Art et Apologétique* (Paris: Bloud et Barral, 1909).

11. J. Gredt, O.S.B., *Elementa philosphiae* (Freiburg: Herder & Co. 5. 1929); B. H. Merkelbach, O.P., *Summa Theologiae Moralis* (Paris: Desclée de Brouwer, 1935–6).

12. R. Fry, *Vision and Design* (Harmondsworth: Penguin, 1937); H. Taine, *Philosophie de l'Art* (Paris: Hachette, 1921); H. Lützeler, *Führer zur Kunst* (Freiburg: Herder, 1938). His three-volume omnium gatherum of art-critical theories, *Kunsterfahrung und Kunstwissenschaft. Systematische und Entwicklungsgeschichtliche Darstellung und*

Dokumentation des Umgangs mit dem bildenden Kunst (Freiburg-Munich: Karl Alber, 1975), pays much attention to 'heteronomous' theological accounts of art, but hardly any author cited is scholastic.

13. M. Cordovani, O.P.; 'Filosofia e arte belle', in *Saggi e lezioni sull'Arte Sacre* (Rome: Istituto Beato Angelico, 1935–1936; A. Ciappi, O.P., 'Filosofia dell'Arte', in ibid., 1936–1937.

14. P. Philippe, O.P., *Le rôle de l'Amitié dans la vie chrétienne* (Rome: Angelicum, 1938).

15. *Tractatus de finalitate artis, liber primus* (Rome: 1939), p. iv.

16. In a second book, he proposed to treat the artist's goal in creating, something he identified with 'the way the work can affect and move human beings'. Lastly in a third book, he intended to look at the 'further end of the work and the activity of art', under which rubric he would say a word about the goodness or badness of the human notions involved in art, whether from the maker's side or the viewer's. This, then, is the question of the morality of art: namely, its relation to the last of all ends which is God. This, he thought, might be considered in a twofold way: *vis-à-vis* God as our Creator (and here artistry enters as, simply, a human act), and *vis-à-vis* God as our Redeemer (and here it enters more distinctively as a Christian act). And that should be a proper point on which to finish, since it belongs to the 'summit' of theology to reflect on any activity in its relevance to God as raising up man to share the supernatural order of Grace, ibid., p. vi.

17. For a brief characterisation in this perspective, cf. A. Nichols, O.P., *The Art of God Incarnate. Theology and Image in Christian Tradition* (London: Darton, Longman and Todd, 1980), pp. 91–94.

18. E. Gill, *Beauty Looks After Herself*, p. 11.

19. *Tractatus de finalitate artis*, p. xxviii.

20. T. Gilby, *Poetic experience*, p. 71, cited in *Tractatus de finalitate artis*, p. xlvii.

21. Ibid., p. cxiv, citing Psalm 117.27.

22. For the text see e.g. *Dominican Prayer Book* (Rome: Curia Generalizia, O.P., 1962), p. 368.

23. Mention could be made here of his translations from the German, notably of hagiological and Mariological writings (L. von Matt and N. Vian, *St Pius X. A Pictorial Biography*, London: Longmans, Green and Company 1955; L. von Matt and W. Hauser, *St Francis of Assisi. A Pictorial Biography*, London: Longmans, Green and Company 1956; H. Rahner, *Our Lady and the Church*, London: Darton, Longman and Todd, 1961), as well of his interest in the *process* of translation, as evinced in his revision and amplification of H. Pope, O.P., *English Versions of the Bible* (St Louis, Mo.: Herder, 1952).

24. 'Scripture at School', *Blackfriars* XXII. 257 (1941), p. 406.

25. Ibid., p. 408.

26. *Five Minor Prophets* (London: Saint Catherine Press, 1953).

27. *Jewish Chronicle* for 3 September 1953.

28. *Five Minor Prophets*, p. xxvii, with reference to Micah 2.5.

29. Ibid., p. lvii.
30. Ibid., pp. lxii–lxiii, with references to 14.1 and 14.6–7.
31. *The Church in the New Testament* (London: Burns, Oates and Washbourne, 1945), p. viii.
32. Ibid., pp. 231–32, with an internal citation of 1 Corinthians 10.17.
33. *St Paul and the Apostolic Writings* (London: Burns Oates and Washbourne, 1950), pp. vii–viii.
34. *Meditations in Advent* (London: Blackfriars Publications, 1955), p. 8.
35. Introit of the Second Sunday of Lent, from the old Roman liturgy.
36. *Meditations in Advent*, pp. 11–12.
37. Ibid., p. 15.
38. *Meditations in Lent* (London: Blackfriars Publications, 1959), p. 1.
39. Ibid., p. 7.
40. Ibid., p. 23.
41. Ibid., pp. 27–28, citing Origen's *Homilies on Joshua*, at *Patriologia Graeca* 12, 843.
42. 'The Character of St Dominic', unpublished typescript, Blackfriars, Cambridge, p. 4.
43. Ibid., p. 11.
44. 'History of the Order', unpublished typescript in the possession of Blackfriars, Cambridge, p. 11.
45. 'Catherine the Dominican', Blackfriars XV (1961), pp. 447–52.
46. Letter 185.
47. Letter 183.
48. 'Catherine the Dominican', p. 449.
49. 'Dominican Saints': unpublished typescript in the possession of Blackfriars Cambridge, p. 11.
50. 'History of the Order', p. 14.
51. Cited O. Hamilton, *Paradise of Exiles. Tuscany and the British* (London: André Deutsch, 1974), p. 163
52. 'History of the Order', p. 15.
53. *Constitutiones Fratrum Sacrae Ordinis Praedicatorum*, ed. jussu N. S. Gillet (Rome 1932), I. 1, 4, i.
54. 'History of the Order', p. 19.
55. 'Dominican saints', p. 14.
56. 'Master-General's Questionnaire', English Dominican Archives.
57. In his learned essay 'St Thomas and Music', he had noted that 'Our musicians are forming us all the time, and either they are building up the republic, or they are sapping its vitality.' See *Dominican Studies IV* (1951), p. 33
58. The same citation would be used by Fr Aelred Squire, writing as a Dominican, for the frontispiece of his *Asking the Fathers* (London: SPCK, 1972), a book which started life as his lectures on ascetical and mystical theology at Blackfriars, Oxford; Fr Aelred subsequently joined the Camaldolese Order as a hermit in the United States.
59. *Roman Catholicism* (Harmondsworth: Penguin Books, 1963).
60. *A Catechism of Christian Doctrine, as Approved by the Archbishops*

and *Bishops of England and Wales, and Directed by Them to be Used in All their Dioceses*, (Ditchling: St Dominic's Press, 1931), ch. 1.

61. *Roman Catholicism*, p. 15.
62. Drawing on Victor White, O.P., 'St Thomas's Conception of Revelation', *Dominican Studies* 1 (1948), pp. 6–7.
63. See further on this: H. Pope, O.P., *English Versions of the Bible*, revised and amplified by S. Bullough, O.P. (St Louis, Missouri: Herder and Herder, 1952).
64. *Roman Catholicism* p. 64, citing Pope Pius XII's encyclical letter on the liturgy, *Mediator Dei*.
65. Ibid., p. 74.
66. Gaetanus (Thomas de Vio); *Commentarium in Thomae Aquinatis Summa Theologiae* IIIa, q. 68, 1–2 and 11.
67. *Roman Catholicism*, pp. 89–90.
68. M. de la Taille, *The Mystery of Faith* (ET London 1941–50); V. McNabb O.P. 'A New Theory of the Eucharistic Sacrifice; *Blackfriars* 4 (1923), pp. 1986–2110; for Jones, it was a 'crucial and great work' about 'the relationship of what was done in the Supper-room with what was done on the Hill and the further relationship of these doings with what is done in the Mass': thus *The Anathemata – Fragments of an Attempted Writing* (London, 1952), p. 37.
69. *Roman Catholicism*, p. 165.
70. 'The man's own private devotion is entirely sunk within his obedience, as he is covered by the vestments and subordinates his own words and gestures to those of the Church', *Roman Catholicism*, p. 182.
71. 'The Spiritual Life: An Historical Approach, I–IV', *Life of the Spirit* XIII. 149 (1958), pp. 212–19; 150 (1958), pp. 270–77; 152 (1959), pp. 349–57; 153 (1959), pp. 394–402.
72. *Roman Catholicism*, p. 227.
73. Ibid., pp. 228–29.
74. 'The Spiritual Life: an Historical Approach, I'. pp. 214–15.
75. 'The Spiritual Life: An Historical Approach, II', pp. 270–71.
76. *Roman Catholicism*, p. 230, with reference to *De natura et gratia* 84.
77. 'The Spiritual Life: An Historical Approach, II', p. 277. See on this A. Nichols, O.P., *Byzantine Gospel. Maximus the Confessor in Modern Scholarship* (Edinburgh: T. & T. Clark, 1993).
78. *Summa Theologiae*. Ia IIae, q. 68, q. 3, cited 'The Spiritual Life: An Historical Approach, III', p. 355.
79. 'The Spiritual Life: An Historical Approach, IV', p. 385.
80. Ibid., Cf. P. Debognie, 'Dévotion moderne', *Dictionnaire de Spiritualité* XX–XXI (Paris: 1955), col. 743.
81. *Roman Catholicism*, p. 231.
82. 'The Spiritual Life: An Historical Approach, IV', art cit., p. 400.
83. *Vida*, 13; cited ibid., pp. 401–402.
84. *Vida*, 8, cited *Roman Catholicism*, p. 236.
85. Ibid., p. 237.
86. Ibid., citing Luke 3.6.

Works by Sebastian Bullough

'Truth and Poetry', *Blackfriars* XIX. 225 (1938), pp. 897–901.

Tractatus de finalitate artis (Rome: Pontifical University of St Thomas, 1939).

'Scripture at School', *Blackfriars* XXII. 257 (1941), pp. 416–23.

The Church in the New Testament (London: Burns, Oates and Washbourne 1945).

Saint Paul and the Apostolic Writings (London: Burns, Oates and Washbourne 1950).

'St Thomas and Music', *Dominican Studies IV* (1951), pp. 14–34.

Five Minor Prophets: Obadiah, Micah, Zephaniah, Haggai and Zechariah (London: Saint Catherine's Press, 1953).

'Recent Popes on Church Music', *Life of the Spirit* XIII. 145 (1958), pp. 14–21.

'The Spiritual Life; An Historical Approach', *Life of the Spirit.*, XIII. 149 (1958), pp. 212–19; 150 (1958), pp. 270–77; 152 (1959), pp. 349–57; 153 (1959), pp. 394–402.

'Catherine the Dominican', *Life of the Spirit* XV. 178 (1961), pp. 447–52.

Roman Catholicism (Harmondsworth: Penguin Books, 1963).

Gerald Vann, O.P. (privately printed, n.d., n.p.)

'Dr. Alexander Geddes, 1737–1802', *Scripture* XVI. 937 (1965).

'The Question of Metre in Psalm 1', *Vetus Testamentum* XVII. 1 (1967).

'Notes on Dominican Saints and Beati', MS, Blackfriars, Cambridge.

'History of the Order', MS, Blackfriars, Cambridge.

7

Gervase Mathew

Anthony Mathew first saw the light of day in Chelsea, on 4 March 1905. He was the second son of Frank Mathew, an Irish lawyer, born in Bombay, and an English mother. The family of Agnes Woodruff were of rather more consequence in the legal world of British India, for her father was advocate-general of Bengal, and her brother a judge of the high court of Calcutta. Frank Mathew fancied himself as a writer, especially on Irish history, romantically conceived, and, since he did not encourage the arrival at his door of barristers' briefs, was able to indulge his talents as an all-round *littérateur*, supported by private money, on a kind of semi-permanent grand tour of the warmer Continental countries.

> To all my comrades, poor and kind, encountered long ago
> I send a greeting now in mind of joys we used to know,
> Remembering how the Dawn awakes the Mountains of Algiers
> And deep in amethystine lakes the silver Moon appears,
> And how the hooded Arab sets his weather-work lateen
> And silent fishers haul their nets by misty Trasimene,
> And songs that hailed the Morning when our lips were salt
>   with spray
> And honest wine with honest men in taverns far away.
> To these who watch a fading sky or – done with toil and mirth –
> Far off in Lacedaemon lie, embraced by kindred earth,
> Or where in Youth I loved to dwell, the Laestrygonian shore,
> I send a brother's last farewell, for we shall meet no more.[1]

Judging by this valedictory poem, a sort of combination of Lawrence Durrell with Chesterbelloc, it was all rather fun. No doubt it gave his younger son his taste for foreign, preferably exotic, travel.[2] Similarly, Katharine Tynan's remark, apropos of Frank's novelistic account of the 1798 Irish Rebellion, *Wood of the Brambles* 'he had a hereditary knowledge of the minds and manners of the roystering Anglo-Irish gentry of the eighteenth century',[3] explains a good deal about the *tenue* of Anthony's elder brother David, subsequently auxiliary bishop of Westminster (1938), apostolic visitor to Abyssinia (1946), apostolic delegate to the British colonies of East and West Africa (1946), and, Ordinary of the Military Vicariate (1953) – as well as his habitual gravitation toward the houses of the recusant aristocracy and gentry. Disappointed in his hope of securing an English diocese (his manner was considered impossibly eccentric), and alarmed by the liturgical reforms of the Second Vatican Council (though far from being a zealot in matters of Church policy at large), Archbishop David took early retirement in 1963. His last years were spent as chaplain to the Camoys family at Stonor Park, Oxfordshire, a house which could claim to have endured as a family home for longer than any other in English history. (The appearance of a photograph of the chaplain, in episcopal choir-dress, as an illustration to the passage in the Book of Judges about a house-Levite attached to a Benjaminite landowner in early Israel, occasioned, however, a threat of litigation against the publishers of *Bible Today*.)

Retirement enabled Archbishop David to lavish much affection on his brother Gervase, then living in nearby Oxford. It is impossible to resist quoting the vignette of the archbishop and the Dominican in the *Dictionary of National Biography*.

> The two brothers, always in correct clerical dress though otherwise distressingly dishevelled and unkempt, were often to be seen in the streets of Oxford, sometimes arm in arm, as they made their way somewhat ponderously to a small French restaurant for a special celebration (at which the sweet trolley was always their great delight), or pottering over to Blackwell's to leaf through the latest book by one of their many friends. The enigmatic silences, the sudden hilarity which ended with the disconcerting abruptness with which it began, and the oracular manner, which the brothers shared, alarmed many people; but many others found in their love for one another and in the absolute simplicity of their religion, a touchstone of fidelity.[4]

Retirement also made it possible for Archbishop David to resume writing. Here he increasingly emulated his father's favoured genre – pen-portraits of notable figures of the Tudor age, though his own writing included a study of the nineteenth-century Liberal Catholic historian Acton, as well as more ambitious projects, such as wide-ranging accounts of England (and Scotland) in the reigns of James I and VI and Charles I, a history of Ethiopia, and a still useful account of post-Reformation English Catholicism.[5]

Given the parental, and notably paternal, background, it is perhaps hardly surprising that the future Fr Gervase's education was somewhat neglected, though he did manage to spend a brief period at the Jesuit College in Wimbledon. None the less, in 1925 he was able to follow his elder brother in gaining a place at Balliol College, Oxford. He read modern history, collected early editions of the Church Fathers and above all began to develop his large circle of friends from whom devotion was demanded, and on whom it was, even more spectacularly, lavished. He joined the Order on graduation in 1928, attracted by the figure of Bede Jarrett, a childhood friend of his mother's. (In their shared circle of servants of the British Raj she had taught him to play tennis.) The enduringness of Jarrett's influence is shown by, *inter alia*, Fr Gervase's concern with the practice and theory of friendship,[6] for spiritual friendship is a major theme of Jarrett's surviving letters,[7] as well as the motif which drew him to the study of the English Cistercian author of a treatise *De spiritali amicitia*, St Aelred of Rievaulx.[8]

More than anyone else in the Province Fr Gervase realised the aspirations of Jarrett for the Oxford priory. Beginning humbly with self-appointed lectures in the 'Outside Aula', now the lower library of Blackfriars, he soon established a reputation for erratic brilliance. Touching on widely scattered themes in Church history, the Fathers, Byzantium and archaeology, his assorted knowledge, irradiated by numerous brilliant insights of the kind that would cause other people much hard work, was recognised by the University's decision to appoint him its first Lecturer in Byzantine Studies. Balliol Hall was his favourite venue for these courses and others which he volunteered to the Faculty of History. More privately, he was an enthusiastic member of the *Inklings*, that sparkling coterie of philosophico-literary Christian apologists – C.S. Lewis, Charles Williams, and J.R.R. Tolkien being the best known, which met regularly for the sharing of ideas in Lewis's rooms in Magdalen, as well as at the Eagle and Child hostelry in St Giles' Street, a few doors along from the Dominican house. The Inklings' influence was especially strong among Anglican undergraduates and budding dons, but it extended further. Fr Gervase's importance to the Inklings can be detected in the fact that, among the contributors to the posthumous *Festschriften* in honour of Williams and Lewis, he is the only writer to appear in both.[9] Lewis, in the preface to the former, alluding to Williams's 'romantic theology' speaks of Fr Gervase's essay as treating a subject which not only had 'always seemed to Williams of deep significance', but, moreover, had been 'the common interest that first brought him and me together'.[10] Ronald Knox's version of Lewis's *Mere Christianity* (though never prescinding, unlike Lewis's work, from a specifically 'denominational' allegiance) would be a work dedicated to Fr Gervase, the series of 'Oxford Conferences' brought together under the title *In Soft Garments*, in 1942.[11]

In the last decade of his life, Fr Gervase had to contend, not only with the trauma of post-conciliar Catholicism in Church and Province, but also with physical ill-health. Still, as the Dominican obituarist reported: 'He lived his life as he always had done, Mass in the morning according to the Dominican rite, helping and rejoicing in his friends, travelling to the sun, and remaining for us an example of the old Province that could not be ignored.'[12] The death of his fervently loved brother, Archbishop David, in December 1975 sapped his will to struggle on with this by no means unpleasant but – for one of his depleted resources – relatively exigent life. Such was the collaboration between them that it would be hard to say which line of what book by David Mathew Fr Gervase did not have a hand in – and vice versa. Fittingly, then, the account of Fr Gervase's literary contribution to be given here opens with their only joint work, *The Reformation and the Contemplative Life*.

A battle for Christendom

Given the topic of their co-authored 1934 book: *The Reformation and the Contemplative Life. A Study of the Conflict between the Carthusians and the State*,[13] the likelihood must be that the initiative was David's. He had tried his vocation in *Carthusia* immediately after his priestly ordination in 1929. Bishop W.G. Wheeler remarked in his panegyric at the elder Mathew's Requiem in Westminster Cathedral on 17 December 1975:

> Here was a discipline and an ethos, unmarred by the vicissitudes of history, which appealed to one who ever proved to be wholehearted in his commitment. It was with great sorrow that he accepted the fact that his life and calling were to lie in other fields. But the spaciousness and tranquillity of Parkminster [the sole English Charterhouse, in Sussex] left an indelible mark on the whole of his life and an understanding of this is essential to a true assessment of him.[14]

On the other hand, Fr Gervase's contribution was sufficient to warrant the interest of the Dominicans' censors, whose names – Robert Bracey, himself a Fellow of the Royal Historical Society, and Leo Moore, appear, along with that of the new provincial, Bernard

Delany, succeeding to Bede Jarrett shortly before, opposite the contents page of the book.

The topic may appear of limited significance, but the brothers' introduction claims for it not only a universal but also a dramatically contemporary importance. For the Carthusian life, in the opening moment of the English Reformation, represented the 'gathered fruit of a theocentric speculation based on the outlook of a world coterminous with integral Catholicism'.[15] Confronting the Carthusians' essentially simple spiritual outlook, which expected Latin Christendom to comport itself as what it was, 'a City of God', were men of a new spirit bent on realising in practice a 'novel but highly synthesised philosophy of the State'. In the context of the 1930s' battle of the Catholic Church for minds threatened by Fascism in Italy and National Socialism in Germany (not to mention her 'descent into darkness' in Bolshevik Russia a decade before), it was not difficult to gauge the bearing of these words:

> The English province [of the Carthusians] is in an especial manner the scene of this conflict; for the supra-national values, based on a consciousness of the undivided Christian spirituality, were here threatened by the new forces incarnate in the King's Vicar, Thomas Cromwell, the first exponent of the modern State Supremacy.[16]

If Cromwell's life work 'foreshadowed an expression of the Totalitarian State', the phrase 'King's Vicar' in the above passage is theologically sinister. Understood as isomorphic with *Christ's* Vicar, the Petrine office-holder for whose place in the Church the Carthusian martyrs died, it conveys the notion of a functionary who is an unholy parody, a minister of Antichrist.

Robert Hugh Benson, the son of an archbishop of Canterbury, had been received into the Catholic Church at Woodchester by Fr Reginald Buckler, O.P. Though he had died prematurely in 1914, still in his forties, he already had a sparkling reputation as preacher, apologist and, above all, novelist. Two precocious and devout boys born in a Catholic household in the reign of Edward VII could hardly have missed an introduction to his fiction. Its main subjects were precisely the English Reformation (as in *By What Authority?* and *Come Rack, Come Rope*) and the Antichrist, or, more generally, eschatology (as in *Lord of the World* and *The Dawn of All*).[17] The novelistic style of, in particular, the opening chapter of *The Reformation and the Contemplative Life* (despite the end-noting of primary sources) and the book's setting within a deliberate framework of negative eschatology (Erastianism as a manifestation of Antichrist) point in the clear direction of Benson's influence.[18]

The work is excellently conceived. Based on Carthusian MSS at Parkminster, the British Museum and Bodley's Library at Oxford, as well as on printed sources, it opens with an evocative account of a day at the London Charterhouse in the spring of 1528. Its motifs are piety towards the liturgy, a delight in nature, and a celebration of *sancta simplicitas*. 'The murmur of the bees rose from above the garden and in the still air of the cell there hung the scent of straw.' But its real hero is straightforward, assured traditional religion – the order of things about to be so roughly shaken by Henry VIII's 'Great Matter'. As the monks' recreation ends:

> With that constant unhurried calm they arranged the habit correctly, letting down the full weight of the tunic that they had fastened for walking. The will of God was obeyed in following the rules of the Order. They knelt on the wood of the *prie-dieu* and composed themselves to their prayer.[19]

The manner of writing changes abruptly with chapter two, becoming business-like and controlled: professional historians at work. The brothers explain the organisation of the Carthusian Order by the early sixteenth century; the crucial role allotted in that organisation to the prior of the Grande Chartreuse (in Dauphiné) and the likely implications of the fact that the prior currently in office was a denizen of the Burgundian Netherlands, come to maturity at just the time when the Holy Roman emperor, Maximilian I, had accepted from the last duke of Burgundy, his father-in-law, the bequest of his rule and jurisdictions, and added these to the imperial dream. It was with the vague hope of a Catholic *pax germanica* behind him that Guillaume Bibauce abandoned the life of a priestly courtier in 1500 and entered the charterhouse of Ghent.

> The Van Eyck altar piece in Saint Jan's at Ghent was now both modern and familiar and the security of doctrine, which the figure of the Paschal Lamb there represented, still unassailed. To the burghers of the Netherlands gazing upon this scene the Heavenly Jerusalem stood unchallenged, the City of God bearing the company of angels, the Faithful Ages and the saints ... The solitude engulfed him and, when he was chosen, nearly a quarter of a century later, to rule the Order, it was only the memories of the dead fifteenth century which remained to serve him as a guide.[20]

What the Mathews show is that the rulers of the isolated Carthusian hermitages were simply too sanguine, as the Protestant revolt began. Dependent for news on the occasional guest, and on the coming of priors to the Grand Chartreuse for general chapter (from which those of England and Saxony – the very areas soon to be devastated by the coming storm – were frequently, on account of distance, dispensed), the head of the Order had very inadequate means of taking stock of the real situation. Added to which, his personal friendship with his fellow countryman the cardinal of Utrecht, become pope in 1521 as Adrian VI, lulled him into a false sense of security. Dr Florisz had been vice-chancellor at Louvain, and in the long summers, kept his parish, Goedereede, in Zeeland. Though he had become tutor to the Archduke Charles (the future Charles V), and thus rose to be bishop, cardinal and even for a while Viceroy of the Spains, he remained a sober, stolid Dutch pastor: knowing him to be chief shepherd of the universal Church, the Carthusians could sleep safe at night. 'It was typical of his life and his pontificate, this determined and unaltered zeal, somewhat pedestrian, as he moved with deliberation along the pathway, while beyond him stretched the sea-won fields and the buttercups of Schouwen.'

Meanwhile, in the Peasants War of 1524–5 we find for the first time a peasant *jacquerie* turning against Catholicism as such. Memories of Hus, and reports of Luther and Zwingli, coalesced, half-understood, with economic grievance. The willingness of the secular arm – in this case, the princes of the Swabian League – to come to the Church's aid renewed a shaken confidence in the continuing attachment to the Church of the Christian prince – and the Christian town council. Meanwhile:

> At the Grande Chartreuse, as the liturgical year moved forward, the ordered change in the Office provided the only alteration of background, while the rye ripened to harvest in the mountain fields which lay shadowed by the heaped pine woods on the steep ridges.

None the less it was by the duly constituted authorities of a merchant city – of the sort which, until then, had made the Carthusians foundations, given them benefactions – that the blow fell. By the action of the city council of Nuremberg in 1525 a charterhouse was for the first time suppressed *on theological grounds* by the secular power. By which date death, disrespectful of reasonable expectation, had left no Hollander pope to give the Carthusians counsel. That a majority of the Nuremberg monks had agreed to abandon their vocation and join the new excommunicate preachers was the worst cut of all.

At this point the Mathews turn their gaze back to the English scene. They point out how in England the kingship was linked with a deep religious tradition, expressed in the coronation ritual To the older monks of the nine charterhouses (founded between 1178 and 1414), the strongly orthodox piety of the early Tudors was more apparent than the present strength of the Crown: they had entered *Carthusia* under the system of Henry VII, the 'early fumbling bureaucracy of Morton and Dudley'.

> Each monk had the knowledge of the world which he possessed when he entered, but since profane events were never discussed this was a static knowledge which grew slowly dim with the years. All that he had left became shadowy and the names of great worldly figures grew the while less significant.

But, so the authors argue, this very absence of mundane knowledge helped the Carthusians to clarity when they had to consider a purely religious question. Their training and outlook equipped them to grasp dogmatic change perfectly, political not at all. An evocation of the 'monastic standpoint' of their prayer-life as they kept vigil around the eucharistic Lord in the hanging pyxes of their churches, has the fervent impressionism of Benson's word-sketching of contemplative and mystical states.

> It seemed that the desire for union with God could not be selfish; it must widen out in an ever-increasing desire of the spirit that God's Will be completely fulfilled. It was a longing, apostolic in its charity, for the union not of one soul only but of all created souls with their Creator. The trammels of worldly detail and care no longer hampered them ... Yet, even so, with their own peace would be bound up a Pauline solicitude for all the Churches; universal in its scope, detached and free. Nothing could any longer seem of value, save that age-long gathering in of men to God, the completed sum of all the souls in Grace, Christ's Mystical Body.[21]

But before focusing on the crisis caused in England by the passing of the Act of Supremacy in 1534, the spotlight turns once again to the international affairs of the Order, as seen through the prism of the general chapters of 1528 and 1532. Anxieties about Reformation stirrings in Strasbourg and Rostock, from the Rhineland to the Baltic margins of the German world, about the Turkish defeat, at the battle of Mohacs, of the (admittedly, ramshackle) Magyar monarchy, and the related threat of further Ottoman advance on the charterhouses of Carinthia and Austria were to a degree soothed by the consoling thought that the English king, whose chief minister Thomas More, was a good friend of the London charterhouse, should be so devoted to the Church. The same year Dom Theodoric Loher, a Carthusian of Cologne, dedicated his edition of his confrère Denys van Leeswen's Gospel commentary to that monarch: *Christi athleta invictissime* 'unconquered athlete of Christ'. Denys' theology, forged in the

'Second Realism' of fifteenth-century Cologne, deeply influenced by the neoplatonised Thomism of the Dominican Rhenish school, was a thousand miles distant from the chief intellectual nourishment of Luther, whether Nominalist or that of the *devotio moderna*.[22]

The climax of the book is formed, naturally, by the accession of Henry VIII to the European revolt against Rome, and the martyrdoms of the English Carthusians which followed. It is intriguing, in view of the shortness of time between publication and David Mathew's elevation to the episcopate, to see how firmly the authors ascribe the twin *débâcles* – schism, judicial murder – to the supineness of the national episcopate. It was the 'over-great confidence placed in the bishops which led the monks to come so suddenly upon their disaster'; 'in their isolation from the world they had trusted the courtier bishops overmuch'. A year elapsed it is true, between the committal of the sole episcopal dissenter, John Fisher of Rochester, and of the Carthusians' friend, Thomas More, to the Tower, and their own sufferings. But they were persuaded that Fisher and More were detained for their refusal to withdraw opinions on the question of the succession – itself, it seemed, purely temporal – put forward during the king's long drawn out 'great matter'. That this was far from the whole story emerged in January 1535 when Henry announced in the Privy Chamber his new title – *et in terra supremum caput Anglicanae Ecclesiae* – at the same time appointing Thomas Cromwell visitor of all the monasteries of the realm with power to dispose of any 'papistical escript'. In mid-april, the Carthusian priors of London, Beauvale and Axholme, were twice interviewed by Cromwell in connection with their request for an exemption from taking the oath of supremacy. On 28 April their trial for high treason opened; the following day it concluded with their conviction. The contrast between the monks, 'with the signs of the fasting and long vigils' upon them, and the king's secretary, the lines of his face 'somewhat blurred by prosperous living', only recently recovered from one of the intermittent bouts of fever which his 'doubtful hold on office could ill afford', is drawn dramatically, but not melodramatically. Cromwell's viewpoint is intelligently, though not sympathetically, stated. The State must be strengthened, even via the whims of so theological a sovereign. Far away in southern France the prior of the Grande Chartreuse was notified, by a priest-agent of the English government, of a little local difficulty. It is not clear whether he understood that the Carthusians had died (much less by how gross a method of execution). A letter preserved among the manuscripts of the British Museum reveals his appreciation of the need for caution in its reminder of the perpetual Carthusian prayer for the king, *ipsam benignissimam regiam majestatem.* 'As far as the Carthusians in England were concerned it was the last Epistle of the Catholic Ages.'[23]

The executions of the English Carthusians were altogether exceptional in terms of Reformation Europe as a whole. The charterhouses of northern Germany and Scandinavia were swept away no less surely – in princely reformations modelled in part on Henry VIII's example. For the Carthusians of Spain and Italy, on the other hand, life continued apparently unchanged. But, the Mathews note, change there had been, and profound change at that. The mid-sixteenth-century religious revolution did not fail to leave its mark both on the Catholic Church and on the wider society she animated. From being a 'firmament', the Church became a 'citadel'; and 'the sense of European unity had vanished'.[24] It was to an eirenic, and quasi-ecumenical mission that Fr Gervase – despite the traditional, even neo-mediaeval, character of his Catholicism would henceforth be committed.

An ecumenical vision: Christendom East and West

Speaking at Blackfriars, Oxford, during the Octave of Prayer for the Unity of Christians in January 1950, on the theme of the spiritual unity of East and West in Christendom, Fr Gervase made this autobiographical aside: 'By chance I have had to combine two kinds of study, working as a Byzantinist and working as a Western medievalist. They are two kinds of study not often combined ...' And explaining how the great difference in 'economic factors' in Byzantium and the mediaeval West led to a wide divergence in social structure and hence in social ideals – for fourteenth-century England lacks the 'cult of the statesman as the wise man [and] zest for the conscious dominance of cool and temperate mind', just as the Constantinople of the same epoch has 'very little of the ideal of knighthood and chivalry' – Fr Gervase goes on:

> So much can be affected by the economic factors in history, but not religious truth. The social structure is different, the purely spiritual ideals are still the same. Notice how easily we could translate back *The Cloud of Unknowing* into medieval Greek, or how easily much of *Piers Plowman* can pass into Slavonic.[25]

Here we begin to detect something of his spirit.

The same lecture-article, 'Eastern Traditions in Christianity', has more of a personal nature besides, throwing light on his literary project. First of all, he points out that, just because his own circle included many friends of other communions or religions, he was acutely aware of the degree of mutual misapprehension there could be, and 'how unlikely it is that that will be done away with within a space of time measurable by the historian'. Added to which, ecumenical 'reunion' smacked to him of a view of the Church incompatible with the doctrine of her indivisibility, whether Catholic or Orthodox. He follows this rather bleak disclaimer, however, with a warm appeal for charity and rebuttal of intolerance. Actually, there can be no dogmatic objection to such phrases as 'the reunion of Christians' or even 'the reunion of Christendom'. It is only the synthesis of the terms 'reunion' and 'Church' which is debatable. He had in mind, evidently, what Ronald Knox had called: 'the pathetic dream of a re-united Church, something not quite Protestant and not quite Catholic, based upon those principles of compromise which are so dear to the English heart.'[26]

In fact, Fr Gervase believed that there was much in common between Catholics and Orthodox at least. His 'master in Byzantine archaeology' had told him that, compared with their own, Byzantine civilisation might as well be in China. But it all depends on what one means by 'one's own'. 'The difference between Haghia Sophia and modern Oxford is no greater than that between modern Oxford and Chartres.' The foundations of Chartres and of Haghia Sophia, in other words, are one. That he came to see when he began his work in iconographic history on location in Greece, annotating the mosaics at Hosios Loukas, and the frescoes of the Vatopedi monastery on Athos. Thinking perhaps of his brother David's Carthusian experience and their common book on the sufferings of the English Carthusian martyrs, he compared Athonite monasticism to that most austere Western brand.

> Both have had their failures and their misfits, but in both the same fruition is being sought, within the framework of the same laws. With the Carthusians and with the monks at Athos there is the same conception of the organised contemplative life, the use of the religious vows, the position of the abbot, the use of the same psalms for the same end, even the similar use of silence. And at a deeper level not only the same liturgy but the same sacraments, the same Christ received in the same Eucharist on Athos and at Parkminster.[27]

Nor did monasticism constitute the only common link, for, just as, in East and West, the fundamentals of the religious life are the same because derived from 'that close spiritual brotherhood which linked St Basil and St Benedict', so the patristic past as a whole is at once spiritually life-giving and doctrinally authoritative for both the major

segments of divided Christendom. Fr Gervase insisted that Thomism
– and its commanding place in the Catholic theology of 1950, at least
as understood by the English Dominicans – made not a jot of difference to this state of affairs. John Damascene, the author of the first
Byzantine 'Summa Theologiae' was Aquinas's predecessor; Denys the
Areopagite is cited getting on for two thousand times in Thomas's
corpus, and there is a famous remark recorded of him that he would
give all Paris for Chrysostom on Matthew. And so 'As long as the
Summa is studied, thoughts from Basil and Nazianzen and Nemesios
will be part of the Western theological inheritance'.

Nor does it stop there. There remains the popular religion of
Orthodox East and Catholic West, viewed by Fr Gervase with both an
anthropologist's eye and the devotion of a practitioner. (He once told
me, in atypically sombre mood, that he was the 'last mediaeval
Catholic'.) He had in mind such things as the veneration of the saints
and their relics, and the frequenting of their shrines – but above all,
the love of the Mother of Jesus. Consciousness of that 'common
Motherhood' of Mary is, Fr Gervase thought, the strongest glue still
holding East and West together. And here 'East' meant more than
simply the Orthodox: for the historic churches of the pre-
Chalcedonian Orient were also children of the Madonna. In the
Ethiopian monasteries that Fr Gervase had visited in his East African
explorations with Archbishop David; there is 'the same unchanging
trust in the care and protection of the Mother of God. "Our Lady
Maryam, the Merciful, the Preserver, the Covenant of Mercy".'

But what, then, of the alleged profound spiritual differences in the
mentality of Orthodox and Catholics which Orthodox apologists and
self-critical Catholics (especially) expatiated on? Fr Gervase did not
think much of them. He mentioned two: the supposedly unique
Orthodox emphasis on *sobornost* – the solidary togetherness of the
Church, her extended conciliarity – and the claimed absence in the
East, and, correlatively, exaggerated emphasis in the West, of devotion to the humiliated Christ. On the first: what was the 'doctrine of
Sobornost', he asked, but that of the Mystical Body of Christ? (Its
continuous presence in the Western theological tradition had recently
been exhaustively charted by the Belgian Jesuit Emil Mersch.) In
more homely, and natively English terms, that great *sobor* of the
Church's household was described with perfect literary propriety by
Langland in *Piers Plowman*'s vision of the 'Common Barn'. And as
to the second: Fr Gervase maintained not only that the icon-painters
of fifteenth-century Novgorod were perfectly familiar with the motif
of the humiliated Christ, but that they had probably derived their
version of it, via painters of the Hanseatic towns, from the 'wounded

battered Christ on the wall-paintings of fourteenth century East Anglia'. (King's Lynn was a Hansa city.) Here too he could draw on Langland:

Piers the Plowman came in all bloody
Bearing his cross before the common people
Like in all limbs to the Lord Jesu.

The two sides of Fr Gervase's scholarly inheritance from these spiritually twin worlds are conveniently displayed in, respectively, *The Court of Richard II* and *Byzantine Aesthetics*.

The mediaeval West

Fr Gervase's interest in the Western Middle Ages centred on fourteenth-century England – not, however, in any insular spirit, for the high culture of the period fed eagerly on pabulum from (especially) France, Italy and Bohemia. *The Court of Richard II* is itself, however, a very 'Oxford' book: suggested by F.M. Powicke, it profited by its author's conversations with such Oxford historians as Maurice Keen (political and social history), Billy Pantin (ecclesiastical history), Nevill Coghill, Peter Dronke and C.S. Lewis (literary history), J.R.R. Tolkien (the history of language), and Walter Oakeshott (art history). Indeed, the only non-Oxonian to whom Fr Gervase acknowledged a substantial debt was John Beckwith, keeper of the mediaeval holdings at the Victoria and Albert Museum. Moreover, as its author admitted, the book was 'shaped by the conditions of life at Oxford':[28] MSS consulted were chiefly in the Bodleian Library. Such restrictiveness of attention was ceasing to be a tolerated vice in English scholarship at the time when Fr Gervase published. It betokened the earlier, pre-war world in which his intellectual formation had taken place. Reviewing a study of French mediaeval art by an English author in *Blackfriars* for 1949, he had summed up the glories and deficiencies of a certain *amateur* quality in the English scholarly tradition of that time:

It is both the strength and the weakness of English art history that it is the child of archaeology. It still lacks much of the technical equipment of the continental schools, the great photograph collections of Paris or Vienna, it has always been based on a detailed first-hand knowledge of the objects themselves and of the monuments studied on the site. It is precisely this intimately personal first-hand knowledge that gives such unique value to Dr Evans's survey of all French art from the tenth to the fifteenth century – sculpture and painting, tapestries and plate and furnishings. Her lucid analyses and descriptions are varied by passages of real beauty and emotional insight – it has long been a tradition in English art history to love what is described.[29]

Mutatis mutandis, the same judgement might be passed on Fr Gervase's own book. It was dedicated to Nevill Coghill (whose brilliant rendition of the *Canterbury Tales* into modern English was even then opening the world of Chaucer to a wider public), and the memory of Maurice Powicke.

The uniqueness of *The Court of Richard II* lies in its attempt to interweave four strands of history: political history, changes in social structure and social ideals, developments in literature and altering art forms. Opening with a richly evocative account of court life and its material setting in the royal palaces of Richard's reign, Fr Gervase moves on to consider court art and aesthetics, and the courtly literature of the time. His determination not to isolate court culture from its wider environment then leads him to attempt accounts of the less accomplished provincial art and a tentative reconstruction, from very slender evidence, of peasant attitudes. Such reflections funnel out naturally enough into a broader picture of social ideals – especially chivalry, marriage and loyalty, within the differentiated mass of the 'community of the realm'. It was conflict of loyalties which generated the crisis in which Richard II's government fell, and so the book can end convincingly with an analysis of Henry Bolingbroke's *coup d'état* of 1399.

There are several overarching themes which give a unity to the treatment of much disparate material in *The Court of Richard II*. One is a delight in an England which was in so multifarious a way open to the European inheritance. The first true court in England – for previously, in Fr Gervase's view, we have only the bare administrative institution of the *curia regis* – drew from Continental Europe by many filaments of connecting thread. There were even, at Richard's court, echoes, however 'transmuted and remote' of Byzantium, caught, Fr Gervase believed, through Naples. Petrarch, to whom the Neapolitan king Robert of Anjou, had been patron, was a profound influence on Chaucer, 'my maister Petrak', 'Fraunceys Petrak the lauriat poete'.[30] Valois France made a more manifest impact: the court art, with its delight in bright primary colours, as the literature associated with it, 'reflected a "Froissart" culture that was essentially heraldic'. Other features ascribed to Parisian models range from livery collars and badges (such as even angel guardians wear in the Wilton Diptych) to the cult of St Edward the Confessor: royal ancestor *par excellence*, and dynastic counterpart of St Louis. Above all, Richard's queen, Anne of Luxembourg, linked him to the imperial court, and accustomed him to its ceremonial, found him relatives from Brabant to Poland, and furnished him, perhaps, with a personal model in her father, the Emperor Charles IV, on whom Fr Bede Jarrett had written some forty years before. Books, cooking and dress were Richard's hobbies, and Fr Gervase delights in their minute description: the account of the de luxe manuscripts, costly recipes and jewelled tabards of this bilingual court has the richness-to-excess of Keats or Huysmans. Yet all this took place at the heart of England: administered as modern Britain is from Whitehall, that fact has its origin in Richard II's transfer of the Court of Chancery to the White Hall of the Palace of Westminster in 1393.

Secondly, Fr Gervase maintains beneath the aesthetic surface of his prose (both as a style of description and in the choice of what is described) an unyielding moral interest and passion. Writing of the new poets, he comments:

> Both in Gower and in Langland the purpose is primarily didactic and the moral values are simple, unchanging and contrasted like black on white or blood upon the snow. Horror alternates with beauty. There is corporate guilt and individual evil. England is conceived as a commune, the *Communitas Regni*, now grown sterile and frustrated because the rhythm of justice and equity which alone brings a commune into being had been broken.[31]

Langland, whose patristic culture Fr Gervase notes, he considers a prophet. His message may be the way to perfection, rather than, as with those of Scripture, salvation, yet maybe 'man can only be saved by trying to become perfect'. The injustice against which Langland rails is, as violated equity, a blinding of that right reason which 'lies in the very nature of created things'. Not that Fr Gervase's appreciation of moral values is restricted to these elemental forms. He also writes sympathetically of such features of the chivalrous ideal as *largesse* (prodigal generosity), *franchyse* (freedom and naturalness of manner), and *cortaysie* (good manners, together with 'gentle heart' and 'fair welcome'). The courtly love tradition receives high marks, too, for its Christianised Ciceronianism. 'Because it is the love of another for the other's sake it finds its expression in giving and serving, not in getting; and is frustrated not when it fails to get but when it ceases to give. Therefore love service is the essential expression of *amour courtois*.'

A third and final theme is the need for almost superhuman prudence (and luck) if historical agents are to actualize the particular set of finite possibilities which the hand of history has dealt them. Ultimately economic forces (in Fr Gervase's view) find expression in changes in social structure, which in turn affect the political organism, just as, through the parallel causal chain of culture, the same forces create new publics with fresh demands. There could be no straightforwardly legal-constitutional answer to the problems which faced Richard. Not only is such an instrument too crude to be a sufficient guide to the statesman's hand, but in the period 'There was no constitution, only groups of precedents pointing different ways'. Recognising the lacunae in Richard's policies, and the bounds that limited his choice of policy, Fr Gervase permits himself a note of valedictory sadness at the departure of so glittering a figure (who was also a Dominican tertiary): 'The scale of the court had altered; the first creative phase in the court culture had ended.'

One area in which the change of dynasty in no way set back that culture was, however, the work of miniature painters. A consideration of one such artist will provide a link to Fr Gervase's second major contribution to mediaeval studies, *Byzantine Aesthetics*.

It was natural that Fr Gervase should linger on the topic of John Siferwas, the Dominican illuminator whose two main works are the Sherborne Missal and the Lovel Lectionary. Fr Bede Jarrett had already touched on Siferwas in the course of his own researches into the mediaeval Province: two of the five documents relevant to the artist's life were unearthed by him. Although Fr Gervase's characterisation of him as one of the king's 'court Dominicans' has been modified by subsequent research – his patrons were abbots, bishops and members of the lesser nobility, and his sympathies by no means wholly Plantagenet (the Lancastrian emblems of the white swan and the greyhound appear in the margins of his Missal) – his importance as the leading English representative of a late mediaeval Dominican involvement with the visual arts has been fully vindicated.[32] Siferwas's work was at once liturgical – and hence theological and devotional – and naturalistic. The elaborate iconographic schemes, in part innovatory, of his Missal, served, among other things, to portray specifically Dominican emphases or themes in doctrine, such as the significance of the Name of Jesus, with its many aspects in the christological titles of the New Testament. They were intended presumably, not only to give glory to God but also to propagate the Order's thinking and spirituality among other groups – the black monks of Sherborne, the premier abbey of Dorset, with its venerable Anglo-Saxon roots and relics, or the church and bishop of Salisbury, the home of the Sarum Use. The contrasting aspect of Siferwas was his bird and flower painting, designed at once to give opulence to his liturgical illuminations and – at least in the case of the birds – to provide accurate information about the species of the created order. Fr Gervase notes the peculiar excellence of the ornithology, but it was left to a later scholar, T.S. Tolley, to ascribe to him a project in creation theology, along the lines suggested by the descriptive and categorising work on flora and fauna of the German Dominican Albert the Great. In Fr Gervase's words, Siferwas: 'combined a zest for the minute with mastery of line, a sense of altering proportions and broken rhythms and an utter sympathy with animal life.' While his suggestion that the 'white hart' of Richard II's costly coronation icon, the Wilton Diptych, may be Siferwas' work has not been widely accepted, the general claim that the Dominican élite were intimately associated with the English Crown from Edward I to the Reformation is well established. Henry IV may have turned to the Carmelites in the moment of establishing his dynasty, but from Henry V onwards the Dominicans recovered their place as court chaplains: the young Siferwas's priory at Guildford continued to enjoy the special patronage of English queens from its foundation in 1275 by Eleanor of Provence until Henry VIII's third wife, Jane Seymour. A strong hint of a certain critical distance from the charms of court life is dropped, however, in the Sherborne Missal's Crucifixion scene, as interpreted by Fr Gervase:

> It is an experiment in dramatic tensions. The composition centres in the far corner where the Good Thief seems to spring triumphant from his cross under the nailed right hand of Christ ... But on Christ's left, fashionably dressed courtiers are talking as they ride by ...[33]

It is time to turn to a different iconographic world within the Christian cosmos, that of the Greek East.

The Byzantine East

Byzantine Aesthetics has, despite its title, almost as ample a vision of mediaeval East Roman society as *The Court of Richard II* has of mediaeval Western. It combines a broad account of the development of Byzantine culture in its social and even economic setting with a detailed attention to many of the outstanding artworks Byzantium left behind. In the appreciation of the latter Fr Gervase's forays abroad can be seen to have paid off handsomely; their geographical spread is attested by the acknowledgements in his Foreword: from Venice to

Moscow with, naturally, a particular emphasis on Greek sites: monastic communities on Athos, Patmos and Sinai as well as at Hosios Loukas and Mistra in the Peleponnese. Here his persuasive eccentricity had gained him entrance and hospitality where few 'Frankish' priests would have found a welcome. Other names who figure here read like a roll-call of the eminent Byzantinologists of the period: Norman Baynes, Egon Wellesz, Dmitri Obolensky, as well as art historians like Thomas Whittemore (the uncoverer of the mosaics of Hagia Sophia), John Beckwith, Emmy Wellesz, and David Jones's interpreter Nicolete Gray.

The rationale of Fr Gervase's broad definition of his subject is explained aphoristically in the book's opening sentence: 'Byzantine art can only become intelligible when considered in relation to the civilisation of which it is an expression.'[34] His approach to both art and civilisation in the Byzantine world proceeds by a simultaneous recognition of continuity and discontinuity. On the one hand, the single most important fact about the Byzantines is their cultural and institutional continuity with the Roman empire of the East; on the other hand, their civilisation never ceased to change and develop, by a movement which can be considered as falling into six main phases. And analogously with their art: as one trend replaced another with such stylistic clarity and chronological well-definedness, the exact dating of Byzantine artworks is, or should be, an easy task. And yet four factors recur constantly, factors Fr Gervase describes in these terms:

> a recurrent taste for classical reminiscence, which expressed a conscious inheritance of a Graeco-Roman past, an essentially mathematical approach to beauty, which led to an emphasis not only on exact symmetry but on *eurhythmos* and balanced movements; an absorbed interest in optics, which led not only to many experiments in perspective but to a concentration on Light – conceived as in itself incorporeal, though finding expression in contrasted colours; and finally a belief in the existence of an invisible world of which the material is the shadow – so that an image presupposes the Imaged just as a shadow presupposes the human body that casts it, and is as closely linked to it.

The first of those factors is intelligible enough. Classical statuary abounded in later Constantinople, arousing artists to the values of monumentality in painting. Classical literature and philosophy, knowledge of which was essential to good education for Byzantine people, conferred prestige on classical art-forms by association. The second recurrent motif, a *mathematical* aesthetics, is harder to pin down. Sometimes, Fr Gervase appears to be using a *metaphor* for a certain

intellectual style: Byzantine civilisation was mathematical in its
'emphasis on the inevitability of due proportion, rhythm and order'.
At other times, he refers to the role of a (quite literally conceived)
geometry in the colour schemes of Byzantine paintings themselves.
The difference between the Byzantine and the earlier Platonist-
Aristotelean conception of beauty, he thinks, was that the Christian
Greeks treated material beauty as symmetry *shot through with life* –
though he admits a third-century anticipation of this conviction in the
pagan philosopher Plotinus. The third constant factor in Byzantine
aesthetic standards is a link between life and light, with colour as
light's materialisation. (Not that visual values were all; tactile values
also counted for much in the 'minor arts'.) Lastly, there is the question of the theological dimension to Byzantine art. Since this has
frequently been made paramount (partly because of the particular
fascination of the Iconoclast crisis of the eighth and ninth centuries) it
might seem odd in a priest-Byzantinist to relegate it to the end of a
list. Fr Gervase's motive was a desire not to let Byzantine civilisation,
as a many-faceted unity, each aspect enjoying a relative autonomy, be
collapsed into its theological life *tout court*. Yet he does full justice to
the mystagogical dimension of Byzantine art: just as for the
Alexandrian approach to exegesis, the water of the literal sense leads
on to the wine of the profounder mystical meaning of Scripture, so for
the Byzantines line and colour had their noblest employment when in
service to the symbols of the Christian Liturgy: the latter being not
only worship but also initiation into new transcendent life.

All Byzantine religion centred round the performance of the
Leitourgia conceived as a sacred drama; not a commemoration but
a re-enactment. The infinity of Godhead taking flesh had given the
Incarnation a reality that pierced through time and space.

If Byzantine art had been long travestied as a style incapable of
learning or forgetting, frozen into formal archaism, this was owed, Fr
Gervase believed, to three factors: the bad press endured by the
Byzantines generally in the early modern West (classically, for the
English, through the scathing comments of Gibbon); the habit of
Italian art historians to dub pre-Giotto painting the work of an ill-
defined *scuola bizantina* (in fact it was provincial Italian, Giotto was
the recipient of the genuine Constantinopolitan impulses of the time);
and the secretion of so many Byzantine masterpieces under layers of
Turkish plaster-work. And those with eyes to see *could* have seen –
at Ravenna and Torcello, Cefalu and Mistra.

The chronological development of Fr Gervase's study – from the
'Third Century Transition' to the fall of Constantinople – deploys in

differing proportions, and with varying emphases, the four basic factors he has identified as together making the distinctive character of Byzantine art. This is done in no wooden fashion, but with a spectacular imaginative freedom. Yet a number of his succinctly expressed insights have stimulated in others more laborious research which has shown them well-founded. *Byzantine Aesthetics* still appears in bibliographies because of its striking *Innerlichkeit* in evoking Byzantine society in its main phases. It is religiously sympathetic to the Byzantine world without being theologically overdrawn. In a word, it interprets Byzantine Christianity by way of Byzantine *culture*. The spiritualisation and inward turn evident in the Imperial portraiture of the anxious Late Antique period; Byzantine Neo-Pythagoreanism with its emphasis on the transcendent significance of number; the marriage of geodesy with optics; the continuity of the East Roman civil service from the late fourth to the middle fifteenth centuries; the shifting of primacy among the senses from hearing to sight in the predominant aesthetic theory under the Amorian and Macedonian dynasties and the appreciation then of precious materials by craftsman and patron alike; the taste for dramatic narrative sequence under their successors the Comneni and Palaeologoi: all this receives the same careful attention as the specifically religious and theological factors – the masterworks of trinitarian, christological and sacramental symbolism at Dura and Ravenna, the Chora church, Torcello and Rome; the illuminated codices with their visual meditations: on the Gospels of Lent, as in the Rossano Codex, or the correspondence of Old and New Testament types and antitypes in its brother of Sinope; the portable panel-paintings of the Holy Ones of Christendom which roused the wrath of the Iconophobes; the theology of the Iconophile doctors; the theological character, in consequence, of much Macedonian church decoration when the sacred images returned; and in Comnenian and Palaeologan painting the

> characteristics in spirituality which Western mediaevalists associate with the Cistercian and Franciscan schools ... already apparent in eleventh and twelfth century Byzantium ... an essentially Christocentric devotion, an emphasis on each physical detail of the Incarnation, the spirit of the Stabat Mater and of the crib.[35]

The 'new emotional range and depth' of late Byzantine art seems mirrored, finally, in Fr Gervase's own concluding chapter on the vanished Byzantine world. In the church of the Brontochion at Mistra 'angels with overlapping wings swerve among wine-red shadowing', while in the nave of the Peribleptos there 'a dark bent Christ strains beneath the Cross or against a ladder among rough splashes of blue light'. Christ the true liturgist celebrates in 'opal robes [falling] from neck to ankle in still and living folds' as the lines of angels, bearing bread and wine, advance towards him. On the walls of the Pantanassa, Lazarus is raised again: see 'the quick unwinding of the sere cloth, the dull ochre shadowing upon the marble, the small white flowers with chocolate leaves.[36] It is as though in recording the end of the Byzantine polity Fr Gervase felt he must atone for the Western neglect, followed by travesty, of its civilisation. In paying this debt, he no doubt saw himself as a successor of the Dominicans who, between the two Union councils, had worked in the great city to keep the Unionist idea alive.

A Dominican view of spirituality

How then did Fr Gervase see the Dominicans themselves? In an article on 'Dominican Spirituality', he pointed out that the greater religious orders could claim each its own school of spirituality – 'a clumsy term for the conscious following of a way to God'. Yet despite the individuality of their sub-traditions – both within the religious life as a whole, and within the wider reality of Catholicism at large – all seek a common end, by a common faith, and, in the case of most of their male members at any rate, the 'bond of priesthood'. Fr Gervase found for this, in the last analysis, a metaphysical explanation to do with the God-world relationship. 'Each will mirror in its finite contrasted achievement the infinite unity of God, since each will be perfect in so far as it participates in the divine and yet remain inevitably separate in so far as it is participant ...'[37] – a point he substantiates by reference to Aquinas's claim that 'what in God exists simply and in a uniform manner is in creatures multiple and divided'.[38]

To put it more concretely: what all spiritualities have in common is threefold: the goal of the vision of God; a source in the love of God by charity; a life in grace. In each case, therefore, success or failure turns on the same crucial factor: intensity in charity – or its loss. What, by contrast, distinguishes one spirituality from another is four-fold: the special purpose for which each order has been created; the choice of means this has necessitated; the influence of the personality of the founder; the impact of the 'cumulative influence of generations striving, however imperfectly, to keep the spirit as well as the letter of the rule'.

The decks duly cleared, Fr Gervase can concentrate on the specific spirituality of the Dominicans. And in the first instance that is: the

contemplative appropriation of truth. An order of apostles was meant
to be and remain 'primarily contemplative'; in it, in a perceptive
phrase, 'action was never to be the purpose of contemplation but
always its natural result'. Contemplation then is the vision of truth;
the apostolate the effort to bring it to others. Donning the historian's
cap, he stresses the accident of circumstance whereby a primarily
metaphysical heresy (Albigensian dualism) led to the founding of an
Order where God was necessarily presented more as truth (intellectually) than as the desired (affectively). This end dictated the means:
study, chiefly theological, being elevated to challenge the pre-
eminence in Christian monasticism of the liturgy as the *opus Dei*; and
an intellectualist rather than voluntarist road to prayer. For, as Fr
Gervase notes, even such radically un-Thomistic Dominicans as the
mystics of the Rhineland school – Meister Ulrich, Meister Dietrich,
and the better known Meister Eckhart, remained passionate adherents
of an 'intellective' theory of prayer. Had they not been lectors in
theology prior to becoming masters of the contemplative life?

But here a worry intrudes. Could not such an approach all too easily
forget the weightier matters of Torah: the adoration, and above all,
the *love* of almighty God? Lectors in sacred theology, like sacristans,
may forget to bow before the altar: a professional obsession with God-
talk, as with orphreys, can corrode the foundations of piety and the
fear of the Lord. That this did not happen to Dominican spirituality
Fr Gervase ascribes to two factors above all: the generosity and zeal
of St Dominic's christocentric devotion, and the genius for integration
which marked his most celebrated follower, St Thomas.

Without derogation from the ideal of assiduous study, Dominic's
'utter concentration upon the following of Christ' continued to
'dwarf all other devotion in the Order', energising its apostolic zeal
in the image of Christ's self-giving on the cross. Of this, Fr Gervase
takes the Rosary to be the symbol: treating it not as a Marian prayer,
but as an act of christocentric commitment to the detailed following
of Christ's life on earth. And in a generation, with the composition
of Aquinas's works, the intellectual doctrine of prayer found its
proper context in a holistic account of the human person before God,
thanks to the concept, now baptised, of the 'hylomorphic' (matter
with form) unity of man, body and soul. Though Thomas had no
desire to innovate in spiritual theology, and was self-consciously a
disciple of Gregory the Great in his teaching on contemplation, none
the less 'he had altered traditional conceptions by integrating them'.
If we ask, How?, Fr Gervase had two answers to give. First:
through the idea of the *desiderium naturale* for the vision of God.
As he explains:

It is from an exigency of nature that man finds his beatitude through intellectual vision. The impulse to know more perfectly is the corollary of love, for the lover is not content with a superficial knowledge of the beloved.

Here we come upon the theme of 'the mind in love', which will be central to Fr Kenelm Foster's understanding of the search for God. And secondly, Thomas's doctrine of the gifts of the Holy Spirit unifies the mystical and the moral: the excellence of the gift of understanding (*intellectus*) lies in the consideration of the Eternal not simply as it is in itself but also as the norm for human action.[39]

The doctrine of the Gifts remains the essential note in Thomist spiritual theory precisely since it provides the unbroken rhythm in the ascent to the divine. The contemplative will possess a higher degree of knowledge as he grows more connatural with the contemplated, and he has grown more connatural through the growth of charity and its corollary, the more patent presence of the Gifts.[40]

Yet in practice, few individuals incarnate the fullness of this apostolico-contemplative norm. The exigencies of human individuality and the historically situated mission of the Order in this or that particular place see to that. The 'interplay of natural talent and obedience' tends to foster a specialisation in which a full Dominican life may be possible for *communities* but only at the cost of the 'canalized energies of their members'. Thus the saints and *beati* of the Order reached holiness in diverse settings: *studia*, 'anchorholds', parish houses, or itinerancy, as well as what may be termed the 'normal' priory.

And this brings us to the question of the organised life of the Order. Though Fr Gervase's name would scarcely have been on everybody's lips were a competent administrator sought, his comments on the Order convey a marked admiration for the gift of administration, which Paul, indeed, lists by the name *kybernêsis*, as a grace volunteered by the Spirit to the churches (1 Cor. 12.28). Noting among Dominicans a lack of 'prudent discretion', Fr Gervase developed more fully a second criticism: a recurring absence of 'disciplined co-ordination'. 'At times Dominican action was to mirror the feudal levy of new Castille riding southward, loosely, with its many leaders to some chance-won foray or to some quite unnecessary defeat ...' – a metaphor put forward to compare and contrast their Order with the Jesuit Society.

If we turn to his essay on the English Dominicans, printed as an appendix to the first edition of David Mathew's *Catholicism in England (1535–1935). Portrait of a Minority: its Culture and*

Tradition, we find this healthy respect for good government fully borne out. Its heroes are Philip Thomas Howard and Bede Jarrett, the giants of the restoration of the English Province in the mid-seventeenth, and its sudden expansion in the early twentieth, centuries, with honourable mention for two intermediate stalwarts, Dominic Williams and Thomas Worthington. Though Fr Gervase does justice, in a few deft strokes, to the 'baroque magnificence' of Cardinal Howard – the 'Rubens setting' of his childhood as Lord Arundel's grandson on a perpetual foreign tour; his trusted position in Charles II's court as Lord Almoner to the queen; the un-Roman gift to the Roman populace, when cardinal, of an ox roasted and stuffed English-style, in place of the more customary, and circumambient Late Renaissance delights offered by the other cardinals to celebrate James II's Catholic triumphs (*tableaux vivants*, Latin odes, illuminated statuary), his true focus of attention is elsewhere. Howard's chief contribution lay in his fourteen years as Vicar of the Province, when he 'restored the provincialate and *a normal administration* and the means to fulfill the obligations of community life and of the choir'.[41] And after describing Howard's (in fact, sometimes short-lived) foundations – the priory at Bornhem, near Antwerp, the monastery of nuns at Brussels, the houses in Tangiers and Rome, Fr Gervase goes on, revealingly: 'An expansion of Dominican activity was followed naturally by an increase in number. The same recipe for success – decisive government, in a positive, expansionist spirit, leading to new recruitment – governs his account of the provincialates of Bede Jarrett, whose biography he was to co-author with Fr Kenneth Wykeham-George. 'His provincialates were marked by unbroken administrative success'. And noting the main landmarks in that course – the foundations in South Africa, in Oxford, in Edinburgh, Fr Gervase went on: 'New work was undertaken constantly, always Dominican work ... He planned, and then he carried out his plans through years of indomitable patience.'

The statements are patently true: but they also disclose a *beau idéal*. It recurs in more muted form in the lesser figures of bishop Dominic Williams, vicar-apostolic of the Northern District under Queen Anne – his 'controlled energy, his sense of detail and his recognition of reality made him a formidable administrator', and of Thomas Worthington, provincial during the administration of Hugh Walpole – his time in office 'marked by an increased efficiency of control'. It is in sharp contrast, that William Perrin, prior of the newly gifted house of St Bartholomew's, Smithfield, under Mary Tudor, and a significant *avant garde* figure of the new Counter-Reformation themes and techniques, puts in only the briefest of appearances (and then as *re-organising* the friars); that the only beatified Reformation period

martyr of the Province, Robert Nutter, is bleakly characterised –
'unwilling to negotiate, ready to plunge into quarrel, always dogged',
and that the spiritual writers Reginald Buckler and Bertrand
Wilberforce, the preacher Vincent McNabb, and the exegete Hugh
Pope receive no mention at all (though the fact that the latter two were
still alive may have caused hesitation).

The portrait of Jarrett in *Bede Jarrett of the Order of Preachers* is
a good deal more rounded, thanks not least to the copious use of the
subject's letters.[42] How much of the work is due to Fr Kenneth
Wykeham-George is hard to say: probably the final embellishments.[43]

A constant feature of Fr Gervase's writing on the English
Dominicans is a patriotic reiteration of their Englishness. In 1535 we
read of the Province: 'It had long possessed its own traditions and a
certain distaste for foreigners, and a quick impatience with the enact-
ments of central authority had been spasmodically apparent.'[44]
Cardinal Howard, we are told, made an 'abrupt refusal to accept a
pension from a foreign prince', and showed 'displeasure at foreign
mannerisms in an English priest'. In the early nineteenth century, the
Province had 'some of the characteristics of the English yeomanry
declining with it'. The Dominicans of 1860, untouched by either the
Oxford converts or the Irish immigration, 'represented the tradition of
a penal England, uncompromisingly steadfast, a little grim'. These
notes gather into a crescendo which reaches its climax in Fr Gervase's
character portrait of Bede Jarrett: 'Traditions of public service
absorbed since childhood gave him a sympathy with all that was
essentially English in the non-Catholic official world'. When we hear
that he was 'intensely English, intensely Dominican', we may begin
to wonder whether this two-phrase formula does not constitute something of a tautology! It is of course virtuous to love one's country –
as that human solidarity which, by a network of indebtedness, has the
prior claim to loyalty of all the blocs of which the race is naturally
composed. It is also highly understandable that one should prefer what
is best known. So international and peripatetic, however, was Fr
Gervase's Dominicanism – he preferred to be on Athos or at Addis
Ababa so long as he was assured of return to Oxford, that some
further explanation of this harping on Englishry should be sought.
Had he not written of the friars, as dispersed by the Henrician and
Edwardine Reformations, that they were 'to be traced at Brechin and
at Louvain and in the island of Chios; they had always been mobile'?
In part there is an echo here of Jarrett's own apologetic deployment
of Englishness: in a Protestant England, and a world where the British
Empire created by that England counted, for Catholics to appear
archetypally as Irishmen or Italians was poor strategy.[45] But Fr

Gervase's use of the term 'English' functions almost as a term of moral approbation. It represents a cluster of virtues of its own: constancy, balance in judgment, humour, the capacity for friendship, truthfulness, candour in personal relations, and in religion a strong, not mawkish, devotion.[46]

We are not surprised, then, to find him contributing, with Jarrett, to a series of essays on approaches to holiness in some English authors under the general title *The English Way*.[47] Fr Gervase's choice – at once, perhaps, a compliment to the Fathers and to the great Provincial – was Bede the Venerable. It is an instructive account, of which the author conveniently summarises the lessons for us at the close: 'The presence of an unseen world around him and the duty of the prescribed devotions had been the motifs in Bede's life.' Maisie Ward's collection of essayists opens by offering a theological rationale of the concern with Englishness:

> Because it [Christianity] is universal it is in every country, but because it is sacramental it is intensely local, found in each country in a special and unique fashion, not a spirit only but a spirit clothed in material form.[48]

How does this programmatic statement work out in Fr Gervase's version of the Northumbrian *doctor Ecclesiae*?

Beginning with Bede's death – of which we have, in the 'Letter of Cuthbert' one of the finest death-bed descriptions in all patristic literature, Fr Gervase announces three themes of his own. And these are: first, the role of the Latin liturgy in Bede's life; secondly, the continuing influence of the pagan inheritance (and not only for the worse); thirdly, the apostolic imperative to share the truth. 'As he lay there he murmured ceaselessly – antiphons from the office for quinquagesima, uncouth Northumbrian verses on man's destiny and the need for prudence, and aphorisms culled for his pupils' sake.' To a reader seeking the plain facts of Bede's life and literary production, the essay is of little worth. But its aim is not to reproduce a section of a manual on patrology, it is to evoke a world. In its course, Fr Gervase succeeds in making a number of points. To begin with, he brings home Bede's avidity to create a culture – a widely informed setting for life – for his readers and disciples:

> He had written of the nature of the rainbow and of the colour of the Red Sea; of clouds and of frost and of the River Nile; of the astrolabe and of blood letting; of the seven wonders of the world, and of the seven stars that hang between the earth and sky. He had learnt so much, he had written so much, he had been interested in so little.

The sudden coldness of that ending alerts us to the ambiguity that runs through all of Fr Gervase's encomium. For example: there is the tension between, on the one hand, eschatological concentration on another world – the wider world of reality whose epiphanic presence Fr Gervase never denies but sees, contrary-wise, as integral to a Catholic sensibility – and, on the other hand, a necessary 'political' attention to the trends of this world. Thus the 'quick play' of Bede's imagination was haunted by the apocalypse when each Christian would 'learn his eternal destiny'; yet the indifference to the political movements of the time prepared the downfall of the civilisation a-building in his work.

> How trivial and remote the chaffering of the Norse traders seemed to them – an occasional galley storm-beached, the rapid bargaining talk. On the background of the life of Jarrow and Monkwearmouth, behind the careful chanting and religious custom, there passed unperceived the northern movements. Threatening the whole new system, bringing in time destruction and the sword, there moved the friendless sea.[49]

Then again, there is the contrast between Northumbria's successful assimilation of both Latin and Greek elements, and the imperfect appreciation, dulled by the Paschal controversy, of the Celtic contribution to these islands: a failure in Catholicity. Though a late twentieth-century neo-Romantic imagination, schooled by the ecological movement, would see things otherwise, what Fr Gervase, writing in 1933, meant by this was – proto-scholasticism.

> The hampered thought and clumsy perverted Latin of the Irish scholars foreshadowed the clear glory of Erigena, and in their delight in dialectic as dialectic they were the precursors of those great schoolmen of the thirteenth century who were to see in every syllogism a theophany of the Incarnate Word.

And yet Fr Gervase could also see in Bede's English theology factors that made for the transcending of such limitation or disunity. His sense of the end of all things might not encourage prescient government for the near-present, yet it could support a philosophy of history. His sense of the 'sacramental concord of created things' combined with 'a complete union of intention and will and desire' in the following of Christ to produce a wisdom that could suffer patiently the reverses of history. Had he known of the Viking invasions to come, 'a half-quenched civilisation beyond Humber', the tenor of his life and work would not have been disturbed. For: 'his life's purpose had been the fulfillment of God's will, and this, implying an overwhelming trust in Providence, involved an entire acceptance of the future.' Moreover, his imperfect sympathy with the Celtic world was softened by his feeling for the individual significance of each human life, as well as by his courtesy.

Two last points may be noted. Fr Gervase's sensibility for artefacts, later to be put to such excellent use in his art historical studies, is already highly developed. His exultation in richness of colour and texture is patent in his references to the artworks of the Anglian Renaissance, 'the old gold and the vermilion, the cloisonné and the green of patined bronze'. It makes him a plausible spokesman for a barbarian voice: the Norsemen who had 'heard of the red twisted gold in the sacrist's keeping and of the embroidered coverlets from Greek-land of the worth of many hides'. More importantly, his Bede is a profoundly christocentric figure, and being christocentric also ecclesiocentric, for the Head is inseparable from the Body.

> If his learning had been inspired by his devotion to God's word his devotion to God's word resulted from his devotion to the Word made flesh – the devotion that is so apparent in the most self-revealing of his books, the commentary upon the Song of Songs, to the golden blossom Christ and the Church his body. Bede's words as he lay dying, 'My soul desires to see Christ my king in his beauty' serve both to summarize and to explain his teaching. For it was his realization of the Incarnation as a present fact that led to his strong loyalty to the Catholic Unity: *indivisa in se, a aliis vero divisa*: in antithesis to the city of hell, the impregnable city of God.[50]

And so the figure of Bede merges imperceptibly into that of the encomium of St Dominic in 'Dominican Spirituality' and with those of the London Carthusians in *The Reformation and the Contemplative Life*. For the historian not to perceive the identity of sanctity is verily not to see the wood for the trees.

It is in a strong feeling for the particularity of things, married to a conviction of the presence of the Eternal – an 'Aristotelian' and a 'Platonist' mind-set rolled into one, that Bede's Englishness, for Fr Gervase, seems to have consisted.[51]

A philosophy of history

A Dominican historian in an age of Thomistic revival must inevitably be a combination of chronicler and metaphysician. The empiricist cast of twentieth-century English culture is inimical to such projects, which are better received in Germanic or Latin Europe. Yet if done well they can be 'empirical' in the best sense, fathoming the *empireia*, the given of experience, to its depths. Fr Gervase was torn by conflicting emotions when he surveyed the cultural history that was his subject. As a professional historian he was committed to the primacy of the specific and contingent: precisely that with which a philosophy of history of a Thomist kind would find business most difficult. As a Dominican committed to the Thomist school he considered it desirable to disengage a series of causal principles at work in the historical process at large, 'an inherent truth in time-forms of development and decay'.[52]

As this formulation suggests, Fr Gervase was influenced in his account of the aims a philosophic history should set itself, by the success of Oswald Spengler's *The Decline of the West* – soon to be followed, in its analysis of patterns of the rise and fall of cultures by the even more widely read indigenous work of Arnold Toynbee, *A Study of History*. However, he offered an original categorisation of historical genres: 'the 'Chronicle', the 'Myth' and the 'Culture Study'. By these capitalised headings he meant to denote, respectively: the technically sophisticated study, based on primary sources, of a highly restricted portion of the past; an ideologically informed explanation of the present by a large-scale interpretation of the past; and, lastly, an investigation of the sources of cultural achievement and decay. It is to the third of these that Fr Gervase found his Thomism relevant. The first he regarded as incapable of philosophical ennoblement since unwilling to make wider connections or draw ramifying analogies: 'at last analysis mediaevalist research remains irremediably nominalist.' The second, exemplified in Cobbett, Gibbon, H.A.L. Fisher, depends on an 'assurance in the efficacy of contemporary values' such that, given the 'self-conscious insecurity of so much modern civilisation', its days are, at least for the present, numbered. The third alone holds out the possibility for a Thomist historian of a kind of writing that would constitute a 'natural development from the school of the great Commentators'. Here Fr Gervase drew on an essay by Raymund Klibansky in an Oxford collection on the philosophy of history where that student of Renaissance culture had distinguished between the time in which things happen (*Geschehenszeit*), the time in which things are 'ordered' (*Ordnungszeit*), and the time of destiny (*Schicksalzeit*) whereby within the time-form of history at large each civilisation manifests a specific conditioning towards some clearly defined end.[53] Just so for St Thomas *tempus ut mensura* (time considered as the 'measure of movement' rather than as mere duration) is the measuring rod for 'the growth of a perfection still realizable and so not yet realized – *actus entis in potentia prout in potentia*'.[54] In point of fact, the exchange of sweeping historiographical generalisations in the debates of the 1930s was more concerned with imperfection than perfection: interlocutors asked whether the source of the collapse of a civilisation should be sought in the light of historical determinism or its main alternative, some form of catastrophe theory. It is a tribute to the optimism of grace which underlies Fr Gervase's writing that he found growth toward perfection the more considerable subject.

Fr Gervase laid his finger unerringly on one necessary condition for the recreation of a Christian culture: and this is the willingness to receive from without but transform from within. Only thus can the two senses of the word 'Catholic' – universal outreach of mission, inward continuity of essence – be simultaneously done justice. Describing how a group of Oxford manuscripts suggest a link between the twelfth-century Byzantine court and the early years of that Western University, he concluded:

> Behind many of the certitudes of mediaeval Oxford lay a Byzantine heritage, texts and the commentaries upon texts and a vision of an intelligible world order. For Oxford came to being through a characteristic common to all thirteenth century Western culture: the power to receive and then transform.[55]

Notes

1. F. Mathew, *A Book of Songs* (London: Elkin Mathews, 1925), p. 35.
2. Fr Gervase's travels issued, however, in gains to scholarship, communicated in 'Recent Discoveries in East African Archaeology', *Antiquity*, XXVII (1953), pp. 212–18; 'The Culture of the East African Coast in the Seventeenth and Eighteenth Centuries in the Light of Recent Archaeological Discoveries', *Man*, LVI (1956), pp. 65–8; 'Chinese Porcelain in East Africa and on the Coast of South Arabia', *Oriental Art*, VII (1956), pp. 50–57; 'The Land of Zanj' in R.A. Oliver (ed.), *The Dawn of African History* (London: Oxford University Press 1961). These publications led to an invitation to co-edit the Oxford *History of East Africa*, I (with R.A. Oliver, Oxford: Oxford University Press 1963), to which he contributed 'The East African Coast until the Coming of the Portuguese', ibid., pp. 94–127.
3. K. Tynan, 'Frank Mathew: A Memory', in Mathew, *A Book of Songs*, p. 8.
4. F. Kerr [O.P.], 'Mathew, David James, 1902–1975', *Dictionary of National Biography*, 1971–1980 (Oxford: Oxford University Press, 1980), pp. 553–4.
5. D. Mathew, *The Celtic Peoples and Renaissance Europe. A Study of the Celtic and Spanish Influences on Elizabethan History, with an*

Introduction by Christopher Dawson (London: Sheed & Ward, 1933), followed up, in its concern for the Anglo-Celtic peoples of the British Island, by two articles on Scotland and Wales in the sixteenth and early seventeenth centuries co-authored with Fr Gervase: namely, 'William Semple's Reports on Scotland in 1588 and 1610', *English Historical Review* XLI (1926), pp. 579–83, and 'The Survival of the Dissolved Monasteries in Wales', *Dublin Review* CLXXXIV (1929), pp. 70–81. Studies of the Tudor and early Stuart periods flowed copiously from his pen: thus *The Jacobean Age* (London: Longmans & Co, 1939; Port Washington, NY: Kennikat Press, 1971); *The Social Structure in Caroline England* (Oxford: Clarendon Press, 1948); *Scotland under Charles I* (London: Eyre and Spottiswoode, 1950); *The Age of Charles I* (London: Eyre and Spottiswoode, 1951); *James I* (London: Eyre and Spottiswoode, 1967); *The Courtiers of Henry VIII* (London: Eyre and Spottiswoode, 1970); *Lady Jane Grey. The Setting of the Reign* (London: Methuen, 1972). Family pride was satisfied by *Sir Tobie Mathew* (London: Max Parrish, 1950): however, Bishop David made an abortive attempt to prove his claim to the Mathew earldom of Llandaff, with a view to 'representing' the Catholic bishops in the House of Lords. *Acton. The Formative Years* (London: Eyre and Spottiswoode, 1946) was a perhaps over-benign account of the Victorian historian, its judgements modified in *Lord Acton and his Times* (London: Eyre and Spottiswoode, 1968). David's naval career as an officer cadet at Dartmouth was reflected in *British Seamen* (London: William Collins, 1943) and *The Naval Heritage* (London: Collins, 1944). His history of Abyssinia was published as *Ethiopia. The Study of a Polity, 1540–1935* (London: Eyre and Spottiswoode, 1947). There may be a rueful element, given his failure to realise a widely made prediction by becoming archbishop of Westminster, in his contribution to the history of the London district in *Richard Challoner, 1691–1781. The Greatest of the Vicars-Apostolic, his Life, Times, Works, Influence* (Westminster: Westminster Cathedral Chronicle, 1946).

6.　'Ideals of Friendship', in J. Lawlor (ed.), *Patterns of Love and Courtesy. Essays in Memory of C.S. Lewis* (London: Edward Arnold, 1966), pp. 45–53.

7.　*Letters of Bede Jarrett*, ed. B. Bailey, A. Bellenger, S. Tugwell (Bath: Downside Abbey and Blackfriars Publications, 1989), especially, pp. 180–82.

8.　B. Jarrett, O.P., 'St Aelred' in M. Ward (ed.)., *The English Way. Studies in English Sanctity from St Bede to Newman* (London: Sheed and Ward, 1933).

9.　'Marriage and *amour courtois* in Late-Fourteenth-Century England', in *Essays Presented to Charles Williams* (London: Oxford University Press, 1947), pp. 128–135; 'Ideals of Friendship', in J. Lawlor (ed.), *Patterns of Love and Courtesy. Essays in Memory of C.S. Lewis* (London: Edward Arnold, 1966), pp. 45–53.

10.　C.S. Lewis, 'Preface', to *Essays Presented to Charles Williams*, q.v.

11. R.A. Knox, *In Soft Garments. A series of Oxford Conferences* (London: Burns Oates, 1942).

12. Gervase Mathew, in *Acts of the Provincial Chapter of the English Province Held at St Thomas' Priory, Hawkesyard 1978* (n.d.), p. 34.

13.. *The Reformation and the Contemplative Life. A Study of the Conflict between the Carthusians and the State*, by David Mathew and Gervase Mathew, O.P. (London: Sheed and Ward, 1934).

14. W.G. Wheeler, 'Archbishop David Mathew, M.A., Litt.D., F.S.A., F.R.S.L., 1902-1975', *Ampleforth Journal* 81/1 (1976), p.5.

15. *The Reformation and the Contemplative Life*, p. 1.

16. Ibid., pp. 1-2.

17. R.H. Benson, *By What Authority?* (London: Burns, Oates and Washbourne, 1909); *Come Rack, Come Rope* (London: Burns, Oates and Washbourne, 1912); *Lord of the World* (London: Burns, Oates & Washbourne, 1908); *The Dawn of All* (London: Burns, Oates and Washbourne, 1911); For his life, see C.C. Martindale, S.J., *The Life of Monsignor Robert Hugh Benson* (London: Longmans, Green & Co., 1916); and for a theological comment on his writing, A. Nichols, O.P., 'Imaginative Eschatology: Benson's 'The Lord of the World', *New Blackfriars* 72. 845 (1991), pp. 4-8.

18. Another possible factor is the trilogy *The Fifth Queen* (1906-1908) by the (somewhat nominal) Catholic convert Ford Madox Ford. It too 'focuses on the clash between an old Catholic order and the new secularisation represented by Thomas Cromwell: thus T. Woodman, *Faithful Fictions. The Catholic Novel in British Literature* (Milton Keynes: Open University Press, 1991), p. 18.

19. *The Reformation and the Contemplative Life*, pp. 13-14.

20. Ibid., pp. 31-2.

21. Ibid., pp. 99-100.

22. An end-note, surely Fr Gervase's, is expansive on this Dominican connection: 'It is significant that throughout the first half of the sixteenth century the Carthusians would seem to have maintained a far closer contact with the Dominicans than with any other body of Religious. The friendship, traditional between the Orders and emphasised by the lives of so many saints, had grown throughout the fifteenth century. The priories of the Strict Observance in the south of Spain had been linked closely with the charterhouse of Porta Caeli since the time of Saint Vincent Ferrer and his Carthusian brother Boniface. At the same time, the revival of Carthusian studies in the Rhineland had been influenced profoundly by the Dominican theologians of Cologne. It was a connection that inevitably affected the Carthusian judgment of the new febrile movements in the schools at a time when the Dominicans were the protagonists of the Old Learning in the North.' Ibid., pp. 292-3.

23. Ibid., p. 263. A modern scholarly account is L.E. Whatmore, *Carthusians under King Henry the Eighth*,=*Analecta Cartusiana* (1983).

24. *The Reformation and the Contemplative Life*, pp. 279-80.

25. 'Eastern Traditions in Christianity', *Blackfriars* XXXI (1950), p. 203.
26. R. Knox, 'The Man who Tried to Convert the Pope' in D. Woodruff (ed.) *For Hilaire Belloc. Essays in Honour of his Seventy-Second Birthday* (London: Sheed and Ward, 1942), p. 18.
27. 'Eastern Traditions in Christianity' p. 201.
28. 'Foreword', *The Court of Richard II* (London: John Murray, 1968).
29. J. Evans, *Art in Mediaeval France [987-1498]*, (London: Oxford University Press, 1948), *in Blackfriars* XXX (1949), p. 386.
30. *The Court of Richard II*, p. 7.
31. Ibid., p. 82.
32. T.S. Tolley, 'John Siferwas' (University of East Anglia doctoral dissertation, Norwich, 1984).
33. Ibid., pp. 45-6.
34. *Byzantine Aesthetics* (London: John Murray, 1963), p. 1.
35. Ibid., p. 145.
36. Ibid., p. 155. At the opposite (chronological) end of Byzantine civilisation, he had noted in Gregory of Nyssa, writing in the fourth century, a special sensitivity to colour; 'The Aesthetic Theories of Gregory of Nyssa', in *Studies in Memory of David Talbot Rice* (Edinburgh: Edinburgh University Press, 1975), pp. 218-19.
37. 'Dominican Spirituality', *Blackfriars* XVII (1936), p. 650.
38. *Summa Theologiae* Ia, q. 47, art. 1.
39. *Summa Theologiae* IIa IIae, q. 8, art. 3, ad ii.
40. 'Dominican Spirituality', pp. 655-6.
41. 'Appendix I. The English Dominicans', in D. Mathew, *Catholicism in England, 1535-1935. Portrait of a Minority: its Culture and Tradition* (London: Longmans, Green & Co., 1936), p. 265. Italics added. On Howard's role in the history of the English Dominican Province, see Appendix 1 of this volume.
42. *Bede Jarrett of the Order of Preachers*, by Kenneth Wykeham-George, O.P., and Gervase Mathew, O.P., With a Foreword by the Very Revd. Hilary J. Carpenter, O.P., Prior Provincial of the English Dominicans (London: Blackfriars Publications, 1952).
43. A suggestion made by Fr Vincent Pizzala, O.P. in conversation with the present author. He had opportunity to study Fr Kenneth's *modus operandi*.
44. 'Appendix I. The English Dominicans', p. 263.
45. The Jarrett Province was Ultramontane, but definitely not Italianate. He wrote: 'The incoming of converts has, on the whole, led to a more intense loyalty to the Holy See, for each convert experiences intense relief in the change from the City of Confusion to the City of Peace and Security, and realises that his precise change is due to the acceptance of papal infallibility. Hence the accession of the converts has but confirmed what we may call 'hereditary' Catholics in their devotion of immemorial antiquity to St Peter and his Vicars. This feeling has indeed sometimes led to an exaggerated aping of Italian practices which have little more to do with loyalty to the Holy See than would have a

habitual diet of macaroni.' *The Church in England in 1922*, (London: Catholic Truth Society, 1922), p. 7.

46. Could he have been influenced by the longest-serving, and most popular, British prime minister of his early manhood? On Baldwin's rich concept of Englishness, and the political capital he made from it, see P. Williamson, 'The Doctrinal Politics of Stanley Baldwin', in M. Bentley (ed.), *Public and Private Doctrine. Essays in British History presented to Maurice Cowling* (Cambridge: 1993), pp. 181–208.

47. M. Ward (ed.), *The English Way. Studies in English Sanctity from St Bede to Newman*, (London: Sheed & Ward, 1933).

48. 'Foreword' in ibid., p. 7.

49. 'St Bede' in ibid., p. 11.

50. Ibid., pp. 16–17.

51. The question, What is essential Englishness? – a query barely intelligible until the early German Romantics – is not exactly easy to answer: see D. Gervais, *Literary England. Versions of 'Englishness' in Modern Writing* (Cambridge: Cambridge University Press, 1993).

52. 'Philosophy and the Meaning of History', *Blackfriars* XVII. 200 (1936), p. 826. To borrow a phrase of William Temple's, he was seeking 'middle axioms', lying between the totalising (and predictive) explanations of 'substantive' philosophies of history and the merely conceptual enquiries of 'analytic' ones. For this distinction see A.C. Danto, *Analytical Philosophy of History* (Cambridge: Cambridge University Press, 1965).

53. R. Klibansky, 'The Philosophic Character of History', in R. Klibansky and H.J. Paton, (eds.), *Philosophy and History. Essays presented to E. Cassirer* (Oxford: Clarendon Press, 1936), pp. 323–38.

54. 'Philosophy and the Meaning of History', p. 824.

55. 'Byzantine to Oxford', in D. Woodruff (ed.), *For Hilaire Belloc. Essays in Honour of his 72nd Birthday* (London: Sheed and Ward, 1942).

Works of Gervase Mathew

'William Semple's Reports on Scotland in 1588 and 1610', with David Mathew, *English Historical Review* XLI (1926), pp. 579–83.

'The Survival of the Dissolved Monasteries in Wales', with David Mathew, *Dublin Review* CLXXXIV (1929), pp. 70–81.

'St Bede', in M. Ward (ed.), *The English Way. Studies in English Sanctity from St Bede to Newman* (London: Sheed and Ward, 1933), pp. 9–23.

'Cajetan', *Blackfriars* XV (1934), pp. 826–29.

The Reformation and the Contemplative Life. A Study of the Conflict between the Carthusians and the State, with David Mathew (London: Sheed and Ward, 1934).

'Dominican Spirituality', *Blackfriars* XVII (1936), pp. 650–57.

'The English Dominicans', = Appendix I to: D. Mathew, *Catholicism in England, 1535–1935. Portrait of a Minority: its Culture and Tradition* (London: Longmans, Green & Co., 1936), pp. 263–69.

'Philosophy and the Meaning of History', *Blackfriars* XVII (1936), pp. 820–26.

'Patristic Revival', *Blackfriars* XIX (1938), pp. 16–22.

'Byzantine to Oxford', in D. Woodruff (ed.), *For Hilaire Belloc. Essays in Honour of his 72nd Birthday* (London: Sheed and Ward, 1942), pp. 108–117.

'The Character of the Gallienic Renaissance', *Journal of Roman Studies* XXX (1943), pp. 65–70.

'Marriage and *Amour Courtois* in Late Fourteenth Century England', in *Essays Presented to Charles Williams* (London: Oxford University Press, 1947), pp. 128–35.

'Ideals of Knighthood in Late Fourteenth Century England', in R.W. Hunt, W.A. Pantin and R.W. Southern (eds.), *Studies in Medieval History Presented to F.M. Powicke* (Oxford: Clarendon Press, 1948), pp. 354–62.

'Justice and Charity in *The Vision of Piers Plowman*', *Dominican Studies* 1 (1948), pp. 360–66.

'Eastern Traditions in Christianity', *Blackfriars* XXXI (1950), pp. 199–203.

Byzantine Painting (London: Faber and Faber, 1950).

'The Collapse of a Civilisation', *Blackfriars* XXXI (1950), pp. 467–70; also in: *The Story of the Christian Church, in a Series of Broadcast Talks* (London: Mowbray, 1951), pp. 24–31.

Bede Jarrett, of the Order of Preachers, with Kenneth Wykeham-George (London: Blackfriars Publications, 1952).

'The Origins of Eucharistic Symbolism', *Dominican Studies* VI (1953), pp. 1–11.

'Recent Discoveries in East African Archaeology', *Antiquity* XXVII (1953), pp. 212–18.

'The Culture of the East African Coast in the Seventeenth and Eighteenth Centuries in the Light of Recent Archaeological Discoveries', *Man* LVI (1956), pp. 65–68.

'Chinese Porcelain in East Africa and on the Coast of South Arabia', *Oriental Art* VII (1956), pp. 50–57.

'Byzantine', in J. Bowle (ed.), *Concise Encyclopaedia of World History* (London: Hutchinson, 1958), pp. 175–86.

'The Land of Zanj', in R.A. Oliver (ed.), *The Dawn of African History* (London: Oxford University Press, 1961), pp., 45–52.

'The East African Coast until the Coming of the Portuguese', in R.A. Oliver and G. Mathew (eds.), *History of East Africa*, I (Oxford: Clarendon Press, 1963), pp. 94–127.

Byzantine Aesthetics (London: John Murray, 1963).

'The Literature of Africa', *New Blackfriars* 46 (1964), pp. 41–43.

'The Christian Background' in *The Cambridge Medieval History, Vol. 4. The Byzantine Empire, Part 1. Byzantium and its Neighbours* (Cambridge: Cambridge University Press, 1966), pp. 42–60.

'Ideals of Friendship', in J. Lawlor (ed.), *Patterns of Love and Courtesy: Essays in Memory of C.S. Lewis* (London: Arnold, 1966), pp. 45–53.

'The Religion of Teilhard de Chardin', *New Blackfriars* 49 (1968), pp. 220–23.

The Court of Richard II (London: John Murray, 1968).

8

Kenelm Foster

Fr Kenelm was born in India, and christened Francis, in 1910. His father was a judge, a convert to Catholicism at Peterhouse, Cambridge, his mother a diligent upholder of family pride as a Digby-Beste. Her great-grandfather, Henry Digby-Beste, a Fellow of Magdalen College, Oxford, had become a Catholic in 1798, a Neo-Gothic harbinger of the Oxford movement. Fr Kenelm would take after his mother in disregarding the advice of Poobah in *The Mikado* to the effect that 'family pride should be denied, and set aside, and mortified'. This did not, however, prevent him from placing a safe distance between himself and his maternal grandmother, in whose Florentine home much of his childhood was spent. In the harsh words of his obituarist in the *Acta* of the English Dominican Province, he 'disliked ... the pious, cloying, but censorious Catholicism that she tried to din into their hearts and minds'.[1] He first met the English Dominicans in the shape of Fr Bede Jarrett, who came to Downside, the young Francis's school, to give the annual retreat. At Christ's College, Cambridge, he was introduced to what would be, after Christ himself, the great love of his life, Dante Alighieri, by no less than Professor Edward Bullough – who has already appeared in these pages in connection with his son, Fr Sebastian. A perfect candidate for doctoral studies, he was too swayed by a second meeting with Jarrett, at Fisher House, to walk along the road that leads to the strictly academic life. Instead, he took up where his elder brother Anthony (later a sculptor of note, under the pupillage of Eric Gill) had left off.[2] He was clothed in the habit of the Order at Woodchester in the autumn of 1934. After ordination, he was assigned – somewhat improbably for one of such a fastidious scholarly and literary temper – to parish duties at Holy Cross, Leicester. Owing perhaps to the continuing tension between those in the Province who favoured integration (but without loss of identity) into the world of University (i.e. Oxbridge) education on the one hand, and, on the other, those who regarded

Hawkesyard, with its purely Catholic diet of Aristotle (dubbed an honorary Papist), Aquinas and Père Lagrange, as their intellectual *beau idéal* for a Friar Preacher, Fr Kenelm was originally inhibited from taking the lectorate – the normal preparation for a teaching career in the Order. Indeed. he was never to teach theology in its study houses. Any injustice in the decision that he should not take the lectorate was soon atoned for, not only by its relatively speedy reversal, but also by the support given his doctoral research in the Modern Languages Faculty at Cambridge. Doctorates were *rarae aves* in the 1940s – not least for Dominicans, not least in (apparently) non-theological disciplines. The generosity paid off in every sense. In 1948 Fr Kenelm was made a lecturer in Italian by the University, a post he retained (and later it was upgraded to that of Reader) until 1978. The following year the University of London accorded him the Edmund Gardner prize for distinguished work in Italian studies. He died suddenly, of pneumonia, in his beloved Cambridge, in the harsh early February of 1986.

Fr Bede Bailey, the archivist of the English Dominican Province, wrote of him what could be said of all the figures studied in this book: 'The 1920s and 30s were his seedbed; there he remained firmly rooted.'[3] And Fr Bede links that assertion to the influence of four indigenous figures on Fr Kenelm's thought and sensibility: Gerard Manley Hopkins (long dead, of course, yet effectively buried in a metaphorical sense also until his rediscovery in that period); Christopher Dawson; David Jones and, a non-Catholic, but one whose name has already figured in these pages in connection with the 'London intelligentsia' of the Church, D.H. Lawrence. He also adds a fifth from that neighbouring culture of most importance for the English Dominicans of this time: the French poet and dramatist Paul Claudel.[4] Fr Kenelm's memorialist furnished a brief perceptive comment on the use to his subject of each of these. Hopkins was 'the modern poet in whom he took the greatest delight, understanding and perhaps sharing the poet's tension between his religion and artistry'. Dawson he considered 'probably the greatest Catholic educator in England since Newman', albeit an insufficiently appreciated one. Lawrence he lauded for his piercing awareness of non-rational modes of being – in plants, animals and also human emotions. Jones he revered for the mind-entrancing disorder of his prose, with its frolicsome images that, none the less, genuinely enlighten the intelligence. They meet Claudel's test of the Christian poet – that he shall depict 'la sainte réalité', reality as flowing from God, and, through grace, returning to him. In Fr Kenelm's own search for that engraced reality, his supreme masters were, however, St Thomas and Dante. To them may be paid Dante's accolade to Aristotle: masters of them that know. And Fr Bede adds a final comment on these sources which sums up the Dominican spirit at its best, and the culture depicted in this study likewise: 'To go with them, all that his mind had accepted from his study of literature, history, art and poetry were integrated into his theology and his understanding of the Word.'[5]

Dante

Dante was Fr Kenelm's chief professional forte: what was his overall *lectura Dantis*, his 'reading' of Dante? It is not accidental that his introductory chapter to *God's Tree. Essays on Dante and Other Matters* is entitled 'Dante as a Christian poet'. Though in no way wishing to reduce Dante's poetic achievement to the deployment of philosophical and theological resources in the service of faith, Fr Kenelm's peculiar contribution to Dante studies, in Britain especially, lay in his masterly understanding of Dante as a Christian intelligence setting itself to poetic work.[6] Yet increasingly he would come to stress, in his exploration of the role of philosophy and theology in Dante's work the tension between the 'two Dantes', humanist and Christian, where the moral virtues are not quite integrated by charity – a tell-tale sign of Dante's eclectic rather than Thomist scholasticism.[7]

Much Dante criticism from the Renaissance humanists to the present century had found repellent the theological component in the *Commedia*, and attempted to disengage the poetry from the religious thought. The more serene, and historically sensitive, approach of mid-twentieth-century scholarship did better in seeking not to dissolve the poem's own most powerful impression, which is that of its own unity. To judge by Natalino Sapegno's review of the broad development of Dante criticism, Fr Kenelm's work belongs in the succession of the mid-nineteenth-century Italian critic F. de Sanctis who in an apt formula called the *Commedia*

> the poem of the Universe, the eternal geometry and the eternal logic of creation incarnated in the three worlds of Christianity: the city of God in which is reflected the city of man in all the reality of a particular time and place, the one being the type, exemplar and judge of the other.[8]

In a characteristically severe self-assessment, Fr Kenelm asserted that his writings had failed to deal 'on a large scale with the sense of the Comedy as a whole'. His reading in mediaeval philosophy

and theology had 'helped him to contribute to the elucidation of
sections or aspects of the Comedy [but] on the poem in general he
has published nothing important'.[9] Prior to assessing the (limited)
truth of this remark, the bibliographical survey in which it occurs
will help to contextualise his efforts within the *English* study of
Dante.

In the late nineteenth and early twentieth centuries, England had
been fortunate in the possession of Dante scholars of the calibre of
Edward Moore, Paget Toynbee, Edmund Gardner and P.H.
Wicksteed. Their scholarship, in Fr Kenelm's view, was 'still touched
by inherited sentiments of admiration and veneration deriving from
the Romantic movement', and its attendant religious revival. Their
work as critics and interpreters of Dante's text survived, however, the
weakening of such stimuli, as it had earlier done the passing of an age
when the English educated class could speak and write Italian at least
as well as French. If the years between the two World Wars were lean
ones in England for Dante scholars, that succeeding age could boast
a number of perceptive non-specialist commentators on Dante, of
whom, as it happens, several have already figured in the presentation
of the intellectual world of inter-war Catholicism in the second
chapter of this study. Fr Kenelm considered that T.S. Eliot had made
Dante's art, in the *Comedy*, more 'accessible to modern sensibility
than was previously the case': and Dante was, after all, Eliot's ideal
poet, his true *miglior fabbro*.[10] Charles Williams's *The Figure of
Beatrice*, he deems 'interesting but highly subjective', while Etienne
Gilson's *Dante et la philosophie* rates the accolade of a 'brilliant raid
into Dante territory'.[11] (Not of course that Gilson was English – but
his reviewers were.) In the 1950s, Fr Kenelm could cite a woman
luminary of the Anglo-Catholic renaissance which fed into its Roman
Catholic sister-movement: this was Dorothy Sayers, who, despite her
ignorance of 'non-English dantology' he admired for her grasp of the
Comedy's crafting as narrative, its theology (and notably of purga-
tory), and the 'absolutely central importance of the Beatrice-image'.
Colin Hardie, Lecturer in Romance Languages at Oxford, University
Orator, and a Catholic member of the Inklings, wins the crown: 'the
most impressive body of work on Dante put out by an Englishman
since 1921'. However, Fr Kenelm distances himself rather from
Hardie's overall presentation of the Comedy as a return to integral
Christianity after a quasi-pagan period of worshipping the Lady-
Philosophy and the Messiah-Emperor, a return which is
simultaneously a reconversion to poetry (as distinct from philosophy
and politics), since, for Dante religious vocation was inseparably –
thanks to its link with Beatrice – a call to write as poet. Fr Kenelm

stood, unfashionably, for a continuity of development throughout Dante's work.

It is not difficult to see, then, how Fr Kenelm could have treated his work as a Dantist as a natural expression of a priestly and Dominican vocation. Dante studies rooted one – not least in England – in a sub-tradition of scholarship of evident interest to the cultural consciousness of the Catholic Church.

Although the *Commedia*, as a 'poetic Christian microcosm',[12] occupies, therefore, the centre of Fr Kenelm's attention, he by no means ignored Dante's other works. Along with his ertswhile pupil, Professor Patrick Boyde, he produced a two-volume edition of Dante's lyric poetry, which, if it leaves technical issues of metre and versification to his collaborator, celebrates the *Rime* both for the pleasure they give sensibility and the light they bring to thought.[13] It is natural that in discussing Dante as a lyric poet Fr Kenelm should lay the accent on the 'pleasure-giving motive'.[14] After all, the special function of a poet lies in the creation of beautiful verbal objects. In the *Convivio* Dante himself analyses such beauty in terms of the way the poet joins music – metrical pattern – to the arts of grammar and rhetoric. And though that analysis applies also to the *Comedy*, there non-aesthetic concerns – moral, political, religious – predominate, whereas in the *Rime*, with their *stil dolce*, the sheer musicality of Dante's art is easier to appreciate. To see Dante in the round, however, both the aesthetic and the non-aesthetic motives must be held together.

> Though he often speaks like an unhappy man, as a poet he must have been singularly happy, his passionate delight in form and construction was only matched by his passionate interest in an immense range of possible themes. The development of his genius was essentially towards the achievement of an ideal balance between the aesthetic and the non-aesthetic sides of human nature; and he stands pretty high, to say, the least, among those who have aimed at that ideal.

In the *canzoni*, indeed, the distinction between erotic and philosophical poetry is often hard to draw. Writing love-poems, Dante, like the early vernacular poets at large, would write about love, and so tend towards philosophy; while, writing about philosophy he was drawn to make sexual love a symbol of philosophic aspirations. The *Rime* as a whole are 'the work of a genius in process of discovering his own powers and needs', something expressed in the 'sheer poetic force' whereby themes are handled, resources of vocabulary and craft deployed. Fr Kenelm recalls Eliot's praise of Dante as well as the latter's indebtedness to the world-view of Christian scholasticism when he concludes his introduction to the interpretation of the lyric verse by writing:

> He combined an astonishing constructive, 'architectural' power with an exquisite sensibility to the sheer expressive quality of words. These two aspects of Dante's genius are not always, one need hardly say, equally in evidence in the *Rime*; now one, now the other at times predominates. But his innate tendency was towards a poetry whose beauty would be a product of both, a harmony of reason and sensibility, each extended to its utmost; a beauty therefore which would at least in part reflect these outshinings of the divine Goodness, in the sensible world and in the mind itself, which Dante thought it the proper business of the human spirit to consider, record and imitate.

Questions of dating of the *Rime* as a whole, and of individual poems in particular (and hence the sequence proper to the *canzoni* collection) obviously underpin (and reflect) Fr Kenelm's convictions about Dante's 'growth'. Essentially, as he views it, that growth took the form of an ever-widening extension of the poet's emotional range, consistent with an ever-developing confidence in his capacity to express the entire gamut of human experience. More specifically, Fr Kenelm finds, in the poetry and prose taken as a whole, a definite tendency to shift from 'private' to 'public' concerns and meanings. Such themes as justice and liberality, the desirability of a union of the human race under a single imperial head; the urgency of a reform of Christ's Bride, the Church: these topics came to loom larger than more intimate emotions.

> With all his intense individuality Dante had a very strong sense of the human community, of the inter-dependence of human minds; for him, to live humanly was to seek reasons for living, and to seek them with others, in a common pursuit, through the interchange of ideas. In a deep sense he did not believe in 'private thoughts'; every thought had a public importance, though the public it concerned might be a small one.[15]

The term of Dante's development as a poet is the *Commedia*. While that poem is not a biographical surd, a sheer thunderbolt in the *trecento* sky, Fr Kenelm never ceased to wonder at its making, even less predictable as that was than, say, *Paradise Lost* in Milton's career, or the *Aeneid* in Virgil's. The fresh assimilation of classical and, especially, Virgilian models and of Christian poetic matter can evidently be ascribed to voracious study in Dante's middle years. But the forming of poetic object on such a scale, and with so rich, yet unified, a complexity of meanings, is less easy to explain.

Fr Kenelm describes the *Commedia* programmatically as 'a poetic imitation of the concrete historical universe, charged with the poet's sense of the terror and the beauty of God.'[16] The two main tracks on which Dante's mind had moved hitherto – one leading from erotic love to the veneration of Beatrice, the other to mastery of scholastic philosophy and natural science, were insecurely connected by allegory. Now, without abandoning the use of allegory as one literary device among others, Dante transforms his entire poetic register by way of a 'huge shift towards the real historical universe as this had come home to the poet through his personal and political experiences and through his reading of history, chiefly Roman and biblical, in the light of the Christian revelation.' And the effect of *that* is at once to people the Comedy with real men and women, in actual space and time, as well as to produce a reflection in miniature of the whole Christian economy of how God is related, salvifically, to humankind. Typologically, but without evacuation of the substance of the individuals,

> its protagonist is the individual Dante *and* all mankind, and Virgil is Virgil *and* the Gentile preparation for the Gospel, and Beatrice is Beatrice *and* a symbol of Christian wisdom, and even, in the great scene at the close of the *Purgatorio*, an image of Christ himself.

In the same early essay, Fr Kenelm tries to sum up the *Comedia*'s spiritual atmosphere in terms of three themes, which he calls 'innocence', 'moral criticism', and 'intellectual discovery. By 'innocence' Fr Kenelm means, in this context, a 'pure receptive attention to ... the world revealed by the senses, a half-expectant wondering awareness, prior to reasoning and calculation ... Whether as delight or as longing this note is struck many times in the *Commedia*, but especially in the early cantos of the *Purgatorio* where Dante portrays the beauty of restored humanity, and nature, first felt in the translucent loveliness of water and sky.[17]

The 'moral criticism' is made, notably, in the name of the virtue, and the demands, of justice, though this criterion, so prominent in the *Inferno*, recedes as Dante's rises higher on his journey towards the vision of God. Fr Kenelm gave particular attention to the question, What is distinctive in Dante's account of human evil? As he points out, the portrayal of evil in the *Inferno* has a strong social and political emphasis.

The phrase Charles Williams applied to Geryon, the symbol of

Deceit, might indeed be applied to all that lower Hell into which Geryon carried Dante: it is 'the City infernalized'. Of the three principles, the World, the Flesh and the Devil, this is the World, depicted by a man of the world who had seen through it. Of all the Hell indeed which Dante sees, only a relatively small part is allotted to the flesh; and the devils might be regarded as mere scenery if their number did not include Satan; whose sin ... underpins in fact, the whole structure.[18]

'Malice' for Dante is a disposition to inflict *ingiuria*; and this is, generally, all the vices that flow from contempt of God, persons, nature, but, more especially – and very frequently – 'injury' means assault on fair dealing, on the just order of things. Possessed of an intensified wickedness when it subverts a bond of trust – a claim on love added to the natural love that links all creatures – *ingiuria* is always to some extent ingratitude, for in every created good violated by sin the divine Goodness has made its appearance. And this explains the pivotal role in Dante's theology of Luciferian wrong-doing. Satan

> preceded Judas in betraying his benefactor; and this term here takes the fullest possible stress, for Satan was the fairest work of God. That is the measure of his ingratitude; which is pride expressed in the rejection of Another's love; and in which, rather than in bare pride, Dante finds the absolute or extreme of evil.[19]

'Intellectual discovery' or 'religious intellectualism' is the last of the hallmarks of the Comedy's spiritual structure. Dante located the goal of living in an *act of knowledge*, the vision of God, to which topic, in its Dantean guise, Fr Kenelm devoted a substantial essay. At the opening of the *Paradiso* Dante remarks that 'as it approaches the end of its desire, our mind goes so deep that memory cannot follow'.[20] Now this is not a question of the recalling of events in past time – though that is how, in the fictional narrative of his journey, Dante depicts the momentary vision of the divine Essence with which the Paradiso will end.

> The poem is *given* as reminiscence. But the event it recalls was intellectual, and precisely under this aspect it cannot now be fully recalled. It is forgotten, or half-forgotten, not as past, but as intellectual; not, obviously, because it happened a long while ago, but because it was a particular sort of experience – whether in time or out of time does not matter for the moment. What matters is that the experience was too great for the mind's power of retention, and so of apprehension after the event, and so of 'memory'.[21]

What Dante has portrayed is what Aquinas, by way of allusion to the experiences of Moses on Sinai and Paul in being 'caught up to the seventh heaven', terms (with the precedent tradition) *raptus* – a momentary glimpse of the divine Essence which will be man's joy hereafter.

> In the *Paradiso* Dante's sight of the divine Essence is ... transitory; he will return to the mortal world after it, like his prototype St Paul. But in the Thomist theology of vision the transience of St Paul's *raptus* (and therefore, we may say, Dante's also) is its only difference from the truly final beatific Vision. The supreme degree of *raptus* also is a sight of God's Essence and therefore requires that supernatural 'light of glory', without which, said St Thomas ... 'the divine Essence cannot be seen by any created intellect'. But the theologian adds that, in the particular case of the *raptus*, the light of glory would affect the intellect, not as an indwelling form, but as a sort of passing disturbance, *per modum cujusdam passionis transeuntis*. And this last phrase might serve as an epitome of the *Paradiso*, provided we add that the disturber is God as seen, and that the disturbance is bliss.[22]

Reference has been made above to 'Dante's theology' – and Fr Kenelm was certainly not slow in underlining the theological (and philosophical) matter in Dante's poetry. Yet he always insists that the proper task of the critic (as distinct from the intellectual historian) lies not in elucidating Dante's ideas, but in showing how those ideas were transmuted into poetic form. His question concerns, What is going on when the process of *poesis* occurs? Could it be said, however, that *part* of Dante's poetic greatness was owed to his being a great-minded theologian? Just that was the thesis of Pope Paul VI in his *allocutio* for Dante's birth-centenary in 1965,[23] and Fr Kenelm's analysis of his letter, *Altissimi cantus*, pays it respectful attention.[24] There is no difficulty about the pope's claim that Dante's *humanitas* seems to wax, not wane, as he moves through heaven towards God, nor in the statement, indebted for its terminology to the inter-war Italian aesthetician Benedetto Croce, that tension between *poesis* and *logos* – the 'whole power and process of elucidating the real' – belongs to the essence of poetry. The enquiry which *Altissimi cantus* stimulated in Fr Kenelm turned rather on the notion that there is a *special affinity* between poetry and theology. He was inclined, on Thomistic grounds, to grant that this is so. For Thomas, all the natural powers and tendencies of the psyche are available for entry and transformation by the grace of God. Charity perfects natural eros, divinely revealed truth finds awaiting it a mind with an inbuilt readiness to receive it. 'The poetic "gift", then, whatever special modification of eros and mind it may entail, would, on this view, be potentially responsive to faith and to some sort of creative appropriation of the wording of faith, that is, of theology.' The idea that poetry and the higher gifts are cognate, and even that poetry brings with it a tacit sense of God's creative presence, is something Fr Kenelm will find more fully articulated by another of his Tuscan heroes, Petrarch.

At many points in his discussion of Dante, Fr Kenelm assumes that, not scholasticism at large, but the theology of St Thomas in particular, furnishes the proper court of appeal in interpreting Dante's reflections on faith. However, in the course of time he arrived at a more nuanced position: though indebted to Thomas in various ways, Dante is not a Thomist *tout court*. Researching his contribution 'Tommaso d'Aquino' to the prestigious *Enciclopedia dantesca*, he realised that the (somewhat anti-clerical) Italian Dantist Bruno Nardi had been correct: 'Dante's universe was not the Thomist one'.[25] The difference in cosmogony and anthropology struck him with special force. The Dantean world, unlike Thomas's, is philosophically unstable, riding in uneasy tandem Aristotle and the Neoplatonists. The poetic unification of materials, driven by a thirst for earthly justice in the *Inferno* and *Purgatorio*, and for intellectual understanding in the *Paradiso*, stood out the more plainly by contrast. Moreover, nowhere – despite opportunities like his eulogy of Thomas the saint – does Dante express a judgment about Thomism as such. He took no part in the contemporary debate about the Thomist synthesis, and remained a scholastic eclectic to the end.

This is not to say, however, that Thomistic elements are indetectable in Dante's corpus. His view of the angels as non-material, his understanding of the unity of substantial form in man, his ascription of pre-eminence to intellect above will: all of these show Thomist – or at least Albertine – influence. His grasp of Aristotle seems to have been mediated by Thomas. Yet other crucial theses of Aquinas – such as the distinction between *esse* and *essentia* in creatures and their identity in God, and the notion of the 'agent intellect' as the distinctive function of the human mind, play no part in his transcription of the real.

Most important for Fr Kenelm is understanding the nature of Dante's veneration for St Thomas, for, as Gilson pointed out, he 'profoundly admired and loved [him]'.[26] In the *Convivio*, Dante associates Thomas with the gift and power of discrimination, conceived as 'a quality both intellectual and moral though rooted specifically in the human reason whose task it is to discern the relations between things'.[27] In the *Paradiso*, Aquinas appears as the figure of saintly intelligence, or at least one important kind of saintly intelligence, that which practises theology while doing full honour to reason. In *Paradiso* X, XI and XIII respectively, Dante has Thomas laud rational discrimination, measure, and sobriety of judgment – the more surprising, then, that in so many areas – the act of creation, the attempt to tie in angelic being with the moving structures of the cosmos, the notion that human beings might, without grace, attain, as the good pagans, a flawless ethical perfection and natural beatitude, he diverged so notably from him. As the Italian version of Fr Kenelm's thoughts on their interrelation closes, '*Strana e pregnante conclusione*'.[28]

And that same nuanced attitude of Dante towards the angelic doctor reflects his careful attitude towards the Order of Preachers as a whole. As Fr Kenelm notes, eulogies of St Dominic and St Francis in the Paradiso convey a view of Dominicanism and Franciscanism at large. 'In both panegyrics the figure of the saint is presented less as a personality than as the representative of an idea destined to become embodied in the Church, the Spouse of Christ, in order to bring it into closer conformity with its Model.'[29] Fr Kenelm argues that the 'heaven of the Sun', where the meeting with Francis and Dominic is situated, reflects in Dante's schema the Spirit's procession from the Son, the spiration of subsistent Love from the Word of God. Its human analogue is 'the perfect coinherence of intelligence and love, realized once and for all in Jesus Christ, the incarnate Word'. In this perspective, Francis appears as image of the love of Christ, Dominic of his wisdom. The inseparability of the two excellences, founded as it is on the trinitarian relations, leads Dante to remarks of the two mendicant founders: 'I shall tell of the one, since to praise one, whichever we take, is to speak of both, for their labours were to one end ...'[30] These are words placed on the lips of Thomas, apropos the encomia which he and Bonaventure, his Franciscan counterpart, are about to pronounce on their fathers in God.

The *opere* [labours] in question are clearly those which each saint accomplished on behalf of *la sposa*, the Church, the promotion of whose spiritual well-being, therefore, was that one *fine* to which both had dedicated themselves, while operating in his own way, in accordance with his own highly personal vocation, and so realizing a certain unique likeness to Christ. For Francis, the *Poverello*, the object of love was the Man-God who chose to make himself poor, and for Dominic the incarnate Word, Teacher of divine Truth. Love of poverty, therefore, is Francis's distinguishing feature, whereas Dominic's is love of faith, especially in the doctrinal sense.[31]

As Francis was married to Lady Poverty, so at the font of baptism, Dominic was espoused to Faith – and Dante links these spiritual unions to the dying Christ's union with the Church, so as to draw out their shared ecclesial significance. After all, Dante had studied both with the Franciscans at Santa Croce in Florence, and with their near-neighbours the Dominicans at Santa Maria Novella. In addition to the Albertine and Thomist elements in his writing, there are no less unmistakable 'Franciscan-sounding' passages, in the *Convivio* as well as the *Commedia* – though only in the latter does the penitential side of Franciscanism appear alongside its contemplative and cosmological aspect. Dante could not be a straightforward *afficionado* of the Dominicans: the pull of the Franciscan vision was too strong for a man who 'yearned for the Church to be reformed along Franciscan lines through the re-awakening within her of the *Poverello's* own love for the supreme Povero who had appeared to him on Mount Verna.' Though, symbolically, Dominic stands for the soul as open to receive the divine Word, Francis for its receptivity to the divine Spirit, the trinitarian parity of persons is somewhat forgotten in Dante's brief biographical re-creations of the two saints.

> Dominic's assimilation to Christ always retains something of a faithful, trusted, tirelessly active servant to his master, whereas in the Francis canto ... what seems undeniably to be suggested is a veritable identification of the Poverello with Christ, to the extent that he becomes in a very special way a living image of the Saviour, an *alter Christus*, in fact; an appellation which, moreover, had already been current for some time among the Franciscans themselves.[32]

But as Fr Kenelm's fellow-Dantist Howard Needler has pointed out, Dante's primary concern is, in any case, that the 'eternal moment' represented by both Francis and Dominic should not continue to be betrayed by the all too human concerns which afflicted subsequent generations of Franciscans and Dominicans.[33]

As one whose theological and philosophical sensibility had been formed by Thomism – and here the texts of Aquinas himself, in the studium, and, in his pre-Dominican days, the example of Jacques Maritain were crucial – it worried Fr Kenelm that Dante had not quite brought off the integration of his pagan and Christian materials, of nature and grace. The problem was especially acute in the *Commedia* 'Because the hero of the Divine Comedy is a Christian, the poem is Christian, but through two-thirds of it the hero is guided by a pagan ....' Paganism is not simply the childhood of Dante's race, nor even the cultural form of nature without Christian grace. It is Dante's *alter ego*, that 'second self' taken by his imagination, in the guise of Virgil, into the 'Other World'.[34] Fr Kenelm had already detected in the *Convivio* a tendency to 'regard human life, properly speaking, as ... directed to ends attainable on earth, and to relegate to a life after death the whole possibility and process of man's divinization ...'[35] Reassuringly, the *Comedy* differs not only in its refocusing of attention on the eternity awaiting man after death, but also in its pervasive insistence on the abiding need for (intellectual and moral) supernatural help. The 'protagonist's submission to the rule and guidance of Virgil and Beatrice, themselves the instruments, ultimately, of God', expresses Dante's recognition of the need to accept divinely appointed guides. However, it remains the case – and Dante's portrayal of the adult inhabitants of Limbo, with its sublime yet natural happiness show this – that his visualisation of the human situation never fully conforms to 'the new pattern imposed by that shift towards other-worldliness and the surrender of autonomy'. Though Dante certainly underwent a conversion from the naturalistic rationalism which had earlier tempted him (for the close of the *Purgatorio* contains a tacit confession of habitual misdirection of mind), what Gilson called '*un petit coin de Dante*' escaped immersion in the river of Lethe where the memory of former sins is washed away.[36]

The Limbo-image in the *Comedy* stands, in principle for human nature considered as 'a thing good in its kind and degree but *incomplete*'. And this incompletion affects – once again, in Dante's theory in the poem – human nature at large, pagan culture and the Empire shorn of its fulfilment in the Church. And yet, when Fr Kenelm looked at the idea of mere human nature as Dante handles that apart from the Limbo-theme, he found, disconcertingly

> a 'nature' whose contact with God (through grace) is minimal, but whose intrinsic excellence, on its own level and for the duration of life on earth can, in principle, be complete. And this completeness in human excellence, if achieved, would be *self*-achieved. Grace as *sanans*, as healing the wound of sin, would not, in principle, be needed.[37]

Although Dante's good pagans need supernatural *gratia elevans* if they are to be raised up to share the life of friendship with God – something he thought was only very exceptionally, and indeed miraculously, bestowed upon them – their moral life is, sheerly by their own efforts, complete.

In this Fr Kenelm finds a defect of thought. The cult of moral virtue is, unfortunately, only too combinable with indifference to God. Had Dante's intelligence been wholly Christian on this point he would have realised that the moral virtues are meant to be offered to God as the way *par excellence* of co-operating with his grace, and thus become themselves grace's organs, no longer simply humanly acquired but divinely infused. And there St Thomas shows his greater refinement of perception.

> Guided by this insight St Thomas could take over the whole achievement of Aristotle, as a philosophical moralist, while giving it an entirely new setting and direction. In Dantean terms this means the difference between Limbo and *Purgatorio*; in which we see repentant man recovering, under grace, the lost or diminished natural virtues, but only in preparation for something that is utterly beyond their own range, a love union with the Infinite. In the *Purgatorio* Aristolelianism is integrated into Christianity; in the Dantean Limbo it is not.[38]

In Petrarch, Fr Kenelm would find some even sharper disassociations of what ought not to be separated, though it can be distinguished. But before looking at that younger contemporary of Dante, it will be well to consider how he approached a more uncomplicated figure: Dante's fellow Tuscan, Catherine of Siena.

Catherine

It is not surprising that Fr Kenelm was attracted to the study of the fourteenth-century Dominican tertiary, St Catherine of Siena. Quite apart from belonging to the same Order, Catherine was, like his other favourite subjects, Dante and Petrarch, a child of Tuscany, and she was also a younger contemporary of Petrarch. Moreover, her writings (or, more likely, 'dictatings') combine a theological depth (recognised by Pope Paul VI when in 1970 he declared her a doctor of the Church) with a spiritual warmth which made her an ideal subject for a writer who loves to see how reason and passion intertwine.

It is as an interpreter of Caterinian *theology* that Fr Kenelm presents himself, the key to that theology being 'the central dogma of Christianity, the union of godhead and manhood in Christ'.[39] And what in his view distinguishes Catherine's comments on the Incarnation from those of a medley of other authors is 'the exceptional clarity, force, sweetness and profundity of her utterances on this great matter'. This did not prevent him giving a lively biography of her; indeed, an account of a theologian of the Incarnation that was not itself enfleshed in time and space would be something of a contradiction.

Fr Kenelm's brief *Vita Caterinae* strikes a balance between her public interventions in the life of the Church on the one hand and her secret, spiritual experience on the other. The origin of both lies in her hold on what she believed to be her Christ-given vocation, intimately linked as this was to (but not initiated by) her entry into the *Mantellate*, a Dominican lay sisterhood, at the age of sixteen.[40] For three years after that event she lived an even more strictly secluded life (in the 'cell' of a room in her family home). Then she understood herself to be summoned out of solitude so that she might practice the second commandment, loving her neighbour as herself.

The 'public interventions' were by no means all extraordinary things: much of her resolve to serve Christ in neighbour took forms where the only element out of the ordinary was the particularly intense *tenderness* with which she served the sick and the poor. Fr Kenelm brings out well the specifically Dominican note in her practice of that commonplace apostolate:

> Many were drawn to her, and not only by her cheerful goodness but also increasingly by her intelligence. She did not seek to be loved but to love; but her Dominican training had not been wasted and she was already clear in her young mind that the way to love lay through knowledge. This truth she had already tested in the matter of loving God; she now had to discover – for her a harder task – the loveableness of human beings. So, as usual, she turned to Christ and begged for the grace to 'perceive the beauty of all the souls she came into contact with, so that she would be the more prompt to work for their salvation'.[41]

It appears that the prayer was answered, because she retained an unshakable conviction that no sin ever is or was necessary in the midst of daily dealings with sinners and outcasts, despairing lepers and condemned criminals.

As she gathered round here a group of disciples – lay and priestly, male and female, most in the vigour of early adulthood, her powers began to be deployed on a wider stage. Fr Kenelm explains this by two factors: her patronage by a religious order of 'unsurpassed intellectual prestige and doctrinal authority', and her own 'spontaneous delight in knowledge and its communication', facilitated as this was by her own first-rate intelligence and the subtle beauty of her Tuscan speech. She caught, in every act of the understanding, a glimmer of the 'sweet primal Truth'. Christ was her Master because, as the Logos incarnate, he *rendered knowable* the Father's glory. When she began to paint on a wider canvas, her theme would be: the unity and reinvigoration of Christendom. Where there was division – between laity and clergy, as in the conflict between the Florentines and the pope, or within the clerical body over attitudes to the Avignon exile of the papacy, and in its wake, the Great Schism of the West, begun in 1378 – she would strive to re-create unity, and where there was debility in the Church body, she would aim to bring new spiritual life – something for which she looked, among other sources, to a potential inflow of converts from Islam through the crusading mission to Muslims which she preached. What Fr Kenelm characteristically stresses in his account of her 'policy aims', and her reactions to the setbacks they suffered, is the *theology of the Church* which underlies them. Why, after all, should we be bothered about the Church? For Catherine the reason is *aimatological* – from the Greek words for 'blood' and 'knowledge'.

> For her the indispensability of the Church consists precisely in this, that it is the medium through which the Blood shed on the Cross for the human race becomes not only the sign of God's re-creating love for sinners but also the vehicle of that love to this and that sinner individually. The Church 'holds the keys of the Blood', the Blood reaches us 'through the ministers of Holy Church'. Indeed, the Church exists, for Catherine, only *in function of* Christ's Blood; but that was enough to prostrate her in reverence before its meanest minister.[42]

And if, in her *The Light and the Rainbow*, the student of Catholic mysticism Hilda Graef found 'so much talk of blood' excessive, Fr Kenelm defended the Tuscan doctor *con spirito* against this (quite unacrimonious) attack.

> Well, each to his taste; but God really did bleed, and all that Catherine does is to dwell on this fact as the supreme image and sign of divine love and the chief motive for ours ... An unconscious poet, she thought with symbols, and the blood became the symbol of symbols in which to express her experience and understanding of Christianity. And I suppose her readers will always divide into those who find her indelicacy in this matter rather repulsive and those who find it (as I do) magnificent.[43]

And if, at the end of her life, not only the Church but also her Order was riven by schism – the Master, a Frenchman, repudiating the validly elected Pope Urban VI, her disciples would none the less be well placed to propagate her spiritual teaching after her death. For her principal follower, Raymund of Capua, to whom she had entrusted her book, the *Dialogo*, would be elected Master of the non-schismatic Dominicans in 1380, two years after her death.

It is in expounding Catherine's spiritual theology that Fr Kenelm really comes into his own. Conscious of the fact that, prior to the papal declaration of her 'doctoral' status in 1970, Catherine (like Teresa of Avila) would have been classed with the mystics, not the theologians, Fr Kenelm is in no way deterred by it. The rationale of Pope Paul's decision, in creating the first female doctors of the Church, goes much deeper than any considerations of 'Christian feminism'. For, if theology is mainly intellectual and even conceptual, mysticism chiefly affective and experimental, still

> the *object* of both is the same, namely the living God whom Jesus has told to love above all things (including our subtlest concepts) and who, having loved us first, can be trusted to love the mind that sincerely seeks him and to guide it into what St Paul called 'the depths of God'. This is the guidance described by Catholic theologians in terms of the gifts of the Holy Spirit, who is the spirit of love; above all the gift of wisdom, without which the cleverest theology remains arid and stunted. In this sense all theology worthy of the name is in tendency 'mystical'. As for mystics in the more usual sense of the term, whether their contact with God will give rise to clearly articulated doctrine will depend, humanly speaking, on their natural gifts and circumstances.[44]

In speaking of Catherine's mystical theology, Fr Kenelm deals relatively briefly (but by no means dismissively) with the preternatural element in her religious experience – the miracles, visions and intermediate phenomena such as knowledge at a distance described by Raymund under the heading of her 'spirit' of prophecy'. He concentrates, as is surely proper for a Dominican, on Caterinian *doctrine*. His starting-point is not, however, a key concept, but a key image – a literal image, an artwork. And that is the *crucifix*. Catherine's doctrine is eminently staurocentric: cross-centred. To understand why this is so requires, however, that we need to grasp two other major themes in her writing: self-knowledge, and the creation of the human person in the 'image' of the Holy Trinity.

Actually these two further themes are in some sense themselves one: for what Catherine knows in knowing herself is not only moral and metaphysical frailty but a being made and remade by God the Creator and Redeemer who is none other than Father, Son and Holy Spirit. This is splendidly expressed in one of her letters:

> I do not see how we can relish ... this truth if we do not know ourselves, for through genuine self-knowledge we discover that we are not, and we find our being in God, seeing that he has created us to his image and likeness ... and we find moreover our recre-

ation inasmuch as God has re-created us ... in the blood of his Son, the blood that shows us the truth of God the Father; whose truth is this, that he created us for the glory of his name and in order that we might have a share in his eternal beauty, being sanctified in him.[45]

Fr Kenelm draws three conclusions from her teaching (prescinding for the moment from its trinitarian dimension). First, because it is the primal *Love* that has left its imprint on the soul, the soul is made for love, and cannot be content until united with Love itself, the divine Essence. Secondly, such is the *eccelenza* of the soul that it can be subject to nothing and no one save God himself. Thirdly, the task of self-knowledge is to see self-love and see it as perverse, since, for such creatures as ourselves, not to love (it, him or her) *in God* is to enact a lie against God and self alike, to 'try to enclose in the finite our natural desire for the Infinite'.[46] Catherine did not have the philosophical formation to elucidate this state of affairs entirely, but she grasped the essential.[47]

Catherine's theocentric anthropology is, as already mentioned, resolutely trinitarian. The forming of man – male and female – in the image of the Trinity enables Catherine to speak in hyperbolic terms of God's entrancement by the beauty of his creature-to-be. The communications thus established by the love-affair of our creation comes to its climax in that other great work of the Holy Trinity: our redemption into the eternal joy which is the sharing of their life. Commenting on Genesis 1.26 (the foundational *imago* text of Scripture), she writes:

And this you did, most high eternal Trinity, so that man might participate in all of you. So you gave him memory, to remember your benefits; and by this he participates in your power, eternal Father. And you gave him intellect, to see and know your goodness, and so participate in the wisdom of the ... Son. And you gave him will that he might love what with his understanding he saw and knew of your truth, and thus participate in the clemency of the Holy Spirit.[48]

But all of this is by way of preamble to grasping the significance of the blood-shedding on Calvary.

The same love which made us was yet more ecstatically displayed when it redeemed us on the cross – which it did in an act of reconciliation corresponding in its principal aspects to the three chief elements in human sinfulness: disobedience, ignorance, egotism. Jesus' act of obedience in dying on the cross reversed Adam's sin, atoning by an act of infinite love for the infinite non-love which is sin's heart. The cross, simultaneously, reveals the true nature of God's love to man's darkened understanding, enabling us to know the Father's truth: his desire to give us his own joy and glory in the life everlasting. As Fr Kenelm explains her soteriology here:

> To 'lift the eye of the intellect' to the Crucified is the first task of every Christian; and this not only for the ascetical reason that Christ has shown that we have to suffer, and how we should suffer if we would be his disciples. Catherine accepts this reason, of course, but she sees in the Blood much more than an example. She sees, or strives continually to see, the *end* beyond all suffering and discipleship; the end that will be the restoration in ourselves of the original unspoiled image of the Trinity, that 'pure tree of human- ity' planted by God 'in the beginning'. In this sense the Blood is the clue to a kind of ultimate self-knowledge.[49]

Lastly, the sacrifice of Christ provides the remedy for the will's disor- der. The more God's love for us in Christ's Passion is known, the more we are found lovable. Faith-borne love desires to be rid of vice and grow in virtue, enabling reason to bring the soul to 'a sweet and glorious order'.[50] The soul's powers are 'clothed' in God's own charity – which is the proper effect of the Holy Trinity, and the only thing we can take with us into eternal life.

As with Dante, Fr Kenelm concludes, a shade reluctantly, one imagines, that Catherine is not a Thomist *de métier*. Apart from the Latin Psalter and New Testament, she knew some Augustine, Cassian, Bernard, and rather less Aquinas. Through the Dominican devotional theologian Domenico Cavalca, she may have appropriated assorted snippets of other church fathers and divines. But this only makes the intense personality of her teaching the more remarkable – and, as he evidently, thought, the more worthwhile.

Petrarch

Petrarch – and the religion of the early humanists generally – had fascinated Fr Kenelm long before the publication of his *Petrarch: Poet and Humanist* in 1984.[51] His interests extended, then, from the Middle Ages into the world of the Renaissance. However, he knew far too much about the thought and culture of the mediaeval epoch to be content with the nineteenth-century definitions of that 'rebirth' by such historians as Michelet and Burckhardt. As a Dante scholar, he could hardly have treated the Middle Ages as 'an interval of darkness between two luminous eras'. On the other hand, Petrarch's contemporaries certainly *thought* they were present at the birth of something new. For Fr Kenelm the distinguishing mark of the Renaissance humanists was that they rediscovered the world of antiquity as distant from that of the Middle Ages but *not* over against the Gospel.

> Petrarch's Antiquity, his golden age, was, roughly, the millenium stretching between, say Plato or Pythagoras and Gregory the Great, with its centre in the Incarnation of the Word – the centre which divided, but did not separate, the pagan world from the Christian. That millenium with its sages and saints, its poets and moralists, became Petrarch's inspiration and the norm by which he judged, not always justly his own age. And the vision of it was his bequest to the humanists who followed him ... the vision of a world prepared, politically by the Roman empire and spiritually by the classical philosophers and poets, for the descent of God's Word; and then living on this divine-human heritage for a few happy centuries before slipping into a barbarous ignorance and oblivion which was now in its turn happily coming to an end.[52]

Precisely because Petrarch knew the classical sources so much better than Dante, he had perforce to give more attention to the problem of conflicting loyalties – pagan and Christian – which they raised.

Moreover, whereas the earlier, mediaeval 'renaissance' of Hellenic (and notably Aristotelian) thought had been, essentially, a recovery of Greek *science and philosophy* by the Christian mind, what was now at issue was the Roman and above all Ciceronian *studia humanitatis*, the study of what makes man man. The new concentration on human moral agency (*virtus*) and the unique human capacity for speech (*eloquentia*) gave *the* Renaissance a different ethos from the previous classical revivals. The Italian *Trecento* saw a resurgence of ancient quarrels between in particular philosophy and poetry, *logos* and *mythos*, already long-standing when Plato expelled the poets from his ideal city. Part of Petrarch's case against scholasticism lies in the schoolmen's neglect of poetry, which was so often the preferred medium of Scripture and the Fathers. He appears to have considered poetry to be itself religiously significant – almost irrespective of its content. As Fr Kenelm interprets him: 'he regarded the poetic gift as a kind of inborn impression on the soul of the Creative Word whence it derives, a sign of our being made to God's image.' It was, he thought, peculiarly incompatible with either atheism or denial of the immortality of the soul.

A second form in which the early humanists expressed their reservations about Aristotelianism concerns the notion of pure knowing:

epistêmê, scientia. Their epistemological ideal (following Augustine) was, by contrast, sapiential: knowledge of the right term of *desire* is what really counts in human life. On both scores, they win Fr Kenelm's sympathy:

> If the Catholic humanists had no other claim but this on our respect it would be worth upholding – that in the face of a culture excessively atomized by the *ratio ratiocinans* they made, as a group, an impressive attempt to re-unite what they found divided, knowledge and virtue and poetry, into a whole and single religious wisdom.

Not that – as a Dominican – Fr Kenelm was insensitive to the line that could lead from a Boccaccio, with his bourgeois mockery of friars and nuns, through Valla, and his frontal attack on religious life as a needless human complication of the 'way of Christ', to Luther, who indeed warmly admired Valla's *De professione religiosorum*. But of these disturbing developments, there is in Petrarch, with his Carthusian and Augustinian friendships, no sign at all.

Fr Kenelm's *Petrarch: Poet and Humanist* gives the lion's share of its attention – and that in frequently technical discussion – to the former. If in *Dante's Lyric Poetry*, he was content to leave matters of (mediaeval rhetoric and verse-style) to Professor Boyde, here he grapples with them on his own account. Petrarch's life was divided between Provence (where his father had taken refuge on his banishment from Florence) and Italy. Though doubtless he knew Provençal his writing is either in the Tuscan of Dante and Catherine, or in Latin which he was taught at Avignon, then home of the Roman Curia. He became deeply read in the Latin poets and moralists, notably Virgil and Cicero. As a vernacular lyric poet, his *canzoni*, in Fr Kenelm's view, surpass even those of Dante.[53] The *terza rime* work called the 'Triumphs', in the same metre, then, as the *Commedia*, he regarded as less successful, though with passages of great beauty, but its subject matter – a portrait of man in terms of 'three fatalities' (Carnal Love, Death, Time) and 'three correlative liberations' (Chastity, Fame, Eternity) was deeply sympathetic to Fr Kenelm's at once sharp and deep philosophical and theological mind.

In the *Canzoniere* Petrarch, who to some degree disprized the vernacular as suited only for the outpourings of the heart, frames poems whose single most pervasive subject is his beloved Laura. The frame, however, Fr Kenelm describes as 'anti-erotic' or even 'anti-amorous', for it is made up, at the beginning, by the Stoic-Platonic sonnet *Voi ch'ascoltate* and, at the end, by a canticle placed on the lips of the Blessed Virgin. Fr Kenelm finds the older Petrarch's embarrassment at his obsessive 'harping' on unsatisfied desire in youth and early middle age slightly overdone. The poems, he thought, 'contained all the moral reflection that any sane judge could require in a book of its kind'. The tension was never fully resolved between two authorial voices: 'Franciscus', lover and poet, and 'Augustinus', Stoic-Christian philosopher. The apparently total repudiation of Laura which is the upshot of the *Canzoniere* (for of two interpretations, Petrarch's love for Laura as spiritual ennoblement, and as a form of idolatry, it is the latter that wins out), is withdrawn in the *Triumpha Eternitatis*, which

> ends with the poet rejoicing in the thought of Laura's physical beauty, both in that which she had possessed on earth, in time, and in that which she will possess, after the Resurrection of the Flesh, in heaven, it being implied that the latter will be somehow the same as the former, only transfigured and enhanced ... the argument [offering] implicitly a certain excuse for what was excessive, and therefore sinful in his past infatuation with her ...[54]

However, in the poetry itself this is only a suggestion, and the poet's despair at the loss of Laura, which Fr Kenelm compares with Cleopatra's on the death of Anthony ('all's but naught, and there is nothing left remarkable beneath the visiting moon'), is assuaged only by the prayer to another woman, whose magnificence of utterance he considers 'superb': 'commend me to your Son, true man and true God, that he may receive my last breath in peace'.[55] Petrarch's subtle account of his continued contact with Laura after death – as 'heavenly visitant, consoler and counsellor' – means, however, that this Marian trope, though genuinely felt, is not the last word. Taken as a coherent song cycle, the *Canzoniere* is owed, after all, to Laura's death in the spring of 1348. Basically, the *Canzoniere* punctuates a celebration of Laura's created glory with danger signals indicating the sins and errors that flow from any quasi-divinisation of her. Faintly, but unmistakably, the book as a whole tells the story of Petrarch's deeper evangelical conversion, with echoes of his revered model, the Augustine of the *Confessions*. The real Laura was innocent, but *Petrarch's* Laura was, in part, self-delusion, and *to this extent* she can symbolise the capacity of the created order in its beauty to act as rival to the 'one transcendent and properly Divine Good'.

In any case, by the late 1340s, Petrarch was writing ever more exclusively in Latin; stimulated by his discovery of Cicero's letters at Verona in 1345, he turned to reflective and descriptive prose. The shift coincided with a deepening of his Christian faith, or at any rate a new determination to witness to it in his writing. The first sign of this is the 1343 *De Vita solitaria*, written to commemorate the entry into the Carthusians of his brother, Gherardo, to whom Petrarch was especially close. The book embodies, it must be said, an already considerable biblical and patristic learning.

> Whereas hitherto – in the *De viris illustribus*, the *Africa*, the *Rerum memorandum libri* – Petrarch had made himself the recorder for his own time of the pagan, principally Roman, world of the past, its men, events, ideas and emotions, turning exclusively to that world for examples of virtue, wisdom and eloquence; now in *De vita solitaria*, for the first time in a work written for the public, he spoke out explicitly as a Christian, with frequent mention of the 'sacred and glorious name of Christ'. One can say that from now on his humanism was inseparably linked, as a fact of consciousness with Christianity, although the integration of the two sets of ideas was usually left implicit.[56]

Fr Kenelm's passionate interest in Petrarch's 'philosophy' lays bare its own root in his comments on the *Secretum*, the most intimate of Petrarch's Latin works. Here the danger identified is not just Laura. Instead,

> it is the fascination of *all* created beauty and *all* human culture, with their power to distract from true self-knowledge and its correlative, a genuine awareness of God, that 'unique and most pure foundation-head of whatever is good', and especially of man's true self and quintessential title to 'nobility', the rational soul.[57]

Culture ou saintetè? – the question asked of the early years of monasticism in Christian Egypt by the French patrologist Père A.J. Festugière, O.P. was always implicit in the work of the Dominican septet described in this study. But all held it possible, in Pascal's words, to 'hold both ends of the chain', and return a resounding '*both* [culture] *and* [holiness]'. In point of fact, Petrarch could hardly have counterposed as simple opposites divine revelation on the one hand and the world of pre-Christian or non-Christian culture on the other. For the Greek philosophers knew something of the existence and unity of God (while lacking the courage to proclaim these truths to a culture darkened by polytheism), the Pythagoreans and Plato rising even to an intuition of the notion of creation. The practical bent and eloquence of the Roman moralists, moreover, and particularly Cicero, Seneca and Horace, are of great utility to the Christian engaged in the moral life.

It is the more surprising that Petrarch could regard scholasticism as a pseudo-philosophy. In the full-scale study Fr Kenelm is able to go more fully into the reasons than was possible on the modest canvas of his earlier essay, and he finds in Petrarch's negative judgment on mediaeval philosophy an *aesthetic* component – philosophy should be kept 'human' by preserving its link with the art of verbal expression, and a *moral* component – it will only be true wisdom if it arises from a deep sense of the limits of human understanding, not from love of dialectic. But of course Petrarch only knew scholasticism in decline; the implication seems to be that, had he been familiar with Thomas Aquinas, he would have judged differently. And certainly the English Dominican Thomists of the first half of the twentieth century seem to have been aware both of the demands of eloquence and of the dangers of an inflated epistemic optimism in theology. For Fr Kenelm, Petrarch, despite his high evaluation of reason, notably in the practical conduct of life, did not really rise above the level of a 'homiletic moralist, gathering from his experience of life the bitter-sweet fruit of self-knowledge'. He suffered from his time's disassociated sensibility – the parallel with T.S. Eliot's critique of modern culture is surely intended in Fr Kenelm's account.

> This diagnosis points to a disconnection between the different parts or powers of the psyche as the basic ailment in fourteenth century culture, a disconnection at once reflected in and exacerbated by the 'professional' separation of philosophy from theology and of this from piety.[58]

Labouring under these difficulties, there was the more honour to him that he brought his intellectual resources so acutely to bear on the Catholic culture of his day. In middle life, he embarked on

> a wide-ranging, highly critical assessment of his own medieval world – a critique not of its fundamental beliefs but of its culture in the sense of its intellectual fashions and pretensions, of certain widespread superstitions, of the actual situation of its two chief transnational institutions, the Church and the Empire (witness the anti-scholastic and anti-aristotelian polemics, the critique of astrology, the diatribes against the illiteracy of the pseudo-cultured, the 'Sine Nomine' campaign against the Avignon Curia, the repeated efforts to get both Pope and Emperor back to Rome).[59]

Both in affable letters and in the invective of his treatises he made himself the 'mediator and champion of a tradition' – the Christianised classicism of St Augustine. What Fr Kenlem doubted, however, was whether Petrarch's could be called a thoroughly Christian intelligence, which has mastered its materials (including, to be sure, the classics) so as to be able to deliver judgments, at once unified and wide-ranging, in the light of the Gospel. Here St Thomas remained for him the 'master of those who know'.[60]

Thomas and the angels

Although, as we have seen, Fr Kenelm could hardly be accused of *insouciance* towards the realm of ideas, his preferred way of contributing to the overall presentation of Thomism was by way of concentrating on Thomas the man. More precisely, he regretted that 'the man within the teacher' had been neglected.

> The writings themselves of St Thomas, in their style and method, are partly the cause of this: so impersonal are they, so thoroughly didactic and abstract, that in their light the writer seems to vanish, like Dante's angel who 'col suo lume se medesmo cela' [hides himself in his own light].[61]

The prestige of the system of doctrine has overshadowed its founder, who appears, consequently, as a kind of 'embodiment of theology' rather than a Christian man. Fr Kenelm did not propose, however, to write a life of Aquinas, but to present a 'selective miscellany' of biographical fragments (the earliest testimonies to Thomas), so that his readers may have a chance to see him with the eyes of those who knew him, before a 'mounting and increasingly official glory had blurred his human countenance ...'

The contemporary testimonies fall, Fr Kenelm explains, into three groups. There are, first, the minutes of the formal canonisation enquiry held at Naples in 1319; secondly, the lives of Thomas by three of his brethren, William Tocco, Bernard Gui, and Peter Calo (dateable to the years 1318–1330), and lastly a sizeable chunk of the *Historia Ecclesiastica* of Tolomeo of Lucca, the Dominican who completed Thomas's *De regimine principum*, a text which hove into view in the context of Fr Thomas Gilby's politological enquiries (see Chapter 5). Incidentally, William of Tocco was, along with Bartholomew of Capua, the chief witness at the 1319 Enquiry. Although the Parisian Faculty of Arts, as early as May 1274 had petitioned the Dominican General Chapter, then sitting at Lyons, for the body of 'so great a cleric, so great a father, so great a teacher', Thomism itself was already meeting with some resistance in more conservative circles both at Paris and Oxford. However, so doughty an opponent of Thomas's anthropology as the Franciscan John Pecham, Archbishop of Canterbury declared Thomas himself a 'man of holy memory'. It is, then, difficult to assess just what role the doctrinal debate played in the movement towards Thomas's canonisation – or, for that matter, the *vitae Thomae* of the Dominican writers. The Dominicans had not been especially quick off the mark in securing the public veneration of their holy fathers. Both in Dominic's own case, and that of Peter of Verona, the second canonised saint of the Order, the initiative was the pope's. In Thomas's case, however, the situation was rather different. 'He had been from the start ... the object of a local cult is South Italy; and scattered about the Provinces of the Order were men devoted to his memory and sure of his holiness; there were records too of miracles and rumours of visions.' In 1317, the Chapter of the Province of Sicily, meeting at Gaeta, commissioned William of Tocco and Robert of Benevento to collect materials pertinent to a petition for Thomas's canonisation to the Holy See. Even before the dossier was ready, John XXII told Tocco that Thomas had enlightened the Church 'more than all the other doctors'. and five years later, at a canonisation ceremony celebrated with more than customary solemnity the octogenarian pope 'associated himself in a particularly emphatic way with the glorifying of Aquinas'.

The 'life of Thomas' which forms the first substantial section of Fr Kenelm's collection is not the most primitive (Tocco's), but that of the Frenchman, procurator-general of the Order at Avignon, Bernard Gui. His reason for preferring Gui (who was largely dependent on Tocco) is frankly stylistic: if the latter was verbose and tiresome, the former is crisp, sober, elegant. Essentially the Tocco life (thus mediated by Gui) provides the south Italian tradition about Thomas, with some memories of Paris and Cologne worked in; Tolomeo's that of central Italy (he was a Lucchese), while that by Calo, a Venetian, is somewhat unplaceable – and anyhow adds little to those already mentioned. Tolomeo interested Fr Kenelm for two reasons: he was more of an intellectual than the other biographers, though an intellectual with political interests (the 'watchful observer of human affairs ... always ready with allusions to texts and books'). He was also prior of Santa Maria Novella in Florence in 1301, on the eve of the crisis which culminated in Dante's expulsion from the city. One might have thought that Fr Kenelm would have preferred Tolomeo's account to all others, and indeed he translates a good half of it.

Lastly, and unannounced in the opening pages of the Introduction, Fr Kenelm throws in for good measure two tiny pieces from the credulous but chatty Gérard de Frachet's *Vitae Fratrum* and *Cronica Ordinis*, as well as the letter from the dons of Paris already mentioned. What may sound like a dog's dinner is really more of a mosaic: for the ample notes with which the translator supplies his texts not only furnish cross-referencing between them but provide, too, enough additional data on the setting of Thomas's life and work for the attentive student to construct a rounded image.

So far as the *direct* evocation of Thomas's spiritual personality is concerned, Fr Kenelm focuses on what may be called his intellectual holiness. He had already noted how little Gui was disposed 'even at his most "secular" moments, to consider the saint's intelligence apart from its loving absorption in God'.

> All the intellectual activity of Thomas is shown as continuous with his prayer, as both the expression of and the means of fulfilling his desire for union with God; and, in a special way, with the God who confronted him, even now on earth – at once challenging faith and stirring intelligence – in the Sacrament of the Altar, to which ... 'he had a particular devotion'.[62]

Fr Kenelm's favourite icon of Thomas is the Fra Angelico figure, in a group before the crucified Christ, painted for the chapter room at San Marco in Florence. It is not 'placidly sagacious' but passionately thoughtful.

> If he is a prodigious master, it is because he himself was mastered – held by a vision of God's presence in the world's being (*esse*) and fascinated by the mystery of God incarnate and crucified. It is hardly possible, surely, to exaggerate either the clarity of this man's awareness of the divine presence in all existence – *esse* ... *proprius effectus Dei* – or, on the other hand, his sense of the complete 'otherness', the utter transcendence of the divine nature with respect to things created ...[63]

A contemplative, yes, but one who made an enormous effort not only into seeing but also into making intelligible what he saw, and so communicating it to others. And Fr Kenelm cites approvingly the dictum of Père Chenu: 'From the beginning of his teaching, Thomas Aquinas was carried by the grace of his Order, which is self-recognizant in him.'[64] It was by a cognate impulse, 'to render intelligible, in terms of rational human discourse, all such vision as could be gained',[65] that Fr Kenelm took on the task of presenting to the modern reader one of the most demanding and apparently inaccessible of the tractates of the *Summa Theologiae* – that on the holy angels.

The 'broad biblical tradition' of angelology has been conserved, but little developed, in Church teaching. The Catholic Church takes their existence 'as read' (read in the Scriptures, indeed), and in line with the inspired writings treats them, in Fr Kenelm's summary of the dogmatic tradition (Nicaea I, Lateran IV, Vatican I, and certain papal affirmations) as 'non-human intelligent beings, some of whom are in

God's favour and service, and some in rebellion against him'.[66] And he suggests that the reason for his restraint lies in the resolve that angelological speculation shall not in any way compete with the primacy of two all-encompassing dogmata, the doctrines of God the Creator and of Christ the only Mediator between God and the world.

In the course of the history of revelation, and its scriptural witness, belief in non-human spiritual powers came into close relation with that history, and so with that revelation, but for that very reason it must accept purification in revelation's light. And such doctrinal correction the Church's tradition in fact provides. On the other hand, Catholicism is not simply concerned to rein in a wild freedom where thinking and feeling about the angels is concerned. Angelology enables us to 'see the material world in due proportion', and so to grasp its limitedness in what Dante called 'the great sea of being'.[67] And here Fr Kenelm made his own (as rather rarely) some words of a contemporary dogmatician, the German Jesuit Karl Rahner. Angelology 'prevents man from foreshortening the dimensions of his environment: he stands in the midst of a wider than human society of salvation and damnation.'[68] And in this perspective, Fr Kenelm acclaims Thomas's treatise on the angels as 'probably the most brilliant piece of speculation on the subject produced by a Western theologian'.[69] Though not without shortcomings, its greatness derives from its summation of St Thomas's thought about created spiritual being, produced as this was in a period of outstanding metaphysical activity.

How should we understand metaphysics, considered as the *Summa Theologiae*'s chief philosophical instrument, not least in the tractate *De angelis*? The first act of intelligence is a tacit apprehension of reality at large, which apprehension in some fashion pre-contains every concept the mind may go on to form, for, as the *De veritate* has it, 'everything intrinsically shares in being'.[70] As Fr Kenelm explains:

By abstracting the formal content of that apprehension and reflecting on it, it is possible to acquire certain insights into the structure of reality which are evidently true, and universally and necessarily so; and which, when critically and systematically drawn out, compose a science. This science, which is metaphysics, represents, then, the analytical unfolding of the content of 'being' considered formally, i.e. in respect precisely of what it conveys *as an idea* and *as this idea*. And this idea itself has emerged from an initial intuitive contact, so to call it, of the mind with real existence. Hence, as regards sensory experience, metaphysics must depend on it so as far as that institution is involved and continues to involve it; but no further, strictly speaking. In this sense and to this extent meta-physics is not an empirical science; it is the formal science of the structures of being.[71]

Not that so far as the angels in particular are concerned Thomas proceeds in a conceptually *a priori* fashion. His aim, rather, is to 'conceive of a realizable type of being *answering to what the Bible says about angels*',[72] as well as to clarify this concept by as full an analysis as his programme of work in the *Summa* can allow. Essentially, he succeeds in marking off a 'zone of non-material and yet fundamentally contingent, because created, existence' from, on the one hand, the human condition (and here the duet of key terms 'form' and 'matter' is vital), and, on the other hand, the divine nature (and there the binary set of 'actuality' and 'potentiality' is crucial).[73]

Fr Kenelm's notes to the text do not only display his own beautiful clarity of mind; they also reveal genial insights into the philosophical and doctrinal intent of Aquinas's writing. Thus, for example, the principle that each angel is its own species can be rendered: 'Each angel in and by himself realizes the fulness of his angelhood; no single man can realize the fulness of humanity.' Or again, on the natural immortality of angels, compared and contrasted with human ensoulment and the God who is very Life:

> At the human level the form, the rational soul, is still a determinant of matter, but prior to this (prior in nature, *not* in time) it participates in *esse* of and by itself and not only as form-in-matter; hence it is called an *anima subsistens*, a subsistent life-principle, to distinguish it from the *animae* of brutes. Yet in so far as it is form-in-matter it is subject to the violent reduction (not complete loss) of existence called death. At the angelic level the form subsists of course, and far more strongly, as the charge of life that it represents is entirely contained in itself, with no threat from that corruption – death – to which forms are subject which energize whatever can only subsist in space and time. But it still receives this immortal *esse* from that absolute source which is existence itself, *ipsum esse subsistens*.[74]

Nor, in the light of the familiar anti-scholastic jibe about the number of angels who can be present on the head of a pin should one overlook Fr Kenelm's careful discussion of 'angels and position in space'. An angel is related to place through the actual or possible application of his power to some body – by *acting* there, if the term *actio* be allowed to include any kind of 'conjunction', *unitio*.[75] In point of fact, Fr Kenelm departs from Thomas by arguing that a plurality of angels *could* be 'in' one place, since there is nothing contradictory about the notion of several spiritual beings each causing some part of a general effect in the physical world. A similar subtlety (in a non-pejorative sense) attaches to the discussion of the angels' relation with time, and especially the lack of proportion between the time-measure of the embodied creature and that of pure spirits.

> We say that an angel moves because he brings about effects in the physical world: that he moves 'in time' because these effects are successive; and we represent that 'time' as discontinuous instants to each of which corresponds, in our world, an effect which may be over in a moment or, for all we know, may last a million years.

And the capacity of angelological theory, in Fr Kenelm's hands, to throw light on certain conditions, or dimensions, of the human being (for a consideration of pure intelligence may assist a grasp of the intellect which belongs to an animated body), is well exemplified in a note on angelic understanding.

> An angel's intelligence ... is not principally concerned with what comes to him from his creaturely lack of full actuality, his imperfection as a unity, his limitation to particularity. All this indeed an angel knows in himself, for it all constitutes in fact what he actually is; but he knows it en route, so to say, towards a more perfect object. His intellect, essentially correlated as it is to actuality and being as such, cannot rest in himself but only in the infinite perfection and actuality of God. The same is true indeed even of human intelligence, aware as it is – and precisely as intelligence – of the attraction of being and truth in general. Intelligence, in short, whether angelic or human, is the power to pass beyond the created subject, to transcend its limits.[76]

But the most impressive tour de force in Fr Kenelm's angels concerns the question of evil – to which he devotes a lengthy appendix. Drawing on the work of the French Dominican M.L. Guérard de Lauriers, Fr Kenelm essays an analysis of what he calls 'evil abstracted from everything adventitious or circumstantial', or again, 'evil in its purest condition: the choice of a mind hitherto absolutely innocent and, in the act of choosing, utterly unclouded by sentiment.'[77] In the case of a pure spirit – to whit, Lucifer,

> the object aimed at in the act of choice – the act that introduces sin – is and must be on the same ontological level as that aimed at by the spiritual nature as such. Now this nature's 'aim' is defined by

the way reality is related to it, and this way is such that reality is related to it, the spiritual nature, as a *totality* ... Hence when [the angel] chooses, it chooses entirely and exclusively according to the intellectual nature which it is – in view of total being. We might say that its choice establishes a universe – complete in itself.

To Fr Kenelm's mind, four notes typify at once great speculative genius, and great art and poetry. They are: width, depth, sympathy and proportion. It was, he thought, more especially in the last of these qualities – a sense of 'tact' that respect for the 'factors that make up the order of being' – that Thomas's particular greatness consisted. Each facet of the real is 'isolated, focused, regarded and then placed; and once placed it is henceforth related, rid of its isolation'.[78]

Intelligence and imagination

Not many students of the Middle Ages and Renaissance could combine analytic conceptual intelligence with imaginative critical flair after Fr Kenelm's style. A clue is that he cultivated the *inter-connections* of intelligence with imagination. As he saw things, the first duty of imagination is to serve the intelligence with 'intelligible data' (the Thomist principle of 'whatever is in the mind was first in the senses'), a mission closely followed by a second (and this more properly poetic) of furnishing examples and analogies to aid a grasp of more difficult truths by way of what is already understood. But thirdly, in 'our present decrepit condition' (he means, out of Eden) imagination has a more paradoxical task, at first sight antithetical to objective understanding but in reality not so.

I mean that the mind can play with images without seeking to understand them or make examples of them; and it claims to do this sometimes for its own good. It needs to bathe in the freedom of fancy from time to time not merely for the sake of repose, but also because it is nourished by the sensible world, and it is through images that it makes itself aware of the wild and independent vastness of this world.

And citing the words of the Psalmist, *Quam magnificata sunt opera tua, Domine,* he continues:

This wild world comes home to us sometimes. Chesterton strove to bring it home to his duller contemporaries; but he was forever outstripping fancy, diving down to the contingency of created being where only intelligence could take him. The artist need not go so far; he can yet awake us ...[79]

And if the image-borne intelligence can thus plumb the relation of 'physics' to metaphysics, of the everyday world to its undergirding mystery, Fr Kenelm was equally concerned that the *historical* and *ethical* orders should likewise be given their due. This was the attraction to him of the early nineteenth-century Italian novelist Alessandro Manzoni, a lover both of reason and of the Church. Had Fr Kenelm lived longer, a full-scale study of Manzoni was his next task. As it was, he left at least two essays. Rejecting with horror the notion that Christian faith involves some loss to rationality, Fr Kenelm's Manzoni explores both rationally and poetically the 'relation between history and morality, man as he has been and man as he should be'.[80] In Manzonian perspective, the poet's aim is to arrive at knowledge of man in his whole social reality, given that the poet, by definition, can boast a special aptitude not only for feeling but also for 'achieving an *idea* of his emotion and so the truth of it'. *Il vero poetico* – in, say, *I promessi sposi*, 'The Betrothed' – is a showing forth of good and evil, and thus is identical with *il vero morale*. For Manzoni, human history is 'borne onward by an inward conflict that cannot be resolved within history itself': the subjective urge to happiness and the objective requirements of justice are reconciled only outside history. How contrasted – *toto caelo*! – the approach of Manzoni's non-believing Enlightenment brother Leopardi, whose 'truth' sets man in opposition to the universe of fact, and counterposes reason to existence. These two paths constitute, Fr Kenelm suggested in an enigmatic conclusion, 'perhaps ... the only possible directions open, in the end, to human thought'.

At the beginning of February 1986 Fr Kenelm took with him, dying, to hospital in Cambridge neither Chesterton nor Manzoni or even Dante but *Hopkins*. He read Gerard Manley Hopkins' poems aloud with peculiar beauty. Among the letters from the Catholic critic Bernard Kelly which he kept to the end, we find an extract from an essay of his correspondent on Hopkins' 'mind and poetry'. A passage of commentary on *The Windhover* might serve as his epitaph:

The intellectual form of chastity ... is precisely the form of Hopkins' mature artistic creation. For the chastity of the intelligence, is in its objectivity, a perfection of its obedience to the subtle modifications of the real. By chastity, then, we do not destroy or distort ourselves and the world, but perfect the fecundity of the world both in itself, in its own intelligibility, and in ourselves as knowing and feeling subjects. The mind, in its act of apprehending the world, sets the senses moving in precisely the same direction as the moderative virtues, towards God; by way of particular truth which is an *aliquid Christi*, by way of beauty also.[81]

Notes

1. 'Kenelm Foster', in *The Acts of the Provincial Chapter of the English Province Held at All Saints' Pastoral Centre, London Colney, 1988* (n.d.), p. 32.
2. For a brother's appreciation, see 'The Sculpture of Anthony Foster', *Blackfriars XXXII*. 372 (1951), pp. 119–23.
3. B. Bailey, O.P., 'In Memoriam. Kenelm Foster, O.P.: 1910–1986', *New Blackfriars* 67, 789 (March 1986), p. 139.
4. An inkling of Claudel's attraction is found in Frank Sheed's summary of the Claudelian theological aesthetic: 'Mysteries ... are an invitation to thought; and while their content is infinite and never to be exhausted, the mind can steadily draw out of them truth, which is its proper food.' F. Sheed, *Sidelights on the Catholic Revival* (London: Sheed and Ward, 1941), p. 102.
5. Ibid. Cf. My essay 'The Spirituality of the Dominicans', in A. Nichols, O.P., *Scribe of the Kingdom. Essays on Theology and Culture* (London: Sheed and Ward, 1994), II., pp. 199–206.
6. 'Dante as a Christian Poet', in *God's Tree. Essays on Dante and Other Matters* (London: Blackfriars Publications, 1957), pp. 1–14, and, much more briefly: 'Poet of Time and Eternity. Reflections on Dante's Seventh Centenary', *The Tablet*, 8 May 1965, pp. 512–13.
7. See 'Religion and Philosophy in Dante', in U. Limentani (ed.), *The Mind of Dante* (Cambridge: Cambridge University Press, 1965), pp. 47–78; and *The Two Dantes and Other Studies* (London: Darton, Longman and Todd, 1977), p. 253. On Dante's relation to St Thomas, see 'Dante e San Tommaso' (Rome: 1975), as well as his fuller articles on this topic in the *Enciclopedia Dantesca*.
8. Cited by N. Sapegno, 'Genesis and Structure: Two Approaches to the Poetry of the *Comedy*, in U. Limentani, *The Mind of Dante*, p. 13.
9. 'Dante Studies in England, 1921–1964', *Italian Studies* XX (1965), p. 10.
10. Ibid., p. 4. Cf. T.S. Eliot, 'Dante', in Eliot, *The Sacred Wood. Essays on Poetry and Criticism* (London: Methuen, 1928; 1960), pp. 159–171; also, under the same title, the fuller study in Eliot's *Selected Essays* (London: Faber and Faber, 1951[3]), pp. 237–80.
11. 'Dante Studies in England, 1921–1964', p. 5.
12. *God's Tree*, p. 4.
13. *Dante's Lyric Poetry* (with P. Boyde, Oxford: Clarendon Press, 1967). Volume I: The Poems, Text and Translation; Volume II: Commentary. He had explained elsewhere that 'By the *Rime* of Dante are commonly

meant all the poems that he wrote apart from the *Comedia*, though sometimes the term is limited by subtracting those contained in the vita Nuova.' 'Recent Work on Dante's *Rime*', *Le Parole e le Idee IV* (1962), p. 255.

14. *Dante's Lyric Poetry*, I., p. xv.
15. Ibid., I., p. xix.
16. *God's Tree*, p. 4.
17. *Purgatorio* I, 19-25; 115-17.
18. Ibid., p. 55, citing C. Williams, *The Figure of Beatrice* (London: Faber and Faber, 1943), p. 132.
19. *God's Tree*, p. 66.
20. *Paradiso* I, 7-9.
21. *The Two Dantes, and Other Studies* (London: Darton, Longman and Todd, 1977), p. 68.
22. Ibid., pp. 72-3, with an internal citation of *Summa Theologiae* IIa IIae, q. 175, art. 3.
23. Apostolic letter of 7 December 1965, printed as an introduction to *Annali dell'Istituto di Studi Danteschi* (Milan: Società Editrice Vita e Pensiero, 1967).
24. 'The Pope and Poetry', *Dante Studies* LXXVII (1969), pp. 147-51.
25. *The Two Dantes, and Other Studies*, p. 57.
26. E. Gilson, *Dante et la philosophie* (Paris: Vrin, 1939), p. 118.
27. *The Two Dantes, and Other Studies*, p. 63.
28. 'Dante e San Tommaso', *Quaderni della Casa di Dante* (Rome, 1974-1975), p. 20.
29. 'Dante and Two Friars', *Paradiso XI-XII*', *New Blackfriars* 66. 785 (1985), pp. 481-2. This article is a translation by Mary John Ronayne, O.P., of Fr Kenelm's Italian original 'Gli elogi danteschi de S. Francesco e di S. Domenico', in *Dante e il Francescanesimo* (*Lectura Dantis Metalliana*, Avagliano Editore, 1987), pp. 321-49.
30. *Paradiso* XI, 40-42.
31. 'Dante and Two Friars', p. 483.
32. Ibid., p. 496.
33. H. Needler, *Saint Francis and Saint Dominic in the Divine Comedy* (Krefeld: Scherpe Verlag, 1969; =*Schriften und Vorträge des Petrarca-Instituts Köln*, XXIII), p. 21.
34. *The Two Dantes*, p. 156.
35. 'Religion and Philosophy in Dante', in U. Limentani (ed.), *The Mind of Dante*, p. 67.
36. E. Gilson, *Dante et la philosophie* (Paris: 1939), p. 100.
37. *The Two Dantes* pp. 248-9.
38. Ibid., p. 253
39. 'Introduction', *I Catherine. Selected Writings of St Catherine of Siena*, Edited and Translated by Kenelm Foster, O.P., and Mary John Ronayne, O.P. (London: Collins, 1980), p. 11.
40. For the contemporary efflorescence of such bodies, see G.G. Meersseman and G.P. Pacini, *Ordo Fraternitatis. Confraternite e pietà*

dei laici nel medio evo (Rome: Herder, 1977, three volumes).

41. 'Introduction', *I Catherine*, p. 18, with an internal reference to Raymund of Capua's *Legenda Maior: The Life of St Catherine of Siena, with an Introduction by Thomas Gilby*, O.P., (London: Harvill Press, 1960), p. 137.

42. 'Introduction', *I Catherine*, p. 23, with citations of *Letters* 17 and 82.

43. 'The Spirit of St Catherine', *Life of the Spirit* XV. 178 (1961), pp. 433–46, with reference to H. Graef, *The Light and the Rainbow A Study in Christian Spirituality from its Roots in the Old Testament and its Development through the New Testament and the Fathers to Recent Times*, (London: Longmans, 1959), pp. 252–3.

44. Ibid., p. 29

45. *Le Lettere di S. Caterina da Siena*, con note di Niccolò Tommaseo, a cura di Piero Misciatelli (Siena: Giantini e Bentivoglio 1922³), No. 102.

46. 'Introduction', *I Catherine*, p. 33.

47. 'Such a perversion must be due to a darkening of the mind, a failure to *see* ourselves in our true relation to God. But what can account for this if not a prior misdirection of *desire* through absorption by, and in, the self and the sensible world? But does not this in turn entail some error of judgement? Further analysis would be needed to untie this knot, but we should not expect it from Catherine; enough for her to have seen – though she could not perfectly explain it – the interplay of error and self-love, of darkened mind and twisted desire, that is at the root of sin'. Ibid.

48. Catherine of Siena, *II Dialogo*, XIII.

49. 'Introduction', *I Catherine*, p. 36, citing *Le Orazioni di S. Caterina da Siena*, a cura di Giuliana Cavallini (Rome: Centro Nazionale di Studi Cateriniani, 1978), X.

50. Ibid. VII.

51. *Petrarch: Poet and Humanist* (Edinburgh: Edinburgh University Press, 1984); of the sub-title of his 'Christ and Letters. The Religion of the Early Humanists', *Blackfriars* XLIV. 514 (1963), pp. 148–56.

52. 'Christ and Letters', pp. 149–150.

53. *Petrarch: Poet and Humanist*, pp. 7–8.

54. Ibid., pp. 42–3.

55. *Canzoniere* 366. 135–7, cited in *Petrarch*, p. 44.

56. Ibid., pp. 8–9.

57. Ibid., p. 141, with references to the text of D. Carrara, in Francesco Petracha, *Prose* (Milan-Naples: Ricciardi, 1955). pp. 160, 186.

58. Ibid., p. 153. The emphasis here on the internal disintegration of the soul is less Eliot's and more an echo of the Christian Jungianism of Fr Victor and Fr Gerald.

59. Ibid., p. 159.

60. Inferno IV. 131.

61. *The Life of Saint Thomas Aquinas. Biographical Documents* (London: Longmans, Green and Co., 1959), p. 1, citing *Purgatorio* XVII. 57.

62. Ibid., p. 20, citing the *Life of St Thomas Aquinas* by Bernard Gui, Chapter 15.

63. Ibid., p. 22, with an allusion to *Summa Theologiae* Ia, q. 45, a. 5.

64. M.-D. Chenu. O.P., *Introduction à l'étude de S. Thomas d'Aquin* (Paris: Librairie Philosophique J. Vrin, 1950), p. 38.

65. *The Life of Saint Thomas Aquinas*, p. 23.

66. *St Thomas Aquinas, Summa Theologiae Volume 9. Angels [Ia 50–64]* (London: Blackfriars in conjunction with Eyre and Spottiswoode; New York: McGraw-Hill Book Company 1968), p. 301. Cited below as *Angels*.

67. Ibid., p. 302, citing *Paradiso* I, 113.

68. K. Rahner and H. Vorgrimler, *A Concise Theological Dictionary* (E.T. London: Burns Oates, 1965), p. 21.

69. *Angels*, p. 303.

70. *De veritate* I, 1.

71. *Angels*, p. xxiii.

72. Italics added.

73. Ibid., p. xxv. A note on p. 9 offers a clear account: 'Matter and form: respectively, the determinable and the determining factors in bodily things; what they are made of and the intrinsic principle 'making' them. They are correlative terms, but by extension 'form' can also be used to mean a matter-less actuality in which the mere potentiality to exist (*esse*) is realized; and the angels, for St Thomas, are such matterless forms'.

74. Ibid., pp. 27

75. Ibid., pp. 45–46, with reference to Ia, q. 52, art. 1, and *Quaestiones quodlibetales* I. 4.

76. Ibid., p. 81.

77. Ibid., p. 311, with reference to M.L. Guérard de Lauriers, O.P., 'Le Péché et la causalité', *Bulletin Thomiste* XI (1962), pp. 553–637.

78. 'The Tact of St Thomas', in *God's Tree*, p. 149.

79. 'On Imagination', *Blackfriars* XXI. 248 (1940), p. 656. He had written of Chesterton in the same issue, 'He was clearly a genius – I like to think that he was the greatest Englishman of his time – but he was of the kind that is given to men to be imitated', Ibid., p. 667, reviewing H. Belloc, *On the Place of Gilbert Chesterton in English Letters* (London: Sheed and Ward, 1940).

80. 'The Idea of Truth in Alessandro Manzoni and Giacomo Leopardi', *Proceedings of the British Academy* LIII (London: Oxford University Press, 1967), p. 240. See also 'Manzoni and the Italians', in *God's Tree*, pp. 85–92.

81. 'The Mind and Poetry of G.M. Hopkins', English Dominican Archive. Later published as *The Mind and Poetry of Gerard Manley Hopkins, S.J.* (Ditchling: St Dominic's Press, 1935; reprinted New York: Haskell House Publishers, 1971).

Works of Kenelm Foster

'Freedom and Spontaneity', *Blackfriars* XXI. 247 (1940), pp. 593–98.
'On Imagination', *Blackfriars* XXI. 248 (1940), pp. 651–60.
'Created Holiness', *Blackfriars* XXII. 251 (1941), pp. 74–81.
'The Adolescent Vision in Dante', *Dominican Studies* I (1948), pp. 127–48.
St Thomas, Petrarch and the Renascence, 'Aquinas Paper' 12 (London: 1949).
Aristotle's 'De Anima' in the Version of William of Moerbeke, with the Commentary of St Thomas Aquinas. Translated with Silvester Humphries, O.P. (London: Kegan Paul, 'Rare Masterpieces of Science and Philosophy', 1951.
'The Sculpture of Anthony Foster', *Blackfriars* XXXII. 372 (1951), pp. 119–23.
Cassell's Encyclopaedia of Literature, 2 vols. (London: 1953). All the articles on Italian literature of the thirteenth century, including Dante and ending with Cino da Pistoia.
'Dante's *Paradiso*: Canto I' (translation), *Life of the Spirit* X (1955), pp. 180–84.
The Mind in Love: Dante's Philosophy (London: Blackfriars Publications, 1956; Aquinas Paper, No. 25.
God's Tree. Essays on Dante and Other Matters (London: Blackfriars Publications, 1957).
The Life of Saint Thomas Aquinas. Biographical Documents (London: Longmans, Green and Co., 1959).
'Lines of Grace', *Blackfriars* XLII. 493 (1961), pp. 238–44.
'The Spirit of St Catherine', *Life of the Spirit* XV. 178 (1961), pp. 433–46.
'St Catherine's Teaching on Christ', *Life of the Spirit* XVI (1961), pp. 310–323.
'Recent Work on Dante's *Rime*', *Le Parole e le Idee* IV (1962), pp. 255–68.
'Beatrice or Medusa, The Penitential Motif in Petrarch's *Canzoniere*', *Italian Studies Presented to E.R. Vincent* (Cambridge: Heffers, 1962), pp. 41–56.
'Continental Versions: Italian' in S.L. Greenslade (ed.) *The Cambridge History of the Bible*, Vol. 1, pp. 110–3, 358–60, (Cambridge: Cambridge University Press, 1963).
Courtly Love and Christianity, 'Aquinas Paper' 39. 1963.
'Christ and Letters'. The Religion of the Early Humanists', *Blackfriars* XLIV, 514 (1963), pp. 148–56.
'Michelangelo's Failure', Blackfriars, XLIV, 519 (1963), pp. 355–63.
Alessandro Manzoni, *La Colonna Infame*. Translated (as *The Column of Infamy*) with an Introduction (Oxford: Oxford University Press, 'The Oxford Library of Italian Classics', 1964).
'Religion and Philosophy in Dante', in U. Limentani (ed.), *The Mind of Dante* (Cambridge: Cambridge University Press, 1965). pp. 47–78.
'Dante Studies in England, 1921–1964', *Italian Studies* X (1965), pp. 1–16.
'Poet of Time and Eternity', *The Tablet* 219 (1965), pp. 512–14.

'Dante, Poet of the Intellect', *New Blackfriars* 46 (1965), pp. 442–46.

'The Idea of Truth in Alessandro Manzoni and Giacomo Leopardi', *Proceedings of the British Academy* LIII (London: Oxford University Press, 1967).

Dante's Lyric Poetry (with P. Boyde). Vol. I The Poems. Text and Translation; vol. II Commentary (Oxford: Oxford University Press, 1967).

'Dante', in H.F. Davis, A. Williams, O.S.B., I. Thomas, O.P., J. Crehan, S.J. (eds.) *A Catholic Dictionary of Theology* (London: Thomas Nelson & Sons, 1967), II., pp. 153–54.

Eros (Medieval Period), in *A Catholic Dictionary of Theology*, pp. 230–32.

'Typology and a Poet', *New Blackfriars* 48 (1967), pp. 205–208.

St Thomas Aquinas, Summa Theologiae, Volume 9. Angels [Ia 50–64] (London: Blackfriars, in conjunction with Eyre and Spottiswoode and McGraw-Hill Book Company, New York, 1968).

'The Pope and Poetry', *Dante Studies* LXXVII (1969), pp. 147–51.

'Cristo', *Enciclopedia Dantesca* II (Rome: 1970), pp. 262–69.

'Dio', *Enciclopedia Dantesca* II (Rome: 1970) pp. 452–57.

'Dante e San Tommaso', *Quaderni della Casa di Dante'*, I (1974–1975), pp. 5–20.

'Summa contra Gentiles', *Enciclopedia Dantesca* V (Rome: 1976), pp. 479–80.

'Teologia', *Enciclopedia Dantesca* pp. 564–68.

'Tommaso d'Aquino', *Enciclopedia Dantesca* pp. 626–49.

'Vangelo', *Enciclopedia Dantesca* pp. 874–77.

The Two Dantes, and Other Studies (London: Darton, Longman and Todd, 1977).

I Catherine, Selected Writings of St Catherine of Siena (with M.J. Ronayne, O.P., London: Collins, 1980).

'Purgatorio XXXII', in K. Foster (ed.), *Cambridge Readings in Dante's 'Commedia'* (with P. Boyde, Cambridge: Cambridge University Press 1981), pp. 138–54.

'Dante's Idea of Purgatory, with Special Reference to Purgatorio XXI, 58–66' in J.H.M. Taylor (ed.), *Dies illa. Death in the Middle Ages* (Liverpool: 1984), pp. 97–105.

'Dante and Two Friars: Paradiso XI–XII', *New Blackfriars* 66 (1985), pp. 480–86.

'Gli elogi danteschi di S. Francesco e di S. Domenico', in *Dante e il Francescanesimo (Lectura Dantis Metelliana*, Avagliano Editore, 1987) pp. 321–49.

9

Conrad Pepler

The origins of Fr Conrad's Catholicism lie in that unique experiment in the marriage of religion and art known in a word as *Ditchling*. Since Ditchling remained in several ways as crucial for his theological approach as it was central in his biography, a word must be said about it here.

In the beginning, however, was Hammersmith. It was in that definitely urban (not suburban) yet river-washed district of London that Eric Gill had encountered Douglas Pepler – later 'Hilary', the name he took at baptism, and father of Stephen Conrad – in 1906, the year before the latter's birth. Eric and Ethel Gill, together with their first child, Elizabeth, had come there in 1905, anxious, in their move to London, to avoid all that savoured of suburbia, since it was essential to Gill's aesthetic that an artist was, essentially, a *workman*. Here Gill took his first assistant, Joseph Cribb, later to become a major sculptor in his own right. Here he maintained his friendship with the calligrapher Edward Johnston, his teacher in writing and lettering at the Central School of Arts and Crafts.[1] Through Johnston (and the painter William Rothenstein[2]) he got to know numerous major figures on the Edwardian cultural scene – artists such as Ambrose McEvoy and Augustus John; the critics Roger Fry, Sydney Cockerell and A. R. Orage; the writers Cecil and Gilbert Keith Chesterton, H.G. Wells, and George Bernard Shaw; the social commentators Sidney and Beatrice Webb, and was attracted or repelled by them.[3] Here too he struck up a friendship with Pepler *père*, a young man with a patchwork quilt of a career to his credit, and seeking to add a new talent, stone-carving.[4]

Pepler came from a Quaker family, and had received his schooling at a famous Quaker academy, the Friends School at Bootham, York. After ventures in commerce, handicraft and surveying, he turned to social work, in the company of no less a one than William Beveridge, founder of the British 'Welfare State'. His chief interest was the welfare of children, to which he devoted his *The Care Committee, the Child and the Parent* of 1912, as well as *Justice and the Child*, published in 1915.[5] But he was far from being a Fabian Society pattern-man. He tried his hand at sociological satire in *The Devil's Devices* (its subtitle 'Control versus Service' betrays his animus against an invasive bureaucracy), and, aided by a preface from G.K. Chesterton, had William Cobbett's *Cottage Economy* reprinted.[6] (It would be a thoroughly practical resource at Ditchling). He wrote verse and plays; he was gifted at puppetry and (especially) mime. His life was to be changed by the encounter with Gill.

In 1907 Gill decided to transfer his workshop from London to Ditchling, a village perched on the northern slopes of the South Downs, in Sussex, the Gills' native country. Although the Distributist movement, of which the Dominican Fr Vincent McNabb was the best-known oracle, favoured life in the country ('Back to the Land') in and for itself, Gill himself had a nuanced attitude on the point. The city is the crown of human civilisation, but without a flourishing country-side round about it the city can hardly exist. And yet, motivated as it was by a desire to disentangle himself from the over-sophistication of the high-art world of London, Gill's move to Ditchling represented in fact a search for metaphysical and human basics. The Indian philosopher of art Ananda Coomaraswamy commented revealingly:

> Gill said himself that he invented a religion and found that it was Roman Christianity: he might also have said that he re-invented a way of working, and found it was that of all traditional societies and Plato's way ... This amounts to saying that Eric's was not a personal point of view, but simply a true one that he had made his own. He was not 'thinking for himself', but assenting to credible propositions; and he was, accordingly, a man of faith.[7]

In 1910 he hinted, in a letter to Rothenstein, at the 'possibility' of a religious renaissance in England, with a religion 'so splendid and all-embracing that the hierarchy to which it will give birth, uniting within itself the artist and the priest, will supplant and utterly destroy our present commercial age'.[8] In the course of the years 1911 to 1913 he came to identify it, as Coomaraswamy reported, with the Church of Rome. According to Donald Attwater, the most ecclesiastically informed of Gill's biographers, the stages were: reading Robert Browning's poem 'Bishop Blougram's Apology'; inscribing the memorial-tablet of the Victorian Catholic poet-derelict Francis Thompson, at Greatham, house of his patrons, the old Catholic family of the Meynells; paying a visit to the Benedictine monastery of Mont-César, Louvain, where, in Attwater's words, 'the bodiless hand of

God, clothed in the materiality of public worship, touched Eric Gill'. Or, in Gill's own words: 'There, at Louvain, after the slow procession of incoming monks and the following short silence when I first, all unprepared and innocent, heard *Deus in adiutorium* ... I knew, infallibly, that God existed and was a living God ...'[9] Instructed by, in turn, Abbot Edmund Ford of Downside and, less grandly, a priest of the diocese of Southwark at Hove, he and his wife were received into the Catholic Church in February 1913. It was a significant moment. Fr Kenelm Foster, identifying as the normative features of Gill's style 'linear beauty, respect for the native character of materials, and a certain rationality in the treatment of subjects' (whether the human figure, sacred and secular, animals, or letters), would write, in the wake of the Second World War, of the consequences of that ceremony on the eve of the First:

> There has been attempted amongst us, during the past thirty years, and in the face of most discouraging odds, the revival of an art at once Christian and rational. We Catholics cannot afford to ignore it; nor can England. And where else if not among Christians, can reason walk with beauty and poverty with freedom?[10]

In the November of that year, the Gills left their house in Ditchling village for the more rural setting of Ditchling Common; the Peplers moved into the property they had vacated. It is to this period that his carving of the great Stations of the Cross at Westminster Cathedral belongs. But this was not his only Catholic commission of the war years. During the opening summer of the Great War, Gill was in Edinburgh to work on the decoration of Canon John Gray's perfectly conceived church of St Peter's, Morningside.[11] Gray and his patron André Sebastian Raffalovitch were Dominican tertiaries and Gill met there the Dominican who was so to influence him: Vincent McNabb. The seed was planted of an idea: a guild of Catholic craftsmen, not only collaborating in their work but following a common rule of life. In the autumn of 1916, Gill and Pepler (the latter not yet a Catholic) visited Fr Vincent at Hawkesyard, where he was prior: Pepler's conversion, and Gill's enrolment as a Third-Order Dominican were the result. The attractions were threefold: the Dominican emphasis on missionary preaching (Gill would later write, 'All art is propaganda'!); the ascetic and contemplative aspects of their Rule and Constitutions; and the philosophy and theology of St Thomas. Between 1919 and 1921 the 'Guild of St Joseph and St Dominic' took shape, both materially (in the form of a circle of workshops and a chapel) and canonically, in the enrolment of qualified persons.[12] They had to be tertiaries and to ply a trade. Each member owned 'his tools, his workshop and the product of his work'. The menfolk met in chapel four or five times daily for the Hours of the Little Office of the Blessed Virgin Mary (as used by the novices, lay-brothers and tertiaries of the Province). As Fr Conrad would remark in a memoir: Ditchling 'did its best to mirror the regular life of a Dominican priory in its liturgical practices'.[13] Hilary Pepler, as a cofounder, was naturally a constituent member of the Guild; his printing at 'St Dominic's Press' would become celebrated.[14] Others, like the poet, painter and engraver David Jones were content to live at Ditchling, and work within its ambience. That ambience was not only liturgical; it was also domestic. Fr Conrad would recall the prominence given to the 'hearth': the family gathering in each cottage, the reading aloud (especially of Dickens) by the light of Aladdin lamps. 'Home the last haven of civilisation' encapsulates an important dimension of the Ditchling ethos; or as Fr Conrad put it, more Thomistically, that 'hearth' could be considered the *'primum analogatum* for other ways of human life to copy'.[15] (He would later try to realize it – analogically – at Spode House.)[16]

Hilary Pepler came to differ from Gill on several points. In the first place, he was much more sympathetic to Distributism – and in that respect closer to McNabb. The Distributist movement as an organised affair was effectively killed off by the Second World War, yet Pepler could write later that Distributism remained for him 'a fundamental conception, but so much so that it cannot be isolated. Like charity, stable society is not possible without it, but it is too universal to organize.'[17] A second cause of their divergence – and ultimately separation, lay in Gill's theory and practice where the interrelation of sexuality, art and ethics were concerned. Though Pepler printed Gill's provocative wood-engraving 'Nuptials of God' (showing the Church, personified as a woman, embracing in erotic fashion the dying Christ on the cross), he came increasingly to share the anxieties aroused by Gill's erotophile images (not to mention opinions – and behaviour!) among those Dominican priests like McNabb and Austin Barker who were close to the Ditchling founders.[18] Writing a quarter of a century ago Attwater had already identified this factor (despite the discretion of all parties on the point), though he referred to it in terms excessively favourable to Gill: 'Pepler was still marked by the puritanism of his upbringing, and he was unable to come to terms with Gill's increasing freedom as expressed in some of his drawings and engravings.'[19] With the publication of Fiona MacCarthy's biography of Gill in 1989, a rather different judgment can be ventured. In her words:

His urge to experiment with social conventions, especially the prevailing sexual mores, became more obviously and more painfully at variance with the Gills' accepted role as the ideal Catholic family, the public demonstration of fidelity and cohesiveness. It can now be seen that Gill's own leanings, in particular his sexually possessive attitude to his own daughters, led directly to his fatal quarrel with Pepler, destroying not only the coherence of Ditchling, so painstakingly built up over the years, but also removing the one person who was on an equal footing, who loved him yet was frank with him.[20]

In comparison with this, their friction over Pepler's shortcomings as a double-entry book-keeper was a bagatelle.

Hilary's second son, Stephen, born in Hammersmith on 5 May 1908, had been baptised, thanks to his father's new found Catholicity, at St George's Retreat (a nursing sisterhood on the edge of Ditchling Common) by Fr Alfred Swaby, one of Cardinal Manning's 'Oblates of St Charles' who received permission to transfer his vows to the Dominicans in 1918. He received confirmation at the hands of the English Dominican bishop Anthony Felix Couturier, then Apostolic Visitor to Egypt, in the priory church at Hawkesyard, where he would return under a different aegis when enrolled by his father in the Dominicans' school. In 1924, however, he abandoned formal education so as to begin a three-year apprenticeship in his father's workshop at St Dominic's Press. At 'Mr Pepler's Printing Shop' – the reference is to Eric Gill's coloured plan now at the William Andrews Clark Memorial Library in Los Angeles – exacting standards of craftsmanship and a positively religious devotion to the value of work obtained. In Hilary Pepler's *The Hand Press*, written and printed by him for the Society of Typographical Arts of Chicago, we read:

> The hand printer should break away from the modern craze for outward uniformity and enjoy a freedom denied to the machinist. Uniformity is a good rule but it is not infallible and it is often a yoke too grievous to be borne. It is, like other rules, a means not an end; for rules were made for men, not men for rules.[21]

On the other hand: 'Rules of taste should be rigidly self-imposed in order to avoid the diffuse and incongruous, they are especially to be desired in the matter of TYPES.' Nor did Pepler rescind the declaration, made originally to a purely Dominican audience, in his earliest essay on the subject in *The Hawkesyard Review* (the priory's 'in-house' journal) for 1918:

> The work of the printer, as all work, should be done for the glory of God. The work of the printer is to multiply the written word,

hence the printer serves the maker of words, and the maker of words serves – or should serve – the Word Which became Flesh.[22]

The 'philosophy' of Fr Conrad's boyhood home, the Ditchling 'Community' – Guild members, however, disliked the word, since communal living as such had never been in prospect – has been described numerous times in print, in connection with Gill, Jones, Hilary Pepler himself, and other figures. Thanks especially to the influence of Vincent McNabb, Ditchling was affected by a radical – agrarian and Luddite – as distinct from moderate Distributism of the kind that might have formed a national programme for public policy.[23] The main aim of the latter variety was simply to restrict the growth both of bureaucracy and of big business. Its chief tenet was the thesis that property – the widely distributed small ownership of the means of production – is a necessary foundation for real freedom in civil society. Linked to the developing social doctrine of the papacy, especially in Leo XIII's encyclical *Rerum Novarum* (1891), it would be too easy to write off Distributism as the Italianate enthusiasm of Anglo-Saxon converts for the more picturesque societies of Southern Europe. In one of its main expositions, Hilaire Belloc's *Economics for Helen*, its *beau idéal*, indeed, was cited as *Denmark*.[24] However, the 'Back to the Land' Distributism of McNabb, which married an agrarian emphasis to an assault on machines as such, counted for more than such social politics in the making of Ditchling. Here for instance is Hilary Pepler pleading (anonymously) for the Catholic bishops in England to take seriously not only their rural flock but also the theologically privileged status of the countryside.

I submit the story of Our Blessed Lord Who chose the country for His dwelling place, a country Maid for Mother, and the hills in which to pray. Whose gospel lives with images of country life – lambs (O Lamb of God), swine, oxen, asses, hens, seed-sowing, harvests, corn and barns. Who chose His first disciples, men with country crafts, and taught them in the country. But even they wavered in the town caught in the net of disbelief and doubt which was Jerusalem. And He who spent His life by farm and lake wept over the city which had killed her prophets. It is most strange that lovers of Our Blessed Lord should think they can succeed where He Himself has failed. The modern Baptist stands by the city cesspool, but the Jordan flows between unpopulated hills – a pure baptismal water given by God to cleanse men of their lusts and usuries.[25]

Missions, or Sheepfolds and Shambles coheres perfectly with the monastic historian Peter Anson's recollection of Ditchling as it was in 1920, when Stephen was twelve years old.

> Twenty-six years ago Folders Lane, which leads from Burgess Hill to Ditchling Common, was a real country lane. There were fields on either side, and no jerry-built bungalows had then begun to transform it into a typical suburban high road. It was easy to realise why ... the Community had chosen this rural spot for their home. It was still unspoilt Sussex. Having reached a cross-roads where the Common begins, I noticed an old purple-red brick farmhouse set in an orchard ... On looking back after a quarter of a century I find that ... what I remember best is the 'atmosphere' of the place. I fell in love with the setting – the people whom I met there, the kindly welcome, and the homeliness of everything ... There was a certain spartan simplicity about the domestic arrangements, and a complete lack of what are known as 'modern conveniences'. Water was drawn from a pump. Meals, though the food was abundant, were somewhat erratic, because all cooking was done on an open fire which burned logs.[26]

But the domestic idyll of Hilary Pepler's family life did not answer to something hard, and more exclusively God-centred, in the young Stephen's personality.

The contemplative and even mystical orientation of his religious life was signalled by his intention, on leaving school, to offer himself to the Carthusian monks of nearby Parkminster, founded in 1873 after ten years of English episcopal negotiation with the Grande Chartreuse and, at the time of its building, 'easily the largest monastic building in England', a veritable city.[27] the Carthusians are – as this study's investigation of the work of the Mathews has already noted – by far the most austere and eremitical order in the Western Church. Pepler *fils* was dissuaded by Dom Gregory Swann, monk of Ampleforth, and persuaded to try his vocations with the Dominicans instead. In 1927, to his parents' silent chagrin, Stephen left them to enter – as Br Conrad – the Woodchester noviciate. He was ordained at Oxford on 30 July 1933, rounding off his studies with the acquisition of the lectorate from the Pontifical Faculty at the Angelicum in Rome. On returning to England, he who had hoped to teach liturgiology – the liturgy would remain a great inspiration for his life, though he was in time saddened by the abolition of the historic Dominican use in favour of the modern Roman rite – was told to teach the history of philosophy instead. Mercifully, the unseated lector, Fr Quentin Johnston, lent him his notes. Fortunately for students and lecturer alike, the Master of the Order, Stanislas Martin Gillet, called him to Rome to teach in the newly founded 'School for Novice Masters' which that enterprising and ambitious cleric had established at Santa Sabina, as well as to be a member of the 'Liturgical Institute' there.

With the entry of Italy into the Second World War on Hitler's side these promising developments were cut short – very short, he left with only habit, breviary and typewriter. Assigned to Oxford, he at once took on a formidable work-load. As the secretary whom he eventually perforce acquired wrote after his death:

> It is not easy to 'convey' the young (30ish) Conrad of 1940 – he was full of zest for life, had a lively (and sometimes basic) sense of humour, was warm, kindly and welcoming to all comers, was sensitive and caring for anyone in trouble and was blest with an apparently inexhaustible energy that left me (and I considered myself no sloth) gasping. In Oxford he said Mass at the earliest permitted time (5.30? 6.00?) and his day (which included of course attendance at conventual Offices since he was organising cantor) rarely ended before midnight. At one point he was concurrently student master, cantor, librarian, editor of both *Blackfriars* and *Life of the Spirit* (i.e. two monthly editorials), gave a large number of retreats etc. around the country and still managed to find time to be 'accessible', to write his own books and to start and supervise Blackfriars Publications at the period when publishing was particularly difficult with paper rationing, printing restrictions, etc, etc. – though at this point even C.P. realised he needed help.[28]

This hectic round (as it must seem) did not prevent him from excogitating a theory of what he was doing – and notably an editorial philosophy for *Blackfriars* and *Life of the Spirit*.

In a Memoir of 1971, looking back, he explained his policy. The aim of *Blackfriars* was an apostolate to culture, that of *Life of the Spirit* the cure of souls. (The two neatly reflect the historic definition of the goal of the Order, 'for the sake of preaching and the salvation of souls'). As he wrote:

> *Blackfriars* I felt was attempting to bring our Lord (for this is the aim of every apostolate and so of every Dominican) into circles where it might be said that 'the Word' existed in the natural order. That is to say, to show the relevance of the Gospels, the Church, Christianity, our Lord himself, to contemporary culture, art, literature, science, politics, etc. etc.

Life of the Spirit, by contrast, was 'trying to intensify the Christian spirit where it already existed', to assist in the deepening of the Christian life, which must mean, in Fr Conrad's christocentric vision, 'to love our Lord with increasing depth and understanding'.[29] Owing to these two distinct finalities, there must be two reviews, reflecting the simultaneous existence of *La Vie intellectuelle* and *La Vie spirituelle* in the Province of France.[30] The editorial office – a 'loghut, but with a surprisingly generous bay window and a Victorian door' (it became open to the elements in the course of the 1970s and gradually disintegrated), was situated in a minute garden where Fr Conrad's feeling for the natural world could feast nevertheless on a particular tree. 'Spreading its branches over the shack was a fully mature "tree of heaven" whose economy of leaves, and red glowing buds in the spring' inspired the activity beneath. (As a very old man, he would find in trees moved by the Cambridge winds 'angels talking', perhaps an unconscious echo of Rilke's First *Duino Elegy*.)

He had thought for a while that, in so academic and graciously conventual a setting as Blackfriars, the editor of the journal of the same name might be in danger of hitting out at phantom problems. Might it not be preferable to go with a lay-brother (for the sake of the common life) and inhabit a 'house of hospitality', on the model of those founded by Dorothy Day in the United States, serving 'down-and-outs' at the poorer end of the Haverstock Hill parish? Though his superiors dismissed the idea as thoroughly impractical, his admiration for Dorothy Day would take shape eventually in a brief biography.[31] Befriended by Belloc and Maritain she had embraced a voluntary poverty worthy of the earliest Franciscans – giving up not only material possessions, but mental and spiritual comforts, not least privacy. The combination of elements in her programme – houses of hospitality for the urban poor, rural communes where new forms of social coexistence could be created on the basis of the Land and the Gospel, the intellectual apostolate of her newspapers – appealed strongly to him. He treasured her saying: 'When we begin to take the lowest place, to wash the feet of others, to love our brothers with that burning love, that passion, which led to the Cross, then we can truly say, "Now I have begun".' But it was not to be.

Fr Conrad's predecessor as editor of *Blackfriars*, Fr Hilary Carpenter, had attempted to fold up the journal during the war, thinking, wrongly, that in wartime people would have more things to do than read. It was in that crisis that the Provincial, Fr Bernard Delany, had placed Fr Conrad at the helm. Fr Hilary's election as Fr Bernard's successor was not, in this perspective, propitious, and in 1949 Fr Conrad was replaced as editor by Fr Illtud Evans. In 1952, concerned that, unlike its French model, Editions du Cerf, Blackfriars Publications was hardly a raker in of gold, Fr Hilary disposed of it, and in the following year appointed Fr Conrad Warden of Spode

House – the conference centre created out of the old Spode House, Armitage Park, at Hawkesyard. Though the move from Oxford was surprising, even controversial, he saw sense in it: the task of organising a Dominican Conference Centre was an extension of his editorial work on *Life of the Spirit*, many of whose contributors would now become his speakers.[32] At a deeper level, two unlike poles of spiritual attraction had mysteriously met. If the pull towards the London poor, the 'house of hospitality', had represented 'mucking in', he had felt no less strongly the drawing power of certain more withdrawn communities (George Scott Moncrieff's island experiment on Oronsay, or the [Anglican] Community of the Glorious Ascension at Clere Priory, in Somerset) where the aim was to create a holy place to which the outside world might be drawn – 'mucking out'. The Hawkesyard of Vincent McNabb and Austin Barker had been a form of 'mucking out', what with its crystalline Thomism and liturgical purism, and its farm, vegetable gardens, orchards and woodlands, so suited to the exponents of 'Back to the Land'. But it was hardly part of the Dominican vocation to be smallholders rooted in the soil: and those whom the cap fitted could not presume on a lifelong assignation to the place. Spode House, providentially, would combine mucking in with mucking out: one would find there Everyman and his wife, yet one would find them away from it all.[33]

Until his retirement in 1981, which astonished him ('I never thought I would be retired'), the wardenship of Spode was his remaining life work. He combined the role of self-effacing patron to an astonishing variety of groups and persons, with a pastoral solicitude, and continuing delight in beauty in all its forms – notably in line and the printed page (an inheritance from Gill and his father), in script (an inheritance from the Ditchling calligrapher Edward Johnston[34] and in the tones of colour and music (an inheritance from his artist mother). The best portrait of Spode as he made it was provided in his *Tablet* obituary by the critic and social commentator Brian Wicker. Recording Spode House's contrast with the newer, more 'flash', conference centres founded after it, Wicker describes it as at once 'spartan, workmanlike, poor' and a place of huge creativity, theological, political, aesthetic, practical. Linking this to Fr Conrad's Ditchling beginnings he writes:

> From the Ditchling years he inherited a recognition of the power of art ... to bring order out of chaos: and especially the chaos of a world riven by past wars and rumours of wars to come. For Conrad war was both a palpable outward fact – the inevitable product of what Ditchling would call 'industrial capitalism' – and an inner

chaos for which the only remedy was a return to 'the tranquility of order' (to use Augustine's phrase, much alluded to at Ditchling), in the form of communal work and community prayer shaped by the traditional offices of a Dominican discipline ... Conrad brought this combination of insights with him to Spode House, and made them come alive, not so much in carved blocks of stone or finely printed books but among living human beings. He was an artist in people.[35]

Retired to Cambridge, he successfully overcame a cancer and continued to practice this 'artistry' in the setting of a 'mixed' community of Dominicans and lay people, mostly graduate students of the university.

Leaving home at 73 indicates that one has entered the period of one's last hours ... For a family man it would be most fitting to die at home surrounded and supported by the family. But for the Dominican who has cut himself off by vow from an earthly home, it is right that he should die away from home. In a very small way he has to try to emulate the Lord who was crucified outside the camp – if Jerusalem was his rightful home he died outside that home. So for me it is necessary to make the most of this opportunity and to be grateful for it, not to grumble or wish I was back home.[36]

His preaching, like that of the apostle John according to Polycarp of Smyrna, became largely reduced to a repetition of the words, 'God is love', and in this returning of all things – humanity, and living nature – to their source certain distinctions important to Catholic theology were occasionally overlooked – unless that is, the formidable figure of Professor Elizabeth Anscombe, who was devoted to him, hove into view before his homily was finished. But he could have replied in some words of Newman, written in 1850, which were found in his office-book after his death:

Time clears up all errors: the untruth of today is driven out by the contrary untruth of tomorrow, and the many-coloured impressions of particular minds are all eventually absorbed by the consistent light of truth.

The roots of religion

Gillesque echoes abound in Fr Conrad's *Riches Despised*, its subtitle framed around a 'dead' metaphor which here must be allowed its life:

'A Study of the *Roots* of Religion'.[37] Its basic theme is the relation between nature and grace: one feature of Gill's personal preoccupations (and the wider problematic of Ditchling) which also had *droit de cité* in the official commonwealth of Catholic theology in the period. There Fr Conrad, in his role as an editor with Blackfriars Publications and *Life of the Spirit*, as well as host to a variety of conferences at Spode House, could claim an expertise which Gill lacked.

Starting from the Thomist adage that grace perfects nature, rather than destroying it, Fr Conrad sets out the primary theme of his book in the form of a conundrum. On the one hand, numerous saints have thought it necessary to 'ape the angels and to fly above nature altogether in order to be true to the invitation of Christ to be perfect', and one can hardly ignore them. How could a theology of engraced nature not 'take into account the great living exponents of the life of grace'? On the other hand, the most resolutely anti-Manichaean of authors, insistent as these are that 'natural inclinations are good, God-given faculties and instincts that must not be denied' (here the shade of Gill rises before us) fail thereby to acknowledge the 'weakness and incapacities of nature'. Translated into a moral programme, such humanists seek 'a balance and poise that is not weighted by the *pondus* [Augustine's term for the influence of the will] of the supernatural love of God'.

In coming to grips with his problem Fr Conrad proceeds, in approved scholastic fashion, by the defining of terms. 'Nature' has an analogically related variety of references, but he treats as primary its meaning as something's 'intrinsic principle of movement'. The question then arises, What is the movement that is proper to *man*? In a phenomenological description of that movement, every writer or speaker gives away what to him or her counts for most in (natural) human living; their implicit anthropology. Fr Conrad's version has the vigour of Gill.

> The nature of man is the *principium*, the *archê*, the source of that great congeries of movements that together are proper to man, the movement towards his own complete weal of health which includes the activity of eating and drinking, and in some way the fulfilment of the desire and power to generate, the desire to see beautiful things and to be nimble and strong.

These movements have their source in a nature which is 'at once both flesh and spirit, animal and rational'. And if, then, Fr Conrad treats nature as a simplicity at the origin of a complexity, much the same could be said of his notion of grace. Pointing out that by a happy fluke of linguistic history, the word for grace in New Testament Greek –

charis – sounds much like the English verbal noun 'caress', he proposes to treat as the 'special divine love' whereby God draws rational creatures beyond their natural condition so as to share in his own goodness: there being but 'one grace flowing out into a variety of divinely assisted activities'. Thus whereas in the post-Augustinian theology of the Latin West, the simple *charis* of the gospels had 'grown up into the rather sophisticated mother of a whole brood of graces' (the numerous sub-divisions of the subject in scholastic thought), Fr Conrad emphasised that such complexity belongs not to God but to human nature and the human condition, where different 'potencies' need correspondingly different manners of perfecting.[38] By contrast, nothing could be basically simpler than grace itself. 'Grace is fundamentally the touch of God's triune, personal love upon a human person, and holiness is the full response of that person who can thus give love for love.'[39] Not that he intends to espouse the kind of personalism which, in a flurry of Franciscanism, would deny the primarily *intellectual* character of the vision of God which is such a hall-mark of the Dominican and Thomist traditions. Though the capacity for the divine vision is not something man himself can activate in any way, it is none the less proper to him; he can be 'raised by God to the order of things where universal truth is a concrete reality'.

Unfortunately, however, the actual human situation is not one where our nature is incapacitated by, simply, the lack of active power to reach its divine goal. Rather has it been 'deflected towards another goal altogether'. In an image beloved of the prophets of Israel (but here given a new severity):

> This is no perfectly malleable clay from which the potter may simply draw forth what shapes he will. The clay is full of lumps that resist the action of the loving hands of the divine potter. The clay must be softened, the lumps ground and crushed to non-existence.

Here 'moulding' is no longer simply the gentle perfecting of an integrated nature but the hard pummelling of a disintegrated one.

But there is more to add. For the grace of God works in a way both delicately attuned to *individual* human beings – it is 'not a sort of universal medicine which cures every man in the street irrespective of his "case history"', and ordered to the deeper incorporation of such individuals into the race as a whole, and, beyond the race, the cosmos.

> The soul of the individual man is the proper subject of grace, and it works through his infinite potentialities of mind and will; but the

individual man is not an isolated point, some choice gem selected by God and removed from the crown of glory in which it is set. Man is perfected by God in so far as man lives and moves in God's universe.

The potential for 'super-perfection' is in fact inseparable from man's role as the 'sinful and disintegrated centre' of a network of creatures. It is only in this cosmic setting, then, that the grace of God goes out to man, heals him and makes him 'lovable and a friend'. What this means for the proper setting of human life, two subsequent chapters – on 'The Peasant Religion' and 'The Industrial Man' – will explore.

Meanwhile Fr Conrad can move to a provisional resolution of his original dilemma. So exigent are the demands made by *gratia sanans* – healing grace – on fallen nature that the latter may be said metaphorically to 'die' or 'be slain'. But the sense of the metaphor is that, in this situation, our powers are painfully detached (though not 'totally separated') from the immediate goals on which they are set. They have become fixed on their own objects *without respect to the final object of all human nature*. Hence: asceticism, mortification, the cross every day. But the eventual outcome (and abiding aim) of this detachment is precisely the 'safeguarding and perfecting of each human power cleansed by grace in such a manner as to be able to function in supernatural life'. By the discipline of the cross the Christian is thus led to a condition which superficially resembles the self-control of the pagan ideal, but is in fact the supernatural condition of being grace-controlled, and therefore, 'God-controlled'.[40]

How, then, does Fr Conrad see that total environing context for human living which is congruent with our nature? In a powerful anticipation of present-day 'theological ecology' he maintains that

> the religion established by Jesus Christ when he founded his Church is a religion with its roots in nature, a religion which fulfils all the wholesome aspirations of the nature of man, not merely as an individual unit, but as a member of the wider concourse of natures we have called 'Mother Nature'.

And putting the point in a deliberately provocative way, he calls Christianity 'a peasant religion offered to the natural man who knows no peasantry'. In a later generation the Cambridge anthropologist Ernest Gellner would indeed predict a bleak future for Catholicism on the world scene precisely because, as a religion tied by many bonds to a pre-industrial world it can hardly adapt (unlike, say, Islam) to a post-industrial successor without losing its soul.[41] But Fr Conrad makes it clear that he is not defining the 'peasant' *over against* the man of high culture, typically the philosopher. His culture is not an alternative to such others; rather is it the 'hidden foundation' of those built upon it. Nevertheless, his peasant is a man of the land (in the spirit of McNabb) and a manual maker (in the spirit of Gill). He is 'the one who tills the soil or works creatively with his hands and finds his wisdom in what he does'. However, the key to Fr Conrad's concept of the peasant lies in his explanation of how such wisdom is possible: what the peasant (so defined) carries out is 'a human activity conjoined with the activity of other natures around'. King David; Peter the fisherman; 'Piers the Plowman' of Langland's mediaeval poem: these figures can be culture-heroes of Judaeo-Christianity because of their relation, then, with 'other natures around'. Enjoying a significant relation with the wider concourse of being is a necessary (though not of course a sufficient) condition for being a type of the Christian man. Christianity pre-supposes Judaism, the one revealed religion hitherto, and, as Fr Conrad shows in his exploration of Jewish life and worship from the Hebrew Bible, Judaism presupposed – purified and reordered, it is true – a deposit of the pagan in its turn.

> All religions before Christianity, even the non-revealed religions of the pagan, were characterised by their sense of the elements into which their own lives were woven. Secondly, they derived from their contact with the world of nature around them a profound sense of dependence upon the hidden divine powers. This was expressed in ways consonant with their natures, and in at least one case [the Jewish] sanctioned and purified by the Creator himself. We must keep in the front of our minds that a supernatural religion must also be a natural religion.[42]

Whence Fr Conrad's Ditchlingesque problem: how can a natural – that is, a 'peasant' religion survive within supernatural religion in a non-peasant age? For Christ 'fulfilled nature and perfected her worship in an order that was above her, but not beyond her'. The language of his parables and indeed of his wider gospel is couched in 'peasant symbolism', a 'language which strikes at once into the heart of a man in touch with the constant movements of "the Creature" as St Paul calls the whole creation'. His atoning sacrifice, his sacraments – all are given in the same mode, one which implies that Christ 'brings salvation to men as a part of the universe, and not as wholly distinct from it'. None of this signifies that Christian salvation must pass by the 'urbane and civilised', a notion Fr Conrad stigmatises as 'a word from hell'. Rather does civilised man himself – if he is *truly* civilised – preserve his natural roots, growing from the soil like the corn. The Word Incarnate both reclaimed man for the natural order,

and regenerated the human being thus once again en-wombed ... And
so in Fr Conrad's soteriology, the perfecting and the transcending of
the natural order bear equal weight: traditional Christianity was at
once entirely natural, in that its pivotal festivals of Christmas, Easter
and Pentecost, made winter, spring and summer (in a daring phrase)
'part of the flesh of the Word'; and entirely supernatural, for

> this was no mere natural religion [but one which] gathers all into
> the point of time when the Precious Blood was shed. This is the
> supernatural religion which, from within the intimate, eternal life
> of the Godhead, is utterly and instantaneously fulfilled.

It nevertheless remains the case that, to appreciate the conceptual and
imagistic content of the faith today, one would fare better in, say
Nigeria. Fr Conrad was, however, well aware that not everyone
would agree when he wrote of modern industrialised man as 'not so
much a materialist, for he shows no respect for the material universe,
but rather impious in the true sense of the word, having turned away
from the Father with a sweeping act of impiety.' To him, this was no
'reactionary rhetoric' but a straightforward statement of the place of
the human being (or lack of it) in the cosmos. The person who ceases
to venerate the earth (the 'cultivation' of which implied a cultus,
reverence for our mother), who is ignorant that animals are given man
for 'his shepherding as well as for his sustenance', and whose forms
of nutrition (later called 'fast foods') make the human body 'a kind of
machine that needs fuel', is really a displaced person in the world.

> We do not wish to fulminate stupidly against industrial process, nor
> to try to prove too much in going beyond our thesis. All we are
> showing here is the change of attitude that has taken place in man's
> mind towards the mysterious and elemental things whence he
> derives his life and with which Christ built his supernatural reli-
> gion.

For what has disappeared for the moderns is the previously existing
'common imaginative background' of humanity.

> In theory it might seem a matter of indifference whether the imag-
> ination were formed by natural things like seeds sown and growing
> into plants – lilies – and sparrows flying or falling. Closer investi-
> gation, however, shows that the imagination cannot be altogether
> rationalised and treated as a mere instrument of human thought and
> willing. It is the bridge to the whole universe, with the rhythm of
> the heavenly bodies, the movements of creatures of every descrip-
> tion coming over that bridge into man and so reaching up to God

in this new world of intellect. It is this natural world which provides the sacraments and the sacraments gain entry into man's spirit through this inner faculty where poetry is created and understood.[43]

And Fr Conrad concludes, apparently hopelessly, that this divorce between natural life and ritual life renders impossible 'any truly Christian art and culture'. So too has the ritual life become separated off from the mystical life whose own process of growth – through purgation, illumination, and union, seems accordingly quite unreal.

In point of fact, he has not abandoned the struggle, but before suggesting a way forward to its triumphant resolution he considers a pseudo-solution: the changing, not of the 'mechanical life of man' but the sacramental life of the Church – altering her symbols to correspond to the mechanised imagination.

> The priest-worker sheds his symbolic and sacramental garb and wearing the same dungarees as his fellows workers so as not to provide any sense of strangeness and to avoid a shock to the imagination, he brings religion into the factory. The kitchen table in the tenement, now the centre of the workers' human life, becomes the place for the Eucharist celebration.

But this is to deny the objectivity of worship, precisely because it ignores the natural needs of humankind. Only by living in wayward contradiction of emotional and imaginative nature could one change the symbols and ways of worship at will. 'Only the alternative course of action remains: We must change industrial man; change the whole temper and tempo of his social order, in order that he may be able to approach God along the way made for his feet to tread.' But how can one do this? One possibility is to let the present (disastrous) course of things run to its natural term, trusting to the ensuing *débâcle* to bring people to their senses. Yet this would be to ignore the demands of 'fraternal correction' of one's contemporaries – and thus the call of charity. Fr Conrad recognises none the less 'a profound truth in the perception that only by suffering and disaster will the evil be righted'. It was the cross that healed mankind's wounds, restoring sanity to the world; it can only be by sacrifice – the cross of Christians – that the same is done for modern culture.

In fact, however, the 'solution' Fr Conrad would tentatively press upon his readers is not so Jeremianic. Rather does it involve the simultaneous pursuit of two complementary strategies. In the first place, the answer he offers is intellectual: a change of view. The perspective he seeks to commend is that of a renewed *Christian cosmology*. This means, first and foremost, rediscovering the world as a *uni-verse* in the etymologically original and philosophically pregnant sense of that word. 'God made the *uni*-verse: that is, he made all things to turn round, to ad-vert or re-vert to the one point or end, which is himself.' Empirical science, apparently unable to speak of any other 'clear centre', effectively abandons the concept of a universe altogether. But this foundational cosmological principle is full of implications for the co-relations of things within the world.

> All things are for God, and therefore they are all subordinated to that one end and among each other they find relative subordinations which co-ordinate and make for an interlocking of all activity and all being within this oneness, the unity of purpose.

Man, however, is not only a part of this complex cosmic rhythm where 'only the principle of self-movement ... provides a clue to the distinction between one living substance and another'. He is also a microcosm of the universe, since four sub-natures cohere within his humanity:

> sheer inanimate matter (one with the rocks and the mountains and the hard beds of the deep sea), the nature of the first living thing (the tree of life), the nature of the things that move in the sea and creep over the face of the earth; the nature, finally, of the noblest creature who can distinguish virtue and follow it, who can desire God and love him.[44]

The privileged status of cosmic microcosm does not, however, render humankind independent of the rest of the universe, but rather makes man at large and individual men and women the more thoroughly dependent – because the most intricately connected to all the realms of being. So man is dependent on subhuman nature, on his fellows (including his ancestors, which dependency moulds his thoughts, dreams and imagery) and on the heavenly host of angels and saints.

All of this should find expression in three kinds of life-experience by individual human beings. First, they should be conscious of the level of nature, of the 'world-wide rhythm of beginning, growth and fulfilment in union with the animals, the plants and the earth itself'. Secondly, that rhythm should be appropriated and turned to the centre of the cosmos, God, in a liturgical and ritual existence. The Christian sacraments are but a more perfect, because supernatural, expression of the same rhythm; from out of which fusing of nature and supernature flowed forth the 'great stream of Christian art, musical, sculptural, pictorial, architectural'.

The Christian ritual was not simply imposed on a Europe converted from paganism; the peasants remained as dependent as ever upon those 'gods of nature', the sun and the moon, the rain and the drying wind, and the Church showed that the wind was the breath of God, the sun shone from his face, and the mother of God stood in the crescent moon.

And then thirdly, there is the level of the spiritual life, emerging as this does from the ritual, as the level of rite has come from the depths of nature herself. Although the 'Presence' or the 'Mystery' is not confined to specifically Christian faith and worship – 'every bush ... is in fact burning and not consumed by the Presence which is closer to it than it is to itself', the natural disposition towards faith and worship (founded ultimately on the ontological relation of finite being to Being itself) produces something of a cacophony when expressed outside of the historic revelation. In particular, it is only with the Incarnation that man can be enveloped in the Mystery of the Triune God. And the characteristic effect of this 'enveloping' is a more *interior* cultus. 'The Word made flesh brings the Presence down into the life of every man with the result that his reverence and worship is more interior than before and more interlocked with his faith.' Hence the great importance of Christian mysticism – which is not an optional extra for certain preternaturally gifted souls, but a testimony to the central effect of the Incarnation itself.

Before exploring Fr Conrad's writings on the mystical, however, we must look at the second strategy he proposes in *Riches Despised* for the return of 'industrial' man to something approximating at least his 'peasant' condition.

The second string to Fr Conrad's bow is practical: and it is made possible by the fact that there remain certain regions of present human living where, though industrialised, human nature still works 'in some deep harmony with all other natures, moving towards the one goal of God's glory'. People must eat: and what and how they eat is of the highest consequence for preserving a link with the natural foundations of worship. Good natural food, eaten with care, ceremoniously, in the social – or, better still, the family – setting: this is an excellent preparation for the Holy Eucharist. Again, the family itself preserves the 'closest and most precious ties with the natural order'. The recovery of breast feeding, and an emphasis on the mother's handling and fondling of the infant, in post-natal practice give grounds for hope. For when the rest of nature is treated as a mere utility, the desecration of the generative instinct is only to be expected. Artificial contraception enters in order to isolate the presence of sexuality from the normal rhythms of birth and life. Or, in a lapidary formulation, 'Birth is in fact prevented while sex is used'. Already at Fr Conrad's time of writing, a rising divorce rate was giving cause for alarm, and here he counselled not an intensified stress on the duties entailed in contractual obligation so much as a fresh look at the attractions of permanent monogamy in the light of the 'motherhood' of nature.

> Under her mantle husband and wife are united in life and in family rearing, and in that occupation the two are kept in touch with a deep-seated instinct which is part of the movement and rhythm of the world.

Then again there is the possibility of smaller scale community or industrial organisation. On a vast scale of human co-existence or work certain jobs are inhuman but in a small community they acquire a certain nobility, whereby people can become proud of menial tasks. The small factory or business can retain the ethos of properly human labour where all who work are treated as persons (an anticipation of Pope John Paul II's personalist theology of work in the encyclical *Laborem exercens*). 'Church work' – the building and furnishing of churches, and the creation of objects for the liturgy – should act as a model, with, if possible, the use of local talent from the artisanal professions and the use of such authentic materials as will delight. Play too must be participatory, not spectatorial merely – which is why Fr Conrad singles out the mime (in whose making his father had excelled) as the ideal of recreation.

No doubt all of these practical proposals were part and parcel of Ditchling life; Fr Conrad is, in fact, resuming the Ditchling ethos for a wider audience. Referring to such community experiments in English Catholicism he in effect writes their swan-song, albeit with discretion.

> We will not here go into the reasons why so many of these attempts have failed. The main reason lies within the very nature of the effort which is anti-social in the sense that such community life necessarily sets itself up against the whole of the tendencies of the industrial society around it. So the effort to live out the ideal produces a very self-conscious set of men and women, and a highly developed self-consciousness necessarily breeds individualism if not eccentricities which militate against the nature of community life.[45]

Lastly, Fr Conrad had a word in season for 'monastic' communities – by which he meant coenobitic institutes of religious leading the ascetic life, whether as monks in the canonical sense, friars, clerks regular or the female analogues of each of these. Pleading for a greater integration of the individual-ascetic and the corporate-liturgical dimensions of religious life, he excoriated anticosmic, illuminist and excessively élitist attitudes not unknown (in his period) in connection with the former, as well as too sharp a disaggregation of worship from the rhythm of work in the latter. (Here he expressed a marked distaste for the Dominican notion of lectorial 'privileges' of choir exemption.) Above all, he thought, what was needed was a serious return to the practice of *lectio divina*: the 'contemplative study of the divine word in the Scriptures and the Fathers' – something which would bring in its train a happy *rallentando*, or slowing of pace, in religious life at large.

A theology of mysticism

In Fr Conrad's spirituality, then, the mystical is contextualised within a wider pattern, both cosmological (created) and soteriological (gracious).

> The foot should be always resting on a realisation of good, from the natural good of the pagan philosophers and mystics, upon the good of the liturgy, the doctrine of the Church, the Scriptures up and up to the heights where 'there is a death in fruition, and a melting and dying into the Essential Nudity, where all the divine names and all conditions and all the living images which are reflected in the mirror of divine truth lapse in the Onefold and Ineffable, in waylessness and without reason.'[46]

The 'mystic heights' represent the culmination of the 'normal way of sanctity'; just as all are called to be saints, so likewise everyone in the Church is invited to ascend there. And yet Fr Conrad quite reasonably hesitates to equate holiness with the mystical. Rather should we say that 'the man who is ... raised to the closest union with God is given the elements or ingredients of the mystic life' – but *not* the 'right to be called a mystic'. For the very word 'mystical', connoting as it does some hidden (*mystikos*) truth, is inseparably linked to the idea of the experience of what is normally concealed. As he concludes:

> it would seem ... that the element of experimental knowledge plays the *formal* part in mysticism, while the love of God, which is the formal element in holiness, is the *material*, the two together completing the essential nature of mysticism. This would account

for the fact of there being many saints who are not mystics, and many mystics who are perhaps only at the beginning of sanctity.[47]

Not the experience of union with God but *the union itself* is the 'substance of the true Christian life'. Fr Conrad points out the notorious difficulty of determining whether some putative mystical experience is authentic: and while approving, so far as they go, the tests St John of the Cross suggests for distinguishing true from false in matters of visions or the 'sense of union or peace with God and man', tends to think that the only secure criteria are *a posteriori*. 'Events alone will show. The lasting and ultimate effects of these experiences will reveal whether they were truly what Catholics call "mystical experiences".' For other categories – those of the 'hysterical' or 'a counterfeit thrown up by the subconscious' are possible locations for their filing. The 'effects' Fr Conrad looked for include humility, sympathy, generosity, a diminishment in self-concern. Mystical experience is a help to the full Christian life, 'one of God's most heartening gifts [but] ... not God himself'. Exceptional graces prepare the Christian for adversity, and propel him or her into a fuller life among the people of God. In other words, the experience of union is ordered to deeper union – and 'it is this divine touch in the substance of the soul, beyond feeling and in some ways beyond concepts, which we are maintaining to be of necessity for attaining the final supernatural goal of human existence.' And if, following the classic study of 'Western Mysticism' by abbot Cuthbert Butler of Downside, Fr Conrad takes the Latin doctors Augustine and Gregory as his guides, adding thereto John of the Cross, his chief aim is to reinstate what he takes to be the authentically biblical, incarnational, sacramental and caritative mysticism of St Thomas.[48] It was because these dimensions are less clear in Sanjuanist teaching (at any rate, if one prescinds from the lyrical poetry of John of the Cross), that, so Fr Conrad felt, Garrigou-Lagrange had not won as many converts as he might to his admirable thesis that all are called to the heights of contemplative perfection. There the life of faith reaches its full term in mature growth, unity, and integration.

But to work out further his ideas on asceticism and contemplative prayer, Fr Conrad turned to entirely native sources, the spiritual writers of the later middle ages in England – perhaps influenced here by Bede Jarrett, since Julian of Norwich, Richard Rolle and the unknown author of *The Cloud of Unknowing* had been among Fr Bede's preferred sacred texts, 'primary sources for much that he taught and wrote'.[49]

The English Religious Heritage – a study of the pre-Reformation spiritual writers in England – was originally published as a series of essays in Fr Conrad's 'own' journal, *Life of the Spirit*. But, as the book's preface tells us, those articles were from the start conceived and worked out as a unitary whole. The book's aim is to help people take the English mystics as spiritual guides. 'They may be mystics but they're certainly English' captures, if cavalierly, the tone of Fr Conrad's introduction. Remarking the easy victory of Spanish and French spiritualities in post-Reformation English Catholic sensibility, Fr Conrad writes:

> St Teresa, St John of the Cross, St Francis de Sales and the vast body of spiritual writers thrown together by the French spiritual controversies, Jansenism and Quietism – these have soaked into English writing which deals with the life of the spirit, while the healthy, robust if a little easy-going spiritual writings of Rolle, Mother Julian, Hilton and the *Cloud* have been left to the academic scholars of middle English and to the rising tide of dabblers in 'mysticism'.[50]

In other words, two categories of reader with faulty perceptions are in view. English Catholics have ignored their 'ancient heritage'. Non-Catholic readers, avid for esoteric religion, have ignored the 'ascetic form and value' of the lives of those who wrote this corpus of texts. It is as an exercise, then, both of ecclesial recuperation and of historical realism, that *The English Religious Heritage* will proceed.

Fr Conrad's first task is to ascertain the *general place* in Catholic literature occupied by the body of texts with which he is concerned – above all, as we shall see, five: the *Ancren Riwle*, Richard Rolle's *Incendium amoris*; the *Cloud of Unknowing*; Julian of Norwich's *Revelations of Divine Love*; Walter Hilton's *Scale of Perfection*. Why his book is entitled 'The English *Religious* – and not *Mystical* – Heritage' soon becomes apparent, for he defines these works in the classifying categories of early modern Latin theology as belonging principally to ascetical – rather than mystical – theological reflection. We must at once note, however, that his distinction of these terms is not dichotomous but nuanced. He rejects the notion of a chasm fixed between them, whereby ascetic theology describes the ordinary Christian life, mystical theology an abnormal life-experience based on a select gift of graces of 'infused contemplation' and a special sense of the divine presence.[51] As a good disciple of Père Réginald Garrigou-Lagrange, O.P., he is clear that contemplation lies *within* the normal progress of the Christian in his or her ascent to God. The distinction between ascetical and mystical is, for him, primarily one of earlier and later in the development of a generous Christian existence; or, to put it another way, it is a distinction between the active attempt to make room for God by self-discipline, and detachment, on the one hand, and, on the other, the passive reception of God's disciplining the soul so as to unite it finally to himself – the position we have already encountered in Fr Sebastian (Chapter 6). However, Fr Conrad insists that the ascetical never ceases to be relevant to the mystical, while the mystical has a pre-existence in the ascetical.[52] In my end is my beginning.

> Ascetical theology should set forth the work of detachment, of cutting away sinful or dangerous ties that prevent a Christian's taking wing and rising to full union with God. This is a labour of great severity; it is specially the lot of the beginner, but in different ways it follows the rising spirit of the Christian in his highest ascents to the very threshold of glory where the Cross no longer tortures. Mysticism is only the converse side of the Christian life of asceticism; beginning meagrely in the life of the first conversion it flourishes in full bloom in the unitive way.[53]

How does he commend to his readers the value of studying the pre-Reformation English religious masters – this primarily ascetic but by no means wholly non-mystical corpus of texts? In two ways. First, these writers are chiefly concerned with the objective form of holiness, rather than the subjective study of experiential states of the soul in its journey to God. Secondly, they fulfil a great desideratum for the formation of a Catholic culture in England. It can be stated in a dictum: 'Something more native to the country is required'.[54]

The psychologico-analytical approach to the spiritual life, dominant when the 'specialisms' of ascetical and mystical theology came to be in the Baroque period, is fraught with danger, so Fr Conrad thought, in an age of embarrassed and complex subjectivism like his own.

In the pre-Renaissance centuries, spiritual teachers focused on 'objective beatitude' ('God is all that matters'), whereas their successors concentrated on 'subjective beatitude' ('My possession of God is all that matters to me'). The English mystics – if one may, despite Fr Conrad's strictures, use that conveniently succinct denomination – belong firmly with an objective and corporate approach to the Christian life. However, here a *caveat* must be entered. Fr Conrad is not really opposed to the introspective or phenomenological map-making of the spiritual life in post-Reformation Catholicism. St Thomas, with behind him St Gregory and Denys the Areopagite, already has a skeletal 'periodisation' of spiritual growth. Garrigou-Lagrange, whose doctrine of Christian perfection was enormously influential among Dominicans in the years 1930 to 1960, had attempted a synthesis of the Carmelite analysts of the spiritual life in Spain's *siglo d'oro* with the wider principles of St Thomas, and Fr Conrad speaks respectfully of the result. 'In the direction of people who aspire to holiness such work is essential; those who are placed in this high responsibility for others' spiritual welfare may not neglect either the Spaniards' work themselves, nor the commentators.'[55] So what *does* Fr Conrad want? A spiritual theology which will combine the subjective analysis of later tradition with the wholesome objectivity of the earlier. After all, in the patristic fountain-head, with a figure like St Augustine, we see the two work happily in tandem – 'at once a subjective concentration on his own soul in relation to God, and an objective, almost a collective, view of the spiritual life, in regarding all mankind in terms of the Mystical Body led to God by the divine Head'.

And moreover, as if to give yet more urgency to this quest, there is the matter of Englishness. At the present time, Fr Conrad writes, the Roman Catholic religion in England is 'largely foreign', both in outward appearances and in inward methods of spirituality. In recent centuries English Catholicism has been nourished by Continental fare, and while 'this food has been good ... it lacks the local ingredients which long experience has taught the locals they need'. Fr Conrad invites, then, what in the 1990s would be termed a 'local theology' of the spiritual life – but one open to the catholic (universal) experience of the whole Church: 'an indigenous spiritual life growing up from the soil of England these several centuries and thrusting out into the universal spirituality of the Church of God'.

Having declared an interest, Fr Conrad can now set the scene for his five authors. The admixture of (sober) Romans to (fiery) Celts accounts, he thinks, for the peculiar character of the Christianity which emerged in England after the age of the conversion: it was at once undemonstrative yet highly imaginative. The strongly monastic ethos of both the Lindisfarne mission of St Aidan and the Canterbury mission of St Augustine left a lasting imprint. And if the Roman monachism, largely coenobitic, had its natural successor in the black monk and white monk communities of the Middle Ages, the Celtic, mainly eremitical, had a posthumous after-life in the numerous anchorites and anchoresses to be found in or near the parish churches of mediaeval England. The life and culture of monastics build necessarily on the wider foundations of the folk Catholicism of the age, just as the later mediaeval mystics he will be discussing 'took for granted the traditional life of the Church in England'. And so a mass of literature less exalted than, say, the biblical commentaries of St Bede or the treatises of St Aelred on the soul, or on friendship, are relevant to their case. Such rough-and-ready works of pastoral direction as the *Oculus sacerdotis* (1314), the *Regimen animarum* and the *Memoriale presbyterum* (both c. 1340) were rightly concerned with laying foundations for piety in the overcoming of basic forms of sinfulness by the grace of the Word and sacraments, and through appeal to the rules and ordinances of God and the Church. At the same time, an elementary training in the liturgy was offered by such texts as *The Lay Folk's Mass Book* and *The Prymer* – a lay adaptation of the Divine Office.

The fourteenth century – with which, in this book, Fr Conrad has chiefly to do, was not a golden age in Western Europe either for civil society or for Church. The relevant sections of the *Dialogues* of the Dominican mystic and reformer Catherine of Siena, do not make pleasurable reading on that point. And yet in a variety of widely spaced settings, from Tuscany to the Rhineland, an efflorescence of vernacular writing on the spiritual life testifies to the survival of the highest standards of Christian existence. 'In the midst of this desolation and disease rose these sweet flowers of Christian sowing.' The devotional focuses most important to popular feeling in England were the Passion and the Holy Name of Jesus. Though Fr Conrad shows a momentary unease that the fourteenth-century mystical flowering may not have attended sufficiently to the mysteric and sacramental Christ – 'the liturgical, hieratic figure hanging serenely on the Cross, or sitting as High Priest and Judge surrounded by a stately and formal nimbus', he can only applaud the way 'an intense, personal and chivalrous love of our Lord in his human nature led these English people to ... (a) life of union with the One and Triune Divinity'.

Though Fr Conrad admits that all forcing of the texts into categories alien to them would kill their spirit, he nevertheless feels that a comparison of Walter Hilton's *Scale* (itself a primitive attempt at a periodisation of the stages of the spiritual life) and the classical twentieth-century Dominican school schema of Garrigou-Lagrange shows the fundamental validity of the latter for ages not its own, and for authors who are not among its sources. And Garrigou-Lagrange's elaboration of the purgative, illuminative and unitive ways which first found expression as Christian vocabulary in Denys provides him with a ladder of his own on whose rungs he can arrange the texts he is to discuss. Thus, prefacing his five studies with an account of Langland's *Piers Plowman* seen as a call to a first conversion which gives entry to the purgative way, Fr Conrad will take the *Ancrene Riwle*, the earliest of his sources, as dealing with the initial stages of that way – the basic virtues and other dispositions which the soul needs to make progress. The purgative way shades off into the illu-

minative, on Garrigou-Lagrange's account, via the 'passive purification of the senses', and of these higher reaches of the purgative way
Fr Conrad takes Rolle's *Emendatio Vitae* as emblem. The same
author's *Incendium amoris* typifies the illuminative way in its 'ordinary' guise, while *The Book of Margery Kempe* (not a central text in
The English Religious Heritage) illustrates, with its powerful visionary component, the 'extraordinary' form of that way. For the unitive
way, which succeeds the illuminative via the 'passive purification of
the spirit', we have the *pièces de résistance* of this entire literature –
Mother Julian's *Revelations of Divine Love* and the *Cloud of
Unknowing* (as well as the short companion pieces to that text by the
same anonymous writer). A fuller consideration of Hilton's *Scale of
Perfection* rounds off the whole work by enabling Fr Conrad to take
an overview of the journey thus set forth.

Fr Conrad considers *Langland* the best gateway to the English
mystics, not only because his call to a good life, and explanation of
salvation for the common man, set out the ordinary Christianity the
spiritual writers of the fourteenth century presupposed. More than
this, a close examination of the poem revealed to Fr Conrad that it
constitutes a practical application of the theologian's theory of a
movement from *incipientes* to *proficientes*, and *proficientes* to
perfecti. For three types of life are shown: Do Well, Do Better, and
Do Best.[56] Yet in all three grades of the Christian life, Langland's
main concern is with *action* – the conversion of England to saving
good by way of social justice based on charity. (Fr Conrad does not
hesitate to claim him as a Distributist *avant la lettre*!) Hence, even
when describing the devout life in its perfect form Langland's contribution is best seen as an exploration of what *first* conversion involves.
In his description of the way to Truth, Langland finds room for all the
elements needful in the first stage of spiritual growth: grace and its
fruit, contrition; fuller instruction in the Christian mystery through the
Creed, and its celebration through the sacraments; such evangelical
moral virtues as humility and purity. Especially attractive is the note
on which Fr Conrad brings his account of Langland to a close: the
christological version of the 'three lives'.

> Our Lord began the life of Dowel [Do Well] when he turned water
> into wine, for wine stands for law and a holy life; he taught us to love
> our enemies and he was then known as the Son of Mary. As Dobet
> [Do Better] his life was one of the ministry, healing, comforting; and
> this included the Crucifixion and Resurrection, and he was known as
> the Son of David. As Dobest [Do Best] our Lord gave Piers [St
> Peter] authority to bind and loose and instituted the authority of the

Church by sending the Paraclete. Here he establishes fully the new law of love – one of the themes of the whole vision – where Truth is completely discovered.[57]

Thus first conversion opens the way to love, and love inaugurates contemplation. The simplicities of the elementary Christian life in its ethical and liturgical aspects contain in advance the entire development of the ascetic and mystical ways, since for fallen man the sanctifying grace which enters our existence with justification is a supernatural revivification. 'It is quite literally an event on a standing with the raising of Lazarus – a miracle', for it means the coming to be of divine friendship in one who was before a sinful creature.

Langland had seen that, if society is to work justly there must be justice in the souls of individuals – implying repentance of sin and the giving over to God of what is 'due'. In Passus XV-XVII we have the poet's reaction to the corruption of Christendom. In a vivid sequence marked by the influence of the liturgical offices of Passiontide, Will returns to the Church – as A.V.C. Schmidt has written, not by the way of 'a "notional" assent to academic arguments but [by] a "real" immersion in prayer and a rediscovery of faith through imaginative and affective means'.[58] The fundaments of a spiritual life flowing from first conversion ('the purgative way' in its basic features) are the topic of Fr Conrad's next text, the *Ancrene Riwle*.

A rule for anchoresses (of all people) one might reasonably expect to turn out a repository of the most esoteric spiritual doctrine. Far from it. The *Ancrene Riwle* 'is in effect an ascetical work designed to instruct beginners in their first retirement from the world'.[59] Though mentioning respectfully the view of Vincent McNabb that the author of this rule of life for anchoresses was a Dominican,[60] Fr Conrad preferred the view of H.E. Allen and Professor C.W. Chambers that it antedated – if not by much – the foundation of the Order.[61] Whatever the similarities between the observances of the primitive Dominican Constitutions and those of the *Riwle*, the spiritual culture of the latter belongs with the monastic world of late twelfth-century Latin Christendom at large – being particularly indebted to Augustine, Gregory, Bernard and Aelred, as well as to the prayers of the Roman liturgy. Fr Conrad lauds it for the wise moderation of its ascetic doctrine, for its doctrine that the fulfilment of religious rule lies in love (based on God's love for man), and for the vivid, homely imagery in which its programme of 'purgative' beginnings is expressed.

But if the rule of love is, in the anonymous author's words, the 'lady or mistress [which] all the others serve', he none the less insists that, initially, ascesis must undertake the disciplining of the will by the following of regulations for ordered spiritual living – what Fr Conrad summarises as 'a rugged life', hard, mortified, austere. If the Abbé de Rancé would frown at the *Riwle*'s sanction of a pet cat, he would not have quarrelled with the anchoresses' ideal, which is far from being mediocre. As Fr Conrad repeatedly insists, the *Riwle*'s gentleness must not be mistaken for naturalism.

In the first stage of conversion, vocal prayer – whether liturgical or not – is of the first importance. In the *Riwle* an elementary form of the Liturgy of the House, the Lady Office (*Officium Parvum Beatae Mariae Virginis,* for which Eric Gill had done a superb edition at St Dominic's Press), constitutes the 'scaffolding of prayer holding together all the moments of the waking hours'.[62] The anchoress's day has its culmination at the outset in the early morning celebration of the Mass. She would have communicated only on the great feasts, some fifteen all told, for 'men esteem a thing less dainty when they have it often', as the *Riwle* remarks. Fr Conrad counsels against thinking that, in an age when weekly and indeed daily Communion is encouraged, such a warning is old hat. Though he agrees that the 'beginner' must nourish his life of prayer above all by the divine actions of Eucharist and penance (sacramental confession with absolution), he opposes any depreciation of devotions in the name of liturgical purism. The *Riwle* moves effortlessly from Office to devotion, to the Holy Cross, to the Real Presence, and to the Mother of Christ in the 'Five Joys of our Lady' which bear a close resemblance to the developed Rosary prayer long associated with the Dominican Order. In each case the body is co-involved, through genuflections, inclinations and the telling of beads, and Fr Conrad wholeheartedly approves the *Riwle*'s statement that, in these ways of prayer, the 'bond-servants', our 'natural senses', serve their lady – the spiritual profit of the anchoress's soul. Purists, in shunning such devotions, lose an opportunity to make progress in the early stages of prayer, for in their concern for liturgical externals they have spurned – ironically – the chance to be 'purified and detached by the spirit of the Mass'.

If the devotions in the *Riwle* presage the later mediaeval prayer-forms of, respectively, the Stations of the Cross, the Blessed Sacrament, and the Rosary of the Blessed Virgin, it is on that latter that Fr Conrad allows himself fullest licence:

> Just as the alternative recitation of the psalms, thrown verse by verse from side to side of the choir, like some sacred ball-game, produces a tranquillity of spirit in which prayer can rise to great heights, so our Lady's Psalter with its repetition and rhythmical

progress through the mystery induces a state in the person using the beads in which the mind can hover freely over the Mysteries seeing always more in them.

But the baptism of the senses, like all manifestations of the baptism begun on Jordan, finished on Calvary, is not had without a death. The beginner's life is called 'purgative' because its main feature is the cleansing of personal evil through death to the disordered self's desires. The mortification of seeing, speaking and hearing leads to the opening of the spiritual eyes and ears, while that of touch or feeling, being all-pervasive through the body, must be especially guarded. Love of ease and comfort is a snare on the path to salvation. The creative and restorative hands of Christ were *pierced* hands, comments Fr Conrad, adding (anatomically inaccurately but with theological truth) that 'through those fissures [they] support the [Crucified's] whole body'.

The main aim of the purification of the exterior senses is the gradual elimination of vanity and curiosity of a dissipating kind. Where hearing is concerned, that raises the issue of silence, which is not only a form of mortification but a way to the 'full flowering of the love of God'. In agreement with the ascetic tradition at large, Fr Conrad regards silence as disposing one in a very direct way to contemplation. He also notes the special stress of the *Riwle* which sees it as intimately connected with the theological virtue of hope. The anchoress, like the sparrow of the Psalmist on the housetops, uses her silence and solitude to sharpen her watchfulness, her expectation of God's future grace.

In general, Fr Conrad's commentary on the *Riwle* seeks at one and the same time to expound its content for religious who may be living much the life of its original recipients and to interpret that content more speculatively for a wider Church public. Nor does he regard this as a denaturing of the text. For on the one hand, the *Riwle*'s solitary remains, paradoxically, a social being: she is to let her mind rove over the needy members of Christ's mystical Body; and on the other, there is a metaphysical depth to be gained by every soul where it can communicate uniquely with God as Creator and as Author of grace.

It is for this reason that watching and retirement of some sort are of the essence of the spiritual life; and once the obvious dangers of self-centred introspection have been pointed out, the principle of the anchoress's life may be applied to every Christian really intent upon growing to the stature of grace.[63]

When the soul begins to be generous in responding to God's work

of salvation, he for his part co-operates by sending her not consola-
tions but temptations and trials. Their point is to show the soul her
weaknesses and the virtues she needs to develop, and because they call
forth – or at least call for – strenuous *activity* on the part of the will
these negatives experiences are not yet what St John of the Cross,
and, after him, Fr Conrad's mentor Garrigou-Lagrange, call the first
of the 'dark nights', the dark night of the senses. For the dark nights
of the Sanjuanist schema and terminology are always a matter of the
passive purification of the soul. It is a mark of Fr Conrad's spiritual
realism – as also of his willingness, under the influence of the English
mediaeval writers, to depart from the ascetical and mystical system of
Garrigou-Lagrange, that he treats such trials as illness, persistent
misunderstanding, ill-use by others, depression, bereavement, neglect
by friends, together with the temptations whereby the seven deadly
sins allure us, as in true continuity with the dark nights. The former,
in point of fact, are the latter's normal preliminary. Although such
trials and temptations are dangerous, they are also (or are meant to
be) salutary. And here he cites the *Riwle* itself:

> It is very necessary that an anchoress of holy and highly pious life
> have the falling sickness ... an infirmity of the body, or tempta-
> tion of carnal frailty, by which she seems to herself to fall down
> from her holy and exalted piety. She would otherwise grow
> presumptuous, or have too good an opinion of herself, and so come
> to nothing ... God so wills it, in order that she may be always
> humble; and, with low estimation of herself, fall to the earth, lest
> she become proud.[64]

In speaking both of trials *and* of temptations as encouragements along
the purgative way, neither the *Riwle* nor Fr Conrad intend to make
light of the malice of sin as such. It is sin which these tests are given
us to eradicate. Under vivid images taken from the mediaeval
bestiary, the *Riwle* describes not lust alone – Fr Conrad notes with the
contemporary Anglo-Catholic lay theologian Dorothy Sayers how
frequently in popular writing today 'immorality' denotes lechery only
– but the nefarious zoological garden of the deadly sins at large.[65] If
the Reformers erroneously judged human nature to be entirely
corrupt, the Catholic Christian may fall into the opposite error – a
failure to recognise the 'tight embrace with which they grip human
nature'. Connected as these are with man's primary instincts and
appetites they are ever present, *becoming more subtle as the soul
grows in attachment to God*. The *Riwle* suggests numerous remedies
for sins, yet a sheerly negative war against vice can end up by making
Stoics of us all. Thus Fr Conrad is happy to find its author bidding

the soul rest on the divine mercy as she strives to overcome the evil fruits of (original and actual) sin. The danger of the purgative way is that self-reform may generate a (purely natural, and therefore misleading) ideal of self-perfection. The *Riwle*, by contrast, becomes more and more christological in its doctrine of virtue as it progresses. 'Fly into his wounds ... with his precious Blood ensanguine thy heart': for our virtues are to be, above all, supernatural – flowing to us through the humanity of Christ. And this can only happen if petitionary prayer to the Saviour is at the centre of our purgation, rather than a programme for self-mastery.

As already mentioned, the *Riwle* does not envisage the dark night of the senses in St John of the Cross's understanding of that phrase – when consolation flees, meditation becomes impossible and darkness falls. Yet the text ends with a prediction that the faithful anchoress will desire to become a co-victim with Christ. Whatever she suffers will seem ever more identified with the Christ who experienced the cross for our salvation. The dryness which ends the purgative way in the Carmelite scheme has its equivalent for the *Riwle* in the 'sticks' of wood which the Widow of Zarephath (1 Kings 17, 8–24) gathered for kindling. Here they serve as a symbol both of the life and labours of the anchoress and of the cross of Christ.

> With these two sticks ye ought to kindle the fire of love within your heart. Look often upon them. Think whether ye ought not joyfully to love the King of Glory, who so stretches out his arm toward you, and bows down his head as if to offer you a kiss.[66]

The illuminative way – the beginning of mysticism proper in the sixteenth (and twentieth) century schema which Fr Conrad made his own – is enlightening, then, because of *love*. The transition from the lowly yet essential wisdom of the *Riwle* to the work of the 'father of English mysticism', *Richard Rolle,* comes about in real life only when the Christian disciple begins to know the love of God (his for God, and God's for him) in actual existence, and not mere words, and when from the seat of this love (the cross), he perceives all else – God, the world, the self – in its light.

Rolle was a Yorkshireman who cut short his studies at Oxford to answer a call to eremitism. After a further period of academic immersion, this time at Paris, he resumed the hermit life from which his writings – of which the *Incendium Amoris* is the most important and influential – took their rise. Though posthumously accredited with sanctity (an Office was composed in his honour), Fr Conrad finds in his literary remains the telltale signs of a *proficiens* rather than a *perfectus*. Certainly, there is little record of the purgative way in

Rolle: he consistently refers to himself as 'the sitter', because he found that posture not only helpful for contemplation but also comfortable! His writings are ardent, radiant: they are eloquent of mystical grace, but in an emotional mode. Or as Fr Conrad puts it, comparing his subject with (once again) the yardstick of St John:

> We could not easily class him among the higher ranks of those who have largely experienced the joy of perfect union in the unitive way. However diligently we may apply the interpretation of metaphor and analogy, his constant insistence on the heat of love in his breast as being also a physical thing limits the scope of the love: he cannot have borne the full impact of the *Todo y Nada* of St John of the Cross.[67]

However, Rolle himself speaks of a three-year period from his 'conversion of life' to what he terms the 'opening of the heavenly door'[68] – and we may surely suppose that this interval was filled with the kind of ethical and spiritual effort of which, for a related public, the *Riwle* had spoken. Nor did the felt experience of divine love supervene directly on the outset of the illuminative way,

> so that, the Face being shown, the eyes of the heart might behold and see by what way they might seek my Love and unto him continually desire. The door forsooth yet biding open, nearly a year passed until the time in which the heat of everlasting love was verily felt in my heart.[69]

Moreover, Fr Conrad admits that, in Rolle's later period, when a certain residual arrogance is eased out by an apostolic charity concerned for the spiritual lives of other religious and with the ministry to plague victims which claimed his own life in 1349, he 'was really stabilised in the life of union and ready for its culmination in heaven'. So Rolle's career testifies to the full process of development of Christian perfection; yet for the bulk of his writings Fr Conrad's decision to let him represent the illuminative way is fairly made.

Rolle's entry into contemplation of the divine Face was followed by the special mystical graces which form the *Leitmotiven* of his spiritual writings: essentially, *calor* (warmth), *canor* (song) and *dulcor* (sweetness).[70] These experiences Fr Conrad treats not as necessary accompaniments of the illuminative way, nor even, by some special adaptation to Rolle's temperament, integral features of it in his case; they are, rather, 'utilities'. That is, the fire, music and sweetness Rolle reported were (divinely provided) means of understanding what is *meant* by love and praise in their fullness. After all, he himself insisted that the inner ravishing of the spirit is the only thing that really counts.

In this interpretation, Fr Conrad is anxious not to be regarded as relegating to the level of the secondary whatever is distinctive in one mystic's personal experience. It is, he thinks, characteristic of the working of grace that it becomes more tailored to individuals as the ascetical and mystical way unfolds.

> Grace is a habit which qualifies the soul so that each soul is possessed of it in its own individual nature, just as knowledge of the same subject will have its different emphasis and colouring in different men. And the more powerful the grace the more individual does it become; for two great theologians who have given their minds to the study of the same great dogmas on which they agree, will express themselves in far more different and variegated ways than two seminarians who have barely assimilated the elements of the science from text-books.[71]

Special feelings or comforts in contemplative prayer – like such wider phenomena as visions, auditions, significant dreams or unmistakable 'coincidences' – are not signs of sanctity, but they may be signs of a vocation to sanctity. They are, if authentic, stimuli to a deeper Christian life, encouragement on the journey toward the heights of union. Normally, then, such experiences are transitory – here Rolle's case seems unusual. Fr Conrad accepts Garrigou-Lagrange's suggestion that the role of these extraordinary experiences, confined as it often is to the beginning of the illuminative way, can be compared to the apostolic experience of the resurrection appearances. On Emmaus road the two unnamed disciples had their eyes opened by a tangible manifestation of the risen Lord. It is unlikely that those eyes 'closed' again, that they ceased to think of him or know him.

> They could say, as Richard Rolle echoed so many centuries later, that their hearts had been burning within them in his company. But the inner reality of that burning heart never disappeared though the feeling had gone when he vanished.[72]

The *Form of Living*, one of Rolle's vernacular works, makes clear the intensity of his 'Emmaus experience':

> The sweetness of him who is in this degree is so comforting and lasting in his love, so burning and gladdening that he or she that is in this degree may feel the fire of love burning in their souls ... Then the soul is Jesus-loving, Jesus-thinking, Jesus-desiring, only breathing in the desire for him, winging to him, burning for him,

resting in him. Then the song of praise and love is come.[73]

At the same time, Fr Conrad underscores Rolle's evident belief that receipt of such graces does not place one beyond the power of sin. Under the heading 'Hesitations in the Face of Love' he mentions a number of forms that sin, at this stage, characteristically takes: self-satisfaction, spiritual complacency, unteachableness, envy of others' spiritual progress, and, above all, the continuing events of weakness of character and personal idiosyncracy. Fr Conrad links Rolle's plea for a total self-giving to Christ in this context with the Carmelite concept of the night of the senses, and the idea of 'acquired contemplation' closely connected with it – at any rate by many commentators influenced by the Carmelite school. Although the vocabulary of purification, intrinsic to the purgative way, recurs here, Fr Conrad stresses that the dark night of the senses, unlike post-conversion purgation, is 'first and foremost a new state of love'. It is the tell-tale sign that the initiative in prayer is passing from the human agent to the divine. While not regarding the *term* 'acquired contemplation' as particularly felicitous, Fr Conrad considers that the claim made by the concept is both psychologically plausible and echoed in Rolle's work.

> [For] as a rule a man will not undergo a sudden and complete change-over from human discursive activity to an equally complete passivity to the divine form of contemplation. There is a period in which the soul cannot meditate or occupy itself with its own considerations in prayer, but when the divine infusion is only perceived as a momentary actual grace bestowed at rare intervals.[74]

In this 'space of life between', the heart must be 'all the time maintaining its effort to gaze at the divine face'.

If it is fair to say that, through the Franciscan doctor St Bonaventure, Rolle had undergone the influence of one of Bonaventure's own preferred sources, the twelfth-century canon Richard of St Victor, then we can expect to find in the work of the Yorkshire hermit traces of the distinction between meditation, acquired contemplation and infused contemplation of (much) later times, for Richard speaks of a threefold quality of contemplation: the 'expansion of the mind', *mentis dilatatio*, the 'raising of the mind', *mentis sublevatio*, and the 'transformation of the mind', *mentis alienatio*. Fr Conrad finds confirmation that Rolle indeed experienced the night of the senses, or the difficult transition period to which the awkward phrase 'acquired contemplation' points, in the problems Rolle reports with gaining spiritual profit from the liturgical offices of the Church. The effect of the new gift God is beginning to lavish on

the soul is to disturb temporarily its participation in the public liturgical life of the Church. Given his high sacramental and liturgiological
doctrine, Fr Conrad could hardly regard this as a satisfactory termi-
nal state! In the unitive way, he predicts, the Catholic in Rolle's
position will rediscover the Liturgy at a higher level of significance
and fruitfulness.

But the objection to Rolle's doctrine (and that of developed mystical theology at large) which he considers at greater length concerns
the danger of *illuminism* and *quietism*, In *The Mending of Life* Rolle
asks not only that the uncreated Light of God may enlighten his mind
with 'clearness unmade', but also that kindled with God's savour, he
'may sit and rest, joying in thee, Jesus'. Should we say, as Fr Conrad
certainly intends to say, that not only acquired but also infused
contemplation is a perfectly normal experience for those who are
growing in grace, then do we not throw open the door to self-delusion and false passivity? To this Fr Conrad has various answers – and
from them we see the extent to which his study of the English mystics
is intended, not only as an historical evocation, but also as a spiritual
exhortation: the book is academic and pastoral in one. First, the
Christian who is generous in his or her response to the everyday
demands of the virtues will not fall into these snares. Secondly, there
must be no question of attempting to infer one's own state of soul
from a combination of reading the mystics on the one hand and introspection on the other. Not only do some Christians never reach these
'passive ways of the spirit', but even of those who do, no two are
alike. Here objectivity is all – which means, first, that a figure like
Rolle is to be studied, not copied, and secondly, that the willingness
to be guided by a confessor or director is crucial. Yet when all is said
and done, there is no Christian discipleship without some risk, and if
the heart of the illuminative way is a prayer caused by God rather than
man then the most likely fault of Christians will be a lack of generosity in responding to this new divine initiative rather than a failure of
prudence in misapplying it. The gifts of the Holy Spirit, which come
in power with the beginnings of infused contemplation, teach their
own supernatural prudence.

The economy of the Spirit is never found without some relation to
that of the Son, and Fr Conrad ends his account of Rolle with the
latter's central teaching, love of the personal Word of God. The mere
quenching of earthly lusts is in itself a purely negative activity which,
were it everything, would finish by making neurotics of us all. The
heart was made for desiring. With Rolle,

it is as though all the rivulets of passing human wishes, the craving

for little luxuries and human comforts, all flow into the one great
stream of the burning desire for Christ himself. He is man and he
is God, and he can fulfil all the passions of human nature by transforming them in some way into a part of divine love. So strong can
this stream become as to convey the soul to the very threshold of
death itself in a flood which is the exact contrary to the desire of
self-destruction in suicide.[75]

In turning from Rolle to *the author of 'The Cloud of Unknowing'*,
and to *Mother Julian*, for an exposition of the unitive way, Fr Conrad
is not rejecting the centrality of the theme of love, but asking for it to
be pressed further. Comparing Rolle and St John of the Cross, he
finds in the former a certain otherness and distance, when the soul
speaks of the reciprocal love of man and God in Jesus Christ, a gap
annulled in the final transformation of love which the latter describes.
Rolle was probably the leader of the mystical movement in fourteenth-
century England. The *Cloud* author, and Julian, 'perhaps being more
hidden ... seem to have drawn still closer to the end of all loving'.

If the Lucan forty days of the resurrection appearances is, in
Garrigou-Lagrange's christological typology of the mystical life, the
archetype of the illuminative way, the 'novena' of days between the
Ascension and Pentecost represents for him the Sanjuanist 'night of
the spirit' ushering in the final, unitive stage of transformation
through the Spirit of Love. The diversity of experience and expression by the saints and mystics notwithstanding (and Fr Conrad holds
that this will become more marked, not less, as the mystical way
unfolds), such a night is, he believes, inevitable, since, as one turns
to look at the sun one is naturally made blind from excess, not insufficiency, of light.

The night is therefore no vacuum; it overflows with the reality of
God's presence, the closeness of God banishes all other reality into
a realm of insignificance. That banishment itself purifies the spirit,
leaves it isolated and desolate until it grows accustomed to the
intensity of God's presence, and the cloud which at first seemed
dark and forbidding turns out to be luminous and radiant with the
transforming splendour of Mount Thabor.

Although the identity of the spiritual director who authored *The
Cloud of Unknowing* is itself unknown, it is clear that he was a theo-
logically learned writer. If his ultimate inspiration was Denys'
Mystical Theology, where the divine presence plunges the initiate into
a 'darkness of unknowing', his proximate source appears to have been
Richard of St Victor who provides him with the terms 'cloud of

unknowing', *nubes ignorantiae*, and 'cloud of forgetting', *nubes oblivionis*. There are lateral links also to St Albert, or at any rate the immensely-popular Pseudo-Albertine *De adhaerendo Deo*, and to St Thomas Aquinas, who evidently numbered Richard among the 'new masters'. The *Cloud* author's last work, *The Epistle of Privy Counsel*, confirms, if further proof were desired, that he had enjoyed a full scholastic training, perhaps at Oxford or Cambridge.

However, he is not writing speculative theology for the novice, like Aquinas, but advanced mystical theology for individuals already living in a 'sphere of considerably elevated prayer'. For most readers, then, Fr Conrad warns, what is set forth in these texts is an ideal, not an experience. True, the seventeenth-century English spiritual writer Dom Augustine Baker treats the kind of prayer set forth in *The Cloud* as identical with the prayer of simple regard found in the state of 'acquired' contemplation – rather than a prayer on the heights of union. Fr Conrad adduces reasons for thinking, contrary-wise, that what these texts describe is 'a settled form of the prayer of quiet ... a divinely induced passivity'. At the same time, he does not deny that there are elements in them which can be profitable to people at a less advanced stage of contemplative growth: to those with a naturally contemplative disposition God may sometimes give touches of passive prayer, to encourage them, even before a consistent form of active prayer has been attained. *The Cloud* itself draws attention to the enormous variety found on the way to sanctity, and Fr Conrad picks up this point in a way not easy to square with his commitment to the classificatory structure found in Garrigou-Lagrange.

> The whole question of the normal way to sanctity as including the contemplative life and virtues has to be qualified in view of this constant experience as expressed so simply in *The Cloud*. The general doctrine is traditional and certainly true that action must prepare the way for contemplation and lead into it (as *The Cloud* also explains). But when the soul is in fact approaching the higher development which might be called the first buds of holiness, the nature of this contemplation will vary enormously, partly from the man's own character and the particular type of action and asceticism in which he has been engaged, and partly owing to God's unpredictable will, for his Spirit breathes where he listeth ... One needs only to read the lives of a few saints to realise how variously holiness, and to that extent contemplation, are realised in the concrete.

And with the reactions of devout readers in mind, he continues:

Those who are dismayed by the description of the contemplative heights in such books as *The Cloud of Unknowing* and *The Dark Night of the Soul* should bear this firmly in mind. They will find their share of contemplation by waiting upon the Lord and fulfilling his will as it is revealed from moment to moment with all the generosity they possess. They will not find it by forcing themselves into a mould for which they were never intended by character of Providence. The fact of their dismay is one of the external signs that God has not called them to this type of contemplation.[76]

Yet this recognition of a plurality of vocational types in no way lessens the special regard Fr Conrad has for the mystical teaching of the *Cloud* author. The 'substance of his work' – his essential message – concerns nothing less than the direct 'touch' of God on the soul, causing in it a 'naked intent': what *The Cloud* itself calls 'a naked intent directed unto God for himself'.[77] It is the combination here of immediacy and objectivity ('naked', 'for himself') which arouses Fr Conrad's admiration and awe.

Although the background of apophatic or negative theology in the dialectical metaphysics of pagan Hellenism (as well as in the Sinai experience of 'thick darkness' recounted by the Hebrew Bible in connection with its single greatest figure, Moses) might make the unwary approach *The Cloud of Unknowing* as, first and foremost, a *philosophical* treatise, the presence within it, as an important preamble to its doctrine of divine union, of a particular concept of moral evil as *sin* should alert the reader to its essentially *theological* character. While the accusation of conscience by any specific sin will properly lead the contemplative to go to the Church's well – the sacrament of penance – for washing, what *The Cloud* has in mind, as befits a treatise for those who are long past the merely purgative state of beginners, is a generalised sense of guilt stemming from the tainting of our natural inclinations by original sin. *The Cloud* counsels, for such a one, the covering of the past in a 'thick cloud of forgetting'. The 'ground and root' of sin, however, can only be destroyed, in the last analysis, by what it terms the 'blind stirring of love'. Where for the person already far along the road of contemplative holiness, the sense of sin (even or, better, *especially* in the absence of any obvious continuing sinful habits) can be so all-encompassing that the very substance of the self seems but a 'lump of sin', *The Cloud* author recommends a method for the perfecting of contrition which is, in Fr Conrad's view, peculiarly apt for the stage of acquired contemplation, as the soul prepares herself for God's take-over. Penitent contemplatives should, the text adjures, 'try to look as it were over their shoulders, seeking another thing; the which thing is God, enclosed in a cloud of unknowing'.

As Warden of Spode House, Fr Conrad greatly encouraged the work of the late Mrs Ursula Fleming, who combined an enthusiasm for Meister Eckhart with a ministry of teaching relaxation as a preparation for meditation. And in *The Cloud*'s teaching here Fr Conrad finds

> the theological counterpart of the same truth. If the man who is tempted relaxes not only all his muscles and limbs (which often become taut at times of the attacks of evil) but also his imagination and his mind, and if he lies back, so to speak, completely at his ease in the consciousness of the supporting presence of God, he will find that the evil suggestions depart. He must be conscious of his own nothingness, his own utter helplessness in the face of these evil powers, and conscious too of the supple power of the Spirit who enfolds him.[78]

The radical humility which the *Cloud* author desires goes far beyond, however, simple repentance of personal sins. Without in any way suggesting that the higher stages of the mystical life entail immunity from sin, he supposes it to be the case *de facto* that there deliberate sins are effectively unknown. The perfect 'meekness' which stems from self-humbling brings with it an all-embracing concentration on the goodness and love of God. The soul now enters a cloud with a positive charge in spiritual metereology where, without attention to anything created, it cries in the darkness for God himself. This is not, as some would suspect, the sinister shadow of the ancient Manichees falling again over a world which God himself had pronounced 'very good' and so thoroughly compatible with himself. *The Cloud*'s point is that none of the acts of God – whether in creation *or in redemption* – are God himself, for what is wanted now is that *no* medium should stand between he who is all and the soul which is nothing. For the time being, only 'a naked intent unto God' suffices. As Fr Conrad explains, citing *The Cloud*'s fifth chapter:

> If thoughts be a distraction, the will has the power to gain direct access to God. The mind is always groping as in a glass darkly in its faith, but the will leaps forward into the very depths of God's naked being by charity. 'Therefore I would leave all that thing that I can think, and choose to my love the thing that I cannot think. For why, he may be well loved, but not thought. By love may he be gotten and holden; but by thought never.'

Such self-abandonment, to be content to rest in love at the very source of being – but without light for the understanding, or sweetness in the affections – is for Fr Conrad the essence of infused contemplation.

Method in prayer is now to pray without a method: what at an earlier time would have been a recipe for disaster has now become (after due consultation with those more experienced in the life of prayer) a spiritual necessity. Though the liturgical prayer of the Church in its diversity (and even prolixity) forms the groundwork of all prayer, this is not the time for many words. No more, *The Cloud* explains, caught in a conflagration, would one wish to shout more than 'Fire!' or 'Out!' So now a monosyllabic prayer – 'God!', 'Love!' – alone accords with what God is doing to the soul. In such unitive prayer, the gifts of the Holy Spirit unfold fully: a man's natural faculties are rendered unconditionally docile to God's leading. Fr Conrad finds for this – in the manner of Garrigou-Lagrange's parallels between the apostolic experience and that of Christian contemplatives – a christological archetype: the obedience of Gethsemane ('not as I will but as thou wilt') is transformed on Calvary into utter surrender ('into thy hands I commend my spirit'). He takes this as emblematic of the way in which the higher stages of the spiritual life, so far from leaving the lower behind, reproduce their virtues, intensified, in a new context.

These comments and others are added because of Fr Conrad's painful awareness that the *Cloud of Unknowing* can be read abusively as non-evangelical, 'leading us out of the Gospels back to the detached life of the pagan mystics of all time'. He points out that the *Cloud* author is speaking here of a contemplative strategy in a very special period of prayer; the same author elsewhere sets aside as pseudo-mystics those who would deny that Christ 'is not only porter himself, but also the door; the porter by his Godhead, and the door by his Manhood'.[79] Similarly, there is no transcending of the Church here. *The Cloud* requires acceptance of her authority and use of her healing sacraments as part and parcel of the way of perfection. And in any case the union of love which it describes, though beyond both imagination and reason, still takes place within the act of faith, which requires the constant stimulation of the Word of God in the apostolic community.[80]

No such difficulties of presentation attend the *Revelation of Divine Love* by *Mother Julian*. Though her 'shewings' were imaginative, 'sensible', her theme, which binds them together, belongs firmly with the unitive way. It is a vision of all things in the love of God, which is the reverse of the coin of union in 'unknowing'. 'Love was his meaning ... Hold thee therein and thou shalt learn and know more in the same. But thou shalt never know nor learn therein other thing without end.'[81] By showing the highest cause of the events of the world, Julian provides the antidote, Fr Conrad thought, to the 'lethal pessimism' which 'leads us to wars and to individual human catastrophes of all sorts'.[82]

Julian was an anchoress attached to a church that itself belonged to the Benedictine nunnery of Carrow, on the outskirts of Norwich. Fr Conrad inclined to the view that she was Benedictine-trained but had been exposed to Dominican preaching. On 8 May 1373, at the height of a serious illness, Julian had the first of the visionary experiences which she was later to interpret, after twenty years of reflection, in her book. It was the morrow of the feast of the Yorkshire pastor St John of Beverley; she believed him to have appeared to her, joining at her bedside her mother and the curate. Fr Conrad, noting how she remarked on the saint's Englishness, summed up the situation: 'She was surrounded thus by her natural neighbours, both saints and sinners, a young Englishwoman apparently delirious and dying in the heart of Norwich'. This social setting of the visions – composed by the co-presence of members of the earthly and heavenly cities – is entirely fitting for, on Fr Conrad's interpretation, the *Shewings* testify to Julian's having reached what he calls the 'apostolic stage' of the unitive way. Passing through purgation and illuminated proficiency into the cloud of unknowing she grasps there a meaning to be communicated to her even-Christians, her fellows in the mystical Body of Christ. *Contemplare et contemplata aliis tradere* is, after all, following St Thomas, the apostolic fullness of Christian perfection.

And her message is a resolution of the 'fundamental problem of God's attitude to evil in view of the all-embracing nature of the love of God'. She affirms that 'Love was his meaning', but must not be regarded as minimising, in quasi-monistic fashion, the evil of the world. This she does not do, declaring sin to be 'in sooth viler and more painful than hell, without likeness, for it is contrary to our fair nature'.[83] Yet she can also affirm that, seen from another perspective, 'sin is behovely':[84] when, in the future, God's will is fully worked out sin will prove to have been the occasion of greater good. What then of the *wrath* of God, so urgent a theme of both Testaments and insisted on by preachers of all ages? For Mother Julian, it is a reality indeed – but *in man*. God's love is changeless as it goes out to creatures and brings them back to himself in a wonderful unity. Pain and suffering are sent by the loving mercy of God for man's purification: if a human being chooses to let them draw him into despair his condemnation is self-inflicted. In permitting sin, foul evil as it is, God has 'no other object than the greater expansion of love and mercy'.[85]

Not that such a theodicy, indebted as it is to her visions of both the public suffering Face of the incarnate Son and of the secret reposeful

Face of the divine Father, exhausts Julian's gospel. There is also her profound theology of the prayer of petition. Like St Thomas Aquinas, she gives much space to that cinderella of prayer-forms, often dismissed as too humble a personage for high spiritual aspiration to notice. The 'asking of worthy things from God' is for Thomas, citing St John Damascene, a definition of the essence of prayer.[86] Julian treats 'beseeching' as a means ordained by God for our reaching spiritual blessings (as well as certain temporal ones). Such prayer makes us pliant to God – but not vice versa, for as Julian realised, our beseeching is not the cause of God's benevolence in our regard. On the contrary, God's generous goodness is the cause of our petition. Fr Conrad stoutly defends her approach.

> The objection to this type of prayer, as well as the idea that it is over active and unsuited to the higher phases of prayer derive from the confusion of regarding it as man caused and man centred. The more a man asks of God the more he realises his dependence on God for everything; the more he asks as a Christian through Christ, the ground of his beseeching, the more unified and single becomes his prayer. He is all the time praying, beseeching, that God's will may be done in his regard; he is more and more moulding his own human will upon the changeless will of God's unfathomable and infinitely tender love.[87]

The conclusion is, paradoxical as it may sound, that petitionary prayer, intensely performed, is typical of the unitive way and indeed leads into the prayer of union itself. Following Julian's teaching, 'the desire for God grows so intense that the words of the petition fade away in the quiet beholding of the Beloved'.

When asking after the 'ground of union' – the foundation of the unitive state, Fr Conrad turns to chapter 48 of Mother's Julian's *Revelations*, with its affirmation that 'our good Lord the Holy Ghost, which is endless life dwelling on our soul, full seemly keepeth us; and worketh therein a peace and bringeth it to ease by grace, and accordeth it to God and maketh it buxom.' This statement he interprets in terms of the theology of St Thomas – the knowledge of faith is perfected by the gifts of the Holy Spirit granting, through an infusion of charity, wisdom, understanding, and science to the contemplative soul, and of St John of the Cross, who offers the 'best description' of the working of the Holy Spirit in the highest states of unitive prayer. The divinisation of the soul's activity lies in its complete docility to the Holy Spirit's action – and so full maturity in the reception of his gifts *is* the 'spiritual marriage', nuptial union with God.

Fr Conrad's conclusion from the Sanjuanist teaching is, however, robustly exoteric, even commonplace: infused contemplation, as in Mother Julian, is nothing other than the sturdiest possible growth of the seed of faith. It is the outcome of submission to the Word of God – a formulation for the mystical life which anticipates that of the Swiss theologians – one a priest, the other a laywoman – Hans Urs von Balthasar and Adrienne von Speyr, themselves writing with one eye on the critique of esotericism in such matters made by their co-national Karl Barth. Like St Thérèse of Lisieux – a saint enormously popular during Fr Conrad's productive period, and to whose doctrine of 'spiritual childhood' he, without naming her, alludes – Mother Julian identifies the transforming union of spiritual marriage with the union by charity of Christ's mystical Body.[88] It is in *love* that God is the ground of the whole Christian life.

Walter Hilton's 'Scale of Perfection', the work of an Augustinian canon much engaged in the direction of anchoresses such as Julian, as well as other contemplatives, constitutes, in *The English Religious Heritage*, a kind of measuring rod for the judgments the book has made. Fr Conrad takes Hilton's interest in the periodisation of contemplative advance to be a consequence of Richard of St Victor's influence. The latter's six 'degrees' of contemplation found their way into Aquinas's theology also.[89] But other Augustinians of Hilton's time were also producing maps of the Way: the Fleming, Blessed Jan Ruysbroek, for example, with his *Seven Steps of the Ladder of Spiritual Love*, composed a little before *The Scale of Perfection*.[90] Ultimately, Augustine was the stimulus, and notably his treatise *De quantitate animae* with its discussion of seven stages in the soul's ascent to God.[91]

The main new *content* added by Fr Conrad's discussion of Hilton to our understanding of the spiritual life is the role of *study*. One might think that, as a Dominican, Fr Conrad would have lingered over Hilton's decision to locate here the first (though dispensable) degree of contemplation. But his account is brief. Learning for Hilton is useful – and for some souls, indispensable – water that Christ can turn into wine. So far as the *form* of Christian living is concerned, *The Scale* confirms the *overall* grid (which we may call Thomistico-Carmelite) that Fr Conrad has used to pattern his materials, and above all the three great stages of purgation, illumination, union. However, Hilton's presentation of those stages in terms of three loves (the love, sufficient for salvation, of those who have faith; love for Christ's manhood as seen by the imagination, and love for his Godhead as perceived in his manhood by 'ghostly sight') reminds Fr Conrad that the scheme in question has a plurality of expressions. Christ is 'lived in each person according to the construction of that personality and the love works through the individual's free will'. And referring to

Victor White's essay on Hilton for the Guild of Pastoral Psychology, Fr Conrad acclaims the latter as not only an acute reader of the human psyche but also a highly christocentric writer, for whom the reformation of feeling which growth in holiness involves is always a matter of the clearer emergence of the image of Christ in each soul.

A sacramental Catholicism

In the course of *The English Religious Heritage* the author expresses an occasional anxiety that the ascetical and mystical writers, concerned as these are with the disciplining, and subsequent efflorescence of personal spiritual life, may not have attended sufficiently to the corporate, liturgical, sacramental life of the Church. Living as he did at a time in the Church when the Liturgical Movement still worked on classical lines – recovering the biblical and patristic riches of the liturgical tradition, albeit in a pastoral, rather than archaeological spirit, he was conscious of no internal strain in the formula 'Sacramental Prayer' which he chose for a collection of essays on this topic.[92]

To Fr Conrad's mind, the somewhat aliturgical quality of much early modern writing on prayer and spirituality in England derived from two sources. In the first place, the 'growing individualism' of the later Middle Ages deflected attention from the corporate acts which are the 'primary sources' of the life of prayer. In the second place, the conditions of penal England left Catholics little option.

> In England the Mass had to be celebrated in attics with as little sound and ceremonial as possible, and the faithful were left to their books of piety to continue the heroic struggle of the faith with fervour and true union with God. Of necessity then, in such countries as ours the liturgy was abandoned as the main source of prayer and was substituted by private forms of devotion that could be practised alone easily hidden from the prying eyes of the pursuivants.[93]

And in any case, the primarily historical bent of the first great liturgical scholars of the country, such as the antiquarian Edmund Bishop; the somewhat confusing plethora of theories about the eucharistic sacrifice which jostled for space in orthodox divinity, and a distrust of excessive concern with rubrical minutiae all conspired to ensure that the pre-Great War early stirrings of the Liturgical Movement would not have much resonance in English Catholicism at large.

If by the years immediately following the Second World War the situation had vastly improved, Fr Conrad ascribed this happy change to three main factors: first, the excellence of the theology of the eucharistic sacrifice produced by two influential writers of the inter-war period, Anscar Vonier, abbot of Buckfast, and the French Jesuit Maurice de la Taille, whom we have had occasion to note already, in connection both with Gerald Vann and David Jones; secondly, the movement for biblical *ressourcement*, with its concern for the bread of the scriptural word to complement the bread of the eucharistic table; and thirdly, its sister movement, the patristic revival, for the Fathers 'thought always sacramentally'.

The upshot is, or should be, a rediscovery of liturgical prayer as the prayer of Christ himself in his sacred humanity, joining the Church, his body, to himself, as he petitions the Father. For the liturgy takes place 'according to his institution, his mind; it is inspired by his grace and his love, and it is designed to draw all men into Christ through whom alone they can approach the Father'.

This christological emphasis may well have owed much to the influ-ence of the topic he took as the subject of his lectoral thesis: *Christ the High-Priest of the Mass*.[94] Here he considered the sense in which Christ, the Church's great High Priest, could be said to offer each celebration of the eucharistic sacrifice. The importance of the subject could hardly be missed, because the Mass is the daily moment when:

> Christ the Priest appears to us and when we approach him to take part with him in his priestly sacrifice and so to receive the effects of [his] Priesthood, above all in the very body and blood of the Victim himself.[95]

Drawing not only on the work of de la Taille but also on other Francophone theologians of the 'Sacrifice of the Altar', Fr Conrad provides a christological account of sacrificial mediation at large prior to pressing home his concern with its eucharistic form in particular.[96]

Thanks to the hypostatic union, Jesus Christ enjoyed a unique 'title' and 'foundation' for his mediatorial activity. Representing at once the Father, through his eternal procession as Son and its continuation as the temporal mission of Jesus of Nazareth, that very human Word of God also had his correlative commissioning from the side of men. Jesus was, firstly, by his union with the Word, the 'New Adam', the new head of humankind. Secondly, all the patriarchs and prophets of the ancient Covenant had desired such a Mediator. And thirdly, at the Annunciation, blessed Mary by her *fiat* had embodied the receptivity not only of Israel but of all humanity to his coming. And yet a priest (for this is what the go-between must be) is an anomaly unless he has something to offer – as the Letter to the Hebrews points out. An offer-ing was found. The unique Priest would carry in oblation a unique Victim: his own manhood. The accepted, glorified Victim of this sacrifice was displayed to humankind in the resurrection of Christ. That offering would remain the centre-piece of the continuing drama of salvation. The worship of the Church revolves around the sacramental renewal of the redeeming sacrifice of the Lord.

What is not so clear in theological tradition is *how* Jesus Christ continues to exercise, in the Holy Eucharist, this high priesthood. '*Either* Christ is the principal priest because he is the principal offerer, offering the sacrifice of his body and blood here and now upon the altar ...' – and this scholastic divinity termed the theory of his 'actual' offering, *or* he constitutes the primordial celebrant of every Mass inasmuch as 'he has left the act of offering in the hands of the Church and her priests, to be offered in his name, as an ambassador offers the gifts in virtue of the king he represents ...' – whence the name of the alternative theory, that of his 'virtual' offering.[97]

Reviewing a great deal of historical material, Fr Conrad records that a number of Church Fathers and ecclesiastical writers hint at an actual offering – Tertullian, Lactantius, Ambrose, Faustus of Riez, Maximus of Turin, Leo the Great, while Cyprian, the Augustinian tradition and the Greeks would more naturally be interpreted as teaching a virtual offering only. If in the thirteenth century, the 'Everest in the history of theology', St Albert was an actualist, St Thomas (probably) a virtualist, the Tridentine Catechism stands, curiously, over against the Decrees of Trent in much the same way. And while voices raised in favour of an actual offering by the ascended Lord are never missing (the conciliar doctors Melchior Cano and Gaspar Casali ['Lerinensis'], the Jesuits Petavius and Gregory of Valencia, the Dominican John of St Thomas, the Salamanca Carmelite John of the Annunciation), virtualism retained the majority vote. In Fr Conrad's own time, de la Taille had attempted a compromise formulation, remarking of Christ that he is the author and institutor of the Mass, commanding its continuance in his name, giving the power to offer it, and being represented in image and person by the priest (a summary of the positive affirmations of virtualism), but adding, in a concession to actualism, that Christ also co-operates in making our oblation efficacious here and now. But, as Fr Conrad comments, the question is, *How*?

Though concluding cautiously that the 'time has not yet arrived' for a definitive view, Fr Conrad clearly tended towards the 'higher' doctrine as the following remarks make plain:

> Christ has sent forth his priests; but this simile does not include the whole truth because it cannot convey the idea of the intimate and hidden presence of this priestly King when his ambassadors offer his Gift throughout the world. The High-Priest actively co-operates

in the sacrifice. The same sentiments of love, obedience and religion which inspired his offering on Calvary remain ever vibrant and supremely efficacious in his glorious soul. Thus the High-Priest presides over the subordinate sacrifices, desiring the salvation of his Church, giving her himself as the unique Victim, empowering the priest to offer in his name. His supreme causality pervades the whole offering.[98]

That this substantial essay is not simply concerned with the theology of the eucharistic sacrifice in and for itself but looks for a deeper awareness of the mystery in which the *worshipping people* are engaged, is evidenced by an early passage relating the topic to the concerns of the Liturgical Movement. When we know how Christ's priesthood 'functions' in the Mass, we 'shall realize more fully the part to be taken by each one of us, be we clerics or lay'. In *Sacramental Prayer*, Fr Conrad stresses, in ascending order of importance, three fruits of liturgical participation: a livelier sense of the cosmic content of this essentially *embodied* prayer; a drawing others nearer to Christ by this *common* praying; and greater possibilities of sanctification through what is – as he explains, for the point is not so obvious – an intrinsically *unitive* kind of praying.

> The variety of words and gestures and actions in the liturgy, while offering an opening to 'activism' and distraction if misused, in itself should lead the prayer deeper into unity, finding eventually the simplicity within this complex system.[99]

Thus the recitation of the Psalter can keep the 'pray-er' 'so constantly before God that all the words begin to have a single meaning'; the absorption of the Word of God in the liturgical readings can stimulate and nourish *lectio divina*; and listening to a gradual or alleluia verse will 'elevate his spirit'.

Before coming to the heart of the liturgical cycle – the celebration of Easter, with its long drawn out prelude of Lent – the essays gathered in *Sacramental Prayer* take further these thoughts about the liturgical environment at large. Some writers on the liturgy are so taken up with outer forms – the media of 'active participation' – as to give the impression of a materialistic monism, whereby the worshipper *is* his body, *simpliciter*. Their critics may swing over to the opposite extreme, so privileging the interiority of the worshipper as to make it quite unclear as to why liturgical prayer is social and public at all. Fr Conrad steers between Scylla and Charybdis: 'The liturgy is external, public worship; yet worship itself is principally an act of soul.' He appeals for support to Hildegard of Bingen, for whom the Holy Spirit teaches that the body

with the soul should sing praises to God through the voice. The imagination is the bridge between the two. And the principal lesson is that
'worship ... is inextricably bound up with *art*', for art is that making of
things to express the 'harmony and skilful rhythm' present in all *God
has made*. 'Culture has always meant the cultivating of God or the gods
– with perhaps the exception of a few decadent eras as is our own.' And
if worship is, through liturgical art, the matrix of culture, so the
liturgy, enabled by the works of culture to possess its full dramatic
power, flows back, through the disciplined imagination, on to the
innermost powers of the soul. The liturgically-trained imagination
makes it possible for us to 'sink back' into 'an habitual worship flowing
out from [our] God-focused interior bodily faculty' in all the interstices
between our daily occupations. And, concerned for what he saw as
'rather too humanistic tendencies within the Liturgical Movement', Fr
Conrad insisted that a man should 'be more ready to learn the language
of the Liturgy, rather than expect the Liturgy to learn his ... '. (Here he
took issue with Romano Guardini's *The Spirit of the Liturgy*, in which it
sometimes seems that the universal, hieratic and restrained ethos of the
Roman rite is to be adapted to 'modern man', rather than modern man,
for his welfare, to it).

Fr Conrad gave pride of place, among the liturgical arts, to music
– and not easy music either. David's dance before the ark may sound
like an unrehearsed *jeu d'esprit*, but like the religious dance of all
primitive peoples it would surely have entailed complex patterns. The
art of music is worship's chief vehicle inasmuch as it 'calls into activity *intelligence*, will, memory and the feelings of man'.[100] Such music
– Byzantine, Gregorian, Renaissance and modern – both, negatively,
purges the spirit, and, positively, opens it up to heights of communion
with God. This dialectic of purgation-and-communion typifies Fr
Conrad's approach to liturgical art – it is no less apparent, for
instance, in his treatment of visual images, from the Madonna to the
Sacred Heart.[101] His theology of worship is never allowed for a
moment to forget his ascetical theology (or vice versa), for a theological humanism, based on the incarnation and the resurrection,
requires, if it is to be Christian, an asceticism of the cross. Only in
their synthesis is there peace.

> Both men [the 'humanist' and the 'ascetic'] have to meet in the
> Paschal Mystery which combines the complete self denial of the
> Cross with the perfection of human life in the Resurrection. The
> humanist must be ready to set aside all the wonders of God's creation
> for God himself, and the ascetic must be made aware of the glory of
> what God has made. The humanist must be ready to accept the truth

of the vast penitential literature which deals with God and the soul alone, while his seeming opponent must begin to appreciate the sanctification of all 'humanities' in the splendour of the Liturgy and the beauty and integrity of Christ's human flesh and spirit.[102]

So from this point of view, as from all others, the mysteries of Lent and Easter form the centre of all. His commentary on the liturgical readings of *Lent* – no longer usable for its stated purpose, except by those parishes and communities following the old Roman rite – presents the 'Lenten spirit and message' as 'summed up in two doctrines, Christian penance and Christ's Passion, which divide the entire forty days into two equal parts ...'[103] and links those 'doctrines' to the sacraments of baptism, penance and Eucharist, expressions *par excellence* of the Lord's death, descent and rising again. His *vade-mecum* for the Lenten season exemplified the merits he had found in the achievement of the Spanish Dominican spiritual theologian Juan Arintero, the 'ploughing back' of the 'conclusions' in ascetical and mystical theology of the Dominican school into the sacramental life, participation in the mysteries of the Church. The divine life is developed, manifested and perfected within the mystical body of the Church by an ever deepening assimilation to Jesus Christ as he is shown forth in the liturgical celebration of his saving actions, and the spiritual and corporal works of mercy of his Church.[104] On the basis of Arintero's work – and the last Spanish Master of the Dominican Order, Anicetus Fernandez, once told the present author that, had Arintero's *Obras completas* been known more widely the Second Vatican Council would never have been necessary! – Fr Conrad foresaw an 'entirely new type of study of "mystical theology"', one which would approach the Word of God in Scripture by the light of one single theme: the 'way to divine union within the total Christ' (Christ and his Church).[105] This was his abiding conviction: almost at the end of his life, in a critique of the 'creation-centred spirituality' of the American Dominican (but now Episcopalian) Matthew Fox, he wrote: 'I would, of course, agree that creation is good in itself and can form the ground of "a theology"; but I would prefer to see any complete theology grounded on the "New Creation" in and through Christ Jesus our Lord.'[106]

The Dominican Use

It is impossible to leave the subject of the Liturgy without a word on the role played in Fr Conrad's outlook by the distinctive Liturgy of the Order of Preachers. Fr Conrad had a special love for the ancient Dominican Use, a variant of the Roman rite abandoned by the Order in the later 1960s. He followed the American Dominican William Bonniwell in holding that the Use was a particularly 'pure' form of the Roman Rite, purer than was customary in many localities in the mid-thirteenth century: it was, he thought, owing to its lack of 'Gallicanisms' that certain Parisian friars made trouble over the Order's liturgy until its codification by Blessed Humbert of Romans (the fifth Master General) in 1256. As to the Divine Office, that remained basically unchanged from 1260 until 1923, when its shape was modified to render it more isomorphic with the modern Roman Office-books of the Rite at large. Fr Conrad hoped (in vain) that the Liturgical Institute created by Master General Gillet in 1939, and of which he had briefly been a member till war intervened, would prove the providential instrument for a revision 'in the wise and pure spirit of Bl Humbert': in other words, a return so far as possible, to the thirteenth-century book.[107]

Given these views, it was inevitable that the effective disappearance of the Dominican liturgy as a whole in the wake of the Second Vatican Council should have greatly saddened him.[108] In the unpublished *Memoir* he wrote in 1976 he describes the old Dominican Use as vital, since the Order, 'as a cell in the Body of Christ [necessarily] had its own method of existing and functioning'. By the time of writing, alas, 'It could surely be said that the prayer of the Dominican Order as a special style in which the brethren were formed into one praying body had disappeared.'[109] The provision of a *proprium* for the Missal and Lectionary, on the one hand, and the Liturgy of the Hours, on the other, did something to remedy this situation by furnishing the reformed Roman Liturgy with a supplement for the Dominican saints and beati (as well as a handful of texts for the temporal cycle).[110] But the point Fr Conrad makes here will not be fully met without some re-creation of the Dominican Use as an organic entirety of text, music and gesture.

Notes

1. P. Johnston, *Edward Johnston* (London: Barrie and Jenkins, 1976); his main work was *Writing and Illuminating and Lettering* (London: Adam and Pitman Publishing, 1906; reprinted in 1983).
2. See W. Rothenstein, *Since Fifty: Men and Memories, 1922–1938* (London: Faber, 1939).
3. R.M.Y.G. [leadowe], *Ambrose McEvoy* (London: Ernest Benn, 1924);

M. Holroyd, *Augustus John: A Biography* (Harmondsworth: Penguin, 1976²); V. Woolf, *Roger Fry: A Biography* (London: Hogarth Press, 1940); Cockerell was Director of the Fitzwilliam Museum, Cambridge, from 1908 to 1937: his 'dialogue' with Dame Laurentia McLachlan of Stanbrook is described in F. Corrigan [O.S.B.], *The Nun, the Infidel and the Superman The Remarkable Friendship of Dame Laurentia McLachlan with Sydney Cockerell, Bernard Shaw and Others* (London: John Murray, 1985); on Orage, founder of the cultural reviews *New Age* and *New English Weekly*, see P. Mairet, *A.R. Orage: A Memoir. With an Introduction by G.K. Chesterton* (London: J.M. Dent and Sons, 1938), and W. Martin *The 'New Age' under Orage* (Manchester 1967); on Chesterton himself the most recent of numerous lives is M. Coren, *Gilbert. The Man Who Was G.K. Chesterton* (London: Jonathan Cape, 1989); his brother is studied in B. Sewell, *Cecil Chesterton* (Faversham: St Albert's Press, 1975); A. West, *H. G. Wells, Aspects of a Life* (London: Hutchinson, 1984); M. Holroyd, *Bernard Shaw* (London: Chatto and Windus, 1988-1992). On the Webbs, see M. Cole (ed.), *The Webbs and their Work* (London: Frederick Muller, 1949). A valuable guide to the whole scene is J. Coates, *Chesterton and the Edwardian Cultural Crisis* (Hull: Hull University Press, 1984).

4. D. Attwater, *A Cell of Good Living. The Life, Works nd Opinions of Eric Gill* (London: Geoffrey Chapman 1969), pp. 33-6.
5. D.C. Pepler, *The Care Committee, the Child and the Parent* (London: Constable, 1912); *Justice and the Child* (London: Constable, 1915).
6. D.C. Pepler, *The Devil's Devices, or Control versus Service* (London: Hampshire House Workshops, 1915).
7. A. Coomaraswamy, Foreword to E. Gill, *It All Goes Together* (New York: The Devin-Adair Company, 1944).
8. Cited in D. Attwater, *A Cell of Good Living*, pp. 47-8.
9. Cited in ibid., p. 49.
10. K. Foster, O.P., 'The Sculpture of Anthony Foster', *Blackfriars* XXXII. 372 (1951), pp. 120, 123.
11. Well-described in B. Sewell, *In the Dorian Mode. A Life of John Gray, 1866-1934* (Padstow: Tabb House, 1983).
12. P. Hagreen, 'The Guild of St Joseph and St Dominic', *Sower* I. 2 (1930). Hagreen was Ditchling's wood-engraver and ivory-carver.
13. Memoir, 1975-1976, English Dominican Archive.
14. Much information on Hilary Pepler and his printing work is available in the *Aylesford Review* for Spring 1965. An account of the books of Dominican interest published by the Press is offered by B. Sewell, O.Carm., 'Dominicana from Saint Dominic's Press', in D.A. Bellenger (ed.), *Opening the Scrolls. Essays in Catholic History in Honour of Godfrey Anstruther* (Bath: Downside Abbey, 1987), pp. 235-43. The Press's liturgical books had a major patron in Jarrett, on the principle that for Catholic worship only the best could suffice. See now for a *catalogue raisonné*, M. Taylor and B. Sewell, *Saint Dominic's Press. A Bibliography 1916-1937. With a memoir by Susan*

Falkner, an introduction by Brocard Sewell, a preface by Michael Taylor, and an appendix by Adrian Cunningham (Risbury: The Whittingston Press, 1995).

15.   'Memoir' 1975–1976, English Dominican Archive. The sacrality of the family – and of birth and the generative processes – as understood by Catholicism were (despite Gill's lapses) vital *credenda* at Ditchling: one could consult Gill's *Birth Control*, with the briefest of forewords from Vincent McNabb (Ditchling: St Dominic's Press, 1919). This booklet was sold by the pair of them at a meeting addressed by Dr Marie Stopes, the *apostola* of contraception.

16.   As brought out in J. Batkin, 'Reflections on Life at Spode with Father Conrad, 1960–1979', English Dominican Archive.

17.   Cited in Attwater, *A Cell of Good Living*, p. 75.

18.   F. MacCarthy, *Eric Gill* (London: Faber and Faber, 1989), pp. 163–4, 211–12.

19.   Attwater, *A Cell of Good Living*, p. 86. Perhaps there were others who took the view so cavalierly expressed by Robert Speaight: 'I must admit that there were one or two skeletons in Eric Gill's cupboard, but I preferred to exhibit the cupboard because it was so beautifully made.' R. Speaight, *The Property Basket. Recollections of a Divided Life* (London: Collins and Harvill, 1970), pp. 376–7.

20.   MacCarthy, *Eric Gill*, p. xi.

21.   *The Hand-Press. An Essay by H.D.C. Pepler. First Printed by the Author at St · Dominic's Press and now Re-printed with Facsimile Reproductions from the Original* (Ditchling: The Ditchling Press, 1953), p. 12.

22.   H.D.C. Pepler, 'The Printing Press', reprinted in M. Taylor and B. Sewell, *Saint Dominic's Press*, p.163.

23.   See D. Quinn, 'Distributism as Movement and Ideal', *Chesterton Review* XIX. 2 (1993), pp. 157–74; 'The Historical Foundations of Modern Distributism', ibid. XXI. 4 (1995), pp. 451–72. On McNabb's contribution, there is much material in *The Chesterton Review* XXII, 1–2 (1996), a special number of the journal devoted to this figure.

24.   H. Belloc, *Economics for Helen* (London: J.W. Arrowsmith, 1924^2), pp. 108–126.

25.   *Missions, or Sheepfolds and Shambles*, by A. Sheep (Ditchling: St Dominic's Press, 1922), p. 10.

26.   P. Anson, *A Roving Recluse* (Cork: Mercier Press, 1946).

27.   E. Cruise, O.S.B., 'Development of the Religious Orders', in G.A. Beck, A.A., *The English Catholics, 1850–1950* (London: Burns Oates 1950), p. 454.

28.   Letter of 13 November 1993 from Clare Lilleyman to Fr David Sanders, O.P. Prior of Blackfriars, Cambridge.

29.   'Memoir' of 1971, English Dominican Archive.

30.   For the model provided by the Province of France, see Fr Conrad's 'Aspects of French Dominican Life', *Blackfriars* XXVIII, 322, (1947), pp. 27–32.

31. *Dorothy Day and the Catholic Worker Movement* (London: Catholic Truth Society, 1980).

32. I owe this point to a letter of 14 January 1994 from Mrs Maureen Tempest.

33. Memoir, 1971, English Dominican Archive.

34. See Johnston, *Writing and Illuminating and Lettering.* Fr Conrad remained concerned for the quality (often deplorable, in contrasting ways, throughout his lifetime) of Catholic iconography – even, or especially, for children. Excoriating gaudiness and sentimentality in religious art for children he recommended as a model Nicolete Gray's *Jacob's Ladder: A Bible Picture Book from Anglo-Saxon and Twelfth Century English Manuscripts* (London: Faber, 1949) for a child's mind is instinctively symbolical, and dried up by literalism. Thus: 'The Bible in Pictures', *Blackfriars* XXXI (February 1930), pp. 79–84. In 1991, Linda Kindersley, a Cambridge artist and letterer, commissioned a young Cambridge history graduate, Lottie Hoare, to write a text for Fr Conrad's own childhood watercolours (at the age of six) of the early English saints: *Stephen's History of Saints* (Cambridge: Cardozo Kindersley, 1992).

35. B. Wicker, 'Conrad Pepler', *The Tablet* 247. 7988 (20 November 1993), p. 1538.

36. Autobiographical notes of 1982, English Dominican Archive.

37. *Riches Despised: A Study of the Roots of Religion* (London: Blackfriars Publications, 1957). The italics are, of course, added.

38. This complexity is well brought out in his essay 'Psychologies of Mysticism', *Dominican Studies IV* (1951), pp. 133–52 where four distinct kinds of psychology – rational, empirical, 'divine-imaging', and sacramental are deemed necessary to do justice to the topic. As he wrote: 'Having considered the Christian soul as the form of an intellective physical being, which is the discipline of rational psychology, the psychologist can go on to regard it as the seat or centre of human experience from which he can develop various types of empirical psychology. But certain facts of the Christian revelation have provided other fundamental aspects of the soul, the two most important being those of the soul as the image of God, both incarnate and triune, and as the subject or recipient of sacramental activity.' Yet more important than discerning their distinction, for Fr Conrad, is bringing them to a 'synthesis': ibid., pp. 133, 152.

39. *Riches Despised*, p. 8.

40. Compare Fr Gerald Vann's interpretation of St John of the Cross in Chapter 4.

41. E. Gellner, *Sword, Plough and Book, The Structure of Human History* (London: Collins, 1988).

42. *Riches Despised*, p. 35.

43. Ibid., pp. 69–70.

44. Ibid., p. 100.

45. Ibid., p. 144.

46. *The Three Degrees, A Study of Christian Mysticism* (London: Blackfriars Publications, 1957), p. 109, citing Jan Ruysbroeck from the anthology *The Spear of Gold. Revelations of the Mystics*, ed. H.A. Reinhold (London: Burns Oates, 1947), p. 312.
47. Ibid., p. 102.
48. 'The Basis of St Thomas's Mysticism', in ibid., pp. 120–45.
49. K. Wykeham-George, O.P. and G. Mathew, O.P., *Bede Jarrett of the Order of Preachers* (London: Blackfriars Publications, 1952), pp. 104–5.
50. *The English Religious Heritage* (London: Blackfriars Publications, 1958), p. 3.
51. As found, so he points out, in, for instance, the Carmelite P. Chrysogono de Jesu Sacramentato's *Asceticae et mysticae summa* (Turin: Marietti, 1936).
52. Fr Conrad's use thus draws close to that of Fr Sebastian Bullough, see Chapter 6.
53. *The English Religious Heritage*, p. 5.
54. Ibid., p. 10. For the place of some of these writers in the literary history of England, see M.A. Knowlton, *The Influence of Richard Rolle and of Julian of Norwich on the Middle English Lyric* (The Hague: Mouton, 1973).
55. Ibid., p. 9. Fr Vincent McNabb, whose training was not Angelicum but Hawkesyard, shared Garrigou-Lagrange's admiration for John of the Cross, but on very different grounds: to him it seemed undeniable that 'the most significant element in the movement created by the sanctity and genius of St Teresa and St John of the Cross is not Carmelite Prayer but Carmelite Poverty. These two strong-souled lovers of Jesus recognised that their beloved Master had put all right things in their right order when, opening His mouth, He said, "Blessed are the poor in spirit, for theirs is the kingdom of heaven." If at any time he identified perfection with prayer, he knew that in the soul's life of prayer the most important element is the soul's life. But this threw him back on the first of the Beatitudes which Our Blessed Lord at the later date reinforced by the principle, "A man's life" (even his life of prayer) "does not consist in the abundance of things which he possesseth."' Thus his 'The Mysticism of St John of the Cross', *Blackfriars* XVI. 180 (1935), p. 11.
56. Ibid., p. 41. Fr Conrad's references were to the modernised text, *The Vision of Piers Plowman by William Langland newly rendered into English by Henry W. Wells* (London: Sheed and Ward, 1935) – a version which conflates the A and B (but not the C text) of the great poem. A (unfinished) is dated to c. 1370, B (completed) to 1378–1379, and C (the final but never finished revision) to c. 1386.
57. *The English Religious Heritage*, p. 64, with reference to *Passus* XIX, 106: ff.
58. A.V.C. Schmidt, 'Introduction', *Piers Plowman. A New Translation of the B-Text* (Oxford: Oxford University Press, 1992), p. xxxiii.
59. *The English Religious Heritage*, p.67.

60. V. McNabb, 'The Authorship of the *Ancren Riwle*', *The Modern Language Review* IX, i (1916).
61. H.E. Allen, *The Origin of the Ancrew Riwle* (Baltimore, Modern Language Association of America, 1918); R.W. Chambers, *On the Continuity of English Prose from Alfred to More and his School* (London: Early English Text Society, 1932), pp. xcvi-c.
62. *The English Religious Heritage*, p. 88.
63. Ibid., p. 115.
64. Cited ibid., p. 119, from the modernised version by J. Morton: *The Nun's Rule, being the Ancren Riwle* (London: King's Classics, 1905).
65. D. Sayers, *The Other Six Deadly Sins* (London: Methuen & Co., 1943).
66. Cited The *English Religious Heritage*, p. 157, from *The Nun's Rule*, pp. 304-5.
67. *The English Religious Heritage*, p. 163.
68. *Incendium amoris* 15.
69. Ibid. The translation is F.M.M. Comper's modernisation of a fifteenth-century Englishing of the original: *The Fire of Love or Melody of Love and Mending of Life or Rule for Living. Translated by R. Misyn from the 'Incendium Amoris' and the 'De emendatione vitae' of R. Rolle, Ed. and done into modern English by F.M.M. Comper. With an Introduction by E. Underhill* (London: Methuen, 1913).
70. O. Davies, *God Within. The Mystical Tradition of Northern Europe* (London: Darton, Longman and Todd, 1988), p. 162.
71. *The English Religious Heritage*, p. 171. This is hardly more than Rolle's own teaching in *Incendium Amoris* II. 6.
72. *The English Religious Heritage*. p. 174. Cf R. Garrigou-Lagrange, O.P., *Les trois âges de la Vie intérieure, prélude de celle du Ciel* (Paris: Editions du Cerf, 1938).
73. Cited G.C. Heseltine, *Selected Works of Richard Rolle, Hermit* (London: Longmans, Green & Co., 1930), p. 37.
74. *The English Religious Heritage*, p. 191: with reference to Gabriele di Santa Maria Maddalena, Discalced Carmelite, *St John of the Cross. Doctor of Divine Love* (ET London: Thomas Baker, 1940), pp. 115-16.
75. Ibid., p. 208.
76. Ibid., p. 246.
77. *The Cloud of Unknowing*, ch. 24.
78. *The English Religious Heritage*, p. 257.
79. *Epistle of Privy Counsel*, ch. 9. R.W. Englert has noted: 'As one moves away from the sacred humanity, a mysterious Jesus seems to reappear as one who affirms the bodiliness of the contemplative in the midst of ghostliness. The overarching presence of this Jesus who knits together action and contemplation, humanity and divinity, conscious-ness and unconsciousness explains the occurrence of Christological language in the most apophatic of contexts.' *Scattering and Oneing: A Study of Conflict in the Works of the Author of 'The Cloud of Unknowing'* (Salzburg: Institut für Anglistik und Amerikanistik,

Universität Salzburg, 1983), p. 116.

80. As Dr Phyllis Hodgson has written: 'The doctrine of *The Cloud* treatises is traditional and orthodox, the counsel is personal, and directed ... to a discipline on the threshold of unitive prayer.' Hodgson (ed.), *The Cloud of Unknowing and Related Treatises* (Salzburg: 1982), p. xxi.

81. *Revelations of Divine Love*, ch. 86.

82. *The English Religious Heritage*, p. 307.

83. *Revelations of Divine Love*, ch. 63.

84. Ibid., ch. 27.

85. *The English Religious Heritage*, p. 340.

86. *Summa Theologiae IIa IIae*, q. 83, art. 1, ad ii.

87. *The English Religious Heritage*, p. 347.

88. Ibid., p. 365, with reference to the *Revelations of Divine Love*, ch. 61.

89. *Summa Theologiae IIa IIae*, q. 180, a. 4, ad iii.

90. J. Ruysbroeck, *Seven Steps of the Ladder of Spiritual Love* (ET Westminster, Dacre Press, 1943).

91. *De quantitate animae, Patrologia Latina* 32, cols. 1073–76.

92. *Sacramental Prayer* (London: Bloomsbury Publishing Company, 1959).

93. Ibid., p. 4. Recent research has in fact queried this: the musical and ceremonial resources of Stuart and Georgian Catholicism in England were considerable. See, e.g., J. J. Scarisbrick and M. Hodgetts, *A History of Catholic Britain* (Birmingham 1990), pp. 80–81, 88.

94. 'Christ the High-Priest of the Mass' (Rome: Angelicum, 1937).

95. Ibid., p. 1.

96. M. de la Taille, *Mysterium Fidei d'après les théologiens depuisl' origine jusqu'à nos jours* (Paris: Beauchesne 1931³); M. Lepin, *L'Idée de la sacrifice de la Messe, d'après les théologiens depuis l'origine jusqu'à nos jours* (Paris: Beauchesne 1926³); A. Michel, 'La Messe chez les théologiens postérieurs au concile de Trente', *Dictionnaire de Théologie Catholique* X.1 (Paris: Librairie Letouzey et Ané, 1932), cols 1143–1316. Fr Conrad also made good use of the indices to the patrologies of the Abbé Migne.

97. 'Christ the High-Priest of the Mass', 44: Italics added.

98. Ibid., p, 419. The passage about Christ's continuing 'sentiments' is indebted to Julian of Norwich.

99. *Sacramental Prayer* (London: Bloomsbury Publishing Co., 1959), p. 14.

100. Ibid., p. 92. Italics added.

101. 'Concerning the Worship of Images' in ibid., pp. 123–140.

102. Ibid., p. 38.

103. *Lent. A Liturgical commentary on the Lessons and Gospels* (St Louis, Mo. and London, B. Herder Book Co., 1944), p. 1.

104. 'A Christian is a social contemplative' (*Lent*, p. 234) is, in effect, the Peplerian summary of Arintero's position.

105. *The Three Degrees*, p. 112.

106. 'Creation Theology', *Mystics Quarterly* XV. 2 (1989), p. 88. See further on the re-creation by Christ 'The Feast of Feasts' in

Sacramental Prayer, pp. 52–60.

107. Reviewing W.R. Bonniwell, O.P., *A History of the Dominican Liturgy* (New York: J.F. Wagner, 1944), in *Life of the Spirit* II. 13 (1946), pp. 30–32.

108. Strictly speaking, no document exists which professes to suppress the rite of the Order, and it might be maintained that in the absence of such, members of the Order are entitled to its use. A General Chapter has no authority to suppress something based on a pontifical decree without a concurrent specific reprobation by the relevant Roman dicastery acting in the name of the pope. In any case, such arguments have now been overtaken by the willingness of the *Ecclesia Dei* commission to include the Missal of the Order of Preachers within the earlier forms of the Latin rite for which they may provide indults – with the permission of the relevant Prior Provincial for each petitioner.

109. *Memoir*, English Dominican Archives.

110. *Proprium Ordinis Praedicatorum, Missale et Lectionarium* (Rome: Santa Sabina, 1985); *Proprium Officiorum Ordinis Praedicatorum* (Rome: Santa Sabina, 1982).

Works of Conrad Pepler

'The Mass: Theory and Practice', *Blackfriars* XVII. 199 (1936), pp. 757–62.

'Christ, the High-Priest of the Mass' (Diss., Pontifical Athenaeum of St Thomas, Rome, 1937).

'Worship and Family Life', *Blackfriars* XX. 234 (1939), pp. 655–66.

'Contemplation and Culture', *Blackfriars* XXI. 246 (1940), pp. 511–22.

'The New Order', *Blackfriars* XXI. 247 (1940), pp. 608–619.

'Christ in History', *Blackfriars* XXI. 249 (1940), pp. 701–711.

'Imagination and Society', *Blackfriars* XXIII. 271 (1942), pp. 390–97.

'The King of Nations', *Blackfriars* XXIII. 273 (1942), pp. 463–69.

Lent. A Liturgical Commentary on the Lessons and Gospels (St Louis, Mo., and London: Herder Book Co., 1944).

'The Dominican Spirit', *Blackfriars* XXVI. 300 (1945), pp. 82–92.

'Aspects of French Dominican Life', *Blackfriars* XXVIII. 322 (1947), pp. 27–32.

'A Study in Integrity. The Life and Teaching of Eric Gill', *Blackfriars* XXVIII. 326 (1947), pp. 198–209.

'Cosmic Praise', *Blackfriars* XXIX. 338 (1948), pp. 33–41.

'The Beauty of God', Blackfriars XXXI. 358 (1950), pp. 14–22.

'Recent work on the Mass', Blackfriars XXXI. 367 (1950), pp. 484–88.

'Psychologies of Mysticism', *Dominican Studies* IV (1951), pp. 133–52.

'More Literature on Liturgy', Blackfriars XXXIII. 387 (1952), pp. 267–71.

Riches Despised. A Study of the Roots of Religion (London: Blackfriars Publications, 1957).

The Three Degrees. A Study of Christian Mysticism (London: Blackfriars

Publications, 1957).

The English Religious Heritage (London: Blackfriars Publications, 1958).

Sacramental Prayer (London: Bloomsbury Publishing Company, 1959).

'Ditchling: A Community of Craftsmen', *Dublin Review* 482 (1959–1960).

'Ditchling: A Community Fifty Years Ago', *Spode House Review* 9, 98 (1973).

Dorothy Day (London: Catholic Truth Society, 1980).

'*In Diebus Illis*: Some Memories of Ditchling', *Chesterton Review* VIII. 4 (1982).

'Looking Back in Wonder, Looking Forward in Hope', *Dominican Ashram* 2. 2 (June 1983), pp. 55–66.

'Looking Back', *New Blackfriars* 66. 775 (1985), pp. 15–20.

10

Epilogue: Critic's retrospect

Professor Adrian Hastings, in chronicling the decline of English Nonconformity in the inter-war years, wrote: 'It was indeed the age of "the social gospel" and a rather rapid fading away of any strong doctrinal undergirding would seem in retrospect the truly disastrous weakness of the period'.[1] Although the Dominican 'culture' described in these pages was the intellectual equal of that of the Free Church colleges (Westminster, Cheshunt, Wesley at Cambridge; Mansfield and Regent's Park at Oxford), that temptation, if felt, was clearly resisted. A Christian culture without a doctrinal foundation is all bosom and no backbone. The seven Dominicans whose work has been outlined here represented – if with peculiar excellence – a Church that was indeed pastoral, but not at the cost of ascetical and mystical effort, of Scripture study, of a liturgical life of depth and dignity, and the impassioned investigation of philosophy and psychology, history, literature and art. These diverse materials and interests could never have been integrated by that network of connections which the word 'culture' implies without the assistance of the doctrinal framework of Catholic orthodoxy. That common faith was not only conscientiously sustained in union with the rest of the Church; it was also theologically interpreted. And here the Thomism – whether explicit or implicit – of the Dominican writers emboldened them to an equal confidence in both faith and reason: for, in company with Thomas, they saw faith as a light, a source of enlightenment, of what the poet Crashaw in his 'Hymn to the Name and Honour of the admirable Sainte Teresa' called 'great drafts of intellectual day'. The revealed truths, as the truth about man's creation and redemption, and its divine Origin and Goal, could not but illuminate all other truths. At the same time, it belonged to the Thomist inheritance to respect critical intelligence, and all its media and tools, some lowly. The logician and poet, the literary critic and art historian, all by utilising the instruments of their own proper trades can dig out jewels that gleam with reflection of

God's glory. Here such Neo-Thomists as Gilson and Maritain garnered riches with an abandon reflecting Thomas's own spirit. As Bernard Gui's *Life* translated by Fr Kenelm Foster, has it:

> Through the fields of secular knowledge he passed, gathering all its flowers. He filled his arms with the fragments of the teaching of the Apostles, those fragments which God himself has commanded be gathered into baskets, lest they be lost to future generations. From the rich barns of the Fathers, stored with the harvest of both Testaments, Thomas gathered into his books ... all that may serve the needs of our time.[2]

Nor is this simply a matter of working in some putative 'spirit' of the Thomist school, but without a care for any of the important elements of Thomism's material content: though such a 'solution' to the problem of what to do with the Thomist inheritance is not without advocates in the Dominican Order today. Contrary to what is often alleged, the Second Vatican Council recommended that theology be based on the perennially valid philosophical heritage issuing through Aquinas.[3] As perhaps the most distinguished post-Conciliar theologian writing in the English tongue, Fr Avery Dulles, SJ, has commented on the pertinent Conciliar texts:

> It is necessary to challenge the nominalist supposition that abstract concepts and terms are mere conventions established for the sake of convenient communication. Theological experience suggests on the contrary that the ecclesiastically approved philosophical categories have been shaped by, and in some way correspond to, the structure of reality itself. Acceptance of this conceptual tradition is a singular asset for the better understanding of revelation. Sound theologies may begin from different philosophical perspectives, but they must in the end converge toward a harmonious articulation of the meaning of revelation.[4]

The question remains as to whether the seven figures described in this book, and the 'culture' they represent occupy a distinctive place on the Thomist spectrum. Do they bring a tonality of their own, a recognisable timbre, to the Thomist symphony? Surely, they do, and its special contribution is its *power of incarnation*. They were not content simply to rehearse fundamental principles of Thomistic ontology, epistemology and ethics – though when they did this, as in Gilby's case, they (significantly) chose to do so in a way which, though sometimes mannered, employed as in his translations of St Thomas a 'King's English' of, frequently, singular power and beauty. Though devotees of philosophical and theological intelligibility, and therefore committed to an abstractive *moment* in the scanning of concrete experience, abstraction in any other sense is peculiarly foreign to their thought, their concerns. Whether it be Victor White on the patterns of the psyche, Gerald Vann on the role of the great revealed symbols in biblical and liturgical spirituality, Thomas Gilby on the life of the imagination, or the well-tempered civic community, Sebastian Bullough on the rationale of beauty, Gervase Mathew on the world of the mediaeval historian, Kenelm Foster on that of the mediaeval man (or woman) of letters, or Conrad Pepler on the roots of the sacraments in a social living close to nature and their flower in the highest mysticism – we are always dealing with a rational and spiritual intelligence which has come successfully to grips with the concrete. Perhaps Maritain – with his own combination of interests in metaphysics and ethics, politics and aesthetics here resembles them, as in some respects he may have been their model. Yet they differ from him in the more imagistic style of their presentation (one thinks of Thomas Gilby's indefatigable search for simile and metaphor), as in their constant returning to a form of exposition which works by way of concrete examples. This may be the characteristically English way of being Catholic and Thomistic. It is the tendency of their writing to settle on the particular (rather than any special speculative thesis of the kind which has set the Thomistic schools of the twentieth century at odds one with another) which defines their specificity as a group. And precisely this turn to the concrete, not simply as a pedagogical method but as the true, native object of understanding, even understanding *sub specie aeternitatis*, gave them the power to shape a common culture – to shed illumination on the psyche and the symbol, the artwork and the political ethos, the artefact or the mentefact from the human and Christian past, the earth and the spirit – and to provide words whereby the presence of the Word in all of these might become articulate in one time, one place: then, in England.

It has been a strength of the English Dominican Province in the post-Conciliar period that it has not turned its back on the Thomistic element in its patrimony.[5] What has not yet occurred, however, is a diffusion of these materials by way of *haute-vulgarisation* and their deployment in a culture-creating fashion. On the analogy of the 1930s and their aftermath, it is this which is necessary if Thomism is to make its contribution to redeeming a certain spiritual and intellectual disarray, or at least flaccidity, in modern Catholicism in England.

There is one further general lesson to be learned. This book opened with a lay voice from the 1930s who identified himself as, in spirit, 'Dominican and Thomist'. It might suitably end with the warning-note he sounded while surveying the contrasted scene of the 1960s.

Observing how Church authority in England has abandoned, to a degree, the 'entrenched dogmatic position' which was its first response toward the 'new trends in the culture', Harman Grisewood went on: 'Their movement since has been more and more towards compromise with the culture, assuming, naively, that any contemporary manifestation of the culture offers to Christianity equal possibilities of engagement with it'.[6] And pointing out that concern for social justice, in its various forms, though eminently needed as well as fully cognate with the Christian message, also has the slightly suspicious advantage of making few demands on faith in the super- natural, Grisewood finds the one thing necessary for a recreation of a Christian culture in the rediscovery of *the objectivity of the Church's worship and the vision of reality which that worship commands*. For religion 'as a means of knowing reality and, more generally as a system which credibly authenticates the reality of all that is, super- natural and natural, is greatly weakened by weakening the cult.'[7] Cult and culture are indeed related terms, and it was on their two – and reciprocally conditioning – foundations that the seven just men described in this study built their city. The *lacunae* of the liturgical reform, as introduced in the later 1960s, are, however, another story.[8]

Frank Sheed, in attempting to answer his own question – 'Why did the bright promise of the twenties, thirties and even forties, fade away into the sadness of the seventies?' – was inclined to conclude that the literary revival of inter war English Catholicism depended too much on its intellectual revival, while the intellectual revival itself was too confined to intellectuals. And the reason for *that* he located in the insufficient formation furnished for the doctrinal consciousness of the laity. Quite simply, the humus was not widely, or thickly enough, spread in which such fine growths could propagate. Unfortunately, the same difficulty dogs the attempt to construct a 'Catholic culture' today.

The principal study of post-Conciliar English Catholicism on the ground, Michael Hornsby-Smith's *Roman Catholics in England*, and its sequel *Roman Catholic Beliefs in England*,[10] chart what the author terms the gradual dissolution of 'the sort of distinctive Catholic sub- culture' which any account of the Church earlier this century would have to describe. Despite the adoption of a professional sociologist's neutral tone, Hornsby-Smith makes sufficiently clear his relief that such a distinctive culture and ethos are, in his view, unlikely to survive in England – owing to 'normative convergences in a predom- inantly secular society'.[11] His colleague Grace Davie, an Anglican, while admiring Hornsby-Smith's work as the fullest sociological survey of any contemporary English religious body, records her dissenting view that what has overtaken large swathes of the erstwhile 'churched' population is not secularisation but 'Christian nominalism'.

The fissiparous nature of institutional Christianity in England had long struck foreign observers. What is new, on Davie's account, is the 'muddle' now typical of credal Christianity within the historic churches – with the probable exception of the Eastern Orthodox, and the traditional and evangelical wings of, respectively, Rome and Canterbury. 'There can', she writes:

> be no getting away from the fact that the drifting of belief away from anything that might be termed orthodoxy is a major challenge to the contemporary churches – a far greater one – in my opinion – than the supposedly secular nature of the society in which we are obliged to live.[12]

The clarification of intuitions for which she thus calls will require as its instrument the reconstruction of a culture at all levels, from the tacit and popular, to the explicit and the literary. The Gospel of the Word Incarnate cannot, on pain of contradiction, be culturally discarnate.

But the difficulty of one is, for another, challenge. This is the as yet unacknowledged task awaiting the Catholic Church in England, for which the saints of her calendar, and the stones of cathedrals and parish churches cry out. The successors of the seven men described in this book will have their part to play.

Notes

1. A. Hastings, *A History of English Christianity, 1920–1985*) London: 1986), p. 118.
2. *The Life of Saint Thomas Aquinas. Biographical Documents* translated and edited with an introduction by K. Foster, O.P., (London: Longmans, Green and Co., 1959), p. 35.
3. *Optatam totius*, 15.
4. A. Dulles, 'Vatican II and Scholasticism', *Commonweal* (May 1990), p. 10. It is because, incidentally, 'transcendental' Thomism – a Thomism self-consciously concerned to be modern in its acceptance of Kant's critique of traditional metaphysics – is agnostic about the role of concepts (as distinct from judgments) that its claim to *droit de cité* in the Thomist commonwealth can be contested: see R. Dennehy; 'The Philosophical Catbird Seat: A Defense of Maritain's Philosophia Perennis', in D.W. Hudson and D.W. Moran (eds.), *The Future of Thomism* (Notre Dame, Ind.: American Maritain Association, 1992), pp. 65–76.
5. Represented in its importance for spiritual theology in, e.g., S.

Tugwell, O.P., *Albert and Thomas. Selected Writings* (Mahwah, NJ: Paulist Press, 1988), and, for theology at large, B. Davies O.P., *The Thought of Thomas Aquinas* (Oxford: Clarendon Press, 1992). The Thomism of the authors described in the present book, however, in its character as a creative criticism of culture is best represented in that subsequent generation (if with sharpened emphasis on politics) by the work of Herbert McCabe, O.P., notably in *Law, Love and Language* (London: Sheed & Ward, 1968) and the essays and addresses collected as *God Matters* (London: Geoffrey Chapman, 1987).

6. H. Grisewood, *The Painted Kipper. A Study of the Spurious in the Contemporary Scene* (London: C.A. Watts and Co., 1970), p. 69.

7. Ibid., p. 70.

8. I may refer here to my *Looking at the Liturgy. A Critical Perspective on its Contemporary Form* (San Francisco: Liturgical Press, 1996).

9. F. Sheed, *The Church and I* (London: Sheed and Ward, 1974), p. 99.

10. M. Hornsby-Smith, *Roman Catholics in England* (Cambridge: Cambridge University Press, 1987); *Roman Catholic Beliefs in England* (Cambridge: Cambridge University Press, 1991).

11. *Roman Catholics in England*, p. 216.

12. G. Davie, *Religion in Britain since 1945. Believing without Belonging* (Oxford: Blackwell, 1994), p. xii.

Appendix 1: The pre-history of the modern English Dominicans

The Dominican Order – more properly, Order of Preachers – is a child of the Latin Christendom of early thirteenth-century Western Europe.[1] It grew out of the efforts of a variety of ecclesiastics, concerned for the situation of the Church in south-west France, to stem the swelling tide of Catharism – a revival of an ancient Oriental dualistic heresy or (so alien was it to historic Christianity) syncretism. For reasons that scholars still dispute, the Cathars of Languedoc were known from the name of the hill-top city of Albi as 'Albigensians' – though Albi, in point of fact, was a solidly Catholic city in the midst of an heretical countryside.[2] Like their early spiritual forebears in the Near East and the Balkans, Albigensians held that there are two divine principles at work in the world, one good, associated with the spiritual principle in man, the other evil, associated with his body and the wider material realm in which the body lives. Plainly, this was a basic belief system utterly corrosive of the Catholic doctrines of the essential goodness of creation, of the Incarnation (for the divine Word was humanised into an *embodied* life), and of the sacraments (material signs which are also means of grace).

The initiatives of bishops, legates, popes, were eventually gathered up and consolidated by a young Spanish canon, Domingo Guzman. Dominic's response to the Cathar challenge was to form *équipes* of preaching brothers, well-read and with their arguments marshalled, dedicated to an ascetic life-style, and based in preaching-houses where the atmosphere was studious, liturgical, and indebted to the monastic 'observances' – silence, the wearing of the habit, attendance at chapter where faults were admitted and encouragement given – which had proved so useful to religious of all traditions in keeping mind, heart and imagination focused on God. By adopting for his disciples the Augustinian Rule, Dominic linked their vocation to the wider tradition of coenobitic monasticism in the Western Church. Approaches made to pope Innocent III met with an encouraging response, and after the drafting of the first 'Constitutions', the Order received full recognition from Innocent's successor, Honorius III, in 1216. The next year Dominic dispersed his brethren to various European centres. In 1220 the Order's first General Chapter was held at Bologna, one of the three great Western University towns of the day (the others being Paris and Oxford), and the place where eventually the great patriarch of the preaching brothers would be buried.

The English Dominican Province has its genesis in the lifetime of St Dominic. Its origin lies in an initiative of the second General Chapter of the Order, meeting at Bologna in spring 1221 under the founder's presidency. Twelve friars were sent to England, arriving at Dover on 5 August, under the leadership of Gilbert of Fresney (possibly identical with a 'Gilbert of England' who was a master of canon law at Bologna University). Although the term 'preaching' in the Dominican context refers to the teaching of Catholic doctrine more fundamentally than to homiletics, the giving of the first Dominican sermon in England was evidently an occasion of note. At Canterbury on the feast of the Transfiguration in the presence of archbishop Stephen Langton it elicited an invitation from the latter to stay in the primatial town, but this was, for the time being refused. Three days later, on St Lawrence's day, the friars reached London. But their real destination was elsewhere, as the most celebrated English Dominican of modern times, Fr Bede Jarrett, explained. The choice of Oxford

> supplies the key-note of the Dominican ideal. These friars arrived in England, strange and unknown, their dress unfamiliar, their fashion of life new and so far untried in these islands; they were welcomed in the ecclesiastical capital of the country, but they passed on. They arrived at the political capital where dwelt the government and the commercial centre; but this too they left. It was the intellectual capital of England that they 'finally reached'. They made their first settlement, not near the Primate nor the King but at the University ...[3]

The Oxford priory was to remain (probably) the largest of the Province's houses, and a *studium generale* of international repute, right up to the dissolution of the monasteries by Henry VIII. In terms of sheer numbers, its position may at times have been challenged by Edward II's foundation of a *studium provinciale*, reserved to English friars, at King's Langley in Hertfordshire. Its primacy in a wider sense might be disputed, moreover, by London, thanks not least to that close connection which developed between the 'Black Friars' – so called from the black cloak and hood worn over the white habit – and the mediaeval English Crown. By the end of the thirteenth century, the Province comprised 48 houses, the lion's share of its ultimate, immediately pre-Reformation, total of 57.[4] With its two clusters of dependent houses, furthermore, in the vicariates of Scotland and Ireland, it was for much of the mediaeval period the most numerous Province of the entire Order.

Though the main brunt of the energies expended in the making of so many foundations was naturally borne by the Dominicans themselves, the work could not have been realised, or sustained, without the generous assistance of the laity. Founders or patrons (the distinction is often unclear) included the Crown and the royal family, the aristocracy and the burgesses or middle class, while countless unrecorded subventions from more humble folk filled up the financial shortfall. This testifies to the important cultural role of the Order, since no religious institution thus valued by all sections of society can fail to make a significant impact in terms of that society's values, norms and predominant images. While their doctrinal preaching took place at all levels, some too unsophisticated to have left literary record, they appear to have been particularly valued by the more intellectually inclined members of the English episcopate, such as Alexander of Stavensby, Bishop of Lichfield, Robert Grosseteste, Bishop of Lincoln, Edmund of Abingdon, who became Archbishop of Canterbury in 1234, and Richard Wych, Bishop of Chichester and one time Chancellor of Oxford University. Used by popes as commissioners and preachers of the Crusades, they were equally employed by the Crown as royal confessors, envoys and ambassadors. Beginning with Robert Bacon, Richard Fishacre and Simon of Hinton, they produced a galaxy of (mainly scholastic) writers. The impression given in some standard surveys that they were relatively unproductive and overshadowed by the sometimes supportive, sometimes antagonistic company of the Franciscans has been dispelled by more recent studies, such as those of the late Beryl Smalley – who once remarked tartly that 'the real intellectual backwardness must be ascribed to the historians of the Friar Preachers'.[5]

The very fragmentary character of the surviving records of the mediaeval Province, whether in writing or masonry, has always made it a difficult task to recreate that lost world: the main prosopographical survey, that of A.B. Emden, is based on the ordination lists in episcopal registers rather than Dominican sources themselves.[6] Emden writes:

> The history of the Friars Preachers of the English Province has suffered irreparably from the loss of the records of its constituent priories and of their provincial chapters at the time of the ruthless

suppression of the Order in England by King Henry VIII and his Parliament in 1538–9.[7]

But the indefatigability of researchers has triumphed where the royal commissaries failed in obliterating all record of the Order's English existence. Reasonably satisfactory results have been obtained by forming a general picture of Dominican life and proceedings internationally, and illustrating these by the scattered evidence for the English Province. This methodology is legitimated by the consideration that

> On the one hand, [the Province] was part of an international organization from which, in the last resort, it received its laws, guidance, and commands. On the other hand, its membership was composed of Englishmen, its immediate superiors were Englishmen, and it lived and did its work in the cities, towns, villages and highways of England.[8]

And so, as William Hinnebusch points out, the two elements, international and national, interacted, the international influencing the national, the national modifying and sometimes restricting the international. But the time would come when, for the repercussion of England's politics on the life of the Order, that term 'restriction' would be euphemism indeed.

It cannot be said that the English Dominicans of the 1530s, confronted by the determinedly Erastian religious policy of the Tudor Crown, showed themselves to be the stuff of which martyrs were made. Some priors, notably those of Bristol and Norwich, tried to temporise in the hope of finding a compromise solution. Others took refuge in still Catholic Scotland, for instance the priors of Newcastle and Cambridge, though the latter moved on to the Netherlandish ecclesiastical metropolis of Louvain – a place that in the following century, as English friars painfully picked up the pieces of their broken institution, would mean much to them. Only one local superior, the prior of York, resisted to the end – or almost to the end if an abortive confession of Romish errors, designed to secure his escape from execution, be genuine. In any case, as a participant in the Pilgrimage of Grace, religious and political factors were in Fr John Pickering's case too inextricably confused for later historians – or the Congregation for the Causes of the Saints – to disentangle. The only clear martyrs of the Province were two figures on its periphery: Blessed Adrian Fortescue, an Oxfordshire gentleman who was a Dominican 'tertiary' (a lay associate of the Order),[9] and Blessed Robert Nutter, a secular priest admitted to the Order while already in prison awaiting trial.[10] The collapse was total. As Jarrett wrote: 'The whole body of friars seem to have melted out of existence, save for a chance reference to an English Dominican in some Flemish or French or Italian convent.[11] Nor was the attempt under Mary Tudor to restore the Dominicans to their former glories any more successful. Given the former Augustinian church of St Bartholomew's, Smithfield, as their sole priory, and with a talented communicator, William Perrin, as prior (and Vicar of the Province), death quickly claimed the superior as it claimed Mary's primate, Reginald Pole, and the queen herself. Royal succession passed to a more astute, less religiose, female who perceived the advantages of a State Church and the impossibility, given the political muscle of groups grown mighty on a diet of Church land, of a monastic restoration. Perrin's successor, Fr Richard Hargrave, fled to Flanders, taking with him the surviving nuns of Dartford (the only pre-Reformation contemplative Dominican monastery for women), and three unnamed friars. As under Elizabeth I's father, the rest are presumed to have conformed to the Church of England. If it is a testimony to the theological, pastoral and administrative training provided by the mediaeval Province, it is not, to the Catholic historian, a source of wider satisfaction to discover that a number of the clerical leaders of the newly schismatic *Ecclesia anglicana* were recruited from its membership.

Such English friars as went into exile for the cause of the faith were soon thinking, however, in what way they might serve the English 'mission' – as perforce to Catholics England had now to be. The realm was officially closed to Catholic priests, and draconian 'penal' laws served the government's intention of driving the Catholic laity (for a good deal of Elizabeth's reign as much as half of the population) into the arms of the Established Church. In 1622 the Master of the Order made Fr Thomas Middleton Vicar of the Dominicans in England, though his attempts to reorganise the Province were mostly carried out from the Clink and Newgate prisons. When the papal agent Gregorio Panzani visited the country in 1635 he calculated there to be a total of seven friars.[12] (With this one must contrast a plausible estimate of eight thousand at the pre-Reformation zenith.) The way of life of this earlier 'septet' – individual missioners serving harassed Catholic communities with both obstinacy and discretion, gaining assistance from the recusant gentry and the embassy chapels of Catholic princes abroad, but also from the pennies of the labouring poor – would be the lot of Dominicans in England for the rest of the seventeenth century and the entirety of its successor.

From 1559 to 1658 there was no common life, either at home or abroad.[13] In the latter year the conventual life was resumed, thanks to the determination – and the contacts, both civil and ecclesiastical – of the Province's most outstanding member in the entire penal period, Philip Thomas Howard of the ducal family of Norfolk, later on cardinal of the Roman church. Taken by his grandfather, Lord Arundel, on an Italian tour (the earl was one of the most discriminating judges and collectors of art in Charles I's highly art-conscious reign), the fifteen-year-old Philip Howard outraged his family by assuming the Dominican habit at Cremona (but for the English Province) in 1645. The pope – Innocent X Pamphilj, who was acquainted with the earl through Rubens – supported their efforts to recover him. But his persistence overbore them, and in 1646 he made profession at the Roman priory of S. Sixtus. His studies and ordination took place (after a stint in Naples) in northern France, from where he put out feelers to English exiles along the Channel coast. This stood him in good stead when, with the consent of the Dominican missioners in England itself, he used his patrimony to purchase an unfinished set of conventual buildings with a chequered history at Bornhem, outside Antwerp, in the Spanish (later, Austrian) Netherlands. The foundation, originally with six members, Philip Howard himself being prior, was a success, and was soon followed by the creation of a monastery of Dominican nuns at nearby Vilvorde. So far as is known, Howard's cousin was the first Englishwoman to adopt that way of life since the Reformation. With some misgivings on the part of his brethren, Howard also started up a school within the precincts of the priory itself. The question which exercised them was: Should not the claustral life be maintained in its fullness as the best possible preparation for the English mission, or, alternatively, might a school very properly be conducted for English Catholic boys (as the Benedictines and Jesuits were doing elsewhere in Flanders and France), since this too was an apostolic contribution to the needs of the Church at home?

In 1661 Howard was made Vicar of the Province, in 1672 vicar-apostolic of England, with the titular see of Helenopolis *in partibus infidelium*, and in 1675, in recognition of his services at the court of Charles II to whose queen he was chaplain, cardinal. Though Howard's other conventual projects eventually failed (his Roman priory of SS. John and Paul, on the Caelian Hill, passing in time to the Passionist Congregation), Bornhem with its dignified cloister and church, its library, and its full liturgical life, not to mention the 'moat full of carp' and rows of linden trees, and marshy meadows', survived, and constituted, in the words of one of the Province's antiquarians, Fr Robert Bracey, 'a real oasis in the desert' for the friars.

Here they could wear the religious habit, lead the monastic life, and openly practise their religion; instead of being forced to live in private houses, without any external sign of their calling, with the fear of penal statutes ever weighing upon them, and with holy ceremonies and ecclesiastical observances reduced to the barest minimum. Here they were indeed exiles, but honoured ones ...[14]

The House of Habsburg looked benevolently on the English Dominicans (whose school indeed would benefit indirectly from the closure by Maria Theresa of its English Jesuit competitors at Bruges). In 1695 the Habsburg government permitted the opening of a small college at Louvain, where the English friars could both study and lecture. Its succession of 16 rectors, ended only by the disruptions of the Revolutionary Wars in 1796, paralleled the 34 priors of Bornhem, and the institutional stability which these Flemish enclaves provided enabled the normal constitutional machinery of the Province to be restored in 1730, with properly elected provincials and regular (quadrennial) chapters. But the purpose of it all was the maintenance and extension of a presence in England, to England. There, however, the impossibility of common life and enterprise, as well as the taint of Jacobitism, necessarily hampered their efforts.[15] There could be no sustained re-creation of a culture, at once Catholic and indigenous, when the most elementary kind of pastoral and sacramental care was the order of the day. Decorated by Louvain, or even the Royal Academy at Brussels, they might be, but their life – even for a bishop, like Dominic Williams, vicar apostolic of the Northern District from 1725 to 1740 – was an unremitting slog aimed at keeping the Catholic Church alive: not *bene esse*, much less *plene esse*, but *esse* plain and simple – sheer survival – was their aim.

The repercussions of the Great Revolution of the West (1789–1815) nearly extinguished even this modest aspiration. If Bornhem was recovered in 1797, the remnants of its community were never able to restore the conventual life, and English boys, their parents understandably unwilling to send their offspring abroad in time of war, no longer came to its school. The coincidence of interest whereby the Anglican Church-State of the English *ancien régime* found itself on the same side as the Catholic Church in the counter-revolutionary struggle relaxed English Protestant attitudes to the recusant clergy sufficiently to enable the friars to open an English school in an Inigo Jones house at Carshalton, Surrey – but not to resume the formal religious life, still accounted too inflammatory of public opinion. By 1810, with no municiate, no formal priory, and no prospects, several of the younger and more energetic English Dominicans had decided the game was up, and emigrated to the United States there to begin a new province, and so pass from our story.

Despite the bankruptcy, in that year, of the Carshalton school, the remnant were emboldened to persevere by the combined efforts of a Yorkshire missioner, Fr Albert Underhill, and the erstwhile head-master of Carshalton, Fr Ambrose Woods, who would shortly become Provincial. At the small Leicestershire market town of Hinckley, where the nearby Turville family had proved supportive, the second created a quasi-noviciate with candidates earlier received as postulants into the mission-house of the first. By 1850 the Province's numbers were reduced again to seven – precisely the number at the time of Howard's first contact with the Order.

The English Catholic revival, with its gift to the Church of imagi-native, sometimes brilliant, converts in an age when entrepreneurialism and religious confidence went hand in hand, was to change all that. On 29 August 1850, as the handful of capitular fathers brooded in chapter at Hinckley on an economically uncertain future, an Oxford convert of some few years' standing, a correspon-dent of John Henry Newman's, arrived to offer them a purpose-built church at Woodchester in Gloucestershire. This William Leigh had destined for any Order dedicated to the choral celebration of the Catholic liturgy. 'His conversion coincided with his move to Gloucestershire, where he hoped to establish a model village which would incarnate in its architecture, social life and pattern of authority the ideal Christian commonwealth.[16] The Dominicans accepted Leigh's offer at a propitious time. First, a Catholic demographic explosion, triggered by the famine-driven immigration from Ireland, was creating new needs and opportunities. Secondly, there had come into office a Master-General Alexandre-Vincent Jandel, who was devoted to the full restoration of the classical Dominican life. He was particularly solicitous for the tiny but reviving Province, sympathetic to his ideas on the monastic character of formation, and coincident in its self-renewal with his own, papally engineered, rise to fame if hardly fortune. (Jandel was a zealous devotee of the principle of community of goods.) By the end of the nineteenth century, the Province could boast a hundred or so members – approximately its tally today.

Increasing numbers, together with the recovery of a classical ideal of the Dominican life (whether in the rigorist version preferred by Jandel, or in the more mitigated scheme urged by his chief rival, Père Henri-Dominique Lacordaire), led to a major shift in the structure and ethos of the Province. In the future, most Dominicans would be living in relatively substantial priories, although, since the needs of a multi-plying Catholic population required it, and the conditions laid down by bishops for new foundations demanded it, these were frequently linked to parish commitments in the larger cities (London becoming a priory in 1868, Newcastle and Leicester in 1882, Pendleton in 1901). To balance the urban-parochial element, however, Woodchester was joined in 1894 by Hawkesyard, Staffordshire – a formal priory engaged in the philosophical and theological formation of the young men who had made their noviciate, the spiritual initiation into the Order and its traditions, in Leigh's Gloucestershire foundation. The age of the individual Dominican missionary in England (from Elizabeth's reign to the early Victorian period) had given way to an age of priories, whether pastoral, monastic, or monastico-academic in overall character. Henceforth, the term 'missioner' would change its sense in English Dominican usage. It no longer referred to a friar living in solitary splendour (more usually, highly straitened circumstances), and had come to mean, rather, one who, whatever his priory of assignation (and therefore normal home) was in principle available for preaching work anywhere in the country. Really, it was only the continued existence of the school, revived at Hinckley in 1825 and moved in 1898 to Hawkesyard; the curious location of the Hinckley community itself (some few miles, merely, from the Dominicans of Leicester), and the burses provided by Louvain at the behest of a Belgian government conscious of the expropriation of English Dominican property, that reminded the friars of the age before William Leigh.

Notes

1. M.-H. Vicaire, O.P., *Histoire de saint Dominique* (Paris: Editions du Cerf, 1957, 2 vols); idem, *Dominique et ses Prêcheurs* (Fribourg: Editions Universitaires, 1977).
2. I owe this point to the kindness of Fr Simon Tugwell, O.P.
3. B. Jarrett, 'The English Dominicans. I. The Foundation', in F. Couturier, O.P., et al., *The English Dominican Province 1221-1921* (London: Catholic Truth Society, 1921), p. 3.
4. W.A. Hinnebusch, O.P., *The Early English Friars Preachers* (Rome: Instituto Storico Domenicano, 1951), p. 56. This total does not include the Scottish and Irish priories, which were of the English Province until the late mediaeval and Tudor periods, respectively.
5. B. Smalley, 'The Religious Orders in England', reviewing Dom David Knowles's work of the same title (Cambridge: Cambridge University Press, 1948), in *Dominican Studies* II (1949), p. 61.
6. A.B. Emden, *A Survey of Dominicans in England, Based on the Ordination Lists in Episcopal Registers, 1268 to 1538* (Rome: Instituto Storico Domenicano, 1967).

7.   Ibid., p. 15.
8.   W.A. Hinnebusch, O.P., *Friars Preachers*, p. 2.
9.   He entered the third Order on the eve of the Province's destruction, in 1533: it was, his biographer writes, 'as if to deepen his commitment to the Church, before the 'breaking of the storm': M. Elvins, *Bl. Adrian Fortescue, Englishman, Knight of Malta, Martyr* (London: Catholic Truth Society, 1993), p. 11.
10. G. Anstruther, O.P., 'The Venerable Robert Nutter, O.P., *Archivum Fratrum Praedicatorum* XXVII (1957), pp. 359–402.
11. B. Jarrett, O.P., 'The English Dominicans. VIII: At the Reformation', in Couturier, *English Dominican Province*, p. 206.
12. The smallness of this number may, however, be the result of excluding foreign-born (and Irish) friars from the count: thus W. Gumbley, O.P., *Obituary Notices of the English Dominicans from 1555 to 1952* (London: Aquin Press, 1955), p. 7.
13. G. Anstruther, O.P., *A Hundred Homeless Years. English Dominicans, 1558–1658* (London: Blackfriars Publications, 1958).
14. R. Bracey, O.P., 'The English Dominicans. IX: The Period of Eclipse', in Courturier, *The English Dominican Province* pp. 226–7.
15. Jacobite support was strongest among the lower clergy, notably the seculars (despite the role in episcopal nomination conceded by the pope to James III). However, the (Irish) Dominican prior of San Clemente Rome, was among those who defied the papal ban on receiving Charles III as king in 1766. On the whole subject, the best account is P.K. Monod, *Jacobitism and the English People, 1688–1788* (Cambridge: Cambridge University Press, 1989), pp. 132–8.
16. A. White, O.P., 'The Forging of the Nation and the British Dominican Pilgrimage', *Signum* 23, 10 (1995), p. 8.

Select Bibliography

G. Anstruther, O.P., *A Hundred Homeless Years. English Dominicans 1558–1658* (London: Blackfriars Publications, 1958).

G. Anstruther, O.P., *The Dominicans of Newcastle upon Tyne* (Newcastle: n.d. but 1948).

A.B. Emden, 'A Survey of Dominicans in England, Based on the Ordination Lists of Episcopal Registers, 1268 to 1538 (Rome: Instituto Storico Domenicano, 1967).

E. Essex, O.P. (ed.), *Dominican Church and Priory, Woodchester*, (n.d.).

W. Gumbley, O.P., 'The English Dominicans from 1555 to 1955', *Dominican Studies* V (1952), pp. 103–133.

W. Gumbley, O.P., *Obituary Notices of the English Dominicans from 1555 to 1952* (London: Aquin Press, 1955).

M. Harrison, O.P., *The Early English Friars Preachers* (Rome: Instituto Storico Domenicano, 1951).

W.A. Hinnebusch, O.P., *The Early English Friars Preachers* (Rome: Instituto Storico Domenicano, 1951).

B. Jarrett, O.P., *The English Dominicans* (London: Burns, Oates and Washbourne, 1921; 1937²).

A.H. Kimberlin, *The Return of Catholicism in Leicester, 1746–1946* (Hinckley, 1946).

M.-H. Vicaire, O.P., *Histoire de saint Dominique* (Paris: Editions du Cerf, 1957); two vols.); *Dominique et ses Prêcheurs* (Fribourg, Editions universitaires, 1977).

A. White., 'The Forging of the Nation and the British Dominican Pilgrimage', *Signum* 23, 10 (1955), pp. 1–16.

A Dominican Centenary, Woodchester, 1850–1950 (Woodchester, n.d. but 1950).

The English Dominican Province, 1221–1921 (London: Catholic Truth Society, 1921).

Appendix 2: Two unpublished letters of David Jones, poet and artist, to Thomas Gilby O.P.

at Northwick Lodge,
Harrow on-the-Hill,
Monday July 1st 1963.

Dear Thomas G.,

Forgive my bothering you, but I want to ask you a question about the Four Causes which you explain with great lucidity in *Barbara Celarent* 156–7, but I'm such a dunderhead when it comes to applying what is said to particular instances.

In 1929 I did some copper-plate illustrations to Coleridge's *Ancient Mariner* and now a new limited edition is in preparation for the U.S.A. and a few sell in Britain, but the point is that the joint publishers, Douglas Cleverdon here and Louis Cowan in New York have asked me to contribute a foreword to this new edition, and after saying I had nothing to say, I was persuaded into trying to make a brief foreword, which has now turned out to be a rather long one, for I'm no good at conciseness.

Anyway, you will remember that in the *Ancient Mariner*, the pivotal incident occurs when the Mariner, from loathing the water-snakes that surface round the becalmed vessel, on observing their beauty blesses them, and this act of love releases him from the dead-bird and the spell begins to be broken. It was the *beauty* of the water-snakes that *caused* this crucial change. Was that beauty the 'material'* or the 'efficient' cause of this most fortunate effect?

You must forgive my stupidity, but I can't see it clearly.

It is not very important except that in writing of this incident I say that it was the snakes' beauty or the Mariner's apprehension of the beauty of these creatures that caused the momentous change. So I would like to have the right adjective qualifying the 'cause'. It would give a sharper edge to what I am trying to say.

I notice that in a footnote to p. 157 of *Barbara Celarent* you say that 'An effect is the dependent of an efficient cause'. But does that apply to my 'beauty' of the water-snakes effectively causing the change whereby the creatures previously anathematized and despised by the Mariner now became the cause of his joy and part of his *anathemata*.

I hope you are well, and will excuse my bothering you with what ought to be clear to me.

I've been somewhat unwell for months now and am subjected to a regimen of innumerable drugs, but I think I'm a bit better than I was a little back. Remember me to anybody I know at Blackfriars; I believe Illtud is still in the U.S., isn't he?

Yours very sincerely,

David Jones

The Rev. Fr. Thomas Gilby O.P.,
Blackfriars
Cambridge

* In a sense the beauty seems to meet the question *in quo*? and in a sort of way corresponds with your definition of that 'in what?' in the case of the pom-pom being made of certain specific material but I feel shaky about this and see that the 'beauty' may be the efficient cause, meeting the question whence and how.

Northwick Lodge,
Harrow on the Hill,
July 4th 1963.

Dear Thomas,

Diolch yn fawr iawn, as my father's countrymen would say. Thanks very much, for your letter, which I treasure. I felt and feel a bit ashamed in bothering you, for that passage in my beastly Foreword is brief and also, though, by inclination, I've a weakness for qualifying clauses,* I want this passage to be as direct as possible. I realized that within the context of my water-snakes-Mariner all the causes were involved and that the final cause was love. But I wanted, if I could, without explanation, to convey to the reader that the visual, seen, natural beauty of the water-snakes[+] moved the heart of the Mariner to bless them and so by this act of love 'put about', not indeed the doomed vessel, but the vessel of the Mariner's soul, as it were.

As you most kindly said I could write further, I think I'll quote verbatim exactly what I wrote including a bit of the context:

> It is here, on the Equator, under a 'hot and copper sky' that the real ordeals begin and continue. We are still in Part 2 of the poem and in Parts 3 and 4 the major horrors occur, with the vessel still becalmed, motionless, rotting, fixed in the 'sultry main' with the teeming water-snakes, creatures found only in tropical seas. It is these very creatures whose tropic beauty [once the Mariner had perceived it**] was the material cause of the Mariner's blessing them, the effect of which can hardly be exaggerated, for thereby the whole situation is transformed. The water-snakes that had been loathesome to the Mariner have now become efficacious as a cause of his joy.

It was on re-reading this that I began to have my doubts as to my use of the adjective 'material' and that was why I decided to write to you, as the use of technical terms, without proper technical understanding, can make one say some very unfortunate things, as for example speaking of 'stays' when you mean 'braces'.

If there is anything at all in the passage quoted over-leaf that gives a wrong impression, or worse, I should greatly appreciate any correction you might suggest. I can't lengthen the passage, really, for the Foreword is already miles too long, and I don't want to labour the matter, but nor do I want to misapply a term.

By the way, switching from scholastic terms to nautical ones, does one say *on* the Line or Equator or *at* the Line or Equator? – or are both used? I usually enquire of my friend Michael Richey when in doubt about sea matters but he's in the U.S.A. for a month or so.

I find on re-reading Coleridge's poem with greater attention all kinds of interesting problems arise. I'm purposely avoiding consulting works by Coleridgean scholars, as I want only to convey my own impressions as a layman when I illustrated the poem 35 years ago and at the present time.

Again thank you very much for your letter and for your replying so promptly. I value it and it confirms what I had imagined were the dangers of using terms without many qualifications. That's why I thought it best to send you the passage as it stands, for your judgment.

It would be *jolly* nice to see you again but I don't suppose you are ever in Harrow*** and what with one thing or another I seem stuck here.++

God bless you.

Yours

David

*   I think that's why I used to enjoy von Hügel years ago!

\+   In fact what you express in your letter 'but do allow for the material cause – no uplift there': I loved that. That's *exactly* what I wanted to get across – that it was a material thing, seen under dread circumstances, yet which had, well, this enormous 'immaterial' effect – as you say 'in the joy in the beauty that uplifts his own' – that seems absolutely 'incarnational'.

**   these six words were later crossed out, perhaps they should be restored, but they seemed to retard the sentence, without clarifying anything much, and I wanted to be as brief as possible.

***   I haven't done much painting of late, but there are one or two things I'd like you to see should you ever be in the vicinity.

\+ \+   though I hope not quite 'stuck' as Coleridge's image of the vessel.

> We stuck, no breath nor motion,
> As idle as a painted ship
> Upon a painted ocean.

I venture to point out in my Foreword that unwittingly Coleridge chose an image not at all pleasing to painters for whom 'stuckness' in a picture, no matter how *static* in feeling, must at all costs be avoided. Poor old Galileo's *Eppur si muove!* is what we cry in the presence of any decent art-work.

Commentary

In these two letters Jones approached Fr Thomas, evidently, as a Thomist metaphysician – though one who had shown a special interest in aesthetics. The Foreword proved much too lengthy for the publishers of the second edition of his illustrations to the *Rime of the Ancient Mariner*. Only a short introductory segment was published. The rest did not see the light of day until Jones's friend and editor Harman Grisewood selected the essay for inclusion in a posthumous collection, *The Dying Gaul*.[1]

The preface to Coleridge's poem on which Jones sought Fr Thomas's advice is an extraordinarily rich reading which stresses not only the many-levelled mythological allusiveness of the *Rime* but also its physical exactitude in sea-going matters. As Jones writes:

> The *Mariner*, as in all incantative poetry, lifts up bodily images, no matter how mysterious, ethereal, metamorphic some of those images may be, or how conceptual the matter of which they are the *signa* ... In poetry everything matters, and the greater the poetry so much the more is this true.[2]

Jones's own concern with the application of Scholastic vocabulary to the poem illustrates his own passion for conceptual, as well as graphic and mythopoeic, precision. That same care for language and idea, led him to write, schooled by Fr Thomas, in his final version of the crucial episode of the Mariner's prayer of praise for the water-snakes: 'The essentially tropic beauty of these water-snakes thus became the material cause, and more, of the Mariner's blessing them.[3] The addition of the words 'and more' to Jones's draft was prompted, presumably, by the consideration that knowledge, on the Thomist-Aristotelian understanding of things, is a transitive reality. Thus the wonderful iridescence of the sea-creatures affected the Mariner not only as a mental image (a material cause in the strict sense, for such a cause is always *intrinsic* to the reality changed) but in all the glorious objectivity mediated by such an image – and therefore through efficient causality as well. One sees, however, why Jones mentioned by name only 'material' causality in this passage, for the word would convey to the modern English speaker the primacy of initiative of the *animals* in the Mariner's change of heart.

In general, the essay offers, as one might expect, a Christian interpretation of Coleridge's text – but one sensitive to the pagan sources and parallels present in, or at any rate pertinent to, its imaginative structure.

> It is evident that this great poem, taken as a whole and in spite of various very differing themes, belongs to the tradition of the wonder-voyages and is evocative of the argosy of mankind and hence cannot avoid evoking the Redeemer, our Odysseus, who in Homer is, at his own command, made fast to the stepped mast.[4]

Indeed, Jones interprets the *Rime* via a passage on the 'voyage of the Redeemer' in his own *Anathemata*,[5] and the same alignment of the artist's own poem with Coleridge's appears in the first letter to Fr Thomas, where he applies to the Mariner's snakes that same ambivalent term, 'anathema', which gives his 'Fragments of an Attempted Writing' their title.

> I knew that in antiquity the Greek word *anathema* (spelt with an epsilon) meant (firstly) something holy, but that in the New Testament it is restricted to the opposite sense. While this duality exactly fitted my requirements, the English word 'anathemas', because referring only to that opposite sense, was of no use to me. I recalled, however, that there was the other English plural, 'anathemata', meaning devoted things, and used by some English writers down the centuries, thus preserving in our language the ancient and beneficent meaning; for 'anathemata' comes from *anathema* spelt

with an eta, of which the epsilon form is a variant ... So I mean by my title as much as it can be made to mean, or can evoke and suggest, however obliquely: the blessed things that have taken on what is cursed and the profane things that somehow are redeemed ...[6]

Jones also found in the *Rime* – and not least in the water-snake section – a moral theology of a peculiarly gracious kind. In Coleridge's 'faultless' theology, the spell that afflicts the Mariner is lifted by an 'interior act of love' when he blesses the creatures unaware.[7] Jones's explanation of the last of the full-page illustrations to the *Rime* – showing as it does a priest censing an altar – characteristically unites this thought with the movement of the Catholic liturgy. Whereas Coleridge has a bell calling the inhabitants of the port to the Office of Vespers, where incense is offered at the Magnificat, Jones adds a reference to the Mass, at once the foundation and the summit of worship.

The pelican feeding her young from her own flesh in the tailpiece requires no explanation. The Latin inscription of that tail-piece is taken from the Roman Mass, the words being part of what the celebrant says while he is censing the altar having censed the Oblations: May the Lord kindle in us the fire of his love and the flame of eternal charity. Words which seemed to tally with the third stanza from the end of the poem, and which express a theme that runs like a thread through the whole mysterious weft and warp of *The Rime of the Ancient Mariner*.[8]

'Illtud' is Father Illtud Evans (1918–72), an English Dominican of London-Welsh origin whose wide-ranging interests and bilingualism would have endeared him to Jones. He became editor of *Blackfriars* in 1951, and was responsible for the merging of that journal with *Life of the Spirit* as 'New Blackfriars' in 1964. Though he died in Athens, his last house of assignation was Blackfriars, Cambridge, Fr Thomas's home.

Michael Richey, a pupil of Gill's in stone carving and lettering, after trying for a while the monastic life, found his vocation in marrying contemplation to solo sailing. He was Executive Secretary and later Director of the Royal Institute of Navigation from 1947 to 1982, and editor of the *Journal of Navigation* from 1948 to 1987. At the time of writing, Michael Richey is one of the last survivors of that ramifying English Catholic circle which this book has described.

There is a good account of David Jones's engravings for the *Rime*, and their critical reception, in David Blamires' study, *David Jones*.

Artist and Writer (Manchester: Manchester University Press, 1971), pp. 47–56. A brief account of David Jones's contribution to the English Catholic culture of the period from the 1930s to the Second Vatican Council may be found in Chapter 2 of the present work, 'The English Catholic Setting'.

Notes

1. D. Jones, *The Dying Gaul and Other Writings, Edited with an Introduction by Harman Grisewood* (London and Boston: Faber and Faber, 1978), pp. 186–226.
2. Ibid., pp. 208, 207.
3. Ibid., p. 197.
4. Ibid., p. 214.
5. Ibid., p. 190; cf. idem., *The Anathemata. Fragments of an Attempted Writing* (London: Faber and Faber, 1952), p. 106.
6. Ibid., pp. 27–29.
7. 'An Introduction to *The Rime of the Ancient Mariner*', in *The Dying Gaul*, p. 193.
8. Ibid., p. 225.
9. See now his own essay, 'David Jones and the Arts of Seafaring', *The Chesterton Review* XXIII, 1–2 (1997), pp. 171–175 – a contribution to an issue of that journal devoted to Jones.

Index of Names